The Garden Lovers'
GUIDE TO
BRITAIN

Kathryn Bradley-Hole is renowned for her perceptive views on British gardening. For this third edition of *The Garden Lovers' Guide*, she has explored every corner of Britain, unearthing the best gardens, nurseries, craftsmen, potters and ornament makers that Britain has to offer.

Currently Gardens Editor of *Country Life*, Kathryn was previously a gardening columnist for *The Daily Telegraph*, for which she received two awards from the Garden Writers Guild. She has also written for *BBC Gardeners' World Magazine* and the Royal Horticultural Society's journal, *The Garden*, and has contributed to many bestselling titles, including the *Reader's Digest New Encyclopedia of Garden Plants & Flowers*. Kathryn's latest books are *Stone, Rock and Gravel* and *The Daily Telegraph Weekend Gardening*. She is married to garden designer Christopher Bradley-Hole.

'A comprehensively inspiring book, well worth buying'
Plants Magazine

'Anyone who enjoys visiting gardens should have a copy'
Active Life

'Kathryn Bradley-Hole writes in a readable, personal style and her remarks are witty and useful... As handbooks go, this one is a great companion.'
Alan Titchmarsh in the *Daily Express*

Gardeners' World

The Garden Lovers' GUIDE TO BRITAIN

KATHRYN BRADLEY-HOLE

Acknowledgements

This guide is my personal selection of the best Britain has to offer, and I have many people to thank for their local knowledge, hospitality, helpful suggestions and enthusiasm for this project. Particular thanks go to Adam Pasco and Séamus Geoghegan of *BBC Gardeners' World Magazine*, Nicky Copeland, Sarah Miles and Khadija Manjlai at BBC Books, all of whom have given me unstinting help and encouragement, and Ben Cracknell who has designed the pages, icons and plans in an invitingly lively style.

My husband, Christopher, has been a 'guide, philosopher and friend' throughout; his support has been invaluable, as always.

Some years ago Sue Clifford and Angela King of Common Ground inspired me by their work. They have made us all aware of the importance of regional disinctiveness and I have tried to reflect some of that inspiration by including plants and people important in each region.

I would also like to thank: Geoff Amos, Stephen Anderton, Richard Ayres, David Beaumont, Peter Blackburne-Maze, Elizabeth Braimbridge, Jenny Broome, Neil and Jerry Campbell-Sharp, Georgina Capel, Nigel Colborn, Simon Dorrell, Valerie Finnis, Daphne Foulsham, Kate Garton, Jackie Gurney, Bob Harrison, Jane and Robert Hasell McCosh, Kathleen Hendry, Stephen Higham, Penelope Hobhouse, Malcolm Hutchinson, Carol Klein, Stephen Lacey, Roy Lancaster, Andrew Lawson, Val Lowther, Jim Marshall, Anya Medlin, Margaret Milton, Peter Pashley, Rosie Reed, Peter Reekie, John Sales, Myra Sanderson, Kathy Sayer, Peter Seabrook, Barbara Segall, Geoffrey Smith, Anne Swithinbank, Christopher Thacker, Alan Titchmarsh, Rona Wallace, Charis Ward, Jim Ward, David Wheeler, Fred Whitsey and all the garden owners, craftsmen, head gardeners and nurserymen and women, who have been incredibly generous with their time and knowledge.

COVER PHOTOGRAPHS
Front: Barnsley House Garden, Gloucestershire (Jerry Harpur)
Back: The author, Kathryn Bradley-Hole (courtesy of the author)

Published by BBC Worldwide Limited,
80 Wood Lane, London W12 0TT

First published in 1998
This third edition published in 2001

© Kathryn Bradley-Hole 1998, 2000, 2001

The moral right of the author has
been asserted.

ISBN 0 563 53434 6

Commissioning Editor: Nicky Copeland
Project Editor and Copy-editor: Sarah Miles
Art Director: Pene Parker
Book Design Manager: Lisa Pettibone
Designed by Ben Cracknell Studios
Maps: © MAPS IN MINUTES™ (1999)
   © Crown Copyright, Ordnance Survey &
   Ordnance Survey Northern Ireland (1999)
   Permit No. NI 1675

Set in Book Antiqua and Frutiger

Printed and bound in Great Britain by
Butler & Tanner Limited, Frome and London

Cover printed by Belmont Press, Northampton

For information about this and other BBC
books, please visit our website on
www.bbcshop.com

Contents

Foreword 6
Introduction 8
How to Use This Book 9

ENGLAND

NORTHERN IRELAND

SCOTLAND

WALES

Foreword

With such a rich heritage of gardens throughout our country, providing a living history of garden design through the ages, it is no surprise that visiting gardens is such a popular pastime.

Gardens have often evolved in the most inhospitable regions, with limited money or resources, taming nature to produce scenes of breathtaking beauty. But in plenty of cases money has been no object, as entire landscapes have been remoulded, lakes excavated and buildings and follies created. The end result? Some of the finest gardens in the world.

Whatever your reason for visiting gardens, there is no better way to get the best from your day out than in the company of an experienced guide, a role Kathryn Bradley-Hole admirably fulfils in this book. Combining her plant knowledge and gardening experience with a love of gardens, their creation and the stories behind them, she uncovers a wealth of gardens we can all enjoy.

The Garden Lovers' Guide spans the entire country, presented by region and county, so that you can plan day trips and holidays, with a location map at the back of the book for quick reference. In addition to the gardens, you will find many nurseries and other places of interest discovered while researching this book, making it the most up-to-date, informative and inspiring guide you will ever own. Kathryn has also picked the brains of leading experts regarding their favourite gardens, and the ones that feed their gardening passion.

Throughout history, people and gardens have been closely linked. We can now marvel at the replanted Privy Garden of William and Mary at Hampton Court, while sharing the gardening interests of our current Royal Family at Sandringham House, Norfolk, and at Highgrove, Gloucestershire. Start visiting such gardens and you will find yourself walking through a living *Who's Who?* of gardening and garden design. Spectacular gardens of the past, designed by Capability Brown, Humphry Repton, Sir Edwin Lutyens and Geoffrey Jellicoe have developed and matured much since their conception, while the gardens of Vita Sackville-West and Gertrude Jekyll, for instance, are often preserved in a form as close as possible to their original. You can also visit contemporary plantsmen and women, from Christopher Lloyd and Beth Chatto to Alan and Adrian Bloom, whose gardens attract visitors in their thousands each year, eager to learn about new plants and the best ways to grow them.

Three things really excite me about visiting gardens, and from my contact with readers of *BBC Gardeners' World Magazine* I know they excite you too. First come the plants, which I try to identify despite their tongue-twisting Latin names, studying their shape and size, their associations with neighbours and their preferences for, say, a shady spot under a tree, or the support of an old rustic arch in the sun. Rather than rely on memory, an enthusiast like me takes a camera and notebook to record every detail. Second are the special features, structures and design, and while some may inspire an odd corner of my own plot, most are there to be enjoyed and marvelled at, and to add to that ever-growing wish list of ideas for my dream garden. And third there are the people, not just fellow visitors but the owners and gardeners. Usually they are busying themselves with some essential chore, but most are happy to share a story about the garden or to pass on a few tips about a plant, which you might have struggled to grow for years, but which flourishes at the touch of their green fingers.

Gardens are as diverse as the interests of their owners and the landscapes they occupy. Some are historical records, still growing the very same plants raised from seed 100 years ago, brought back by the great plant hunters. Others may have been transformed from the most unpromising sites, being turned into the nearest images of paradise we will find on earth. And some have been carved out of a passion for a particular plant, becoming the site of a National Collection, a living museum of international importance.

With new gardens being created and opened all the time, visiting gardens is always full of surprises. Since gardens develop and mature, never standing still, seeing them at intervals through the year allows you to follow these subtle changes and bold, seasonal transformations. Thousands of pounds are raised for charity from many open gardens, much under the National Gardens Scheme, with teas and plant sales adding to the overall enjoyment.

The value of any garden is in the eyes of the visitor. To some it involves learning about new plants, new plant associations or design features, while for others it is simply the sheer enjoyment, relaxation and contemplation, an escape from the hustle and bustle of the artificial word that surrounds us and a chance to rekindle our relationship with the natural world.

I am sure you will enjoy *The Garden Lovers' Guide*, turning to it again and again to explore some of the hundreds of gardens described within its pages, and getting to know many of them personally on your own gardening adventures.

Adam Pasco

Introduction

Welcome to the new, completely revised and updated edition of *The Garden Lovers' Guide to Britain*. The total number of places to visit now exceeds 600. The first and second editions have been very warmly received and I think you will agree that the additions we have made to the *Guide* are well worth having. We have included detailed plans to some of the most interesting places featured, useful specialist category lists at the back of the book and discount entry vouchers for 40 gardens.

Rather than simply providing factual text on what you will find in any given garden, the *Garden Lovers' Guide* endeavours to give you a flavour of the atmosphere and character of the gardens and some of their owners. It also, uniquely, sets the gardens into the context of their region. Gardens on acid soils in the wet maritime climate of south Cornwall, for example, tend to be very different from those on high ground in the limestone Cotswolds, or indeed from those in the flatter, drier landscape of East Anglia. Some gardens (such as The Earth Centre at Doncaster) have made use of their location in heavily industrialised areas and drawn inspiration from it. If you're not already familiar with the different flavours to be found in each region, I urge you to take a look at the county and regional introductions that set the scene for each area.

For *The Garden Lovers' Guide* I have travelled the length and breadth of the United Kingdom, covering many thousands of miles. I have met, along the way, a marvellously diverse range of people, all of whom share a common fascination and love for plants and gardens. I immediately think of Mark Robson, in Northumberland, who has been making a wondrous plantsman's garden at Bide-a-Wee Cottage, his parents' home, since he was 15 years old. I think of Maitreya, a former Zen Buddhist monk, who has settled in Nottinghamshire and built by hand a tranquil Japanese garden that reminds him of his homeland. And of nurserywoman Jekka McVicar, who was a rock musician before she became captivated by culinary and medicinal herbs. I also think of Major Tony Hibbert, who retired in 1980 to Cornwall's south coast, only to begin an unexpected new career in his twilight years, restoring with gusto the all-but-lost Victorian garden of Trebah to its sub-tropical glory.

The Garden Lovers' Guide features, almost exclusively, gardens and nurseries that are *regularly* open, with just a few exceptions to this rule. It is therefore intended as a handy, glove-box guide in which you can quickly find places of interest in your area, or when taking a break elsewhere. Many of the National Trust's and National Trust for Scotland's gardens are included, and I cannot stress too often the usefulness of having an NT membership card, which allows free entry to their numerous properties in exchange for the comparatively small annual fee (current fees – single person £31, couple £52.50, family £58). Certain gardens opening for the National Gardens Scheme (and Scotland's Gardens Scheme) are also included in this *Guide*. These organisations, which raise huge sums of money for Macmillan Cancer Relief and other worthy causes, deserve all possible support, and their well-known 'yellow books' are handy references to thousands more gardens, which open perhaps just one or two afternoons a year for charity.

Lastly, I very much welcome your helpful comments on this third edition of *The Garden Lovers' Guide*. Your observations and contributions will help ensure that it continues to provide useful, entertaining information for everyone who loves plants and gardens.

How to Use This Book

Structure

The Garden Lovers' Guide is divided into the countries of England, Wales, Scotland and Northern Ireland, and sub-divided into counties. Wales and Scotland, which have recently undergone extensive fragmentation (from the old counties into numerous unitary authorities), are arranged regionally, which will make more sense to the visitor. Within each county (or region) there is a scene-setting introduction, followed by main entries, which are organised alphabetically according to the nearest town or village. The index at the back of the book can also be used to locate a garden or nursery, when only the name is known.

Among the main entries there are boxed sections highlighting other places or features of note, including plants or people of local significance, locally made crafts from pots to trugs and a selection of special nurseries. At the end of each region the 'And also...' section is a round-up of other places worthy of mention.

Plans

Some of the entries show plans of the gardens, which will help you organise your visit. The original plans were provided by the gardens themselves and should be used only as a rough guide, as they are not drawn to scale.

Maps

The maps at the back of the book give approximate locations for all of the main entries in the *Guide*. When planning a tour of a region, however, you will also need a good road atlas showing more local detail than can be presented here. The maps are also useful because they show other nearby gardens, some in an adjacent county.

Garden Highlights

Throughout the *Guide*, certain outstanding gardens and nurseries have been awarded a 'Must See' plaque. These places should not be missed when touring a particular region, whatever the season; the plaques are especially useful for pinpointing the best places to visit if time is limited.

Other gardens are highlighted with an 'Exceptional in ...' plaque. As the vast majority of gardens opening to the public are at their best in the summer, these seasonal highlight plaques are designed chiefly to pinpoint gardens which peak in other seasons. There are, however, a small number of places which have been designated 'Exceptional in Summer'. These gardens offer well above average interest in the high season and are worth making a priority at that time.

There is a helpful summary of these highlighted gardens on the opening page of each county, including those which are worth a visit in winter. Please note that many of the spectacular spring gardens are also excellent in autumn and vice versa. See individual descriptions for further details.

Entries

Full addresses, telephone numbers, web site addresses, entrance fees (where applicable), directions and opening times are listed for each entry. Seasonal openings, such as 'March–Oct', are inclusive and run from the start of the first month to the end of the last. We have gone to great pains to ensure that details are up to date, and every entry has been checked with the owners at the time of going to press.

However, if you are making a special journey to a garden or nursery, or planning a detailed itinerary, it is worth ringing beforehand to ensure that opening times have not suddenly been altered. Changes of ownership, a change of address, or route alterations due to road improvements can occur with little warning.

In order to make the most of each visit, facilities such as refreshments, plants for sale, gift shops, wheelchair access, mail order services and whether a National Plant Collection (NPC) is held are clearly shown at the start of each main entry. If a garden is featured in the 2 for 1 voucher scheme at the back of the book, this is also marked here.

     ♿ Access   Gift Shop   Café   Plants for Sale

      Nursery   NPC   Mail Order   2 for 1 Voucher

Lists

After the garden entries you will find comprehensive specialist lists, including a guide to the National Plant Collections. I have also added my personal 'Six of the Best' – gardens that excel in a particular category, whether for family visits or for garden size and situation.

Vouchers

Included with this edition are 2 for 1 free entry vouchers for 40 gardens, all of which are described in the *Guide*. With this fantastic offer, one adult can enter each garden free when accompanying another full-paying adult. All you have to do is cut out the voucher and present it upon entry to the garden it refers to. Please do double-check all opening times before visiting just in case they have changed without warning.

Entrance Fees

Charges for visiting gardens can vary greatly. The higher costs are given for tickets letting you into a stately home and the gardens. It is more usual, however, that cheaper tickets for the latter alone are available. As this is a garden visitors' guide, the emphasis is on the gardens, but where I have found the house to be particularly interesting, I have given it a mention too, and listed the ticket price for the interior. While the entrance fees quoted were correct at the time of going to press, on occasion you may find slight increases have been made at the start of the season.

Wheelchairs

Where available, wheelchair access has been noted at the start of each entry. Such notification indicates that the garden, or a significant part of it, can be negotiated by someone in a chair. It does not necessarily mean that there are full facilities, such as toilets, for disabled visitors, though they usually are present in the larger, more commercially run gardens, especially those attached to stately homes and National Trust properties.

Dogs

For various reasons dogs are practically never admitted to gardens, but sometimes guide dogs for the blind are permitted. It is worth checking ahead if you do have a guide dog.

Readers' Reports

We welcome your comments, good and bad, on any of the gardens, nurseries and other suppliers listed in the *Guide*, which will be helpful in compiling future editions. Also, if you know of any garden or nursery not currently in the *Guide* which warrants a mention, please send full details (including its complete name, postal address and telephone number), explaining why it should be included, and I shall follow it up. Send your letters to:

Kathryn Bradley-Hole
The Garden Lovers' Guide to Britain
BBC Worldwide
80 Wood Lane
London W12 0TT

ENGLAND

Avon district

The area we have come to know as Avon over the last 20 years has recently been split up into four unitary authorities. However, for the purposes of the *Guide* it is convenient to keep Avon intact as an exceptionally rewarding region for garden visitors, plant enthusiasts and anyone who enjoys limestone landscapes and towns.

Taking in the elegant spa town of Bath and the historic sea port of Bristol, this area encompasses the lower reaches of the River Avon. It is rewarding for visitors who enjoy handsome architecture and gardens. Other highlights include Bath's sweeping Royal Crescent and Roman baths, built around a hot spring. Occupying fertile ground between the Mendip Hills to the south and the Cotswolds to the north, Avon is also a region which enjoys a fair share of interesting nurseries, so come armed with a cheque-book and plenty of car-boot space.

Exceptional in Autumn
American Museum, Bath
City of Bath Botanical
  Gardens, Bath

Worth a Visit in Winter
University of Bristol Botanic
  Garden, Bristol

BATH

The American Museum

Claverton Manor, Bath BA2 7BD TEL. 01225-460503 OWNER Trustees of the American Museum in Britain HOURS Late March–Oct, Tues–Sun, 1–6p.m. (museum 2–5p.m.), Bank Holiday Suns and Mons, 11a.m.–5p.m. ENTRANCE £6, OAPs £5.50, children £3.50 (grounds £3.50, OAPs £3, children £2.50) DIRECTIONS 3m SE of Bath, off A36 or via Bathwick Hill, Bath WEB www.americanmuseum.org

🚹 ᕍ Access 🚹 Gift Shop 🚹 Café

Claverton Manor is a handsome Georgian mansion of local stone in a glorious hillside setting, overlooking the valley of the River Avon and the picturesque Limpley Stoke Valley. Within its 55 acres, sloping lawns run up to the house, where a small parterre is laid out beside the stone terrace. This is the Colonial Herb Garden, with box-edged beds infilled with traditional dyers', culinary and medicinal herbs that were used by early American settlers. There are climbing roses and sun-loving shrubs against a tall balustraded wall near the house, but the main gardens and arboretum are set apart, further down the hill. The Mount Vernon Garden is enclosed by white palisade fencing and is a replica of George Washington's flower garden at Mount Vernon in Virginia. Filled with irises, columbines, salvias, geraniums, shrub roses and much else, it includes many of the plants that America's first president may have grown. Its brick-edged gravel paths lead to an attractive octagonal garden house, a reproduction of a similar building where Washington's step-grandchildren were schooled at Mount Vernon.

The arboretum is of special interest for its large collection of trees and shrubs of North American origin, including scarlet oaks, American hybrid magnolias, silver and sugar maples and many American roses. The garden's most unusual ornament is an Indian teepee of the Cheyenne tribe, a conical tent stretched over poles, decorated with buffalo designs.

While you are here, it is worth touring the manor, where there are fascinating exhibits of American domestic design (including quilts, stencils and Shaker furniture).

BATH

City of Bath Botanical Gardens

Royal Victoria Park, Upper Bristol Road, Bath BA1 2NQ TEL. 01225-482624 OWNER Bath and North-east Somerset Council HOURS Open all year, daily, dawn–dusk ENTRANCE Free DIRECTIONS On N side of Victoria Park in Bath city

 ᕍ Access

This garden was originally known as the Broome Botanical Garden at its inception in 1887, when it was named after an amateur botanist who had donated a collection of 2000 plants. It lies at the north-western corner of the city's Royal Victoria Park, forming a separate, richly planted area of lawns and beds, dissected by numerous wiggly paths.

Within its nine acres, there is a one-acre woodland garden known as the Great Dell, where hydrangeas and other woodland shrubs are gathered, and where Tenby daffodils light up its sloping, grassy banks in spring. Other specialist plant collections are displayed in a heather garden, a rock garden, a shrub-rose garden and an area devoted to the prickly shrubs in the genus *Berberis* (extending to around three dozen different kinds). Natural springs draining from the limestone hills above Bath city feed this pleasant garden's waterfall, stream and curved pool. There is also a grand herbaceous border stretching 150ft, a herb garden and a scented walk. Autumn shows off the brilliant colours of the garden's massive tree and shrub collections as numerous species turn to brilliant reds and golds.

Organic Herbs by Post

Jekka McVicar performed in a rock band and was a self-confessed hippie, 'every parent's nightmare', before she became hooked by the beauty and usefulness of herbs. After a brief spell working for a commercial herb nursery, she started a small business in the mid-1980s, growing and selling plants from her home. Business mushroomed, and today **Jekka's Herb Farm** offers one of the largest selections of herbs and wildflowers in England, and her stand at the larger RHS flower shows is always worth investigating. (Recently I tried the delicious Vietnamese coriander, *Persicaria odoratum*, which Jekka recommends using with pineapple dishes, or for adding piquancy to salads.)

The nursery is not open to visitors, but its mail order catalogue is extensive and includes useful brief descriptions of the plants on offer. And there are plenty of them, around 500 different varieties, mostly sold as small plants, though some are available as seed. All are grown organically, to the standards of the Organic Food Federation. For a catalogue, send 4 × 1st-class stamps to **Jekka's Herb Farm, Rose Cottage, Shellards Lane, Alveston, Bristol BS35 3SY (tel. 01454-418878)**.

Prior Park

Ralph Allen Drive, Bath BA2 5AH TEL. 01225-833422 OWNER The National Trust HOURS Open all year, Feb–Nov, daily (closed Tues, Easter–Nov), 11a.m.–5.30p.m. (opens 12 noon, Oct–Nov) or dusk if earlier; Dec–Jan, Fri–Sun, 12 noon–dusk ENTRANCE £4, children £2 (£1 off entrance fee with valid ticket for public transport or bicycle hire) DIRECTIONS 1m from city centre, by hired bicycle or public transport only as there is no parking nearby (bus 2, and Mon–Sat bus 4, from the bus station). Phone to book access for disabled.

Prior Park is for the enthusiast of the English 18th-century landscape garden, who will find it sublime, and for anyone wanting to stretch their legs on a hilly parkland walk. It also provides an airy escape from the traffic-filled streets of Bath, which can be seen in glorious views across the valley. At 28 acres it is comparatively small and intimate for a landscape garden, being largely the work of Alexander Pope, followed by Capability Brown (*q.v.*). After years of neglect the park was given to the National Trust in 1993 and has since been extensively restored at a cost of half a million pounds; its lakeside and woodland walks were opened up, and its fine features (including a handsome, colonnaded Palladian bridge) repaired.

The property was the creation of Ralph Allen, a larger-than-life gentleman and philanthropist of Bath (upon whom Henry Fielding based the wise and generous character of Squire Alworthy in *Tom Jones*). He made a fortune by reorganising the cross-country postal system and supplying the growing spa town with honey-coloured stone from his quarries at Combe Down and Bathampton. Architectural buffs will be enraptured by the classical stone house (now a school, closed to the public) with its rusticated arcades terminating in further large buildings. Allen intended it to be a seat where his stone could be seen 'to much greater Advantage, and in much greater Variety of Uses than it had ever appeared in any other Structure'. Fortunately, in spite of two massive fires (in 1836 and 1991), the restored house is as imposing as ever and its park is well on the way to providing it with gracious surroundings.

Garden Bygones

David Bridgwater, Heather Cottage, Lansdown, Bath BA1 9BL (tel. 01225-463435), sells antiques, specialising in traditional garden architecture, ornaments and old garden tools, including metal watering cans, glass cucumber straighteners and other fascinating gardening accessories. Visitors by appointment only.

Hand-made Terracotta Pots

Bill Donaldson, of **Willow Pottery, Toghill House Farm, Hanswell, nr Wick (tel. 01225-891919)**, is a potter with a passion. After taking a degree in fine art at Leeds University, he worked with a clay producer, setting up a pottery in the heartland of the industry at Stoke-on-Trent. But in the mid-1980s he moved to Bath to set up his own pottery and has since developed a distinctive style, based on English traditional wares and motifs of the English countryside. Hares, dragonflies and bees ornament his early ranges, large fig pots are rimmed with appropriately figgy decoration, while his citrus pots are decorated with lemons.

Well-made, hand-thrown pots such as these are fired at very high temperatures to cope with our climate. You will also find traditional Long-Toms, rhubarb forcers and alpine pans, and it is difficult to leave without weighing down the car boot with a selection of these tactile containers. Donaldson also sells other handmade items and organises garden lectures. Open Mon–Sat, 9a.m.–5p.m., Sun, 10a.m.–4p.m. M4 Jct 18, then A46 towards Bath, right at 1st roundabout, pottery on left after ¹/₂m.

BRISTOL

University of Bristol Botanic Garden

Bracken Hill, North Road, Leigh Woods, Bristol BS8 3PF TEL. 0117-9733682 OWNER The University of Bristol HOURS Mon–Fri, except Bank Holidays, 9a.m.–5p.m., other times by appointment only ENTRANCE Free, except for prior arranged tours, £3 per person DIRECTIONS From Clifton, cross the suspension bridge and take 1st right (North Road), garden entrance on left after ¼m; from M5 exit at Jct 19, then last on left before the bridge WEB www.bris.ac.uk/depts/botanicgardens

Set on a hill among substantial suburban houses near the famous suspension bridge, this unusual five-acre garden is a hidden-away gem in the city, and extraordinarily peaceful. Its sheltered position and extensive walling provide an ideal home for many plants of borderline hardiness, with plant collections from Australia, New Zealand and southern Africa. Although its function is primarily as a botanic garden for the university (and thus the layout is piecemeal), it is intimate enough and sufficiently packed with plants to provide an afternoon's entertainment for any keen gardener. There are bamboos and bulbs, a collection of hebes and wonderful glasshouses filled with orchids, bromeliads, succulents and other tropical greenery.

TOCKINGTON

The Kitchen Garden and Old Down House

Oldown Country Park, Tockington, Bristol BS32 4PG TEL. 01454-413605
OWNER Mr and Mrs Robert Bernays HOURS Open all year, May–July and Sept,
Tues–Sun and Bank Holiday Mons, 10a.m.–5p.m.; Aug, daily, 10a.m.–5p.m.;
Oct–April, Tues–Sun and Bank Holiday Mons, 10a.m.–4p.m. ENTRANCE £3.75
DIRECTIONS 10m N of Bristol, follow brown Tourist Board signs to Oldown from
A38 at Alveston WEB www.oldown.co.uk

⬛ ♿ Access ⬛ Gift Shop ⬛ Café

Within easy reach of Bristol and Bath, this is a popular venue for family
outings, attracting over 100,000 visitors per year. What do they come
to see? The country park's main attraction is a highly productive one-
and-a-half-acre kitchen garden, but one with a difference. It isn't just a
visual experience – this is a pick-your-own establishment, with popular
soft fruits in great variety, so you can weave your way through the rows
picking raspberries, currants, strawberries, blackberries, gooseberries
and a few seasonal vegetables. It is an interesting enterprise, enabling
the old Victorian walled garden to be commercially viable, while still
being used as it was originally intended.

Apart from the quantities of sticky fruits to hand, children enjoy
the farm and meeting the animals and there are also lengthy woodland walks and fine views of the Severn bridge. The private gardens
around Old Down House (part of the property) are opened on one
or two afternoons each year, for the National Gardens Scheme charity.

The Cheddar Pink

Seedling trees and shrubs eke out a precarious living on the sheer
limestone cliffs of Cheddar Gorge, England's own Grand Canyon.
The chasms and caverns of this part of the Mendip Hills provide an
awesome spectacle popular with visitors, while the springy, thyme-
speckled turf above is the lone wild habitat of the Cheddar pink,
Dianthus gratianopolitanus (syn. *D. caesius*), one of Britain's most
endearing wildflowers. Its clove-scented, deep rose-pink flowers were
keenly sought by plant collectors and alpine gardeners during the
18th and 19th centuries. The Cheddar pink might easily have become
extinct but for some tenacious and out-of-reach plants surviving in
the most inaccessible crevices of the Gorge. Gardeners can find
nursery-raised stocks of this now protected species through specialist
alpine nurseries, including **Arne Herbs** (*q.v.*) at Chew Magna in
this region.

And also...

Arne Herbs, Limeburn Nurseries, Limeburn Hill, Chew Magna, Bristol BS40 8QW (tel. 01275-333399/web www.arneherbs.co.uk), offers around 600 culinary, aromatic and medicinal herbs by post (catalogue £2). A garden has recently been added to the Nursery. Visitors are welcomed, but an appointment is advisable. (Try to avoid visiting on Tuesdays or Saturdays if possible.) From A37 or A38 follow signs to Chew Magna, from village take road to Bishopsworth, nursery on left after 300yds.

Blackmore & Langdon, Stanton Nurseries, Pensford, Bristol BS39 4JL (tel. 01275-332300/web www.blackmore-langdown.com), specialises in phlox, begonias and, above all, delphiniums, for which stately plants the nursery has been famous since the early 1900s (July is therefore a rewarding time to visit). The catalogue (send a s.a.e.) lists old and new varieties, with informative notes, and there are also useful plant supports available by mail. Open Mon–Fri, 9a.m.–5p.m., Sat–Sun, 10a.m.–4p.m. From A37 take B3130 towards Bristol Airport, nursery on left after ½m.

Cadbury Garden and Leisure Centre, Smallway, Congresbury, Bristol BS49 5AA (tel. 01934-875700), covers 14 acres of a former salad nursery and offers large stocks of typical garden centre ranges of plants and sundries, well displayed. Open Mon, 9.30a.m.–6p.m.; Tues and Thurs–Sat, 9a.m.–6p.m.; Wed, 9a.m.–8p.m; Sun, 10.30a.m.–4.30p.m. M5 Jct 21, follow signs towards Bristol and at 2nd traffic lights turn left.

Anyone with a penchant for passion flowers should visit the **Passiflora National Collection, Greenholm Nurseries, Lampley Road, Kingston Seymour, Clevedon BS21 6XS (tel. 01934-833350)**, where nurseryman John Vanderplank cultivates over 200 species and varieties, both ornamental and edible, under glass. As well as hardy varieties, there are many suitable for the unheated conservatory or greenhouse and more tender specimens that require extra winter warmth. For mail order catalogue send a s.a.e. and £1 in stamps. Open Mon–Sat, 9a.m.–1p.m. and 2–5p.m. M5 Jct 20, follow signs to Clevedon, then Yatton, then Kingston Seymour.

Bedfordshire

The soil of rich clay which is a feature of this county gave rise to its centuries-old chief industries, brick-making and wheat-growing. It is a landscape of gentle undulations, sandwiched between a flat plain to the north and a southern boundary of chalk hills. However, more people rush through this county *en route* to somewhere else than pause to look at it, which has been the case since the Romans extended Watling Street (now the A5) to link St Albans with Wroxeter and Wales. The M1 slices its way through the south of the county, leaving its tranquil gardens relatively unexplored.

Exceptional in Spring
The Swiss Garden, Old
   Warden

OLD WARDEN

The Swiss Garden

Old Warden Park, Old Warden, Biggleswade SG18 9ER TEL. 01767-627666
OWNER Shuttleworth Trust (leased to Bedfordshire County Council) HOURS
March–Sept, Sun and Bank Holiday Mons, 10a.m.–6p.m.; Mon–Sat, 1–6p.m.
(last adm. 5.15p.m.); Jan, Feb and Oct, Suns only and New Year's Day,
11a.m.–3p.m. ENTRANCE £3, concessions/children £2, family ticket £8 (no dogs
allowed) DIRECTIONS 2½m from Biggleswade, signposted from A1 (2m away)
and from A600 (4m away) WEB www.bedfordshire.gov.uk

⬤ ⅄ **Access** ⬤ **Gift Shop** ⬤ **Plants for Sale**

The Swiss Garden

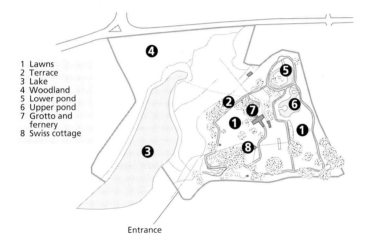

1 Lawns
2 Terrace
3 Lake
4 Woodland
5 Lower pond
6 Upper pond
7 Grotto and
  fernery
8 Swiss cottage

Entrance

'Romantic' is the adjective most usually applied to the nine-acre Swiss
Garden with its quaint Victorian cottage, dainty wrought-iron bridges
and wistful walks among cherry blossom and seas of daffodils. Spring
is a wonderful time to visit because the pastel colours lend the garden
a softness at this time, echoed by the meandering waters of the three
irregular ponds.

It is an introspective garden, hidden from the outside world by
gloomy shrubberies and large specimen conifers, many of the views
angling inwards to the garden's *pièce de résistance*, a tiny, hilltop
thatched cottage, appearing to be single-storey on one side, but with
two storeys visible from the other, where there is a partly concealed
basement set in the hill. It is worth inspecting the building at close
quarters to admire the patterned twigwork and pine cone decorations
under the eaves of the verandah's roof, and the detailed craftsmanship
within the cottage itself. There are statues, urns, ornamental islands

and marvellous specimen trees, but the other key feature at the garden's centre is the grotto and fernery – cool, damp and atmospheric, illuminated by shafts of sunlight through a moss-encrusted glass roof. The grotto is a cave-like structure of porous tufa stone, providing convenient cavities populated by ferns and ivies; the fernery is an important early example of cast ironwork with glass, dating from the early 1830s.

It is said that the garden was created by the 3rd Lord Longley, of the East India Company, for his mistress, and that it is haunted. Certainly, in spite of changing fortunes and recent restoration projects, this garden has managed to maintain its many attractive features and an eerie atmosphere of times past.

SILSOE

Wrest Park

Silsoe, Luton MK45 4HS TEL. 01525-860152 OWNER English Heritage HOURS April–Oct, Sat–Sun and Bank Holiday Mons only, 10a.m.–6p.m. (closes 5p.m. in Oct), last adm. 1hr before closing ENTRANCE £3.50, concessions £2.60, children £1.80 (under 5s free), family ticket £8.80 DIRECTIONS ¾m E of Silsoe village, off A6

Gift Shop   Café

You could be forgiven for thinking you had been transported back to 18th-century France when visiting Wrest Park; its mansion is a 19th-century copy of a French chateau, set in palatial grounds with formal box parterres and a long canal leading directly to a baroque pavilion, half a mile's walk from the house.

There are several distinct ages of garden design woven into the fabric of the park's 90 acres: the Long Water canal dates from the late 17th century, and is flanked by an early 18th-century woodland garden criss-crossed by straight rides, with smaller paths snaking their way through the trees, especially beautiful in spring and at leaf-fall in autumn. Capability Brown (*q.v.*) worked at Wrest in the mid-18th century, but his contribution was confined to far parts of the woodland garden, where he softened the contours of the formal canals surrounding the garden to provide a more naturalistic effect.

By the end of the same century Horace Walpole made no bones about the garden's outmoded formality, claiming it was 'very ugly in the old-fashioned manner, with high hedges and canals, at the End of the principal one of which is a frightful Temple...' New gardens, including the formal parterres, were added around the house when it was rebuilt in the 1830s, to the Francophile taste of its then owner.

Few visitors today would find the park ugly, or frightful, as Walpole did, and its peaceful greenery provides a perfect backdrop to its collections of statues and the elegant Chinese bridge. Do not miss the crumbling Bath House, a delightful fake ruin dating from 1770, sited at the water's edge, or the splendid French-style orangery which, in its heyday, is said to have housed the largest orange trees in England.

Whipsnade Tree Cathedral

Whipsnade, Dunstable OWNER The National Trust HOURS All hours ENTRANCE Free DIRECTIONS On W side of Whipsnade village, N of the village road; from M1, exit at Jct 9 and use A5, follow signs to Zoo and then Tree Cathedral

While Whipsnade is best known for its zoo, the village possesses an unusual horticultural landmark. This extraordinary man-made woodland dates from the 1930s and is laid out in cathedral plan, with a nave and transepts, chancel, chapels and an outer cloister, all formed by trees. The brainchild of Edmund Kell Blyth, it was planted to commemorate the loss of his two boyhood friends during World War I. Inspired by a visit to the newly built Liverpool Cathedral in 1930, Blyth embarked upon a plan to create his own cathedral, entirely of trees.

There is a chapel for each season: one of cherry trees for Easter, whitebeams (formerly elms) for summer, beech and cherry for autumn, and spruce firs for winter. The semi-circular chancel is of silver birch, and the cloister walk (with central dewpond) is formed from ash trees. The cathedral nave is of limes, while deodar cedars were chosen for the north transept, and horse chestnut for the south.

And also...

Bloms Bulbs, Primrose Nurseries, Melchbourne, Bedford MK44 1ZZ (tel. 01234-709099/web www.blomsbulbs.com), produces an explosively colourful, free catalogue for mail order bulbs listing over 400 varieties, with tulips a speciality.

Over 100 varieties of herbs and wildflowers are on sale at **The Seed Sowers Training Project, Stables Christian Centre, Bolnhurst, Bedford MK44 2ES (tel. 01234-376237)**. The five-acre grounds include a woodland walk, shop and refreshments. Open April–Oct, Sat, 2.30–5p.m. Entrance free. On B660, 7m N of Bedford, or 7m from A1, exit at Eaton Socon.

Toddington Manor, Toddington LU5 6HJ (tel. 01525-872576), is a garden of rich, traditional planting for the summer, with generously wide double herbaceous borders extending for 100 metres. Within the walled garden there is a substantial aromatic herb garden, long beds of peonies and delphiniums, glasshouses with orchids, fruit trees and walls garlanded with climbing roses and clematis. The attractive rose beds feature floribundas producing a long season of white and yellow flowers, punctuated by fragrant philadelphus. A stream runs through the garden to fill ponds within the grounds, which feature some splendid mature trees, wildflower meadows, orchards and woods. A great deal of work has been done here since 1979 to turn this garden into a stylish showpiece. Open May–Aug, Mon–Sat, 12 noon–5p.m. Entrance £3.50, OAPs £2.50, children £2. Signposted from Toddington, 1m NW of village.

Willington Garden Centre, Sandy Road, Willington, Bedford MK44 3QP (tel. 01234-838777/web www.frostgroup.com), is a substantial, well-stocked garden centre that has developed out of a 100-year-old nursery on the same site, and is still run by the same family. Open daily, Jan–Feb and Nov, 9a.m.–5p.m.; March, Sept–Oct and Dec, 9a.m.–5.30p.m.; April–Aug, 9a.m.–6p.m. From A1, take A603 towards Willington.

Berkshire

Royal Berkshire takes in the vast park and ancient Windsor Castle, home of kings and queens. The county's landscape is varied, with the great meanderings of the River Thames snaking across the middle, through a broad plain of fertile pastures, and is speckled with glorious gardens. The swooping uplands of the Chilterns line the northern boundary, and in the west racehorses gallop the chalk downs around Lambourn, where Bronze Age remains pepper the grassy hills.

Exceptional in Spring

Frogmore, Windsor Great
  Park
The Savill Garden, Windsor
  Great Park
The Valley Gardens, Windsor
  Great Park

Worth a Visit in Winter

The Living Rainforest,
  Newbury
The Savill Garden, Windsor
  Great Park

Period Plants Nursery

Elm Farm, Hamstead Marshall, Newbury RG20 0HR TEL. 01672-811738/
07767-411611 OWNER K. Bott and S. Zundel HOURS Open by appointment only
ENTRANCE Free DIRECTIONS S of the River Kennet, between Hungerford and
Newbury, in village of Hamstead Marshall, almost opposite the White Hart
Inn; from A4 follow signs to Hamstead Marshall
🌑 Plants for Sale 🌑 Nursery 🌑 Mail Order

If you're fascinated by the historical side of gardening, then this new
nursery will interest you. Its creators, Katy Bott and Sue Zundel, share
a passion for old plants and have decided to specialise in those that
were grown in British gardens before their cut-off date of 1700. They
offer specific collections of plants, such as medieval culinary herbs
(10 varieties, including angelica, lovage and savory); strewing herbs
– that were strewn on the ground in olden days and walked upon to
release their aromas; old-fashioned columbines; and low hedging
plants suitable for making Tudor-style knot-gardens. The general list
offers over 120 species and cultivars and makes interesting reading
as most entries are accompanied by notes of their historical uses.

A formal garden, laid out in a pattern of narrow beds, helps to
display the organically grown nursery stock. The plants are grouped
as much as possible into separate periods of plant history: one area
represents plants of the 10th to 12th centuries; another has 13th to
15th centuries; a third deals with the 16th century and the last deals
with the 17th century, including introductions by the John Tradescants (*q.v.*). Part of the enterprise's *raison d'être* is as an educational
aid for schools and Katy and Sue will be running a series of special
events and talks during 2000 for the general public (telephone for
details).

The Living Rainforest

Streatley Road, Hampstead Norreys, Thatcham, nr Newbury RG18 0TN
TEL. 01635-202444 OWNER Worldwide Land Conservation Trust HOURS Open all
year, daily, 10a.m.–5.15p.m. (last adm. 4p.m. in winter, 4.30p.m. in summer)
ENTRANCE £4.50, OAPs £3.50, under 16s £2.50, under 5s £1, family ticket £12
(all profits go to conservation work) DIRECTIONS M4 Jct 13 then go N on A34
and turn E onto B4009 WEB www.livingrainforest.org
🌑 ♿ Access 🌑 Gift Shop 🌑 Café 🌑 Plants for Sale

When it is cold or wet outside, a chance to retreat into the humid,
enveloping warmth of a tropical glasshouse is particularly seductive,

especially when the orchids or the giant waterlilies are in bloom. This glass-enveloped landscape covers 20,000 sq.ft and is as much an educational establishment as a practical home for tropical plants.

It is divided into three distinct, climatic areas with the temperature, humidity, ventilation and shade all monitored by computer. The Lowland Tropical area is the warmest, offering the deep shade and high humidity that nurtures lush, large-leaved anthuriums and alocasias. Fabulous orchids thrive in Amazonica, a brighter, less humid section, which is also home to *Victoria amazonica*, the extraordinary waterlily whose leaves can achieve an 8ft span in one season. The coolest house is Cloudforest, with temperatures similar to those of the Himalayan foothills, nurturing ferns, bromeliads and more orchids.

If you have children in tow, this is one garden they will really enjoy. Besides the spectacular plants, there are birds, fish and small mammals, demonstrating the symbiotic relationship between the flora and fauna of the rainforests.

The Loddon Lily

Resembling huge snowdrops, bearing sturdy, white bell-flowers on 2–3ft-high stems, the summer snowflake (*Leucojum aestivum*) is a captivating wildflower seen on some damp, southern river banks in May. It grows so plentifully on the sodden banks of the River Loddon in Berkshire that it has long enjoyed the popular title Loddon lily, forming white carpets among stands of willow. 'I have rarely seen anything more beautiful than a colony of the summer snowflake on the margin of a tuft of rhododendrons at Longleat,' declared William Robinson (*q.v.*) in his influential book *The Wild Garden* towards the close of the 19th century. 'Both the spring and summer snowflakes (*L. vernum* and *L. aestivum*) are valuable plants for wild grassy places, and the last grows freely in the good soil in the islets in the Thames near Wargrave.' At around the same time it was recorded that the flowers were used extensively for decorating Wargrave Church and that large quantities were gathered for sale in the streets of Oxford and for posies in local May Queen processions.

Robinson selected his own superior form of this handsome flower, naming it 'Gravetye Giant'. It is distinguished by its stout, strong stems and rich green, strappy foliage. Suppliers of 'Gravetye Giant' include Avon Bulbs (*q.v.*) and Hadspen Garden and Nursery (*q.v.*), both in Somerset.

Frogmore

Windsor Castle, Windsor SL4 1NJ TEL. 01753-869898 OWNER H.M. The Queen HOURS Open 1 Tues–Thurs in mid-May, 10a.m.–6p.m. and Aug Bank Holiday Sat–Mon, 10a.m.–4p.m. ENTRANCE May: garden and mausoleum £3, children free; house £3.60, OAPs £2.50, children £1.30; Aug: house, garden and mausoleum £5.20, OAPs £4.20, children £3.20 (no under 8s allowed in house) DIRECTIONS Entrance via Park Street gate into Long Walk (follow AA signs) WEB www.royalresidences.com

🚻 ⅙ Access 🚻 Café

'When we have done Broiling at Ascot, you shall cool yrself at Frogmore, where it looks very Ruralistic at present,' wrote Queen Charlotte (wife of George III) to Lord Harcourt in 1793. In those days it was the venue for lavish entertaining, but is now largely kept out of the public eye, being a private home where the present Queen comes to relax and enjoy its peace. Queen Victoria also loved Frogmore, and she and Prince Albert are buried here, in an imposing marble mausoleum. Queen Victoria's mother lies in a smaller mausoleum in the grounds.

Nevertheless, its fame isn't just as a royal graveyard. Thirty-five-acre Frogmore has a delightful, small park of immaculately kept, gentle hillocks and bulb-filled lawns, sloping easily down to a meandering canal that winds its way through the gardens. Little stone bridges cross the waters, and there are attractive pavilions dotted about the grounds, including a pretty, hexagonal teahouse draped in Chinese wisteria. Nearby are two ancient holm oaks under which Queen Victoria used to set up a tent, where she painted in summer. Although Frogmore gardens are opened rarely, for charity, they have tranquil beauty, immaculate upkeep and are well worth visiting.

The Savill Garden

Wick Lane, Englefield Green, Egham, Surrey TW20 0UU TEL. 01753-847518 OWNER The Crown Estate HOURS March–Oct, daily, 10a.m.–6p.m., Nov–Feb, daily, 10a.m.–4p.m. ENTRANCE April and May, £5, OAPs £4.50, children £2; June–Oct, £4, OAPs £3.50, children £1; Nov–March, £3, OAPs £2.50, children £1 (under 5s free at all times) DIRECTIONS 3m W of Egham by A30 and Wick Road, signposted; from M25 Jct 13 (3m away) follow Egham Road; from M4 Jct 6 take A308 through Old Windsor WEB www.savillgarden.org.uk

🚻 ⅙ Access 🚻 Gift Shop 🚻 Café 🚻 Plants for Sale

Only 35 of Windsor Great Park's 4500 acres are taken up by this popular garden which is one of my favourite spring-time haunts.

It is a woodland garden *par excellence,* with magnolias, rhododendrons, pieris and dogwoods under tree canopies of oaks and pines.

The garden also features a large collection of daffodil cultivars, individually grouped and well labelled, but even more attractive are the grassy slopes when covered with hoop-petticoat narcissi (*N. bulbocodium*) and patches of the dainty *Narcissus cyclamineus.* Informal gravel paths wind through the Dry Garden, where there are further colourful plantings of spring bulbs and Mediterranean plants. In the damper valleys, bright yellow kingcups and lysichitons line the bogs and streams among unfurling fern fronds. One of the garden's finest trees, an unusual Chilean *Podocarpus* in the herbaceous area, was quite unintended; it was a discarded nursery seedling that took root here 60-odd years ago. A modern glasshouse was added in 1995 to house more tender rhododendrons, and plants of the southern hemisphere.

Mrs Sinkins and her Pinks

The old-fashioned pink, *Dianthus* 'Mrs Sinkins', is a popular variety bearing attractively ragged, white flowers with a heady, clove scent. Its origins go back to the Slough of more than 100 years ago, when John Thomas Sinkins ran the Slough Poor Law Institution, with his wife, Catherine, as matron. John was a flower fancier who bred a new garden pink which caught the eye of Charles Turner, of the Royal Nurseries, in Slough.

Sinkins let the nursery raise the plant commercially on the condition that it was named after his wife. Supplies of *Dianthus* 'Mrs Sinkins' were made available to gardeners from the early 1870s onwards. Although its flowering period is brief, compared to more modern varieties, it is still valued, and appears in the coat of arms for Slough Borough.

WINDSOR GREAT PARK

The Valley Gardens

Windsor Great Park, Windsor SL4 2HT TEL. 01753-847518 OWNER The Crown Estate HOURS Open all year, daily, 8a.m.–7p.m. or sunset if sooner; possible closure in bad weather ENTRANCE April–May £5 for car and occupants (coin machine); all other times of year £3.50 DIRECTIONS 3m W of Egham by A30 and Wick Road, signposted

This is a huge garden within Windsor Great Park, extending to around 200 acres on the northern shores of Virginia Water lake.

Mature trees planted in the 1750s date from the time of William, Duke of Cumberland, the son of George II, and now provide some of the majestic framework to be enjoyed on the wooded slopes.

Rhododendrons flourish on the local, acid soil of Bagshot sand where they can be found in great variety decking the hillsides in drifts of shocking pink and orange, purple and delicate yellow. The Punch Bowl – a natural amphitheatre of great beauty – is the main area for spring's kaleidoscopic azalea show. The soil is also suitable for heathers displayed in vast numbers in the Heather Garden, beyond the pinetum. As well as native species and varieties, there are imported heathers that bring colour into the gardens at every stage of the year. There are also important collections of hollies, dwarf conifers and magnolias within the gardens.

And also...

Dorney Court, Dorney, Windsor SL4 6QP (tel. 01628-604638). This quaintly creaking Tudor manor of pink bricks and old oak timbers oozes character surrounded by wonderful yew topiary and ancient Buckinghamshire woods. Open July–Aug, Mon–Thurs, 1–4.30p.m.; other times by appointment only. Entrance £5, children £3 (under 9s free). M4 Jct 7 and follow signs. Of more interest to gardeners, however, is the **Bressingham Garden Centre (tel. 01628-669999)** in the grounds, featuring a wide range of plants raised by Blooms of Bressingham, notably perennials and conifers (open daily, March–Oct, 9a.m.–6p.m.; Nov–Feb, 9a.m.–5p.m.). Entrance free.

Foxgrove Plants, Foxgrove, Enborne, Newbury RG14 6RE (tel. 01635-40554), specialises in snowdrops which are sold 'in the green' (when in leaf) so that they have a better chance of establishing than if sold as dry bulbs (catalogue published each Feb £1). They also offer a range of alpines and small hardy plants (catalogue £1). There is no mail order service, but orders can be placed to collect from the various RHS shows around the country. Open all year, Wed–Sun and Bank Holiday Mons, 10a.m.–5p.m.; closed in Aug. From A34 take A343 towards Newbury, then Essex Street and Wheatlands Lane.

Waltham Place, Church Hill, White Waltham, Maidenhead SL6 3JH (tel. 01628-825517/824605/web www.waltham-place.org.uk), has 40 acres of organic gardens, including walled gardens, bluebell woods, fine specimen trees and a lake. Open April–Sept, Mon–Fri (closed Bank Holiday Mons), 10a.m.–5p.m. (guided walks and groups by appointment all year). Entrance £3.50, children £1. M4 Jct 8/9, take A404(M), come off at next exit, follow signs to White Waltham, left onto B3024, gardens on left.

Buckinghamshire

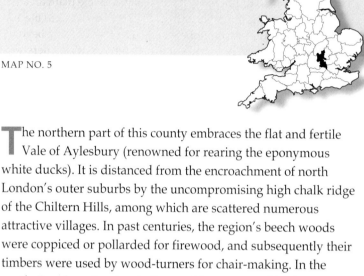

The northern part of this county embraces the flat and fertile Vale of Aylesbury (renowned for rearing the eponymous white ducks). It is distanced from the encroachment of north London's outer suburbs by the uncompromising high chalk ridge of the Chiltern Hills, among which are scattered numerous attractive villages. In past centuries, the region's beech woods were coppiced or pollarded for firewood, and subsequently their timbers were used by wood-turners for chair-making. In the south, Burnham Beeches is the most famous wood in the Chilterns. Many of its trees are stout and ancient pollards, of massive girth and enormous character, bearing twisted and misshapen trunks.

Must See

Chenies Manor House, Amersham – wonderfully effective seasonal flowers nurtured by the owner

Stowe, Buckingham – heroic 18th-century landscape on the grand scale

Turn End, Haddenham – artistically arranged, intimate town garden

Worth a Visit in Winter

Waddesdon Manor, Aylesbury

Stowe, Buckingham

Cliveden, Taplow

AMERSHAM

Chenies Manor House

Chenies, nr Amersham WD3 6ER TEL. 01494-762888 OWNER Mrs MacLeod Matthews HOURS April–Oct, Wed–Thurs, 2–5p.m. (last adm. to house 4.15p.m.); also Bank Holiday Mons, 2–5p.m. ENTRANCE House and garden £5, children £3; garden only £3, children £1.50 DIRECTIONS In Chenies village, off A404 between Amersham and Rickmansworth; from M25 Jct 18 follow signs to Amersham for 2m

🟦 ♿ Access 🟦 Gift Shop 🟦 Café

When Elizabeth and Alistair MacLeod Matthews bought the red-brick Elizabethan manor in the 1950s, practically nothing remained of the four-acre Tudor garden that had once surrounded it. They therefore made their own gardens of topiaries and colourful flowers, in the spirit of Tudor formality if not in detail, for this garden has its own style and is not a slave to historical dogma. Neat lawns beside the house lead to a trelliswork screen of dark green ivy, beyond which is a brilliantly colourful sunken garden, filled with tulips in spring and with dahlias and other bedding flowers in summer.

There is an interesting physic garden of medicinal and culinary herbs, a turf maze, a productive and very attractive kitchen garden, a pleached lime tunnel and a narrow *allée* lined with velvet-smooth cypress hedging, proving that × *Cupressocyparis leylandii* need not be a monstrous hedger, provided it is regularly tamed with shears. The White Garden, especially effective in the twilight of summer evenings, is planted with white cosmos and marguerites, grey-leaved and variegated plants and stout topiary birds in yew. All is immaculately maintained by Elizabeth MacLeod Matthews and one helper.

AYLESBURY

Waddesdon Manor

Waddesdon, nr Aylesbury HP18 0JH TEL. 01296-653211 (infoline); 01296-653203 (administration) OWNER The National Trust HOURS Early March–Christmas, Wed–Sun and Bank Holiday Mons, 10a.m.–5p.m.; sculpture in the garden uncovered week before Easter, weather permitting; house open (by timed ticket, no children under 5), April–Oct, Thurs–Sun and Bank Holiday Mons (also Weds in July–Aug), 11a.m.–4p.m. ENTRANCE Grounds £3, children £1.50, family ticket £7.50 (free from early Nov–Christmas); house £7, children £6, under 5s free DIRECTIONS 6m NW of Aylesbury on A41, entrance in Waddesdon village WEB www.waddesdon.org.com

🟦 ♿ Access 🟦 Gift Shop 🟦 Café

The manor, built by Baron Ferdinand de Rothschild in the 1870s, is a magnificent French-style chateau, the stuff of fairy tales perched on a cold – and formerly bare – Buckinghamshire hilltop. Baron Ferdinand, it is said, had a special strain of Percheron cart-horse bred to transplant full-grown trees to the new site, with teams of 20 horses used to draw the vast trees along the village High Street.

The north front of the house faces a long, straight carriage drive, leading to a circular pool with an elaborate fountain centrepiece. The south side features Italianate terraces and parterres in a symmetrical design, with bedded-out spring and summer flowers and golden topiaries. This area will hold special interest over the next five years, as each year a leading artist will be invited to create schemes for two of the flowerbeds in the Victorian parterre. So far we have had artist John Hubbard (in 2000) and the couturier Oscar de la Renta (in 2001) successfully providing a modern twist to the Victorian passion for carpet bedding.

The former 'Daffodil Valley' on a western slope, once a breath-taking sight in spring, is now an area for wildflowers including orchids, primroses and cowslips, since the daffodils succumbed to an eelworm-propagated virus. Don't miss the grand aviary near the valley, built by Baron Ferdinand in the French 16th-century style. There are also miles of parkland walks among great trees and shrubberies.

The Waddesdon Dairy and Water Garden, part of the estate, is a luxurious venue hired out for private functions, but its interesting water and rock garden, a well-restored Victorian feature, is opened a few days each year for the National Gardens Scheme charities.

BUCKINGHAM

Stowe Landscape Gardens

Stowe, Buckingham MK18 5EH TEL. 01280-822850 OWNER The National Trust HOURS March–Oct and Dec, Wed–Sun and Bank Holiday Mons (also Tues in July–early Sept), 10a.m.–5p.m.; last adm. 4p.m. (3p.m. in Dec) ENTRANCE £4.80, children £2.40 (under 5s free), family ticket £11.90 DIRECTIONS M40 Jct 9, then A421 to Buckingham, then N on A422, turn right towards Dadford and follow signs

🌿 Gift Shop   🌿 Café

It is said that England's greatest contribution to world art is the landscape garden. And Stowe is great. Like Castle Howard (*q.v.*) in Yorkshire, it is a heroic landscape on the grandest scale, with a ½-mile beech and chestnut avenue leading from the Buckingham entrance to a triumphal arch, from where you can look upon the 325-acre garden laid out around the magnificent mansion which is now Stowe School. The list of landscapers who helped is impressive: Sir John Vanbrugh, Charles Bridgeman and William Kent were involved in the early work; Lord Cobham, the owner, involved himself in the development of the grounds and employed the young Capability Brown (*q.v.*) who became head gardener in 1741 (at the age of 25) and laid out the Grecian Valley. Stowe's waters, vistas, numerous garden buildings and undercurrents of allegory make an exhilarating visit, beautiful and atmospheric in every season.

HADDENHAM

Turn End

Townside, Haddenham, Aylesbury HP17 8BG TEL. 01844-291383/291817
OWNER Peter and Margaret Aldington HOURS Some Suns in June for NGS charities, 2–6p.m., groups by appointment at other times ENTRANCE £2, children 50p DIRECTIONS 7m SW of Aylesbury, from A418 go to Haddenham, then from Thame road turn at Rising Sun into Townside and on left
 ⛺ ♿ Access ⛺ Plants for Sale

This is a really delightful, small, private garden with oodles of atmosphere, and the owner's love for the place imbued in every pot and plant. From some viewpoints it looks Mediterranean, with tile-topped rendered walls and dry gravel paths. Other parts convey timeless English woodland, carpeted with primroses and bluebells. Elsewhere, a fairly dark, enclosed area wedged behind outbuildings turns out to be a formal courtyard planted with a box-edged parterre, seasonally laced with single-colour bedding plants. A broad sweep of lawn meanders across the site bringing green spaciousness into the picture.

Just over thirty years ago the owner, an architect, won a prestigious architectural award for the courtyard development which includes his home and two others (not open). The garden developed piecemeal as the Aldingtons were able to buy up adjacent parcels of land. 'The aim when we started out was to make a labour-saving garden – an abysmal failure, as it turned out,' says Peter. His passion for plants took hold and he lavishly planted roses and clematis, bearded irises, peonies, euphorbias, troughs and pots of alpines, violas, fritillaries and countless spring flowers. It is carefully managed profusion, planted with a most artistic eye.

Bernwode Plants

Large quantities of herbs and unusual hardy perennials are the speciality of **Bernwode Plants, Kingswood Lane, Ludgershall, Aylesbury HP18 9RB (tel. 01844-237415), 11m W of Aylesbury, then 1m SE of Ludgershall off the Wotton road, from A41 follow signs towards Brill**. I first met Derek and Judy Tolman 14 years ago, when they had recently quit city life in favour of the Good Life to set up their nursery. Its list is now extensive and has recently expanded to include a selection of old apple cultivars and other fruits. Plants are available by mail and the catalogue (send 8 × 1st-class stamps or £2) is exceptionally well produced, with many interesting descriptions, especially where plants have historical interest. Open March–Oct, Tues–Sun and Bank Holiday Mons, 10a.m.–5p.m. or dusk if earlier.

TAPLOW

Cliveden

Taplow, Maidenhead SL6 0JA TEL. 01628-605069 OWNER The National Trust HOURS Mid-March–Oct, daily, 11a.m.–6p.m.; Nov–Dec, daily, 11a.m.–4p.m. Closed Jan–Feb ENTRANCE £6, children £3 (under 5s free), family ticket £15 DIRECTIONS 2m N of Taplow off A4 on B476; from M4 Jct 7 take the A4, then follow signs

🅿 ♿ Access 🛍 Gift Shop ☕ Café

In this well-heeled area embracing the upper Thames, fabulous houses lie behind high gates and, towering over them all, like a temple of Mammon, sits Cliveden, perched on its chalk eyrie in 10 acres of gardens. The house (now a luxurious hotel) was built by Sir Charles Barry in 1850, but was bought by William Waldorf (1st Viscount) Astor in 1893. Astor brought a balustrade from the Villa Borghese in Rome, several ancient Roman sarcophagi, vast urns and statuary, and laid out a serene topiary garden and an oriental-style water garden. An intimate rose garden hidden in the woods was designed by Sir Geoffrey Jellicoe.

A broad, lawned platform below the house is planted with a formal box parterre, infilled with seas of mauve nepeta, and grey santolina and senecio which, while somewhat uninspired, does not detract from the main point of this area – its spectacular views of the Thames and surrounding landscape. There are plenty of shady walks on hot summer days, and rough steps descend the cliff to the river.

West Wycombe Park

West Wycombe HP14 3AJ TEL. 01494-513569 OWNER The National Trust HOURS April–Aug, Sun–Thurs, 2–6p.m. (last adm. 5.15p.m.) House open June–Aug only ENTRANCE £2.60, children £1.30 (£4.60, children £2.30, family ticket £11.50, includes house, June–Aug) DIRECTIONS From M40 Jct 4 take A4010 towards Aylesbury, then left onto A40, through West Wycombe village, Park on left

⬛ ♿ Access

Here is an 18th-century landscape garden of sublime tranquillity, dotted with classical statues and pavilions, and an exquisite music temple, serenely reflected in the waters of a large lake. There are plantations of fine trees contrasting with open lawns, quaint timber bridges cross the streams, and you can be thrilled by the sound of a magnificent, flint-enclosed, gushing cascade.

Can it be that this park is the creation of the same man who founded the infamous Hell-Fire Club? It is. 'Fornication, adultery, whore-mongering, drunkenness, blasphemy, gambling, and atheism were thought, by the pious, to be increasing at an alarming rate in the 18th century,' explains Eric Towers in his book *Dashwood: the Man and the Myth*. At the same time, Sir Francis Dashwood, from 1735 until his death in 1781, worked on his 350-acre garden, creating a formal landscape in the early years which was overlaid with softer contours as the naturalistic influences of Capability Brown (*q.v.*) became *de rigueur*. Little has altered since, although the National Trust's summer evening concerts are not quite the Bacchanalian revelries the park witnessed in its youth.

Ascott

Wing, nr Leighton Buzzard LU7 0PR TEL. 01296-688242 OWNER The National Trust HOURS April and Sept, Tues–Sun, 2–6p.m.; garden only May–Aug, Wed and last Sun in month, 2–6p.m. Open some Bank Holiday Mons ENTRANCE £4, children £2 DIRECTIONS From A505 take A418

⬛ ♿ Access

This 35-acre garden is so redolent of the Victorian age when it was created that you might expect to see ladies tightly waisted and bustled, taking a leisured perambulation (with parasol in hand) through the park.

It was laid out in the late 19th century by Leopold de Rothschild, with the help of the Veitch Nursery of Chelsea. It is famous for its trees, topiaries and formal seasonal bedding, all signature features of the Victorian era. One area, hedged in golden-leaved yews and golden holly, draws in the yellows of the cornfields lying in the Vale of Aylesbury beyond the garden's boundaries. Another topiary area conveys the sentiments of the age with a sundial (its gnomon in green and golden yew) surrounded by the hedged inscription 'Light and shade by turn but love always'. The Roman numerals of the sundial are fashioned in clipped box.

Developments continue in this beautifully maintained garden, including an astrological garden (again laid out with topiary plants), relevant to the birth dates of Sir Evelyn and Lady de Rothschild.

And also...

Bekonscot Model Village, Warwick Road, Beaconsfield HP9 2PL (tel. 01494-672919/web www.bekonscot.org.uk), is huge fun. It is the oldest model village in the world, covering one and a half acres, and is planted with over 8000 conifers and 2000 miniature shrubs; 200 tons of stone have been used to make its rockeries. It offers a nostalgic glimpse of English village life in the 1930s in a series of cameo scenes, with cricket on the village green, the local hunt riding by and the sounds of the choir emanating from the church, all within a quaint garden setting. Open mid-Feb–Oct, daily, 10a.m.–5p.m. Entrance £4.50, concessions £3.50, children £2.75, family ticket £12.50. M40 Jct 2 and follow signs.

Buckingham Nurseries and Garden Centre, Tingewick Road, Buckingham MK18 4AE (tel. 01280-813556/web www.buckingham-nurseries.com), specialises in trees, shrubs and conifers suitable for hedging (whatever sort of hedge you want, you will almost certainly find it here). The prices are very reasonable, especially for bare-rooted plants available for autumn–winter planting. The Nursery provides a free catalogue. Open all year, Mon–Wed and Fri, 8.30a.m.–6p.m., Thurs, 8.30a.m.–7.30p.m., and Sun, 10a.m.–4p.m. (closes at 5.30p.m. in winter). M40 Jct 9, then A421, nursery 1m W of Buckingham.

Cambridgeshire

MAP NO. 6

This small, relentlessly flat county is part of the East Anglian fenlands, a region of dark, alluvial soil and lonely marshes, criss-crossed by drainage ditches, with the level horizon intermittently broken by the shimmering silhouettes of willows. The Romans first tried to drain the fens, but it was not until the arrival of Dutch engineers in the 17th century that the landscape became useful pasture, speckled with windmills driving huge pumps. The River Ouse winds a lazy route across the county, dividing north from south. The historic university city is crammed with beautiful buildings and bicycles, the favoured mode of transport by students and staff alike.

Must See

Anglesey Abbey, Lode – grand scale 20th-century garden, beautifully maintained

Crossing House Garden, Shepreth – unique railway-side setting

Worth a Visit in Winter

Cambridge University Botanic Garden, Cambridge

Anglesey Abbey, Lode

Cambridge University Botanic Garden

Cory Lodge, Bateman Street, Cambridge CB2 1JF TEL. 01223-336265 OWNER University of Cambridge HOURS Open all year, daily, 10a.m.–6p.m. (5p.m. in Feb and Oct, 4p.m. in Nov–Jan) ENTRANCE £2, children/OAPs £1.50, disabled and helpers free DIRECTIONS Entrance on Bateman Street, 1m S of city centre, and off Station Road WEB www.botanic.cam.ac.uk

🟥 ৬ Access 🟥 Gift Shop 🟥 Café 🟥 NPC

Any time of year is a good time to visit this diverse garden, set in a rectangular site of nearly 40 acres in the city's southern suburbs. Its many mature trees, including handsome cedars and pines, bring height and a sense of enclosure into this level site, and its winding paths ramble pleasantly through a series of areas, including herbaceous beds, systematic order beds (where plants are grouped according to their botanical families) and an ecological area. The best features are the rock and water gardens (with a beautiful madrona tree) beside a naturalistic lake, and the clutch of glasshouses nurturing desert and Mediterranean plants, tropical flowering plants, palms and rainforest trees, orchids and cacti. The glasshouses make a warmly welcoming refuge in winter, but outdoors the mid-winter gardens are colourful with stems of dogwoods, willows and brambles among bright-foliage conifers.

The Manor

Hemingford Grey, nr Huntingdon PE28 9BN TEL. 01480-463134 OWNER Mrs D. S. Boston HOURS Open all year, 10a.m.–6p.m. House visits by appointment only ENTRANCE Garden only £1, children 50p (parties can book to see the house, £4 and £1.50) DIRECTIONS At Hemingford Grey, off A14, 3m SE of Huntingdon. Park in village and enter via towpath on River Ouse

Foreign visitors to Hemingford Grey have been known to call this four-and-a-half-acre garden a 'delicious slice of England'. The house was built around 1130 and is reputedly the oldest, continuously inhabited house in the country, with much of its moated Norman structure intact. It became famous in the 1950s, when Lucy Boston wrote a series of children's books about Green Knowe (modelled on Hemingford Grey), that acquired a worldwide following.

Lucy Boston died in 1990, aged 97, but her daughter-in-law, Diana Boston, is working hard to maintain the Green Knowe legacy in the house and garden. The latter boasts herbaceous borders in traditional style, with an old-fashioned mix of delphiniums, pinks, lavender, phlox and, especially, roses. Lucy Boston planted only roses that were known prior to 1900, and around 200 of them are still here. Garden visitors enter via a small gate, attracted by the cascades of mid-summer roses in bloom. There are also splendid yew topiary 'cottage loaves', with cross finials on top.

LODE

Anglesey Abbey and Garden

Lode, Cambridge CB5 9BJ TEL. 01223-811200 OWNER The National Trust HOURS March–Oct, Wed–Sun and Bank Holiday Mons, 10.30a.m.–5.30p.m., last adm. 4.30p.m. (house open 1–5p.m.). Also garden only, Nov–Feb, Thurs–Sun, 11a.m.–4p.m. or dusk if earlier ENTRANCE £6.25, children £3, but Sun and Bank Holiday Mons £7, children £3.50; garden only £3.85 (£3.25 in winter), children £1.75 DIRECTIONS In village of Lode, 6m NE of Cambridge on B1102, signposted from A14 2m away

🔲 ♿ Access 🔲 Gift Shop 🔲 Café 🔲 Plants for Sale

Anglesey Abbey

1 Coronation Avenue	7 Cross Avenue
2 Lode Mill	8 Formal garden
3 Pilgrim's Lawn	9 Anglesey Abbey
4 East Lawn	10 Herbaceous garden
5 South Park	11 Emperors' Walk
6 Temple Lawn	

Entrance

Ninety-eight acres of windswept Cambridgeshire fenland may seem an unpromising site for a garden, but the Anglesey estate, sold in 1926 to Huttleston Broughton, the first Lord Fairhaven, had two things in its favour: the romantic remains of an Augustinian abbey, and the tremendous vision of its new owner who had the means to lay out a magnificent park.

Be prepared for a good long walk, if you want to see it all. Vast avenues and vistas were created to provide the perfect setting for the owner's collection of 18th- and 19th-century statuary. The Emperors' Walk, for example, runs a straight quarter mile. It was formed to display a dozen busts of Roman emperors carved from Carrara marble. The Coronation Avenue of magnificent chestnut trees extends for more than half a mile.

There are also fine flower gardens, including a D-shape traditional herbaceous border, wonderful at mid-summer, sheltered by tall beech hedges. A formal area of symmetrical beds, enclosed by precision-cut yew hedges, is fragrant with bedded-out hyacinths in spring, which are replaced by blocks of scarlet and golden dahlias for a late summer display. Bulbs, berries and colourfully-stemmed shrubs have been added to brighten up winter visits.

Fenland Sweet Peas

Fragrant sweet peas were in great demand 100 years ago. **Unwins Seeds, Histon, Cambridge CB4 9LE (tel. 01945-588522)**, is one of the nurseries which has specialised in these flowers since the early 20th century, when William Unwin, an enthusiast, issued his first modest seed list of home-raised varieties. Their list today includes over 50 varieties, covering all available colours and shades. The free colour catalogue also covers a wide seed list of other flowers and vegetables. Mail order only.

SHEPRETH

Crossing House Garden

Meldreth Road, Shepreth, Royston SG8 6PS TEL. 01763-261071 OWNER Mr and Mrs D.G. Fuller and John Marlar HOURS Open all year, daily, dawn–dusk ENTRANCE Donation DIRECTIONS 8m S of Cambridge, ½m W of A10, follow signs to Shepreth

Here is one railway level crossing where you will never get bored while waiting for the express trains between Cambridge and London to fly past. The commuters on board get a jolt, too, when they reach Shepreth, for the colourful Crossing House Garden looms into view, with its tapestry of flowers strung along the railwayside.

Margaret and Douglas Fuller came to The Crossing House in 1959, when Douglas was appointed crossing keeper. Nowadays the crossing is automatically operated, but the Fullers have remained in their eccentric, wedge-shape plot and continue to tend the quarter-acre garden crammed with all manner of decorative trees and shrubs, roses, perennials and colourful annuals (they reckon to have around 5000 different plants). There are beds, a lawn edged with dwarf box, topiary in box and yew, three small greenhouses packed with orchids and alpines, and much more. Fortunately, the Fullers like trains although Margaret preferred the days of the steam engines 'when people waved out of the windows'.

SHEPRETH
Docwra's Manor

Shepreth, Royston SG8 6PS TEL. 01763-260235/261557 OWNER Mrs John Raven HOURS Open all year, Wed and Fri, 10a.m.–4p.m.; also 1st Sun of month April–Oct, 2–4p.m. and NGS charity open days ENTRANCE £3, £4 for special openings, extra for tour DIRECTIONS In Shepreth village, opposite war memorial
🚗 ♿ Access 🚗 Plants for Sale

Plants have a free rein in this delightfully informal two-and-a-half-acre garden, made over the last 40 years by the late John Raven (a scholar and botanist) and his wife, Faith. An enormous range of plants is gathered here, with particular emphasis on those hailing from dry habitats such as the Mediterranean. The garden is divided into a series of enclosed areas, separated by walls and hedges which provide some wind shelter; within, self-sown plants enhance the garden's feeling of natural abundance. The emphasis on species, rather than garden hybrids, is refreshing and instructive.

WISBECH
Peckover House

North Brink, Wisbech PE13 1JR TEL. 01945-583463 OWNER The National Trust HOURS Late March–early Nov, Sat–Thurs, 12.30–5p.m.; house Wed, Sat–Sun and Bank Holiday Mons (also Thurs, July–Aug), 1.30–4.30p.m. ENTRANCE £3.80, children £1.50 (on garden only days £2.50, children £1.25) DIRECTIONS On N bank of River Nene, in Wisbech (B1441), ¾m from A47 (limited parking available 10 mins from house)
🚗 ♿ Access 🚗 Café 🚗 Plants for Sale

Graceful Georgian houses lining the River Nene at Wisbech belonged to merchants who traded on the then navigable waters, when the town was a thriving port. Peckover House is a classic example, formerly belonging to a prosperous Quaker family, and its garden is a rare and spacious survival of a Victorian layout, covering two acres. Within you will see a rustic summerhouse, yew topiaries, fine specimen trees, including an old *Ginkgo biloba*, and fan palms on broad lawns, summer bedding and a fine orangery complete with ancient orange trees. The potted plant displays of ivies, ferns, aspidistras, primulas, geraniums, gloxinias and Malmaison carnations are a notable Victorian feature in the glasshouse.

Fragrant Fields of Hyacinths

Picture a vast plain, with pastel rainbow stripes running like colourful ribbons into the distant horizon. For a brief spell in late March and early April, this transformation occurs on the dark, peaty fenlands of Waterbeach, when the National Collection of hyacinths is in bloom, its heady perfumes fleetingly carried away by the winds. Farmer Alan Shipp turned to hyacinths in the mid-1980s, and part of his 100-acre holding is now devoted to these exotic bulbs, instead of the more prosaic wheat, sugar beet and potatoes that surround them.

Today's garden hyacinths trace their ancestry to the wild *Hyacinthus orientalis* of Asia Minor, first grown in Europe in 1573 by botanist Carolus Clusius in Vienna. On moving to Holland, Clusius took his bulbs with him and within the space of 100 years they had spawned a lucrative industry. Two hundred years after Clusius planted his first bulbs there were 351 cultivars for sale and by the mid-1800s 2000 varieties had been bred. Now there are only perhaps 240, for many old strains are extinct, and the **National Collection, 9 Rosemary Road, Waterbeach CB5 9NB (tel. 01223-571064)** extends to 111. They can be seen on just one open weekend, usually at the end of March. Entrance fee £1. The open day is not held at this address, but is signposted from the A10.

And also...

Bulbeck Foundry, Reach Road Industrial Estate, Burwell CB5 0AH (tel. 01638-743153/web www.bulbeckfoundry.co.uk), manufactures English lead statuary, such as fountains, urns, planters and troughs in a range of traditional designs and also undertakes restoration work of lead antiques. Catalogue free on request. Open Mon–Fri, 8.30a.m.–5.30p.m., but phone before visiting. From A14 take B1102 to Burwell, left in village towards Reach, on left.

Elton Hall, Elton, Peterborough PE8 6SH (tel. 01832-280468). The gardens contain herbaceous borders, old roses and fine trees. Open

Spring Bank Holiday Sun and Mon; June, Wed; July and Aug, Wed–Thurs, Sun and August Bank Holiday, 2–5p.m. (parties by appointment on other days, April–Sept). Entrance (house and garden) £5, children (15 and under) free (garden £3). Off A605 near A1. The **Bressingham Plant Centre (tel. 01832-280058)** at Elton Hall opens daily, 9a.m.–5p.m. (6p.m. in summer), offering alpines, conifers, climbers and herbaceous perennials in the old walled kitchen garden. Entrance free.

Columbines, granny's bonnets, granny's nightcaps – call them what you will, aquilegias are enchanting flowers of damp meadows, woodlands and alpine pastures, tremendously varied in shape, colour and size. John Drake keeps a National Collection of them in his attractive, windy garden outside Cambridge at **Hardwicke House, Fen Ditton CB5 8TF (tel. 01223-292246)**, open by appointment and for the National Gardens Scheme. Entrance £3.

The Herbary, Mile End Road, Prickwillow, Ely CB7 4SJ (tel. 01353-688392), sells fresh-cut culinary herbs, edible flowers and speciality leaf-salads by mail, amounting to around 20 varieties. The price list is free.

Monksilver Nursery, Oakington Road, Cottenham CB4 8TW (tel. 01954-251555), is a plant connoisseur's dream nursery full of rare and choice plants, tantalisingly seldom open to visitors but redeemed by a mail order catalogue (8 × 1st-class stamps). Herbaceous perennials, particularly pulmonarias, lamiums, mildew-resistant monardas and galeobdolons feature, with new plants from recent Far Eastern expeditions, and unusual shrubs. Open March–June, Fri–Sat only, 10a.m.–4p.m. M11 to end, then A14 towards Huntingdon, take 1st turning towards Oakington, over flyover and through Westwick, after 1m nursery on right.

Wimpole Hall, Arrington, Royston SG8 0BW (tel. 01223-207257/web www.wimpole.org), is the largest country house in Cambridgeshire, an imposing 18th-century mansion set in park landscaped first by Charles Bridgeman (in the 1720s) followed by Capability Brown (*q.v.*) and Humphry Repton (*q.v.*), with a model farm attached. There are many wonderful trees in the 350-acre park, and its colourful parterre garden was recently restored by the National Trust. Garden open mid-March–Oct, Tues–Thurs, Sat–Sun and Bank Holiday Mons, 10.30a.m.–5p.m., (Tues–Sun in July–Aug), house open 1–5p.m. Also garden only, Nov–March, Sat–Sun, 11a.m.–4p.m. Entrance £2.50, children free (£5.90 and £2.70 for hall and garden). M11 Jct 12, off A603 between Cambridge and Sandy.

Cheshire

The fertile Cheshire plain is rich farming country, with hedged and tree-lined pastures, watered by countless small canals and meres. Much of the county is spread over low ground, with gentle undulations here and there, and trees grow well in this region of rich soil and relatively high rainfall. It changes character to the east, where steep moorland rises on the edge of the Pennine range and sheep graze the hillsides. The ancient and prosperous city of Chester was founded by the Romans, who built the foundations of its two-mile city wall.

Must See
Tatton Park, Knutsford – classic Victorian garden in tranquil park
Bridgemere, Nantwich – huge garden centre with fascinating display gardens

Exceptional in Spring
Dunham Massey Hall, Altrincham
Cholmondeley, Malpas

Worth a Visit in Winter
Tatton Park, Knutsford
Bridgemere, Nantwich
Ness Botanic Gardens, Neston
Lyme Park, Stockport

ALTRINCHAM

Dunham Massey Hall

Dunham Massey, Altrincham WA14 4SJ TEL. 0161-941 1025 OWNER The
National Trust HOURS Garden April–Sept, daily, 11a.m.–5.30p.m. (last adm.
5p.m.), Oct–Nov, daily, 11a.m.–4.30p.m.; park all year, daily ENTRANCE Garden
£3.20, children £1.60; park only £3 per car DIRECTIONS M56 Jct 7, 2m SW of
Altrincham, off A56, signposted

🞄 ⚇ Access 🞄 Gift Shop 🞄 Café 🞄 Plants for Sale

The 30 acres of fine gardens are embraced by a 350-acre park within
a vast estate. The gardens demonstrate the layered effect of different
periods: there is an Elizabethan mount, a moat lake, an 18th-century
orangery, well-preserved Victorian pleasure grounds with extensive
shrubberies and an Edwardian parterre.

Its appeal lies in the skilful blending of these elements, especially
the streamside and woodland plantings. The rhododendron collection, ribbons of cobalt blue meconopsis and contrasting swathes
of pink persicaria are some of the spring-into-early-summer enchant-
ments. The standard of upkeep is also exceptionally high.

DUTTON

Bluebell Cottage and Lodge Lane Nursery

Lodge Lane, Dutton, nr Warrington WA4 4HP TEL. 01928-713718 OWNER Rod
and Diane Casey HOURS Garden May–Aug, Fri–Sun and Bank Holiday Mons,
10a.m.–4.30p.m.; nursery mid-March–mid-Sept, Fri–Sun and Bank Holiday
Mons, 10a.m.–5p.m., at other times by appointment only ENTRANCE £2,
children free, nursery free DIRECTIONS From M56 Jct 10 take A49 towards
Whitchurch, turn right at lights onto A533 towards Runcorn, then take 1st left

🞄 ⚇ Access 🞄 Plants for Sale 🞄 Nursery

Bluebell Cottage seems to have something for everyone. It features
herbaceous borders cut as island beds in the lawn and beside the
whitewashed, slate-roofed cottage there are wonderful shelved
displays of potted pelargoniums and a gravelled area with troughs
of saxifrages. The one-and-a-half-acre garden also features a pond
and bog garden, a scree garden planted with euphorbias, thrift and
sempervivums, and plenty of seats strategically placed to take in
different views. You can also stroll beside a delightful three-acre
wildflower meadow (at its best in June and early July), which leads
to a natural woodland.

The Lodge Lane nursery next door is stocked with more than 2000
different perennials and shrubs, and is particularly rich in achillea,
allium, aster, campanula, geranium, penstemon, nepeta and salvia.

'You are unlikely to find a wider choice of perennials in any other nursery in the county,' say proprietors Rod and Diane Casey, who have been developing the nursery and garden since 1993.

KNUTSFORD

Tatton Park

Knutsford WA16 6QN TEL. 01625-534437 OWNER The National Trust HOURS April–mid-Oct, park daily, 10a.m.–6p.m., garden Tues–Sun, 10.30a.m.–5p.m.; late Oct–March, park Tues–Sun, 11a.m.–4p.m., garden Tues–Sun, 11a.m.–3p.m. ENTRANCE Park £3.50 per vehicle, garden £3, children £2; house and garden £4.60, children £2.60 DIRECTIONS 3½m N of Knutsford, 4m S of Altrincham, 5m from M6 Jct 19 or follow signs from M56 Jct 7. Well signposted on A556. WEB www.tattonpark.org.uk

🎖 ᕴ Access 🎖 Gift Shop 🎖 Café 🎖 Plants for Sale 🎖 2 for 1 Voucher

This 60-acre garden is a sumptuous period piece, summing up many of the gardening ideals of the 19th century. Its neo-classical mansion of pinky-grey sandstone gazes over terraced lawns to a swanky Italianate parterre (probably designed by Sir Joseph Paxton) filled with seasonal bedding plants. There are two very fine glasshouses – an orangery built in 1818 that is still used for nurturing citrus fruits, and a handsome fernery which houses a collection of prehistoric-looking dicksonia tree ferns from the antipodes. There are further formal flower gardens, with mixed shrub and herbaceous borders, rose beds and neatly clipped yews.

The most celebrated part of Tatton Park is its Oriental Garden, laid out in 1910 by Japanese landscapers, with a still, dark pool fed by four streams. A great deal of money and effort has been invested in its restoration. It is richly planted with azaleas and acers, ferns, irises, willows and mosses. Flat stone bridges cross the waters, leading to a ceremonial tea-house with a thatched roof. It is a place of abundance and tranquillity, surrounded by some of the magnificent trees of the park. Since 1999, Tatton Park has also hosted a spectacular summer show for the Royal Horticultural Society in late July.

MALPAS

Cholmondeley Castle

Malpas SY14 8AH TEL. 01829-720383 OWNER The Marchioness of Cholmondeley HOURS April–Sept, Wed–Thurs, Sun and Bank Holiday Mons, 11.30a.m.–5p.m. ENTRANCE £3, children £1.50 DIRECTIONS Off A49 Tarporley–Whitchurch road

🎖 ᕴ Access 🎖 Gift Shop 🎖 Café 🎖 Plants for Sale

Cholmondeley

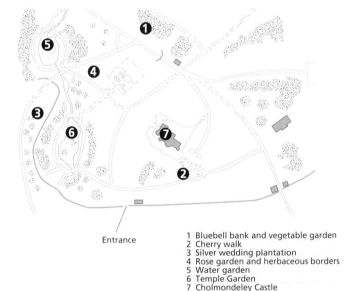

Entrance

1 Bluebell bank and vegetable garden
2 Cherry walk
3 Silver wedding plantation
4 Rose garden and herbaceous borders
5 Water garden
6 Temple Garden
7 Cholmondeley Castle

Cholmondeley Castle is an early 19th-century gothic creation of pink and grey sandstone, with pointed windows and battlemented roof. It sits on the summit of a gently rising hill, surrounded by 30 acres of tree-filled gardens, looking benevolently onto its own cricket-ground and 300-year-old cedars. There are some formal gardens near the house, with roses and herbaceous borders, but the woodland and water gardens are the really enchanting part of Cholmondeley.

There are magnolias and weeping beeches, thickets of bamboo and glorious rhododendrons and azaleas. Late spring is the best time to see them, when you will also be enchanted by the pocket-handkerchief tree, *Davidia involucrata*, in bloom, in a sea of white narcissi and bluebells. The Temple Garden is like a willow-pattern design come to life, with islands in a serpentine lake, bridges and waterfalls, twisty-branched cedars and tiered Scots pines – not consciously oriental, but conveying the tranquillity of an Eastern garden. The traditional kitchen garden is run organically, with neat rows of vegetables and caged fruits, and there is a section offering home-grown azaleas and other ornamental plants for sale.

Recent developments in the gardens include several new island beds near the house, containing displays of various ornamental grasses – an interesting feature for summer and autumn.

NANTWICH

Bridgemere Garden World

Bridgemere, Nantwich CW5 7QB TEL. 01270-521100 OWNER John Ravenscroft
HOURS Open all year, daily, 9a.m.–8p.m. (5p.m. winter) ENTRANCE Free
DIRECTIONS On A51 S of Nantwich, follow signs from M6 Jct 15 or 16 WEB
www.bridgemere.co.uk

 ⚇ Access Gift Shop Café Plants for Sale Nursery

The owners claim Bridgemere offers the greatest gardening day out
in Europe; that is a lot to live up to, but it is certainly the most
impressive garden centre I have seen anywhere, well organised with
a huge range of stock, including many choice and unusual plants.
Beyond is a large area devoted to 20 display gardens, including well-
landscaped rock and water gardens, a sumptuous rose garden,
gardens of herbaceous flowers and annuals, rhododendrons, winter
gardens, and several Chelsea flower show exhibits, rebuilt here. There
are also huge displays of conservatory and house plants.

NESTON

Ness Botanic Gardens

Ness, Neston CH64 4AY TEL. 0151-353 0123 OWNER University of Liverpool
HOURS March–Oct, daily, 9.30a.m.–dusk; Nov–Feb, daily, 9.30a.m.–4p.m.
ENTRANCE £4.70, concessions £4.30, children under 18 free if accompanied,
unaccompanied £3.50. Guide dogs only DIRECTIONS Signposted off A540
Chester–Hoylake road and from M53 Jct 4 WEB www.merseyworld.com/
nessgardens

⚇ Access Gift Shop Café Plants for Sale

This interesting garden is owned and run by Liverpool University,
yet it retains much of the ambience of the private, domestic garden
that it once was. It was started in 1898 by Arthur Bulley, a Liverpool
cotton broker and founder of the seed merchants Bees of Chester. A
keen collector of plants from distant parts of the world, Bulley
launched the plant-hunting careers of George Forrest and Frank
Kingdon-Ward by helping to finance their seed-collecting expeditions
to western China. Consequently, oriental trees and shrubs, including
magnolias, rhododendrons and Himalayan birches are well
represented here, and Kingdon-Ward's exquisite blue Himalayan
poppies, *Meconopsis betonicifolia*.

The undulating site at Ness enjoys fine views across the Dee
estuary to the Clwyd hills, and its 62 acres embrace a variety of soil
types. There is a good collection of roses, an azalea border, a vast

herbaceous border, a large rock garden and one of the best heather gardens in the country which is at its most brilliant in late summer.

The Marton Oak

The great oak at Marton, three miles north of Congleton on the A34, is one of the largest old oak trees in the country and perhaps it takes the record for being the strangest. Its trunk long ago split vertically into four separate pieces, with a girth totalling 58ft at the foot of the tree. According to local lore, when the tree split it made a convenient pound in which a local farmer kept his bull. It now provides an unusual enclosure for a Wendy house, which has been erected right inside the trunk at ground level.

NORTHWICH

Arley Hall

Arley, Great Budworth, Northwich CW9 6NA TEL. 01565-777353 OWNER Viscount Ashbrook HOURS Mid-April–Sept, Tues–Sun and Bank Holiday Mons, 11a.m.–4.30p.m., Oct, Sat–Sun, 11a.m.–4.30p.m. ENTRANCE £4.50, OAPs £3.90, children £2.25, family ticket £11.25 DIRECTIONS 5m W of Knutsford, signposted from M6 Jct 20 and M56 Jct 10 WEB www.arleyestate.zuunet.co.uk

🍏 ⅄ Access 🍏 Gift Shop 🍏 Café 🍏 Plants for Sale 🍏 2 for 1 Voucher

On my first visit to Arley Hall I had the great good fortune to be shown its grounds by the late Lady Ashbrook, who had run the 14-acre gardens since 1939, and by Tom Acton, her head gardener, who arrived in 1940. Both of them knew every plant, and the experience of seeing the gardens through their eyes (each of them having been there for more than 50 years) was unforgettable.

Most of the garden's present layout was done by Lady Ashbrook's great-grandparents in the 1840s. They made Arley's famous double herbaceous borders in 1846, when Queen Victoria had been on the throne less than 10 years. 'It was called the Alcove Walk,' said Lady Ashbrook, 'because the term "herbaceous border" hadn't yet been invented.' The two rows of mixed perennial flowers are almost certainly the first herbaceous borders ever planted and they have changed relatively little over 150 years.

They are reached via the straight Furlong Walk, which runs for one eighth of a mile above a ha-ha overlooking the fine park. The rest of the gardens are less labour-intensive than in Victorian days, but still include topiarised holm oaks, a herb garden, scented garden, roses and shrubberies, a vinery, and woodland grove of ornamental shrubs and trees (especially rhododendrons), underplanted with spring bulbs. An annual garden festival is held here over a weekend in July, when the borders are going full tilt.

NORTHWICH

Stonyford Cottage Garden

Stonyford Lane, Cuddington, Northwich CW8 2TF TEL. 01606-888128 OWNER Mr and Mrs F.A. Overland HOURS Garden open by appointment only; nursery open Tues–Sun and Bank Holiday Mons ENTRANCE £2, children 50p DIRECTIONS 6m W of Northwich, turn right off A556 Northwich to Chester road, following signs to Norley and Kingsley (*not* Cuddington signs), entrance is ½m on left WEB www.gardenchoice.co.uk

🌿 ♿ Access 🌿 Plants for Sale 🌿 Nursery

When the present owners moved to Stonyford Cottage they were faced with a bog, a swamp and a large, silted-up pool, and decided that water should form the main feature of the garden. They brought in a tracked excavator to dredge the pool and the land on either side was dressed with the lifted silt. Silver birches and alders have sprung up at the waterside and the emphasis is on shade- and moisture-loving, bold foliage plants such as ligularia, *Rheum palmatum*, the gigantic leaves of *Gunnera manicata* and hostas in wide variety.

Two bridges cross the lake to reach an island and a third bridge leads to further woodland plantings beyond the water. Higher ground closer to the house is home to plants requiring less soggy conditions, such as salvias and penstemons. Because the garden is in a frost pocket, many of its loveliest herbaceous plants need the protection of several layers of fleece to prevent blackening of their unfurling leaves in spring. The nursery on the same property specialises in herbaceous perennials, for both damp and dry ground.

NORTHWICH

Wood End Cottage

Grange Lane, Whitegate, Northwich CW8 2BQ TEL. 01606-888236 OWNER Mr and Mrs M.R. Everett HOURS By telephone appointment, and one afternoon in July for the NGS charities ENTRANCE £2, children 50p DIRECTIONS Turn S off A556 (Northwich by-pass) at traffic lights by Sandiway Post Office, then turn left to Whitegate village, then opposite school follow Grange Lane for 300yds

🌿 Plants for Sale

The half-acre garden gently undulates and is attractively bordered by a stream. Among the summer highlights in the borders are 69 different clematis, plus delphiniums, campanulas and phlox, thriving in a light, sandy loam which is regularly enriched with farmyard manure and leafmould.

Shade- and moisture-loving plants embroider the banks of the stream and adjacent areas under mature trees, and the presence of flowing water lends the garden exquisite tranquillity. This is a richly stocked plantsman's garden, with many unusual plants grown from seed, so the plant stall Christine Everett erects every year for her charity open day is always popular with visitors.

STOCKPORT

Lyme Park

Disley, Stockport SK12 2NX TEL. 01663-762023 OWNER The National Trust HOURS Park daily; gardens late March–Oct, daily, 11a.m.–5p.m (Wed–Thurs, 1–5p.m.); Nov–mid-Dec, Sat–Sun only, 12 noon–3p.m. ENTRANCE Garden £2.50, children £1.25 (under 5s free), car £3.50 DIRECTIONS 6½m SE of Stockport on A6, just W of Disley

🌿 ৬ Access 🌿 Gift Shop 🌿 Café

The grounds of Lyme Park are still for ever etched in millions of viewers' minds as Pemberley, home of Mr Darcy in the BBC's popular adaptation of *Pride and Prejudice*. According to Vicky Dawson, the property manager, visitors of all nationalities want to know where Mr Darcy went for a dip and whether they can see his wet shirt. (Alas, we can't.)

The property is one of the National Trust's most dazzling jewels, with a huge Palladian mansion and six acres of fabulous gardens within a 1300-acre landscaped park grazed by red and fallow deer. It also enjoys breathtaking views of the Pennines and the lowland Cheshire plain. There is a formal, patterned Dutch garden with ivy-edged beds, infilled with bright spring and summer bedding. A sunken garden on the north side is more discreetly planted with trees and shrubs. An early 19th-century orangery houses a splendid fig tree and two enormous camellias, dating from Victorian times, plus a scattering of other fragrant and leafy conservatory stalwarts. Outside are terraced beds and a rose garden, leading on to less formal grounds with lawns and woodland. The lake and lime avenue are remnants of a 17th-century garden that has been absorbed into the gentler contours of the great 18th-century park.

13 Yew Tree Cottages

Beacomfold, Compstall, Stockport SK6 5JU TEL. 0161-427 7142 OWNER Mr and
Mrs M. Murphy HOURS Open several afternoons during June–Aug, also for
private visits by prior appointment in May–Aug, and some Suns for NGS;
phone for details ENTRANCE £2, children £1 DIRECTIONS 6m E of Stockport, use
M60 Jct 25. Follow signs to Romiley and Marple Bridge on B6104, turn into
Compstall village at Etherow Country Park sign, then take 2nd left after
Andrew Arms public house (parking restricted but within walking distance
of village car parks)

🌱 Plants for Sale

Situated at the north-eastern tip of the county, this is one of the
highest and smallest gardens in the *Guide*. Covering a one-third-of-
an-acre site, high on the west-facing slope of a glaciated valley, it
endures a fairly constant cool wind and, say the owners, the plants
tend to be a good couple of weeks later into bloom than those grown
by their friends in more sheltered parts of Cheshire.

The Murphys have been here for 27 years and have developed the
property as a series of small, enclosed spaces of relaxed cottage-style
planting. The emphasis is on roses, clematis, penstemons and hardy
geraniums, at their best in June and July. Part of the garden is across
the lane, on the site of an old orchard. Its picturesque situation is
popular with walkers because the adjacent cotton mill now houses
facilities for a country park, with marked walks through moorland
and woods. The yew tree that gave the cottages their name was felled
200 years ago, but Mike Murphy has planted another in its place.

And also...

**Cheshire Herbs, Fourfields, Forest Road, nr Tarporley CW6 9ES (tel.
01829-760578)**, is a specialist herb nursery selling pot-grown plants
(around 180 different herb varieties), with a small shop on the
premises selling herb-related products and gifts. Herb seeds only are
sold by mail order (catalogue on request). Open all year, daily,
10a.m.–5p.m. Off A49 at junction with A54.

Spring and autumn are the best times to visit **Granada Arboretum,
Jodrell Bank, Macclesfield SK11 9DL (tel. 01477-571339)**. Occupying
a level site of 35 acres, it has National Collections of malus (crab apples
particularly) and sorbus (mountain ash). There are also many alders,
birches, pines and other trees and a large collection of heathers.
Open mid-March–Oct, daily, 10.30a.m.–5.30p.m., Nov–early March,
Tues–Sun, 11a.m.–4.30p.m. Entrance £4.90, concessions £3.50,

children £2.50, family ticket £14.50 (includes visits to science centre and planetarium). Off A535, between Holmes Chapel and Chelford.

Late May, rhododendron time, is when **Hare Hill Garden, Garden Lodge, Over Alderley, Macclesfield SK10 4QB (tel. 01625-828981)**, is at its most splendid. Covering 12 acres, it has a walled former kitchen garden, now grassed over and planted with flower borders and tender shrubs trained on the walls. Unusual hollies feature in its woodland. Open Easter–Oct, Wed–Thurs, Sat–Sun and Bank Holiday Mons, 10a.m.–5.30p.m.; also daily, mid-May–early June, for rhododendrons. Entrance £2.50, children £1.25. Off B5087, between Macclesfield and Alderley Edge.

Little Moreton Hall, Congleton CW12 4SD (tel. 01260-272018), owned by the National Trust, has a one-and-a-half-acre formal garden surrounding one of the most celebrated timber-framed houses in England (the property was used in the TV filming of Daniel Defoe's *Moll Flanders*). Its knot garden is based on an Elizabethan design and there are historic herbs, vegetables and herbaceous flowers. Open late March–early Nov, Wed–Sun and Bank Holiday Mons, 11.30a.m.–5p.m.; mid-Nov–Dec, Sat–Sun, 11.30a.m.–4p.m. Entrance £4.50, children £2.25, family ticket £11. Follow signs from M6 Jct 16 or 17, 4m S of Congleton.

Peover Hall, Over Peover, Knutsford WA16 9HW (tel. 01565-830241), has five walled gardens within its 15 acres. They include a White Garden with box topiary, a lily-pond court, a rose garden, herb garden and pink-flower garden, surrounded by an 18th-century landscape garden with fabulous trees and pretty pavilion. There is also a woodland dell with rhododendrons and magnolias, and a pleached hornbeam walk by the churchyard. Do not miss the magnificent stables with carved stalls and an ornate plaster ceiling. Open April–Oct, Thurs and Mons (but not Bank Holidays), 2–5p.m. Entrance £2, children £1. Signposted from A50 near Knutsford.

Stapeley Water Gardens, London Road, Stapeley, Nantwich CW5 7LH (tel. 01270-623868), displays huge ranges of waterlilies and other aquatic plants in both outdoor and indoor water gardens. Although a tourist spectacle, it is also somewhere to buy anything and practically everything to make ponds and water features at home. Open all year, daily, April–Oct, 9a.m.–6p.m. (9a.m.–8p.m., Wed, 10a.m.–4p.m., Sun); Nov–March, 9a.m.–5p.m. (9a.m.–7p.m., Wed, 10a.m.–4p.m., Sun). Entrance free, except Palm Garden £3.85, OAPs £3.25, children £2. M6 Jct 16, then A500, then A51 towards Nantwich, then follow signs to Water Gardens.

Cornwall

MAP NO. 1

Resembling a long, bony foot stepping gingerly into the deep Atlantic, the rugged Cornish peninsula sits in splendid isolation in England's extreme south-west. Its wind-blasted cliffs are carpeted with tough heathers and thrift; the 'nut-smell of gorse and honey-smell of ling / Waft out to sea the freshness of spring,' as John Betjeman observed.

Plunging, sheltered valleys provide homes for spectacular exotics such as Australasian tree ferns and lofty rhododendrons and magnolias from the slopes of the Himalayas. For centuries the county's wealth stemmed from tin-mining and shipping, and the coastal area around Falmouth is rich in famous sub-tropical gardens that have been maturing for 100 years or more. Cornwall celebrates its horticultural diversity in its own Festival of Gardens, when around 60 properties open to the public (some for only a day or two) from mid-March to the end of May.

Must See

Trebah, Falmouth – Himalayan hillsides relocated to Cornish coast

The Lost Gardens of Heligan, St Austell – major restoration revived this Victorian showpiece

Tresco Abbey, Tresco – island of exotic plants

Exceptional in Spring

Glendurgan, Falmouth

Trengwainton, Penzance

Caerhays Castle Garden, St Austell

Worth a Visit in Winter

Trebah, Falmouth

Trelissick, Truro

FALMOUTH

Glendurgan Garden

Mawnan Smith, nr Falmouth TR11 5JZ TEL. 01326-250906/01872-862090 (information line) OWNER The National Trust HOURS Late Feb–Oct, Tues–Sat and Bank Holiday Mons (closed Good Friday), 10.30a.m.–5.30p.m. (last adm. 4.30p.m.) ENTRANCE £3.70, children £1.95 (under 5s free), family ticket £8.75 DIRECTIONS 4m SW of Falmouth, ½m SW of Mawnan Smith on road to Helford Passage

🌿 Gift Shop 🌿 Café 🌿 Plants for Sale

Both Glendurgan and its next-door-neighbour, Trebah (*q.v.*), were created in the 1830s by the Fox family, Quaker merchants with shipping interests in Falmouth. The 26-acre gardens descend dramatically from their respective hilltop houses, through sheltered valleys to the Helford waters beyond. Glendurgan boasts a pair of vast tulip trees, a highly unusual laurel maze, glorious spring displays from magnolias, rhododendrons, primroses, bluebells and daffodils and woodland walks down to the hamlet of Durgan (where there are National Trust cottages to rent), at the water's edge.

Poolside gunneras with their vast, spiny parasol leaves are another feature of Glendurgan, and winding paths on each side of the steep valley allow intermittent, focused views of the garden spread out below. The recently built visitor centre cum entrance will be welcomed by many, although I felt it, and the rather manicured garden paths, slightly diminished the garden's previously more spirited atmosphere.

FALMOUTH

Trebah Garden

Mawnan Smith, nr Falmouth TR11 5JZ TEL. 01326-250448 OWNER Trebah Garden Trust HOURS Open all year, daily, 10.30a.m.–6.30p.m. (last adm. 5p.m.) or dusk if earlier ENTRANCE £4.50, OAPs £4, children £2.50; Nov–Feb £1.75, OAPs and children £1 (RHS and NT members free at all times) DIRECTIONS 4m SW of Falmouth, 1m SW of Mawnan Smith (signposted from A39/A394 Treliever Cross roundabout; 500yds W of Glendurgan Garden) WEB www.trebah-garden.co.uk

🌿 ♿ Access 🌿 Gift Shop 🌿 Café 🌿 Plants for Sale

When Major Tony Hibbert and his wife bought Trebah in 1980, they envisaged spending their retirement 'sipping gin and tonic on the terrace and doing a spot of sailing' in the Helford estuary at the bottom of the garden. The local Gardens Trust soon informed them, however, that they possessed an important historic garden with many rare plants thought lost in the undergrowth for 40 years. Sportingly, the Hibberts began restoring their 26-acre ravine, which descends 200ft from the 18th-century house down to a private beach.

It is now, says Tony, 'like a corner of the Himalayas only better cared for', with a stream cascading over waterfalls, ponds of giant Koi carp surrounded by exotic waterside plants, towering rhododendrons of scarlet and pastel shades, and two acres of brilliant blue and white hydrangeas. Trebah has glades of 100-year-old giant tree ferns, which form the biggest collection in Europe, and also boasts vast clumps of 18ft-high *Gunnera manicata* with leaves 10ft across. Unlike many gardens regularly open to the public, Trebah is allowed a hint of wildness and eccentricity, which contributes greatly to its appeal. There are garden trails and a thrilling Tarzan's Camp for children, and a good plant sales area.

CELEBRITY CHOICE

Roy Lancaster
Plant hunter, author and
television presenter

'For me there are two great things in the world: mountains and the sea. Mountains are my favourite – you have to climb them, to explore them. And that is why I like **Trebah** (*q.v.*). It's not mountainous, of course, but the depth of the valley is very much like a mountainside, and it has very good mountain flora, especially its Himalayan and Chinese content – the big rhododendrons, bamboos, a huge *Davidia involucrata*, one of my favourite trees. It's a primeval world. It is also about foliage, and scale. To stand by the house at Trebah and look down the valley, glimpsing what appears to be the sea at the bottom, is very exciting. Then there is the huge gunnera grove in the valley. The path through it is very carefully cleaned up around the plants so you can see the huge rhizomes, very primeval-looking indeed, and I love the lurid green light that shines through the gigantic leaves when you are standing under them. The plant content at Trebah takes in so many elements I've enjoyed in wild places. It's a rough, jagged garden, and one I love visiting.'

MARAZION

St Michael's Mount

Marazion, nr Penzance TR17 0HT TEL. 01736-710507 OWNER The National
Trust and Lord St Levan HOURS Castle April–Oct, Mon–Fri, 10.30a.m.–5.30p.m.
and most weekends (last adm. 4.45p.m.), Nov–March, Mon, Wed and Fri
(subject to weather and tide, ring in advance to check); gardens April–May,
daily, 10.30a.m.–5.30p.m. Also open for charity most summer weekends
(June–Oct), when NT members are asked to pay for admission ENTRANCE
April–May, gardens only £2, castle and gardens £4.50, children £2.25, family
ticket £12 DIRECTIONS ½m from the shore at Marazion, ½m S of A394. Foot
access over cobbled causeway at low tide (unsuitable for wheelchairs and
prams, etc.). In summer there is a ferry, weather permitting (for ferry info.
tel. 01736-710265)

🍽 Gift Shop 🍽 Café 🍽 Plants for Sale

Limited access adds to the Mount's air of isolation and mystery. The
Revd William Borlase wrote in 1762 that it was 'Anciently only a
monastery, in tumultuous and warlike times a fort and a monastery
together, since the Reformation a fort only, and now neither fort nor
monastery, but a neat comfortable and secure dwelling house'.

The forbidding granite house sits on top of the rocky outcrop, and
much of the garden is made from small terraces reached by narrow,
ascending paths on the cliff face. Head gardener Alan Cook and his
team must feel they are almost gardening at sea, cast away on this
precipitous island where much of the gardening has to be done by
abseiling down the cliff faces.

Although exposed to constant winds and salt-laden air, sub-
tropical flowers abound throughout the year, having rooted
themselves into the rocky crevices. Pelargoniums, fuchsias, osteospermums, hebes and euryops thrive on the usually frost-free slopes;
Hottentot figs (*Carpobrotus edulis*) and around 30 different mesembryanthemums broadcast their vivid, daisy-like flowers from the
crevices. Red-hot pokers have spread like wildfire on the lower
slopes, and spring sees the island under a quilt of wild daffodils.

PENZANCE

Morrab Gardens

Morrab Road, Penzance TEL. 01736-362341 OWNER Penwith District Council
HOURS Daily all year, 9a.m.–dusk ENTRANCE Free DIRECTIONS In Penzance town
centre, close to the seafront

🍽 ⚿ Access

Penzance enjoys views of Mount's Bay and St Michael's Mount (*q.v.*)
from its long promenade, while its narrow streets and Regency squares

boast some charming architecture. *Morrab* is Cornish for 'seashore' and these three-acre gardens, close to the town centre and seafront, were developed by Penzance Corporation in 1889 as a public amenity following a nationwide competition. It was won by a London landscaper who received a prize of £21 and the pleasure of seeing his designs realised.

Morrab Gardens retain much of their Victorian aura, with winding paths and plenty of traditional benches on which to eat sandwiches and take in the view. Large cabbage palms, Abyssinian bananas, sophoras and libertias are among the exotic features of this surprising and pleasing urban park.

Magnolia Magic

Exquisite and fragrant-flowered magnolias are among the oldest plants on earth, having changed little in 100 million years. They thrive in the acidic soils and humid, rain-speckled atmosphere of Cornwall, the oldest specimens offering their glorious, waxy-petalled blooms from lofty branches, best seen in the great valley gardens which often allow good views from above. The first magnolia, *M. virginiana*, arrived in England from Virginia in 1688. The shiny-leaved evergreen *M. grandiflora* followed in the early 18th century, but it was not until 1789 that the first Chinese magnolias reached these shores and nearly 100 years later that *M. stellata* arrived from Japan. Among the most spectacular plants in this genus are *M. campbellii*, brought from China in 1864, and *M. sargentiana robusta*, with pendent, large-petalled flowers 9in in diameter, one of many outstanding species introduced by the plant-hunter E.H. Wilson (*q.v.*) in 1908. *M. denudata*, with elegant, pure white, goblet flowers, has been cherished in China for at least 1400 years, being grown in temple gardens as a symbol of candour, purity and the feminine (Yin) principle.

PENZANCE

Trengwainton

Exceptional in Spring

Madron, Penzance TR20 8RZ **TEL.** 01736-362297 **OWNER** The National Trust **HOURS** March–Oct, Sun–Thurs, 10a.m.–5p.m., last adm. ½hr before closing **ENTRANCE** £4, children (under 16) £2, family ticket £10 **DIRECTIONS** 2m NW of Penzance, ½m W of Heamoor on B3312, or ½m off A3071

🌿 ♿ Access 🌿 Gift Shop 🌿 Café 🌿 Plants for Sale

Large, rare magnolias, camellias and rhododendrons planted earlier this century contribute to the magnificence of Trengwainton. A gurgling stream runs close to the carriage drive, its banks planted with skunk cabbages whose smell is an acquired taste, strongest in spring when the cowled flower spikes appear. These banks also feature white arum lilies, masses of primulas – crimson *P. pulverulenta* and *P. japonica*, and yellow *P. helodoxa* – and shady tree ferns from Australia.

The 25-acre south-facing site, looking over Mount's Bay (with a view of St Michael's Mount in the distance), particularly favours tender plants such as the vivid blue Chatham Island forget-me-nots. Brick-walled gardens, built in the 19th century, feature unusual, sloping beds, built to raise early produce for the kitchen. They now provide a sheltering home for plant rarities.

POLRUAN

Headland

Battery Lane, Polruan-by-Fowey PL23 1PW TEL. 01726-870243 OWNER Jean Hill HOURS May–Aug, Thurs, 2–6p.m. ENTRANCE £2, children £1 DIRECTIONS 8m E of St Austell; use passenger ferry from Fowey, then 10 mins walk up the hill; or follow signs to Polruan (on E of Fowey estuary), park in car park overlooking harbour and turn left on foot down St Saviour's Hill

This is a marvellous, craggy, gale-swept garden, enclosed by the sea on three sides and situated on the steeply sloping terrain of a former stone quarry. The house (not open) was built in 1921, and the abundant local slate was put to good use in creating wiggly paths, retaining walls, seats, steps and attractive archways. They lead you to stunning views of the south Cornish coastline in one direction and the white-painted cottages of Fowey, across the estuary, in the other.

The salt-laden air, carried on persistent winds, ensures that only certain specialised plants can grow here – those that relish life beside the seaside, such as *Fuchsia magellanica*, escallonias, sea buckthorn and Monterey cypress, which provide some wind-filtering shelter for many other species. Although it is blowy, the climate here is also mild, providing an excellent home for succulents such as aeoniums, candy-pink lampranthus, Hottentot figs (*Carpobrotus edulis*), echeverias and sempervivums. *Gladiolus byzantinus* forms carmine thickets in early summer; red-hot pokers, valerians, wallflowers, hydrangeas, yuccas and Dracaena palms add to the exotic ambience.

It is a remarkable feat to have made such a splendid garden, which the present owner has worked on improving for nearly a quarter of a century. You have to 'go with the flow', says Jean Hill; the terrain and the maritime situation dictate what can and cannot be done. Even so, there is enough shelter in one spot for a productive kitchen garden with soft fruits and a selection of vegetables. Cream teas are served and if you can tackle the 100 steps down the cliff-side, there is also a small, sandy beach on the premises.

REDRUTH

Burncoose Nurseries

Gwennap, Redruth TR16 6BJ TEL. 01209-860316 OWNER C.H. Williams
HOURS Daily all year, 8.30a.m.–5p.m. (Sun 11a.m.–5p.m.) ENTRANCE £2, children
£1 DIRECTIONS 3m S of Redruth on A393 towards Falmouth, between Lanner
and Ponsanooth (signposted) WEB www.burncoose.co.uk
🌿 ♿ **Access** 🌿 **Café** 🌿 **Nursery**

This is a must for plant lovers. Well-displayed, well-grown shrubs and trees in stock include many rare and slightly tender species unlikely to be found elsewhere in British nurseries. Varieties of camellia, leptospermum, magnolia, hydrangea and pittosporum are very well represented, as are Japanese acers and bamboos. A peaceful, 15-acre woodland garden (awash with bluebells in spring) adjoins the nursery, featuring broad collections of acid-loving shrubs and around 25 species of bamboo.

ST AUSTELL

Caerhays Castle Garden

Exceptional in **Spring**

Caerhays, Gorran, St Austell PL26 6LY TEL. 01872-501144/501310 OWNER F.J.
Williams HOURS Mid-March–May, daily, 10a.m.–4.30p.m. (house mid-March–
end April, Mon–Fri, 1–4p.m.) ENTRANCE House and garden £8, garden only
£4.50, children £1.50 DIRECTIONS In Caerhays village, 10m S of St Austell on
the coast by Porthluney Cove (parking at beach car park), from A390 take
B3287 and follow signs WEB www.caerhays.co.uk
🌿 **Café** 🌿 **Plants for Sale** 🌿 **NPC**

A thrilling place for springtime woodland walks, where it is essential to peer into the treetops and discover pale-pink magnolia flowers the size of dinner plates, all the more glorious against a clear blue sky. (A National Collection of magnolias is held here.)

The romantic, early 19th-century gothic castle of Caerhays was built for the Trevanions by John Nash. However, John Trevanion's fortune ran out before the landscaping could be completed and he fled to Paris to escape his creditors. Subsequently, the wealthy Williams family, with mining interests in the county, bought the castle and began to plant the garden. It is now famous for being intimately connected with the intrepid explorations of E.H. Wilson (*q.v.*) and George Forrest (*q.v.*) who brought back wondrous new shrubs and trees from the Far East. Like so many Cornish gardens, its woodland stretches down to the sea, and is filled with plants which date particularly from 1896, when J.C. Williams retired from politics to garden in earnest.

The 100-acre garden's impressive collection includes vast magnolias dating from this period (notably *M. campbellii* ssp. *mollicomata* and *M. veitchii*) and the famous *williamsii* hybrid camellias, bred by J.C. himself, who also did valuable work in hybridising daffodils and rhododendrons.

ST AUSTELL

The Eden Project

Bedelva, St Austell TEL. 01726-811911 OWNER Eden Project HOURS Open all year, daily, 10a.m.–6p.m. (last adm. 5p.m.), phone for details of late openings, mid-July–early Sept ENTRANCE £9.50, OAPs £7.50, students £5, children £4 (under 5s free), family ticket £22 DIRECTIONS Signposted on roads near St Austell WEB www.edenproject.com

🌿 ⅋ Access 🌿 Gift Shop 🌿 Café

This extraordinary site is the vision of Tim Smit, enterprising restorer of the Lost Gardens of Heligan (*q.v.*), which are nearby. But whereas Heligan is a celebration of Victorian horticulture and leisure, the Eden Project is an invention totally in keeping with the 21st century.

The vast, white-walled crater of a former Cornish clay-pit, which produced high quality kaolin for making porcelain china for perhaps 150 years, has been re-landscaped since 1998 to provide the setting for a series of futuristic geodesic domes, resembling glass bubbles, held in a honeycomb-like framework. What impresses most is the enormous scale of the site – and its inventiveness (like a James Bond film set). Glass has not been used, since the modern material is transparent Teflon foil, as thin as cling-film, but strong enough to take a man's weight. The domes (known as biomes) house massive-scale plantings of species from tropical and temperate zones, providing exciting and educational visiting. The Humid Tropics biome, for example, is 165ft high – taller than Nelson's column – and linked to a chain of smaller biomes.

Further landscaping and botanical displays can be found in the outdoor areas and an infrastructure of roads and visitor facilities is part of the £74 million project, half of which has been funded by lottery money from the Millennium Commission. It's an entertaining place, but the plants will need another couple of years before they look at home here.

ST AUSTELL

The Lost Gardens Of Heligan

Pentewan, St Austell PL26 6EN TEL. 01726-845100 OWNER Tim Smit and John Nelson HOURS Open all year, daily, 10a.m.–6p.m. (last adm. 4.30p.m.), closes at 5p.m., Oct–Feb; groups by prior arrangement only ENTRANCE £6, OAPs £5.50, children £3 (under 5s free), family ticket £17 DIRECTIONS A390, then B3273 towards Mevagissey and follow signs WEB www.heligan.com

🔲 ♿ Access   🔲 Gift Shop   🔲 Café   🔲 Plants for Sale

These 'lost' gardens were buried under brambles and the rampant evergreenery of rhododendrons when Tim Smit, a former archaeologist turned rock music producer, first visited (machete in hand) 10 years ago.

The 80-acre gardens were probably begun in the earliest years of the 17th century and were extended and enhanced through the 18th and 19th centuries. However, with the start of the First World War, they suddenly became like Sleeping Beauty's castle – engulfed in thickets and brambles. The estate's teams of male staff went away to fight in the trenches (and didn't return). The property had been untouched since 1914 when the Tremayne family packed up and left and the house was commandeered by the War Department. Extensive restorations since 1991 have seen the reinstatement of magnificent walled kitchen gardens (complete with melon and pineapple pits), a vinery, a grotto, an extensive rockery, an Italian garden with pool, a summerhouse, a 300ft herbaceous border and much more.

An adjoining lost valley of 30 acres, with lakes and an old mill-pond, was the next area to be reclaimed and can be visited via winding woodland paths and bridges. The property is now very well known and receives large numbers of visitors, having been the subject of entertaining television series and a book. The Eden Project (*q.v.*) is another of Tim Smit's awesome projects and is quite close by.

ST IVES

The Barbara Hepworth Museum and Sculpture Garden

Barnoon Hill, St Ives TR26 1TG TEL. 01736-796226 OWNER The Trustees of the Tate Gallery HOURS Open all year, March–Oct, daily, 10a.m.–5.30p.m.; Nov–Feb, Tues–Sun, 10a.m.–4.30p.m. ENTRANCE Museum and garden only £3.75, concessions £2, OAPs/children free; Tate Gallery only £3.95, concessions £2.50, OAPs/children free; combined ticket £6.50, concessions £3.50 DIRECTIONS In the centre of St Ives (signposted). Parking in public car parks some distance away WEB www.tate.org.uk

🔲 Gift Shop   🔲 Café

From the 19th century onwards the picturesque fishing village of St Ives, clustered on a steep hillside, became a colony for artists seeking inspiration from the landscape and the sea (don't miss the new Tate Gallery nearby on the seafront, which also serves good food in its roof terrace café).

The sculptress Barbara Hepworth is among the many famous people who took up residence in St Ives; her studio is now a fascinating museum, with many of her nature-inspired sculptures displayed among the cabbage palms and exotic flowers in her quarter-acre walled garden.

'Here in Cornwall,' she wrote, 'I have a background which links with Yorkshire [her birthplace] in the natural shape of stone structure and fertility, and it links with Italy because of the intensity of light and colour. Here I can carve out of doors all the year round – a background for which I am grateful – for I have always been preoccupied with man's position in landscape and his relation to the structure of nature.'

The garden presents a marvellous, atmospheric Mediterranean-style setting for Hepworth's work, with winding paths threading through thickets of bamboo, flowering cherries, camellias, myrtles, a ginkgo tree and ground-covering geraniums. Hepworth's bright studio opens into the garden and is kept as it was at her death in 1975, with work in progress on a trestle table surrounded by tools and plaster-stained overalls hanging on pegs behind.

TRESCO

The Tresco Abbey Gardens

Tresco, Isles of Scilly TR24 0QQ TEL. 01720-422849 OWNER Mr R. A. Dorrien-Smith HOURS Open all year, daily, 10a.m.–4p.m. ENTRANCE £6.50, accompanied children free; weekly tickets (7 days) £10 DIRECTIONS From Penzance Heliport by helicopter (for reservations tel. 01736-363871), from St Mary's island by launch or by steamer from Penzance to St Mary's (tel. 01736-334220) WEB www.tresco.co.uk

Gift Shop · Café · Plants for Sale · 2 for 1 Voucher

Cast away at sea, 28 miles from the craggy cliffs of Land's End, the Isles of Scilly endure and are enriched by their tempestuous maritime surroundings. Augustus Smith, a young landowner from Hertfordshire, took out a lease on these remote isles in 1834 and immediately built his new home, Tresco Abbey (alluding to the nearby ruined Benedictine priory). The house exterior was described by a visitor in 1843 as having 'a very respectable, if not picturesque appearance, with just enough workmanship to prevent it looking commonplace, but not enough to give it that cold, formal, workhouse-like appearance which is the great defect of more magnificent mansions'.

Smith also started in haste on the 16-acre gardens, and a vast range of exotic plants from the southern hemisphere is now grown here, including scarlet banksias from Western Australia, king proteas from South Africa (regularly in bloom), together with New Zealand flame trees, silver trees from Cape Province, and metallic-turquoise puyas from Chile. They thrive under the warming influence of the Gulf Stream and the south-facing slope on which the gardens lie.

According to Mike Nelhams, the curator, wind shelter is the critical factor. It is provided by thickets of cypresses, pines, eucalyptus and evergreen oaks to supplement Smith's original plantings of Monterey cypress which are reaching the end of their life. A steep, stone stairway (lined with Canary Islands palm trees and hedgehog-like furcraeas from Mexico) cuts through the middle of the garden, ascending the hill to provide access to the garden's richly planted terraces. Succulent aeoniums cover rocky cliff walls, joined by brilliant mesembryanthemums and spiny agaves. A recently made Mediterranean garden and a fascinating collection of ornate figureheads salvaged from ships wrecked long ago add to the allure of this unique place. A day trip is interesting, but a longer stay (there are self-catering cottages, a hotel and an inn on the island) reveals more of the island's charms.

TRURO

Trelissick

Feock, nr Truro TR3 6QL TEL. 01872-862090 OWNER The National Trust
HOURS Mid-Feb–Oct, Mon–Sat, 10.30a.m.–5.30p.m., Sun, 12.30–5.30p.m.
(5p.m. in Feb, March and Oct), last adm. ½hr before closing. Woodland
walks and park only, throughout year ENTRANCE £4.50, children £2.25, family
ticket £11, car park £1.50 (refundable on entry to garden) DIRECTIONS 4m S of
Truro, on both sides of B3289, above King Harry Ferry (for cars and
pedestrians)
🚫 ♿ Access 🚫 Gift Shop 🚫 Café 🚫 Plants for Sale 🚫 NPC

The blissfully peaceful 30-acre garden of Trelissick is set on a majestic eminence above a broad estuary known as the Carrick Roads, a deep-water anchorage for Falmouth Harbour. Large ships and tankers often provide curious eye-catchers from the upper slopes of the garden.

Trelissick's undulating park was planted in the 1820s by Ralph Allen Daniel, who was so rich (from tin-mining) that he was known as 'Guinea-a-minute' Daniel. It is said he could ride all the way to Truro without leaving his property. Fruit trees were added by a later owner, but most of the present garden is early 20th-century planting and features massed hydrangeas, rhododendrons and camellias (*de rigueur* in this county), underplanted with cyclamen and erythroniums, a dell with bog-loving plants and fine tree ferns. A National Collection of *Photinia* (Asian and American shrubs also known as Christmas berry) is held here. The extensive woods are streaked magenta by the abundant foxgloves in late spring. Near the entrance, a splendid gothic water tower with pointed roof and circular rooms would suit latter-day Rapunzels, and can be rented from the Trust.

Old Garden Artefacts

Keith Webb and Mary Porter run **Farm and Garden Bygones** at **Padstow Antiques, 23 New Street, Padstow PL28 8EA (tel.01841-532914), just above St Petroc's Hotel, at the end of the one-way system**. Their stock includes a large range of old granite troughs, millstones and staddle stones, old garden tools, wooden barrows, statuary and plenty of old terracotta oil jars imported from Spain, Greece and Morocco. Open all year, Mon–Sat, 10a.m.–5p.m., but Keith says phone first if you're making a special visit as they close the shop when they're out buying new stock.

And also...

Around 3000 different plants are offered at the **Duchy of Cornwall Nursery, Cott Road, Lostwithiel PL22 0HW (tel. 01208-872668/web www.duchyofcornwallnursery.co.uk)**. The emphasis is on the acid-loving or slightly tender plants that thrive in Cornwall, including hydrangeas, myrtles, echiums and Australasian shrubs. The nursery is well run and prints a mail order catalogue, £2. Open all year, daily, Mon–Sat, 9a.m.–5p.m., Sun, 10a.m.–5p.m. Signposted from A390 at Lostwithiel.

The garden at **Lamorran House, Upper Castle Road, St Mawes TR2 5BZ (tel. 01326-270800, or evening 01872-530204)**, is the passion and creation of Robert Dudley-Cooke, who has filled his steep, four-acre hillside with intimate glades featuring over 500 azaleas, 250 rhododendrons, sumptuous collections of plants from the southern hemisphere, Italian-style masonry and tranquil pools. Open

April–Sept, Wed and Fri, 10a.m.–5p.m., 1st Sat in each month and by appointment. Entrance £3.50, children free. Take A3078 to St Mawes, turn right at top of village and follow signs.

Like so many Cornish gardens, rhododendrons play a key part at **Pencarrow, Washaway, Bodmin PL30 3AG (tel. 01208-841369/web www.pencarrow.co.uk)**. There are around 700 different rhododendrons, in fact, scattered through the 50 acres of woodland and park, where they are joined by a good collection of camellias. There is a lake and an ice house, and nearer the imposing stone mansion there are formal lawns and flower gardens. The garden possesses a significant collection of conifers dating from the 19th and early 20th centuries. Also look out for the Victorian rock garden, made from boulders gathered on Bodmin Moor. Open March–Oct, daily, 9a.m.–6p.m. (house open Sun–Thurs only). Entrance £3, children free (house and garden £6, children £3). Groups by appointment only. Signposted from A389 Bodmin to Wadebridge road and B3266 at Washaway, 4m NW of Bodmin.

I have heard good reports of **Pine Lodge, Cuddra, St Austell PL25 3RQ (tel. 01726-73500)**, a 30-acre garden and tranquil park which will be of great interest to the plant lover. Around 6000 different plants, thoughtfully labelled, are displayed in the garden's various settings, which include herbaceous borders, marsh gardens, fish-ponds, a pinetum, a Japanese garden, formal gardens, a lake with black swans, woodland walks and shrubberies. Open late March–Oct, daily, 10a.m.–5p.m. Entrance £4, children £2. Just E of St Austell, off A390 between Holmbush and Tregrehan (signposted).

Trerice, at Kestle Mill, Newquay TR8 4PG (tel. 01637-875404), on 12 acres of land, is a small and secluded Elizabethan manor, surrounded by herbaceous borders and cottage garden plants, and an orchard planted in formal 17th-century style. The former stable hay loft contains a fascinating museum of early lawnmowers. Open April–Oct, Sun–Mon and Wed–Fri (also Tues, July–mid-Sept), 11a.m.–5p.m. (4.30p.m. in Oct). Entrance (garden) free, (house) £4.30, children £2.15, family ticket £10.75. From A30 take A3058, follow signs from Kestle Mill.

Cumbria

MAP NO. 7

The dramatic landscapes of the Lake District are unforgettable, with high, volcanic peaks in the central region reflecting in deep meres under ever-changing skies. The heathy uplands of the fells are the domain of tough sheep and the resourceful curlew, while abundant local sandstones and slates have fashioned farmsteads and field boundaries for many centuries. It is a region of high rainfall, and of such scenic beauty that the most famous lakes and towns are tourist honeypots, best avoided in high season. The 70ft waterfall of Aira Force tumbles down a wooded gorge to feed the lovely lake of Ullswater; a spring walk nearby, among the daffodils, inspired William Wordsworth to write his best-known poem.

Must See

Holker Hall, Grange-over-Sands – carefully designed and beautifully maintained

Levens Hall, Kendal – thrilling and historic topiary gardens

Exceptional in Autumn

Holehird, Windermere

Rydal Mount

Rydal, Ambleside LA22 9LU TEL. 015394-33002 OWNER Rydal Mount Trust
HOURS March–Oct, daily, 9.30a.m.–5p.m.; Nov–Feb, daily, except Tues,
10a.m.–4p.m. ENTRANCE £1.75; house and garden £4, concessions £3.25,
children £1.25 DIRECTIONS 20m from M6 Jct 36 on A591, 1m N of Ambleside,
14m from Kendal

🔲 Gift Shop 🔲 2 for 1 Voucher

The home of William Wordsworth from 1813 until his death in 1850,
the slate-roofed white cottage sits snugly in the hillside enjoying
distant views of Windermere from the upper windows, where the
poet had his study. Wordsworth was a keen gardener who designed
not only the four and a half acres surrounding his home, but also
the gardens of many friends and neighbours.

At Rydal Mount, still much as he designed it, Wordsworth followed
his philosophy that a garden should be informal, harmonise with the
surrounding landscape and include 'lawn, and trees carefully planted
so as not to obscure the view'. There are long terrace walks following
the contours of the rising ground behind the house and further walks
winding through woodland and shrubberies. Wordsworth also built
a rough-stone rustic summerhouse on the upper terrace, from where
you can still enjoy views of Rydal Water and distant heather-clad hills.
The garden retains much of the atmosphere of an early 19th-century
residence in the picturesque style, and its enthusiastic curators, Peter
and Marian Elkington, have uncovered further walks and water-
courses that had long been lost in dense undergrowth. A handsome
fern-leaved beech is one of many fine trees planted by the poet.

Charney Well

Hampsfell Road, Grange-over-Sands LA11 6BE TEL. 015395-34526 OWNER
C. Holliday and R. Roberts HOURS Open 2 days in June for NGS, 11a.m.–
4.30p.m.; groups also welcome in late June by prior arrangement ENTRANCE
£2 on NGS days, children free DIRECTIONS From A590, take B5277 to Grange-
over-Sands, continue uphill to mini-roundabout and turn right, turn right
again at crossroads, then left up Hampsfell Road (car parking 5 mins walk
away) WEB www.charneywell.com

🔲 Café 🔲 Plants for Sale 🔲 NPC

This very original, steeply sloping garden (unsuitable for wheelchairs
or the infirm) is arranged on different levels, enjoying fine views of
Morecambe Bay to the east, and the warming influence of the Gulf
Stream, due to its proximity to the coast.

The owners, who had previously had little experience of gardening before coming here in 1988, became intoxicated by their half-acre of south-facing hillside and the ranges of exotic plants that it could nurture. Crocosmias and day lilies romped away so well they had to be removed before they smothered everything else. European fan palms (*Chamaerops humilis*), cabbage palms, acacias and callistemons thrive. Among the sub-tropical specialities, plants from the southern hemisphere are well represented and a new rockery has been added, featuring yuccas, grasses and alliums. But it is the phormiums (New Zealand flax) that have really captivated the owners, who have now planted 200 of them, representing a National Collection of around 30 species and cultivars.

Despite the limitations of thin, freely-draining soil over limestone bedrock, the plants thrive in their random groupings, which you can weave among via paths and terraces, soft underfoot as they are thickly mulched with wood-bark. There is a strong emphasis on foliage and evergreen textures that brings pleasure throughout the year.

GRANGE-OVER-SANDS

Holker Hall

Must See

Cark-in-Cartmel, Grange-over-Sands LA11 7PL TEL. 015395-58328 OWNER Lord and Lady Cavendish HOURS April–Oct, daily, except Sat, 10a.m.–6p.m. or dusk if earlier (last adm. 4.30p.m. when house closes) ENTRANCE £3.65, children over 6 £2.10, family ticket £10.75 DIRECTIONS 4½m W of Grange-over-Sands off B5278, signposted; 15m from M6 Jct 36 on A590, then signposted WEB www.holker-hall.co.uk

🔴 ⅙ Access 🔴 Gift Shop 🔴 Café 🔴 2 for 1 Voucher

By any standards this unusual and spectacular garden is thrilling, because you are instantly aware of its high quality in design and maintenance. From a modest garden entrance you come into the Elliptical Garden, a symmetrical, formal area laid out in 1993. Local materials such as slates and cobblestones from the nearby coast are used in the hard landscaping and planting is of mixed shrubs and herbaceous perennials. There are ripples of blue catmint and fascinating delphinium 'cages' made yearly from hazel rods cut on the estate.

The Summer Garden features a tunnel of Portuguese laurel casting shade along the central path, topiarised above clean stilt trunks. There are fragrant shrubs, lilies, roses and lavender, and the box-edged beds are filled with seasonal flowers. In contrast, the wildflower meadow beyond is home to 24 species of perennial native wild-flowers, a glorious sight before hay cutting.

Long grasses and wildflowers are encouraged to great effect elsewhere among the numerous specimen trees that have been planted over the centuries. A fountain is surrounded by the lofty, twisted trunks of *Rhododendron arboreum* (hugely decorative when its deep pink petals carpet the ground), which was planted by Lord Burlington around 1840. A magnificent stepped water cascade is a fairly recent addition, inspired by an ancient Indian water garden in Rajasthan, and across the lawns is the small, intimate rose garden, a formal area with trellised gazebos supporting climbing varieties. There are many unusual trees and shrubs here, making this is a garden to return to as new projects are executed.

Seeds of Wonder by Mail

If you enjoy growing plants from seed, you will be endlessly tempted by the ranges offered by **Chiltern Seeds, Bortree Stile, Ulverston LA12 7PB (tel. 01229-581137)**. Around 4500 items are available, covering all manner of annuals, herbaceous perennials, trees, shrubs, conifers, British wildflowers and herbs. There are also exotic seeds such as Japanese cut flowers, rare and oriental vegetables, Australian and New Zealand plants, and many oddities that can be grown from seed as house or conservatory plants. Although unillustrated, the catalogue (a 50p donation is asked for) of over 300 pages is a great read, with tempting descriptions and cultivation notes.

KENDAL

Levens Hall

Kendal LA8 0PD TEL. 015395-60321 OWNER Mr C.H. Bagot HOURS April–mid-Oct, Sun–Thurs, 10a.m.–5p.m. (house, 12 noon–5p.m.) ENTRANCE £4.50, children £2.20, family ticket £13 (house and garden £6, £3 and £17.50) DIRECTIONS 5m S of Kendal by A591 and A6; from M6 use Jct 36, then follow signs WEB www.levenshall.co.uk

🅿 ♿ Access 🌱 Gift Shop 🌱 Café 🌱 Plants for Sale

The astonishing topiary garden draws most visitors to Levens. There are yews and box trees cut into all manner of quixotic shapes – huge pyramids, top hats, tipsy leaning spirals, chubby little birds and many other non-representational bulging forms that have evolved over the centuries. The surprisingly cosy grey stone hall dates from the 13th century, with later additions. The upper windows give an interesting perspective on the topiaries below.

The topiaries have grown out of formal, box-edged parterres that were laid out in the 17th century, and the spaces between the box hedges are filled with seasonal bedding plants in bold blocks of colour, adding a vivid counterpoint to the greenery of the topiary. Historically, it is interesting because it is a very rare example of the work of Guillaume Beaumont, a French landscaper much in vogue in the late 17th century. His large beech hedges remain intact, as does the ha-ha (a dry ditch, forming a concealed boundary), which is thought to be the first in this country. Golden-leaved yew topiaries were added in the Victorian age. Elsewhere in the five-acre garden there are pleasing herb and rose gardens, herbaceous borders and an orchard which is magnificent at blossom time, when the fruit trees rise out of a sea of scarlet 'Apeldoorn' tulips.

KENDAL

Sizergh Castle

Sizergh, nr Kendal LA8 8AE TEL. 015395-60070 OWNER The National Trust HOURS April–Oct (May–Oct in 2000), Sun–Thurs, 12.30–5.30p.m. (last adm. 5p.m.), castle 1.30p.m.–5.30p.m. ENTRANCE £5, children £2.50, family ticket £12.50 (garden only £2.50, children £1.20) DIRECTIONS 3¼m S of Kendal, NW of interchange A590/A591; from M6 Jct 36, take A590, then A591 and follow signs

◾ ♿ Access ◾ Gift Shop ◾ Café

According to Malcolm Hutchinson, Sizergh Castle's long-serving, loquacious head gardener, you should see the gardens in reverse order to the one suggested in the official guide. You will be surprised as each new vista unfolds as you walk through the rose garden and the formal lawns of the Dutch garden towards the castle and lake. The magnificent rock garden then becomes the climax of the visit, as it should. It dates from 1926, when such conceits were deeply fashionable. Built with beautiful weathered local stones, it covers nearly one acre of ground and is planted with Japanese acers, handsomely gnarled and character-ful in their maturity, accompanied by assorted small conifers, primulas and a huge collection of hardy ferns.

PENRITH

Acorn Bank Garden

Temple Sowerby, Penrith CA10 1SP TEL. 017683-61467 OWNER The National Trust HOURS April–Oct, daily, 10a.m.–5p.m. ENTRANCE £2.50, children £1.20, family ticket £6.20 DIRECTIONS 1m N of Temple Sowerby, 6m E of Penrith, from Penrith use Jct 40 of M6, then A66 and follow signs from village

◾ ♿ Access ◾ Gift Shop ◾ Café ◾ Plants for Sale

Around 250 different herbs are grown in the two and a half acres of sunny, sheltered walled gardens at Acorn Bank, in the broad vale of the River Eden. The herb garden is a small part of the walled area, but is home to an interesting, well-labelled collection of medicinal and historic herbs, including woad, which the ancient Britons used to dye blue, tattoo-like patterns on their skin, and Florentine irises, whose roots are used in perfumery. Also within the walled area is an orchard of local old apple varieties such as 'Keswick Codlin' growing in long grasses and meadow flowers. Wildflowers, especially daffodils, populate the glorious oak woodland walks on steep banks rising up from Crowdundle Beck. It is a peaceful gem of a garden, not far from Wetheriggs Country Pottery (*q.v.*) and Larch Cottage Nurseries (*q.v.*).

PENRITH

Dalemain

Dalemain Estate, Penrith CA11 0HB TEL. 017684-86450 OWNER Mr R.B. Hasell-McCosh HOURS April–early Oct, Sun–Thurs, 10.30a.m.–5p.m. (house 11a.m.–4p.m.) ENTRANCE £3.50, children free if accompanied (house and garden £5.50, children £3.50, family ticket £14.50) DIRECTIONS On A592 3m SW of Penrith; from M6, 4m away, use Jct 40, then A66, left at roundabout onto A592 WEB www.dalemain.com

  Access   Gift Shop   Café   Plants for Sale   2 for 1 Voucher

A smart Georgian facade of pink sandstone greets visitors to Dalemain, although behind it lies an Elizabethan manor house, a medieval hall and a 12th-century peel tower, a strategic tower typical of the Border lands. An amalgamation of periods and styles exists in the four-acre gardens, too, for the early knot garden near the house is surrounded by 17th-century terraced walks, around which lies an 18th-century park. The garden's Tudor gazebo looks over ancient woods to Dacre Beck and an old coach road; there are high brick and stone Tudor walls enclosing an orchard, beside which are gently sloping lawns and flower borders which have been largely replanted in the last four decades.

Overlooking the park, the first terrace you encounter has a long herbaceous border which terminates in the shade of a vast silver fir tree, *Abies cephalonica*, almost certainly one of the first of its kind to have been planted in this country. The wild garden below features mown paths through massed daffodils and rhododendrons, and breathtaking drifts of blue Himalayan poppies in late May which thrive in the sheltered site and acid soil.

Within the walled garden, some of the gnarled apple trees that were purchased in 1782 still bear fruit while a path beside them is being developed into a rose walk, with old-fashioned varieties planted over rustic arches, and in long beds to either side. The garden's development in the decades after the Second World War was largely the work of the late Sylvia McCosh, who documented much of her work at Dalemain in two enjoyable books, *Between Two Gardens* and *North Country Tapestry*. Inspired by these writings, her daughter-in-law, Jane Hasell McCosh, is now actively involved in maintaining and replanting the gardens, which look forward to a rosy future.

PENRITH
Hutton-in-the-Forest

Penrith CA11 9TH TEL. 017684-84449 OWNER Lord and Lady Inglewood HOURS Gardens daily, except Sat, 11a.m.–5p.m.; house May–Sept, Thurs–Fri, Sun and Bank Holiday Mons, 12.30–4p.m. ENTRANCE £2.50, house and gardens £4.50, children £2.50, family ticket £12 DIRECTIONS 6m NW of Penrith on B5305, 3m W from Jct 41 of M6 on B5305 towards Wigton

🌼 **Gift Shop** 🌼 **Café**

Traditional herbaceous borders in the opulent Edwardian style are backed by yew hedges running through the delightful walled garden at Hutton-in-the-Forest. There are old-fashioned purple lupins, bearded irises, campanulas, phlox, lady's mantle and oriental poppies. Beyond the walls, the gardens drop away in terraces from the mansion house, merging into woodlands and the medieval Forest of Inglewood.

There are stout topiaries, planted a century ago, while the Low Garden is a spectacular Victorian plantation of yews and other conifers, with large rhododendrons, cut through by formal rides. This area, the ponds and cascade beyond became neglected and over-grown during the 20th century and they are gradually undergoing restoration and some replanting.

WINDERMERE
Brockhole

Lake District Visitor Centre, Brockhole, Windermere LA23 1LJ TEL. 015394-46601 OWNER Lake District National Park Authority HOURS Open all year, daily, 10a.m.–dusk (visitor centre open April–Nov only, 10a.m.–5p.m.) ENTRANCE Car park fee only: £3 for 3 hours, £4 for day (£1 in winter); pre-booked coaches free DIRECTIONS 1½m N of Windermere on A591 towards Ambleside, 12m from M6

🌼 **Gift Shop** 🌼 **Café** 🌼 **Plants for Sale**

In its layout, if not in the detail, this is one of the best preserved gardens of the renowned Windermere-based garden designer, Thomas Mawson, set in a glorious position on a southwest-facing hillside above the great waters of Windermere itself. Created for one William Henry

Adolphus Gaddum, a Manchester silk and textiles magnate, the property comprises 10 acres of intensively maintained gardens, 10 acres of wildflower meadows and a further 10 acres of woodland, featuring mostly native species that were planted to create a shelter belt. The gardens descend from a white hilltop house (built between 1898 and 1901) in a series of imposing terraces leading to the lake.

Brockhole's initial moment of glory was short-lived. From the 1940s to 1960s the property was used as a convalescent home and the grounds lost much of their character. Much work has been undertaken in the last two decades to turn its fortunes around and today the gardens flourish with sumptuous seasonal borders and plenty of inspired planting. There are substantial spring and summer borders with plants in the pink–blue–purple–white range, including peonies, penstemons, alstroemerias and cranesbill geraniums. The autumn border glows with the warm colours of rudbeckias, red-hot pokers, sedums, asters and nerines. Attached to the house is an orangery, with a well-trained grapevine spanning the roof above cool-greenhouse plants, such as begonias, agaves and pelargoniums.

Brockhole is extremely popular in summer, but a spring, autumn or even a winter visit, minus the crowds, can be equally rewarding as the planting has been designed for year-round effect.

WINDERMERE

Holehird

Exceptional in Autumn

Patterdale Road, Windermere LA23 1NP TEL. 015394-46008 (tel. unmanned in winter) OWNER Windermere Council, leased to Lakeland Horticultural Society HOURS Daily, dawn–dusk ENTRANCE Donation DIRECTIONS 1m N of Windermere by A592; from M6 (12m away) take A591 to Windermere, then A592 (¾m away)
⬛ ♿ Access ⬛ NPC

The Lakeland Horticultural Society has its base at Holehird, three and a half acres of sloping grounds which enjoy spectacular views of Lake Windermere and some of England's highest mountains beyond. The walled garden covers just over one acre of thoroughly well-tended borders and lawns, maintained by the Society's volunteer members. Beyond lies a magnificent rock garden which makes full use of the natural stone outcrops on the high ground. The plantings of heathers are particularly effective, and are best seen in high summer and autumn. There are National Collections of astilbes, hydrangeas and *Polystichum* ferns and there is also a large collection of hostas. The gardens also have several characterful specimen trees.

Alpines in the Pennines

There is a wonderful, scenic drive from Penrith up to **Hartside Nursery Garden, nr Alston CA9 3BL (tel. 01434-381372), down a stony track, 1¼m SW of Alston, on E side of A686, use Jct 40 of M6**, with a chance to pause for excellent organic food at the bakery in Melmerby, on the way. The road winds its lonely route through the high moors of the Pennines, offering magnificent views of the Vale of Eden, which you leave behind as you climb. In fact, Hartside is very close to the Northumberland border and this inland site, around 1100ft above sea level, makes it perhaps the highest and bleakest nursery in the country.

Expect exceptionally hardy plants from this family-run nursery which specialises in unusual alpines, primulas, dwarf conifers, ericaceous shrubs and ferns, which can withstand local winter temperatures as low as -80°F. It isn't what you would call a neat nursery, with weeds threading their way among the pots in the small display area, where there are plenty of rarities. Owners Sue and Neil Huntley are enthusiastic growers who exhibit at many of the top RHS shows around the country. They alao have a mail order catalogue – send 4 × 1st-class stamps. Open March–Oct, Mon–Fri, 9.30a.m.–4.30p.m.; Sat–Sun and Bank Holiday Mons, 12.30–4p.m.

And also...

Graythwaite Hall, Ulverston LA12 8BA (tel. 015395-31248), is a pleasant place to visit in late spring when its tree-packed slopes are brightly jewelled with rhododendrons in bloom. The local garden designer Thomas Mawson was hired to landscape six acres of grounds around the house from 1889 to 1895, which he did in the contemporary Arts and Crafts style. There are formal terraces near the house and a woodland garden with a stream leading to a naturalistic pool. Open April–June, daily, 10a.m.–6p.m. Entrance £2, children free. M6 Jct 36, then A590 towards Barrow, at Newby Bridge take road towards Ambleside.

Anyone looking for sculptural inspiration for their garden will enjoy rambling in **Grizedale Forest Park, Grizedale, Hawkshead, Ambleside LA22 0QJ**. Maps can be bought at the Visitor Centre (tel. 01229-860010) pinpointing the fascinating wood and stone sculptures by artists such as Giles Kent, Richard Harris, Andy Goldsworthy and Sally Matthews. Open daily, dawn to dusk (Visitor Centre daily,

10a.m.–5p.m. in summer, Mon–Fri, 10a.m.–4p.m. in winter). From M6 Jct 36 take A590 towards Barrow and follow signs, 3m S of Hawkshead.

The imposing stone and stained-glass entrance to **Larch Cottage Nurseries, Melkinthorpe, Penrith CA10 2DR (tel. 01931–712404)**, leads into a fascinating sales and display area with naturalistic pools, a herb garden, pergola walk, Japanese dry garden and arcaded stone 'ruins'. Plants for sale include a large range of cottage garden perennials, shrubs, alpines, roses and aquatic plants. Open daily, 10a.m.–5.30p.m. Entrance free. M6 Jct 40, then A66 towards Brough, then A6 towards Shap and follow signs.

Muncaster Castle, Ravenglass CA18 1RQ (tel. 01229-717614), has an aura of gothic chill. Visit in spring, when its important collection of rhododendrons is in bloom, some of them cascading down a deep ravine. During the 19th century, Muncaster's was considered the largest collection of species rhododendrons in Europe and had a further injection of plants in the 1920s and 1930s, when many more new species were introduced and others were bred here. Substantial investment is currently under way to restore the 77 acres of gardens to their former glory and prominence. The grassed Terrace Walk, with panoramic views of Eskdale and the fells beyond, is memorable. Muncaster Castle also has an owl centre, which is the headquarters of the World Owl Trust. Open daily, 11a.m.–6p.m. Entrance £5, children £3, family ticket £15. (Castle open March–Oct, Sun–Fri, 12.30–4p.m., £6.50 and £4 (under 5s free), family ticket £18.) M6 Jct 36, then A590 towards Barrow, then A5092 and A595 towards Ravenglass. **2 for 1 Voucher**

At **Wetheriggs Country Pottery, Clifton Dykes, nr Penrith CA10 2DH (tel. 01768-892733)**, you can see the only surviving steam-powered pottery in the country, with its nearby clay pit, settling pans, steam house, pug-mill and beehive kiln. Much of the stock is glazed domestic ware, still made to traditional designs that have been produced here for over 135 years. The greatest interest for gardeners, however, lies in the terracotta hand-thrown flowerpots, alpine pans, strawberry and herb pots, rhubarb forcer jars and Long-Toms. You can also order 9in and 12in Victorian flowerbed edging tiles, still made to the original designs. The arch design tiles were used for gardens backing onto the Settle–Carlisle railway, while another pattern features a shamrock, thistle and rose, reflecting the region's proximity to Scotland and Ireland. Open daily, 10a.m.–5.30p.m. (may close weekdays in winter). From M6 Jct 40, take A66 towards Appleby, then A6 towards Shap, left towards Clyburn, then 1½m on left (signposted locally).

Derbyshire

MAP NO. 5

Some of the country's most awesome landscape belongs to Derbyshire. The Pennine range, England's mountainous backbone, starts here on its northward journey to the Scottish border. There are the grouse-grazed highlands of the Peak District, with purple heather-clad moors and spectacular crags, tranquil reservoirs like inland seas and hillside pastures contained in a mesh of stone walls. In the south, heavy industry and mining have played their hand, bringing riches to some. Derbyshire boasts several of England's stateliest homes, the most glorious of which is Chatsworth, near the market town of Bakewell, home of the eponymous almond tart.

Must See

Chatsworth, Bakewell –
   splendid grandeur in an
   unrivalled setting
Hardwick Hall, Chesterfield
   – among the finest herb
   gardens in Britain

Tissington's Famous Flower

Among the speedwells, *Veronica gentianoïdes* makes an excellent front-of-border perennial, sending up spikes of late-spring/early-summer blooms of clear, pale blue above a clump of glossy, green foliage. Its desirable white-flowered form, 'Tissington White', has its origins in the Peak District village of Tissington, where it was found in the front garden of an estate cottage. The plant had spread to line both sides of a path, and was locally known as Prince of Wales feathers. A few years ago it almost disappeared when the garden was tidied up for a new occupant. Fortunately, a few plants were rescued by local plantswoman Anne Liverman, who recognised its garden-worthiness and brought it into cultivation. A few nurseries now stock it, including **Tissington Nursery, Tissington, Ashbourne DE6 1RA (tel. 01335-390650/web www.tissingtonnursery.co.uk)**, where Derek Watkins filled me in on its history. The nursery, in the walled former kitchen garden of Tissington Hall, is open March–Oct, daily, 10a.m.–6p.m. From A52 take A515 towards Buxton, then 4m after Ashbourne, turn right into Tissington village.

ASHBOURNE

Dove Cottage

Clifton, Ashbourne DE6 2JQ TEL. 01335-343545 OWNER Mr and Mrs S.G. Liverman HOURS Open by appointment for groups, also on a few Suns for charity in May–Aug, 1–5p.m. (please ring for exact dates) ENTRANCE £2 on charity days, children free DIRECTIONS 1½m SW of Ashbourne off A515, in Clifton go right at crossroads, then 1st left, house is 200yds on left by River Dove (well-signposted on charity days)
🌿 Plants for Sale

The River Dove, which starts high up in the Peak District National Park, runs a long and wiggly course that marks the boundary of Derbyshire and Staffordshire. And a short way south-west of Ashbourne (home of the excellent mineral water) it also forms the most picturesque of boundaries, beside the garden of Dove Cottage.

The very attractive stone house built in 1750 (not open) is home to horticultural expert Anne Liverman, who dispenses good gardening advice to her listeners on Radio Derby and whose plant stalls at regional fairs are always sought out by gardeners 'in the know'. Needless to say, her three-quarters-of-an-acre garden is packed with plants chosen with a discerning eye. There is emphasis on hardy perennials and shrubs which perform well and give long seasons of colour; favourites include alliums, astrantias, hardy geraniums, euphorbias, hostas, Jerusalem sage, lilies and berrying viburnums. *Veronica gentianoïdes* 'Tissington White' (*q.v.*) was discovered locally by Mrs Liverman and enjoys a prime position in the front garden.

A selection of pear trees lining the stone wall of the front garden pre-dates the Livermans' arrival at the property more than two decades ago. They were planted in the 1950s by an earlier owner, who put all the names in a book, which is passed on each time the house is sold.

BAKEWELL

Chatsworth

Bakewell DE45 1PP TEL. 01246-582204 OWNER Chatsworth House Trust
HOURS Mid-March–Oct, daily, 11a.m.–6p.m. (10.30a.m. in June–Aug), last adm. 5p.m. ENTRANCE £4.50, OAPs £3.50, children £2, family ticket £11 DIRECTIONS 8m N of Matlock, signposted from M1, off B6012 WEB www.chatsworth-house.co.uk
🌳 ♿ Access 🌳 Gift Shop 🌳 Café 🌳 Plants for Sale 🌳 2 for 1 Voucher

Gardening on the grand scale does not come much grander than at Chatsworth, the home of the Duke of Devonshire. The palatial mansion sits in a 100-acre garden, surrounded by a vast estate with glorious views of the surrounding hills. This garden says power, money, grandeur and water, which gets spectacular treatment in several different areas.

Most stunning is the great cascade, a broad stairway of water which tumbles gently down a grassy hill, from various spouts and dolphins arranged on, and around, a handsome pavilion at the top of the slope. The water re-emerges elsewhere in the garden to feed the sea-horse fountain on the south lawn and then another fountain before reaching the river. More water dribbles down an artificial, natural-looking, 45ft-high waterfall known as Wellington. There is also a fake willow tree (modelled on one dating from 1692) which spurts surprise showers from its branches at the discreet turn of a nearby valve, and the great Emperor Fountain and canal, a centrepiece dating from 1702, which throws up a 200ft vertical jet.

Capability Brown (*q.v.*) made substantial alterations to the formal 17th-century gardens, and by the time Horace Walpole visited in 1768 he found them 'much improved ... many of the foolish waterworks being taken away ...' Astonishingly, the water supplying the cascade and the Emperor Fountain is supplied by natural pressure from four large reservoir lakes, all man-made, on the plateau above the woods. There is much else to see here too: rose gardens, flower borders, Paxton's rockeries and a long wall of glasshouses, a fine maze, magnificent trees, a wonderful woodland garden, serpentine hedges and a kitchen garden. For me, it is still the water that captivates, but everyone should find something magical here.

Dressing Well In Derbyshire

Well-dressing is a decorative floral custom unique to a cluster of Derbyshire villages, particularly in the Buxton region, known for its famous spring water. The custom is believed to have originated in pagan times, although the first record of well-dressing (or its revival) dates from the early 1600s, at Tissington.

In limestone areas such as this, where water drains quickly through the porous stone, villages and homesteads were typically situated around reliable water sources. Decoration of the wells became a way of giving thanks for the precious gift of water and ensuring supplies for the future.

The dressing of wells is a skilled art, whereby villagers create pictures, usually of biblical scenes, from flower petals, mosses, lichens, leaves, bark and other natural materials, to make vivid and colourful designs. Traditionally, the men build the board base, onto which the flowers and other materials are pressed into soft clay by the village women. The ornaments last for up to a week, adorning wells in villages such as Tissington, Worksworth, Monyash, Tideswell, Eyam and Whitwell.

CHESTERFIELD

Hardwick Hall

Doe Lea, Chesterfield S44 5QJ TEL. 01246-850430 OWNER The National Trust HOURS April–Oct, daily, 12 noon–5p.m.; house Wed–Thurs, Sat–Sun and Bank Holiday Mons,12.30–5p.m. ENTRANCE House and garden £6.20, children £3.10, family ticket £15.50; garden only £3.30, children £1.60, family ticket £8.20; car park £2 DIRECTIONS Signposted from Jct 29 of M1, 3m away

🔥 ♿ Access 🔥 Gift Shop 🔥 Café 🔥 Plants for Sale

Bess of Hardwick, Countess of Shrewsbury, is one of history's larger-than-life characters – a sort of Pamela Harriman, in spades. Born plain Elizabeth Hardwick in 1527, the daughter of an obscure Derbyshire squire, married four times, on each occasion to a husband wealthier and more powerful than the last, she outlived them all. At the time of her death she was the richest woman in England after the Queen, with 100,000 acres and an annual income of £10,000, a huge fortune at the time.

We have her to thank for beautiful 'Hardwick Hall, more glass than wall', around which lies just the skeleton of her early 17th-century garden. But no matter; the present eight-acre gardens are formally laid out, in sympathy with the building, rather than being historically correct. There are wonderful yew hedges and hornbeam avenues, one of the largest and most beautifully planted herb gardens in Britain, a nuttery, old fruit trees, Gertrude Jekyll-style abundant flower borders, and fine parkland trees. It is a place to enjoy many times, not least up to the hall's rooftops where the initials ES are still proudly silhouetted in fretted stone against the sky. There are plants for sale but only at weekends.

TICKNALL

Calke Abbey

Ticknall DE73 1LE TEL. 01332-863822 OWNER The National Trust HOURS April–Oct, Sat–Wed, 11a.m.–5.30p.m. (last adm. 5p.m.); house 1–5.30p.m. ENTRANCE £3, children £1.50; house and garden £5.40, children £2.70, family ticket £13.50; parking charge of £2.60 is refundable on entry to house, but not to garden DIRECTIONS 10m S of Derby, off A514 at Ticknall

🚻 ♿ Access 🚻 Gift Shop 🚻 Café

Magnificent limes line the sweeping drive through the 25-acre park at Calke Abbey and the setting, of gently undulating pastures, curvaceous lakes and ancient woodland, is captivating, full of the atmosphere of times past. The olden days are even more evident in the house (which must be seen); it is a time capsule that had been barely disturbed for 100 years when the National Trust took over the property, and they have gone out of their way to keep it that way, largely resisting the temptation to spruce it up.

Outdoors, the walled flower and kitchen gardens are hidden away up the hill, where they would not intrude on the 18th-century landscape. In the 1770s Sir Henry Harpur even built a tunnel between the servants' quarters in the house and the walled garden, so there would be no vulgar views of staff fetching food for the kitchen. Here there are flowers, Victorian bedding schemes and vegetables, but the high point is the exceedingly rare auricula theatre, of tiered shelves set in the garden wall, for displaying auriculas in bloom in spring, followed by pots of pelargoniums in summer.

The Bloody Cranesbill

It seems unkind, or at least inaccurate, to call this spectacular native geranium 'bloody', for its cheerful flowers are actually a strikingly extrovert magenta, on a low, spreading hummock of a plant.

In bloom for a long period through the summer, *Geranium sanguineum* is a signature plant of Derbyshire's dales and other limestone regions. Its deep pinkness is set off beautifully by the greyness of the stones among which it creeps, and the leaves take on burnished tints as cooler weather arrives with the autumn. Many named garden cultivars have been bred from the species, offering a range of flower tints from dark to pale pinks, red-veined and pure white varieties, such as the popular *G. s.* 'Album'. The cultivar 'Cedric Morris' bears particularly large, magenta flowers and *G. s.* var. *striatum* bears pretty, candy-pink petals pencilled with contrasting red veins. Easy to grow and propagate and ideal for borders and rock gardens, the bloody cranesbill and its cultivars are widely available through nurseries specialising in hardy perennials.

And also...

Plantsman-explorer Roy Lancaster alerted me to the treasures on sale at **Bluebell Nursery, Annwell Lane, Smisby, Ashby-de-la-Zouch LE65 2TA (tel. 01530-413700/web www.bluebellnursery.com)**. Its catalogue (send a cheque for £1.30 and 2 × 1st-class stamps) is full of obscure shrubs and trees, such as *Sinocalycanthus chinensis*, a rare Chinese relation of American allspice, and the red-and-white-flowered *Mahonia gracilipes*, a dwarf, suckering shrub, also from China. A young, four-acre woodland garden is now open. Open all year, March–Oct, Mon–Sat, 9a.m.–5p.m., Sun and Bank Holiday Mons, 10.30a.m.–4.30p.m.; Nov–Feb, Mon–Sat, 9a.m.–4p.m. Leave M42 at Ashby-de-la-Zouch, take A511 towards Burton upon Trent, after 1m turn right and follow signs.

Dam Farm House, Yeldersley Lane, Ednaston, Ashbourne DE6 3BA (tel. 01335-360291), has, I am told, a wonderful, plant-packed three-acre garden made since 1980 by Jean Player, a scion of the Loder family which has made several of the great gardens of Sussex. There are mixed borders, a scree garden, and rare plants propagated for sale to interested visitors. Open April–Oct, private visitors and groups by appointment, also for several Suns in summer for the National Gardens Scheme. Entrance £3, children free. On Yeldersley Lane, 5m SE of Ashbourne.

Elvaston Castle Country Park, Borrowash Road, Elvaston DE72 3EP (tel. 01332-571342), is interesting because of its history and connection with William Barron, a pioneer of tree transport. No expense was spared in making the gardens between 1830 and 1850, when thousands of mature specimen trees and large, fully formed topiaries were brought in from great distances. Open all year, daily, dawn–dusk (garden opens 8.45a.m.). Entrance free (75p–£1.35 charge for parking). M1 Jct 24, take A50, then A6 and follow signs.

Haddon Hall, Bakewell DE45 1LA (tel. 01629-812855/web www.haddonhall.co.uk), is a thoroughly romantic medieval castle (used in filming Zeffirelli's *Jane Eyre* in 1995), with lofty gardens dating from the 17th century. 'A gloomy and solemn silence pervades its neglected apartments, and the bat and the owl are alone the inmates of its remaining splendour,' claimed Rhodes's travel guide *Peak Scenery* in 1819. Today, restored, it is noted for its roses planted into stepped, south-facing limestone terraces descending to the fast-flowing River Wye. Open April–Sept, daily, 10.30a.m.–5p.m., Oct, Mon–Thurs, 10.30a.m.–4.30p.m. Entrance (hall and gardens) £5.90, concessions £5, children £3, family ticket £15. Off A6, between Bakewell and Matlock.

For all manner of greenhouse and propagating equipment, including staging, potting benches, propagators, heaters, watering systems and cloches, you will seldom need to look further than **Two Wests and Elliott Ltd, Unit 4, Carrwood Road, Sheepbridge Industrial Estate, Chesterfield S41 9RH (tel. 01246-451077/web www.twowests.co.uk)**. The two Wests – Christopher and Josephine – started the business in 1975; Elliott is the black labrador who graces the pages of their comprehensive mail order catalogue (free on request). Open most Sats for collection only, 9a.m.–12 noon. Off A61, between Chesterfield and Sheffield, follow signs to Sheepbridge Industrial Estate.

Devon

MAP NOs 1–2

A county of rich, rolling pastures, edged by two wonderful coastlines and encompassing the rugged moorland expanses of Dartmoor, Devon is varied and endlessly scenic. Its south-eastern coast is particularly favoured with sandy beaches and a mild climate, ingredients that have led it to be called the 'English Riviera'. The National Trust owns, and preserves for the nation, a good deal of property in Devon – around 5500 acres of Dartmoor, more than 80 miles of coastline, and a cluster of magnificent houses and gardens. Here, perhaps more than anywhere, the cost of a membership card can quickly repay itself while you see the best of what Devon has to offer.

Must See

Marwood Hill, Barnstaple – essential viewing for plant connoisseurs

Castle Drogo, Drewsteignton – outstanding design by Lutyens, richly planted

Rosemoor, Great Torrington – rapidly expanding to interest all keen gardeners

Exceptional in Spring

Killerton, Broadclyst

Dartington Hall, Dartington

Exceptional in Summer

The Garden House, Yelverton

Exceptional in Autumn

Coleton Fishacre, Kingswear

Overbecks, Salcombe

Knightshayes, Tiverton

Worth a Visit in Winter

Marwood Hill, Barnstaple

Killerton, Broadclyst

Dartington Hall, Dartington

Castle Drogo, Drewsteignton

Rosemoor, Great Torrington

Overbecks, Salcombe

BARNSTAPLE

Marwood Hill Gardens

Barnstaple EX31 4EB TEL. 01271-342528 OWNER Dr J. A. Smart HOURS Open all year, daily, dawn–dusk ENTRANCE £3, children free DIRECTIONS 4m N of Barnstaple, signposted from A361 (Barnstaple–Braunton road) for cars and coaches, or B3230 for cars only

🌿 ♿ Access 🌿 Café 🌿 Plants for Sale 🌿 NPC

Marwood Hill

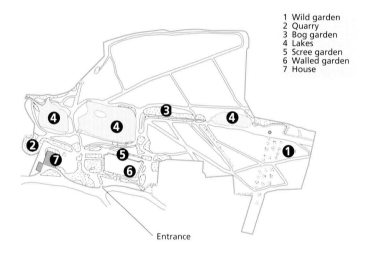

1 Wild garden
2 Quarry
3 Bog garden
4 Lakes
5 Scree garden
6 Walled garden
7 House

Entrance

Marwood Hill is renowned for its huge range of plants and breathtaking spectacles of spring and summer blossom. However, I visited a couple of years ago in early November and found the garden still flourishing, with many plants gloriously in bloom (including the National Collection of *Tulbaghia*) and the added bonus of fantastic autumn tints from its large collection of trees and shrubs.

It is a plantsman's garden, informal in layout, spread over 20 acres of sloping ground. The owner, Dr Jimmy Smart, has been developing the garden for nearly 50 years. Now in his 80s, Dr Smart was frantically potting up roots of assorted agapanthus in the potting shed when I called and the speed with which he accomplished the task would put many a young nurseryman to shame. Much of the garden is now mature too, with fine trees covering the south-facing hillside that sweeps down to a series of stream-fed lakes.

The old walled garden near the entrance is an intensively active nursery and plant sales area and includes a camellia greenhouse. Its stone walls are clothed in tender shrubs such as abutilon and *Cestrum* 'Newellii', and choice climbers such as the prolifically flowering, cowslip-scented *Clematis rehderiana*. Beyond the walls a scree garden is packed with alpines, and terraced beds in the upper garden are crossed by narrow turf paths among small shrubs and herbaceous plants in variety. I had never seen *Euphorbia stygiana* before, but its thick, waxy leaves and fat but spreading stems make it an appealing subject for a garden in sub-tropical mode. It is the sort of place where you can get distracted by all sorts of things before even reaching the pools and stream in the valley bottom.

By the water are grassy walks among ferns and assorted eucalyptus, beds of hostas and heathers, and a wonderful weeping form of Bhutan pine. The richly planted bog garden has a large stand of gunnera at one end. The soggy banks of the stream are where you will find candelabra primulas in variety, plus the National Collections of *Astilbe* and *Iris ensata*, the rather flat-bloomed Japanese irises in lovely pastel shades.

The north-facing slope on the far side of the bog garden is home to even more trees and shrubs, with mown paths suggesting a route up the hill for the energetic, plant-thirsty visitor. By the way, teas are served at Marwood Hill, but only on Sundays and Bank Holidays, from April to September, or for parties by prior arrangement.

BROADCLYST

Killerton

Exceptional in Spring

Broadclyst, nr Exeter EX5 3LE TEL. 01392-881345 OWNER The National Trust HOURS Garden open all year, daily, 10.30a.m.–dusk; house open mid-March–end Oct, Wed–Mon (daily in Aug), 11a.m.–5.30p.m. ENTRANCE Garden £3.70, children £1.80 (reduced fees Nov–Feb); house and garden £5.70, children £2.60, family ticket £13 DIRECTIONS 7m NE of Exeter, use M5 Jct 28, then B3181 towards Broadclyst

🅿 ♿ Access 🅿 Gift Shop 🅿 Café 🅿 Plants for Sale

The 21-acre garden at Killerton is enjoyable in all sorts of ways. Its summer beds and borders near the house are exuberantly planted with peonies, shrub roses and assorted Mediterranean plants, with plenty of late-flowering perennials taking over for end-of-season colour. Its woodland gardens beyond are crammed with all manner of beautiful trees, many of them grown from seed brought back from plant-hunters' expeditions in the 19th and early 20th centuries. In spring, the rhododendrons, azaleas and magnolias are remarkable, and the woodland banks are host to carpets of primroses, bluebells, cyclamen and narcissi. The Bear's Hut, near the rock garden, is a delightful rustic building with a patterned floor partly made from the knuckle-joints of long-deceased deer. The peach-coloured house is lovely, too; its elegant rooms are light and spacious, and there are historic costume exhibitions. You can also eat well here in the restaurant (open same days as the house).

CELEBRITY CHOICE

Anne Swithinbank
Television presenter and panellist
on Radio 4's *Gardeners' Question Time*

'I thoroughly recommend **Bicton** (*q.v.*), especially for family visits. My husband and I have been there with my parents and our children, and it really does have enough to interest all three generations. If you take the train ride, which is fun, you can see all the grounds, including the pinetum with its meta-sequoias and a beautiful umbrella pine, *Sciadopitys verticillata.*

The children love the ducks and the adventure playground, and the fountain has always been working – you feel that someone really looks after the place. The planting everywhere is very well executed: the summer bedding is good and the containers well planted. There's a collection of passiflora, and the conservatory is lovely, from an architectural point of view. It's nice to go where there is some diversion, and where there are things to interest other members of the family who may not be as much into the plants as I am.'

BUDLEIGH SALTERTON

Bicton Park Botanical Gardens

East Budleigh, Budleigh Salterton EX9 7BJ TEL. 01395-568465 OWNER Mr and Mrs Lister HOURS Open all year, daily, Easter–late Oct, 10a.m.–6p.m., winter, 10a.m.–5p.m. ENTRANCE £4.75, OAPs £3.75, children £2.75, family ticket £12.75 DIRECTIONS On A376 2m N of Budleigh Salterton, signposted from M5 Jct 30 WEB www.bictongardens.co.uk

🌿 ⅋ Access 🌿 Gift Shop 🌿 Café 🌿 Plants for Sale 🌿 2 for 1 Voucher

The blatantly commercial entrance to Bicton Park can be a little off-putting if you are coming expecting to see tranquil gardens; but do not be deterred, because the 64-acre grounds beyond are magnificent, with interesting features remaining from the different styles which have prevailed over the centuries.

The early 19th-century Palm House is one of the finest in the country, a filigree web of iron and glass, extraordinarily complex in the design of its three-domed roof. It is home to a range of tropical plants, as are the other, more prosaic glasshouses at the top of the walled Italian Garden. Here are broad lawns with formal flowerbeds displaying some of the best – and best-cared-for – seasonal bedding schemes you will see anywhere. The sculpted grass banks and water canal at the further end are survivors from a formal design of the early 18th century, and around the canal lie the park and splendid pinetum. There are urns and statues, the pretty, early-Victorian Shell House made of flint stones (reached via an unusual rock garden), and many fine and unusual trees. The miniature-gauge railway and extensive children's play facilities ensure that enjoyment can be had here by people of all ages.

A Pleasant Selection of Salvias

Plantswoman Christine Yeo is passionate about salvias (sages) in their seemingly endless forms and holds the National Collection at **Pleasant View Nursery, Two Mile Oak, nr Denbury, Newton Abbot TQ12 6DG (tel. 01803-813388), 2m from Newton Abbot, off A381 at Two Mile Oak Cross towards Denbury**. It is a collection that has been gathered over the past 20 years and amounts to over 200 different varieties.

Salvias belong to the Labiatae family, together with other herbs such as rosemary, lavender, mint and thyme. They have aromatic and sometimes very attractive foliage, and the range of flower size and colour is diverse, including vivid cobalt blue, pale sky blue, mauves and purples, pink, scarlet, orange, yellow and white. Hardy species tend to start flowering from May and may repeat-flower later in summer; half-hardy and tender species generally bloom from July onwards, continuing until November or later, if the season is mild. Most perform best on light, well-drained and slightly limy soil in a sunny position; very few will tolerate moist conditions or wet combined with frost. Both plants and seeds are available from the nursery and by mail (send 5 × 2nd-class stamps for a catalogue); Christine Yeo has also written an excellent, colour-illustrated booklet on salvias (£5.95 for Vol 1, £6.95 for Vol 2, plus 50p p&p). Open mid-March–Sept, Wed–Fri, 10a.m.–5p.m. (closed 12.45–1.30p.m. for lunch); garden open May–Sept, Wed and Fri only, 2–5p.m. Entrance (garden only) £2, children 25p. The nursery also sells a variety of shrubs.

DARTINGTON

Dartington Hall

Dartington, Totnes TQ9 6EL TEL. 01803-862367 OWNER Dartington Hall Trust
HOURS Gardens open all year, daily, dawn–dusk ENTRANCE Donation (£2 a
head suggested) DIRECTIONS 2m NW of Totnes, E of A384, leave A38 at
Buckfastleigh

🌳 ♿ Access 🌳 Café

Although the Hall dates from the 14th century, the 28-acre garden
has a curiously Art Deco, asymmetrical quality to it, but that is not
so surprising, as much of the present layout dates from the 1920s and
1930s. Spring is the most enchanting time when the long camellia
walk is in bloom, the banks are awash with flowering hellebores,
crocuses and daffodils, and when the splendid magnolias reach their
peak of loveliness.

It is a fascinating garden; grand in its execution, with giant turf
steps ascending the hillside, and a magnificent stone stairway links
the woods (and a Henry Moore statue) above with the lawns below.
Around the Hall, the treatment is formal, with straight paths, flower
borders and clipped yews. It becomes wilder and more woodish as
you leave the Hall behind; good use is made of the undulating terrain
and its lovely views of the Devon countryside.

Several well-known, 20th-century designers contributed to its
making, including H. Avray Tipping in the late 1920s, followed by
the American landscape architect Beatrix Farrand; in the 1940s and
1950s garden designer Percy Cane became involved.

DREWSTEIGNTON

Castle Drogo

Drewsteignton EX6 6PB TEL. 01647-433306 OWNER The National Trust HOURS
Open all year, daily (except last weekend in Oct), 11a.m.–5.30p.m. (castle
April–Oct, Sat–Thurs) ENTRANCE Castle and gardens £5.70, children £2.80,
family ticket £14.20; garden/grounds only £2.90, children £1.40, Nov–March
£1 (by honesty box Jan–March) DIRECTIONS 5m S of A30 Exeter–Okehampton
road via Crockernwell, or A382

🌳 ♿ Access 🌳 Gift Shop 🌳 Café 🌳 Plants for Sale

Castle Drogo is in a very dramatic setting, enjoying panoramic views
of the rugged northern fringes of Dartmoor. Although it is a medieval
fortress in spirit, the stern, granite house was built by Sir Edwin
Lutyens from 1910 to 1930 for Julius Drewe, a wealthy client who
had made his money from a chain of grocery stores.

Castle Drogo

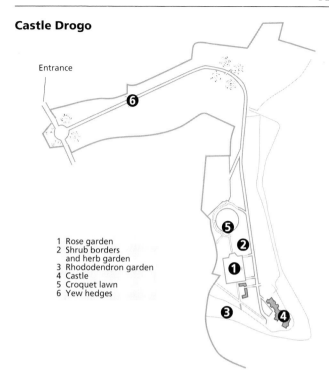

Entrance

1 Rose garden
2 Shrub borders
  and herb garden
3 Rhododendron garden
4 Castle
5 Croquet lawn
6 Yew hedges

To see the 12-acre garden in the correct sequence you should walk up the driveway to the castle and then double back, first taking in the rhododendron valley to the north-west, if you are here in spring. The main gardens are laid out in a series of ascending terraces, with an arrow-straight path leading directly through the centre. Crisp yew hedges enclose them, echoing the stout walls of the castle. From granite steps and a pretty gateway you enter the rose garden, a formal area of hybrid tea and floribunda roses, on either side of which are marvellous herbaceous borders. Shady loggias in the corners are interestingly fashioned from parrotia trees, trained over wire ropes and iron girders.

The next level features a corridor walk through spring-flowering shrubs, acers and shrub roses, leading to a huge, circular croquet lawn enclosed by yew. Lutyens' genius is present throughout the gardens; in his treatment of the hierarchy of spaces, their perfect proportions and the winding paths through the borders – a brilliant counterpoint to the overall linear design. The detail planting was by another early 20th-century designer, George Dillestone.

Do visit the castle, which is wonderfully bright and airy, despite its low proportion of windows, another example of Lutyens' brilliance.

GREAT TORRINGTON

Rosemoor Garden

Great Torrington EX38 8PH TEL. 01805-624067 OWNER The Royal
Horticultural Society HOURS Open all year, daily, 10a.m.–6p.m. (closes at
5p.m., Oct–March) ENTRANCE £4.50, children (6–16) £1 DIRECTIONS 1m SE of
Great Torrington on A3124

🌿 👤 Access 🌿 Gift Shop 🌿 Café 🌿 Plants for Sale 🌿 NPC

This is the stronghold of the Royal Horticultural Society in the south-
west. Rosemoor is, in fact, two gardens, the early section being chiefly
an eight-acre woodland garden with rhododendrons and other choice
shrubs and trees that thrive on acidic soil, with more formal plantings
near the house, made by Lady Anne Palmer in the 1960s. The second,
32-acre garden adjoins it (via a subterranean passage), and has been
laid out in recent years since Lady Anne gave the property to the
Society in 1988.

There are fine rose gardens, herbaceous borders, a cottage garden,
a gravel garden, demonstration kitchen gardens, water and bog gardens,
a herb garden and colour-themed areas. The Society holds regular
courses, lectures and demonstrations throughout the year, and the set-
up is particularly well planned for visitors, with a well-stocked shop
and plant centre and licensed restaurant. Lady Anne's garden holds
important National Collections of dogwoods and hollies.

KINGSWEAR

Coleton Fishacre

Coleton, Kingswear, Dartmouth TQ6 0EQ TEL. 01803-752466 OWNER The
National Trust HOURS End March–Oct, Wed–Sun and Bank Holiday Mons,
10.30a.m.–5.30p.m. (house 11a.m.–4.30p.m., last adm. 4p.m.), also garden
only in March, Sat–Sun, 11a.m.–5p.m. ENTRANCE £3.80, children £1.90; house
and garden £4.80, children £2.40, family ticket £12. Coaches only by prior
appointment DIRECTIONS 3m from Kingswear, off Lower Ferry Road,
signposted from A379

🌿 Café 🌿 Plants for Sale

Sailing, sunshine and south Devon's fashionable resorts brought
Rupert D'Oyly Carte, son and heir of the musical impresario partner
to Gilbert and Sullivan, to this region. In 1925 he had a delightful
house built of local stone, on an enchanting, south-facing valley.
Around it the 22-acre garden is laid out in a series of beautifully
planted terraces.

This garden offers a very satisfying blend of architectural and
natural elements. There are dry-stone walls, circular waterlily pools

and a narrow water-rill near the house; but all of that soon gives way to a free-form, organic pattern of winding paths and shrubberies. Countless little streams feed luxuriant waterside plantings of irises, ferns and oriental primulas. Rhododendrons thrive, and the mild climate nurtures a huge collection of half-hardy plants from Australasia and South Africa. The Rill Garden is brilliant in high summer, with bright orange and scarlet-flowered cannas joined by salvias and assorted African daisies. Coleton Fishacre is tucked away down narrow lanes but is well worth seeking out for its beauty and tranquillity.

SALCOMBE

Overbecks Museum and Garden

Exceptional in Autumn

Sharpitor, Salcombe TQ8 8LW TEL. 01548-842893 OWNER The National Trust HOURS Garden open all year, daily, dawn–dusk; museum April–end July and Sept, Sun–Fri, 11a.m.–5.30p.m.; Aug, daily, 11a.m.–5.30p.m.; Oct, Sun–Thurs, 11a.m.–5p.m. ENTRANCE £3, children £1.50 (museum and garden £4.20, children £2.10, family ticket £10.50) DIRECTIONS 1½m SW of Salcombe, signposted from Marlborough and Salcombe (small car park near house, charge refundable when paying admission – please note nearby roads are steep and single-track and are therefore unsuitable for coaches or large vehicles)

⬛ ♿ Access ⬛ Gift Shop ⬛ Café ⬛ Plants for Sale

The garden occupies a steeply sloping, six-acre site with spectacular views of the Salcombe estuary. Because of the mild climate there is more than a touch of the French Riviera in its planting, with fan palms, banana trees, cannas and eucalyptus contributing magnificent foliage. A collection of orange and lemon trees stands in containers in the parterre during the summer, increasing the Mediterranean ambience. Hydrangeas, day lilies, red-hot pokers and sunflowers contribute to its glorious late-summer spectacle. Spring sees glories of a different kind, from blazes of daffodils, primroses, anemones and *Cyclamen repandum* in the grassy slopes, to the broad, luscious pink flowers of a 100-year-old *Magnolia campbellii*.

'It is so warm and beautiful here. I grow bananas, oranges, and pomegranates in the open garden, and have 3000 palm trees, planted out in my woods and garden,' wrote Otto Overbeck, the scientist who lived here, in 1933. It is probably the banana trees that fascinate visitors most of all. *Musa basjoo*, a Japanese species, produces large flowers and small hands of inedible bananas. The plants at Overbecks succeed in producing fruits, but also bear leaves of up to 15ft in length. (In Japan, they are grown for their fibre, not for the fruit.) Do put aside time to see inside his house (the museum bit of the property), which displays 19th-century photographs of local interest, model boats and ship-building tools, natural history displays of shells, animals and old toys.

Flowerpots and More

If you are touring the north Devon area, it is well worth calling at **Brannams Pottery, Roundswell Industrial Estate, Barnstaple EX31 3NJ (tel. 01271-343035), on the south-west side of Barnstaple, close to the roundabout junction of B3232 and A39 towards Bideford and well signposted from A361 before Barnstaple**. It is a huge pottery, but don't be intimidated by the industrial scale – visitors are welcome.

There are guided pottery tours to see pot-throwing (you can even try making your own), a pottery museum with displays documenting the history of Brannams Pottery (founded in 1879) and a restaurant offering light meals and snacks. A huge range of terracotta pots is sold. Some are cheap-and-cheerful, machine-made and imported items, but there are also thick, swagged pots, traditional Long-Toms, bulb bowls, square planters and ornately decorated troughs. Brannams also imports a range of salt-glazed and decorated oriental pots which make ideal containers for acers, hostas and bamboos.

The pottery shop (which stocks a huge range of domestic/kitchen ware) includes a 'seconds' area with assorted garden pots where you may pick up a bargain. Open all year Mon–Sat, 9a.m.–5p.m. (also open July–Aug, Sun, 10a.m.–4p.m.). Entrance: adults £3.50; OAPs £2.90; children (over 5) £2.25; family ticket £8.50; groups of 12 or more: adults £3 each, OAPs £2.50 each, children £1.75.

TIVERTON

Knightshayes Court

Exceptional in Autumn

Bolham, Tiverton EX16 7RQ TEL. 01884-254665 OWNER The National Trust HOURS April–Oct, daily (house not open Fri, except Good Friday), 11a.m.–5.30p.m. ENTRANCE £3.90, children £1.90 (house and garden £5.50, children £2.70, family ticket £13.70) DIRECTIONS 2m N of Tiverton, from M5 Jct 27 take A361 towards N. Devon and follow signs

🔲 ♿ Access 🔲 Gift Shop 🔲 Café 🔲 Plants for Sale

Passions for golf and gardening do not often go hand-in-hand; each activity demands too much time for them to co-exist. But the wonderful garden at Knightshayes proves the exception to the rule. It was largely the inspiration of Lady Heathcoat-Amory who, as Joyce Wethered, was distinguished in the 1920s as the finest woman golfer in the country – four times British Open Champion and five times English Champion. (Henry Cotton declared that 'no golfer, male or female, has stood out so far ahead of his or her contemporaries'.) However, from the 1950s, Lady Amory exchanged the hickory shafts of her golf clubs for the elm of her garden spade and delved into the woodland of her husband's home at Knightshayes Court.

The existing canopy of oak and beech was thinned out (at around two acres per year) to make a spectacular and exotically planted 30-acre garden in which the Amorys developed lovely rambling walks among rhododendrons, Japanese acers, magnolias and assorted rare trees and shrubs, underplanted by carpets of bulbs. Especially breathtaking in both spring and autumn (and coolly green, with subtle floral highlights through the summer), Knightshayes' woodland garden is among the best of its type in the country.

Beside the house (a Victorian pink-sandstone monstrosity), formal terraces are planted with sun-loving shrubs above rolling lawns and parkland. Several yew-hedged compartments contain assorted mini-gardens featuring alpines, perennials and a serene, circular lily-pool. Hedging is used exceptionally well at Knightshayes, and one memorable hedgetop sports a topiarised scene of fox and hounds, dating from the 1920s.

UMBERLEIGH

Glebe Cottage Plants

Pixie Lane, Warkleigh, Umberleigh EX37 9DH TEL/FAX 01769-540554 OWNER Carol Klein HOURS Feb–Nov, Wed–Fri, 10a.m.–1p.m. and 2–5p.m. ENTRANCE Free for nursery, £1.50 for garden, children free DIRECTIONS Between Umberleigh and South Molton, south of B3227, from M5 Jct 27 take A361 towards Barnstaple, at South Molton take B3226 towards Crediton, then follow signs to Chittlehamholt and nursery
🌿 Plants for Sale 🌿 Nursery

So often it is the small, hidden-away nurseries that prove the most rewarding and Glebe Cottage Plants is no exception. It is remotely located, down a long and narrow, typical Devon lane made long ago for the odd farm cart. Tall hedgerows thick with brambles and ferns (and primroses in spring) prevent you from looking anywhere but forwards (or backwards) until you reach a farm gate and a further track which leads down a sloping pasture to the nursery.

Vermilion-haired nurserywoman Carol Klein is renowned for her fabulous and beautifully arranged plant displays which frequently win gold medals at Chelsea and other major flower shows. Her forthright and engaging style has also earned her a second career as a television gardening expert.

Carol's nursery is a haven for plant lovers, for she seeks out the unusual, especially where hardy perennials are concerned. 'To get in our list, a plant has to be garden-worthy, interesting and beautiful,' says Carol. Hear, hear. There are pulmonarias, anemones and hardy geraniums in variety, and a substantial list of penstemons, including many that were favoured by plantswoman Margery Fish of East Lambrook Manor. Carol counts Margery Fish and Beth Chatto (*q.v.*) among the most important influences on her own gardening style, which is naturalistic and uncorseted, with special pleasure taken in self-sown plants.

In her earlier career, Carol taught fine art, and her strong sense of colour and form are put to good use in her own, steeply sloping, one-acre garden beside the nursery, which is partly terraced and sunny, partly woodland, with rambling paths among spring flowers. There is an excellent nursery catalogue (£1.50 plus A5 s.a.e.) but mail order is no longer offered, so arrive with plenty of car-boot space. If you are after something in particular, it is wise to phone ahead in the off-peak season as many plants are kept at a holding nursery elsewhere.

YELVERTON

Buckland Abbey

Yelverton PL20 6EY TEL. 01822-853607 OWNER The National Trust HOURS April–Oct, Fri–Wed, 10.30a.m.–5.30p.m.; Nov–March, Sat–Sun, 2–5p.m. (last adm. 45 mins before closing) ENTRANCE £4.70, children £2.30, family ticket £11.70, grounds only £2.50, children £1.20 DIRECTIONS Follow signs from A38

🅿 ♿ Access 🛍 Gift Shop ☕ Café

The abbey was founded by the Cistercian order and later became the home of Sir Francis Drake. Beyond its 13th-century barn is a delightful walled herb garden featuring 52 box-edged compartments of random pattern, each one containing a different herb, and stone paths winding through. The main abbey gardens are chiefly sloping lawns, dotted with specimen trees.

Spring-flowering shrubs including camellias, rhododendrons, magnolias and azaleas, so typical of many gardens in the South-west, make this three-acre garden a pleasant place to wander earlier in the year, well before the herb beds get into their stride. Beside the abbey walls, a new formal garden has been laid out in Elizabethan style, with trellis work and box-edged beds.

YELVERTON

The Garden House

Exceptional in Summer

Buckland Monachorum, Yelverton PL20 7LQ TEL. 01822-854769 OWNER The Fortescue Garden Trust HOURS March–Oct, daily, 10.30a.m.–5p.m. ENTRANCE £4, OAPs/students £3.50, children £1 DIRECTIONS 10m N of Plymouth, W of Yelverton off A386 (signposted) WEB www.thegardenhouse.org.uk
🍂 Café 🍂 Plants for Sale

This renowned garden, of eight acres and still expanding, was begun at the end of the Second World War by one Lionel Fortescue, a retired schoolmaster of bluff reputation, but clearly someone with an artistic eye. Its tipsy walled garden contains the ruins of a house that had been built for the abbot of Buckland Abbey (*q.v.*). The position was, in some ways, less than idyllic however, being on a north-facing slope, nearly 500ft above sea level and exposed to tempestuous weather. Fortescue added hedges and terraces to break up the walled area into smaller, wind-filtered spaces and planted frantically, with a huge variety of both shrubby and hardy perennial plants.

Since the early 1980s (after Fortescue's death) the garden has been in the care of Keith and Ros Wiley, who have extended the garden into new plantings beyond the walled area. These include a rocky scree inspired by the wild landscapes of Crete, featuring drifts of thymes among other rock-loving (but not necessarily Cretan) flowers. Many new trees and shrubs have been planted in the grounds and another area is devoted to wildflowers. Plants are carefully selected for the harmonising effects of their foliage and blooms, both well cared-for and well labelled. There is also a well-stocked nursery, but no mail order or catalogue. Buckland Abbey (which serves refreshments) is close by.

And also...

Ann and Roger Bowden, Sticklepath, Okehampton EX20 2NL (tel. 01837-840481), live 700ft up, on the northern edge of Dartmoor, where they specialise in hostas, of which they hold a National Collection amounting to over 500 different varieties. A large number (but not all) are on sale in their excellent mail order catalogue (send 3 × 1st-class stamps), which is sumptuously illustrated. You can visit the nursery by appointment only, and their garden of hostas at Cleave

House opens several times in summer for the National Gardens Scheme (see the yellow book for details), 10.30a.m.–5p.m. Entrance £1.50, children free. On former A30 towards Exeter, 3½m E of Okehampton, on left in village.

Devon Violet Nursery, Rattery TQ10 9LG (tel. 01364-643033), is, as you would expect, devoted to growing *Viola* species and cultivars and holds the National Collection – around 110 different kinds, including Parma violets and Japanese violets, the latter of which are not available elsewhere in Europe. Send a s.a.e. for their list. Mail order is available for orders of six plants or more. Open by pre-arranged appointment, and for one special open weekend in March, for which there is a 50p entry charge. Off A38, through Rattery, then on left.

Full use is made of the water running through **Docton Mill, Lymebridge, Elmscott, Hartland, Bideford EX39 6EA (tel. 01237-441369/web www.doctonmill.co.uk)**. It makes an idyllic and natural-istic garden of mixed shrubs, bulbs and waterside perennials. The eight-acre garden is at ease with its tranquil setting in a quiet valley near the sea. Open March–Oct, daily, 10a.m.–6p.m. Entrance £3.25, OAPs £3, children £1. Signposted from A39 between Bideford and Hartland.

There is no mail order from **Peveril Clematis Nursery, Christow, nr Exeter EX6 7NG (tel. 01647-252937)**, but a visit is well worthwhile. There are varieties you will not find anywhere else (including many that were bred here) and some lovely, rare species clematis. Nurseryman Barry Fretwell offers well-grown and very reasonably priced stock, and the garden beside the nursery shows many clematis in action, draping walls, trees, shrubs and timber structures, often prettily paired with contrasting roses. Open March–Oct, daily, except Thurs, 10a.m.–1p.m., 2–5p.m., Sun 10a.m.–1p.m. only. M5 Jct 31, then follow signs for Morton Hampstead, then take B3193 towards Christow.

Plant hunter and speciality seed merchant Ray Brown runs **Plant World Botanic Gardens, St Marychurch Road, Newton Abbot TQ12 4SE (tel. 01803-872939)**. The display gardens are ingeniously divided into world habitat zones, and unusual plants are available from the specialist nursery. Open Easter–Sept, daily, except Wed, 9.30a.m.–5p.m. Entrance (garden only) £1.50, children free. Follow signs from Penn Inn roundabout on A380, near Newton Abbot.

Suttons Consumer Products Ltd, Wood View Road, Paignton TQ4 7NG (tel. 01803-696321/web www.suttons-seeds.co.uk), is an old-established seed merchant with a large and sumptuously illustrated colour catalogue of flower and vegetable seeds and garden sundries. An autumn catalogue of spring bulbs, perennial plants and soft fruits is also available. Catalogues free on request.

If you never know what to do with all those windfalls, or regularly have a glut of berry fruits, it is worth considering ways of using or preserving the produce. **Vigo Ltd, Station Road, Hemyock EX15 3SE (tel. 01823-680230)**, sells a range of traditional fruit presses and crushers (ideal for making apple and pear juice), and a stainless-steel Finnish juice steamer for currants and other berry fruits, all by mail order, catalogue on request. Open weekdays, 9a.m.–5p.m. Please phone before visiting.

Dorset

MAP NO. 2

This small county embraces green and undulating chalk downs, such as the anciently forested Cranborne Chase, and windswept sandy heathland, immortalised as Thomas Hardy's brooding Egdon Heath, 'a thing majestic without severity, impressive without showiness, emphatic in its admonitions, grand in its simplicity'.

Its coast is balmy, with cosy seaside resorts, such as fossil-rich Lyme Regis, where Jane Austen enjoyed the bay, 'animated with bathing machines and company', and John Fowles's French lieutenant's woman cogitated on the Cobb. Queen Victoria recommended the 'very salubrious air' of pine-encrusted Bournemouth to Disraeli, and its riverside gardens are just a fraction of the town's commitment to horticultural display. Dorset's gardens reflect its varied terrain, from the flint-and-cob walls and yew hedging in the chalkands, to the exotic bedding displays of the coastal resorts.

Must See

Cranborne Manor Gardens, Cranborne – fragrant and wild flowers in a romantic, historic setting

Exceptional in Spring

Abbotsbury Sub-tropical Gardens, Abbotsbury

Exceptional in Summer

Sticky Wicket, Buckland Newton

Kingston Maurward, Dorchester

Compton Acres, Poole

ABBOTSBURY

Abbotsbury Sub-tropical Gardens

Exceptional in Spring

Bullers Way, Abbotsbury, nr Weymouth DT3 4LA TEL. 01305-871387 OWNER
The Hon. Mrs Townsend HOURS Open all year, daily, 10a.m.–6p.m. (Nov–Feb,
10a.m.–4p.m.), last adm. 1hr before closing ENTRANCE £4.70, OAPs £4.50,
children (under 16) £3.20 (under 5s free) DIRECTIONS 9m SW of Dorchester,
9m NW of Weymouth, just off A35 on B3157 WEB www.abbotsbury-
tourism.co.uk

🌑 ♿ Access   🌑 Gift Shop   🌑 Café   🌑 Plants for Sale   🌑 2 for 1 Voucher

Abbotsbury

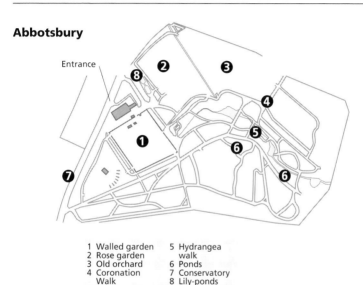

1 Walled garden
2 Rose garden
3 Old orchard
4 Coronation
　Walk
5 Hydrangea
　walk
6 Ponds
7 Conservatory
8 Lily-ponds

If you approach Abbotsbury from the Bridport coast road to the west,
you won't fail to spot a dense jungle standing proud of the
surrounding grasslands in the coastal plain below. This is
Abbotsbury's 20-acre sub-tropical garden, a haven of hothouse plants
growing in the protecting embrace of a hollow in the chalk and
limestone hills.

Inside, the shrieking peacocks and aviary of tropical birds bring
complementary sounds to the exotic surroundings of fan palms,
phormiums and yuccas. Among the garden's prize specimens is a
Caucasian wingnut tree, the largest in Britain. The valley garden has
woodland walks which are dazzling at azalea time; in summer they
maintain a cool atmosphere under the canopy of mature palms, oaks
and eucalyptus.

Streams filled with waterside plants meander lazily through a chain of ponds and simple timber bridges, and through seemingly endless jungle. By late summer the hydrangea walk is in its element, and by climbing a series of log steps to the Coronation Walk, you can admire the carpet of changing colours from above. An excellent range of plants, particularly Australasian and mild-climate species, is on sale in the plant centre.

BOURTON

Chiffchaffs

Chaffeymoor, Bourton, Gillingham SP8 5BY TEL. 01747-840841 OWNER Mr and Mrs K.R. Potts HOURS End March–Sept, Wed and Thurs, some Suns and Bank Holidays, 2–5p.m. Also open for coach parties by appointment (and teas by prior arrangement). Nursery open March–Nov, Tues–Sat, 10a.m.–1p.m. and 2–5p.m. ENTRANCE £2, children 50p DIRECTIONS 3m E of Wincanton. Leave A303 (Bourton bypass) at sign marked Bourton and continue to W end of village. Take lane signposted Chaffeymoor. Chiffchaffs and Abbey Plants ¼m on right
🟫 Plants for Sale 🟫 Nursery

Ken and Gudrun Potts's four-acre garden and nursery sit right on the borders of Dorset, Somerset and Wiltshire, and have developed around ancient stone cottages with views over the Blackmoor Vale to Bulbarrow Hill. Fine trees include the paperbark maple, a weeping wych-elm and a dawn redwood, for Ken Potts was a forester before he became a nurseryman.

Most of the garden is on free-draining greensand and the woodland dell, with its pockets of natural peat, has been developed with acid-loving shrubs. Giant gunneras thrive, unfurling their vast leaves. Around the house, stone walls and crunchy gravel paths wind through colourful borders of cottagey plants, helianthemums and old-fashioned roses, against an evergreen framework. Many plants seen in the gardens are sold in the Abbey Plants nursery that the Potts run on the same site.

BUCKLAND NEWTON

Sticky Wicket

Exceptional in Summer

Buckland Newton, Dorchester DT2 7BY TEL. 01300-345476 OWNER Peter and Pam Lewis HOURS June–Sept, Thurs, 10.30a.m.–8p.m., also for groups by appointment (please write for details) ENTRANCE £2.50, children £1 DIRECTIONS 11m N of Dorchester, 2m E of A352 or take B3143 from Sturminster Newton, garden is at T-junction midway between church and school
🟫 Plants for Sale

This garden is much newer than many others in the county, having only been created since 1987 by its owners, Peter and Pam Lewis. Their two acres are planted with lovely blends of herbaceous flowers, skilfully mixed to present colour-themed areas that will attract butterflies, bees and other wildlife. You may find purple spikes of *Liatris spicata* sharing a bed with deep crimson drumsticks of *Allium sphaerocephalon*, opium poppies and pink phlox; or mounds of lavender, irises, blue grasses and silvery artemisia woven around crunchy gravel paths.

It is an abundant, fragrant plot in the cottage-garden tradition. Herbs such as purple-leaved orach, fennel, anise hyssop and giant parsley, so useful in the kitchen, are also beautifully grown for their ornamental impact. Refreshments are served.

CRANBORNE

Cranborne Manor Garden and Garden Centre

Cranborne, Wimborne BH21 5PP TEL. 01725-517248 OWNER The Viscount Cranborne HOURS March–Sept, Wed only, 9a.m.–5p.m.; garden centre open all year, daily, 9a.m.–5p.m., Sun 10a.m.–5p.m. ENTRANCE Garden only £3, OAPs £2.50 DIRECTIONS From A354, midway between Salisbury and Blandford, take B3081 SE and follow signs for Cranborne. House is on left as you enter Cranborne; entrance is via the Garden Centre WEB www.cranborne.co.uk
🌺 Plants for Sale 🌺 Café

This, I must confess, is one of my all-time favourite gardens; it seems to have everything, in perfect scale. The manor house is one of the prettiest in the country, being not too grand, and is exquisitely proportioned. The original manor was built in 1207 as a hunting lodge for King John and was remodelled in Tudor times. It passed to Robert Cecil, 1st Earl of Salisbury, in the early 17th century and his descendants still live here.

A fine beech avenue runs down a gentle slope from the road to the twin pepperpot gate-houses. The house sits snugly in its 11-acre grounds, which were laid out in Robert Cecil's time under the instructions of John Tradescant the Elder, who brought back rare plants and bulbs from the Continent. A Jacobean mount (built for viewing the owner's rolling acres), and the walled and hedged enclosures, reflect the intimate garden style prevailing at that time.

Broad stretches of grass under fruit and forest trees are spangled with narcissi, cowslips, primroses, orchids and fritillaries in their thousands through spring. A rose-and-wisteria-covered pergola runs beside the old kitchen garden; there are pleached limes, a garden of old roses and pale flowers, and a herb garden with windows cut into an old yew hedge to give views of the countryside beyond.

The River Crane, from which Cranborne gets its name, runs along the northern edge of the garden; it is a winter bourne that dries out in summer. Pause to admire the nearby ancient flint-and-cob walls.

Part of the old walled garden has been turned into a well-stocked garden centre, specialising in old-fashioned roses, herbs, fruit trees and garden ornaments.

Discreet Plant Labels

If you despair of remembering the names of the plants in your garden, but do not want to fill it with garish white plastic labels, you will be pleased to know about **MacPennys Nursery, 154 Burley Road, Bransgore, nr Christchurch BH23 8DB (tel. 01425-672348)**. Their labels are a discreet black, with a scratchable surface onto which you etch the name with a fine metal scriber. Labels come in various sizes including a range with hanging wires for trees and shrubs, and are available by mail order. MacPennys is also a long-established nursery, with a broad general range of plants for sale, including some rare and unusual varieties (also available by mail, send an A4 s.a.e. and 60p in stamps for a catalogue). Nursery open daily, Mon–Sat, 9a.m.–5p.m., Sun, 10a.m.–5p.m. (July–March, 2–5p.m.). The adjoining four-acre woodland garden, converted from an old gravel pit, is also open for charity, by donation. From A31 take road to Burley, then right at war memorial, nursery 2½m on left.

DORCHESTER

Hardy's Cottage

Higher Bockhampton, nr Dorchester DT2 8QJ TEL. 01305-262366 OWNER The National Trust HOURS April (or Easter if earlier)–end Oct, Sun–Thurs, 11a.m.–5p.m. (or dusk if earlier) ENTRANCE £2.60, no reduction for children or parties DIRECTIONS 3m NE of Dorchester, ½m S of A35, cottage is 10 mins walk through woods from car park (nearer disabled car parking by arrangement with Custodian)

🌿 ₺ Access 🌿 Gift Shop

This is the humble cottage, probably dating from the mid-18th century, where Thomas Hardy was born in 1840, and from where he walked a round trip of six miles to school and back each day. The low, thatched cottage with traditional thick brick-and-cob ('cob' being chalk and straw) walls, was built by Hardy's great-grandfather and has remained, we are told, virtually unchanged. It is worth strolling through the interior, with its low ceilings, small windows and head-ducking doorways.

Outdoors, the deep front garden on a two-acre plot of poor, heathland soil, has been planted in a suitably bucolic, cottage-garden style. A narrow path leads up to the cottage door, the latter prettily framed – you will have guessed – with roses and honeysuckle. An underlying formal pattern of beds and paths is lost in the profusion of seasonal herbs and flowers.

The lupins, columbines, foxgloves and peonies of spring and early summer give way to late-season asters and Japanese anemones. A small orchard supports old varieties of apple. Large mounds of clipped box, a cottage-garden favourite for centuries, echo the shorn, rounded shape of the thatched roof that frowns over the upstairs windows. It is chocolate-box pretty, the sort of thing you see in the romanticised watercolour paintings of Helen Allingham, who was in fact a contemporary of Hardy's.

Despite being just three miles from Dorchester, the cottage maintains its air of seclusion, for it is hidden away in bluebell woodlands and cars must park 10 minutes' walk away (although special arrangements can be made in advance for visitors with wheelchairs who want to see the garden).

DORCHESTER

Kingston Maurward Gardens

Exceptional in Summer

Dorchester DT2 8PY TEL. 01305-215003 OWNER Kingston Maurward College HOURS Mid-Jan–mid-Dec, daily, 10a.m.–5.30p.m. or dusk if earlier ENTRANCE £3.75, children £2 DIRECTIONS E of Dorchester off A35, turn off at roundabout at end of bypass WEB www.kmc.ac.uk

🌿 ♿ Access 🌿 Gift Shop 🌿 Café 🌿 Plants for Sale 🌿 NPC

You have to go to the east side of the pleasant market town of Dorchester (known as Casterbridge in Hardy's novels) to find Kingston Maurward gardens, home of the Dorset College of Agriculture and Horticulture. There is a National Collection of *Salvia* here (amounting to around 75 species and 30 cultivars), and late summer is the perfect time to enjoy them, from the deep gentian blues of *S. guaranitica* to the festive magenta 'lipsticks' of *S. involucrata* and scarlet Mexican *S. microphylla*.

The 35 acres of gardens surround a classical Georgian mansion built originally of brick (in 1720), but entirely clad with local Portland limestone at the end of the same century. The grounds also date from that elegant period, but parts were remodelled after the First World War. They now feature broad flagstone terraces, formal pools, urn-topped and balustraded stone walls and an Edwardian-style sense of enclosure, as you move from one garden area to the next.

Kingston Maurward certainly makes eye-popping visiting, with its modern rose gardens, dahlias in great variety and sunny borders packed with explosive seasonal colours of bedded-out annuals and tender perennials. They include phygelius, argyranthemums, nemesias, cleomes, verbenas and much else, and the gardens are also home to a National Collection of *Penstemon*. As well as the variety of formal gardens enclosed by high hedges and walls, Kingston Maurward has parkland walks with broad lawns and bulb-filled meadows, a five-acre lake, nature and tree trails, and an animal park, so there is much here to entertain visitors of all ages. The standard of upkeep is good, too, making the grounds an excellent advertisement for the college courses on offer.

Sexy Hand-made Pots

Jonathan Garratt's fascinating yard at **Hare Lane Pottery, Cranborne BH21 5QT (tel. 01725-517700), 2m E of Cranborne towards Alderholt**, is crammed with pots of all shapes and sizes, with familiar Long-Toms and alpine pans, as well as a range of beautiful one-off pots in his own design. Garratt draws inspiration from prehistoric and traditional pots from France, West Africa and the Far East to make some striking and innovative containers with attractively textured patterns. The pots divide, he says, into two kinds, 'one is about function, the other about sex and romance'. Your average Bill-and-Ben flowerpots clearly fall into the functional category; the sensual shapes, primitive patterning and rich glazes of his other ranges are useful too, but more tactile and interesting. Garratt also sells garden art now.

The clay is dug from a local pit and the kiln is fired around eight times a year. The kiln holds a month's work, and takes 17 hours to fire, entirely with wood; it then cools for four days. Pot colours vary according to the heat in the kiln, from warm reds and oranges through brown to purple-black. 'I don't produce a price-list, maddeningly for everyone,' says Garratt, 'because I sell chiefly from here and change the designs very frequently.' Open all year, daily, but telephone to check times. A31, at Ringwood take road towards Verwood, then right towards Horse Centre, then left towards Cranborne.

DORCHESTER

The Scented Garden

Gardens Cottage, Littlebredy, Dorchester DT2 9HG TEL. 01308-482307 OWNER Chris and Judy Yates HOURS Open for NGS June–July, Tues, 2.30–8p.m., also groups by appointment ENTRANCE £1.50, children 20p DIRECTIONS 10m from both Dorchester and Bridport, 1½m S of the A35 (car parking on Littlebredy village green by round bus shelter, 400yds from garden)

🌿 Plants for Sale 🌿 NPC

This one-acre garden holds one of Britain's National Collections of lavender – over 100 varieties – growing in the former walled kitchen garden of an ancient manor. The proprietors, Chris and Judy Yates, operate in a low-key way, raising small quantities of plants for their own interest and for other like-minded enthusiasts. (Plants are not available by mail, but can be ordered from their list, and picked up by prior appointment.) In some ways their walled garden is the ideal place in which to grow lavender; on a south-facing slope, it is sheltered from frost and wind and enjoys the milder climate of the extreme south of England. The topsoil lies over chalk, which is very free-draining and has the lime content which lavenders prefer.

There is often confusion over lavender names, especially where nursery labelling is concerned. *Lavandula vera*, *L. officinalis* and *L. spica* are all names that have been used for what is actually *L. angustifolia*, the hardy 'old-English' lavender. Its popular name dates from when England was an important producer of the finest lavender oil, from fields on south-facing slopes south of London (Lavender Hill in Battersea recalls the local industry). To add to the confusion, the terms *L. vera* and *L. spica* have also been used for the so-called 'Dutch' lavender, a hybrid which is now classified as *L. × intermedia*. It is the camphorous-smelling *intermedias* that are grown in France for oil production, particularly a fine cultivar named 'Grosso'. This is a handsome choice for gardens, too, bearing plenty of large, purple-blue flowers, a little later than the *angustifolias*.

Like so many good plant collections, the Yates's grew out of an innocent curiosity to find out more. As they had grown sweet peas and roses in earlier gardens for many years, lavender seemed to be a natural companion for their already fragrant selection of plants.

CELEBRITY CHOICE

Penelope Hobhouse
Gardening author and
internationally renowned garden designer

'I love **Athelhampton** (*q.v.*) near Dorchester. It has a wonderful, formal design – a sequence of garden rooms – dating from the 1890s by Inigo Thomas. The atmosphere and architecture of the garden are superb – as a garden I like and admire it a lot. The pyramidal yews set into lawns are wonderful, and they inspired me to plant some like them in my own garden.'

EDMONDSHAM

Edmondsham House

Edmondsham, nr Wimborne BH21 5RE TEL. 01725-517207 OWNER Mrs J. Smith HOURS Easter Sun and Mon, May and August Bank Holiday Mons and Weds in April and Oct, garden only, April–Oct, Wed and Sun, all 2–5p.m. Also group visits by appointment ENTRANCE House and garden £3, children £1, garden only £1.50, children 50p DIRECTIONS 1¼m from Cranborne, between Cranborne and Verwood, off B3081

🌶 ♿ Access 🌶 Plants for Sale

A stone's throw from Cranborne, the handsome, gabled house at Edmondsham stands on the site of a manor which was once seized by William the Conqueror, who gave part of it to his queen, Matilda. There are some fine specimen trees in the six-acre grounds and a former medieval cock-fighting pit, but for me the chief interest is the kitchen garden, where head gardener Andrew Haynes conquers plant pests entirely organically.

Within the brick-and-cob-walled enclosure there are wall fruits and ancient espaliered apples, arched tunnels of runner beans and neat lines of chemical-free vegetables and salads. The dense rows of pot marigolds look wonderfully cheerful in their brilliant gold and orange hues, but their real purpose is to keep the cabbage root fly away. Since Andrew began planting his brassicas in small gaps between the marigolds, they have not been troubled by these pests. He is also a great believer in the efficacious effects of liquid feed made from the rotting leaves of Russian comfrey (despite its rank odour), and will gladly pass on nuggets of organic gardening lore to those who are interested.

A straight path running through the walled garden is flanked by deep herbaceous borders planted for a long season of colour; in high summer watch out for the large, bright blue trumpets of *Nicandra physalodes*, a very unusual but highly poisonous relative of the tomato. Its sturdy, black stems, handsome foliage and lantern-like seedheads are also very attractive.

POOLE

Compton Acres

Canford Cliffs Road, Poole BH13 7ES TEL. 01202-700778 OWNER Red Sky Leisure HOURS March–Oct, daily, 10a.m.–6p.m. (last adm. 5.15p.m.) ENTRANCE £5.95, OAPs £5.45, students £4.95, children £3.25 DIRECTIONS 1½m W of Bournemouth by A35 and B3065, well signposted WEB www.comptonacres.co.uk

🌿 ❧ Access 🌿 Gift Shop 🌿 Café 🌿 Plants for Sale 🌿 2 for 1 Voucher

Compton Acres offers 9½ acres of sheer, unadulterated garden tourism. It is a theme park of a garden, chiefly laid out between the two world wars. The south coast visitors love it, and so do I, because it is executed with great conviction. The bold colours of the planting are invigorating, from the spring azaleas and coppery foliage of the Japanese garden to the corseted bedding schemes around the Italian lily-pool with gushing fountains.

The Heather Dell, under wind-pruned pines, gives just a hint of what was once here; the garden is built on the sandy heathland that has all but disappeared under 20th-century development. The house was built in 1914 but immediately after the First World War its rich new owner, Thomas William Simpson, created several gardens linked by winding paths on the south-facing slopes overlooking Poole's yacht-speckled harbour. No expense was spared, either, in transforming its rough slopes of heather, bracken and briars into a lush and terraced landscape. The bill came to £220,000 (more than £2 million in present-day terms). Statues of bronze, marble and lead, ornate fountains and exotic trees and shrubs were imported to transform the site. The Japanese garden was designed and built by Japanese craftsmen, with genuine oriental artefacts including a stepped temple, imperial tea house, dragon gates and stone lanterns. Recent additions popular with visitors are the new deer sanctuary and a sculpture garden. Compton Acres is a place to enjoy the thrill of gardens in all their variety, and marvel at the singlemindedness of its makers.

PUDDLETOWN

Athelhampton House and Gardens

Athelhampton, nr Puddletown, Dorchester DT2 7LG TEL. 01305-848363
OWNER Patrick Cooke HOURS March–Oct, daily except Sat, 10.30a.m.–5p.m.,
Nov–Feb, Sun, 10.30a.m.–5p.m. (or dusk if earlier) ENTRANCE Gardens only
£3.75, children free; house and gardens £5.75, OAPs £5.50, concessions £3.95,
under 16s free DIRECTIONS 1m E of Puddletown, leave A35 at Northbrooke
junction and follow signs WEB www.athelhampton.co.uk

🟢 ♿ Access   🟢 Gift Shop   🟢 Café   🟢 Plants for Sale

Athelhampton

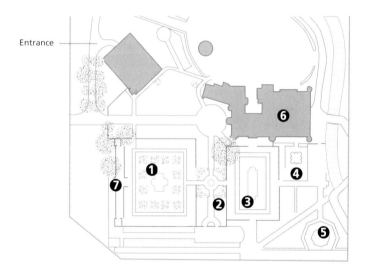

1 Great Court formal garden
   and pond
2 Lion's Mouth
3 Private garden with fish-pond
4 White garden
5 Cloister Garden and pool
6 House
7 Great terrace

Puddletown is deep in Thomas Hardy country and doubled as
Weatherbury in *Far From the Madding Crowd*. Hardy's father was the
local stonemason and carried out repairs at Athelhampton; the manor
provided the setting for some of the writer's work. The fine 12-acre
gardens are due to Alfred Cart de Lafontaine, a rich bachelor who
bought the estate in 1891; he promptly employed Inigo Thomas, an
advocate of formal garden design, to lay out the 20-acre grounds.

Thomas created a masterly series of self-contained spaces entirely
in sympathy with the house and its surroundings. From the Corona

– a circular area enclosed by scalloped walls of rich, ochre Ham stone topped by slender obelisks – tempting gateways lead into other spaces: to the house forecourt, the private garden with its croquet lawn and central canal, the pool garden known as the Lion's Mouth and to the Great Court. The latter features a dozen vast yew pyramids on smooth lawns. Beyond, a raised terrace has a pavilion at each end, decorated with stone faces: a smiling one in the west signifying the joy of summer and a scowling one in the east for winter. Later additions include a Cloister Garden of pleached limes around an octagonal pool, and a garden of white and pale flowers.

The 15th-century house is built on the legendary site of King Athelstan's palace and suffered a fire in 1992, but has fortunately been sympathetically restored.

WIMBORNE

Knoll Gardens

Stapehill Road, Hampreston, nr Wimborne BH21 7ND TEL. 01202-873931 OWNER J. and J. Flude, N. Lucas HOURS Early Jan–mid-Dec, Sun–Thurs, 10a.m.–5p.m. ENTRANCE £4, OAPs £3.50, students £3, children £2, family ticket £9 DIRECTIONS Between Wimborne and Ferndown off Ham Lane, B3073, signposted WEB www.knollgardens.co.uk

🌳 ఉ Access 🌳 Gift Shop 🌳 Café 🌳 Plants for Sale 🌳 NPC
🌳 2 for 1 Voucher

Knoll Gardens is a strange place, piecemeal rather than designed, but with plenty to interest the plantsman or gardener, for it crams over 4000 different species into a compact six-acre site, without feeling cramped.

An immaculate gravel entrance drive leads past impressive displays of fuchsia- and pelargonium-filled hanging baskets; inside, lawns and winding paths lead under mature oaks, eucalyptus and robinia trees to various themed areas. The water garden is a bold feature with lily-ponds and cascades, and beyond is a bedded-out formal parterre with dragon fountain. A straight strip of lawn, bordered either side with a thick ribbon of scarlet begonias, gives the impression of a formal carpet rolled out for an official function.

The garden's National Collection of phygelius, the Cape figwort, began nearly 30 years ago, when the popular hybrid, *P*. 'African Queen', was raised here. It is displayed in the brilliant summer borders, among dahlias, cannas and marguerites; there are also many interesting shrubs, including ceanothus in variety, and *Crinodendron patagua* from Chile, with white bell flowers. Trehane Nursery (*q.v.*) is next door.

And also...

There are pond plants in abundance at **Bennett's Water Gardens, Putton Lane, Chickerell, Weymouth DT3 4AF (tel. 01305-785150)**, with its eight acres, and some 150 varieties of waterlilies, which comprise a National Collection. Many of the waterlilies are displayed in a Giverny-style setting, which features a Japanese-style bridge replicating Monet's famous one. The flowering season is from June to September, with early summer a good time to visit if you want to stock up with pond plants and other aquatic supplies. There are also tropical water plants for conservatory pools and a tearoom, open through the season. Stocks are available by mail. Send 3 × 1st-class stamps for catalogue. Open April–Sept, Tues–Sun and Bank Holiday Mons (Tues–Sat in Sept), 10a.m.–5p.m. Entrance (gardens only) £4.95, OAPs £4.75, children £2.75, family ticket £13.50. A354, then B3157, 2m W of Weymouth, signposted.

Global Orange Groves UK, Horton Road, Horton Heath, nr Wimborne BH21 7JN (tel. 01202-826244), specialises in citrus fruits for the conservatory or greenhouse. Stocks are available by mail. Spanish peaches, apricots and olive trees are also now available. Send a s.a.e. for catalogue. Open daily all year, 10.30a.m.–5p.m. M27, then A31, turn right at Ashley Heath roundabout into Horton Road.

C.W. Groves & Son, West Bay Road, Bridport DT6 4BA (tel. 01308-422654/ web www.cwgrovesandson.co.uk), is a traditional, family-run nursery-turned-garden centre, which has been trading since 1866. As well as providing a good general range of plants, Clive and Diana Groves specialise in violas, particularly Victorian varieties, which are only sold by mail (send a s.a.e. for the catalogue). The show garden features some of the nursery's stock, and there is a demonstration vineyard, roses and asparagus beds. Open daily all year, 8.30a.m.–5p.m. (Sun, 10.30a.m.–4.30p.m.). Off A35, Bridport bypass.

In 1880 General Pitt Rivers laid out **The Larmer Tree Victorian Pleasure Gardens at Rushmore Estate, nr Tollard Royal, Salisbury SP5 5PT (tel. 01725-516228/web www.rushmore-estate.co.uk)**, for the recreation of people in neighbouring towns and villages. The chief interest is the eclectic collection of buildings he acquired and arranged around a broad lawn. They include an Indian room, a Roman temple, an open-air theatre and a richly carved building from Nepal; the surrounding 13-acre gardens are being developed and restored. Open Easter–Oct, phone for details. Entrance £4, OAPs £3.50, students £3, children £2, family ticket £9.75. Follow signs from A354.

Parnham House, Beaminster DT8 3NA, recently sold into new ownership, used to be famous for the timber workshops of John Makepeace, where hand-crafted furniture was made in the 14-acre park with its silent, wooded landscape. The formal gardens are dominated by stout cones of yew, marching around the lawns below the terrace in front of the house. Parnham boasts attractive herbaceous borders, too: one a cool collection of pinks, blues, silvers and whites, the other red-hot with dahlias, achilleas and schizostylis, both planted by Jenny Makepeace in 1984 and '85. Closed in 2002 and limited openings only in 2003 (write to Lander King for details). From A303 take A356 to Crewkerne, through town, staying on A356 towards Dorchester, then right onto A3066 towards Bridport, house is on right, ½m beyond Beaminster.

Trehane Nursery, Stapehill Road, Hampreston, nr Wimborne BH21 7ND (tel. 01202-873490), is renowned for camellias and blueberries. Both plants need a free-draining acid soil to thrive, and this part of Dorset has it in abundance. The nursery is in a sheltered spot with a stream running through, fed by natural springs; the water has a pH of 4.8, ideally suited to these plants. You can buy plants but there is also a mail order service. Open all year, Mon–Fri, 8.30a.m.–4.30p.m., also Sat–Sun in spring, 10a.m.–4p.m. and at other times by appointment. Next door to Knoll Gardens (*q.v.*).

Durham

This is a land of fortresses on rocky outcrops, steeped in histories of border wars, and princes and powerful bishops. Old Durham city, with its vast and splendid Norman cathedral (where the Venerable Bede was laid to rest), lies within a hairpin loop of the River Wear. To the south-west, the Tees Valley embraces some of the country's finest landscape and a sprinkling of attractive, unspoilt villages. Upper Teesdale is famed for its traditionally managed pastures, a wealth of natural limestone flora, and the unique Teesdale violet.

Exceptional in Spring

University of Durham
  Botanic Garden, Durham

Worth a Visit in Winter

University of Durham
  Botanic Garden, Durham

DURHAM

East Durham and Houghall Community College

Houghall, Durham DH1 3SG TEL. 0191-386 1351 OWNER East Durham and
Houghall Community College HOURS Open all year, daily, 12.30–4p.m.
ENTRANCE Free DIRECTIONS 1m SE of Durham city, S of A177

🌿 ♿ Access 🌿 Plants for Sale 🌿 NPC

The college grounds extend to 24 acres of training grounds for
students, encompassing many different horticultural disciplines.
There are smooth lawns displaying formal parterres of traditional
seasonal bedding, glasshouses, rock and heather gardens, woodland
plants, herbaceous grounds, a water garden and an arboretum. The
college is also home to two National Collections of plants: meconopsis
(30 species and cultivars, including the brilliant blue-petalled
Himalayan poppies) and *Sorbus aria*, the whitebeam tree (35 different
species and cultivars).

The college works in collaboration with other gardens in Durham
city, such as Old Durham Gardens, just across the river, for which it
has been grafting old varieties of apple, to grow in the gardens that
are currently being restored. The pleasant woodlands around the
college and its grounds have various walks, including a track leading
to the Botanic Garden (*q.v.*) and an interesting discovery trail which
leads visitors through the remains of the lost village of Houghall.

DURHAM

University Of Durham Botanic Garden

Hollingside Lane, Durham DH1 3TN TEL. 0191-374 7971 OWNER Durham
University HOURS Open all year, daily, March–Oct, 10a.m.–5p.m.; Nov–Feb,
11a.m.–4p.m., except in bad weather ENTRANCE £1.50, concessions 75p,
children free DIRECTIONS A167 to Cock o' the North roundabout, follow signs
to Durham, then signs to garden

🌿 ♿ Access 🌿 Gift Shop 🌿 Café 🌿 Plants for Sale

Just a mile from the city's centre, this garden covers around 18 acres,
principally used for academic teaching and research. A striking feature
near the entrance is the Prince Bishop's Garden, featuring recent,
carved statues of six of the county's most prominent historical figures.
(Alas! All are male – the north is clearly a stronghold of male
chauvinism – but surely Cicely Neville, the Rose of Raby, should be
there? She was the wife of Richard of York who bore two kings,
Edward IV and Richard III.) Beyond lie the glasshouses, featuring
climates for desert plants and those hailing from the humid tropics.

There is a small rose garden and adjoining alpine garden, and a garden of heathers and conifers set in wavy ground whose topography was produced by hundreds of years of ridge-and-furrow ploughing.

The main features, however, are the woodland garden of primulas, giant lilies and blue poppies among the rhododendrons which are best seen in spring, and the North American Arboretum at its most colourful in autumn. Unlike other botanic gardens, where plants are normally grouped according to their botanical families, in this arboretum the trees are planted in groups that would be found growing together naturally in the wild. Thus, those of California are grouped together, separate from those of Canada. A Himalayan dell features white-stemmed birches of the Far East, graceful Bhutan pines and deodar cedars.

Rare and Unusual Plants

Dirk van der Werff is a plant enthusiast who has used his hobby to found a fascinating and invaluable subscription-only journal for plantaholics. Seven years ago he thought of producing an occasional newsletter giving out obscure plant information to like-minded people. *New, Rare and Unusual Plants: A Journal for Plant Enthusiasts* is the result, now in its sixth year of production. It is distributed quarterly for a global market of around 1660 subscribers.

'Information was scarce about [new] plant species which had been collected, where new cultivars appearing in nurseries had come from and old named plants which had been rediscovered,' says Dirk. 'I try to act as a signpost as much as anything else – directing people to where they can find more plants.'

The A5 journal, partially illustrated with colour photographs, is packed with features by nurserymen, plant hunters and others, covering such topics as: the best Japanese anemones, new thyme cultivars, the latest in hardy geranium breeding and new plants from America.

When not hard at work in his own garden or producing this great little journal, Dirk works as a picture editor for a regional evening newspaper. Subscription enquiries should be directed to Aquilegia Publishing, 2 Grange Close, Hartlepool TS26 0DU, tel/fax 01429-423165. E-mail:dirk@plant-magazine.com

And also...

Pockerley Manor, at The North of England Open Air Museum, Beamish DH9 0RG (tel. 0191-370 4000/web www.beamish.org.uk), features quarter-acre terraced gardens re-created to look as they might have done 200 years ago. Three terraces descend the hill, featuring a formal parterre, a vegetable garden of historic varieties and an orchard. The discovery of the 1820 lists of Gateshead nurseryman William Falla, who at that time ran one of the largest commercial nurseries in Britain, provided invaluable data on locally grown plants. Open mid-April–Oct, daily, 10a.m.–5p.m. (last adm. 3p.m.). Entrance £12, OAPs £9, children £6. A1(M) Jct 63, then A693 towards Stanley and follow signs.

Essex

Essex has many different faces. There is the urban sprawl in the south and west that has encroached from north-east London, there are the broad mudflats and silty marshes of the Thames estuary, and the famous old seaside resorts of Southend, Clacton and Frinton-on-Sea. Inland Essex, away from the docks and industrial sprawl, is surprisingly rural – much of it low, level ground with the skyline pierced by the silvery silhouettes of great willow trees. The Stour Valley, on the boundary with Suffolk, is scenic country, often painted by John Constable. Nowhere does this region present real hills, although there are subtle undulations to the north of the county, an area which boasts many pretty villages. Colchester, however, stands on a ridge and was strategically important in Roman times.

Must See
Beth Chatto Gardens,
  Colchester – Influential
  planting by a *grande dame* of
  gardening

Exceptional in Summer
Glen Chantry, Wickham
  Bishops

Miss Willmott and her 'Ghost'

Sea hollies, or eryngiums, are popular herbaceous plants, valued for their spiky flowers which make excellent specimens when dried. Some species have an unusual, metallic-blue sheen to both stems and flowers, others are green or grey, but attractively statuesque. *Eryngium giganteum* is a desirable biennial sea holly, gleaming silver-grey and often called 'Miss Willmott's Ghost'.

The name refers to Miss Ellen Willmott (1858–1934), a headstrong heiress with formidable horticultural knowledge, especially where roses were concerned. She lived at Warley Place, near Brentwood, where her considerable fortune was lavished on the garden and thousands of pounds were spent yearly on new plants. (In its heyday, Warley Place was internationally famous and employed 104 uniformed gardeners and displayed unrivalled plant collections, beautifully grown.)

It is said that the eponymous eryngium earned its name from the way that Miss Willmott scattered its seeds in the gardens of people she visited. The resulting plants were, so to speak, her slowly germinating calling-cards.

The fortune, alas, expired before Miss Willmott did, and Warley Place and its awesome gardens no longer exist, except as a woodland nature reserve.

CHELMSFORD

Hyde Hall RHS Garden

Rettendon, Chelmsford CM3 8ET TEL. 01245-400256 OWNER The Royal Horticultural Society HOURS Late March–Oct, daily, 11a.m.–6p.m. (5p.m. in Sept and Oct) ENTRANCE £3, children (6–16) £1 DIRECTIONS 6m SE of Chelmsford, signposted from A130

🌼 ♿ Access 🌼 Gift Shop 🌼 Café 🌼 Plants for Sale 🌼 NPC

This is a real enthusiasts' garden, begun in 1955 by Dick and Helen Robinson, who passed the property on to the Royal Horticultural Society in 1992. It has always been a garden of richly diverse horticulture: in its eight acres there are pools, woodland areas and mixed borders of shrubs, roses, trees and bulbs. There are substantial collections of roses, irises, South African plants, conifers and daffodils as well as National Collections of crab apples and viburnums.

When the Robinsons came to the windswept, upland farm, there were precious few trees and no garden at all. It was developed gradually, in a piecemeal way, and the spaciousness of the site has allowed it to convert, without too much trouble, into a major horticultural attraction. Development continues under the Society's direction and the lower pond has been enlarged to provide enhanced displays of waterlilies and naturalistic swathes of waterside plants. As part of its mission to provide horticultural education, Hyde Hall now accommodates an extensive horticultural library.

The Farmhouse Garden is a new formal area of brick paths and symmetrical beds, lined with dwarf box edging. The curator calls it 'sophisticated cottage-style planting', with infills of silver- and purple-leaved small shrubs, a range of kniphofias (red-hot pokers), geums, salvias and eryngiums. The emphasis in this sunny area is on 'hot' colours, with the oranges and purples given depth by startling blues.

COLCHESTER

The Beth Chatto Gardens

Elmstead Market, Colchester CO7 7DB TEL. 01206-822007 OWNER Beth Chatto
HOURS March–Oct, Mon–Sat, 9a.m.–5p.m.; Nov–Feb, Mon–Fri, 9a.m.–4p.m.,
closed Bank Holidays ENTRANCE £3, accompanied under 14s free DIRECTIONS
7m E of Colchester, ¼m E of Elmstead Market on A133, from A12 take A120
towards Harwich, then A133 towards Elmstead Market and follow signs WEB
www.bethchatto.co.uk

🔴 Café 🔴 Plants for Sale 🔴 Nursery 🔴 Mail Order

Beth Chatto is one of the most inspiring of gardeners and anyone who gardens in difficult conditions (especially in drought areas) can be uplifted by a visit here. From 1960 onwards, on waste ground considered unfit for farming, Beth began to make a garden following ecological principles by choosing plants to suit the prevailing conditions. She was inspired by her late husband's detailed knowledge of wild plants and their habitats.

The result is a wonderful, six-acre garden, still evolving, with moisture-loving plants providing an exquisite foliage tapestry around pools and springs. Elsewhere, there are richly planted borders where the soil is fertile but well drained; areas of dry shade under trees are planted with appropriately undemanding subjects and bulbs. Mrs Chatto's new woodland garden, featuring early-flowering perennials, is seen at its best in May. The relatively recent Gravel Garden is especially instructive, as it is never watered, and this is in drought-ridden East Anglia. It is a beautiful, flower-filled tapestry of colours through the seasons. Key plants here include pink and mauve alliums, poppies, mulleins, assorted grasses, lavenders, sages, verbenas and African lilies. The adjoining nursery is another feast, with a huge range of well-grown plants, which are also available by mail (the excellent, descriptive catalogue costs £2.50). Light refreshments are served from April to September.

COLCHESTER

The Cottage Garden

Langham Road, Boxted, Colchester CO4 5HU TEL. 01206-272269 OWNER Alison Smith HOURS March–Aug, Mon–Sat, 8a.m.–5p.m., Sun, 9.30a.m.–5p.m.; Sept–Feb, Mon and Thurs–Sat, 8a.m.–4p.m., Sun, 9.30a.m.–4p.m. ENTRANCE Free DIRECTIONS Take A134 N out of Colchester, then follow signs to Boxted, over bridge over A12 and another bridge over stream, then right into Langham Road WEB www.thecottagegarden.com
🌿 Plants for Sale

This is a privately owned garden nursery, established nearly 20 years ago and offering wider-than-average ranges of garden-centre plants and sundries. One section is devoted to antique and hand-crafted artefacts, including willow baskets, sundials, stone troughs, old garden tools, hand-thrown pots, nesting boxes and weather vanes. The plants on offer include around 350 varieties of shrubs and 400 hardy perennials, herbs, alpines and bulbs.

GREAT DUNMOW

The Gardens of Easton Lodge

Warwick House, Easton Lodge, Great Dunmow CM6 2BB TEL. 01371-876979 OWNER Mr and Mrs B. Creasey HOURS Easter–Oct, Fri–Sun and Bank Holiday Mons, 12 noon–6p.m.; Feb–March (for snowdrops), daily, 12 noon–4p.m. (subject to weather) ENTRANCE £3.80, concessions £3.50, children under 12 £1.50 DIRECTIONS From A120 take B184 to Great Dunmow (signposted) WEB www.eastonlodge.co.uk
🌿 ♿ Access 🌿 Café 🌿 Plants for Sale

The owners prefix the property as 'The Forgotten' Gardens of Easton Lodge, but perhaps not for too much longer, for a fascinating project of repair and restoration is now under way. But first, a little background. Originally an Elizabethan estate with 800 acres of deer park, it was home to the fabulously rich Daisy, Countess of Warwick, who was a mistress of the Prince of Wales during Queen Victoria's reign. Daisy employed Harold Peto (*q.v.*) to landscape the gardens in 1902, which he did by providing balustraded raised beds, a rectangular pool, a brick-and-stone pavilion, lawns with arched pergolas and trelliswork, a fantastic Italian garden with 100-ft-long lily-pool surrounded by Ham stone terraces and balustrades, a maze, a tree-house and a Japanese garden with a tea-house by the lake. Alas, after the Countess's death in 1938 the property deteriorated, and in the war the park was obliterated to make an airfield for bombers. The main house was demolished and the gardens abandoned in 1950. Part of Peto's heroic scheme has now been restored (including the terraced beds, formal pool and pavilion) and scrub and tree clearance has revealed the crumbling remains of the Italian garden. All is done on a very tight budget with much help from volunteers and it will be fascinating to see more of this extraordinary garden reappear.

GREAT SALING

Saling Hall

Great Saling, Braintree CM7 5DT TEL. 01371-850243 OWNER Mr and Mrs Hugh Johnson HOURS May–July, Wed, 2–5p.m., parties by written permission ENTRANCE £2.50 for NGS charity DIRECTIONS M11 Jct 8, then A120 and follow signs for Great Saling

This is the lovely, Dutch-gabled home of the erudite wine and tree expert Hugh Johnson, whose books on both subjects are best sellers. 'Trees are tremendously exciting; there is something about the permanence of wood that really appeals to me, rather like maturing wines,' Hugh told me.

Beside the house and its splendid conservatory the gardens are walled and formal, with topiarised box and juniper trees, ancient apples and rectangular beds infilled with glorious mixtures of herbaceous plants and shrub roses. Further from the house the planting is more relaxed, with a large area of almost level ground planted as an arboretum. There is a slender Japanese garden with acers and a stream, a Shinto shrine, and sensuously curvaceous mounds of clipped box huddled together; there is also an informal pool, ornamented by a group of Himalayan birch trees, with gleaming white stems. The plant collection, particularly of trees and shrubs, is extensive, and the 12-acre grounds include an ancient duck-pond and a moat.

HARLOW

The Gibberd Garden

Marsh Lane, Gilden Way, Harlow CM17 0NA TEL. 01279-442112 OWNER Gibberd Garden Trust HOURS Easter–end Sept, Sat–Sun and Bank Holiday Mons, 12.30–6p.m., also small groups by prior appointment on weekdays ENTRANCE £3, concessions £2, children free

 ♿ Access

The garden covers nine tranquil acres on a gently sloping site, with wooded glades, streams and pools, a waterfall and carefully placed sculptures. It was the home of Sir Frederick Gibberd, the modernist architect who designed Harlow New Town after the end of the Second World War. His other renowned commissions include the early buildings for Heathrow Airport, Liverpool's Roman Catholic cathedral and the Northumbrian reservoir, Kielder Water. Gibberd was an art collector with a discerning eye. The modern sculptures displayed are encountered as you progress through the garden which is laid out rather like a series of rooms. (If you're interested in this aspect of Gibberd's patronage, other works of art from the Gibberd Collection are housed on the first floor of the Town Hall in Harlow, including work by Graham Sutherland, John Nash and Elizabeth Blackadder, open weekdays only, no entry charge.) Light refreshments are served at the garden·

SAFFRON WALDEN

Audley End

Saffron Walden CB11 4JF TEL. 01799-522842 OWNER English Heritage HOURS April–Sept, Wed–Sun and Bank Holiday Mons, 11a.m.–5p.m.; house, 12 noon–4p.m. ENTRANCE £4, concessions £3, children £2, family ticket £10, house and garden £6.75, concessions £5.10, children £3.40, family ticket £16.90 DIRECTIONS M11 Jct 8, then B1383, 1m W of Saffron Walden

 ¿ Access Gift Shop Café Plants for Sale

Audley End is a splendid Jacobean mansion set in a fine 99-acre, 18th-century park that was transformed from an earlier, formal layout by Capability Brown (*q.v.*). It is regarded as one of his most successful pastoral landscapes, with woodland groves, an elegant bridge by Robert Adam, temples and wonderful vistas. The River Cam weaves through its rolling lawns; many characterful trees enhance the silhouette of this garden on level ground. A magnificent Victorian parterre of flowers in geometrically arranged beds beside the house dates from 1830. The beds make a formal pattern cut into the lawn and were restored in recent years, having disappeared due to lack of labour for their upkeep in the Second World War. Now they provide a brilliant summer spectacle of mixed herbaceous perennials, bulbs and tender bedding plants, including lychnis and acanthus, sisyrinchiums, violas, lilies and peonies.

The latest project has been to restore the walled kitchen garden to its original 19th-century appearance. The idea is to run it as a fully working organic garden producing choice fruit, vegetables and flowers through the seasons, in collaboration with the Henry

Doubleday Research Association of Ryton Organic Gardens (*q.v.*). Its 170-ft-long five-bay vine house, one of the largest in the country, dates from 1802 and is an elegant forcing-house for exotic plants as well as tender fruits.

The Saffron Walden Crocuses

The picturesque and ancient town of Saffron Walden is famous for its colour-washed houses and decorative plasterwork (pargeting). It is also intimately connected with crocuses, for it derives its very name from the saffron crocus, *Crocus sativus*. These corms are among the oldest of all cultivated flowers. They ornamented vases of ancient Crete, *c*.1500 B.C., and saffron features in the Greek herbal of Dioscorides. Saffron was used medicinally and for dyeing wool, and the Romans may well have brought it to England. There is no record of its being grown here commercially until the 14th century, however, when many small fields around Saffron Walden were used for the purpose.

According to one account, a pilgrim in the Holy Land 'stole an head of Saffron, and hid the same in his Palmers staffe…and he brought this root into this realme, with venture of his life'. Cultivation ceased to be commercial from the 1750s, when cheaper Spanish imports could be bought, but the flower remains significant locally, and is displayed in the town's coat of arms and in carvings in the parish church.

WICKHAM BISHOPS

Glen Chantry

Exceptional in Summer

Ishams Chase, Wickham Bishops CM8 3LG TEL. 01621-891342 OWNER Mr and Mrs Staines HOURS End March–early Oct, Fri–Sat, 10a.m.–4p.m. ENTRANCE £2, children 50p DIRECTIONS 9m NE of Chelmsford off A12, take the Witham turn-off, 2m SE of Witham; turn left off B1018 towards Wickham Bishops, past golf course, over river bridge and left up track by Blue Mills

🌿 Plants for Sale 🌿 Nursery 🌿 2 for 1 Voucher

Most of the wonderful two-and-a-half-acre garden at Glen Chantry is informally arranged, with broad areas of grass winding between large island beds which are packed with choice plants. Amazingly, the garden was started by Sue and Wol Staines just over 20 years ago, on a very dry and windswept site in the driest corner of England. The soil is free-draining and stony, and to compensate for the relatively low rainfall, the beds are heavily mulched annually with composted waste and manure.

Planting is in bold drifts, with ornamental grasses used creatively for their foliage colours and wispy effects. There are hostas and hellebores, irises, peonies, poppies and a huge range of plants bringing continued changing effects all year round. Special features include a wonderful rock garden flowing away from the house down to a richly planted bog garden and lily-pool, and a more formal white garden. The adjoining nursery opens when the garden does, and specialises in a developing range of the more unusual perennials and alpines. There is an excellent catalogue (send 4 × 1st-class stamps), but no mail order.

C E L E B R I T Y   C H O I C E

Peter Seabrook

Author, journalist and presenter of
Peter Seabrook's Gardening Week on BBC1

'I am always very impressed with **Glen Chantry** (*q.v.*) because it has a variety of interesting features on a scale that makes sense to most gardeners. The garden demonstrates good horticultural skills, and the way the plants are grown makes a refreshing change. Within the small garden there is a rockery, a water feature, a shade border and several shrub roses. It is on a hillside, with less-than-perfect soil, but the planting associations are very well thought out, especially the way the tulips are imaginatively mixed with other plants.

And also...

Cants of Colchester, Nayland Road, Mile End, Colchester CO4 5EB (tel. 01206-844008), is the oldest of Britain's rose nurseries which has raised countless well-known varieties, including the highly successful 'Just Joey'. Bare-rooted plants are sold by mail, Nov–March (free catalogue on request) and container-grown roses are available to callers, May–July. Open July–Sept, Mon–Sat, 9a.m.–1p.m. and 2–4.30p.m.; Oct–June, daily, 9a.m.–1p.m. and 2–4.30p.m. Rose fields open June–Sept, dawn–dusk. From A12 take A134 towards Sudbury.

Crowther Nurseries and Landscapes, Ongar Road, Abridge RM4 1AA (tel. 01708-688581), is a smallish nursery and garden centre with popular ranges of plants and sundries. It also has an adjoining demonstration garden which is linked to the BBC Radio Essex gardening programmes, and regular gardening talks are given here by broadcaster Ken Crowther, who is also the proprietor. Open all year, daily, 9a.m.–5.30p.m. Entrance free. M25 Jct 26 at Waltham Abbey, follow signs to Abridge.

Flora Exotica, Pasadena, South Green, Fingringhoe, Colchester CO5 7DR (tel. 01206-729414), offers carnivorous plants, by mail order only (send £1 or 4 × 1st-class stamps for catalogue). Stock includes a wide range of hardy and tropical orchids and many rare and unusual herbaceous plants.

Langthorns Plantery, High Cross Lane, Little Canfield, Dunmow CM6 1TD (tel. 01371-872611), stocks an enormous range of plants, especially hardy herbaceous perennials. Alpines, trees and shrubs are also supplied. There is a £1.50 catalogue, but no mail order. Open all year, daily, 10a.m.–5p.m. (or dusk if earlier). Entrance free. M11 Jct 8, then A120 towards Colchester for 5m, signposted from A120.

Ken Muir Ltd, Honeypot Farm, Rectory Road, Weeley Heath, Clacton-on-Sea CO16 9BJ (tel. 0870-747 9111/web www.kenmuir.co.uk), specialises in fruit, particularly strawberries (his Chelsea show displays are too tempting for words), raspberries, blackberries, currants and a range of tree fruits, especially by mail. Send 3 × 1st-class stamps for a catalogue. Open all year, daily, 10a.m.–4p.m. A133 towards Clacton, then left at roundabout towards Frinton, then right onto B1441, after 1½m turn right at White Hart, farm on left.

Suffolk Herbs, Monks Farm, Coggeshall Road, Kelvedon CO5 9PG (tel. 01376-572456), produces a fantastic, free mail order catalogue of herb, wildflower, vegetable, green manure crop and ancient grain seeds (e.g. quinoa, grown by the Incas); also Chinese and oriental vegetables, organic seeds and products, and a small range of gardening tools.

Warley Rose Gardens, Warley Street, Great Warley, Brentwood CM13 3JH (01277-221966/web www.warleyroses.co.uk), is a specialist rose grower offering a broad range (over 400 varieties), including climbers and ramblers, hybrid teas and floribundas, shrub, miniature and patio roses. Free catalogue on request. Open all year, Mon–Sat, 9a.m.–5.30p.m. Rose fields in bloom, July–Sept. On B186, just off A127 and near M25 Jct 29.

Gloucestershire

MAP NO. 2

The limestone hills of the Cotswolds give Gloucestershire much of its character. They have provided the pleasing undulations in the landscape, and also the wonderful stone that has built many of the county's handsome villages and churches. There are stately homes and royal residences dotted about its dignified countryside, and Gloucestershire certainly has a healthy slice of good gardens, making visiting weekends worthwhile in every season. Designers, architects, artists and others sympathetic with the Arts and Crafts movement of the late 19th and early 20th centuries found the unpretentious vernacular architecture of the Cotswold villages to their taste, and gardens such as those at Snowshill and Rodmarton Manors exemplify the style brought outdoors.

Must See

Hidcote Manor, Chipping Campden – a keystone garden of the 20th century

Painswick Rococo Garden, Painswick – intimate landscape garden with edible highlights

Exceptional in Spring

Barnsley House Garden, Barnsley

Exceptional in Summer

Sudeley Castle, Winchcombe

Exceptional in Autumn

Westonbirt Arboretum, Tetbury

BARNSLEY

Barnsley House Garden

Barnsley, nr Cirencester GL7 5EE TEL. 01285-740561 OWNER Mr Charles Verey
HOURS Feb–Dec, Mon and Wed–Sat, 10a.m.–5.30p.m. ENTRANCE £3.75, OAPs £3,
children free DIRECTIONS 4m NE of Cirencester on B4425 in Barnsley village;
M4 Jct 15, then A419 to Cirencester, then B4425 WEB www.opengarden.co.uk
🌣 Access 🌣 Gift Shop 🌣 Plants for Sale

This is the famous four-acre garden of the late *grande dame* of
gardening, Rosemary Verey, garden adviser to the Prince of Wales,
Elton John and others. My first visit some years ago coincided with
laburnum time (at the end of May), when Mrs Verey's famous
laburnum tunnel was in full bloom, underplanted by alliums, dark
columbines and contrasting foliage of deadnettles, and it was
breathtaking. It is still the time I like best in this garden, when the
late spring bulbs are joined by early perennials. The peonies, lupins
and poppies beautifully mix with sturdy topiaries and formal
hedging.

There are mixed borders, strong vistas and contrasting sweeps of
lawn, a Tudor-style knot garden, a shrubby and flowery wilderness
and, across the farm track, a formal and beautifully kept kitchen
garden/potager. Some of the planting has been rationalised since
Mrs Verey's day, to make it less labour-intensive, but the garden's
place in 20th-century horticultural history is assured.

BROADWAY

Snowshill Manor

Snowshill, nr Broadway WR12 7JU TEL. 01386-852410 OWNER The National
Trust HOURS April–Oct, Wed–Sun and Bank Holiday Mons (all Mons in July
and Aug), 11a.m.–5.30p.m. (house 12 noon–5p.m.) ENTRANCE (House and
gardens – timed ticket system for house) £6, children £3, family ticket £15;
(gardens only) £3.50, children £1.75 DIRECTIONS 3m SW of Broadway,
approach only from turning off A44 by Broadway Green. New car park and
entry (500yds away) – no entry from Snowshill village
🌣 Gift Shop 🌣 Café 🌣 Plants for Sale

To foreign eyes, and even British ones, Snowshill Manor seems the
quintessential English country garden, backed by stone walls, filled
with cottage garden plants in great profusion. Poppies, lady's mantle
and penstemons spill over its narrow gravel paths, aubrieta tumbles
off the walls, and roses and vines run rampant. White pigeons flutter
above the mossy, stone-tiled roof of the substantial medieval

dovecote, and beyond are sneak views of the beautiful, rolling Cotswold pastures.

It is a highly architectural garden, its two acres having been planned in the first instance by M.H. Baillie Scott, an architect working in the Arts and Crafts style in the 1920s, whose intentions were simplified and made less formal by the owner, Charles Wade, who was also an architect. Its little walled enclosures, corridors and flights of steps were laid out with precision, and the incidental timber work – doors, benches, niches and so on – were (and continue to be) picked out in a bold French blue that complements both the flowers and the honey-grey local stone. There are daffodil-packed lawns rolling down the hill in a smooth, green counterpoint to the formal stonework, and everything is now managed organically, in sympathy with the bucolic flavour of the place.

CHIPPING CAMPDEN

Hidcote Manor Garden

Hidcote Bartrim, Chipping Campden GL55 6LR TEL. 01386-438333 OWNER The National Trust HOURS May–Oct, Sat–Mon and Wed–Thurs (Sat–Thurs in June–July), 10.30a.m.–5.30p.m. (4.30p.m. in Oct), last adm. 1hr before closing or dusk if earlier ENTRANCE £5.70, children £2.80, family ticket £14 DIRECTIONS At Hidcote Bartrim, signposted from B4632 Stratford–Broadway road

⬛ ♿ Access ⬛ Gift Shop ⬛ Café ⬛ Plants for Sale

Hidcote Manor is one of Britain's most famous and influential gardens, made in the early years of the 20th century by Major Lawrence Johnston. Its impact on 20th-century garden-making has been profound and new evidence of how the garden looked when Major Johnston was alive is going to be the basis of some substantial alterations to its planting over the next 10 years.

Having been given the hamlet of Hidcote Bartrim, the manor house and 280 acres of farmland by his mother in 1907, Major Johnston set about creating his 10-acre garden masterpiece. It is divided into hedged rooms and green corridors in a thoroughly disciplined way, but within each area the chosen planting conveys a different feel. The restful green simplicity of grass and plain hedges of one area lead to intensive, colourful planting in another. There is a famous White Garden (which was in fact pink in Major Johnston's day), with topiary birds; an equally famous pair of red borders featuring seasonal red flowers and bronze foliage, terminating in handsome brick gazebos; a circular pool garden almost entirely filled with water; a garden of fuchsias; a Long Walk serenely grassed and hedged; woodland and stream gardens crossed by winding paths and much more. Each season has its merits, so return often – there are always new surprises and the restoration of the rock garden will add another dimension.

'Chinese' Wilson and his Plants

If you have *Clematis armandii*, *C. montana rubens*, kiwi fruits, a paperbark maple (*Acer griseum*), or the deeply fragrant *regale* lilies in your garden then you have reason to thank Ernest 'Chinese' Wilson (1876–1930), who was born at Chipping Campden. These are just a few of the beautiful plants that he introduced to our shores following his intrepid expeditions to the Far East in the early years of the 20th century. Wilson's journals note the perilous nature of his task in searching out new plants: 'Well, if they take a fancy for my head during the night I do not see what is to prevent them from taking it,' he recorded on a trip to the mountains of Formosa. 'Gathered around several fires were two score half-naked ex-head-hunters, armed with bows and arrows, long knives and guns, who had struggled all day...carrying our belongings.' Wilson nearly lost his life in collecting *Lilium regale*, but ironically, having survived landslides, armed rebellions and snowstorms during his expeditions, he died in a car crash on a suburban highway near Boston. **The Ernest Wilson Memorial Garden, Leasbourne, Chipping Campden GL55 6AF (tel. 01386-852630)**, features a collection of his plants. Open all year, daily, dawn–dusk. Entrance by donation. At the north end of High Street in Chipping Campden.

CHIPPING CAMPDEN

Kiftsgate Court

Chipping Campden GL55 6LW TEL. 01386-438777 OWNER Mr and Mrs J. Chambers HOURS April–May, Aug–Sept, Wed–Thurs, Sun and Bank Holiday Mons, 2–6p.m.; June–July, Wed–Thurs, Sat–Sun, 12 noon–6p.m. ENTRANCE £4, children £1 DIRECTIONS 3m NE of Chipping Campden, see directions for Hidcote Manor (*q.v.*), next door
🌱 Plants for Sale

Famous for the rampant 'Kiftsgate' rose, which effortlessly clambers through large trees and over a tithe barn, showering everything in white blossoms in July, this is a six-acre garden of dramatic statements. Its house sits at the top of a steep escarpment, peering through the trees to the Vale of Evesham. The garden runs downhill in a series of terraces and zigzag walks, with enclosed areas at the top padded out by lush plantings of shrubs and seasonal flowers, giving way to more natural fusion with the landscape as the paths progress down the steep slope. There are other lovely roses here, including a long path hedged either side by pink-and-white *Rosa gallica* 'Versicolor' (a.k.a. *Rosa mundi*) which terminates by a seat, interestingly framed by an arch fashioned in trained and pruned whitebeam. It is a pleasant, living, family-run garden, as it has been for three generations, and there are some interesting plants for sale near the entrance. Light lunches are served in June and July.

CIRENCESTER

Cerney House Garden

North Cerney, Cirencester GL7 7BX TEL. 01285-831300/831205
OWNER Sir Michael and Lady Angus HOURS April–Sept, Tues–Wed and Fri, 10a.m.–5p.m., also one Sun in May for charity, other times for parties by prior appointment ENTRANCE £3, children £1 DIRECTIONS 3½m N of Cirencester off A435 Cheltenham road, go left opposite Bathurst Arms, follow road up hill past church, and turn in through gates on right
🌿 ♿ Access 🌿 Gift Shop 🌿 Plants for Sale

This exuberant and very richly planted gem, in carefree cottage-garden style, is hidden away in a wooded Cotswold valley. The creation of a mother-and-daughter team (with some part-time practical helpers), the three-and-a-half-acre garden has lawns, a wildflower meadow, a walled Victorian garden which is its centre-piece, mature beechwoods and a park.

The walls, of brick and Cotswold stone, used to shelter a productive kitchen garden for the house, but vegetables these days are grown in a limited area, as the rest is given over to ornamental plantings. There are roses drenching rustic arbours, low hedges of lavenders and partially colour-themed herbaceous borders (such as a cheerful orange-yellow scheme featuring day lilies, solidago and crocosmias). There is also a herb garden beside a rustic wooden gazebo at one end of the walled area.

Hardy cranesbill geraniums and lady's mantle (*Alchemilla mollis*) are used in broad bands to make sweeping edgings to gravel paths. In mid-spring the beech woods are awash with bluebells. The wildflower meadow, a fairly recent creation, supports an increasing population of typical limestone flowers, such as meadow cranesbill, vetches and pyramidal orchid. All of the garden is managed organically, with lashings of home-made compost and goats' manure regularly applied to the beds.

Fabulously Fragrant Carnations

There are many different carnations, but none compares with the sumptuous, peony-like blooms and heady, clove fragrances of the Malmaison race, admired in the 19th century but only recently brought back from obscurity by enthusiast Jim Marshall. **Marshall's Malmaisons, 4 The Damsells, Tetbury GL8 8JA (tel. 01666-502589)**, specialises in these plants, which produce tall stems and classic cut flowers, ideal for ornate arrangements.

The Malmaison carnation originated in France, but its cultivation was perfected in Britain. The variety 'Souvenir de la Malmaison' (also known as 'Old Blush') was so named because it resembled the flowers of the Bourbon rose of that name. Other early varieties include 'Princess of Wales', with rose-pink flowers, 'Duchess of Westminster', also a strong pink, 'Tayside Red', and 'Thora', a pale blush, fading to white. They like the cool, airy conditions of a well-ventilated conservatory or glasshouse. Water sparingly over winter, and use a weak liquid feed from April when new growth has started. Shade is needed to avoid bleaching the flowers once buds begin to open. Most Malmaisons will propagate by stem cuttings taken from March to September. Jim Marshall's collection is open by appointment only. Send 1 × 1st-class stamp for a list. You can also visit the National Collection housed at Crathes Castle Gardens (*q.v.*) in Moray and Aberdeenshire.

CIRENCESTER

Rodmarton Manor

Rodmarton, Cirencester GL7 6PF TEL. 01285-841253 HOURS Mid-May–Aug, Wed, Sat and Bank Holiday Mons, 2–5p.m. (other times by appointment only) ENTRANCE £3, house and garden £6, children £3 DIRECTIONS A433, take road towards Rodmarton, manor on right WEB www.rodmarton-manor.co.uk
🍽 ⅙ Access

Rodmarton Manor is the quintessential Cotswold country house, with a correspondingly typical Cotswold garden. The house was built between 1909 and 1920 by one Claud Biddulph, to replace a dilapidated 15th-century manor on the same estate. Mr Biddulph used the Arts and Crafts architect Ernest Barnsley to design both the house and its garden, using local stone and local craftsmen. The project was, in part, a philanthropic scheme, devised to provide long-term work for scores of local craftspeople, ensuring that their hard-won skills did not die out in an increasingly mechanised age.

From a large, circular lawn in front of the house, the garden's entrance is through a modest gateway in the high garden wall. Within, there are enclosed areas, laid out like rooms of differing character, separated by dry-stone walling and hedges – a feature Rodmarton has in common with its exact Cotswold contemporaries, Hidcote Manor (*q.v.*) and Snowshill Manor (*q.v.*). Subsequent generations of Biddulphs have added details, or rationalised the labour-intensive planting here and there. But the garden still boasts magnificent herbaceous borders in the classic style (with an exquisite stone summerhouse closing the vista), wonderful topiary and hedging in box and yew, and sunny terraces featuring boldly planted pots of agapanthus and other summer flowers.

One enclosure features a 'troughery', where ancient farm troughs mounted on the piers of saddle-stones are home to a recently refurbished collection of alpines. A long, axial path at the southern end of the garden leads past a succession of garden rooms, including the 'cherry orchard' (now home to silver poplars and birch), a croquet lawn with a rock garden at one end, tennis and swimming areas and a wild garden planted with spring bulbs. A substantial walled kitchen garden is only partially productive these days, but includes an historic collection of dahlias, jolly in the late season.

DURSLEY

Owlpen Manor

Uley, Dursley GL11 5BZ TEL. 01453-860261 OWNER Mr and Mrs N. Mander
HOURS April–Sept, Tues–Sun and Bank Holiday Mons, 2–5p.m. ENTRANCE £2.50,
children £1 (house and garden £4.50, children £2, family ticket £12.50)
DIRECTIONS 6m SW of Stroud, 3m E of Dursley off B4066. 1m E of Uley
(signposted) WEB www.owlpen.com

The village of Uley, snuggling into the south-western reaches of the scenic Cotswolds, is well away from the main 'beaten track' of the tourist coaches, but is very pretty, with its 18th-century (and earlier) stone cottages, built to serve the once-thriving weaving industry in the area. And just east of the village, splendidly gabled and mullioned, Owlpen Manor is the typical English Cotswold country house. Like so many of these Gloucestershire properties, it is hidden away in a picturesque valley, below its yew-garlanded church and a rising wood of beeches. The pretty and formal, two-acre terraced gardens date from the 16th and 17th centuries, and maintain the spirit of ages past. They feature yew topiaries, box parterres, old roses and herbs; interest is added by the nearby medieval tithe barn, old mill and millpond. A restaurant on the premises serves meals when the gardens are open.

LONGHOPE

Willow Lodge Garden

Longhope, Gloucester GL17 0RA TEL. 01452-831211 OWNER John and Sheila Wood HOURS May–Aug, most Suns and Mons, 1–5p.m., groups and private visits welcome by prior appointment at other times ENTRANCE £2, children free DIRECTIONS Entrance directly on the A40, 10m W of Gloucester and 6m E of Ross-on-Wye, parking in field beside garden

🔲 ♿ Access 🔲 Plants for Sale

Close to the Herefordshire border in one direction, and the flat plain of the Severn valley in the other, this is an intriguing, four-acre, private, plantsman's garden showing a collector's unquenchable appetite for trees and shrubs, among other things. The arboretum is still in its infancy, but occupies a grassy slope planted with over 300 different species and cultivars. (Clearly, some thinning-out will be required at a later date.) I was particularly taken with a deep-pink-flowered bramble labelled *Rubus odoratus*, with thornless stems and large, palmate leaves. My *Hillier's Manual of Trees and Shrubs* indicates that the fruits (perhaps raspberry-like?) are edible – even better.

The ornamental gardens (suburban-domestic, rather than formal or country-style), follow narrow, winding paths through gaps in hedges, or under arches, into small, themed areas. They include herbaceous beds, an alpine walk, pools and a stream, a bog garden and a small, organic vegetable plot. Many plants are labelled, but the owners are usually close at hand to advise on visitors' queries. 'John and Sheila Wood welcome you to Willow Lodge,' announces their small leaflet, handed to you on arrival, and clearly they do. The place is well set up for visitors' comfort, with nice teas and ample parking close by.

PAINSWICK

Painswick Rococo Garden

Must See

Painswick GL6 6TH TEL. 01452-813204 OWNER Painswick Rococo Garden Trust HOURS Mid-Jan–end Nov, Wed–Sun and Bank Holiday Mons (daily in May–Sept), 11a.m.–5p.m. ENTRANCE £3.60, OAPs £3.30, children £1.80 DIRECTIONS ½m from Painswick, on B4073 (signposted) WEB www.rococogarden.co.uk

🔲 Gift Shop 🔲 Café

Painswick is a splendid small town with a handsome hotel and wonderful churchyard (famous for its 99 ancient, clipped yews, autumn cyclamen and late-winter snowdrops). The Rococo garden is a gem on the edge of town with a pleasing atmosphere and well worth visiting. Bishop Pococke, a visitor to Painswick in 1757, sums up rather neatly what you will see: '...the garden is on an hanging ground from the house in the vale, and on a rising ground on the other side and at the end; all are cut into walks through wood and adorn'd with water and buildings, and in one part is the kitchen garden.' But the garden had long been lost in woodland and undergrowth when, in 1983, its owner Lord Dickinson began to rootle around trying to find its early 18th-century layout and buildings.

Now, almost fully restored, its 10 acres offer splendid walks along snaking or straight paths to investigate its pools, temples, alcoves and pastel-coloured gothic retreats. There is a pretty orchard on sloping lawns and a stroll through the garden is rewarded with dramatic vistas and surprise views. The Exedra Garden is a flowery area of narrow beds with cottage-garden flowers, enclosed by rabbit-proof fencing and swagged ropes bearing roses and honeysuckle.

The kitchen garden is very fine. Informative labels accompany the crops, for example, 'Celeriac: grown for its enlarged roots – introduced 16th century'. Its triangular beds are in a formal arrangement, enclosed by espalier-trained apples and pears which adorn the fencing. Both fruits and vegetables are grown, as far as possible, using varieties that were available in the 18th century.

Plants are for sale at the Pan Global Plants nursery next door.

Old Artefacts and Useful Salvage

If you're in the Stroud area and like rummaging among garden antiques and rescued materials, call in at **Minchinhampton Architectural Salvage Company, Cirencester Road, Chalford, Stroud GL6 8PE (tel. 01285-760886), off A419 between Stroud and Cirencester**. There are traditional building materials on sale, such as granite setts, clay bricks and pavers, chunks of stone, etc. Also an ever-changing stock of popular garden items such as staddle stones (formerly used to keep the hay harvest off the ground, away from rats), rope-twist glazed edging tiles (around £3.50 each plus VAT), stone troughs for alpines, sundials, garden seats, tables and other salvaged bits and pieces which may be just what you have been looking for, but hadn't seen for sale anywhere else. Open all year, Mon–Fri, 9a.m.–5p.m., Sat, 9a.m.–3p.m., Sun, by appointment only.

TETBURY

Hodges Barn

Shipton Moyne, Tetbury GL8 8PR TEL. 01666-880202 OWNER Mrs Charles Hornby OPEN 6 Suns for National Gardens Scheme and by prior appointment only ENTRANCE £4 DIRECTIONS 3m S of Tetbury on Malmesbury side of Shipton Moyne, a few hundred yards after leaving village

You really get the feeling of a well-loved, personally looked-after garden at Hodges Barn. It is renowned for its extensive use of climbing and shrub roses (the late Charles Hornby was passionate about them), and Amanda Hornby will often be seen tending the gardens herself, which she does with limited help, or offering helpful advice to visitors. The Barn itself (now a sumptuous home, not open) was originally an elaborate dovecote, built in 1499 to provide food for a nearby mansion house which no longer exists. The eight-acre gardens surrounding it are divided by ancient, Cotswold-stone field walls and mature hedges. Spring ushers in naturalised bulbs and blossoming cherries, crab apples and magnolias. The many roses take over from early summer, joined by relaxed plantings of herbaceous flowers and fragrant shrubs. There are skilfully planted pots of hydrangeas, fuchsias and scented-leaf plants beside the loggia, and a woodland area backing onto sheep pastures devoted to choice shrubs and more shrub roses.

TETBURY

Westonbirt Arboretum

Westonbirt, Tetbury GL8 8QS TEL. 01666-880220 OWNER Forestry Commission HOURS Open all year, daily, 10a.m.–8p.m. (or dusk if earlier). Visitor Centre open all year, daily, 10a.m.–5p.m. ENTRANCE £4.25, OAPs £3.50, children £1, family ticket £10 DIRECTIONS 3m S of Tetbury on A433

🟥 ♿ Access 🟥 Gift Shop 🟥 Café 🟥 Plants for Sale 🟥 NPC

Wear stout shoes for a jaunt at Westonbirt (it covers 600 acres) which you can enjoy in any season. There are 18,000 trees, representing 4000 species brought from all over the world, and every visit will inspire new impressions. Spring sees the magnolias, rhododendrons, azaleas, dogwoods and wildflowers (especially bluebells) in bloom.

In summer the shade of broad-leaved trees and open lawns provide endless picnic venues, and the air is heady with lime-blossom. Autumn is the peak visiting season for tinted-leaf displays rivalling (and, some say, improving upon) New England in the fall; this is when the leaves of acers, exotic oaks, sweet gum, dogwoods, etc., turn to brilliant golds and scarlets with the onset of colder weather. In winter the deep green and golden silhouettes of the conifers bring a startling contrast to the twiggy, hazy outlines of their unclothed neighbours. There are 17 miles of trails, and the arboretum holds National Collections of acer (maples) and salix (willows).

Westonbirt's plans to host a three-month-long major garden festival, in the style of Chaumont, in France, each summer from June 2002, will surely put these grounds onto the summer agenda of many keen gardeners.

WESTBURY ON SEVERN
Westbury Court

Westbury on Severn GL14 1PD TEL. 01452-760461 OWNER The National Trust HOURS April–Oct, Wed–Sun and Bank Holiday Mons (daily in July–Aug), 10a.m.–6p.m., groups and visits during other months by appointment only ENTRANCE £2.90, children £1.45 DIRECTIONS 9m SW of Gloucester on A48
🚻 ♿ Access 🚻 Gift Shop

If you have ever wondered what a formal, 17th-century Dutch garden is like, then it may surprise you that you don't need to go to Holland to find out. This is a rare (in England) example of the style, laid out on level ground with water canals, yew hedges and topiary. The five-acre garden was established between 1696 and 1705, and has undergone extensive restoration since the 1970s due to some fortunate coincidences. The discovery of the account books, from the 1690s, of Maynard Colchester, the garden's creator, included lists of the plants that were purchased at the garden's outset Added to this, an engraving by Kip, dating from 1712, provided a detailed plan of the garden as it was originally conceived. Plantings appropriate to the period have been reintroduced and the rebuilt brick pavilion, which is a most attractive feature, reflected at the end of a long canal of water, enables you to get a better view of the flat plan of the garden. There is also a walled garden featuring old fruit and flower varieties.

WINCHCOMBE
Sudeley Castle and Gardens

Winchcombe GL54 5JD TEL. 01242-602308/604357 (recorded information) OWNER Lord and Lady Ashcombe and the Dent-Brocklehurst family HOURS Garden March–Oct, daily, 10.30a.m–5.30p.m.; castle April–Oct, daily, 11a.m.–5p.m. ENTRANCE £5, concessions £4, children £2.75; castle and garden £6.50, concessions £5.50, children £3.50, family ticket £18 DIRECTIONS 8m NE of Cheltenham, on B4632 (A46), use M5 Jct 9 WEB www.stratford.co.uk/sudeley
🚻 Gift Shop 🚻 Café 🚻 Plants for Sale

Sudeley Castle oozes history; it was Crown property during the Wars of the Roses, and after the death of Henry VIII was given to Thomas Seymour who married Henry's widow, Katherine Parr. Queen Elizabeth was entertained here in the 1590s and Charles I stayed at the castle during the English Civil War.

The 15-acre gardens are romantically exuberant, but take their inspiration from the formal and symmetrical patterns of original Tudor garden plans. Wisterias and species roses feature in the Tithe Barn Garden; the White Garden displays roses in abundance with white-flowered spring bulbs and summer perennials; the Queen's Garden is enclosed by fantastic yew tunnels, 160 years old, and has formal beds of old roses and herbs. Spring bulbs ornament a garden dedicated to an ancient mulberry tree, and there are further knot gardens and roses, and a Henry Doubleday Victorian vegetable garden specialising in historic kitchen-garden cutivars.

And also...

Batsford Arboretum, Batsford, Moreton-in-Marsh GL56 9QB (tel. 01386-701441/web www.batsford-arboretum.co.uk), offers wonderful walking through 50 acres of diverse trees which have been planted on its undulating hillside since the 1880s. An especially good place for autumn jaunts, the arboretum is also speckled with interesting statuary, including subjects brought from the Far East. Open March–mid-Nov, daily, 10a.m.–5p.m. (last adm. 4.30p.m.), also weekends in Feb for snowdrops. Entrance £4, concessions £3, children £1. The garden centre by the car park is open all year, and is well stocked with shrubs, trees, alpines and flowering plants. Signposted from A44.

Art and nature come together in the **Forest of Dean Sculpture Trail**. There is a marked route of around five miles through the vast forest that blurs Gloucestershire's border with Wales. It is clearly not a garden but, like Grizedale Forest (*q.v.*) in Cumbria, can give anyone a new perspective on using natural materials in a decorative way in the garden, albeit in reduced scale. Open all year. Entrance free. M5 Jct 11, then A40 towards Ross-on-Wye, at 4th roundabout turn left onto A48 towards Chepstow, then right onto A4151 towards Cinderford, then left onto B4226 towards Coleford and follow signs.

There are around 3000 different pots on display at **The Old Bell Pottery, High Street, Lechlade GL7 3AD (tel. 01367-252608)**. Some are thrown on site by potter Keith Broley, others he has bought from suppliers across Britain, Europe and the Far East, and displayed in

his pot and topiary garden, at prices ranging from under 50p to over
£400. Open all year, daily, 9.30a.m.–8p.m. or dusk if earlier. Off A361
Swindon–Burford road.

The four-acre garden of **The Priory, Kemerton GL20 7JN (tel. 01386-725258)**, is renowned for its richness of colour, especially in late
summer, from herbaceous borders packed with sumptuous dahlias,
rhubarb chard, heleniums, Michaelmas daisies and crocosmia. There
is a pale border of graduated hues, with silver foliage plants and
feathery cosmos, and a renowned red border of sultry, deep purple
foliage including ricinus and cotinus, and deep red dahlias in
profusion. The hidden-away June garden features old roses and pastel-coloured perennials. Open June–late Sept, Thurs only, 2–6p.m., Oct
by appointment only. Entrance £2 (£1.50 in June), children free. M5 Jct
9, to Tewkesbury, then B4080 and follow signs to Kemerton.

At **Ruardean Garden Pottery, Ruardean, Forest of Dean GL17 9TP
(tel. 01594-543577/web www.ruardeanpottery.com)**, master potter
John Huggins specialises in frost-proof terracotta plantpots for the
garden in a large range of styles. Also hand-made rhubarb and sea
kale forcing jars with lids, for blanching the stems in the traditional
way. Mail order is available (send s.a.e. for a catalogue). Open all
year, Mon–Sat, 9a.m.–5.30p.m. (also Suns, March–Sept, 1–5p.m.).
Turn off A40 at Huntley, turn right at Cinderford.

Hampshire

Mostly scenic but partly industrial (in its southern ports), embracing the high chalk hills of the North and South Downs, with vast tracts of forested heaths and fertile lowland farms, Hampshire is like England in miniature. There are houses built of solid ironstone and others fashioned from flints and local clay bricks. The famous chalk streams running off the Downs provide some of the best trout fishing in the land, lying in some of the loveliest landscape. The New Forest is home to wild deer and itinerant ponies, and much of its 90,000 acres makes rewarding walking, whether on open heath or through beech and oak woods. Hampshire's gardens are just as varied, too, and its fertile soils have found favour with a number of notable nurseries.

Must See
Longstock Park, Stockbridge
 – generously planted
  waterscape on level ground

Exceptional in Spring
Exbury Gardens, Exbury
Longthatch, Warnford

Exceptional in Summer
Mottisfont Abbey, Romsey

Exceptional in Autumn
Apple Court, Lymington
Furzey Gardens, Lyndhurst
Sir Harold Hillier Gardens,
  Romsey

Worth a Visit in Winter
Sir Harold Hillier Gardens,
  Romsey

Hinton Ampner

Bramdean, nr Alresford SO24 0LA TEL. 01962-771305 OWNER The National Trust HOURS Garden April–Sept, Sat–Wed, 11a.m.–5p.m.; house April–Sept, Tues–Wed (also Sat and Sun in Aug), 1.30–5p.m. ENTRANCE £4, children £2, house and garden £5, children £2.50 DIRECTIONS On A272, 1m W of Bramdean village, 8m E of Winchester. Leave M3 Jct 9 and follow signs to Petersfield

🌳 ♿ Access 🌳 Café

The 18th-century brick mansion of Hinton Ampner is set in wonderful grounds, with outstanding views of its own park and very fine Hampshire countryside. The 12-acre gardens have formal terracing near the house with lawns, excellent topiary and lovely flower borders. In front of the house the stairway balustrades are garlanded with pink roses, and self-sown erigerons and lady's mantle provide a relaxed counterpoint to the austerity of the terrace. There are long, grassy walks terminating in statues, and well-thought-out routes that lead to intimate areas and surprise views. The Dell at Hinton Ampner is a former chalkpit planted with assorted trees and shrubs that were initially chosen for their ability to thrive in the strongly alkaline conditions of the pit. Beyond it is a fragrant philadelphus walk with tall box hedging and assorted flowering shrubs. All in all, a very enjoyable place to spend an afternoon.

The Vyne

Sherborne St John, Basingstoke RG24 9HL TEL. 01256-883858 OWNER The National Trust HOURS Easter–Oct, Sat–Wed, 11a.m.–5p.m., house 1–5p.m. (11a.m.–1p.m., pre-booked guided tours only); Feb–March (grounds only), Sat–Sun, 11a.m.–4p.m. ENTRANCE £3, children £1.50; house and garden £6.50, children £3.25, family ticket £16.25 DIRECTIONS From A340 take A33, then A339 and follow signs

🌳 ♿ Access 🌳 Gift Shop 🌳 Café

Close to the urban sprawl of Basingstoke (but a world apart in its peaceful country setting), this is a popular venue for those wanting a gentle stroll at the waterside or through woodland. The house, a brick-built Tudor mansion, forms a dashing centrepiece, set in neat, smooth lawns which roll gently down to a long, narrow lake and brook. There are really only two routes (or is it one route?): you can go east, around the lake and back again, or go west, around the lake and back again. But the woods, north of the brook, are dissected by broad, grassy paths. They extend to around 175 acres, chiefly oak, with hazel coppices, larches and some Douglas fir plantations. April to May is bluebell time here, followed by magenta drifts of foxgloves in May and June. Autumn in the woods shows a spectacular variety of fungi, for those who are practised in spotting them (woodland walks of different lengths are usefully marked). Part of the west end of the garden is devoted to a wild garden based on ecological principles.

Closer to the house, a new 'Edwardian' garden has been planted next to the 17th-century summerhouse. There are herbaceous borders (planting plans are thoughtfully supplied nearby) and rose beds beside the house entrance. The park itself is dotted with some magnificent trees, especially oaks, and a fine liquidambar. At the east end of the garden, the 'one hundred guinea oak' is thought to be well over 500 years old. Its name derives from when the owner, Mr Chute, in the early 19th century, was offered £100 for the tree's wood by a passing timber merchant. The owner decided to sleep on the offer, but the next day the merchant increased his bid to 100 guineas (the equivalent of nearly £3000 today). Chute decided that if the value of the tree had increased by five per cent in one night, then it was worth keeping. So it still stands, 200-odd years later.

EXBURY

Exbury Gardens

Exceptional in Spring

Exbury, nr Southampton SO45 1AZ TEL. 023 8089 1203 OWNER E.L. de Rothschild HOURS End Feb–early Nov, daily, 10a.m.–5.30p.m. (sunset if earlier) ENTRANCE Feb–mid-March and mid-June–Nov £3.50, OAPs £3, children £2.50 (under 10s free); mid-March–mid-June £5, OAPs £4.50 (Tues–Thurs £4), children £4 DIRECTIONS M27 Jct 2, then A326 and B3054 towards Beaulieu and follow signs WEB www.exbury.co.uk

🔴 ♿ Access 🔴 Gift Shop 🔴 Café 🔴 Plants for Sale

Late April and early May is the peak time to visit Exbury's 200 extraordinary acres. This is when you will see most of the garden's thousands of rhododendrons and azaleas in bloom, and the sight is breathtaking. The gardens were made by Lionel de Rothschild (*q.v.*), a scion of the famous banking family, in the years between the two World Wars. The local mild climate, natural oak wood and light, acidic soil proved ideal for rhododendrons, and Lionel de Rothschild spared no expense in making a garden that was to contain around one million plants, with 22 miles of irrigation pipes and sprinklers to avoid problems in a drought. He took great interest in the plant-hunting expeditions to the Far East by George Forrest, Frank Kingdon-Ward and others, and bred 1210 rhododendrons himself, the best 462 of which were named and registered.

Wear comfortable shoes and set aside a day to enjoy Exbury's 20 miles of rambling pathways, its pools, springs and quiet glades. Early spring sees many camellias and the large-leaved rhododendrons such as *R. sinogrande* and the Exbury-raised 'Fortune' in bloom; in May fragrant azaleas are joined by flowering dogwoods, candelabra primulas and fresh-leaved acers. There is a small, summer garden of roses, but autumn is good for foliage tints in the woodlands. There is also a two-acre rock garden, lovely in April, with dwarf rhododendrons and associated plants.

CELEBRITY CHOICE

Alan Titchmarsh

Presenter of BBC2's *Gardeners' World*
from his home at Barleywood, Hampshire

'The National Trust's property at **Hinton Ampner** (*q.v.*) is, if you like, my local stately home. The brick Georgian house is a beauty and the garden complements it rather well. It is just 20 minutes' drive away from my home, so when I go there I like to dream a little of what it must have been like to be lord of all you surveyed. Its garden has been rejuvenated in recent years, with lovely, luxurious plantings. There are great beds of dahlias and more informal, lush planting, a dell garden, some very good yew topiary and, above all, wonderful views of rolling fields of pasture and wheat. I'd visit Hinton Ampner even if it had no garden at all, just for the views. This garden has a very satisfying component of formal and informal elements, and there's so much there, it takes a while to explore.'

FLEET

West Green House

West Green, Hartley Wintney RG27 8JB TEL. 01252-844611 OWNER Ms Marylyn Abbott (leased from The National Trust) HOURS End April–end Aug, Wed–Sun and Bank Holiday Mons, 11a.m.–5p.m., Sept, Sat–Sun, 11a.m.–5p.m., all other times by appointment only ENTRANCE £3 (entry is free to National Trust members on Weds), children under 12 free DIRECTIONS 1m W of Hartley Wintney, 10m NE of Basingstoke, 1m N of A30

🌿 Gift Shop 🌿 Café 🌿 Plants for Sale

The elegant Georgian brick mansion has seen turbulent times – most recently in 1990, when it was partially destroyed by an IRA bomb. Marylyn Abbott is an energetic Australian and a gardening expert in her own right, and she has undertaken the latter part of the restorations to both house and garden.

The ornamental gardens include both formal and fun elements: the Alice in Wonderland Garden features clipped box and ivy topiaries, including characters such as the White Rabbit and Mad Hatter from the children's stories. Brick walls on three sides and yew hedging on the fourth enclose the former kitchen garden, which is now both productive and highly decorative. Old box hedges contain beds of exuberant herbaceous plantings, lined by gravel paths. The west side continues to be the kitchen-garden element, with two extremely elegant fruit cages, vegetable and herb beds and neat brick paths. The flavour is of well-ordered exuberance, pinned down by the neatness of the clipped trees and trim hedges, and clearly a great deal of thought and time goes into the planting and its maintenance. The recently restored neo-classical park beyond the walled enclosure is a setting for follies, fine trees, a lake and a water garden. Refreshments are served and lunch can be provided for groups if arranged in advance.

LYMINGTON

Apple Court

Hordle Lane, Hordle, Lymington SO41 0HU TEL. 01590-642130 OWNER Diana Grenfell and Roger Grounds HOURS April–Oct, Thurs–Tues, 10a.m.–1p.m. and 2–5p.m. ENTRANCE £2.50, children 50p DIRECTIONS N of A337 at Downton crossroads, between Lymington and New Milton (signposted) WEB www.applecourt.com
Nursery   NPC

Neutral, loamy soil and the mild situation – just one mile inland from the south coast – encourage plants to grow voluptuously at Apple Court. Within its two-and-a-half-acre walled domain, the layout is quite formal, basically split into four different areas, dissected by lawned paths. Next to the house is a spring border, a grassery (displaying collections of ornamental grasses, now much in vogue) and a winter garden. From here you can venture into the yew-enclosed white garden, a brilliantly executed formal area with an open, circular lawn surrounded by a stilt-hedge of pleached hornbeams, which provides a series of 'framed pictures' of the well-stocked borders, glimpsed between the hornbeams' trunks.

But the main reason people come here is for the specialist collections – of hostas, day lilies and grasses – which form the nucleus of the adjoining nursery. Formally arranged beds in the third corner of the garden hold the day lily collections, variously gathered into their colour groupings of purples, blue-red to pink, yellow and white, amber to brown and pure reds – breathtaking at high summer. Adjoining the area is a shady hosta walk. The cross-axis is lined with a lime walk at one end and swagged ropes bearing climbing roses at the other, with plenty more floral interest beneath. Although the emphasis is on herbaceous plants, there is a great deal to see here in any season, and a winter visit is worthwhile for discovering which grasses, if you desire them, can give a good show through the off-season.

LYNDHURST

Furzey Gardens

Exceptional in **Autumn**

Minstead, nr Lyndhurst SO4 37GL TEL. 023 8081 2464 OWNER Furzey Gardens Charitable Trust HOURS Open all year, daily, 10a.m.–5p.m. (or dusk in winter) ENTRANCE £3.50, OAPs £2.80, children £1.75, family ticket £9 (half price in winter) DIRECTIONS At Minstead, 8m SW of Southampton, 1m S of A31, 3½m NW of Lyndhurst

🌿 **Gift Shop** 🌿 **Plants for Sale** 🌿 **2 for 1 Voucher**

Furzey

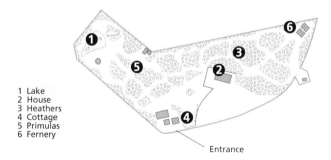

1 Lake
2 House
3 Heathers
4 Cottage
5 Primulas
6 Fernery

Entrance

Furzey is an eight-acre garden of great subtlety and charm. It was made in the 1920s out of rough heathland, in the middle of the New Forest. The planting style is of very informal shrubberies and open lawns covering the garden's south-facing slopes, using a large variety of acid-soil-loving plants. The late spring show of azaleas is spectacular, with flowers in pink and tangerine hues. There is a good collection of birch trees, including *Betula lenta*, with toffee-coloured peeling bark, and the heather collection is extensive, bringing colour all year round. On the lower ground there is a lovely pond with rustic bridges and a stream, with associated waterside plants such as skunk cabbages and candelabra primulas.

Early spring sees the grass carpeted in snowdrops, crocuses and daffodils and the autumn tints of the shrubberies are spectacular, with plants such as enkianthus and amelanchier turning to brilliant reds and golds.

ROMSEY

Mottisfont Abbey and Garden

Mottisfont, nr Romsey SO51 0LP TEL. 01794-340757/341220 OWNER The National Trust HOURS Late March–early Nov, Sat–Wed and Good Friday, 11a.m.–6p.m., also Fri in late May–Aug, except June, daily, 11a.m.–8.30p.m. ENTRANCE £6, children £3, family ticket £15 DIRECTIONS 4m NW of Romsey, ½m W of A3057; M3 Jct 8, then A303, take road towards Stockbridge, then A3057 to King's Somborne, 2m past village on right

🔲 ⚬ Access 🔲 Gift Shop 🔲 Café 🔲 Plants for Sale 🔲 NPC

These are really lovely gardens in one of Hampshire's most idyllic locations, beside a fast-flowing tributary of the River Test. The clear waters skirt a lawn which is host to a vast plane tree – the largest of its kind in the country and, according to some authorities, probably also the largest tree of *any* kind in this country. There are wild areas frothed up with cow-parsley in spring, and more formal gardens beside the abbey, designed in the 1930s by Sir Geoffrey Jellicoe, featuring a pleached lime avenue underplanted with early bulbs.

However, the walled, former kitchen garden is the famous, early summer feature of the 25-acre gardens. Within its red-brick walls lie four square lawns around a central fountain, flanked by herbaceous borders and a collection of old-fashioned roses, in the process of being restored and replanted. Knee-high box edging lines the perimeter gravel paths and lends a note of order among the unruly profusion of shrub roses. Their June flowering is accompanied by white-flowered foxgloves to terrific effect. Another walled garden beyond features further rose and herbaceous plantings.

ROMSEY

The Sir Harold Hillier Gardens and Arboretum

Exceptional in Autumn

Jermyns Lane, Ampfield, nr Romsey SO51 0QA TEL. 01794-368787 OWNER Hampshire County Council HOURS Open all year, daily, 10.30a.m.–6p.m. (or dusk if earlier) ENTRANCE £4.25, concessions £3.75, children free DIRECTIONS 3m NE of Romsey, M3 Jct 11, then A3090 and follow signs WEB www.hillier.hants.gov.uk

🌿 ♿ Access 🌿 Café 🌿 Plants for Sale 🌿 Nursery

Within the 160 acres of undulating ground there is a staggering collection of around 12,000 different plant species and varieties (with the emphasis on trees and shrubs), and a total of approximately 42,000 plants. Although it is lovely at all times of year, I have emphasised its autumn and winter appeal as this is one of the most interesting and rewarding gardens you can visit out of season. There are the fantastic ranges of leaf tints and berries setting fire to the autumnal landscape; winter highlights include the scents of mahonias, the beauty of sculptural trees, colourful bark, shapely conifers and the icing effect of hoar-frost on grasses and assorted twiggery.

There is a long herbaceous border for summer interest, a water and bog garden, a scree bed and collection of heathers. The renowned nurseryman, Sir Harold Hillier, began planting his arboretum in 1953, and its standing as one of the most important hardy plant collections in the world is unchallenged.

SELBORNE

Gilbert White's House (The Wakes)

High Street, Selborne, nr Alton GU34 3JH TEL. 01420-511275 OWNER Oates Memorial Trust HOURS Daily, 11a.m.–5p.m. ENTRANCE £2.50; house and garden £4.50, concessions £3.50, children £1 DIRECTIONS On B3006 between A31 and A3, 4m S of Alton

🌿 ♿ Access 🌿 Gift Shop 🌿 Café 🌿 Plants for Sale

The Wakes was the home of the Revd Gilbert White (1720–93), celebrated naturalist and author of *The Natural History and Antiquities of Selborne*. This seminal work gives uniquely detailed information on the local landscape and the flora and fauna within it, and has been published in 100 editions, in five languages. White enjoys less fame as a gardener, but in fact his five-acre garden is also one of the best documented of the 18th century, due to the meticulous records he kept for 42 years, most notably in *The Gardener's Kalendar* and subsequently in *The Naturalist's Journal*.

Gilbert White's House

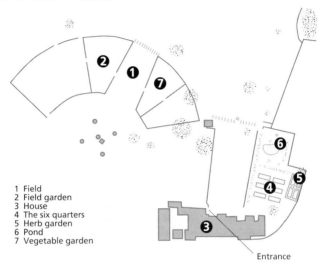

1 Field
2 Field garden
3 House
4 The six quarters
5 Herb garden
6 Pond
7 Vegetable garden

Entrance

In 1990 a decision was made to restore the gardens which had all but vanished since White's day, through the ravages of time and various changes of ownership. White embraced the views of his contemporary, William Shenstone, where gardens were concerned, believing the ground should be divided into three separate areas comprising a kitchen garden, a parterre or flower garden, and a 'landskip' or picturesque garden with follies, woods and vistas. White's orchard has recently been replanted with Portugal quinces, Dutch medlars, red filberts and old varieties of apples and pears that White had once grown. Vegetable and flower gardens have also been recreated more or less according to White's specifications, and herbs and cottage garden flowers are once again being cultivated near the house. (The house is interesting, too, with natural history exhibits and furnishings in period style.) The vegetable garden, although small, is packed with unusual fare grown chiefly from seed types that would have been known to Gilbert White. The gardener produces a helpful and interesting leaflet regularly through the seasons, noting points of interest. Some of the produce is sold to visitors, when available.

There is a lovely walk nearby, created with zigzag paths by White and his brother in 1753, ascending the hill to Selborne Common, a wooded area of outstanding natural beauty.

STOCKBRIDGE

Longstock Park Nursery and Gardens

Longstock, nr Stockbridge SO20 6EH **TEL.** 01264-810894 **OWNER** John Lewis Partnership **HOURS** Nursery and walled garden: Mon–Sat, 8.30a.m.–4.30p.m. (and Sun, 2–5p.m. in April–Sept); water gardens: 1st and 3rd Sun of each month, 2–5p.m. **ENTRANCE** Nursery/walled garden free; water gardens £3, children 50p **DIRECTIONS** From A303 take A30 to Stockbridge and follow signs **WEB** www.longstocknursery.co.uk

  ♦ Access   Café   Plants for Sale   Nursery

I had the great fortune to tour Longstock's gardens and nursery one happy mid-summer day in the company of Roy Lancaster and the garden's estimable curator, David Stuart. The nursery, which is open daily, has a broad and discerning range of plants, including many different kinds of waterlilies, bog primulas, clematis, penstemons, irises, hardy geraniums, buddleias and viburnums. Adjacent is a beautiful walled garden with a 100yd-long traditional herbaceous border, and an equally long rose pergola, decked with climbing roses and many choice clematis. Notable in this area was *Phygelius* 'Winchester Fanfare', of soft, pinky colouring, growing 6ft or so, trained to the wall; Roy was ecstatic to see *Ostrowskia magnifica* (an unusual, white-flowered relation of the campanula) blooming in the border. Beyond is a large collection of buddleias (viewable by appointment).

The famous seven-acre water gardens of Longstock are nearby, occasionally open to the public. There is nothing quite like them, but the effect is rather as if you had walked into a studio full of Claude Monet's paintings of waterlily pools. Neatly cut turf paths wind around a series of pools and streams, and wooden plank bridges criss-cross the clear waters. The banks are filled with astilbes, ferns, mimulus, hostas and primulas, the whole effect being utterly peaceful and enchanting. The Longstock estate was bought in 1946 by John Lewis, who passed it on to the John Lewis Partnership.

WARNFORD

Longthatch

Lippen Lane, Warnford, Southampton SO32 3LE **TEL.** 01730-829285 **OWNER** Peter and Vera Short **HOURS** March–July, Wed, 10a.m.–5p.m., and some Suns for the National Gardens Scheme, 2–5p.m. (phone for details, or see the NGS yellow book), also by appointment with the owners **ENTRANCE** £2, children free **DIRECTIONS** 1m SW of Meon on A32, turn right at George and Falcon, right at T-Junction and on right

  ♦ Access   Café   Plants for Sale   NPC

This enchantingly peaceful garden is renowned for its hellebores in spring, accompanied by other early plants such as primulas and pulmonarias among the damp woodland plantings. It is a three-and-a-half-acre plantsman's garden beside the River Meon, with tranquil pools and riverside plantings, and many unusual trees and shrubs, around a thatched 17th-century house (not open). Its fine lawns form a calm backdrop to herbaceous borders and island beds and there is also an alpine area. Hinton Ampner (*q.v.*) is nearby.

Lionel de Rothschild's World of Plants

Lionel de Rothschild, the charismatic creator of Exbury's famous rhododendron grounds, grew up among fine gardens. He was born at Ascott (*q.v.*) in Buckinghamshire, and from an early age was interested in flowers. Although he was famous for his home-raised rhododendrons, they were not his only passion. During the 1920s and 1930s he also planted an arboretum at Exbury, which he intended should display every hardy tree that could be grown. (His adviser was W.J. Bean, the famous tree expert and curator of Kew Gardens.) There were also acres of greenhouses on the estate, where pride of place was given to a huge orchid collection. Lionel became almost as famous for his orchids as for the rhododendrons, his hybrid cymbidiums being particularly prized.

And also...

Braxton Gardens, Braxton Courtyard, Lymore Lane, Milford-on-Sea SO41 0TX (tel. 01590-642008), is set within a two-acre walled garden and courtyard, with a lily-pool and dovecote, around the red-brick barns of a Victorian farmyard. Besides the knot garden and broad range of herbs, there are old-fashioned roses. Herbs and herb products are sold in the shop and adjacent plant centre. Open mid-March–Oct, daily, 10a.m.–5p.m. Phone to check opening times in winter. Donations to National Gardens Scheme. M27 Jct 1, then A337 to Everton, then B3058, gardens on left.

You can buy all manner of fruit at **Family Trees, Sandy Lane, Shedfield SA32 2HQ (tel. 01329-834812)**, which stocks good ranges of dessert apples, pears, plums and peaches, both trained and untrained, as well as hedging, old roses and some woodland trees.

The catalogue is free on request. Open mid-Oct–May, Wed and Sat only, 9.30a.m.–12.30p.m. Between Wickham and Botley, ½m from A334.

Arthur Nash, 46 Mulfords Hill, Tadley RG26 3JE (tel. 01189-815591/web www.arthurnash.freeservebusiness.co.uk), makes and sells besoms (those useful lawn sweepers that look like witches' brooms), either direct or by mail order, but telephone to check opening times before calling. M3 Jct 6, then A340.

Nine Springs Aquatic Nursery, The Weir, Whitchurch RG28 7RA (tel. 01256-892837), has been operating since 1984 on the site of former watercress beds. It specialises in true aquatics, emergents and marginal plants. Open by appointment.

Priory Lane Nursery, Freefolk Priors, Whitchurch RG28 7NJ (tel. 01256-896533), offers good ranges of herbaceous perennial plants, such as hardy geraniums, phloxes and penstemons. There is a catalogue (send 8 × 1st-class stamps) and mail order service, spring and autumn only. Open March–Oct, daily, 10a.m.–5p.m. M4, then S on A34 for 10m, exit towards Whitchurch, after 3m left at White Hart, after 1½m left in Freefolk, plant shop on right.

The Tudor House Garden, Tudor House, Bugle Street, Southampton SO14 2AD (tel. 023 8063 5904), is a well-made, thoroughly researched reconstruction of a formal Tudor garden with knot, fountain, secret garden and plantings of appropriate herbs and flowers, all confined to a very small plot. Open all year, April–Sept, Tues–Fri, 10a.m.–4.45p.m.; Sat, 10a.m.–3.45p.m.; Sun, 2–4.45p.m. (closed 12 noon–1p.m. every day); Oct–March, Tues–Sat, 10a.m.–3.45p.m. (closed 12 noon–1p.m. on Sat only), Sun, 2–4.45 p.m. Entrance free. From M27 take road to Southampton and follow signs to Old Town and Waterfront, then park where possible and walk.

Damian Grounds at **Hortus Ornamenti, 7 The Wren Centre, Westbourne Road, Emsworth PO10 7RN (tel. 01243-374746/web www.hortusornamenti.co.uk)**, designs and produces very high-quality, hand-made garden tools and accessories, such as trowels, weeding forks and hoes, in stainless steel with smooth, comfortably shaped handles in beech-wood or walnut, from around £30 per item, plus postage. They make luxurious, special presents for keen gardeners; catalogue on request (mail order only).

Herefordshire

Sitting on the border of Wales, and enjoying startling views of the mountains, Herefordshire is deeply rural, with strong farming traditions on its gentle green hills. You notice how well trees grow here on the fertile soils, whether they are massive oaks sprung out of hedgerows, or more exotic species planted in the region's fine gardens. The proliferation of springs, generally mild climate (warm in summer to ripen fruit) and frequency of rain has also encouraged a thriving cider industry for many centuries. The most famous producer is Bulmers (founded in 1887), and as Percy Bulmer's mother once wisely said, 'If you are going into business, let it be food or drink – they never go out of fashion.'

Exceptional in Spring
Bryan's Ground, Presteigne

Exceptional in Summer
Arrow Cottage Garden,
  Weobley

Abbey Dore Gardens

Abbey Dore, Hereford HR2 0AD TEL. 01981-240419 OWNER Mrs C. Ward
HOURS Garden only April–Sept, daily, except Wed and Mon (open Bank
Holiday Mons), 11a.m.–6p.m. Other times by appointment to see hellebores
ENTRANCE £3, children 50p DIRECTIONS 3m W of A465, midway between
Hereford and Abergavenny, follow signs from A465
🔲 ⅅ Access 🔲 Café 🔲 Plants for Sale

Meeting Charis Ward was the highlight of my tour of Herefordshire.
She is a formidable plantswoman and great company. She also clearly
commands the respect of her neighbours, the army, since they ceased
practising helicopter manoeuvres on the afternoon of my visit, at her
request. (Perhaps they had decided to brush up on spying, instead,
as the helicopters started up again the moment I got back to my car.)

The gardens spread for five acres along both banks of the River
Dore in a peaceful, wooded valley. The entrance is through a stable
yard, into a former walled kitchen garden, which is now largely given
over to herbaceous plants, especially euphorbias, peonies and hardy
geraniums – their pastel colours mingle in big, blowsy drifts,
contrasting with a formal orchard beyond. A right-hand turn leads
to the lawn beside the house, planted with two prominent
wellingtonia trees, and a lower lawn, enclosed by mixed plantings
of trees, shrubs and perennials.

Most beguiling on a hot afternoon is the shady River Walk, among
dogwoods, hostas and ferns, to the music of birdsong and the fast-
flowing Dore. There are also double borders featuring a progression of
purple-, golden- and grey-leaved plants with colour-coordinated
flowers, and a meadow area with a pond and rock garden. The house
(not open) was an inn until the mid-19th century, when it was converted
into a gentleman's residence. The Wards have lived here for 30 years;
when not rearranging the plants in her beloved garden, Charis Ward
disappears indoors to rearrange her Persian rugs, her other passion.

Hampton Court Herefordshire

Hope under Dinmore, Leominster HR6 0PN TEL. 01568-797777 OWNER Robert
van Campen HOURS Open all year, daily, 11a.m.–4p.m. (closes at 5p.m.,
April–Oct) ENTRANCE April–Oct £4, OAPs £3.75, children £2 (gardens only); £5,
OAPs £4.75, children £3 (gardens and river/woodland walks); Nov–March £2,
children £1 (gardens and river/woodland walks) DIRECTIONS Between
Leominster and Hereford, off A417, just S of junction with A49
🔲 ⅅ Access 🔲 Café 🔲 Plants for Sale

A castellated mansion dating partly from the 15th century (not open) and its 20-acre gardens lie at the heart of this historic 1000-acre estate. The present owner brought in David Wheeler and Simon Dorrell, of Bryan's Ground (*q.v.*), to redesign the gardens, which they have done in grand style over the last four years.

The new gardens include a sunken garden with a pool, waterfalls and a hermitage, from which a tunnel extends to a tower at the centre of a yew maze. Long double herbaceous borders lead to two Victorian walled gardens, including ranges of glasshouses – one has an extensive water garden with two moated, oak-framed pavilions, water cascades, rose gardens and herbaceous borders. The other is home to a newly planted orchard of local apple varieties and a box-edged vegetable garden.

Beyond is a bowling alley leading to a Dutch canal garden with a summerhouse, topiaries and spring bulbs. The original ha-ha in the park has been extended to provide views of the reinstated lake, replanted areas in the park and the new gatehouse.

Hereford's Apple Heritage

'Foxwhelp', 'Brown Snout', 'Bloody Turk' and 'Sheep's Nose' may sound like the province of the doctor and vet, but they are in fact some of the old varieties of cider apple that once flourished in Herefordshire's orchards, and which are now rare.

The region's tradition of cider-making began long before Roman times; throughout history it was drunk in castles, manors and farms, and was a popular substitute for imported wine during the Napoleonic Wars. You can still see cider orchards dotted about the countryside, but much of the old orchard land is now used for arable farming and the tradition of producing local farmhouse cider has virtually disappeared. There are, however, several local initiatives to find and replant old varieties and you can taste some of the results at **Dunkertons Cider Mill, Luntley, Pembridge, Leominster HR6 9ED (tel. 01544-388653), signposted from Pembridge, nr Leominster and from A44**, which also serves delicious food. Open Mon–Sat, 10a.m.–6p.m. (restaurant closed Jan–Feb). If you want to grow your own old-fashioned cider crop, contact Deacon's Nursery (*q.v.*) on the Isle of Wight, or Keepers Nursery (*q.v.*) in Kent, for trees by mail order.

PRESTEIGNE

Bryan's Ground

Stapleton, Presteigne LD8 2LP TEL. 01544-260001 OWNER D. Wheeler and
S. Dorrell HOURS Limited in 2002 (reopening properly 2003), phone for details
ENTRANCE £2.50, children 50p DIRECTIONS From Presteigne town centre take
unclassified road heading N over River Lugg, then first right, for 1m. Bryan's
Ground is a yellow house set back from the road

⬤ ♿ Access ⬤ Gift Shop ⬤ Café ⬤ Plants for Sale

Bryan's Ground

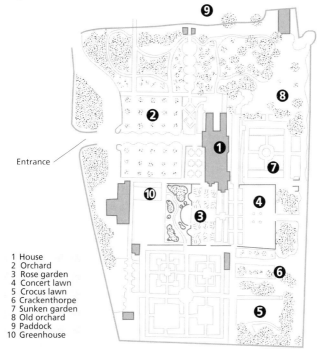

Entrance

1 House
2 Orchard
3 Rose garden
4 Concert lawn
5 Crocus lawn
6 Crackenthorpe
7 Sunken garden
8 Old orchard
9 Paddock
10 Greenhouse

The house that David Wheeler and Simon Dorrell moved into in 1993
is in the style of the Arts and Crafts architect, Voysey, and is what they
describe as 'Surrey stockbroker-style, transported, incongruously, to
the borders of Wales'. Literally to the border, for their boundary, the
River Lugg, is also the national boundary; they can paddle over to Wales
at the end of their garden. The river bank provided flat, smooth, worn
cobblestones which are effectively used in an unusual stone-and-twig
parterre beside the front door. In front is an orchard of apple trees, bred
locally, brilliantly underplanted with masses of *Iris sibirica*.

When they arrived, much of the garden was already divided into 'rooms' by stout yew hedges, put in by the Arts and Crafts architects who built the house. Within them, and in the walled kitchen garden, David and Simon have made new, symmetrical gardens in what you might call the Tudor-style with a twist. The rose garden is very formal, with beds cornered by pyramidal yews trained in wooden obelisks. The walled garden layout is derived from plans in Thomas Hill's book, *Gardener's Labyrinth*, of 1577, its potager enclosed by fancy trellis with carved birds on top, à la Hill. There is a marvellous restored greenhouse, a box-edged sunken garden, a wood and much more.

Around three of their 25 acres are being developed as garden, the rest is pasture. Each part of the garden has a different name: Crackenthorpe, for example, is a narrow strip of lawn flanked by two borders of sumptuous purples and reds, leading to a delightful pavilion Simon built with salvaged masonry from demolition work at Cardiff docks. In all, Bryan's Ground is a plant-filled, beautifully executed garden, made with liberal doses of humour as well as plantsmanship.

A World of Carnivorous Plants

The mysterious world of carnivorous plants has largely eluded me, or it did until I met Paul Gardner, of **JMP Plants, Brampton Lane, Madley, Hereford HR2 9LX (tel. 01981-251659), just off A465 from Hereford; take B4349 to Madley**. Paul has a train-spotter-like passion for insect-eating plants, and an infectious enthusiasm, developed over the 10 years that he has been growing them. Here are Venus fly-traps, sundews, pitcher-plants and butterworts in great variety – ideal fly-catchers for house and greenhouse, provided you bear in mind their needs. They all thrive when standing in peaty soil in rainwater (or distilled water), simulating the bogs which are their habitat; hard, alkaline water is poisonous to them. Cutting off the flower buds maintains the plants' vigour, but you shoud never feed with fertilisers; the plants get their food by digesting flies.

Contrary to popular belief, Venus fly-traps are not short-lived, but often die because people are tempted to trigger the hairs in the trap to watch it close. If there is no fly to digest, the plant is weakened. Anyone keen on natural control in the greenhouse or conservatory should try *Pinguicula moranensis caudata*, a Mexican butterwort, 'the best control I know for whitefly, midges and compost flies', Paul adds. A tip: do not ask what happens to the indigestible remains of flies caught in pitcher plants – you will be shown them! Open by appointment only. Entrance free. Plants also by mail order.

That's A-Maze-ing!

Symonds Yat is a popular haunt of tourists and walkers who enjoy the spectacular setting, on a sharp bend in the River Wye, where it runs through a rocky gorge. Here, you will also find **The Amazing Hedge Puzzle and Museum of Mazes, The Jubilee Park, Symonds Yat West, nr Ross-on-Wye HR9 6DA (tel. 01600-890360/ web www.mazes.co.uk), leave the A40 at Whitchurch, follow signs to Symonds Yat West and on left**. It was built by two brothers, Lindsay and Edward Heyes, from fast-growing Leylandii cypress trees, on the site of an old orchard they inherited around 20 years ago. The cypresses require more frequent trimmings than yew would need, but the brothers manage to keep the eight-sided, intricate maze in densely green, sharp-edged condition. If you manage to puzzle your way to the centre, you can rest within an iron-roofed, classical-style pavilion. According to Lindsay Heyes, they have built 'a labyrinth of love, of the kind that was popular between 1560 and 1650; the idea is that you enter our maze with your friend or lover, your brother or sister, then you split up and try to find each other again. When you do, there is great laughter and embracing.' The sense of relief is tempered, of course, by the piquancy of needing to find your way out again…   Open Easter–end Sept, daily, 11a.m.–5p.m. (closes 6p.m. in school holidays), March and Oct, Sat–Sun, 12 noon–4p.m. (one week in Oct for school half-term holiday, daily, 12 noon–4p.m.). Entrance £3.50, concessions £2.50, children £2, family ticket £10.

WEOBLEY

Arrow Cottage Garden

Ledgemoor, Weobley HR4 8RN TEL. 01544-318468 OWNER Mr and Mrs L. Hattatt HOURS April–Sept, Wed–Sun, 1–5p.m. ENTRANCE £3 (garden is unsuitable for children) DIRECTIONS 10m NW of Hereford between A4110 and A480, 1½m E of Weobley

🌿 Plants for Sale

It is always exciting to see good new gardens being brought into the visiting arena. This exceptionally well-stocked and manicured plantsman's garden is also laid out with cunning precision to make the best use of its two acres. The owners, both keen gardeners, have divided their plot, on very gently sloping ground, into themed mini-gardens of great style.

A natural stream runs through, crossed by a dainty, blue-painted bridge. To one side, a gravelled area with a stone-paved, central circle provides an open arena for a startling jet of water erupting from the centre like a geyser. More water runs down a 170ft, gently stepped rill, rigidly enclosed between high hedges. The productive kitchen garden is enlivened with colour-themed flowers to tone in with the vegetables and herbs. There are richly planted borders, a white garden, old shrub roses, a well-built summerhouse and intriguing statues and sculpture, such as the faces modelled on the primitive figures of Easter Island. A great deal of thought and energy has gone into making the garden (only redesigned since 1994), but the owner is careful to point out that it is not suitable for children, even accompanied by adults (one gets the sense that their antics would not be tolerated). Refreshments are served.

And also...

Brobury House, Brobury HR3 6BS (tel. 01981-500229), has woodland gardens in an idyllic position above the River Wye. A programme of development is under way for the garden, including renovating its Victorian greenhouses, creating a major wildlife pond and opening up some fine views. There are also holiday cottages to let. Open all year, daily, 10a.m.–5p.m. Entrance £2.50, children £1. Between A438 and B4352 on Bredwardine Bridge.

How Caple Court, How Caple, Hereford HR1 4SX (tel. 01989-740626), must have been cherished by its owners 100 years ago, but less so since. It possesses a Lutyens-style Edwardian garden of stone terraces laid out with herbs and roses, on a handsome wooded hill above the River Wye. Its once lavish water and woodland gardens are undergoing slow restoration after years of neglect, but the terraces and long vista by the house are charming in mid-summer. Open all year, Mon–Fri, 10a.m.–5p.m. (also Sat–Sun in April–Oct, 9a.m.–5p.m.). Entrance £2.50, children £1.25. A40, then A449 at Ross-on-Wye, then B4224. 🌿 **2 for 1 Voucher**

Pools, pumps, bog plants and waterlilies are available in huge variety at **Kenchester Water Gardens, Church Road, Lyde, Hereford HR1 3AB (tel. 01432-270981)**. There are also extensive display gardens showing different uses of water. Open all year, daily, March–Sept, 9a.m.–6p.m., Oct–Feb, 9a.m.–5.30p.m. (Sun all year, 11a.m.–5p.m.). Entrance free. On A49 N of Hereford.

Pembridge is an attractive medieval village and at **Pembridge Terracotta, Pembridge, Leominster, Hereford HR6 9HB (tel. 01544-388696/web www.gardenpots.co.uk)**, hand-made clay pots are fashioned on the premises, with a wide range of pots for the garden.

Mail order service and free catalogue available. Open all year, Mon–Fri, 9a.m.–5p.m., Sat–Sun, 10a.m.–5.30p.m. (closed Sun in Jan and Feb). Off A44 at Pembridge.

Rushfields of Ledbury, Ross Road, Ledbury HR8 2LP (tel. 01531-632004/web www.rushfields.co.uk), specialises in herbaceous perennials, including euphorbias, hardy geraniums, osteospermums, penstemons and primroses. Catalogue £1. Open all year, Wed–Sat, 11a.m.–5p.m., or by appointment. M50 Jct 2, then A417 to Ledbury.

Hertfordshire

MAP NO. 3

Once a rural county of cornfields and respectable, small country houses as immortalised in E.M. Forster's *Howards End*, Hertfordshire's close proximity to London has made its land valuable for roads and housing. Its sprawling towns are very much part of the city's commuter belt, and fast trains cut their way through the new towns and suburbs. The chalk ridge of the Chiltern Hills runs along its western and north-western edge, giving way further south to more gentle undulations. Its eastern borders are flatter, however, like neighbouring Cambridgeshire and Essex. The cathedral town of St Albans was know as Verulamium in Roman times, when it was the third largest town in the country. It remains richly historic, with a pleasing blend of the old and new.

Must See
Hatfield House, Hatfield – stately grounds, well-designed, organically managed

Exceptional in Summer
The Gardens of the Rose, St Albans

Exceptional in Autumn
The Beale Arboretum, Hadley Wood

Worth a Visit in Winter
Benington Lordship, Benington

BENINGTON

Benington Lordship

Benington, Stevenage SG2 7BS TEL. 01438-869668 OWNER C.H.A. Bott HOURS
Open by appointment only, phone for late winter snowdrop openings
ENTRANCE £3.50, children free DIRECTIONS In Benington village, off A602
Stevenage–Hertford road and follow signs

Barely four miles away from busy Stevenage town centre, Benington
Lordship is still enshrouded in a landscape of gentle hills and golden
cornfields, and has an atmosphere of times past. Much of its seven
acres dates from Victorian and Edwardian designs and plantings,
with leafy green shrubberies and winding walks among tall conifers
leading to spectacular twin herbaceous borders beside the walled
kitchen garden. Grassy slopes lead to a lake of waterlilies, and there
is a rock garden fed by a spring, home to bog primulas and sun-loving
shrubs. It is a peaceful place for an afternoon's visit, with glorious
pastoral views and surprises around each corner. February's snowdrops are spectacular (phone near the time for snowdrop dates, as
they depend on the weather). The bulbs run through the ruins of a
Norman castle and dry moat, in a part of the garden which is also
devoted to winter-flowering shrubs.

HADLEY WOOD

The Beale Arboretum

Exceptional in Autumn

West Lodge Park, Cockfosters Road, Hadley Wood EN4 0PY TEL. 020 8216
3904 OWNER Beales Hotels HOURS April–Oct, Wed, 2–5p.m. ENTRANCE £1.50,
children free DIRECTIONS Off A111 midway between M25 Jct 24 and
Cockfosters Tube station

🌳 & Access 🌳 Café

When Ted Beale came to West Lodge Park in 1945, he opened the
small mansion house as a quality family-run hotel (which it still is)
and developed his passion for trees. The arboretum is now more than
50 years old and contains more than 800 different species and
cultivars, making visits particularly rewarding during autumn, when
the foliage has multicoloured tints. The hornbeam collection includes
nine named varieties of *Carpinus betulus*, including fastigiate and
weeping forms. Many plants are grouped together with their
relations, as they would be in a botanic garden, so that comparisons
can be easily made between varieties. Broad lawns run between them
on gently undulating ground. This is filled out here and there with
shrubby dells to provide some mystery.

In 1676 the diarist and gardener John Evelyn visited West Lodge Park and reported: 'It is a very pretty place, the house commodious, the garden handsome and our entertainment very free.' He also admired the fact that no 'house, barne, church or building' could be seen, despite the park's proximity to London. Times have changed, and the suburban sprawl tightens its grip around the park, but Mr Beale has planted 24 more acres to complement the existing 10, so even better things can be expected in the future.

Clarence Elliott's Catmint

The pretty and ubiquitous catmint *Nepeta* 'Six Hills Giant' is widely available from nurseries and garden centres nationwide, but it has its origins in Hertfordshire. It was brought into cultivation by Clarence Elliott (1907–1969), who had a well-known establishment, the Six Hills Nursery, on the Great North Road at Stevenage. Elliott was a specialist alpine grower and a founder-member of the Alpine Garden Society, but he was also interested in old cottage garden plants. He spotted an unusual form of catmint, with taller stems and larger flowers than were typical, in a local garden in the mid-1930s. The ease with which it could be propagated meant that stocks were soon ready for sale. *Nepeta* 'Six Hills Giant' quickly found favour as an accommodating herbaceous plant with soft stems of grey-green, aromatic foliage and lavender-blue flowers, growing up to 3ft tall. It flourishes in a sunny position, in well-drained, especially alkaline soil, and makes a good accompaniment to other flowers in the herbaceous border and to pastel-tinted roses. Propagation is by division of the rootstock in spring, or by softwood cuttings in summer.

HATFIELD

Hatfield House

Hatfield AL9 5NQ TEL. 01707-287010 OWNER The Marquess of Salisbury HOURS Easter–Sept, daily (East Gardens closed on Fri): park, West and East Gardens 11a.m.–5.30p.m.; house 12 noon–4p.m. ENTRANCE Park £2, children £1; house and park £7, children £3.50; park and West Gardens £4.50, children £3.50; park, West and East Gardens £6.50; house, West and East Gardens £10.50 DIRECTIONS In centre of old Hatfield, entrance opposite Hatfield Station; signposted from A1(M) Jct 4 WEB www.hatfield-house.co.uk

  点 Access   Gift Shop   Café   Plants for Sale

The 42-acre gardens around Hatfield's famous Jacobean mansion house are laid out formally, with geometrically arranged flowerbeds and much use of yew and box hedging, and yew topiaries. They are largely the inspiration of the present Marchioness of Salisbury, who is one of the country's leading experts on 17th-century gardens. Lady Salisbury has been actively involved in rejuvenating the gardens since she arrived in 1972 and, since that time, they have been run entirely organically. The intention has been to create gardens that are in sympathy with the period of the house, rather than slavishly imitating the period, and the results are superb.

The West Gardens comprise hedge-enclosed flower gardens filled with spring bulbs, herbaceous perennials and shrub roses, planted for a long season of colour. There is also a delightful fragrant garden with seats under bowers of honeysuckle, beside cowslip-scented *Clematis rehderiana*, a herb garden, and a virtuoso Tudor-style knot garden. The East Gardens have further formal flower gardens and topiaries, and lovely woodland walks around the lake.

The John Tradescants

Gardener, nurseryman and plant collector John Tradescant the Elder (*c.*1570–1638) introduced many new plants to Britain, from his travels in Europe and Russia. In 1609 he came to work for Robert Cecil, who was busy building his new house at Hatfield (*q.v.*). Salomon de Caux, a French expert in fountains, was brought in to create elaborate formal gardens, while Tradescant was sent abroad in search of novelty plants. In 1611 he returned with fine flowers, including martagon lilies and a double hepatica. Later, Tradescant went collecting abroad to stock his own London nursery. His son, also named John, continued to bring in new plants from overseas, especially from the New World. Some of their notes and bills survive in the Hatfield House archives.

ST ALBANS

The Gardens of the Rose

Chiswell Green, St Albans AL2 3NR TEL. 01727-850461 OWNER The Royal National Rose Society HOURS June–Sept, daily, 9a.m.–5p.m. (Sun and Bank Holiday Mons, 10a.m.–6p.m.) ENTRANCE £4, OAPs and disabled £3.50, children £1.50 DIRECTIONS Signposted from M1 Jct 6 and M25 Jct 21A WEB www.roses.co.uk

🔥 ♿ Access 🔥 Gift Shop 🔥 Café 🔥 Plants for Sale 🔥 2 for 1 Voucher

This is the headquarters and trial ground of the Royal National Rose Society and *the* place to see roses, especially more modern hybrid teas and floribundas. The 26-acre gardens are something of an anachronism, having a formal, old-fashioned air slightly at odds with today's more relaxed views about planting. You will find large beds cut out of the broad lawns to display blocks of single varieties. Nevertheless, it is instructional to see which ones bloom over a long season, which varieties are still putting on a brilliant show in August, into autumn, and to take note of the berries of different species of shrub roses. There are some old roses too, grown in their own area, and some beds feature herbaceous flowers such as delphiniums and catmint. Climbers and ramblers are well represented, forming an avenue walk between the car park and the main house, and they are joined by clematis, to pretty effect, on a long, curving pergola.

And also...

The gloriously colourful world of dahlias can be viewed in September by visiting the trial grounds at **Aylett Nurseries, North Orbital Road, London Colney, St Albans AL2 1DH (tel. 01727-822255/web www.martex.co.uk/hta/aylett)**. This is a large, comprehensively stocked garden centre with dahlias a speciality (free catalogue on request). Open Mon–Fri, 8.30a.m.–5.30p.m, Sat, 8.30a.m.–5p.m., Sun, 10.30a.m.–4.30p.m. M25 Jct 21A or Jct 22, follow signs to St Albans.

Crown Topiary, 234 North Road, Hertford SG14 2PW (tel. 01992-501055/web www.crowntopiary.co.uk), covering five acres, specialises in producing and supplying topiary figures made from yew, box and Chinese privet. Architectural shapes predominate but flights of fancy, such as eagles, swans, pitchers, armchairs, etc. are also usually available. Illustrated price list on request. Commissions undertaken, subject to materials. Open by appointment only.

The name **R. Harkness & Co. Ltd, The Rose Gardens, Cambridge Road, Hitchin SG4 0JT (tel. 01462-420402/web www.roses.co.uk)**, is synonymous with some of the most popular hybrid tea roses bred this century, although the nursery also stocks good ranges of floribunda, patio and climbing roses. One of their most successful recent introductions has been 'Octavia Hill', a glamorous, fragrant, old-fashioned-looking rose that makes a small bush of really delightful, pink blooms. Mail orders are dispatched in winter; catalogue free on request. Open Mon–Fri, 9a.m.–5.30p.m. On A505 Cambridge Road between Hitchin and Letchworth.

Hopleys Plants, High Street, Much Hadham SG10 6BU (tel. 01279-842509/web www.hopleys.co.uk), is well worth visiting for its broad range of shrubs, hardy and half-hardy perennials. Many new plants have been raised or introduced to the nursery trade and our gardens by Hopleys, and penstemons, salvias and osteospermums are among their specialities. Mail order is available (send 5 × 1st-class stamps for a catalogue). Open March–Dec, daily, except Tues, 9a.m.–5p.m. (Sun, 2–5p.m.). Entrance (garden only) £1.50. M11 Jct 8, then B1004 to Much Hadham.

The Van Hage Garden Company, Great Amwell, Ware SG12 9RP (tel. 01920-870811/web www.vanhage.co.uk), is an old-established garden centre which offers plenty of interest for gardeners. It carries very broad, well-grown ranges of plants. There are refreshments, display gardens including a new maze, animal gardens for children and a miniature steam railway. Open all year, Mon–Sat, 9a.m.–6p.m., Sun, 10.30a.m.–4.30p.m. Entrance free. At junction of A414 and A1170, 1m from Ware.

Isle of Wight

MAP NO. 2

This small island, just 22 miles long and 13 miles at its widest, appeals more to those who enjoy messing about on boats than to gardeners. It is a long-popular holiday destination for families who appreciate the sandy beaches and tailor-made resorts. Since the mild climate provides agreeable conditions for growing a wide range of plants, gardeners have the opportunity to be adventurous. The number of visitors swells dramatically through the summer season, reaching a climax at the start of August when Cowes Week sees the coastline skirted by the triangular handkerchiefs of countless competing sailboats.

Osborne House

York Avenue, East Cowes PO32 6JY TEL. 01983-200022 OWNER English
Heritage HOURS April–Oct, daily, 10a.m.–6p.m. (closes at 5p.m. in Oct); house,
10a.m.–5p.m. (last adm. 1hr before closing) ENTRANCE Grounds £3.50, OAPs
£2.60, children £1.80; house and grounds £6.90, £5.20 and £3.50 DIRECTIONS
1m E of Cowes off A3021

🌿 ♿ Access 🌿 Gift Shop 🌿 Café

The vast, Italianate mansion of Osborne House was built by Queen
Victoria and Prince Albert as a quiet retreat from the pressures of
Court and Empire. The Queen and her Consort also designed the
formal Italian-style gardens, which have been the subject of gradual
restoration over recent years. There are grand terraces and stairways,
broad lawns and fine sea views. A Swiss-chalet-style cottage full of
curios, where teas are also served from April to September, can be
reached by taking a Victorian carriage ride through the grounds.

The most recent project in rejuvenating the gardens is within the
formerly neglected walled kitchen garden. Its design – formal and
traditional, but with contemporary touches rather than being a slavish
restoration – features fan-trained pears, gages and apricots on the
walls, parallel rows of Victorian period flowers for cutting and
bringing into the house, and clouds of perennial and annual flowers
in a four-square symmetrical arrangement.

Deacon's Nursery

Moorview, Godshill PO38 3HW TEL. 01983-840750 OWNER B.H.W. and G.D.
Deacon HOURS Daily, except Sun, 8a.m.–4p.m. (Sat in winter, 8a.m.–12 noon)
DIRECTIONS 9m S of Cowes at Godshill, by A3020 WEB
www.deaconsnurseryfruits.co.uk

🌿 Plants for Sale 🌿 Nursery 🌿 Mail Order

This is chiefly a mail order nursery, although you can also call in to buy.
Its speciality is fruit, particularly old and rare varieties of apple for
dessert, cooking or cider-making. It also sells perry pear, striped
Canadian pear, medlar, quince, plum, gage, damson, cherry and other
stone-fruit trees. Buying fruit can be a hazardous business if you are
not absolutely certain which rootstock (which determines the tree's size
and productivity) your trees should be on. Enquire here, however, and
you can be sure of getting the right information and advice from these
specialist growers. Trees are lifted and dispatched during the dormant
season, from mid-Oct onwards. A free catalogue is available on request.

The 'Howgate Wonder' Apple

Valued for its large, red-striped fruit and abundant cropping ability, 'Howgate Wonder' is a local apple, raised in 1915–16 by Mr G. Wratton of Howgate Lane, Bembridge, on the far eastern end of the island. It was subsequently offered commercially from the early 1930s and received the Royal Horticultural Society's Award of Merit in 1949.

As it produces a vigorous-growing tree, 'Howgate Wonder' should be grafted onto a dwarfing rootstock if grown in the confined space of a small garden. The substantial size and attractive appearance of this late-keeping cooking apple has made it popular as a show-bench variety, but in cooking its flesh has a tendency to break up. It is often planted in the company of 'Bramley's Seedling' apples as a good pollinator and is hardy enough to be grown successfully in many northern gardens. 'Howgate Wonder' is stocked by many specialist fruit growers, including Deacon's Nursery (*q.v.*) in the south of the island.

VENTNOR

Ventnor Botanic Garden

The Undercliff Drive,Ventnor PO38 1UL TEL. 01983-855397 OWNER Isle of Wight Council HOURS Open all year (temperate house March–Oct, daily, 10a.m.–5p.m.; Nov–Feb, Sat–Sun, 11a.m.–4p.m.) ENTRANCE Free DIRECTIONS Signposted from A3055 WEB www.botanic.co.uk
⬛ ♿ Access ⬛ Café ⬛ Plants for Sale

This is not really a botanic garden, although it has a diverse collection of plants. Its position in the Undercliff, a protective, six-mile ledge in the Downs, gives the property good protection from cold north and east winds. Consequently, plants of the southern hemisphere, particularly those of Australasia, grow well. There are cabbage palms and fan palms, silver-leaved astelia and spiky drifts of tall blue echium.

Fine large trees dating from Victorian plantings grace the park, but most of the ornamental planting started only in 1969. In the 1970s Sir Harold Hillier, of the Hillier Nurseries in Hampshire (*q.v.*), provided many of the garden's more obscure shrubs and trees, particularly ones of borderline hardiness which he supplied free on condition that he could use them as stock plants to provide him with propagating material. There are wafts of Victorian sub-tropicality in the choice of plants and further examples are grown in the temperate house.

And also...

Barton Manor Gardens and Vineyards, East Cowes PO32 6LB (tel. 01983-292835), were once part of the Osborne estate and Prince Albert planted some of the trees, including a cork grove. There are herbaceous borders, a maze of roses and a woodland garden, covering 10 acres. Open June–Sept, 1st Sun in month, 10a.m–5p.m. Entrance £3, OAPs £2, children under 15 (accompanied) £1. On A3021.

Mottistone is a delightful stone village with a well on the green, and a lovely bluebell wood opposite the church to enchant visitors in May. **Mottistone Manor Garden, Mottistone PO30 4ED (tel. 01983-741302)**, has rose gardens, fruit trees and herbaceous borders. Open April–Oct, Tues–Wed, 11.30a.m.–5.30p.m., Sun and Bank Holiday Mons, 2–5.30p.m.; house August Bank Holiday only, 2–5.30p.m. (guided tours 10a.m.–12 noon for NT members). Entrance (garden only) £2.60, children £1.30. At Mottistone, 2m W of Brighstone on B3399.

Kent

Crowded and urban in the north-west, forested and wealden at its centre, flat and open towards its chalk-edge coast, Kent is a region of variations and variegations, known since time imme-morial as the Garden of England. Its apple and cobnut orchards, hop fields and vineyards testify to a bounteous county; the wealden villages among oak woods display pretty half-timbered houses, coveted by London's commuters. There are castles galore here, a legacy of less settled times, but today Kent looks more benignly on its continental neighbours. Its proximity to the coastline of France has left the county scarred by fast roads and rail, leading to several ferry ports and the cross-channel tunnel.

Must See
Church Hill, Charing Heath – riot of hardy plants in a tranquil setting

Hever Castle, Edenbridge – huge lake and lavish 'Roman' garden

Sissinghurst Castle Garden, Sissinghurst – influential historic garden, well maintained

Exceptional in Spring
Scotney, Lamberhurst

Exceptional in Summer
Penshurst Place, Penshurst

Exceptional in Autumn
Brogdale Horticultural Trust, Faversham

Worth a Visit in Winter
Bedgebury National Pinetum, Goudhurst

CANTERBURY

Goodnestone Park

Nr Wingham, Canterbury CT3 1PL TEL. 01304-840107 OWNER The Lord and
Lady FitzWalter HOURS Late March–late Oct, Mon, Wed and Fri, 11a.m.–
5p.m., Sun, 12 noon–6p.m. (groups by appointment at other times) ENTRANCE
£3.30, OAPs £2.80, students £1.50, children (under 12) 50p DIRECTIONS 5m E of
Canterbury on A257, turn S on to B2046, signposted; from M2 take A2, then
B2046

🌿 ♿ Access 🌿 Café 🌿 Plants for Sale 🌿 2 for 1 Voucher

Goodnestone (pronounced Gunston) is a lovely 18th-century park,
on undulating ground speckled with oak trees, cedars and chestnuts.
Its six-acre garden surrounds an elegant mansion, where Jane Austen
often visited and danced. In front of the house, a broad, lawned
terrace is planted with informal groups of shrub roses, and there are
many more roses within the lovely walled garden which is filled with
summer flowers. The gardens offer many delightful walks, and there
is a beautiful woodland garden on an outcrop of acid soil, where
camellias, rhododendrons, azaleas and magnolias flourish and
provide shelter for woodland herbaceous plants – especially attractive
in spring, and for autumnal foliage tints.

CHARING HEATH

Church Hill Cottage Gardens

Must See

Charing Heath, Ashford TN27 0BU TEL. 01233-712522 OWNER Margaret,
Michael and Jeremy Metianu OPEN April–Sept, Tues–Sun and Bank Holiday
Mons,10a.m.–5p.m. (nursery Feb–Nov) ENTRANCE £2, children free DIRECTIONS
M20 Jct 8 or Jct 9, then A20, turn onto Charing Heath road (Maidstone side
of Charing). Turn right at Red Lion, right again after 100yds towards church.
Garden is 300yds on right

🌿 Plants for Sale 🌿 Nursery 🌿 2 for 1 Voucher

Over the last 19 years Margaret and Michael Metianu have turned
one and a half acres of rough, sheep-grazed heathland into one of
the most enchanting and plant-packed gardens in the county.
Informal, wavy-edged beds and borders were made each year,
adding a bit at a time, and Margaret simultaneously began building
up a nursery specialising in the cottage garden plants growing in the
garden. Their son has now joined them in running the nursery, and
the garden has become renowned for its great beauty and tranquillity.

Hardly any annuals are used, and just a few half-hardy perennials;
the emphasis is on really good hardy perennials, among choice shrubs
and scattered trees. The soil throughout most of the garden is, says

Margaret, 'fairly neutral, of poor fertility and very free-draining – marvellous to work, because it's very light, but certain things, such as roses, do not grow well in most parts'. There are hardy geraniums in great profusion, campanulas, eryngiums, sultry 'Arabian Night' dahlias, verbenas and much else. A relaxed feeling is achieved by allowing self-sown flowers plenty of leeway to do their own thing. It is a place to tempt me back to Kent in any season, to enjoy the garden, poke about the nursery and while away time in the most pleasant way – talking plants – with the enthusiastic Metianus.

Specialist Plants at Copton Ash

It is easy to drive straight past Tim Ingram's **Copton Ash Gardens and Nursery, 105 Ashford Road, Faversham ME13 8XW (tel. 01795-535919, evenings only), 1m S of Faversham, leave M2 at Jct 6: on A251 Faversham–Ashford road (north of M2) opposite eastbound slipway for M2**. The garden is hidden away behind a row of ordinary houses and you park in the limited space of the drive. The garden covers about one and a half acres and is packed with around 3000 different plant species. The specialist nursery has developed from the garden, and its unusual plants, particularly those suited to the relatively warm, dry climate of the south-east, are a speciality. There are, for example, five different species of bupleurum offered, 11 of eryngium and many different helianthemums, penstemons, Australasian and South American plants. Open March–Oct, daily, except Mon and Fri, 2–6p.m. and at other times by appointment.

DEAL

Walmer Castle Gardens

Walmer, Deal CT14 7LJ TEL. 01304-364288 OWNER English Heritage HOURS Open all year, Jan–Feb, Sat–Sun (gardens also open Mon–Fri), 10a.m.–4p.m.; March and Nov–Dec, Wed–Sun, 10a.m.–4p.m.; April–Oct, daily, 10a.m.–6p.m. (or dusk if earlier); closed when Lord Warden (the Queen Mother) is in residence ENTRANCE £4.80, concessions £3.60, children £2.40, family ticket £12 (garden free Mon–Fri, Jan–Feb) DIRECTIONS S of Walmer on A258

🔲 ♿ Access 🔲 Gift Shop 🔲 Café

The Walmer fortress was built by Henry VIII as part of his coastal defences against threat of invasion by France or Spain. For the past

300 years its use has been primarily as a domestic residence, however, and it is one of the homes of Queen Elizabeth the Queen Mother, one of whose titles is Lord Warden of the Cinque Ports.

The 10-acre gardens are partly walled and include abundant herbaceous borders backed by characterful and bulging yew hedging, a traditional kitchen garden with rows of flowers for cutting, and fruit trees. There are also shrubberies, wildflower areas, a park with stately trees, and a recently made formal garden. The latter features a central canal and yew pyramids on the lawns, surrounded by flower borders, designed by Penelope Hobhouse.

EDENBRIDGE

Hever Castle

Edenbridge TN8 7NG TEL. 01732-865224 OWNER Broadlands Properties Ltd HOURS March–Nov, daily, 11a.m.–6p.m. (castle 12 noon–6 p.m.), last adm. and winter closing time 5p.m. ENTRANCE £8, OAPs £6.80, children £5.40 (under 5s free), family ticket £20.40 (garden only £6.30, £5.40, £4.20 and £16.80) DIRECTIONS 3m SE of Edenbridge, signposted from M25 Jct 5 or Jct 6 WEB www.hevercastle.co.uk

 Access Gift Shop Café Plants for Sale

Several times I have had the opportunity to enjoy Hever's magical evenings at mid-summer, for the 70-odd acres of grounds are host to a season of theatre each year, when performances can be preceded by picnics at the lakeside. And what a lake it is. In the early years of the 20th century the American newspaper tycoon William Waldorf Astor employed 1000 men to transform the landscape; 800 of them excavated the 35-acre stretch of water, which provides a serene counterpoint to the more formal areas. At one end of the lake Astor made a four-acre Italian garden, with a confection of steps, colonnades and a loggia, in opulent classical style. The Italian garden houses Roman artefacts along one side, and a spectacular pergola along the other, draped in all manner of vines and climbers. There are also rose gardens, a rock garden, a very good yew maze, lots of topiary, beds of rhododendrons and a traditional dahlia border. And then there is, not least, the double-moated castle itself, which dates from the 13th century. Henry VIII courted his second wife, Anne Boleyn, here, for it was her childhood home. It sits in island splendour, linked by a bridge to a veritable village of outbuildings that have served the estate for centuries.

FAVERSHAM

The Brogdale Horticultural Trust

Brogdale Road, Faversham ME13 8XZ TEL. 01795-535286 OWNER Brogdale Horticultural Trust HOURS Open all year, daily, 10a.m.–5p.m. (telephone to check opening times for Dec–Feb). ENTRANCE Free, guided tours £3, concessions £2.50, children £2 DIRECTIONS 1m SW of Faversham, M2 Jct 6, left to A2, left onto A2, left into Brogdale Road, museum on left WEB www.brogdale.org.uk

🔲 ♿ Access 🔲 Gift Shop 🔲 Café 🔲 Plants for Sale 🔲 NPC

Brogdale's 150 acres provide a fascinating living museum of fruit. It has national collections of cherries, apples (around 2300 different kinds), pears (around 400 different varieties), plums, hazelnuts, grape vines and currants. Its function was, and is, as a research station, testing new cultivars and conserving the old.

Brogdale has an instructional and institutional layout, and is worth visiting if you have a special interest in fruit or are just inquisitive to know more. Its Apple Day events in October offer entertainment, question-and-answer sessions and all manner of advice on fruit, including identifying unlabelled fruit from your garden. The shop is a marvellous source of fruit for sale when in season, and the huge collections here provide the chance to sample rare and unusual varieties that you won't find in other shops.

GOUDHURST

Bedgebury National Pinetum and Forest Gardens

Nr Goudhurst, Cranbrook TN17 2SL TEL. 01580-211781/211123 OWNER Forestry Commission HOURS Open all year, daily, 10a.m.–7p.m. (closes earlier in winter) ENTRANCE £3, OAPs £2.50, children £1.20 (under 5s free), family ticket £8 DIRECTIONS Off A21 on B2079 Flimwell–Goudhurst road, 10m SE of Tunbridge Wells

🔲 Gift Shop 🔲 Café 🔲 NPC

This is an extraordinary place, ideal for crisp winter walks or misty autumn days. Yet winter visitors are not here purely for the trees, although they are reason enough. Within Bedgebury's 300 acres you may well come across mushroomers foraging for fungi, botanists botanising in the bogs and undergrowth, and you may even catch sight of flocks of birdwatchers, twitching away behind long lenses that are trained on the visiting crossbills, which gorge on various pine cones and kernels.

There was already a comprehensive collection of conifers on the Bedgebury Estate when the Royal Botanic Gardens, Kew (q.v.), and the Forestry Commission pooled resources to maintain it in 1925. These days it is administered solely by the Forestry Commission and it remains one of the finest collections of conifers in Europe.

Here you can see conifers in all their variety, from dainty dwarf kinds to fully mature hemlocks, cedars and pines. The tallest tree here is a grand fir, 150 years old and as many feet tall. Close to it and very nearly as tall are several Leyland cypresses, a reminder of the potentially massive size of these popular hedging trees. It's good to see conifers in a setting that can match their own majesty. The undulating, rugged landscape suits them well and incense cedars stand as tall pillars on the hillside like isolated ruins of classical temples. There are also deciduous trees scattered through the pinetum and a broad range of rhododendrons thrives in the acidic soil conditions, bringing some floral colour to the slopes in the first half of the year.

LAMBERHURST

Scotney Castle Garden

Lamberhurst, Tunbridge Wells TN3 8JN TEL. 01892-891081 OWNER The National Trust HOURS March–Nov, Wed–Fri, 11a.m.–6p.m., Sat–Sun, 2–6p.m. (12 noon–5p.m. in March), Bank Holiday Suns and Mons, 12 noon–6p.m. ENTRANCE £4.40, children £2.20, family ticket £11 DIRECTIONS On A21, S of Lamberhurst

🔹 ♿ Access 🔹 Gift Shop

The classic view of Scotney is the old, partially ruined castle with its bulging round tower, seen from across the waters of its moat. It seems the perfect setting for the dalliance of lovers: the ruin casually draped with wisteria, vines and roses, and fragrant herbs scenting the partially enclosed courtyard. West and north-west of the castle, the sloping gardens display naturalistic plantings of ornamental trees and shrubs. Thickets of rhododendrons, viburnums and azaleas light up the hillside with kaleidoscopic colours in spring, while the coppiced trees of the woodland are awash with bluebells. Early in the year, snowdrops light up the grassy slopes, followed by primroses and daffodils; autumn sees the foliage tints of parrotia, acers and many other fiery-leaved trees and shrubs. Within its 20 acres there is much to see and enjoy, and always the unfailingly romantic atmosphere, especially late in the day after the bulk of visitors has disappeared.

Port Lympne

Lympne, nr Hythe CT21 4PD TEL. 01303-264647 OWNER Mr D. Aspinall HOURS
Open all year, daily, 10a.m.–5p.m. (or 1hr before dusk in winter)
ENTRANCE £9.80, OAPs/children £7.80, family ticket £28 for 2 adults and 2
children, £32 for 2 adults and 3 children (includes house, garden and animal
park) DIRECTIONS 3m W of Hythe, on B2067; M20 Jct 11 and follow signs WEB
www.howletts.net

🌿 ♿ Access 🌿 Gift Shop 🌿 Café 🌿 Plants for Sale

Port Lympne

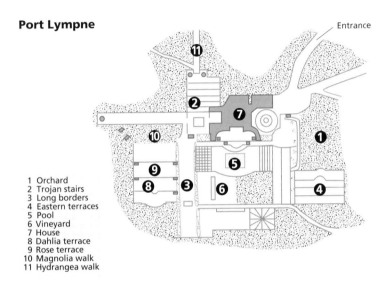

1 Orchard
2 Trojan stairs
3 Long borders
4 Eastern terraces
5 Pool
6 Vineyard
7 House
8 Dahlia terrace
9 Rose terrace
10 Magnolia walk
11 Hydrangea walk

Port Lympne provides a fantastical cocktail of zoo, garden and
eccentrically decorated house, adding up to a highly enjoyable outing
for all ages and inclinations. From the garden visitor's point of view,
it is certainly a novelty to walk through 100yds of hydrangeas to the
accompanying sound of baying wolves, or to hear the distant roar of
rare Barbary lions while admiring the dahlia borders.

The 15 acres of gardens (within a 300-acre animal park) were
originally designed by the wealthy art patron and political host, Sir
Philip Sassoon, being laid out from 1919 onwards. From the hydrangea
walk you reach the top of the 125-step Trojan stairs, offering wonderful
views over the flatlands of Romney Marsh. The stairs lead down to a
formal garden of roses, cotton lavender and Hupeh crab apples (which
have beautiful spring blossom) and further terraced gardens, divided

by walls and hedging. Within the hedged compartments there are bedded-out areas – one in an intriguing chessboard design, another laid out with beds in contrasting stripes. There is a terraced vineyard, a pair of long, mixed borders, a magnolia walk, rose terrace, dahlia terrace and herbaceous border, and surrounding picnic areas.

By the time you have reached the end of the lower terraces, the animals are close at hand – lions, hyaenas, small cats, bison, gibbons and monkeys, etc. It is also well worth looking inside the eccentrically decorated house, which has a delightful Moorish patio with marble floor and five fountains, and a tented room of exotic murals by the celebrated artist Rex Whistler.

PENSHURST

Penshurst Place

Penshurst, Tonbridge TN11 8DG TEL. 01892-870307 OWNER Viscount de l'Isle HOURS April–Oct, daily, 10.30a.m.–6p.m.; March, Sat–Sun only, 10.30a.m.–6p.m. ENTRANCE £6.50, concessions £6, children £4.50, family ticket £18; garden only £5, £4.50, £4 and £15 DIRECTIONS SW of Tonbridge on B2176, in Penshurst village; M25 Jct 5, then A21 towards Hastings, turn off at Hildenborough and follow signs WEB www.penshurstplace.com

🔲 ♿ Access 🔲 Gift Shop 🔲 Café 🔲 Plants for Sale

The county of Kent possesses an excessively generous helping of castles and historic houses, many of which are set off by pleasing grounds. Penshurst Place is among the very best of them – an ancient, battlemented house with thick walls of stone and seemingly endless enclosed gardens, formally laid out but displaying a summertime abandonment under a siege of flowers.

The garden covers eleven acres, sub-divided by a mile of yew hedges into mostly formal areas, such as the symmetrically laid-out Italian garden of neat box beds and polyantha roses around a central lily-pool. There are avenues of fruit trees and parallel herbaceous borders; a 'Union Jack' garden of red and white roses lined by hedges of blue lavender; a formally laid-out cobnut orchard, and smooth lawns pinned down by stout topiary. Flowers, particularly roses, dominate the high season, but spring bulbs and apple blossom make early visits memorable, and autumn sees a magnificent ripening of fruits and foliage. The 100yd-long bed of peonies is spectacular at that expectant moment when spring is retreating in favour of summer.

Sissinghurst Castle Garden

Sissinghurst, nr Cranbrook TN17 2AB TEL. 01580-710700 OWNER The National
Trust HOURS Easter–mid-Oct, Tues–Fri, 1–6.30p.m. (last adm. 5.30p.m.),
Sat–Sun, 10a.m.–6.30p.m. (last adm. 5.30p.m.); timed ticket system means
that at busy times visitors may need to wait to enter the garden ENTRANCE
£6.50, children £3, family ticket £16 DIRECTIONS M25 Jct 5, then A21 S towards
Hastings, after 19m and before Lamberhurst turn left onto A262 and follow
signs to Sissinghurst

  & Access   Gift Shop   Café   Plants for Sale

This world-famous garden was made by the influential gardener and
writer Vita Sackville-West and her husband, Harold Nicolson, from
1930 onwards. Its appeal lies in the disciplined framework of walls
and hedges (chiefly Harold's department), filled out by wonderfully
exuberant plantings of old roses, perennials and cottage garden
flowers (Vita's inspiration). The setting itself is wildly romantic: the
Nicolsons took on the remains of an Elizabethan mansion with twin
towers and rambling, low outbuildings, crumbly, red-brick walls and
open courtyards.

Harold's restrained classicism produced a design of bold vistas
and allées, complementary to the period of the house, but not slavishly
emulating a Tudor layout. By sectioning off the six acres into variously
themed areas, the Nicolsons were able to experiment with contrasting
atmospheres in different parts of the garden. Vita's innovative White
Garden is a poetic composition of white and off-white flowers, set off
by green, grey and blue-tinted foliage plants, such as ferns, artemisias,
sea kale and grasses. It is soothing, cool, restrained. By contrast, the
cottage garden makes the heart beat faster with hot, strong colours –
vivid yellow, orange and scarlet poppies, arctotis, cannas and red-hot
pokers, against the dark greenery of yew. The rose garden is heady
with old-fashioned blooms, sweetly scented and chiefly in shades of
pink, joined by complementary blue, mauve and white flowers.
Harold's spring garden features massed bulbs in variety, beneath an
avenue of pleached limes.

Although the Nicolsons departed a long time ago, their inspiration
lives on, through the talents and skills of succeeding head gardeners.
There is so much to see and enjoy here that any time of year will be
rewarding; visits early or late in the day are usually less crowded,
however; due to the narrow and uneven paths, wheelchairs are
restricted to two at one time, and prams and pushchairs are not
admitted.

TUNBRIDGE WELLS

Groombridge Place

Groombridge, Tunbridge Wells TN3 9QG TEL. 01892-863999 OWNER
Groombridge Asset Management HOURS April–late Oct, daily, 9a.m.–6p.m.
ENTRANCE £7.50, OAPs £6.50, children £6.50, family ticket £25 DIRECTIONS On
B2110, 4m SW of Tunbridge Wells

🌿 &. Access 🌿 Gift Shop 🌿 Café 🌿 Plants for Sale

The pretty, moated house (not open) at Groombridge is set beside
several delightful, terraced, formal gardens rising up a gently sloping
hill. Near the house lie formal lawns, a knot, a sculpture and an
oriental garden, the latter featuring ancient Japanese acers. The
'Drunken' garden displays tipsy topiaries, leaning at odd angles;
there is a rose garden, a white garden and a walled kitchen garden.
An exciting development in this 164-acre site is the Enchanted Forest
woodland garden, where wiggly paths and water gardens ramble
through mature woodland. There are bridges crossing the stream at
intervals, and new plantings of moisture-loving plants, at their most
colourful in spring. As well as being an interesting garden in its own
right, Groombridge Place caters for family interests as a whole, with
falconry displays from one of England's largest birds-of-prey
sanctuaries, canal boat rides and an award-winning children's
garden.

YALDING

Yalding Organic Gardens

Benover Road, Yalding, Maidstone ME18 6EX TEL. 01622-814650 OWNER The
Henry Doubleday Research Association HOURS Easter–Sept, Wed–Sun and
Bank Holiday Mons; also April and Oct, Sat–Sun only; all 10a.m.–5p.m.
ENTRANCE £3, children free DIRECTIONS 6m SW of Maidstone, ½m S of Yalding
on B2010, leave M20 at Jct 4 WEB www.hdra.org.uk

🌿 &. Access 🌿 Gift Shop 🌿 Café 🌿 Plants for Sale 🌿 2 for 1 Voucher

This five-acre garden is a southern offshoot of the Henry Doubleday
Research Association's gardens at Ryton (*q.v.*), in Warwickshire. It is
laid out in a series of attractive demonstration gardens, all cultivated
entirely organically, and offers both interesting insights into garden
making in earlier centuries and a great deal of practical information.

There is a woodland and wildflower walk, a medieval physick
garden of culinary and medicinal herbs, a Tudor-style knot garden
of interwoven low hedging, a 19th-century cottager's garden of mixed
flowers, fruit and vegetables, and another Victorian garden in a more

Yalding

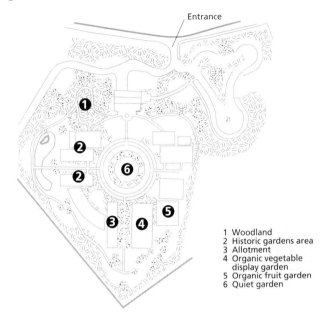

Entrance

1 Woodland
2 Historic gardens area
3 Allotment
4 Organic vegetable
 display garden
5 Organic fruit garden
6 Quiet garden

suburban style. There are sumptuous double herbaceous borders in the spirit of Gertrude Jekyll (*q.v.*), allotment gardens, organic vegetable and fruit displays, etc. Yalding shows how everyone can make a really beautiful garden in an ecologically friendly way, working in harmony with nature and not against it.

And also...

J. Bradshaw & Son, Busheyfields Nursery, Herne, Herne Bay CT6 7LJ (tel. 01227-375415), is an old-established family nursery, specialising in a wide range of climbing plants, particularly honeysuckles (around 100 species and cultivars) and clematis, both of which are held here as National Collections. For the mail order catalogue send a large s.a.e. Open March–Oct, Tues–Sat, and Bank Holiday Mons, 10a.m.–5p.m. A299, then A291 towards Canterbury, nursery is 1m after Herne.

Dr Simon Charlesworth, of **Downderry Nursery, Pillarbox Lane, Hadlow, Tonbridge TN11 9SW (tel. 01732-810081/web www.downderry-nursery.co.uk)**, specialises in producing lavenders, and has more than 60 different species and cultivars. There are also very interesting display gardens, including a maze (of lavender hedges) fashioned in a pattern used at Chartres Cathedral. Send 3 × 1st-class stamps for a catalogue. Many plants are sold as rooted cuttings and liners. Open May–Oct, daily, 10a.m.–5p.m. M20 Jct 4, then A228 towards Tonbridge, then A26, turn right into Common Road, then 3rd right and right at pub.

Herbs, wildflowers, cottage-garden and aromatic plants are on sale and displayed in the show gardens at **Iden Croft Herbs, Frittenden Road, Staplehurst TN12 0DH (tel. 01580-891432/web www.herbs-uk.com)**. Open all year, Mon–Sat, 9a.m.–5p.m.; also Sun and Bank Holidays, March–Sept, 11a.m.–5p.m. Entrance to gardens £2, children 50p. Signposted from A229.

For the largest range of fruit trees in the country, contact **Keepers Nursery, Gallants Court, East Farleigh, Maidstone ME15 0LE (tel. 01622-726465/web www.fruittree.co.uk)**, which offers over 600 different varieties, among them large ranges of apples, pears, quinces, medlars, walnuts, cobnuts and stone fruits (including damsons and nectarines). A propagation service is also available if, for example, you want to duplicate a special tree in your garden (most propagation is carried out by budding from late July–August, with young trees usually ready for delivery 18 months later). Send 2 × 1st-class stamps for a mail order catalogue. Open by appointment.

Madrona Nursery, Pluckley Road, Bethersden TN26 3DD (tel. 01233-820100), has a wonderful selection of plants across a selective range of shrubs and trees, hardy perennials, conifers, grasses, bamboos and ferns. The emphasis is on the interesting and unusual, well grown and reasonably priced. Also plants by mail (free catalogue). Open late March–late Oct, Sat–Tues, 10a.m.–5p.m. M20 Jct 8, then old A20 to Charing, turn right to Pluckley, then left to Bethersden, nursery on right.

Rayment Wirework, Unit 7, Hoo Farm, Monkton Road, Minster-in-Thanet CT12 4JB (tel. 01843-821628/web www.raymentwire.co.uk), manufactures elegant, hand-painted wirework structures for gardens and conservatories. Their range includes plant holders and fancy hanging baskets, intricate gazebos and ornate furniture, in styles inspired by 19th-century French designs. Mail order catalogue on request. Open Mon–Fri, 8a.m.–5.30p.m. Off A2/M2.

Lancashire

Here is a land of contrasts, renowned for its central role in the Industrial Revolution, with a roll call of hard-working cotton towns – Bolton, Blackburn, Oldham and Manchester – and hard-playing seaside resorts, such as Blackpool, Southport, Lytham St Anne's and Morecambe (famous for its shrimps). The north of the region is a land of high fells, while the spine of the Pennines runs down the eastern boundary. The Forest of Bowland is not really a forest, but a former royal hunting ground and an area of wild beauty and subtle heathland colours among high moors. Its fertile valleys provide good grazing for cattle – the name Bowland deriving from the Celtic buland, meaning cattle pasture.

Exceptional in Spring
Fletcher Moss Botanical
  Gardens, Manchester

Exceptional in Summer
Catforth Gardens, Preston

BARROWFORD
Pendle Heritage Centre

Park Hill, Barrowford, Nelson BB9 6JQ TEL. 01282-661702 OWNER Mr J. Miller
HOURS Garden open all year, daily, 10a.m.–5p.m. (museum will reopen in early
2002) ENTRANCE £1.20, concessions and children 80p; garden and museum
£2.20, concessions and children £1.50 DIRECTIONS Come off M65 at Jct 13, 1m
from roundabout at junction, then signposted
🌿 Gift Shop 🌿 Café

This six-acre local history centre with old stone buildings, a small
farm and country trails has a brick-walled garden, restored to look
as it would have done in the late 18th century, using only plants that
were then available. Its triangular-shape beds are planted with herbs
and salad flowers. Two large, box-edge beds contain assorted flowers
and standard gooseberry bushes, with *Rosa gallica officinalis*, the Red
Rose of Lancaster. Two further beds contain vegetables and fruit,
with espalier pear trees trained on wires beside the path. All plants
are organically grown.

There is a steep woodland walk among wildflowers offering views
of the beautiful local countryside. The farm buildings include a fine
cruck barn, dating from the 16th century, its frame formed from a
single oak tree split in half, then roughly shaped to form the inverted
V that provides the basic structure of the building. Gawthorpe Hall
(*q.v.*) is nearby.

BURNLEY
Gawthorpe Hall

Padiham, Burnley BB12 8UA TEL. 01282-771004 OWNER Lancashire County
Council (on lease from The National Trust) HOURS Gardens all year, daily,
10a.m.–6p.m., hall late March–early Nov, Tues–Thurs, Sat–Sun and Bank
Holiday Mons, 1–5p.m. ENTRANCE Gardens free, hall £3, concessions £1.50,
children £1.30 (under 5s free), family ticket £8 DIRECTIONS 2½m NW of
Burnley, N of A671 just E of Padiham town centre WEB
www.lancashire.com.lcc/museums
🌿 Café

The early 17th-century stone house (restored in the mid-19th
century) displays a collection of works on loan from the National
Portrait Gallery. Its surrounding Victorian gardens were designed
by Sir Charles Barry, who had carried out the restoration work on
the house. He laid out a formal parterre of sunburst pattern and
gravel paths, and a small formal rose garden. Beyond, rhododendrons and bright-foliage shrubs bring spring colour to the
woodland walks.

Fletcher Moss Botanical Gardens

Millgate Lane, Didsbury, Manchester M20 1AA TEL. 0161-445 4241
OWNER Manchester City Council HOURS Open all year, daily, 9a.m.–dusk
ENTRANCE Free DIRECTIONS 5m S of Manchester city centre, S of A5145 close
to village of Didsbury, on Millgate Lane

⬛ ♿ Access ⬛ Café

This unusual rock garden of 21 acres is over 100 years old and is still
one of the finest in the north of England. It was begun in 1889 by
Robert Wood Williamson, a solicitor and keen alpine gardener, whose
extensive knowledge of these plants was due to the fact that he joined
his father (a professor of natural history and botany) on geological
expeditions to the mountainous regions of Europe.

You descend the steeply sloping, south-facing garden by narrow,
informal paths that wind along and down a series of rocky terraces.
They are home to many spring flowers and bulbs, such as cyclamen,
crocuses and dwarf narcissi, and small shrubs. There are gentians,
saxifrages, phloxes and other typical rock-garden flowers crammed
into the rockwork, and a small stream feeds several pools on its
descent to a larger pond at the bottom.

The house and garden were sold early this century to a wealthy
neighbour, Fletcher Moss, who gave the property and gardens to the
city of Manchester in 1920. Parts of the grounds were developed for
leisure facilities, but the rock garden has survived. In 1958 part of the
garden was dedicated to the intrepid plant hunter Frank Kingdon-
Ward, who was born just two miles away in the village of Withington.
Interestingly, his father, Marshall Ward, was a pupil of, and later
assistant to, Robert Williamson's father.

Catforth Gardens

Roots Lane, Catforth, Preston PR4 OJB TEL. 01772-690561/690269 OWNER Mr
and Mrs T.A. Bradshaw and Mr W. and Miss S. Moore HOURS Phone for
details ENTRANCE Phone for details DIRECTIONS 5m NW of Preston, turn S off
B5269 to Catforth, Roots Lane is S of village (signposted)

⬛ ♿ Access ⬛ Plants for Sale ⬛ NPC ⬛ 2 for 1 Voucher

A dozen years ago, next-door neighbours Christine Moore and Judith
Bradshaw combined their horticultural interests to open a nursery
together. It specialises in hardy herbaceous perennials, and the
gardens of their respective houses – and a third in the paddock,
planted in 1994 – are also open.

The style is abundant, informal planting with hardy perennials given full rein, especially the cranesbill geraniums, which now amount to a National Collection of the genus. Any season promises rewarding visiting for those interested in plants: in spring, it is the pulmonarias, euphorbias, earliest geraniums and dicentras which provide little jewels of colour. The Farmhouse Garden features an alpine scree, cottage-garden flowers through the season, and a water garden. The Paddock Garden features flowers for high summer in colour-planned areas of hot and cooler colours, a rose and herbaceous garden, and three pools of waterlilies, joined by flowering marginal plants.

A Lost Landscape for Bolton Wanderers

Up on the western, heather-clad moors of Rivington Pike is **Rivington Terraced Gardens, Rivington, nr Bolton (tel. 01204-691549/web www.unitedutilities.com), 7m NW of Bolton, 1m NW of Horwich; M61 Jct 6, then follow signs from A673 to Rivington or Grimeford, walk from Rivington Hall and Hall Barn**. The Edwardian landscape architect Thomas Mawson laid out a public park and a private garden at Roynton Cottage for the soap industrialist, William Lever (who became Lord Leverhulme). Mawson resisted any thoughts of stamping a formal garden onto the landscape; instead he laid out the 45 acres of grounds with lawns and winding paths among plantations of exotic and native trees and ericaceous shrubs, sympathetically following the contours of the hillside. Although he was famous for creating grander gardens in the Arts and Crafts style, Mawson declared: 'Of all the gardens which have administered to my professional enjoyment, none comes into competition with Roynton.'

Decades of neglect have taken their toll on the gardens and their abandoned buildings, but the naturalistic rockwork is impressive, with ornamental pools and miniature waterfalls, and the views are outstanding. Open all year, daily. Entrance free.

And also...

Over 150 different models of vintage garden machinery are displayed at **The British Lawnmower Museum, 106–114 Shakespeare Street, Southport PR8 5AJ (tel. 01704-501336)**. The museum workshop restores vintage mowers belonging to enthusiasts, as well as the machinery in its own collection. Open all year, Mon–Sat, 9a.m.–5.30p.m. (closed Bank Holidays). Entrance £1, children 50p. M57 Jct 7, then A565 and follow signs.

Holden Clough Nursery, Holden, Bolton-by-Bowland, Clitheroe BB7 4PF (tel. 01200-447615/web www.holdencloughnursery.co.uk), specialises in raising choice, really hardy plants suited to northern gardens. It is a long-established traditional nursery, with a large range of interesting plants, including alpines, grasses, heathers, perennials and shrubs; mail order is available (catalogue £1.40). Open all year, Mon–Sat, 9a.m.–12 noon and 1–5p.m. and occasional Sun afternoons in spring. A59, then follow signs to Sawley and Bolton-by-Bowland, after 2m take sharp left at Copy Nook Hotel following signs to Holden, after ¼m fork left, nursery is on right.

Silverdale is in beautiful limestone country overlooking Morecambe Bay, where you will find **Reginald Kaye Ltd, Waithman Nurseries, Silverdale, Carnforth LA5 0TY (tel. 01524-701252)**. There are many rare alpines and rock plants, dwarf trees and conifers, hardy ferns, bog and woodland plants (catalogue 60p, but no mail order). A garden is now open on the site for which there may be an entrance fee. Open Wed–Sat, 10a.m.–5p.m., Sun 2.30–5p.m.

Vegetables are larger than life when grown from seed supplied by **W. Robinson & Sons Ltd, Sunny Bank, Forton, nr Preston PR3 0BN (tel. 01524-791210)**. This is the home of the 'Mammoth' strain of seeds, a speciality which grew out of an earlier family business in market gardening. Robinson's 'Mammoth' onions, leeks, tomatoes and beans (such as the 30in-long 'Liberty' runner beans) are favourites with exhibition growers. Catalogue available on request. Open June–Feb, Mon–Fri, 8a.m.–5p.m., and March–May, daily, 9a.m.–5p.m. M6 Jct 33, 2m S on A6.

Acid, sandy soil at the National Trust's **Rufford Old Hall, Rufford, nr Ormskirk L40 1SG (tel. 01704-821254)**, provides ideal conditions for rhododendrons in the gardens surrounding a magnificent Tudor hall. There are 14 acres of woodland gardens of shrubs and bulbs, topiaries in the lawns and a small orchard featuring old northern varieties of apple. There is also a tearoom and shop. Hall open April–Oct, Sat–Wed, 1–5p.m., last adm. 4.30p.m.; garden same days as hall, 12 noon–5.30p.m., also Nov, Sat–Sun, 12 noon–4p.m., and Dec, Wed–Sun, 12 noon–4p.m. Entrance £4, children £2; gardens only £2, children £1 (free in Nov and Dec). M6 Jct 27, then follow signs to Rufford.

Stydd Nursery, Stonygate Lane, Ribchester, Preston PR3 3YN (tel. 01254-878797), specialises in old-fashioned roses, plus some modern shrub and species roses, climbers and ramblers. Also half-hardy perennials and conservatory plants. Open Mon–Fri, 1–4.30p.m., Sat–Sun, 10a.m.–4p.m. M6 Jct 31, then A59 and follow signs to Ribchester.

Leicestershire and Rutland

Rutland (originally Rota's Land, owned by Queen Edith, wife of Edward the Confessor, and first recorded in the year 851) is a tiny county, just 15 miles long and 11 miles wide. It had been swallowed up by Leicestershire but recently regained its independent status. Leicestershire engulfs its western boundary, and the entire region is known for its fertile farms, an age-old tradition of hunting and Melton Mowbray, the home of crusty pork pies, and Stilton cheese. From the gardener's point of view, the region is also the home of Barnsdale, the television gardens of the late and greatly missed Geoff Hamilton.

BELVOIR

Belvoir Castle

Belvoir, nr Grantham NG32 1PD TEL. 01476-870262 OWNER The Duke of
Rutland HOURS Easter weekend, 1st week and all Suns in April; May–Sept,
daily; Oct, Sun only, all 11a.m.–5p.m. ENTRANCE Castle and gardens £7, OAPs
£5.50, children £3.50, family ticket £17; rose and statue garden £3.90,
children £1.50; spring garden (by pre-booked appointment for parties only
and on a few other days – phone for details) £5, OAPs £4.50 DIRECTIONS By
Belvoir village, 6m W of Grantham, use A1 (signposted) WEB
www.belvoircastle.com

🍃 Gift Shop   🍃 Café   🍃 Plants for Sale

The impressive castle stands in a commanding position above the
Vale of Belvoir (pronounced Beaver), its name meaning beautiful
view. The castle is packed with notable art treasures and fine
furniture; outside, the four-acre Statue Gardens with their 17th-
century sculptures descend the hillside below the castle in a sequence
of terraces and slopes. As well as the fine views, there are modern
roses, a woodland garden, record trees – the tallest bird cherry and
yew tree in Britain – and recently introduced contemporary sculpture.

The Duchess of Rutland's private Spring Garden (open by
appointment) has recently been restored, and is a pretty woodland
of flowering trees, shrubs and bulbs, set in a natural amphitheatre,
hidden away in the woods.

OAKHAM

Barnsdale

The Avenue, Exton, Oakham, Rutland LE15 8AH TEL. 01572-813200
OWNER Nick and Sue Hamilton HOURS March–Oct, daily, 10a.m.–5p.m., last
adm. 3p.m.; Nov–Feb, Sat–Sun, 10a.m.–4.30p.m.; nursery open all year, daily,
10a.m.–5p.m. (closes 4p.m., Nov–Feb) ENTRANCE £5, children free DIRECTIONS Off
A606 between Oakham and Stamford, turn off at Barnsdale Lodge Hotel,
gardens on left WEB www.barnsdalegardens.co.uk

🍃 ♿ Access   🍃 Gift Shop   🍃 Café   🍃 Plants for Sale   🍃 Nursery

Over a period of 17 years the gardens at Barnsdale became familiar
to millions of viewers of the BBC's flagship gardening programme.
The home of the late Geoff Hamilton, Barnsdale covers eight and a
half acres of a variety of demonstration gardens, all specially made
for *Gardeners' World* and themed series, such as *The Ornamental
Kitchen Garden*.

Since 1997 the gardens have been open to the public on a regular
basis, and you can wander through 25 different areas, such as the
Gentleman's Garden, featuring brick paths and terracing, topiary and

trelliswork; the Artisan's Garden, with everything home-made on a tight budget, yet executed with panache; the *Daily Express* garden of herbs and wattle arches; the Elizabethan Kitchen Garden of raised beds and painted finials; and the Paradise Gardens, one with red-brick walls and a conservatory, the other featuring random stepping-stone paths and rustic seating.

Barnsdale Plants Nursery adjoins the gardens, and is run by Geoff Hamilton's son, Nick. It offers a very wide selection of plants propagated from the gardens and specialises in well-grown herbaceous perennials and shrubs, all in peat-free compost.

And also...

Gandy's Roses Ltd, Station Road, North Kilworth, nr Lutterworth, Leicestershire LE17 6HZ (tel. 01858-880398), is an old-established family business, with around 600 varieties of roses available, including a substantial number of climbers. You can buy direct from the nursery, which also stocks shrubs, conifers and fruit trees, and by mail for dispatch during the dormant season (free catalogue available on request). Open daily, Mon–Fri, 9a.m.–5p.m., Sat, 9a.m.–4.30p.m., Sun, 2.30–4.30p.m. (rose fields open July–Sept, free). M1 Jct 20, then A4034.

Goscote Nurseries, Syston Road, Cossington, Leicestershire LE7 4UZ (tel. 01509-812121/web www.goscote.co.uk), was begun by Derek Cox in 1964. It is renowned for its extensive stocks of trees – around 210 different varieties – but also sells shrubs, clematis, conifers and rhododendrons, available by mail or direct from the nursery (send 5 × 1st-class stamps for the catalogue). Open all year, Mon–Sat, 9a.m.–5p.m., Sun, 10a.m.–5 p.m. (4.30p.m. in winter). M1 Jct 21A, then A46 and A6 towards Loughborough, exit at Rothley, right onto B5328, nurseries on left.

The Herb Nursery, Thistleton, Rutland LE15 7RE (tel. 01572-767658), offers herbs, herbaceous plants and wildflowers in variety, with around 500 different plants available. Scented-leaf pelargoniums are a speciality and there is a display garden featuring plants available from the nursery. There is a catalogue (send an A5 s.a.e.) but no mail order. Open daily, 9a.m.–6p.m. (or dusk if earlier). Between Stamford and Grantham, 1m from A1, 7m from Oakham.

If you are keen on dahlias or chrysanthemums, it is worth knowing about **Philip Tivey and Sons, 28 Wanlip Road, Syston, Leicestershire LE7 1PA (tel. 01162-692968)**, which has been specialising in these flowers for over 40 years, producing some of its own varieties. The nursery exhibits at the Royal Horticultural Society's shows and others, including the splendid Harrogate Autumn Show, which is always a riot of colourful blooms. (Send a s.a.e. for catalogue.) Open all year, Mon–Sat, 9a.m.–4p.m. M1 Jct 21A, follow signs to Syston, right at 1st roundabout after junction with A46, then left at 3rd roundabout into Syston Road, on left.

Lincolnshire

MAP NO. 6

Although it is a large county, Lincolnshire is off the beaten track for most tourists; it is completely bypassed by arterial routes linking the north and south of England and its unremarkable landscape – much of it very flat – has proved best suited to arable farms and extensive production of flower bulbs. The broad horizons are punctuated here and there by little more than the odd church tower, under vast skies. The city of Lincoln, perched on a rare hill, was a Celtic settlement before the Romans arrived and named it Lindum Colonia; its triple-towered cathedral is magnificent. Stamford is an attractive town of stone architecture, brought to fame as television's *Middlemarch*.

Exceptional in Summer
Hall Farm, Gainsborough
Gunby Hall, Gunby

GAINSBOROUGH

Hall Farm

Exceptional in Summer

Harpswell, Gainsborough DN21 5UU TEL. 01427-668412 OWNER Mr and Mrs M. Tatam HOURS Open all year, daily, 9.30a.m.–5.30p.m. (opening times subject to change in winter; telephone before visiting) ENTRANCE £1.50 DIRECTIONS On A631

🌑 ♿ Access 🌑 Nursery

This is surely one of the most generously spirited gardens (or at any rate, owners) in the entire *Guide*. Hall Farm is known far and wide for its seed collection day, held (usually) on the first Sunday in September, when visitors can come armed with scissors, secateurs and paper bags to gather seeds from the garden's extensive range – free of charge (bar the entrance fee, of course). Anyone who ever gets the urge to snap off the odd desirable seed-head from a plant when visiting someone else's garden can do it here on the appointed day without subterfuge or feelings of guilt.

The one-acre garden is laid out around the farmhouse and beside a thriving nursery which Pam Tatam has developed in recent years to satisfy her own curiosity and passion for plants. Much unusual stock is grown from seed, and also from cuttings, so if you're not seed-minded yourself, you will find a terrific range of plants ready-grown to buy in pots. Old-fashioned roses – around 100 varieties – are a feature of the gardens. There is also a sunken garden with box-edged beds and colourful seasonal flowers, a pond, a courtyard garden, a spectacular pair of long herbaceous borders and a recently made walled gravel garden.

GRANTHAM

Belton House

Grantham NG32 2LS TEL. 01476-566116 OWNER The National Trust HOURS End March–early Nov, Wed–Sun and Bank Holiday Mons, 11a.m.–5.30p.m; house, 12.30–5p.m. (last adm. 4.30p.m.) ENTRANCE £5.60, children £2.80, family ticket £14 DIRECTIONS Leave A1 at Grantham, then 3m NE on A607 towards Lincoln

🌑 ♿ Access 🌑 Gift Shop 🌑 Café

Belton House is serene, elegant and surprisingly entertaining. It will be familiar to many as Rosings, the stately home of Lady Catherine de Bourgh, in the BBC's serialisation of *Pride and Prejudice*.

The gardens cover 36 acres within a 1000-acre wooded deer park. When gardening writer J.C. Loudon visited with his wife, in May 1840, he declared: 'We have always understood [Belton] to be one of the best kept places in England, and we certainly found it so, though the family had been absent some months, and were not expected till July.'

There are splendid trees, including a handsome Lebanon cedar, the biggest sugar maple in Britain, and fine avenues of lime and Turkey oak. The Italian garden features urns, a fountain pool and clipped yews, presided over by an exquisite early 19th-century conservatory. The Dutch garden features green and golden yews, and bright seasonal bedding. A new maze has been laid out based on a book of mazes from Belton House Library.

The adventure playground and mini-railway will keep children amused. The house is worth seeing, too, for its beautiful carvings. Look out for the 18th-century exercise chair in the library, made for Lord Tyrconnel. Its cushion contains a huge spring, on which his lordship could bounce up and down.

Beautiful Bletillas

I must admit, the genus *Bletilla* had completely passed me by until I saw them displayed at a recent Hampton Court Palace Flower Show, but what delightful plants they are. The showpiece was set up by National Collection holders **Richard and Arline Evenden, of Pinchbeck, Spalding PE11 3PJ, tel. 01775-767857**, who do not run a commercial nursery, but say they sometimes have a few surplus plants from their collection of around 21 species and cultivars, available as an offshoot from their hybridising programme. (Open strictly by prior appointment, May–July.)

So what are bletillas? They are reasonably hardy orchids with quite showy, but graceful, pink or white flowers. They hail from Japan, Taiwan, China and northern Burma. The Chinese species are used in traditional Chinese medicine and it is thought that wild stocks may be substantially depleted because of their medicinal qualities. Bletillas favour neutral to alkaline, humus-rich soils and grow well in full sunlight to light shade. Most species, and all of the hybrids, appear to be fully hardy in the UK, say the Evendens, but late frosts will scorch the early shoots. They will soon recover without damage to the flowers.

You can also grow them in pots of either loam- or peat-based compost, with occasional weak liquid feeds of tomato fertiliser to encourage flowering. In herbaceous beds they will soon produce large clumps which may resist slugs, but will attract aphids to the flower spikes.

Primula Specialists

The genus *Primula* is a large one, with around 400 species of perennial, mainly alpine, herbaceous plants. They occur in many different habitats, right across the northern hemisphere, and also in the Falkland Islands and the southern tip of South America. British natives include the pale yellow common primrose, which ornaments damp woodlands in early spring, and the cowslip of meadow pastures. Popular garden forms include the ubiquitous, jewel-bright bedding polyanthus, and the easy-to-grow candelabra strains that flourish by damp streams. For the enthusiast, there are many challenging alpine species available with exacting requirements, as well as the surreal but enchanting types known as auriculas.

Mary and Michael Robinson have been growing primulas in huge variety for over 20 years at **Martin Nest Nurseries, Grange Cottage, Harpswell Lane, Hemswell, Gainsborough DN21 5UP (tel. 01427-668369), 6m E of Gainsborough on A631.** You can buy from the nursery, which also has a small demonstration garden, or by mail (send 3 × 2nd-class stamps for the catalogue). Open daily, 10a.m.–4p.m.

GUNBY

Gunby Hall

Gunby, nr Spilsby PE23 5SS TEL. 01909-486411 OWNER The National Trust HOURS End March–Sept, Wed, 2–6p.m. Last adm. 5.30p.m. Closed Bank Holidays. Garden also open Thurs 2–6p.m. (house and garden by prior written appointment with Mr and Mrs J.D. Wrisdale on Tues, Thurs and Fri) ENTRANCE Garden only £2.60, children £1.30 (under 5s free); house and garden £3.70, children £1.85 DIRECTIONS 2½m NW of Burgh le Marsh, 7m W of Skegness on S side of A158

Roses are the main event on the seven acres of Gunby Hall in the summer. They clamber up walls, scramble over pergolas and jostle among traditional herbaceous flowers, and in the kitchen garden provide cut flowers. Even the house, a red-brick mansion built in 1700, is clothed with the stems of fragrant, old-fashioned varieties, such as 'Climbing Lady Hillingdon' (amber) and creamy 'Alister Stella Gray'.

The exuberance of summer flowers is almost overwhelming in the two walled gardens. They contain sumptuous borders beside the straight paths, more roses, a well-stocked large herb garden, greenhouses, and a pretty, blue summerhouse. There are fruit trees, espaliered and pinned to the walls, vegetable beds and cages of soft fruits.

Antique Ali-Baba Jars

Visitors to the Chelsea Flower Show in 1997 will recall the display of huge antique anforas (oil jars, also known as amphoras) displayed by **Victoria's Collection, Maltby House, London Road, Louth LN11 9QP**. Anforas date back to ancient Mediterranean lands, where traditionally they were used to ferment wine or store olive oil. They can be as large as 13ft high and 6½ft in diameter, weighing as much as 4400lb.

Such large jars are very rare and expensive, costing from £17,500–£20,000 each, and are usually found in remote locations, buried underground. Victoria's Collection specialises in unearthing them and giving them a new lease of life as spectacular ornaments for larger gardens. There is also a display garden. Open all year, Mon–Fri, 9a.m.–5p.m., Sat–Sun by appointment only, closed for 2 weeks at Christmas. Off A16 between Louth and Skegness.

And also...

Baytree Nurseries, High Road, Weston, Spalding PE12 6JU (tel. 01406-370242), is a large, well-stocked and well-run garden centre. It includes demonstration gardens, a restaurant and the usual range of garden-centre fare. Open daily, 9a.m.–6p.m. in summer (5.30p.m. in winter). Off A151 between Holbeach and Spalding.

Doddington Hall, Doddington LN6 4RU (tel. 01522-694308), is a red-brick Elizabethan mansion, with five-acre gardens laid out in sympathetically formal style. There are knots and parterres, irises, roses, herbaceous borders and a wild garden with turf maze, stream and fine trees. Open May–Sept, Wed, Sun and Bank Holiday Mons, garden only, end Feb–April, Sun only, 2–6p.m. Entrance (garden only) £3.10, children £1.05, (house and garden) £4.60, children £3.10, family ticket £12.75. Off A46 Lincoln bypass.

Potterton and Martin, Moortown Road, Nettleton, Caistor LN7 6HX (tel. 01472-851714), specialises in producing a broad range of alpines and rock plants, also available by mail (send £1 in stamps for catalogue). Open daily, 9a.m.–4.30p.m. M180 Jct 4, then A18 to Brigg, then A1084 towards Caistor, turn right onto B1434, then left onto B1205, nursery on right.

Clive Simms, Woodhurst, Essendine, Stamford PE9 4LQ (tel. 01780-755615/web www.clivesimms.com), is a mail order fruit nursery, specialising in unusual fruiting plants and uncommon nut trees (send 2 × 1st-class stamps for catalogue). Not open to visitors, except by appointment to collect stock.

Lincolnshire's bulb industry puts on a glorious technicolour display at **Springfields Gardens, Camelgate, Spalding PE12 6ET (tel. 01775-724843/web www.mistral.co.uk/springfields)**, for the spring season. Plenty of large, swirly beds displaying massed daffodils, tulips, hyacinths and other bulbs, between broad lawns. Open mid-March–mid-May, daily, 10a.m.–5p.m. Entrance £3.50, OAPs £3. On A16 Spalding bypass.

London and Middlesex

England's great capital city is blessed with numerous wonderful parks and squares, its 'green lungs' that help provide all Londoners and visitors with the opportunity for a green walk in green shade. There are less well-known gardens in London too, such as the rarely opened but richly planted Eccleston Square, and the ancient Physic Garden at Chelsea, started by the Society of Apothecaries in 1673. The internationally important botanic gardens at Kew and the historical grounds of Hampton Court, Ham House and Richmond Park are listed in this *Guide* under Surrey, as their postal addresses dictate, although these days they stand on London's south-west perimeter.

Exceptional in Spring
Myddelton House, Enfield
Eccleston Square, London
  SW1

Exceptional in Summer
Queen Mary's Rose Garden,
  London NW1
Chelsea Physic Garden,
  London SW3

Worth a Visit in Winter
Capel Manor, Enfield
Kensington Roof Garden,
  London W8

BRENTFORD

Syon Park

Brentford, Middlesex TW8 8JF TEL. 020 8560 0881 OWNER The Duke of Northumberland HOURS House April–end Oct, Wed–Thurs and Sun, 11a.m.–5p.m.; gardens open all year, daily, 10a.m.–5p.m. ENTRANCE Gardens £3, concessions £2.50; house £6.25, OAPs £5.25 DIRECTIONS Between Brentford and Isleworth, on N bank of Thames, use A4, then A315; close to Gunnersbury Tube station WEB www.syonpark.co.uk

🌑 ᠁ Access 🌑 Gift Shop 🌑 Café 🌑 Plants for Sale

Syon Park and Kew Gardens (*q.v.*) face each other across the River Thames. Syon is the London home of the Duke of Northumberland, and it never ceases to surprise me that most of the views from the house and park are incredibly rural; you might easily be hundreds of miles from the city when you look over the water meadows to Kew.

Capability Brown (*q.v.*) landscaped Syon Park from 1767 to 1773, adding serpentine lakes and unusual trees. Many of the largest trees here date from his original plantings. It is a delightful park to wander in at any season. In spring it is pretty with magnolias and Japanese cherries in bloom and maples bursting into leaf. In autumn there are the mellow shades of foliage reflected in the lake. Herons fly overhead almost as regularly as the aeroplanes heading for Heathrow, but the peace is more often broken by the shrieking of the resident peacocks. The rose gardens stand beside the house on the site of some early formal gardens that were swept away by Brown.

The park's most impressive architectural feature is the conservatory, which dates from the 1820s and houses tender shrubs, fragrant freesias and carnations. It has a massive glass dome, flanked by curved wings that embrace a formal garden. One wing features a fernery, with mossy rocks and a fish-pond, while the opposite end goes climatically to the other extreme with a mini-desert, home to weird and wonderful cacti, aloes and aeoniums. The garden centre is large and comprehensively stocked with plants and sundries.

ENFIELD

Capel Manor

Bullsmoor Lane, Enfield, Middlesex EN1 4RQ TEL. 020 8366 4442 OWNER Capel Manor College HOURS Open March–Oct, daily, 10a.m.–6p.m. (11a.m.–6p.m., Sat–Sun); end Oct–March, Mon–Fri, 10a.m.–6p.m. (or dusk if earlier) ENTRANCE £4, concessions £3, children £1 DIRECTIONS Off A10 by Jct 25 of M25 (signposted)

🌑 ᠁ Access 🌑 Gift Shop 🌑 Café 🌑 NPC 🌑 2 for 1 Voucher

Capel Manor is a horticultural college which runs a wide range of courses, both vocational and for the interested amateur. The 18th-century former manor house is surrounded by 30 acres of gardens, much of its area divided into plots to demonstrate certain styles, or periods of garden history. They include a Tudor knot garden, a formal 17th-century garden, a Victorian maze, a garden for the disabled, a Japanese garden and a plantsman's garden. There are alpines, roses, herbaceous borders, flower-arrangers' flowers, woodland gardens, a fragrant Sensory Garden with the sounds of running water, fruit and vegetable plots, greenhouses and conservatories. The college strives admirably to be relevant to modern-day gardeners by the emphasis on small-scale domestic areas, rather than the more scientific, botanical garden approach.

Gardening Books in Notting Hill

Garden Books, 11 Blenheim Crescent, London W11 2EE (tel. 020 7792 0777), close to Ladbroke Grove and Notting Hill Gate Tube stations, between Portobello Road and Kensington Park Road, is, as its name suggests, a bookshop devoted to gardens and gardening. As well as holding a huge range of new and recently published books covering all aspects of plants, flowers, gardens of the world, botany, garden design and garden history, it also holds a range of antiquarian and second-hand books, so you might be lucky and find something here that you had always wanted but which is out of print. The shop will also post books worldwide on request. Free mail order list available. Open all year, Mon–Sat, 9a.m.–6p.m.

ENFIELD

Myddelton House

Exceptional in Spring

Bulls Cross, Enfield, Middlesex EN2 9HG TEL. 01992-702200 OWNER Lee Valley Regional Park Authority HOURS Open all year, Mon–Fri, 10a.m.–4.30p.m., also Easter–Oct, Sun and Bank Holiday Mons, 2–5p.m. ENTRANCE £2, concessions £1.40 DIRECTIONS Off A10 on to Bullsmoor Lane, signposted at Bulls Cross WEB www.leevalleypark.com
🌑 ᵭ Access 🌑 NPC

Myddelton House is revered because of its connection with Edward Augustus Bowles (1865–1954), a plantsman of great renown whose classic books, *My Garden in Autumn and Winter, My Garden in Spring* and *My Garden in Summer*, were published around the start of the First World War. The third son of a well-to-do Enfield family, Bowles was due to join the Church on graduating from Cambridge University, but he returned to his parents' home after a family bereavement and stayed there for the rest of his life, tending plants instead of a parish. At Myddelton he built up a renowned plant collection, many plants bearing his name or being named by him. Bulbs were one of his specialities, particularly crocuses (*Crocus chrysanthus* 'Siskin', 'Yellowhammer' and 'Snowbunting' were raised by him). Anemones, snowdrops and cyclamen were also favoured, and the National Collection of irises is held here (*Iris reticulata* 'Cantab' is a Bowles introduction).

The Regency house (not open) was refurbished in the mid-19th century, but Bowles never altered it. Professor William Stearn, who knew Bowles, once told me that 'it was a real museum piece, there was no electric light, just candles or incandescent lamps; dining there was a memorable experience. A very big, polished dining table was always adorned with flowers from the garden, and the butler served us in a room where Bowles's ancestors had entertained the essayist, Charles Lamb.'

The garden, which covers four acres, suffered serious neglect for 30 years after Bowles's death, but has undergone gradual restoration in recent years. A visit in any season is rewarding, because of the diverse range of plants. Bowles had a sense of humour and gathered a collection of 'demented plants', such as the corkscrew hazel with contorted stems, into an area he nicknamed the 'Lunatic Asylum'.

LONDON NW1

Queen Mary's Rose Garden

Inner Circle, Regent's Park, London NW1 TEL. 020 7486 7905 OWNER Royal Parks Agency HOURS Open all year, daily, Jan, 7a.m.–5p.m.; Feb, 7a.m.–6p.m.; March, 7a.m.–7p.m.; April, 7a.m.–9p.m.; May–July, 7a.m.–9.30p.m.; Aug, 7a.m.–9p.m.; Sept, 7a.m.–8p.m.; Oct, 7a.m.–5.30p.m.; Nov–Dec, 7a.m.–4.30p.m. ENTRANCE Free DIRECTIONS Situated within Regent's Park, N of Marylebone Road, close to Baker Street and Regent's Park Tube stations
🅿 ⅙ Access 🅿 Café

The rose garden is a circular area of formal beds dissected by lawn paths, richly fragrant through the long flowering season and host to around 60,000 roses. A breathtaking sight, of course, in summer and a popular venue with nearby office workers at lunchtime, as well as local residents and passers-by. Generally the beds are clearly labelled and display well-grown uniform plants – mainly of the hybrid tea and floribunda types – plus climbers and ramblers trained onto swagged ropes. There are herbaceous borders nearby, and an enchanting rock and water garden, with a water cascade, weeping willows and an island in the lake. This is part of the great green 'lung' of central/north London known as Regent's Park. The historic and fascinating London Zoo, with its renowned Modernist Penguin Pool, is quite near, and there are the broad walks and shady trees of the park itself to enjoy at leisure.

The London Plane

Stroll through any of London's great parks or historic squares and you will see a sight that is so familiar it will probably pass unnoticed. It is the vast, often buttressed bole and seasonally leafy canopy of the London plane tree, *Platanus × acerifolia* (syn. *Platanus × hispanica*).

Though as much a part of London as the black cab, the red bus and the Changing of the Guard, this tree is not native to Britain. It is a hybrid of the oriental plane, *P. orientalis*, and the American buttonwood, *P. occidentalis*. *P. orientalis* hails from the Levant and is one of the world's biggest and longest-living trees. The Greeks planted it in groves to shade their peripatetic philosophers; Xerxes, King of ancient Persia, stopped his marching army of 1,700,000 to admire a particularly fine specimen.

The hybrid London plane has been grown here for well over 200 years, and its success in the capital is due to the smoothness of its leaves, which are easily washed clean by rain, and its habit of shedding bark, which also relieves it of suffocating dirt and soot. There are very large specimens in Hyde Park and Berkeley Square, but the biggest London plane in the country is at Mottisfont Abbey (*q.v.*) in Hampshire, which stands over 130ft tall, with a 40ft girth and a canopy that covers a third of an acre of ground.

LONDON SE1

Museum of Garden History

Lambeth Palace Road, London SE1 7LB TEL. 020 7401 8865 OWNER The Museum of Garden History HOURS March–mid-Dec, Sun–Fri, 10.30a.m.–4p.m. (5p.m. on Sun) ENTRANCE Free, donations requested DIRECTIONS On S side of River Thames, at roundabout junction of Lambeth Palace Road and Lambeth Road, close by Lambeth Bridge, nearest Tube station is Lambeth North WEB www.museumgardenhistory.org

🌿 ♿ Access 🌿 Gift Shop 🌿 Café 🌿 Plants for Sale

This museum has fascinating permanent displays of antique gardening tools and old lawn mowers, and an area devoted to the life and work of the renowned Edwardian gardener/writer Gertrude Jekyll (*q.v.*). Outdoors is a knot garden of low box hedging laid out to a 17th-century pattern. It was designed by the Marchioness of Salisbury, of Hatfield House (*q.v.*), and celebrates the work of the two John Tradescants (*q.v.*), who are buried on this churchyard site. The plants used in the Museum's gardens are those which were known in the 17th century in this country, particularly species discovered by the Tradescants on their plant-hunting trips overseas.

The Westminster Shows

If you are based in London, you do not need to go haring off to far-flung nurseries to find interesting, unusual plants. At the Royal Horticultural Society's Westminster shows, which are held more-or-less monthly throughout the year, the nurseries all come to you. Many of the country's best growers exhibit at these shows, held in the **Royal Horticultural Halls, Vincent Square and Greycoat Street, London SW1 (tel. 020 7316 4107)**, close to Victoria Tube station. Run over two days, the shows also have lively amateur competitions for the best displays of, for example, camellias, daffodils, fruits, dahlias, chrysanthemums, autumn foliage, etc.

The nursery stands always do brisk trade (regulars among the RHS membership form a polite queue outside, then rush in at the start of the first day). There are also exhibits of botanical art in the January, February and November shows. Small sundries and gardening books old and new are also sold. Open 11a.m.–7p.m. (first day), 11a.m.–5p.m. (second day). Entrance £5 (first day), £3 (second day – children free).

LONDON SW1

Eccleston Square

Pimlico, London SW1V 1NP **MANAGED BY** Eccleston Square Garden Committee **TEL.** 01483-211535 (National Gardens Scheme) **HOURS** Open rarely, in spring and summer for NGS charities (telephone for this year's dates) **ENTRANCE** £2, children £1 **DIRECTIONS** In central London, just off Belgrave Road, a few minutes' walk from Victoria Main Line and Tube stations

⬛ ♿ **Access** ⬛ **Plants for Sale** ⬛ **NPC**

Eccleston Square is a typical central London square of elegant town houses surrounding their own private, shared, green space. The gardens of the square cover three acres and are opened only rarely, but if you happen to be in the area on one of their charity Sundays, it is well worth popping in. The gardens committee (led by well-known plant photographer Roger Phillips) is very active and has demonstrated by example what can be grown successfully in the dry, dusty and fume-laden conditions of the city centre. Camellias do particularly well, says Roger Phillips, because they show very good tolerance of drought conditions, 'much, much better than rhododendrons in this situation', he advises. The camellia collection in Eccleston Square adds up to aroud 110 different varieties. There is also a National Collection of ceanothus, displaying around 57 varieties, and many different climbing and shrub roses. There are irises and assorted unusual shrubs and perennials and many wildflowers including poppies, marsh-mallows, larkspurs and wild impatiens, which has exploding seed pods.

LONDON SW3

Chelsea Physic Garden

66 Royal Hospital Road, London SW3 4HS TEL. 020 7352 5646 OWNER Chelsea Physic Garden Company HOURS Early April–late Oct, Wed, 12 noon–5p.m., Sun, 2–6p.m., also daily during Chelsea Flower Show week in late May and Chelsea Festival week in late June, and some Suns in Feb, 11a.m.–3p.m. ENTRANCE £4, concessions/children £2 DIRECTIONS Entrances in Swan Walk and Royal Hospital Road, Chelsea, signposted from Sloane Square Tube station WEB www.cpgarden.demon.co.uk

🌑 ♿ Access 🌑 Gift Shop 🌑 Café 🌑 Plants for Sale 🌑 NPC

This three-and-a-half-acre walled garden faces onto the Thames Embankment and enjoys an exceptionally mild climate (its ancient olive tree regularly bears fruit in quantity). It was founded in 1673 by the Society of Apothecaries and is the second-oldest botanic garden in England (Oxford University's is the oldest). Formed as a place where the medicinal properties of plants could be studied, it is still involved in botanic and medicinal research, and much of it is laid out in 'order beds' where plants belonging to the same botanical family are grouped together.

A lot of the planting is herbaceous and therefore the garden is at its prettiest and most billowing in summer; there is a National Collection of rock-roses (*Cistus* species) held here and the rock garden is a listed monument. It is one of the earliest rock gardens, made from black basaltic lava-stones brought back from Iceland by Sir Joseph Banks in 1772. Visually, its effect is more currant bun than alpine chasm, but that is how it must stay.

There are many unusual plants here, including Australasian collections under glass, dyers' plants and displays connected to various prominent plant hunters and botanists. Recently the garden's role has extended to educational projects for children. The English Gardening School, which runs courses in gardening, botanical painting and garden design, is based in the main building.

Tools, Trugs and Trinkets

The gardeners of Hampstead and its environs have their own neighbourhood shop of trugs and trinkets and, as you would expect in this area, the emphasis is on genteel decoration along with a little light weeding. **Judy Green's Hampstead Garden Store, 11 Flask Walk, London NW3 1HJ (tel. 020 7435 3832),** very close to Hampstead Tube station, stocks a wonderfully eclectic range of gifts for gardeners, from the practical – tough gloves and steel trowels – to the ornamental, such as painted bird-boxes and Grecian urns. There are wire baskets and willow trugs, clay Provençal melon pots, florists' buckets and galvanised metal watering cans, raffia, labels, antique hand tools and much else besides. Free mail order catalogue available. Open all year, Mon–Sat, 10a.m.–6p.m., Sun, 12 noon–6p.m.

LONDON W8

Kensington Roof Garden

99 Kensington High Street, Kensington, London W8 5ED TEL. 020 7937 7994 OWNER Virgin Group HOURS Variable, as closed intermittently for functions; telephone to check gardens are open before attempting to visit ENTRANCE Free DIRECTIONS Entrance in Derry Street, off Kensington High Street (access by lift), close to High Street Kensington Tube station

This extraordinary and varied garden is perched on the roof of what used to be the Derry & Toms department store, a landmark shop in Kensington's High Street from the late 1930s until the 1970s. Fortunately, the idiosyncratic gardens survived the various changes of ownership of the store below. You can still see – almost unbeliev-able for the situation – a Moorish garden with central canal and fountains, complete with exotic plants, inspired by the ancient gardens of Southern Spain, a formal, Tudor-style garden with low hedging, and an English woodland scene with tranquil shade. Live flamingoes step through the garden pools among thriving palms and other mature trees. It is a make-believe garden well worth seeing if you are in the area. The gardens adjoin a restaurant and private members' club, however, and are not open to the public when there are functions on, so do phone to check you can visit before travelling any distance.

And also...

Chiswick House, Burlington Lane, Chiswick, London W4 2RP (tel. 020 8995 0508), is a famous Palladian villa, built by Lord Burlington in the 1720s. Its 62 acres of historic grounds, recently substantially restored, include avenues and vistas, a circular pool and a Victorian garden, with formal flowerbeds spectacularly bedded out each spring and summer, beside a fine conservatory. Open all year, daily, 8a.m.–dusk, house 10a.m.–6p.m. (restricted hours in winter). Entrance (garden only) free; house £3.30, concessions £2.50, children £1.70. Take E3 bus from Turnham Green Tube station or 10 mins walk from Chiswick Main Line Station.

Clifton Nurseries, 5a Clifton Villas, Little Venice, London W9 2PH (tel. 020 7289 6851/web www.clifton.co.uk), is a small (one-acre), very stylish, urban garden centre packed with a well-chosen range of nursery stock, including topiary plants in variety and very good ranges of conservatory plants. It also has a good stock of ornamental and terracotta pots, garden furniture and garden antiques. Open all year, Mon–Sat, 8.30a.m.–6p.m.; Sun, 10.30a.m.–4p.m. Off Warwick Avenue (A5) and close to Warwick Avenue Tube station.

Columbia Road Market, Columbia Road, London E2 (tel. 020 7377 8963), is a chaotic, noisy street market with many stalls selling garden plants, house plants and cut flowers at bargain prices. A good place to get quantities of summer bedding plants for pots and containers. Open Sun, 8a.m.–2p.m. Close to Bethnal Green Tube station.

Fenton House, Windmill Hill, London NW3 6RT (tel. 020 7435 3471), is owned by the National Trust and its delightful one-and-a-half-acre walled garden has been developing in recent years. It is laid out formally, on three levels with lawns, herbaceous borders, an orchard and a productive kitchen garden, with naturalised bulbs in the long grass. Open March, Sat–Sun, 2–5p.m.; April–Oct, Sat–Sun and Bank Holiday Mons, 11a.m.–5p.m., Wed–Fri, 2–5p.m.; last adm. 30 mins before closing. Entrance £4.10, children £2.05, family ticket £10.25. Close to Hampstead Tube station.

Holland Park, Kensington, London W8/W11 (tel. 020 7602 9483), is a popular and well-worn urban space with undulating lawns and specimen trees. By far its most interesting feature is a one-acre traditional Kyoto garden composed of carefully placed rocks with a water cascade and pool, and oriental plants. It was designed by Japanese garden designers and laid out in 1991 as a permanent reminder of the Japanese Festival that year. Tranquil and reflective. Open all year, daily, 7.30a.m.–sunset. Entrance free. Close to High Street Kensington Tube station.

Kenwood House, Hampstead Lane, London NW3 7JR (tel. 020 8348 1286), is a fabulous, neo-classical house redesigned by Robert Adam in the 1860s. Its 112 acres of landscaped grounds are equally splendid, with meadow walks and ornamental lakes, landscaped by Humphry Repton (*q.v.*). Its popular, evening, open-air concerts at the lakeside are one of the pleasures of London life in summer. Park open all year, daily: summer, 8a.m.–8p.m.; winter closes at 4.30p.m.; house: April–Sept, 10a.m.–6p.m., Oct, 10a.m.–5p.m., Nov–March, 10a.m.–4p.m. Entrance free. Use Archway or Golders Green Tube stations or Hampstead Heath Main Line station.

Norfolk

An important textile industry based on woollen goods contributed to the wealth of Norfolk in earlier centuries. As a result, the county's beautiful countryside is dotted with fine flint churches, built in thanksgiving for the prosperity the land brought, but now more often seen in splendid isolation, far from any human habitation. 'Very flat, Norfolk,' remarked one of Noël Coward's characters in *Private Lives*. Much of it is, especially around the reed-fringed waters of the Broads, making this a county popular with cyclists. Other parts enjoy a very gently contoured landscape, and the fertile soil nurtures many gardens and nurseries.

Exceptional in Spring
Fairhaven Gardens, South
   Walsham

Exceptional in Summer
Bressingham Steam Museum
   and Foggy Bottom Garden,
   Bressingham

Exceptional in Autumn
The Old Vicarage, East
   Ruston

Worth a Visit in Winter
Blickling Hall, Blickling

BLICKLING

Blickling Hall

Blickling, Norwich NR11 6NF TEL. 01263-738030 OWNER The National Trust HOURS Early April–Oct, Wed–Sun (also Tues in Aug), 10.15a.m.–5.15p.m. (last adm. 4.30p.m., gates close at 6p.m.); house 1–5p.m. (last adm. 4.30p.m.); garden only Nov–Dec, Thurs–Sun, 11a.m.–4p.m., Jan–March, Sat–Sun, 11a.m.–4p.m.; park and woods, daily all year, dawn–dusk ENTRANCE £3.80, children (accompanied) £1.65, house and garden £6.70, children £2.85 DIRECTIONS On N side of B1354, 1½m NW of Aylsham on A140

🟩 ♿ Access 🟩 Gift Shop 🟩 Café 🟩 Plants for Sale

Blickling Hall provides the quintessential National Trust day out. The spectacular house, a 17th-century stately pile, is surrounded by 43 acres of sumptuously planted, traditional gardens and enchanting woods. The east front of the house looks onto a parterre of four square beds, each fringed with roses and catmint, with yew topiaries in each corner. The beds nearest the house are filled with herbaceous perennials in pink, white, blue and violet hues (especially lovely around mid-summer), while further beds display rich yellows, glowing orange and scarlet tones, brilliant in late summer.

There are gravel walks through smooth lawns, shrubberies with azaleas, hydrangeas and dogwoods, classical ornaments and lovely trees in the park, and great lumpy bolsters of ancient yew hedging the entrance.

EAST RUSTON

The Old Vicarage

Exceptional in Autumn

East Ruston NR12 9HN TEL. 01692-650432 OWNER Graham Robeson and Alan Gray HOURS March–late Oct, Wed, Fri–Sun and Bank Holiday Mons, 2–5.30p.m., groups by appointment ENTRANCE £3.80, children £1, season ticket £12 DIRECTIONS Near Stalham, take A1151 from Norwich and turn off towards Bacton (do *not* follow signs to East Ruston) WEB www.e-ruston-oldvicaragegardens.co.uk

🟩 ♿ Access 🟩 Café 🟩 Plants for Sale

Discipline and strong, formal lines underpin this lavish 12-acre garden, made in earnest for the last dozen or so years by its inspired and determined owners. Set just three miles inland from the North Sea and the wind-battered north-east Norfolk coastline, the garden has little protection from the breezes and gales that characteristically blow across this generally flat county.

The towers of distant flint churches are used as eye-catchers in the landscape and as an excuse to plant straight avenues of trees or

The Old Vicarage

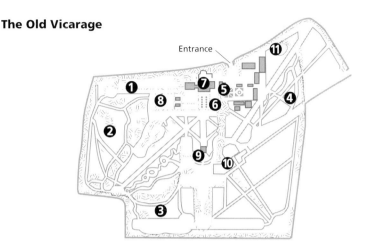

Entrance

1 Holm oak walk
2 Church meadow
3 Cornfield
4 East meadow
5 Walled garden
6 Tropical border
7 House
8 Sunken garden
9 Pavilion and
    mediterranean garden
10 Vegetable garden
11 Pond

sheltering hedges. The garden is divided into a logical sequence of more intimate rooms, *à la* Hidcote (*q.v.*), by trim hedging and finely detailed brick walling. Crisp, green spaces of smooth lawns and topiarised trees provide a cool, monochrome counterpoint to other areas that are richly planted and very colourful. For example, the walled forecourt is a gravelled area with relaxed plantings of fennel, sages, self-sown evening primrose, phormiums, cistus, euphorbias, aeoniums, echeverias, agapanthus, hollyhocks and much else besides.

Rainfall is low in this part of the country, the climate reasonably mild due to its proximity to the sea, and the soil a pleasant-to-work, sandy loam. A tropical area is devoted to exotic cannas, salvias, lantanas, gazanias, red-hot pokers and more. There is also a holm oak walk, a waterlily pool, a sunken garden of sun-loving lavenders, thymes and hebes, lots of topiary work and long vistas that draw the eye into the blue distance. In the more far-flung reaches of the property, there are meadow areas seeded with wildflowers and fine grasses, so you may see poppies and cornflowers creating a blissful sea of red and blue, merging into a mauve haze around the distant tower of East Ruston church. Certainly a place to visit at any time, but perhaps most exciting as high summer approaches the autumn and the unusually exotic elements can be enjoyed at their best.

HEACHAM

Norfolk Lavender

Caley Mill, Heacham, King's Lynn PE31 7JE TEL. 01485-570384 OWNER Norfolk Lavender Ltd HOURS Shop and gardens open all year, daily, 10a.m.–5p.m. ENTRANCE Free DIRECTIONS 13m N of King's Lynn on A149 WEB www.norfolk-lavender.co.uk

🔲 Gift Shop 🔲 Café 🔲 Plants for Sale 🔲 Nursery 🔲 NPC

It is as though a little piece of sunbaked hillside has been plucked from the Provençal landscape and transported to this lowland farming area beside The Wash. The 100 acres of lavender fields are at their most beautiful in summer, when they turn into ripples of dusky-mauve while the bushes are in bloom.

This is the largest lavender farm in Britain where the cut flowers are distilled for lavender oil; many associated products are sold on the premises. One of the four National Collections of lavender is held here, and there are also herb gardens and rose gardens to visit. Harvesting usually begins in mid-July and lasts five to six weeks. The rows are cut mechanically, usually four acres per day. It is worth joining one of the instructive tours of the farm (run daily from Spring Bank Holiday to September); you can even sample lavender in the café, for example, in their lavender and lemon scones.

LODDON

Reads Nursery

Hales Hall, Loddon NR14 6QW TEL. 01508-548395 OWNER T. and J. Read HOURS Open all year, Tues–Sat, 10a.m.–5p.m. (or dusk if earlier); also Sun and Bank Holiday Mons, May–Oct, 11a.m.–4p.m. ENTRANCE £1.50, children free DIRECTIONS From Norwich, take A146. Bypass Loddon and continue on A146 past Hales for 1m. Turn right at sign Kirby Cane 1¼/Hales Hall. After 150yds go right (signposted Hales Hall) WEB www.readsnursery.co.uk

🔲 ♿ Access 🔲 Plants for Sale 🔲 Nursery 🔲 NPC 🔲 Mail Order

There are three reasons to visit this nursery: fruit, interesting conservatory plants and the barn. Reads has been going for well over 100 years and it offers unrivalled selections of fruit, especially traditional varieties, available by mail as well as on-site (send 4 × 1st-class stamps for the catalogue). There are quinces and kiwi fruit, pineapple-guava and olives. There is also an extensive array of figs with 34 different varieties, constituting the National Collection of these exquisite fruits.

Reads also specialises in citrus, with oranges and lemons in variety, and limes, grapefruit, kumquats, limequats and tangelos (a cross between the grapefruit and mandarin, sometimes known as ugli fruit). The conservatory plants account for half of the catalogue (with more than 70 different varieties of bougainvillea), and the fragrant glasshouses are as thrilling as any you will see in a botanic garden, with the added piquancy that most of what you see is for sale.

Lastly, there is Hales Hall Barn. At 184ft long, with stepped gables and a wonderful ribcage of timbers supporting its newly thatched roof, it is one of the largest and most spectacular barns in the country, dating from around 1480. The one-and-a-quarter-acre nursery also offers topiary and hedging plants in box and yew.

The Perennial Blooms of Bressingham

You cannot be interested in plants for long without coming into contact with the Blooms' nursery, in the village of Bressingham. Its founder, Alan Bloom (born 1906) grew up in the company of distinguished plant collectors and hybridists such as Amos Perry, E.A. Bowles and Walter Ingwersen, and he was inspired to look out for new plants that showed improvements on existing cultivars.

At **Bressingham Steam Museum, Bressingham, Diss IP22 2AB (tel. 01379-688585), on the A1066**, Alan Bloom also developed the concept of informally shaped island beds cut out of the lawn (as opposed to long borders backed by a wall or hedge) for growing herbaceous perennials. The method produced sturdier plants and drastically reduced the need for staking. You can see Alan Bloom's perennial beds (and around 5000 different plant varieties) in the six-acre Dell Garden, open April–Oct, daily, 10.30a.m.–5.30p.m. (closes at 4.30p.m. in Oct).

Alan Bloom considers that *Achillea* 'Moonshine', *Agapanthus* 'Bressingham Blue', *Aconitum* 'Bressingham Spire' and *Crocosmia* 'Lucifer' are among his personal favourites of the 170 new plants he has introduced to horticulture during his long life. His son, Adrian, opens **Foggy Bottom Garden** (next door), April–Oct, Tues–Fri and Sun, 12.30–4.30p.m. and one weekend in early March (phone for details), where ornamental conifers are displayed in great variety, among grasses, heathers and perennial flowers. Entrance to both gardens £7, OAPs £6, children £5, family ticket £23.

Nigel Colborn

Author, novelist and panellist
on BBC Radio 4's *Gardeners' Question Time*

'I was really bowled over when I visited **The Old Vicarage** (*q.v.*), at East Ruston. It's a magnificent garden – the owners have obviously invested a lot of money in it. I love the way that it combines traditional garden statements – such as classical vistas and the "borrowed landscape" of the distant church – with really quirky, crazy ideas. It all works so well; it's done with boldness and courage, and nothing has been done by half. You can see the freshness of approach in the planting, too. They have used grasses wonderfully well in the borders, and there is a great tropical border with cannas and dahlias and eucomis. The containers have some really original planting in them, too, with bronze-leaved aeoniums, and I noticed a wonderful, rusty-brown rudbeckia which apparently they had selected from some they have grown from seed. It is the most inspiring garden I have seen in ages.'

NORWICH

The Plantation Garden

4 Earlham Road, Norwich NR2 3DB TEL. 01603-621868 OWNER The Plantation Garden Preservation Trust HOURS Open all year, daily, April–Oct, 10a.m.–6p.m.; Oct–April, 10a.m.–4p.m. ENTRANCE £1.50, accompanied children free; groups by arrangement DIRECTIONS On Earlham Road, between Crofters and Beeches Hotels, near St John's Roman Catholic Cathedral (no parking at garden) WEB www.plantationgarden.co.uk

This extraordinary garden is a rare survivor of the Victorian age, bearing many of the hallmarks of late 19th-century style. It was the creation of successful Norwich cabinet maker and upholsterer, Henry Trevor, and in its heyday boasted fine Italianate terraces, formal bedding areas and a magnificent tropical palm house within its 2½ acres. The garden was then a frequent venue for public occasions, as Trevor's obituary of May 1897 reveals: 'His beautiful and well kept grounds he put to the most generous uses. For purposes of flower shows, bazaars and charitable gatherings of any kind and another, the Plantation was continually in demand.'

After Trevor's death, the garden disappeared from public view and for several decades in the 20th century became all but lost in a dense undergrowth of brambles and self-sown sycamores, revealing only tantalising glimpses of masonry beneath smothering curtains of ivy.

In 1980 a group of local enthusiasts formed a Trust and assembled volunteers to unearth the lost garden, which they have very largely succeeded in doing over the last two decades. Now, it is possible once again to enjoy the fascinating mosaic walls of mixed flints and assorted masonry (such as ornate chimney mouldings) and the cast-concrete balustrades that Henry Trevor assembled in his lifetime. The palm house was demolished long ago, but the garden retains a magnificent tiered gothic fountain, nearly 30ft tall, and a Victorian rockery with masonry. Its neat lawns have returned and formal flowerbeds have been cut into them once more, following the pattern shown in some rare photographs of the garden. Although it is in the centre of Norwich city, The Plantation Garden is a haven of tranquillity, surrounded by mature trees and shrubberies and exuding much of the atmosphere of its bygone age. Don't expect pristine tidiness if you visit, for it is managed on a shoestring budget by volunteers, but it is well worth seeing this garden for the extraordinary way it has survived and undergone a new lease of life.

SANDRINGHAM

Sandringham House

Sandringham, King's Lynn PE35 6EN TEL. 01553-772675 OWNER H.M. The Queen HOURS Early April–early Oct, daily (but closed late July–early Aug), also weekends in Oct, all 11a.m.–4.45p.m. ENTRANCE House, museum and garden £6, concessions £4.50, children £3.50, family ticket £15.50; museum and garden only £5, concessions £4, children £3, family ticket £13 DIRECTIONS 9m NE of King's Lynn on B1440, signposted from A148 WEB www.sandringhamestate.co.uk

  ⬛ ᵭ Access ⬛ Gift Shop ⬛ Café ⬛ Plants for Sale

King Edward VII is said to have remarked that if he had not been King, he would like to have been a gardener. As Prince of Wales he spent the winters at Sandringham, with Princess Alexandra, herself a keen gardener.

During their time, thousands of new trees, shrubs and flowers were imported to ornament the woodlands, watery dells and flower gardens. Pansies in particular were a great favourite of the Princess, who devoted a garden to them. Today's visitor will see a simplified version of the original 60-acre gardens, made to be more labour-saving, but still reflecting the Edwardian age. There are lakes, a grotto and a large rock garden, a woodland with decorative flowering shrubs, fine trees and broad lawns.

Sandringham has long been open to the public, and its popularity as a tourist attraction caused King George VI to commission a private garden area, designed by Sir Geoffrey Jellicoe. Here, behind tall hedges and elegant avenues of pleached lime, lies a series of formal garden rooms with box-edged beds of flowering plants.

Controlling Pests Nature's Way

Biological control of garden and greenhouse pests uses natural predators, instead of chemicals, to deal with a wide range of problems. **Green Gardener, 41 Strumpshaw Road, Brundall NR13 5PG (tel. 01603-715096/web www.greengardener.co.uk)**, produces an informative catalogue (send 2 × 1st-class stamps) of natural pest controls available by mail order and offers expert advice on how to use predators for maximum effect in the right seasons. There are controls to counter aphids, whitefly, red spider-mite, mealybugs, scale insects, slugs and vine weevils, as well as Enviromesh fabrics for effective barrier protection against carrot fly, cabbage root fly and other creatures.

SAXTHORPE

Mannington Hall

Nr Saxthorpe, Norwich NR11 7BB TEL. 01263-584175 OWNER Lord Walpole HOURS May and Sept, Sun, 12 noon–5p.m.; June–Aug, Wed–Fri, 11a.m.–5p.m., Sun, 12 noon–5p.m. ENTRANCE £3, OAPs £2.50, children (under 16) free DIRECTIONS 18m NW of Norwich, 3m NE of Saxthorpe, from A140 take B1149, then minor roads (signposted)

🌿 ♿ **Access** 🌿 **Gift Shop** 🌿 **Café** 🌿 **Plants for Sale** 🌿 **2 for 1 Voucher**

If you are into roses, you will love Mannington Hall and its 20-acre garden. Ramblers cascade over post-and-rail enclosures, climbers cling to flinty walls, shrub roses colonise a large area devoted to their kind, while more disciplined bushes behave themselves in neat beds close to the house. The Hall itself is gloriously romantic, with flint elevations, stone-mullioned windows, gothic arches and a crenellated roofline. If that is not enough, there is a moat surrounding it, packed with waterlilies, and wildflowers do their thing in outlying parts of the grounds. There are rhododendrons in the woods and a relaxed wilderness sets off the ruins of a Saxon church. The walled garden is devoted to Heritage roses, all wild species and old-fashioned varieties.

SOUTH WALSHAM

Fairhaven Gardens

School Road, South Walsham, Norwich NR13 6DZ TEL. 01603-270449 OWNER
Fairhaven Garden Trust HOURS Open all year, daily, 10a.m.–5p.m. (9p.m. on
Wed and Thurs, May–Aug) ENTRANCE £3.50, concessions £3, children £1.25
(season ticket £12.50, family season ticket £30), wildlife park £1 DIRECTIONS
9m NE of Norwich on B1140 WEB www.norfolkbroads.com/fairhaven

🌿 &. Access 🌿 Gift Shop 🌿 Café 🌿 Plants for Sale

The Norfolk Broads are unique; they are mainly freshwater lakes,
quite shallow, linked by rivers, streams and dykes to form around
200 miles of navigable waterways between Norwich and the north-
east coast of Norfolk. They were created by peat extraction in late
medieval times and are part of the man-made landscape. It is unusual
to find a garden in this region, which is more widely associated with
reedbeds and marshland, but the 180-acre Fairhaven is one of the
strangest and most appealing water gardens in the country, best
visited in spring. It is a blissfully quiet woodland, wrapped around
the large stretch of water known as South Walsham Inner Broad,
where the odd sailboat may go scudding by.

A network of water channels runs through the wood with its
thousands of primulas, and astilbes, ligularias and skunk cabbages
lining the banks. Simple timber bridges cross the waters here and
there and masses of primroses and bluebells colonise the woodland
floor. There is a splendid oak tree, believed to be 900 years old,
encrusted with self-sown ferns.

WELLS-NEXT-THE-SEA

Holkham Hall

Wells-next-the-sea NR23 1AB TEL. 01328-710806 OWNER The Earl of Leicester
HOURS Late May–late Sept, Sun–Thurs, 1–5p.m.; park open all year, daily;
nursery gardens open March–Oct, daily, 10a.m.–5p.m. ENTRANCE Park and
garden free; hall and Bygones Museum £6, children £3 DIRECTIONS Signposted
from A149 WEB www.holkham.co.uk

🌿 Gift Shop 🌿 Café 🌿 Plants for Sale 🌿 Nursery

This is a vast stately home, set in a 3000-acre deer park that was
worked on by William Kent in the mid-18th century, followed by
Capability Brown (*q.v.*) and then Humphry Repton (*q.v.*). It is a place
where you can really stretch your legs and enjoy the undulating,
sheep-grazed park, its fine trees and great lake. There is an 18th-
century, six-acre walled garden, richly planted with herbaceous
flowers, shrubs and climbers, where there is also a well-stocked

garden centre. The Bygones Museum on the property features over 4000 items from the past and is therefore a popular visitor attraction in its own right with visitors to this scenic north-Norfolk coast area.

And also...

The famous nursery of **Peter Beales Roses, London Road, Attleborough NR17 1AY (tel. 01953-454707/web www.classicroses.co.uk)**, produces an extensive range of classic and old-fashioned roses (around 1000 species and varieties), many of which are illustrated in the excellent catalogue (free). You can also visit the rose fields (free), or buy from the nursery itself. Open all year, Mon–Fri, 9a.m.–5p.m.; Sat 9a.m.–4.30p.m.; Sun (except Jan) 10a.m.–4p.m. Off A11 between Thetford and Norwich.

Chris Bowers & Son, Whispering Trees Nursery, Wimbotsham PE34 8QB (tel. 01366-388752), is a specialist fruit nursery. There are tree fruits and nuts in variety, with extensive ranges of soft fruit including raspberries, strawberries, currants, gooseberries and blueberries and much more (mail order catalogue £2). Open all year, daily, 10a.m.–4p.m.; closed 1–2p.m. at weekends. From A10 follow signs to Wimbotsham.

Bradenham Hall, Bradenham, Thetford IP25 7QF (tel. 01362–687243), was the family home of the Victorian author H. Rider Haggard who wrote *King Solomon's Mines* (1885) and *She* (1887). The 20-acre gardens feature glorious daffodil displays in spring, a comprehensive arboretum and large, old-fashioned rose gardens, marvellous herbaceous borders and a kitchen garden. Open (gardens only) April–Sept, 2nd, 4th and 5th Sundays in each month, 2–5.30p.m. Entrance £3, children free. From A47, turn off towards Wendling and follow signs to Bradenham.

Linda Laxton runs **British Wild Flower Plants, Burlingham Gardens, 31 Main Road, North Burlingham, Norwich NR13 4TA (tel. 01603-716615/web www.wildflowers.co.uk).** The nursery specialises in wildflowers grown as plugs or in pots; species include cowslips, scabious, ox-eye daisies, harebells, cuckoo flowers, teasels, bedstraws and vetches. Plants are not gathered in the wild, but are grown from seed, with details of the original seed source (catalogue free on request). Open Mon–Fri, 10a.m.–4p.m. and at other times by appointment.

Congham Hall Hotel, Lynn Road, Grimston, King's Lynn PE32 1AH (tel. 01485-600250), is a country house hotel in 40 acres of park and gardens, with a fine herb garden, featuring around 500 different varieties. Many herbs are for sale. Open April–Sept, Sun–Fri, 2–4p.m. (closed Sat). Entrance free. Signposted from A148.

Elsing Hall, Elsing, nr East Dereham NR20 3DX (tel. 01362–637224), is a romantic, moated manor house (not open) dating from the mid-15th century, with stone-mullioned windows and knapped-flint walls. It provides the central focus for lovely gardens, fragrant with roses that drape the walls and fill out the borders. There are wildflower meadows, relaxed plantings and many decorative trees. Open June–Sept, Sun only, 2–6p.m. and at other times by appointment. Entrance £3, children free. From A47 Dereham bypass, take B1110 and follow signs to Lyng.

Four Seasons Nursery, Forncett St Mary, Norwich NR16 1JT (tel. 01508-488344/web www.fsperennials.co.uk), is never open to visitors but it produces a catalogue (free on request) of exceptionally interesting and attractive hardy herbaceous plants. John Metcalf, the joint proprietor, has an artistic eye for plant associations and knows a good plant when he sees one. Plants are dispatched in autumn and spring.

Raveningham Hall, Raveningham NR14 6NS (tel. 01508-548222), sits in splendid parkland, with lawns near the house flanked by borders of shrubs and herbaceous perennials. Unusual and half-hardy plants feature in the gardens and in the excellent nursery, which is located in the walled kitchen garden and its large greenhouses (send 3 × 1st-class stamps for the catalogue). Open Easter–Sept, Suns, Bank Holiday Mons and Wed, 2–5p.m. Entrance £2.50, OAPs £2, children free. Off A146, signposted from Hales.

The Romantic Garden Nursery, Swannington, Norwich NR9 5NW (tel. 01603-261488/web www.romantic-garden.co.uk), specialises in box topiary and ornamental standard (mop-headed) trees and shrubs, particularly half-hardy subjects suitable for mild gardens and conservatories, available by mail (send 4 × 1st-class stamps for the catalogue). Open all year, Wed, Fri, Sat and Bank Holiday Mons, 10a.m.–5p.m. A1067 from Norwich, turn right at Attlebridge and follow signs for Swannington.

Northamptonshire

This small county in the East Midlands is famous for its bootmakers, and it is worth using up a bit of shoe leather in treading some of its lovely gardens. Featuring low-lying land to the east, the ground sweeps up into chalk and limestone country to the west, taking in the northern fringes of the Cotswolds. The area has a beauty comparable with the neighbouring limestone areas of Oxfordshire and Gloucestershire, but is quiet and sparsely populated. In the 1720s Daniel Defoe considered Northampton to be 'the handsomest and best built town in all this part of England', after it had been rebuilt following the ravaging fires 50 years previously.

Must See
The Menagerie, Horton –
  inventive design with
  delightful follies

Exceptional in Summer
Cottesbrooke Hall,
  Cottesbrooke
Coton Manor, Guilsborough

CANONS ASHBY

Canons Ashby House

Canons Ashby, Daventry NN11 3SD TEL. 01327-860044 OWNER The National
Trust HOURS April–Oct, Sat–Wed incl. Bank Holiday Mons, 1–5.30p.m., or dusk
if earlier (12 noon–4.30p.m. in Oct) ENTRANCE £5, children £2.50, family ticket
£12.50 DIRECTIONS 8m S of Daventry, 5m E of Byfield, by local roads off A361
Daventry–Banbury road (signposted); use M1 Jct 16 or M40 Jct 11 and follow
signs, also signposted from A5

🖌 Gift Shop 🖌 Café

The House sits so cosily in its rural setting, with the medieval priory
church to one side and nine-acre walled gardens to the other, that it
conveys a timelessness and serenity seldom matched in other
properties. Its gardens are in a restrained, early 18th-century style,
with lawned terraces, straight, formal paths, some topiaries and a
collection of old fruit varieties. Wildflowers colonise areas of long
grass, and the house itself is worth seeing – an exquisite, well-
proportioned 16th-century manor, with later alterations, in the local,
ochre-coloured limestone.

COTTESBROOKE

Cottesbrooke Hall

Exceptional in Summer

Cottesbrooke, Northampton NN6 8PF TEL. 01604-505808 OWNER Capt and
Mrs J. Macdonald-Buchanan HOURS Easter–Sept, Thurs, 1st Sun in month and
Bank Holiday Suns and Mons, 2–5.30p.m. (last adm. 5p.m.); garden only also
open Tues–Wed and Fri ENTRANCE £3, children £1.50 (house and gardens
£4.50 and £2.25) DIRECTIONS 10m N of Northampton, from A14 take A508
towards Brixworth, turn right at roundabout and follow signs WEB
www.cottesbrookehall.co.uk

🖌 Café 🖌 Plants for Sale

Prepare to be impressed by Cottesbrooke Hall. Its driveway sweeps
through the park for two miles, passing over an elegant stone bridge
that crosses a stretch of water. Around the stately house there are 25
acres of gardens within the vast park; they are variously divided by
walls and hedges into several intimate areas, some featuring
exuberant herbaceous plantings, others with contrasting greenery of
trees and lawns. There is a Dutch garden with formal box parterres
enclosing seasonal bedding; a relaxing pool garden, with distant
views along a lime avenue; a long terrace walk, flanked by herbaceous
borders containing some interesting plants; a rose garden, a garden
of statues and a lovely wild garden washed by a stream, with spring-
flowering shrubs and bulbs and a Japanese bridge.

GUILSBOROUGH

Coton Manor

Exceptional
in Summer

Nr Guilsborough NN6 8RQ TEL. 01604-740219 OWNER Mr and Mrs I. Pasley-Tyler HOURS April–Sept, Wed–Sun and Bank Holiday Mons, 12 noon–5p.m. ENTRANCE £3.50, OAPs £3, children £2 DIRECTIONS 10m NW of Northampton, between A428 and A5199 (signposted)

🌳 ⚬ Access   🌳 Gift Shop   🌳 Café   🌳 Plants for Sale   🌳 Nursery

Coton Manor

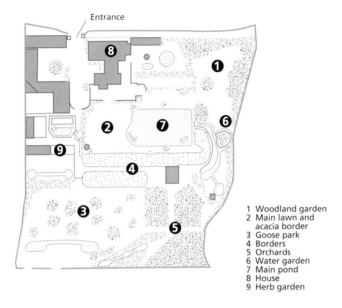

Entrance

1 Woodland garden
2 Main lawn and acacia border
3 Goose park
4 Borders
5 Orchards
6 Water garden
7 Main pond
8 House
9 Herb garden

Coton Manor is a friendly farmhouse of local honey-coloured stone, with mullioned windows and a steeply pitched roof. The 10-acre gardens that frame it on two sides are among the most pleasing you will see anywhere, with exceptional ranges of plants and a high standard of upkeep. I bumped into Susie Pasley-Tyler while she was immersed in a small sea of sisyrinchiums, her wheelbarrow on the turf path alongside rapidly filling up with prunings and tidyings from one of the herbaceous borders. This is a hands-on family garden, as it has been for three generations.

Upon her mother-in-law's death in 1990, Susie and her husband, Ian, took over the manor and began some regenerative work in the garden, and the results are impressive. Roses and summer flowers billow around the footings of the manor and lady's mantle fills cracks in the stone paving. More roses and flower borders near the house are contained by yew hedges, with woodland and water gardens beyond. There are further borders in the lower gardens, and grassy slopes leading to a five-acre bluebell wood – captivating in May. Beyond the recently made herb garden is a nursery worth browsing in for interesting plants, while more are for sale beside the stable yard café, where excellent home-made food is served.

Sweet Peas of Althorp

Fragrant and dainty, with old-fashioned cottage-garden appeal, sweet peas are among Britain's most popular flowers. The famous Spencer strain of sweet peas originated in Northamptonshire in the gardens of Althorp (ancestral home of the late Diana, Princess of Wales). Mr Silas Cole was head gardener to Earl Spencer at the turn of the 20th century, running the 50 acres of gardens at Althorp, with their 14-acre kitchen garden. He noticed an exceptional plant arising out of his stocks of sweet peas (some of which had the pink-flowered 'Prima Donna' as a parent) and named it 'Countess Spencer'. The flowers were particularly large and wavy, and Spencer sweet peas were soon in great demand.

HORTON

The Menagerie

Horton, Northampton NN7 2BX TEL. 01604-870957 OWNER Mr Alex Myers HOURS April–Sept, Mon and Thurs, 2–5p.m., last Sun in month, 2–6p.m. ENTRANCE £3.50, children £1.50 DIRECTIONS 5m SE of Northampton off B526, turn left 1m S of Horton through gate in field (watch out for small sign)
🟥 ♿ Access 🟥 Café 🟥 Plants for Sale

The late Gervase Jackson-Stops, architectural adviser to the National Trust, rescued and restored The Menagerie, a former folly with enchanting rooms and plasterwork, and laid out the four-acre garden with talented Kew graduate, Ian Kirby. Alas, neither of them lived long enough to enjoy this exquisite property for long, but the garden is now open on a regular basis and is worth travelling some distance to see. It commands a hilltop position, with avenues radiating out from the house; the central one of limes leads to a spiral mount, with one on each side in hornbeam terminating in fountain pools. There are two unusual garden buildings, one with a classical front, the other gothic, which, on their far sides, turn into rustic hovels in 18th-century Picturesque style. The planting is exuberant, with choice perennials, abundant roses and flowering shrubs. There is a wetland garden of local native plants and the Vernal Garden features massed spring bulbs and hellebores under spring-flowering trees and shrubs.

The Menagerie was originally the private zoo of Lord Halifax whose Horton Hall (now demolished) had stood on the opposite hill. Jackson-Stops installed a fantasy grotto of rock and shellwork beneath the building, but it is only possible to see it (and the house) by written appointment.

And also...

Castle Ashby, Northampton NN7 1LQ (tel. 01604-696187/web www.castleashby.co.uk), is a handsome Elizabethan mansion, now used as an all-purpose centre for functions, etc. It has a wonderful 200-acre park landscaped by Capability Brown (*q.v.*) with lakes and temple, a Victorian terrace with unusual, carved lettering in the balustrade, a fine orangery and an Italian garden. Open daily, 10a.m.–dusk, with occasional closures during events. Terrace garden by appointment only. Entrance £2.50, OAPs/children £1.50. M1 Jct 15, then A45 and A428 and turn left.

Northumberland

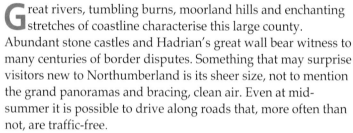

MAP NO. 8

Great rivers, tumbling burns, moorland hills and enchanting stretches of coastline characterise this large county. Abundant stone castles and Hadrian's great wall bear witness to many centuries of border disputes. Something that may surprise visitors new to Northumberland is its sheer size, not to mention the grand panoramas and bracing, clean air. Even at mid-summer it is possible to drive along roads that, more often than not, are traffic-free.

It isn't an easy part of the country for gardeners, however. There can be frosts until June, which often return as early as September. Summer is a glorious, fleeting moment which is celebrated in a galaxy of outstanding gardens.

Must See

Herterton House, Cambo – colour harmonies blended on an intimate scale

Bide-a-Wee Cottage, Stanton – inspired plantsman's cottage garden in an old quarry

Exceptional in Spring

Belsay Hall, Belsay

Exceptional in Summer

Hexham Herbs, Hexham

Worth a Visit in Winter

Wallington Hall, Cambo

BELSAY

Belsay Hall

Exceptional in Spring

Belsay, Newcastle upon Tyne NE20 0DX TEL. 01661-881636 OWNER English Heritage HOURS Open all year daily, April–Sept, 10a.m.–6p.m.; Oct, 10a.m.–5p.m.; Nov–March, 10a.m.–4p.m. ENTRANCE £3.90, concessions £2.90, children £2 DIRECTIONS In Belsay village off A696

🌳 ♿ Access 🌳 Gift Shop 🌳 Café 🌳 Plants for Sale

The Hall is an austerely neo-classical mansion, built from sandstone quarried out of the property's own grounds, with 30 acres of far-flung, unusual gardens, attractively planted. From terraced formal gardens near the house – featuring a symmetrical arrangement of rose beds and sun-loving plants such as lavenders, cistuses, eryngiums and alliums – there are views across sloping parkland to a beautiful rhododendron dell, at its peak in June.

From the formal gardens an informal path winds its way through the woods, past heather banks, a croquet lawn and a wildflower meadow to the Hall's most extraordinary area – the great quarry garden. When the ochre-coloured sandstone was excavated to build Sir Charles Monck's mansion in the early years of the 19th century, the resulting quarry, with its rugged cliff-faces, seemed to be the ideal place to make an atmospheric garden. The rock faces provide a spectacular backdrop to plantings of towering rhododendrons, surprising fan palms, ferns, gunnera and woodland species. A path winds its sinuous way through the bottom of the long quarry, leading eventually to another historical surprise – the picturesque ruins of 14th-century Belsay Castle.

CAMBO

Herterton House

Must See

Hartington, Cambo, Morpeth NE61 4BN TEL. 01670-774278 OWNER F. and M. Lawley HOURS April–Sept, daily except Tues and Thurs, 1.30–5.30p.m. ENTRANCE £2.40, children £1 (under 5s free) DIRECTIONS 2m N of Cambo, just off B6342

🌳 Plants for Sale 🌳 Nursery

It would be difficult to leave Herterton House without a boxful of souvenir plants (quaintly wrapped in newsprint) from the Lawleys' small but intriguing nursery, but there is more: the adjoining gardens, covering one acre around their farmhouse, are among the best to be seen in the country.

Facing the lane, in front of the low, Elizabethan farmhouse, the Lawleys (both of whom are artists) have planted a formal topiary garden of English evergreens – ivy, box, yew and holly, enlivened with golden-leaved and variegated forms. To one side, a fascinating cloistered herb garden displays plants valued by medieval physicians and dyers: there is clary (a time-honoured eye remedy), betony (a cure-all since the days of antiquity), periwinkle, sweet rocket, heartsease, gromwell and woad.

Behind the house, full rein is given to colourful summer flowers, planted in graduated schemes of complementary tones. According to Frank Lawley the scheme symbolises the passing of time, from 'pale colours in the morning (near the house), through the richest, brightest colours at mid-day (in mid-garden), to the deep reds and purples at the far end, signifying dusk and night-time'. The effect is captivating, and the Lawleys have made another enclosed garden beyond – a box parterre, filled with bright annuals.

CAMBO

Wallington Hall

Cambo, Morpeth NE61 4AR TEL. 01670-773600 OWNER The National Trust
HOURS April–Oct, garden and grounds daily, 10a.m.–7p.m. (or dusk if earlier); house Wed–Mon, 1–5p.m. ENTRANCE £3.80, children (over 5) £1.90; house and grounds £5.20 and £2.60, family ticket £13 DIRECTIONS From A1 take A696 past Newcastle Airport, Ponteland and Belsay; Wallington signposted 6m after Belsay

🔲 ♿ Access   🔲 Gift Shop   🔲 Café   🔲 Plants for Sale

It is Wallington's magnificent walled garden, hidden away in the woods, that leaves a lasting impression. Its flower gardens drop down a gentle slope in a series of differently planned areas.

A long terrace to one side skirts the famous conservatory, built in 1908 as an indoor garden to provide interest through the chilly Northumbrian winter. Now it is beautiful all year, with summer displays of abutilons, vast fuchsias (including a splendid specimen planted when the conservatory was new) and a wonderful scarlet 'Duke of Buckingham' pelargonium, which clambers up the wall. Below the terrace lie mixed borders of shrubs and flowering perennials, and a naturalistic pool surrounded by moisture-loving plants.

Wallington's great house (under renovation until 2004, but open to the public to see work in progress) in its 100-acre park dates from 1688 and is famous for its murals depicting scenes of Northumbrian history and for a charming collection of dolls' houses. Among summer's outdoor events are popular theatrical productions performed in the spacious grounds.

FORD

Ford Nurseries

Castle Gardens, Ford, Berwick-upon-Tweed TD15 2PZ TEL. 01890-820379
OWNER Chris Potter HOURS March–Oct, daily, 10a.m.–6p.m., Nov–Feb,
Mon–Fri, 10a.m.–dusk DIRECTIONS 10m N of Wooler, off A697, or 13m from
A1 on B6353 WEB www.fordnursery.co.uk

🌿 ♿ Access 🌿 Plants for Sale 🌿 Nursery 🌿 Mail Order

Over 1600 different plants are raised within the walled former kitchen
garden of historic Ford Castle (open to the public). Few nurseries are
as handsomely situated, with the castle as a backdrop and views of the
Cheviot Hills. Hardy geraniums, hebes (over 50 hardy varieties), alpines
and penstemons are some of the specialities raised by Hazel Huddleston
and her partner, who propagate on-site everything they sell.

HEXHAM

Hexham Herbs

Exceptional in Summer

The Chesters Walled Garden, Chollerford, nr Hexham NE46 4BQ TEL. 01434-
681483 OWNER Mrs Susie White HOURS April–Oct, daily, 10a.m.–5p.m., phone
for winter openings ENTRANCE £1.50, children (under 10) free DIRECTIONS
6m NW of Hexham, ½m W of Chollerford, on B6318 (signposted)

🌿 ♿ Access 🌿 Gift Shop 🌿 Plants for Sale 🌿 Nursery 🌿 NPC

One of the oldest and most picturesque towns in the north of England,
Hexham is popular with tourists because of its famous 12th-century
abbey and proximity to Hadrian's Wall. Mary Russell Mitford,
visiting in 1806, described the town as a 'shocking, gloomy place',
but few visitors today would agree, as they potter among its antique
shops and stone houses perched above the River Tyne.

Hexham's allure for gardeners is chiefly due to the eponymous
herb nursery at nearby Chollerford, up the beautiful North Tyne
valley. Kevin White (an ex-policeman) and his wife, Susie, have been
running Hexham Herbs nursery and garden since 1986.

As well as housing the National Collection of thyme, with more
than 120 species and cultivars, this fragrant garden, humming with
bees in summer, also boasts one of the largest ranges of culinary and
medicinal herbs in the country (900 in all), 300 of which are potted
up for sale. Note the clipped box and billowing lavender hedges
which line the crunchy gravel paths, and do not miss the hidden-
away gardens within the walled framework.

The site of a Roman road crosses the nursery and inspired the
Whites to create an enclosed Roman garden featuring edible, sacred
and curative herbs grown in Britain by the occupying legions.

Common houseleeks were believed to have been a gift from Jupiter, to protect homes from lightning and fire. No doubt there were also plenty of aromatic poultices prepared for chilled and footsore soldiers, in addition to bay leaves for garlanding conquering heroes.

Hand-made Terracotta

The Potting Shed, 1–3 Broadgates, Hexham NE46 1QN (tel. 01434-606811/web www.thepottingshed.co.uk), is in the centre of the town, close to the bus station, opposite Lloyds Bank in Broadgates. It offers an array of traditional terracotta pots, including parsley pots and strawberry pots, all hand-made on the premises and fired to a high temperature for frost resistance. A tiny but bright sales area has been squeezed in beside the workshop. Open all year, Mon–Sat, 9a.m.–5p.m.

HOLY ISLAND

Lindisfarne Castle

Holy Island, Berwick-upon-Tweed TD15 2SJ TEL. 01289-389244 OWNER The National Trust HOURS April–Oct, Fri, 9.30a.m.–4.30p.m.; house Sat–Thurs, hours according to tides ENTRANCE £4.25, children £2.10, family ticket £10.50 DIRECTIONS A1 to Beal junction, then follow signs

If you're in the vicinity of Berwick-upon-Tweed, close to the Scottish border, then a day-trip (or longer visit) to Holy Island and its romantically isolated castle is very worthwhile. (Check the tide tables carefully – the causeway is submerged and impassable for two hours before high tide and for nearly four hours after.) The island is so named because of its links with early Christianity and the settlement of monks from Iona in the 7th century, followed by a Benedictine order which built the (now ruined) 11th-century priory.

Lindisfarne Castle sits on a rocky crag in the south-eastern corner of this tiny island. It was built as a military fort in Tudor times but extensively remodelled and refurbished by Sir Edwin Lutyens (*q.v.*) in 1903 for Edward Hudson, a successful publisher who founded *Country Life* magazine. When Hudson bought the castle, he had envisaged surrounding it with a luxuriant water garden, something that remained a pipe dream. However, its old, one-eighth-of-an-acre walled kitchen garden was remodelled by Lutyens (into a trapezoid shape, to make it look larger than it is from the castle windows) and replanted by Gertrude Jekyll (*q.v.*), then at the height of her design career. This bleak, walled enclosure surrounded by coarse, sheep-grazed pastures and habitually beaten by winds off the North Sea must have been a challenge. She produced two planting plans during 1911 and it is the second one, a colourful flower garden, which was carried out.

Today, the restored garden contains a blend of Jekyll's plants – sweet peas, hollyhocks, *Stachys byzantina*, 'Belladonna' delphiniums, mallows, clarkias and pot-marigolds, among others. Alstroemerias, heleniums, sunflowers and eryngiums also weave their magic through the small enclosure, which is threaded with pleasingly cottagey, random stone paths.

Thomas Bewick

Trees, plants and birds are among the miniature subjects delicately carved onto boxwood blocks by Northumberland's greatest artist, the naturalist Thomas Bewick (1753–1828). His exquisite engravings, vignettes of rural life, are displayed in his birthplace at **Cherryburn, Station Bank, Mickley, Stocksfield NE43 7DD (tel. 01661-843276), in the Tyne valley, 11m W of Newcastle upon Tyne, 400yds off A695 (signposted)**. Open April–Oct, daily, except Tues and Wed, 1–5.30p.m. (last adm. 5p.m.). Entrance £3, children £1.50 (NT members free).

HOWICK

Howick Hall

Howick, nr Alnwick NE66 3LB **TEL.** 01665-577285 **OWNER** Howick Trustees Ltd
HOURS April–Oct, daily, 1–6p.m. **ENTRANCE** £2, OAPs/children £1 **DIRECTIONS** 6m NE of Alnwick, off B1339, from A1 follow signs to Longhoughton, then 2m N off B1339

The elegant mansion was once the home of the 19th-century Prime Minister and social reformer Earl Grey, after whom the tea is named. Commanding a low-lying position close to the sea and sheltered by woods, the Hall has a microclimate quite unexpected in this region. Consequently, the 25-acre gardens boast many tender plants more likely to be seen on the milder coasts of west Scotland or Cornwall.

Howick Hall

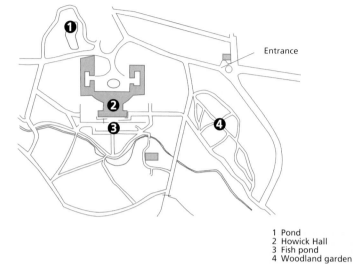

1 Pond
2 Howick Hall
3 Fish pond
4 Woodland garden

There are fine displays of rhododendrons, glorious terraced gardens and floral borders near the house, and unusual plants recently collected in the Far East. The wave of agapanthus, a brilliant blue spectacle on the terraces in high summer, has special significance, comprising many of the original plants that were bred to make the popular Headbourne hybrids.

ROTHBURY

Cragside House

Rothbury, Morpeth NE65 7PX TEL. 01669-620333 OWNER The National Trust
HOURS April–Oct, daily, except Mon (but open Bank Holiday Mons),
10.30a.m.–7p.m. (last adm. 5p.m.), house 1–5.30p.m. (last adm. 4.30p.m.);
garden only Nov–Dec, Wed–Sun, 11a.m.–4p.m. ENTRANCE House, garden and
grounds £6.70, children £3.40, family ticket £16.80; garden and grounds
£4.20, children £2.10, family ticket £10.50 DIRECTIONS 1m NE of Rothbury, off
B6341
🌳 ♿ Access 🌳 Gift Shop 🌳 Café 🌳 Plants for Sale

Rothbury endears itself with a splendid walk along ancient tracks through pink heather above the town, with distant views of the Cheviots on the outward journey and the Simonside Hills on the return, followed by a hearty lunch at the Sun Kitchen teashop in the main street. After that I was prepared to tackle Cragside, a vast 900-acre estate cloaked in a dark mantle of Wagnerian coniferous forest.

A monument to Victorian invention and wealth, Cragside boasts an extraordinary hilltop mansion designed by the architect Richard Norman Shaw. (Don't miss the awesome, gothic interior.) Built for Lord Armstrong, one of the great pioneers and industrial inventors of the 19th century, it was the first house in the world to be lit by hydro-electricity, one of Armstrong's own inventions.

A rock garden, recently replanted with heathers and alpines, tumbles down the hillside below the house, and the forested gardens are cut by a deep gorge. On the opposite hill is the walled garden, recently restored. Its glasshouses feature extraordinary rotating pots which help exotic fruits evenly ripen, while a slope above the lawns displays an impressive example of Victorian carpet bedding, closely planted with succulents for decorative effect.

Capability Brown

Lancelot 'Capability' Brown, the great landscape gardener of the 18th century, was born in 1716 at Kirkharle, a picturesque hamlet in the beautiful Wansbeck valley, and went to school at nearby Cambo. It is easy to see how those early years influenced his taste in garden design; the Brown landscape is visible all around, with its natural hills and gentle folds, dotted by copses of fine trees and watered by gentle burns.

Brown worked on Sir William Loraine's estate at **Kirkharle** for six years, enhancing the grounds with plantations of oak, beech and chestnut, before moving south to work for William Kent at **Stowe** (*q.v.*), in Buckinghamshire.

As he gained renown, his landscaping advice was widely sought by country house owners who engaged him to sweep away the old formal gardens, replacing them with more fashionable, rolling turf and naturalistic 'landskip'. **Blenheim** (*q.v.*), **Chatsworth** (*q.v.*), **Petworth** (*q.v.*) and many other great parks were remodelled by Brown (around 120 in all). His works in Northumberland include improvements to the park at **Wallington** (*q.v.*) and, most importantly, for the Duke of Northumberland at **Alnwick Castle, Alnwick NE66 1NQ (tel. 01665-510777/web www.alnwickgarden.com)**. Open end March–Oct, daily, 10a.m.–5p.m. (castle opens at 11a.m.). Off A1 at Alnwick.

Bide-a-Wee Cottage

Stanton, nr Netherwitton, Morpeth NE65 8PR TEL. 01670-772262 OWNER
Mark Robson HOURS End April–Aug, Sat and Wed, 1.30–5p.m., parties by
arrangement ENTRANCE £2 DIRECTIONS A1 from Morpeth, then left towards
Stanton, after 5m turn right at T-junction, go up hill, garden on right

🌿 Plants for Sale 🌿 Nursery

Bide-a-Wee Cottage

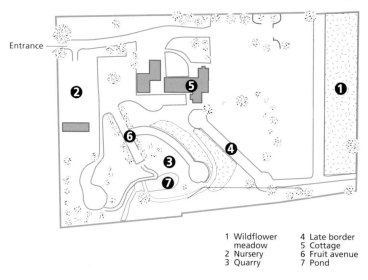

1 Wildflower meadow	4 Late border
2 Nursery	5 Cottage
3 Quarry	6 Fruit avenue
	7 Pond

Mark Robson was 15 when he began making the quarry garden beside
his parents' cottage near Morpeth. Now in his early 30s, he regularly
opens the two-acre garden, by popular demand; the gardening
grapevine doesn't allow such horticultural treasures to remain hidden
for long.

Mark began by gardening in a natural style among the bare rock
faces of the quarry, and at the lowest level he made an informal pool,
fed by a natural spring. Its edges are planted with large-leaved
gunneras and peltiphyllum, astilbes and yellow loosestrife; ferns and
foxgloves clasp the rocky crevices.

A note of formality is introduced where a broad turf path runs
between a short avenue of 'Scotch Bridget' apple trees. This is an old
but rare variety, particularly suitable for northern gardens. Mark
grew his trees from cuttings, on their own roots, and says 'Scotch
Bridget' is 'a good cooker and eater'.

Under the fruit trees two glorious summer borders are ablaze with red-hot pokers, scarlet campions, shasta daisies and puffs of fine-leaved dill, with a froth of lady's mantle tumbling onto the path. A sunny terrace beside the house supports statuesque cardoons and cotton-thistle, threaded with shimmering pink sidalcea. The garden's structure is underpinned by Mark's exceptionally well-laid stone walls.

Wildflowers are very much a part of Mark's planting philosophy. Everywhere he has woven them into this extraordinary garden with more exotic choices and there is also a meadow devoted to them. Almost everything has been grown by Mark from seed, and some of his most unusual plants are potted up for sale during open days.

And also...

Chillingham Castle, Chillingham, nr Wooler NE66 5NJ (tel. 01668-215359/215210), has a fine parterre and long herbaceous border beside the castle, with pleasant woodland walks for springtime. There are also rooms to rent in the castle, ideal for touring the locality. Open Easter–Sept, Wed–Fri and Sun–Mon, 12 noon–5p.m. (last adm. 4p.m.). Entrance £4.50, OAPs £4, children £1 (under 12s free). From A1 take B6348 and follow signs.

Kirkley Hall, Ponteland NE20 0AQ (tel. 01661-860808), is a horticultural college with demonstration gardens of well-labelled plants, and a three-acre walled garden of herbaceous perennials and climbers in great variety. There is also a wide range of greenhouse plants under commercial production. Open all year, Mon–Fri, 10a.m.–3p.m. Entrance free. From A1 turn left onto Airport Road towards Ponteland, then turn right, college on left.

Nottinghamshire

MAP NO. 5

Nottinghamshire is famous for its lace, which has been made here for hundreds of years, and for Sherwood Forest, home of Robin Hood. The Forest is greatly reduced in size from what was formerly a great royal hunting ground stretching north from Nottingham. Picturesque Newstead Abbey was founded in the centre of the old forest and enjoys a glorious setting on the River Leen. Much of this north Midlands county is industrial, especially north of the River Trent; in contrast, the southern region undulates gently in fertile farmland, which is characterised by large fields and arable farms.

Must See
Felley Priory, Nottingham –
  much to interest plant
  connoisseurs

NEWARK

Pureland Relaxation and Meditation Centre

North Clifton, nr Newark NG23 7AT TEL. 01777-228567 OWNER Mr Maitreya
HOURS April–Oct, Tues–Fri, 10.30a.m.–5.30p.m.; Sat–Sun and Bank Holidays,
10a.m.–5.30p.m.; lantern-lit evening garden, Fri–Sun in Aug and 1st
2 weekends in Sept, 7–10p.m. ENTRANCE £3.50, concessions £2.50,
children £1.50 DIRECTIONS At North Clifton, midway between Newark and
Gainsborough, off A1133; from A1 turn off at Markham roundabout onto
A57 towards Lincoln, after bridge turn right towards Newark, centre on right
🌑 Café

This is certainly one of the most unusual gardens in this *Guide*. The
Centre is run by Mr Maitreya, a former Zen monk, who conducts
courses in relaxation, revitalisation and meditation. He began to
transform the one-and-a-half-acre flat field beside his home in 1980,
gradually converting it into a Japanese-style garden of water, winding
paths, clipped trees and little hills. Missing the hilly and mountainous
landscape of Japan, his homeland, Mr Maitreya started to create his
own, in miniature. Earth excavated for the ponds was used to make
'hills' and large stones were placed in harmonious positions. Japanese
traditional garden elements include water, carp, bridges, moss,
stepping-stones, bamboo, clipped evergreens, maples, cherry trees
and stone lanterns. There is a recently made Zen garden of rocks and
chipped marble, and a Japanese-style teahouse for tea ceremonies.
The garden radiates tranquillity, aided by the soothing sounds of
water and wind chimes, and there are many seats placed at vantage
points which are very popular with visitors who, I noticed, end up
sitting in them for hours.

NOTTINGHAM

Felley Priory

Must
See

Underwood NG16 5FL TEL. 01773-810230 OWNER The Hon. Mrs Chaworth-
Musters HOURS All year, Tues–Wed, Fri, 9a.m.–12.30p.m., every 3rd Sun,
11a.m.–4p.m.; March–Oct, every 2nd and 4th Wed, 9a.m.–4p.m. ENTRANCE £2,
children free DIRECTIONS From Jct 27 of M1, take A608 (direction Eastwood
and Heanor) for ½m, look out for discreet sign to nursery and garden on left
🌑 ♿ Access 🌑 Café 🌑 Plants for Sale 🌑 Nursery

This is a garden with everything. It has enormous interest for the
plantsman, for there are many unusual trees, shrubs, bulbs and
perennials throughout the grounds (the owner is a keen, hands-on
gardener). Disciplined structure is provided by walls, mature yew
hedges (which are attractively topiarised with top-knots at regular

intervals) and treillage enclosures; the borders are abundant and thoughtfully planted and the rose garden is spectacular through summer, with late-flowering clematis providing colour once the roses have finished. The garden's layout is in sympathy with the priory house (not open), which has medieval origins, but it has a rewarding vigour and flair. In the depths of the three-acre garden is a delightful lily-pool, with bog irises and shrub roses lighting up the banks.

The Nottingham Crocus

Two species of crocus are associated with Nottingham: *Crocus vernus*, the spring crocus, and *C. nudiflorus*, an autumn crocus. Though they are not indigenous, being natives of southern Europe and the Middle East, their links with the region go back many centuries. They are thought to have been brought back to England either by knights returning from the crusades or by the Cluniac monks of the Lenton Priory, who may well have cultivated *C. nudiflorus* in their herb gardens, as a cheap and available substitute for the saffron crocus.

The Gardeners' Chronicle of March 1872 noted that in spring the flood meadows of the River Trent, near Nottingham, were awash with the silver-lilac blooms of *C. vernus*: 'at the present moment enlivening the Nottingham meadows with thousands of its purple blossoms. Hundreds of "young men and maidens, old men and children" may be seen from the Midland Railway picking the flowers for the ornamentation of their homes. Any stranger fond of flowers who visited Nottingham now for the first time would feel surprised to see large handfuls of Crocuses in the windows of the poorer and middle-class inhabitants. Crocuses in mugs, in jugs, in saucers, in broken teapots, plates, dishes, cups – in short, in almost every domestic utensil capable of holding a little fresh water; and very beautiful they look…'

Since then, intensive use of land for building and agriculture has seen the rapid demise of these harbingers of spring and autumn, although they have survived in isolated areas such as churchyards and golf courses. Nottingham crocuses thrived in the Trent meadows because they were 'Lammas Lands' – hay meadows that were harvested at particular times of year, allowing the flowering and seed-setting of these blooms. The two species thus survived and spread over the area for hundreds of years. Attempts are now being made to reinstate the flowers locally at sites where they may flourish undisturbed.

NOTTINGHAM

Newstead Abbey Park

Ravenshead NG15 8GE TEL. 01623-455900 OWNER Nottingham City Council
HOURS All year, daily, 10a.m.–dusk, house April–Sept, 12 noon–5p.m. (last
adm. 4p.m.) ENTRANCE Gardens only £2, OAPs/children £1.50; house and
gardens £4, OAPs £2, children £1.50 DIRECTIONS 11m N of Nottingham, by A60;
from M1 exit at Jct 27 and follow signs WEB www.newsteadabbey.org.uk
🌑 &Access 🌑 Gift Shop 🌑 Café

This property is famous as the home of the poet Lord Byron, who
inherited the title and estates of his great-uncle (the 5th Lord Byron)
when he was just 10 years old. Newstead was originally an
Augustinian priory in the late 12th century, but came into the
possession of Byron's family in 1539, following Henry VIII's
dissolution of the monasteries.

   The plan of the 25-acre, early 18th-century formal gardens remains,
but not the detail, and there is a large walled garden, geometrically
arranged with a series of terraces and sloping lawns, enclosing a
rectangular sheet of water, 300ft × 100ft. Beside it are smaller walled
gardens and a herbaceous border. There is also an enclosed iris
garden and a substantial, formal rose garden. The park's great lake
is a magnificent feature, visible from the drive. Its waters flow down
a cascade into a spectacular Japanese garden, dating from 1907. It
was laid out by a Japanese landscape architect and is a masterly
composition of winding paths, waterfalls, pools and stone ornaments,
engulfed by bamboos and evergreen shrubs, acers and flowering
cherry trees.

And also...

Hodsock Priory, Blyth, Worksop S81 0TY (tel. 01909-591204), is
famous for its sheets of snowdrops and aconites early in the year.
They are joined by other winter bloomers, such as *Iris unguicularis*,
hellebores and fragrant winter honeysuckle, in grounds extending
over five acres, with a half-mile woodland snowdrop walk. Open for
4 weeks in Feb–March, daily, 10a.m.–4p.m. (dates depend on the
weather, so telephone prior to visiting). Entrance £3, children 50p
(under 6s free). A1(M) to Blyth, then signposted from B6045.

**Mill Hill Plants, Elston Lane, East Stoke, Newark NG23 5QJ (tel.
01636-525460/web www.come.to/mill.hill.plants&garden)**, is a small
nursery offering a selection of herbaceous plants – particularly
bearded irises – and shrubs. The pretty half-acre garden alongside is
open so customers can see how plants will look when mature. There

is also a National Collection of berberis, extending to around 80 different forms of this prickly, spring-flowering shrub. Open March–Oct, Fri–Sun and Bank Holiday Mons, 10a.m.–5.30p.m. and at other times by appointment. Entrance (for NGS) £1.50, children free. From A1 follow A46 towards Leicester, then at East Stoke turn left towards Elston, nursery on right.

Anyone interested in wildflowers should beat a path to **Naturescape, Lapwing Meadows, Coachgap Lane, Langar NG13 9HP (tel. 01949-860592)**. Here is a wildflower farm with visitor centre, covering 40 acres of flowers grown for seed available by mail (send 4 × 1st-class stamps for catalogue). The flower fields are best at mid-summer, and there are demonstration habitats including a wildlife pond with associated water-margin plants, a bee garden, woodland edge habitat, dry-stone wall and wildlife hedge. There is also a nursery stocking plants for these habitats. Open April–Sept, daily, 11a.m.–5.30p.m. Entrance free. A52 E from Nottingham, just after junction A46 turn right towards Langar, after 4m turn left to centre.

Oxfordshire

MAP NOS. 2, 5

Oxfordshire is a fortunate county with a pleasant, gently undulating landscape, watered by the valleys of the Thames and the Cherwell, both rivers (the Thames is called the Isis at Oxford) running through its fine university city. Oxford began as a frontier town, defending Wessex against the Danes in Saxon times. Its university is the oldest in England, as is its botanic garden. The city of 'dreaming spires' and many of Oxfordshire's fine market towns and villages are built of warm-tinted local stone which adds to their architectural appeal. Much of the wealth of the county was based on a thriving wool trade on the edge of the Cotswolds; Witney, on the River Windrush, 10 miles west of Oxford, is a prime example. A wealthy town in the Middle Ages, it is still famed for its woollen blankets and possesses a fine Blanket Hall built in the early 18th century.

Exceptional in Spring
Greys Court, Henley-on-
   Thames

Exceptional in Summer
Waterperry Gardens,
   Wheatley

Exceptional in Autumn
Upton House, Banbury
Blenheim Palace, Woodstock

Worth a Visit in Winter
Rousham House, Steeple
   Aston
University of Oxford Botanic
   Garden, Oxford

Brook Cottage

Well Lane, Alkerton, Banbury OX15 6NL TEL. 01295-670303/670590 OWNER
Mrs D. Hodges HOURS April–Oct, Mon–Fri, 9a.m.–6p.m., other times and
groups by prior appointment only ENTRANCE £3, OAPs £2, children free
DIRECTIONS 6m NW of Banbury, leave M40 at Jct 11, take A422 to Wroxton,
after 1½m turn left to Alkerton

🌿 Plants for Sale 🌿 2 for 1 Voucher

This 4-acre private garden, lovingly made and gradually extended
by its owners since 1964, is the sort of place which leaves overseas
visitors in awe at the greenfingeredness of 'the English'. Well, it
would certainly impress anyone with its careful but informal
blending of spaces, set out on a west-facing hillside to encompass a
huge variety of plants and atmospheres, in relaxed cottage style. A
shady courtyard garden by the house is home to hostas and
campanulas threaded among the flagstone paving, joined by ferns,
foxgloves and a climbing 'Lady Hillingdon' rose spread over the
dark, honey-coloured limestone walls.

The garden is set on a determined slope, with grassy banks rising
behind the house and lawns sloping away below, bordered on one
side by a spring, running in a narrow rill down to a spacious water
garden. Astilbes, sedges, Siberian irises and primulas form large drifts
in the damper areas of soil. There are terraced areas, an alpine scree,
richly planted herbaceous borders (including a white border and a
yellow border), and hedges or shrubs and trees skilfully used to
separate individual areas of the garden. Peonies and clematis relish
the alkaline, clay-loam soil, and there are around 200 different shrub
and climbing-roses. Paths are narrow, steeply sloping in places,
leading you to unexpected views, and there is much to enjoy in
every season.

Broughton Castle

Broughton, nr Banbury OX15 5EB TEL. 01295-276070 OWNER The Lord Saye
HOURS Mid-May–mid-Sept, Wed, Sun and Bank Holiday Mons (incl. Easter);
also Thurs July–Aug; all 2–5p.m. ENTRANCE £4.50, OAPs/students £4, children
£2; garden only £2 DIRECTIONS 2½m SW of Banbury on B4035, use M40 Jct 11
WEB www.broughtoncastle.co.uk

🌿 ♿ Access 🌿 Gift Shop 🌿 Café 🌿 Plants for Sale

The 17th-century traveller, Celia Fiennes, was born at Broughton
Castle, and I sometimes feel she was a kindred spirit, touring houses

and gardens up and down the land and writing them up in her journals. The 14th- to 16th-century fortified manor of soft, brown Hornton stone was certainly a gracious starting point, for it enjoys one of the loveliest settings imaginable, moated by a brook which becomes the River Cherwell downstream.

The entrance gives no hint of the exuberant gardens which lie behind the castle. The walled Ladies' Garden has a formal, central pattern of four fleurs-de-lys formed by low box hedging, infilled with roses and pointing out to mixed borders which enjoy the shelter of the walls. Beyond are two spectacular, colour-themed herbaceous borders, one richly planted in blues, yellows and greens with grey foliage highlights; the other a symphony of deep reds and mauves, tempered by pink and blue hues. The American landscape architect Lanning Roper simplified the gardens, while enriching their planting, nearly 30 years ago, and improvements continue in the range and quality of plants grown here.

BANBURY
Upton House

Exceptional in Autumn

Nr Banbury OX15 6HT TEL. 01684-855365 OWNER The National Trust HOURS Late March–late Nov, Sat–Wed, garden 11a.m.–5p.m. (opens 12.30p.m., Mon–Wed); house 1–5p.m. (last adm. 4.30p.m.) ENTRANCE £6, children £3, family ticket £15; garden only £3, children £1.50 DIRECTIONS By A422, 7m NW of Banbury, 12m SE of Stratford-upon-Avon

🅿 ♿ Access 🅿 Café 🅿 Plants for Sale 🅿 NPC

Anyone with the remotest interest in art should look inside the house, for it holds an awesome collection, with works by Bosch, Bruegel, Canaletto, Constable and Stubbs. Indeed, from the house it is difficult to know whether there is much of a garden since the view is of a vast lawn, flanked by large yew, pine and cedar trees, with sheep-grazed pastures rising up the hill beyond. Go to the far edge of the lawn, however, and a series of terraced and walled gardens fans out below: part flower gardens, part kitchen garden, all lavishly planted, leading down to a big pond at the bottom.

You can descend the terraces via a steep stairway, or by winding back and forth along the turf paths which run beside the long borders. There is an important National Collection of asters (Michaelmas daisies), adding interest to late-summer/early-autumn visits; there is also a richly planted bog garden to one side, and a pair of herbaceous borders ascending the sloping ground the other side of the kitchen garden. A thrilling 35-acre garden in any season; produce from the kitchen area is occasionally offered for sale.

FARINGDON

Buscot Park

Faringdon SN7 8BU TEL. 0845-345 3387 OWNER The National Trust HOURS
House and grounds April–Sept, Wed–Fri, 2–6p.m., also every 2nd and 4th
Sat–Sun in each month, 2–6p.m.; grounds only Mon–Tues, also 2–6p.m.
ENTRANCE House and grounds £5, grounds only £4, children half price
DIRECTIONS Between Lechlade and Faringdon on A417 WEB www.buscot-
park.com

🍂 Café 🍂 Plants for Sale

The high point of this 100-acre park is its formal and dramatic water
garden, which descends a gentle slope to finish in a great lake. It was
designed by Harold Peto (*q.v.*) in 1904 and runs in a series of formal
pools and rills, occasionally crossed by little footbridges, all encased
by box hedges and fastigiate trees. Other avenues cut through the
woodland, offering pleasant walks, although there are one or two
fussy areas added more recently which seem out of step with the
grandeur of the place. There is also a richly planted walled garden
with mixed borders of shrubs and herbaceous plants and one area is
devoted to old shrub roses and collections of fruit.

HENLEY-ON-THAMES

Greys Court

Rotherfield Greys, Henley-on-Thames RG9 4PG TEL. 01491-628529 OWNER The
National Trust HOURS April–Sept, garden Tues–Sat and Bank Holiday Mons,
2–6p.m.; house Wed–Fri and Bank Holiday Mons, 2–6p.m. ENTRANCE Garden
£3.20, children £1.60, family ticket £8; house and garden £4.60, children
£2.30, family ticket £11 DIRECTIONS 3m W of Henley-on-Thames, between
A4130 and B481

🍂 ♿ Access 🍂 Café

The seven-acre gardens at Greys Court lie a little apart from the main
house, filling out and giving coherence to a set of old walls and ruins.
Among its pleasures are the fabulous, gnarled wisterias forming a
long tunnel showered in pale mauve spring-time blooms; formal box
parterres walled in by bricks and flints; a decadent long border
devoted to the brief flowering of many scores of peonies; and, my
favourite bit, a serene, cobbled walk under the spreading branches
of cherry trees that spring from the grass on either side. There are
old roses, a kitchen garden, a turf maze and lovely old trees too. It is
an idiosyncratic garden that has evolved over recent decades, given
enchantment by the fragments of past centuries.

Sultry Snakeshead Fritillaries

The snakeshead fritillary, *Fritillaria meleagris*, is a quietly glamorous wildflower of damp meadows, ideally suited to low-lying ground beside the Windrush and Cherwell rivers in Oxfordshire. Its popular name hints at the slightly sinister ambience of its deep purple, nodding flowers borne on the slenderest of stems. Other vernacular names such as leper's bells, shy widows and sulky ladies also suggest this flower's dark, mysterious qualities.

Vita Sackville-West wrote in her poem *The Land* that the 'snaky flower' was sullen, dangerous and foreign-looking, 'scarfed in dull purple, like Egyptian girls Camping among the furze, staining the waste with foreign colour… An Egyptian girl, with an ancient snaring spell'. Its origins are uncertain, but *F. meleagris* was certainly a well-known and plentiful flower in April and May until 20th-century farming methods with land draining, ploughing and fertilisers severely reduced its numbers.

The most famous site where this flower survives in profusion is Magdalen College Meadow, Oxford, on the banks of the River Cherwell. Until a few years ago, the banks flooded reliably between November and March, providing ideal conditions for the fritillary to flourish, as it has done here for centuries. Winter flooding has not occurred in recent years of low rainfall, but the meadow is still damp enough for the bulbs to have multiplied in great numbers. Part of their successful management is due to the way the flowers are left to set seed before the hay is cut in July. The meadow is then grazed by fallow deer, the trampling of their hooves providing an ideal seed bed. Fritillaries also have a long association with the Oxfordshire village of Ducklington, beside the Windrush, and Iffley, just south of Oxford, where the flowers are celebrated on Fritillary Sunday, at the height of their flowering season.

STEEPLE ASTON

Rousham House

Steeple Aston OX25 4QX TEL. 01869-347110 OWNER C. Cottrell-Dormer
HOURS Garden all year, daily, 10a.m.–4.30p.m.; house April–Sept, Wed, Sun and Bank Holiday Mons, 2–4.30p.m. ENTRANCE Garden only £3, house and garden £6, no children under 15 DIRECTIONS 2m S of Steeple Aston off A4260 and B4030, use M40 Jct 9

 ♿ Access

Rousham possesses 'the sweetest little groves, streams, glades, porticos, cascades and river imaginable' – Horace Walpole's words, written in 1760, but still apt today. This important, early 18th-century, 25-acre landscape garden has pleasing, pastoral views and was laid out by William Kent in the 1730s, overlying a more formal design laid out a generation before. Its recommended route passes grottoes, cascades and the carved image of a dying gladiator, with waterside walks leading to a handsome stone loggia. There is also a fine walled garden with herbaceous borders, ancient espaliered fruit trees and an old dovecote beside the box-edged rose gardens. 'Rousham is uncommercial and unspoilt with no tea room and no shop,' says the leaflet. 'Bring a picnic, wear comfortable shoes and it is yours for the day.' Sound advice for a most enjoyable walk through Arcady. Daffodil time here is lovely, although summer is best for the walled gardens.

WHEATLEY

Waterperry Gardens

Waterperry, Wheatley OX33 1JZ TEL. 01844-339226 OWNER School of Economic Science HOURS Open all year, daily, 9a.m.–5p.m. (closed Thurs–Sun in 3rd week of July) ENTRANCE £3.50, concessions £3, children £2 (under 10s free), Nov–March everyone £1.75 DIRECTIONS 9m E of Oxford, 2½m N of Wheatley; M40 Jct 8A to Wheatley, then follow signs WEB www.waterperrygardens.co.uk
🔲 ♿ Access 🔲 Gift Shop 🔲 Café 🔲 Plants for Sale

This was once the Waterperry Horticultural School for Women (now closed) which was opened in 1932 by Miss Beatrix Havergal and her partner, Avice Sanders. Many well-known gardeners (including Valerie Finnis, Mary Spiller and Sissinghurst's former head gardeners, Pamela Schwerdt and Sibylle Kreutzberger) were trained here, and the highest possible standards of horticulture were instilled in its pupils. Parts of Miss Havergal's legacy continue, such as the spectacular 200ft herbaceous border below a south-facing wall – wonderful from early summer well into autumn. There are also shrub and heather borders, herb beds, a rock garden, well-trained fruit trees, many demonstration beds of assorted herbaceous plants, a knot and a rose garden.

The plant centre at the 83-acre estate's entrance has a reasonably wide stock at competitive prices, and there is often produce from the gardens on sale. Waterperry also features an interesting museum of gardens and agriculture. Any keen gardener will find much of interest and entertainment here.

Euphorbias Galore

In Evelyn Waugh's *Brideshead Revisited*, Lord Sebastian Flyte is overcome by an urge to see the ivies, in all their variety, at **University of Oxford Botanic Garden, Rose Lane, Oxford OX1 4AZ (tel. 01865-286690/web www.botanic-garden.ashmole.ox.ac.uk)**. It is the oldest botanic garden in Britain, and besides ivies there is a National Collection of euphorbia species.

Apparently, euphorbias were so named by Dioscorides, who had learned of the plant via King Juba of Mauretania; the genus was named after the king's physician, Euphorbus. There are at least 2000 species of euphorbia and they are extremely diverse in their distribution and hardiness. Some are typical desert succulents, resembling cacti, while others are hardy and valued as ornamental garden plants. Gertrude Jekyll admired *E. characias* for its contribution to the herbaceous border in spring, and euphorbias continue to enjoy favour in many people's gardens. It should be remembered, however, that the white latex 'sap' is extremely irritant, liable to blister the skin on contact, and possibly carcinogenic. Wear gloves when pruning and handling them. Anyone interested in these unusual plants can see wide ranges of both hardy and greenhouse types in the four-and-a-half-acre University gardens. Open all year, daily, 9a.m.–5p.m. (4.30p.m. Oct–March), last adm. 4.15p.m.; greenhouses open 10a.m.–4p.m. Entrance by donation, except April–Aug, £2, children under 12 free. Use Park and Ride bus, alight on the High Street opposite Magdalen College.

WOODSTOCK

Blenheim Palace

Woodstock OX20 1PX TEL. 01993-811091 OWNER His Grace the Duke of Marlborough HOURS House, gardens and attractions mid-March–Oct, daily, 10.30a.m.–5.30p.m. (last adm. 4.45p.m.); park all year, daily, 9.45a.m.–4.45p.m. ENTRANCE House and gardens £10, OAPs/students £7.50, children £5, family ticket £26; park only £6.50 per car, £2 per pedestrian, children £1 (winter £5, £1 and 50p) DIRECTIONS 8m N of Oxford on A44, Blenheim is clearly signposted; leave M40 at Jct 9, then A34, then A44 to Woodstock

🌿 ♿ Access 🌿 Gift Shop 🌿 Café 🌿 Plants for Sale

Blenheim Palace is the ultimate stately home – Britain's answer to Versailles and quite breathtaking in its opulence. The birthplace of Sir Winston Churchill, it was built by Sir John Vanbrugh and Nicholas Hawksmoor for the 1st Duke of Marlborough and paid for by the nation, following the Duke's victory at the Battle of Blenheim in 1704.

Outdoors it is spectacular, too, with a 2000-acre park landscaped by Capability Brown (*q.v.*) overlaying a more formal, earlier plan. Some of the formal symmetry was put back in the early 20th century, however, when terraced Italian-style gardens with patterned beds of box were added to the east side of the palace, and elaborate water parterres with fountains were reinstated to the west. There is an impressive eight-acre walled kitchen garden (the sole survivor of the pre-Brown layout) with a recently planted maze, and a rose garden and arboretum. At Blenheim you can see how some of the major talents of earlier centuries have interwoven to create a truly great landscape.

And also...

Ball Colegrave Ltd, Milton Road, West Adderbury, Banbury OX17 3EY (tel. 01295-810632/web www.ballcolegrave.co.uk), is a commercial supplier of seeds to the horticulture industry. Its four-acre trial grounds, rarely open to the public, are well worth seeing on the special open days in August, by anyone with an interest in the latest developments in plant breeding, particularly bedding plants destined for the market. The displays are brash, bright, instructive and well maintained. Open for one NGS day in Aug. Entrance £3.

The Burford Garden Company, Shilton Road, Burford, Oxford OX18 4PA (tel. 01993-823117/823285), is a large, well-stocked garden centre. Its plant displays include around 450 different roses, 75 clematis and 300 varieties of herbaceous plants, with ornamental trees and imported topiaries. Open all year, daily, March–Dec, Mon–Wed and Sat, 9a.m.–6p.m., Thurs–Fri, 9a.m.–7p.m., Sun, 11a.m.–5p.m., Jan–Feb, Mon–Wed, 9a.m.–5.30p.m., Thurs–Sat, 9a.m.–6p.m., Sun, 11a.m.–5p.m.

Clock House, Coleshill, Swindon SN6 7PT (tel. 01793-762476), has an unusual five-acre garden featuring the ground plan of Coleshill House (burnt down in the 1950s) planted in box and lavender, to show where the walls and windows had been. There is also a large greenhouse, a fine lime avenue and wonderful views of the Vale of the White Horse. Open April–Sept, Thurs only, 2–5p.m., also for certain NGS days and by appointment. Entrance £1.50. B4019 between Faringdon and Highworth, then to top of Coleshill village.

Kelmscott Manor, Kelmscott, Lechlade GL7 3HJ (tel. 01367-252486), is famous for having been the summer home of 19th-century designer William Morris, for 25 years. It will be of interest to anyone with a fascination for the Pre-Raphaelite movement or Arts and Crafts design (Morris's stylised floral designs continue to be influential 100 years on) and the entry ticket includes a tour of the house. The small, enclosed garden was painted in watercolour by Rossetti's model, Maria Spartali Stillman (1844–1927). The standard roses and profusion of plants which she painted (and which inspired Morris) have been reinstated during recent restorations. Open April–Sept, Wed, 11a.m.–1p.m. and 2–5p.m.; June–Sept, 3rd Sat in month, 2–5p.m.; July–Aug, 1st and 3rd Sat in month, 2–5p.m. Also Thurs–Fri in April–Sept for private groups. Entrance £7, concessions/children £3.50, garden only £2, concessions/children free. Off A417, follow signs to Kelmscott.

Mattocks Roses, Nuneham Courtenay, Oxford OX44 9PY (tel. 0845-758 5652), shares premises with a large and well-stocked branch of Notcutts Garden Centre, which is where you should park to visit the Mattocks rose fields which are open late June–Sept for no charge, across the road. It is always instructive to see demonstration fields in bloom if you are considering buying some new roses. Their ever-popular County series of roses now includes 'Oxfordshire', bearing pretty, shell-pink blooms over a long season on a low-growing bush. Catalogue free on request. Open all year, Mon–Sat, 9a.m.–5.30p.m. (Thurs in April–Dec, 9a.m.–8p.m.), Sun and Bank Holidays, 10.30a.m.–4.30p.m. M40 Jct 8, then A40, then A4142, then A4074, then B4015.

The Nursery Further Afield, Evenley Road, Mixbury, Brackley NN13 5YR (tel. 01280-848808 (day), 848539 (eve)), is a small nursery and display garden, surrounded by silvery willows, tucked away on the edge of Mixbury village. It specialises in hardy geraniums and holds a National Collection of day lilies (*Hemerocallis*), and has a small range of other unusual hardy perennials. Open April–early Oct (closed Aug), Wed–Sat, 10a.m.–1p.m. and 2–5p.m. and some open days for NGS (phone for details). Entrance free. From A43 follow signs to Evenley.

Shropshire

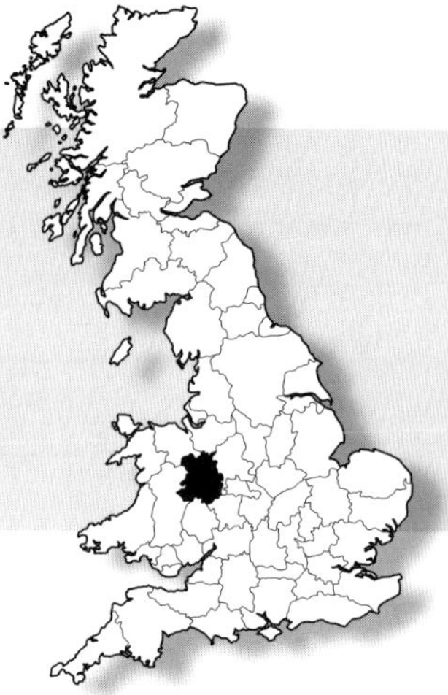

MAP NO. 5

The poet A. E. Housman recalled his homeland as 'the country for easy livers, the quietest under the sun'. This was not always so, however; the county's strategic position on the border with Wales made it the scene of bloody battles for centuries. It is also one of the oldest lived-in regions of Britain; 5000 years ago Stone Age peoples populated the hilly and forested region of Clun, on the westernmost fringes, and to the south a Bronze Age trade route ran across the Clee Hills to join the River Severn. The world's first iron bridge, 196ft long, was built in 1779 to straddle the Severn gorge at Telford, and it remains a potent symbol of the Industrial Revolution which followed.

Must See
Hodnet Hall, Hodnet –
   amazing waterscape with
   seven lakes

Exceptional in Spring
The Dorothy Clive Garden,
   Willoughbridge

Exceptional in Summer
David Austin Roses,
   Wolverhampton

HODNET

Hodnet Hall

Hodnet, Market Drayton TF9 3NN TEL. 01630-685202 OWNER Mr and Mrs A.
Heber-Percy HOURS April–Sept, Tues–Sun and Bank Holiday Mons,
12 noon–5p.m. ENTRANCE £3.50, OAPs £3, children £1.50 DIRECTIONS 12m NE of
Shrewsbury on A53, use M6 Jct 12 or M54 Jct 3 WEB
www.shropshiretourism.com

🌿 & Access 🌿 Gift Shop 🌿 Café 🌿 Plants for Sale

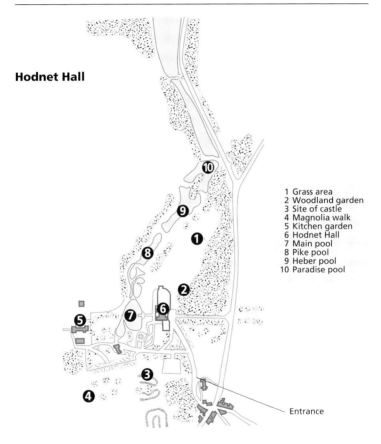

Hodnet Hall

1 Grass area
2 Woodland garden
3 Site of castle
4 Magnolia walk
5 Kitchen garden
6 Hodnet Hall
7 Main pool
8 Pike pool
9 Heber pool
10 Paradise pool

Entrance

Two things about Hodnet Hall are etched forever on my memory:
the fantastic waterscape, created from a chain of big lakes, and the
bizarre experience of taking tea with a snarling tiger (albeit a stuffed
one), under the glassy gaze of hundreds of severed heads of assorted
antelopes, buffalos and rhinoceros. The late-Victorian hall sits on a
plateau, looking down into the main pool; half a dozen more lakes
ascend the gentle valley to the west. Grassy banks either side are

awash with daffodils, rhododendrons and cherry blossom through the spring, followed by astilbes and hydrangeas. There are acers in variety, with Japanese forms elegantly bowing to cast their reflections at the water's edge, and, with a variety of shrubs and trees, they bring a spectacular glow to autumn. It is a really splendid and unusual garden, laid out with imagination in the 1920s and well maintained today. If I lived nearby, its 70 acres would be a regular haunt. Hawkstone Historic Park and Follies (*q.v.*) are nearby (and signposted from Hodnet).

Heart of Oak

Vast forests once covered much of Shropshire, the most significant tree being the oak, because it offered seemingly inexhaustible supplies of stout, hard-wearing timbers for ship- and house-building in medieval and Tudor times. Oaks also provided fodder for the furnaces of the ancient iron industry. Black-and-white oak-framed buildings are still a feature in the region, with one of the most celebrated houses being **Boscobel, Bishop's Wood, Brewood ST19 9AR (tel. 01902-850244), 8m N of Wolverhampton on an unclassified road between A41 and A5**, on the Staffordshire border. The small two-acre garden is in formal, 17th-century parterre style.

The property's name derives from the Italian, *bosco bello*, as it was in the midst of a beautiful wood. King Charles I hid in an oak tree here after the Battle of Worcester in 1651, while Cromwell's men searched the forest. That oak didn't survive in the long term (pieces of it made valuable souvenirs even during the 17th century). Open April–Oct, daily, 10a.m.–6p.m.; Nov, Wed–Sun, 10a.m.–4p.m., early–mid-Dec, Sat–Sun, 10a.m.–4p.m. Entrance £4.40, concessions £3.30, children £2.20, family ticket £11.

WILLOUGHBRIDGE

The Dorothy Clive Garden

Willoughbridge, Market Drayton TF9 4EU TEL. 01630-647237
OWNER Willoughbridge Garden Trust HOURS April–Oct, daily, 10a.m.–5.30p.m.
ENTRANCE £3, OAPs £2.50, children £1 (under 11s free) DIRECTIONS 7m NE of Market Drayton, 1m E of Woore, by A51 between Nantwich and Stone WEB www.dorothyclivegarden.co.uk

 Access Café

Much of the tranquillity and appeal of this eight-acre garden is due to its water, whether tumbling down a rocky cascade, or supporting flat plates of lilies, spread out luxuriantly in the still pool. If Claude Monet could visit, he would marvel at the garden's subtle range of textures and colours, and the tremendous variety of plants arranged on its gentle slopes.

The lime-free soil supports festive displays of rhododendrons, a glorious clash of pinks and purples, reds and yellows, followed by a feast of hybrid azaleas in salmon, orange and lemon, with intoxicating fragrance. There is a great deal to satisfy plantsmen here – many unusual bulbs, perennials, camellias and conifers for interest through the seasons. The scree and rock garden above the lake are especially good. The garden was made by Colonel Clive from the 1940s onwards as a tribute to his wife.

WOLLERTON

Wollerton Old Hall

Wollerton, Hodnet, Market Drayton TF9 3NA TEL. 01630-685760 OWNER Mr and Mrs J. Jenkins HOURS Easter–Sept, Fri, Sun and Bank Holiday Mons (Fri only in Sept), 12 noon–5p.m. ENTRANCE £3.50, children £1 DIRECTIONS 11m NE of Shrewsbury, ½m NE of Hodnet, off A53 (follow the brown signs); from M54 exit at Jct 3 onto A41 towards Ternhill, turn left at Ternhill roundabout onto A53 and follow signs

⬛ ♿ Access ⬛ Café ⬛ Plants for Sale

This is a formal, three-acre garden, divided into hedged or walled rooms and inspired by the geometrical garden styles of the 17th century. It has very strong lines of axis, the chief one from the house leading through a symmetrical knot garden enclosed by beech hedges into a sunken rill garden, with a lime allée and further gardens beyond. Its design is appropriate for the house, which is the sole remaining wing of what had been an Elizabethan mansion; it also suits the flat lie of the land, for the subdivisions by hedges help to filter cold Shropshire winds. There are delphinium borders, a garden of 'hot' red and yellow flowers (best in August), a white garden and, beyond the walls, a semi-wild garden of shrubs and trees in grassland sloping down to the valley of the River Tern. Within the formal structure, planting is exuberant and imaginative.

WOLVERHAMPTON
David Austin Roses

Bowling Green Lane, Albrighton, Wolverhampton WV7 3HB TEL. 01902-376300 OWNER David Austin HOURS Open all year, Mon–Fri, 9a.m.–5p.m., Sat–Sun, 10a.m.–6p.m. (closes at dusk, mid-Oct–mid-March) ENTRANCE Free DIRECTIONS Between A41 and A464, about 8m W of Wolverhampton, Bowling Green Lane leads off Albrighton High Street WEB www.davidaustinroses.com

🌺 Nursery 🌺 Mail Order 🌺 Café

You can buy roses galore at this famous nursery, which also produces an excellent colour catalogue (free). A group of formally planned display gardens for roses has been laid out over the last dozen years, showing over 900 roses in ideal conditions. 'The gardens reflect our view of what a rose should be and how it should be used,' says David Austin. They are mainly old-fashioned and shrub types, together with plenty of David Austin's own-bred English roses. There is also a garden of modern roses.

The gardens are surrounded by neat conifer hedges, with borders edged in box and yew. Also worth viewing in summer is the herbaceous garden, featuring many of the plants listed in the beautifully illustrated catalogue, *Claire Austin's Handbook of Hardy Plants* (available free). David Austin's daughter has developed a parallel business here, selling hardy perennials of many species, but she specialises in those utterly mouth-watering flowers of early summer – peonies and bearded irises.

And also...

Eerie caves, cliffs, castle and concealed grottoes contribute to the thrills of **Hawkstone Historic Park and Follies, Hodnet Road, Weston-under-Redcastle, nr Shrewsbury SY4 5UY (tel. 01939-200611/200300/web www.hawkstone.co.uk)**. Pathways ramble through hilly woods leading to various follies and monuments. In the 18th century, when the romantic landscape was laid out, a hermit with the beard of an old goat dwelt in the caves for 14 years. Open Jan–March, Sat–Sun, 10a.m.–dusk; April–May and Sept–Oct, Wed–Sun, 10.30a.m.–6p.m. (opens 10a.m., Sat–Sun in Sept–Oct), last adm. 4p.m.; June, daily, 10.30a.m.–4p.m. (4.30p.m., Sat–Sun); July–Aug, daily, 10.30a.m.–4.30p.m. Entrance Mon–Fri £4.50, concessions £3.50, children £2.50, family ticket £12; Sat–Sun in summer £5, £4, £3 and £14; Sat–Sun in winter £3.50, £2.50, £2 and £10. Off A49 between Shrewsbury and Whitchurch, signposted from A49 and A442.

The present six-acre gardens at **Preen Manor, Church Preen, Church Stretton SY6 7LQ (tel. 01694-771207)**, were begun only 20 years ago, but have a growing reputation for their stylish planting and imaginative use of the site. Highlights include a chess garden, gravel garden, fern garden, potager and gallery of pots arranged over brick-and-cobble steps. Teas available. Not suitable for wheelchairs. Open for groups of 15 or more by appointment, and for several days in summer through the National Gardens Scheme. Entrance £3, children 50p. Signposted from B4371.

Somerset

MAP NO. 2

Somerset is a county of contrasts, from the flat, watered plains of the Levels to the limestone Mendip Hills, with heather-draped Exmoor in the west. The soft, deep ochre-coloured limestone of Ham Hill has provided building material for countless pretty villages in the south of the county. When I think of Somerset I also picture the small, productive apple orchards that have produced cider for many centuries. A visit to Perry's Cider Mills, Dowlish Wake, near Ilminster, is instructive, but intoxicating, for you can taste a whole range before you buy!

Must See

Forde Abbey, Chard – water, woods and flowers around ancient abbey

Hestercombe, Cheddon Fitzpaine – prime Lutyens garden of Edwardian formality

Exceptional in Spring

Greencombe, Porlock

Tintinhull House Garden, Tintinhull

Exceptional in Summer

Cothay Manor, Wellington

Hadspen Garden, Castle Cary

CASTLE CARY

Hadspen Garden and Nursery

Nr Castle Cary BA7 7NG TEL. 01749-813707 OWNER N. and S. Pope and
N. Hobhouse HOURS First Thurs in March–last Sun in Sept, Thurs–Sun and
Bank Holidays, 10a.m.–5p.m. ENTRANCE £3, university students £1.50, children
50p DIRECTIONS 3½m NW of Wincanton, 2m SE of Castle Cary, by A371

🌑 ♿ Access 🌑 Café 🌑 Plants for Sale 🌑 NPC

Sandra Pope and her husband, Nori, had a specialist rose nursery on
Vancouver Island, off Canada's Pacific coast, before they packed their
bags and came to Hadspen in 1987. The five-acre, old kitchen garden,
with its curved wall and south-facing slope, had been partially
restored by Penelope Hobhouse in recent years, and presented a great
opportunity for laying out a display garden and nursery; it was also
an ideal canvas on which to practise their theories on colour harmony.

A large, rectangular lily-pond had formerly been the water cistern
for the 18th-century Hadspen House nearby, and the Popes have
planted the sunny, terraced walk beside it with plants reminiscent
of sun-baked Mediterranean hillsides. The teahouse garden beyond
the pool features cool blues and whites in the partial shade of trees,
while long, double borders of yellows and creams of varying hue line
one of the main paths through the garden.

The two-acre curved walled area (Sandra's domain) is devoted to
deep reds and oranges, with darkly toned roses, dahlias and *Helichrysum
bracteatum* progressing into delicate half-tones of pastel pinks and pale
apricots. This border always gives endless pause for thought; it's
cleverly, painstakingly arranged, but appears artless and relaxed.

Two rows of slender beech trees provide shade for Hadspen's
famous hosta collection which predates the Popes' arrival; the lower
gardens also house a hydrangea border and the National Collection
of rodgersia. There is a catalogue of nursery stock sold on site, but no
mail order.

CHARD

Forde Abbey

Chard TA20 4LU TEL. 01460-221290 OWNER Mr M. Roper HOURS Garden open
all year, daily, 10a.m.–4.30p.m.; house April–Oct, Tues–Thurs, Sun and Bank
Holiday Mons, 1–4.30p.m. ENTRANCE £4.20, OAPs £3.95, children free; house
and garden £5.40, OAPs £5.10, children free DIRECTIONS 7m W of Crewkerne,
4m SE of Chard, between B3167 and B3162, near Winsham (signposted from
A30 and A358) WEB www.fordeabbey.co.uk

🌑 ♿ Access 🌑 Gift Shop 🌑 Café 🌑 Plants for Sale

For several miles the River Axe forms part of the wiggly boundary separating Somerset from Dorset, and Forde Abbey is a wonderful, hidden-away property, sitting right on that divide. It was founded by Cistercian monks over 800 years ago, in an idyllic situation between the Blackdown Hills and the rising ground of Dorset's North Downs. (Do see the house, if it is open when you visit – the monastery still stands, although it is handsomely overlaid by further developments made in the 16th and 17th centuries.)

Water is an essential part of the 30-acre gardens, although not, as you might expect, by utilising the river. A spring elsewhere on the property feeds a four-acre rectangular pool known as the Great Pond, which in turn feeds lesser ponds and pretty cascades, bringing water all the while to a rectangular canal (the Long Pond), close to the west end of the Abbey. The pools make tranquil, reflective and light-enhancing features that set off the garden's plants beautifully. Herbaceous borders and clipped yew trees beside the Long Pond help to link the Abbey to its garden. A silted-up piece of land by the Great Pond has been developed by the present owners into an abundantly furnished bog garden, at its best in early summer when its irises, candelabra primulas and hostas are in bloom. They are joined by the strange-smelling lysichitons, umbrella-leaved gunneras and rheums, astilbes, rodgersias, peltiphyllums and much more, with a gravel path and decking ramp running through the area in a pleasingly casual way. Don't miss the Beech House, a living, green folly fashioned from pleached saplings, complete with a green roof and little windows.

Forde Abbey also possesses an arboretum with some wonderful trees, and a thriving walled kitchen garden (its pumpkins are entered annually in the local show), which dates back to the days of the Cistercian monks. This is also where you will find a well-stocked nursery with some unusual plants for sale.

CHEDDON FITZPAINE

Hestercombe

Cheddon Fitzpaine, nr Taunton TA2 8LG TEL. 01823-413923 OWNER Hestercombe Gardens Project HOURS Open all year, daily, 10a.m.–6p.m. (last adm. 5p.m.) ENTRANCE £4, concessions £3.80, children (under 15) £1 (under 5s free) DIRECTIONS 3m NE of Taunton, near Cheddon Fitzpaine, use M5 Jct 25 (signposted) WEB www.hestercombegardens.com
🌿 Gift Shop 🌿 Café 🌿 Plants for Sale

On a clear summer's day it is possible to capture wafts of the confident Edwardian age along with the lavender-perfumed air in this famous 50-acre garden; you might expect to bump into Helen Schlegel in *Howards End* in cambric blouse with leg-o-mutton sleeves, poised under a shady parasol. Hestercombe was one of the great success stories of the collaboration of Sir Edwin Lutyens (*q.v.*), the designer, and Gertrude Jekyll (*q.v.*), who planted it. Here are Lutyens's signature stone walls, circular steps and narrow water rills; there is a long, handsome pergola for climbing roses and beautifully detailed patterning of local stone. Jekyll's plantings (restored in recent years, largely according to her plans) feature generous drifts of herbaceous perennials – irises and delphiniums, grey-leaved lamb's ears and red-hot pokers and, of course, plenty of roses.

The plan for the main gardens is formal and symmetrical, making the most of the southern views of the Taunton Vale and distant Blackdown Hills. A new, interesting development is the restoration of a much older garden on the north side of the house: an 18th-century 35-acre landscape park that was laid out from 1750 to 1786 by the then owner, the euphoniously named Michael Coplestone Warre Bampfylde. Its great cascade is reminiscent of one that Bampfylde created at Stourhead (*q.v.*) for his great friend, Henry Hoare.

CURRY MALLET

Mallet Court Nursery

Curry Mallet, nr Taunton TA3 6SY TEL. 01823-481493 OWNER J.G.S. and P.M.E. Harris HOURS Open all year, Mon–Fri, 9a.m.–5p.m.; weekends only by appointment DIRECTIONS 5m SE of Taunton, in village of Curry Mallet, take A358 towards Ilminster, then A378 towards Langport, then turn right to Curry Mallet

🌿 Plants for Sale 🌿 Nursery 🌿 Mail Order

If you like trees you'll love Mallet Court Nursery, which sells more than 800 varieties, many of them unobtainable elsewhere. Proprietor James Harris (known as 'Acer' Harris due to his predilection for Japanese maples) is a lawyer and self-confessed collector of stamps, coins and Roman artefacts, and especially of trees. He helps finance botanical expeditions collecting seed in far-flung places in return for a share of the spoils and the results are among the saplings in his densely stocked nursery. Oaks are another speciality as well as broad selections of hollies and magnolias; whatever tree you are searching for, it is probably here. A catalogue (£1 plus s.a.e.) lists trees available by mail order between November and March.

Barrington Court

Barrington, Nr Ilminster TA19 0NQ TEL. 01460-241938 OWNER The National Trust HOURS March and Oct, Fri–Sun, 11a.m.–4.30p.m., April–June and Sept, Sat–Thurs, 11a.m.–5.30p.m., July–Aug, daily, 11a.m.–5.30p.m. (last adm. 5p.m.) ENTRANCE £5, children £2.50, family ticket £12.50 DIRECTIONS Use M5 Jct 25 or A303 to Ilminster, then 5m NE on B3168

🌿 ⅋ Access 🌿 Café 🌿 Plants for Sale 🌿 Gift Shop

The fine Elizabethan house, with its gables and barley-twist chimneys, was leased by the National Trust in the early 20th century to the Lyle family (of Tate & Lyle sugar). The Lyles commissioned Gertrude Jekyll (*q.v.*), by then in the twilight years of her career and with very poor eyesight, to design the gardens. The 11-acre gardens, laid out in a series of hedged and walled 'rooms', feature some of her best work, although only around half of her schemes were actually carried out.

The property is deeply romantic, in a beautiful setting of lawns and well-treed parkland, with chestnut avenues and sheep-grazed cider orchards, and it boasts some fine architecture among its farm buildings, particularly the 200-year-old cattle stalls. The formal gardens lie beside the house and include colour-themed areas (not all by Jekyll), roses, sumptuous iris beds and a huge, productive walled kitchen garden. The lily garden, with its lovely waterlily pool, has rectangular, raised beds featuring planting in a 'hot' colour scheme combined with Jekyll's signature bergenias. There is a long pergola (not Jekyll's) richly clothed in clematis, golden hops and wisteria, and an oak bridge leads over a 'moat', achieved by diverting a nearby stream.

Kelways Ltd

Barrymore Farm, Langport TA10 9EZ TEL. 01458-250521 OWNER Mr C. Johnson HOURS Open all year, Mon–Fri, 9a.m.–5p.m., Sat, 10a.m.–5p.m., Sun, 10a.m.–4p.m. DIRECTIONS In Langport, 10m E of Taunton, on B3153; from M5 Jct 25 take A358, then A378 to Langport WEB www.kelways.co.uk

🌿 ⅋ Access 🌿 Plants for Sale 🌿 Nursery 🌿 Mail Order

This famous nursery has been operating since 1851 and is now thriving again, under new ownership and management. Astonishingly, around 600 herbaceous peonies are grown here, many being rare Victorian varieties dating from the nursery's glory days, and there is a large range of bearded irises, too. May and June are the best months for seeing the peony and iris fields awash with pastel hues; the once-famous four-acre Peony Valley has recently been re-sited in a weed-free field, and is building up steam to become one of *the* early summer sights of Somerset, with around 500 different varieties.

The Kelways free colour catalogue features a range of these choice plants, plus an interesting selection of day lilies. The plant centre stocks around 100 each of irises and peonies at any one time, but others can be ordered for dispatch during the lifting seasons – August and September for irises, and November to February for peonies.

PORLOCK

Greencombe

Porlock TA24 8NU TEL. 01643-862363 OWNER Joan Loraine HOURS April–July and Oct–Nov, Sat–Wed, 2–6p.m. ENTRANCE £4, children 50p. No dogs DIRECTIONS On minor road to Porlock Weir, ½m W of Porlock
🌿 Plants for Sale 🌿 NPC

Greencombe

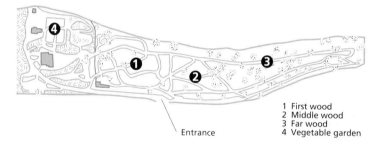

1 First wood
2 Middle wood
3 Far wood
4 Vegetable garden

Entrance

The three-and-a-half-acre garden at Greencombe clings snugly to a wooded hillside on the northern edge of Exmoor, gazing out over the Severn. On a clear day, you can see the coast of South Wales on the horizon and the undulating shadow of the Brecon Beacons beyond, formed of the same ancient red sandstone on which Greencombe itself is built.

There has been a garden here for over 50 years, the first 20 of which were due to one Horace Stroud, a keen plantsman. He was followed by the present owner, Joan Loraine, who retired from a globe-trotting career as a schoolteacher in the colonies to tend more diminutive charges, her National Collection of erythroniums, or dog-tooth violets. They peak in April, while other springtime features include drifts of snowflakes, hellebores and primulas that complement the glorious woodland scenes of magnolias, rhododendrons and Japanese acers.

According to Joan Loraine, it is 'a lunatic place in which to garden', facing directly north, in the shadow of a steep hill with little soil overlaying the sandstone. Fortunately, that does not stop her from tending the garden, or the rest of us from enjoying its special atmosphere and tranquillity.

Local Willow Crafts

The flat, wet lowlands of the Somerset Levels provide fertile grazing for cattle and a rich habitat for marshland birds. Willow trees flourish here, too, in sodden fields that yield forests of canes (withies) for the thriving local industry of basket-making. Gardeners will find it well worth exploring this ancient and mysterious fenland to seek out the village of Stoke St Gregory, about 7m W of Langport, in the heart of 'withy country'.

The **English Hurdle Company, Curload, Stoke St Gregory, Taunton TA3 6JD (tel. 01823-698418/web www.hurdle.co.uk), 1¾m from East Lyng off the Taunton–Glastonbury road (A361), from M5 Jct 24 take A385, then A361 towards Glastonbury, turn right towards Stoke St Gregory,** specialises in willow hurdles, plant climbers, arches and arbours, hand-made on the premises. They also sell by mail (catalogue free on request). Open Mon–Fri, 9a.m.–5p.m., and Sat, 9a.m.–1p.m. At **P.H. Coate and Son, Meare Green Court, Stoke St Gregory, Taunton TA3 6HY (tel. 01823-490249/web www.coates-willowbaskets.co.uk), signposted to the Willows and Wetland Visitor Centre from Durston on the Taunton–Glastonbury road (A361),** you can buy flattish, trug-like baskets, intended for cut flowers, but even more useful for carting about secateurs, twine, trowels, hand-forks, tough gloves, etc. Mon–Fri you can watch the skilled basket-makers at work; there is also an interesting visitor centre showing the history of this local rural craft. Open all year, Mon–Sat, 9a.m.–5p.m. Tour £2.50, concessions £2.25, children £1.25.

SOUTH PETHERTON

Avon Bulbs

Burnt House Farm, Mid-Lambrook, South Petherton TA13 5HE TEL. 01460-242177 OWNER C. Ireland-Jones HOURS Mail order only WEB www.avonbulbs.co.uk

🌿 Nursery 🌿 Mail Order

'Raising plants is in the blood,' says Chris Ireland-Jones, who grew up in Zimbabwe, where his parents farmed tobacco. After training in agriculture and a brief spell in printing Chris bought the nursery (then based at Bradford-on-Avon) and moved it here in 1990 where it goes from strength to strength, and frequently wins gold medals from the Royal Horticultural Society.

Bulbs make perfect mail-order plants, being easy to pack and post while dormant. The colour catalogue (send 4 × 2nd-class stamps) lists many tempting varieties, including around 20 different fritillaries, 25 cyclamen and 25 alliums. (I have some spectacular *Lilium regale* bought from Chris, which dependably produce whopping 6ft stems packed with fragrant flowers.)

Twenty different snowdrop species are offered 'in the green' (i.e. while in leaf) in springtime, when they have a better replanting success rate. Look out, too, for some wonderful exotics, such as *Arum palestinum*, surely Cruella de Ville's own flower, bearing deeply sinister, maroon-black, cowled blooms with a velvety texture. Unusual tulip species are another speciality. If you intend to visit, though, it's essential to phone before travelling any distance because the stock is seasonal.

TINTINHULL

Tintinhull House Garden

Farm Street, Tintinhull, nr Yeovil BA22 9PZ TEL. 01935-822545 OWNER The National Trust HOURS April–late Sept, Wed–Sun and Bank Holiday Mons, 12 noon–6p.m. ENTRANCE £3.80, children £1.80 DIRECTIONS ½m south of A303 on edge of Tintinhull village
🌿 Café

This intimate garden, attached to a substantial, beautiful house in the local honey-coloured limestone, covers little more than one acre but packs in a great deal, being divided into separate rooms in early 20th-century style. It was laid out in the 1930s by Phyllis Reiss, a keen amateur gardener, but became especially famous during the tenure of Penelope Hobhouse, the gardening writer and designer, who lived here from 1979 to 1994.

Penelope says it appeals because it is 'a marvellous, educational garden. Each of its parts can be closely related to the size of many modern gardens, and any one of them can be looked at as though it is a single garden.'

There are hot borders of yellow and red flowers blended with purple foliage, a white garden arranged around a circular fountain, and lawned areas bordered by artistically arranged shrubs, perennials and spring bulbs. A long, flagstone path running straight from the main door of the house to the end of the garden is a bold, inspired creation and is tremendously effective. But for me, the most engaging area is the kitchen garden. It is thoroughly traditional and workman-like, with neat rows of vegetables and salads set off by big clumps of euphorbia, with sweet peas garlanding the bean-poles, and scarlet and orange day lilies complementing the bright yellow flowers of courgettes. The garden can get very crowded, so it's best to plan your visit carefully, and for this reason I have highlighted its appeal in spring, which is as good as its summer season, but in a different way.

WELLINGTON

Cothay Manor

Exceptional in Summer

Greenham, Wellington TA21 0JR TEL. 01823-672283 OWNER Mr and Mrs A. Robb HOURS May–Sept, Wed–Thurs, Sun and Bank Holiday Mons, also some charity days, 2–6p.m. ENTRANCE £3.50 DIRECTIONS 5m W of Wellington, from A38 at Beambridge Hotel turn right towards Thorne St Margaret, continue straight for ¾m and at next crossroads turn right again towards Thorne St Margaret, at end of lane turn left and entrance is on right

🌳 ♿ Access   🌳 Plants for Sale

Before coming to Cothay Manor (open to groups by prior appointment only) a few years ago, Mary-Anne Robb had done great things at her previous home, Chisenbury Priory, in Wiltshire (which, incidentally, still opens one afternoon a year, for the NGS charities). Now, on the Devon-Somerset border, Mrs Robb is weaving her greenfingered magic once more, around a property which has been declared (by Christopher Hussey, no less) as 'the finest example of a small classic medieval Manor left in the kingdom today'. (Take the 'small' bit with a pinch of salt – it has a Great Hall, Oratory, Great Chamber and other fascinating rooms and outbuildings.)

What concerns us, though, is the five-acre garden and further seven acres of meadow. The River Tone meanders through the grounds and is woven into a plan which was laid out in the 1920s, with yew hedges creating enclosures of different ambience. Within this framework, Mrs Robb has been wearing the hat of 'interior decorator', making a 'white-and-grey room, and a purple-and-scarlet room'. She has also lavishly planted herbaceous borders, a scree bed, a cottage garden and a bog garden. All are framed by fine mature trees. The meadows are planted with specimen trees and shrubs and burst into bloom in spring with thousands of tulips, camassias and alliums among the grasses. Plants propagated from the gardens are on sale in a small nursery during visiting hours and teas are served.

CELEBRITY CHOICE

Fred Whitsey

Gardening correspondent for
The Daily Telegraph

'I have always very much admired the garden at **Tintinhull** (*q.v.*). It is, in my opinion, one of the most important gardens in the country and was made, like so many other really good gardens, by an amateur, Mrs Phyllis Reiss, whom I knew.

Tintinhull combines three essential elements for a good garden. Firstly, it has a very coherent design; it is divided into "rooms" and their proportions seem exactly right to me. Secondly, it has very well-considered use of colour schemes. And thirdly, it is full of good plantsmanship; there is, within its comparatively small space, a very large collection of plants and they are so cleverly arranged. It only came into prominence in the 1950s, when it was handed over to the National Trust by Mrs Reiss, but we have her to thank for its inspired arrangement and planting.'

And also...

Kim Woodward and Rupert Ashmore make and sell Ashmore Trugs from their workshop at **Aviaries Farmhouse, Shepton Montague, Wincanton BA9 8JD (tel. 01749-812998)**. Rupert makes a variety of high- and low-sided styles in solid pine and Kim paints them in pale blue, yellow, turquoise or antique/distressed finish (the most popular), but the range is also available unpainted. Kim paints special commissions to order. Trugs are also available by mail, for which there is a free colour catalogue.

Broadleigh Gardens, Bishops Hull, Taunton TA4 1AE (tel. 01823-286231/web www.broadleighbulbs.co.uk), sells bulbs by mail order only (send 2 × 1st-class stamps for a catalogue). The January catalogue features bulbs in growth, such as galanthus, cyclamen and some herbaceous plants; June's catalogue concentrates on dwarf and unusual bulbs. You can also visit the bulb fields in season and collect pre-booked orders. The nursery and garden are open all year, Mon–Fri, 9a.m.–4p.m. Entrance by donation.

Lower Severalls Nursery, Crewkerne TA18 7NX (tel. 01460-73234), is a handsome stone farmhouse draped with fremontodendron and clematis, and is surrounded by cottage-garden borders. Herbs fill out the display areas beyond, and scented geraniums, culinary herbs and salvias are among the specialities in this appealing nursery. Open March–Oct, Mon–Wed and Fri–Sat, 10a.m.–5p.m. (Suns also in May–June, 2–5p.m.). Entrance £2, children free. Off A30, 1m from Crewkerne towards Yeovil (signposted).

Scotts Nurseries, Higher Street, Merriott TA16 5PL (tel. 01460-72306) grows a vast range of stock, especially apples. Since apples have been a speciality for well over a century, local and ancient varieties are well represented. They also grow extensive ranges of roses, shrubs, trees and climbers, available at the garden centre and also through their mail order catalogue (free on request). Scotts' jewel-bright rose fields are a local tourist attraction in August (ask at the garden centre for directions). Open Mon–Sat, 9a.m.–5p.m., Sun, 10.30a.m.–4.30p.m. Leave A303 or A30, following signs to Merriott and then nursery.

Staffordshire

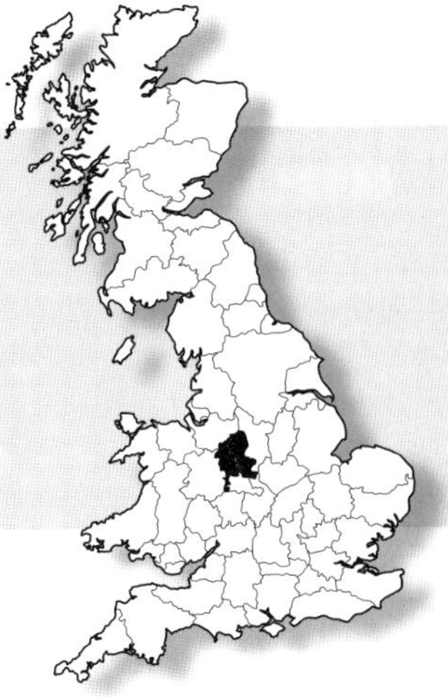

MAP NO. 5

The M6 motorway slices straight through Staffordshire, linking the industrial conurbations of Birmingham and the Black Country to Liverpool and Manchester. Away from the urban and industrial areas, the 17,000 acres of Cannock Chase embrace miles of beautiful countryside, heath and woodland, threaded with streams and dotted with the remains of Iron Age hill forts. It was once a medieval hunting forest, but these days people are only out hunting for picnic spots, or a bit of peace and quiet.

Must See
Biddulph Grange, Biddulph
  – a round-the-world trip in
  one Victorian garden

Exceptional in Autumn
Alton Towers, Alton

Worth a Visit in Winter
Biddulph Grange, Biddulph

ALTON

Alton Towers

Exceptional in Autumn

Alton, Stoke-on-Trent ST10 4DB TEL. 08705-204060 OWNER Tussauds Group
HOURS April–Oct, daily, 9.30a.m.–5p.m. (some later closings in summer)
ENTRANCE £23, OAPs £10, children £19, family ticket £59 DIRECTIONS 18m E of
Stoke-on-Trent, 20m from M6 Jct 15 or 16 and M1 Jct 23A (signposted
everywhere) WEB www.altontowers.com

🅿 ⌁ Access 🅿 Gift Shop 🅿 Café

'The work of a morbid imagination joined to the command of
unlimited resources', was gardening pundit J.C. Loudon's summary
of Alton Towers in 1822, but then he had an axe to grind because his
own proposals for the garden had been rejected. Today, mention of
Alton Towers is most likely to conjure images of funfairs and dare-
devil rides, but the gardens around the fairground are spectacular,
too, set against the gothic backdrop of the ruined hall.

The park covers 500 acres, with a large rock garden cascading
down a valley, out of which rise spires of assorted conifers, with
sprinklings of golden- and crimson-leaved trees lighting up the
landscape. It is an eccentric and romantic place, with delightful
garden features, including ornamental pools and a Chinese pagoda
fountain, a long walk through a succession of arches fashioned out
of sculpted yew, and a very splendid conservatory with beautiful
detailing in its curved, domed roof. Do not miss the chance of a cable-
car ride from the theme park, gaining an unusual aerial view of the
grounds.

Lord Anson's Blue Pea

When Admiral Lord Anson (of Shugborough, *q.v.*) returned from his
four-year voyage round the world, he inadvertently brought with
him horticultural treasure, as well as great material riches. Green
food was scarce during the long voyages, but the sailors found an
edible pea at Port San Julian, Patagonia, and the ship's cook brought
home a few seeds. The plant's bloom was a gem, with sweetly
scented, warm blue flowers on a climbing stem with grey-green,
slightly fleshy foliage. Lord Anson's pea, *Lathyrus nervosus*, is a
perennial of borderline hardiness, and grows best in rich, well-drained
soil in a sunny, sheltered position.

BIDDULPH

Biddulph Grange Garden

Grange Road, Biddulph, Stoke-on-Trent ST8 7SD TEL. 01782-517999 OWNER
The National Trust HOURS End March–Oct, Wed–Fri, 12 noon–5.30p.m.,
Sat–Sun and Bank Holiday Mons, 11a.m.–5.30p.m. (or dusk if earlier); also
Sat–Sun in Nov–Dec, 12 noon–4p.m. (or dusk if earlier) ENTRANCE End
March–Oct £4.50, children £2.40, family ticket £11.50; Nov–Dec free
DIRECTIONS ½m N of Biddulph, 3½m SE of Congleton, 7m N of Stoke-on-Trent,
access from A527 Tunstall–Congleton road (signposted)

🌿 Gift Shop 🌿 Café 🌿 Plants for Sale

Occasionally I come across an old garden that is so extraordinary I
wish its maker were still around, so that I could find out more about
his or her inspirations and intentions in making it. Biddulph Grange
is such a garden; it was made in the mid-19th century, at a time when
Britain was rich: from industry at home, and exploiting its Empire
abroad. With explorations opening up distant corners of the world,
new plants were coming to Britain by the shipload, and new images
of culture in other lands caused equal excitement.

At Biddulph Grange you can thus take a mini-world tour. You
may go through a Chinese water garden via a Scottish glen; enter a
half-timbered cottage, but find the exit is an Egyptian tomb guarded
by sphinxes; you may stroll down a stepped pathway lined with
hundreds of dahlias from Mexico, or wander among a grove of
rhododendrons from Nepal and Sikkim. The house was built with
Italian villas in mind, and there are monkey puzzles from Chile, all
the rage in Victorian gardens after their rediscovery in 1844.

This is certainly a garden for all seasons and all tastes. The area
called China is especially thrilling. It has a willow-pattern bridge and
an ornate temple lined with tiny brass bells, both brightly painted,
and nearby a fabulous, gilded water buffalo, gazing out from the
shade of a painted canopy. For sheer drama, this 15-acre garden is
not to be missed, and is hugely enjoyable in every season.

MILFORD

Shugborough

Milford, nr Stafford ST17 0XB TEL. 01889-881388 OWNER The National Trust
HOURS End March–late Sept, Tues–Sun; Oct, Sun only, 11a.m.–5p.m. ENTRANCE £2
per vehicle for park and gardens (inc. NT members); house £4.50, concessions
£3, family ticket £12 DIRECTIONS 6m E of Stafford on A513, entrance at Milford.
Signposted from M6 Jct 13 WEB www.staffordshire.gov.uk/shugborough

🌿 ♿ Access 🌿 Gift Shop 🌿 Café

This is the ancestral home of the 5th Earl of Lichfield, photographer of society debutantes and Pirelli calendar babes. The 900-acre property is now owned by the National Trust and administered by the local council, but its creation has romantic origins.

Much of its redesign in the 18th century was due to an injection of money, resulting from Admiral Anson's capture of a Spanish treasure ship. The local village, with its cottages, fields, mills and roads, was removed for the benefit of the park, while the old village millpond was elevated to the status of a grand lake. Chinese and classical buildings were dotted about the landscape (even on land which did not belong to the Ansons) and scenes were created throughout the grounds to invoke 18th-century ideals of 'delicious melancholy' in their beholder.

Forming suitably grand surroundings around a very palatial mansion, it is a garden of level, open spaces, magnificent old trees and water, retaining some 18th-century 'melancholy', overlaid with Victorian terraces and attractive flower gardens.

And also...

Cottage Garden Roses, Woodlands House, Stretton, nr Stafford ST19 9LG (tel. 01785-840217/web www.cottagegardenroses.com), is run by Teresa Scarman, whose nursery specialises in old-fashioned roses. Here you will find Gallicas – such as 'Belle de Crécy', 'Belle Isis' and 'Camaïeux' – with a short but spectacular flowering season in June, desirable *centifolias*, such as 'Chapeau de Napoléon', and Damasks such as *Rosa damascena* var. *bifera*. The latter was admired by the ancient Romans for its ability (exceptional in those days) to flower again at summer's end. There are also China roses, wild species which are suitable for garden use, and a selection of classic climbers and ramblers. There is an excellent colour catalogue (£2) for buying roses by mail. Open daily, 9a.m.–5p.m. M6 Jct 12, then A5 and follow signs.

Moseley Old Hall, Moseley Old Hall Lane, Fordhouses, Wolverhampton WV10 7HY (tel. 01902-782808), features a reconstruction of a small, 17th-century garden. It is very formal, with a vine-covered tunnel, and a box parterre, the design of which was taken from Thomas Hill's influential book, *The Gardener's Labyrinth*, of 1577. There are old-variety fruit trees, musk roses and naturalised wildflowers in this disciplined but engaging garden. Open late March–Oct, Wed, Sat–Sun, Bank Holiday Mons and Tues following, 12 noon–5p.m. (house opens at 1p.m.), last adm. 4.30p.m.; Nov–mid-Dec, Sun only, 12 noon–4p.m. (house opens at 1p.m.). Entrance (house and garden) £4.20, children £2.10, family ticket £10.50. M6 Jct 11 or M54 Jct 1, then A460, 4m N of Wolverhampton.

Suffolk

MAP NOS 3, 6

S ince Anglo-Saxon times, this has been known as the county of 'southern folk', the 'north folk' living in Norfolk. At the time of the Domesday Book (in 1086) this was the most densely populated region in England; its fens were drained and forests cleared to make way for arable farming and the raising of sheep. The wool industry brought wealth to Suffolk; its merchants built their timbered houses and fine churches in countless villages and towns, with especially lovely examples at Lavenham and Long Melford. The pounding North Sea continually erodes the sandy beaches and low cliffs of the coast, while further inland the atmosphere is quietly pastoral, much as it was in John Constable's day.

Must See
Helmingham Hall,
  Stowmarket – intimate
  fragrant plots around Tudor
  moated manor

Shrubland Hall Gardens

Coddenham, nr Ipswich IP6 9QQ TEL. 01473-830221 (for booking in to the health clinic only: 01473-830404) OWNER Lord de Saumarez HOURS April–early Sept, Sun only, 2–5p.m.; also Bank Holiday Mons, 2–5p.m. ENTRANCE £2.50, OAPs/children £1.50 DIRECTIONS 4m N of Ipswich, turn off A14 to B1113 at Claydon

There are two ways you can get fit at Shrubland Hall; you can check in as a patient at its health clinic and spend a few days following a regime of raw-food diets and remedial treatments or you can spend an afternoon pacing its grand gardens, running up and down the 100-step Italianate staircase. (The Hall is not open to the visiting public.)

The gardens were laid out by Sir Charles Barry, after he completed the Houses of Parliament in 1860. The owners, inspired by their visits to the great Italian gardens, commissioned Barry to create a series of terraces and stairways to descend from their hilltop house. In its heyday, Shrubland was renowned for its gaudy bedding schemes laid out in endless elaborate parterres. Most of them were swept away by the influential gardener William Robinson (*q.v.*) in the 1880s. Robinson abhorred formal, unnatural bedding and he endeavoured to soften the stonework of the terraces in a mantle of roses and vines.

Hidden in the 50-acre grounds are several notable features, including an Algerian summerhouse of larch poles and bamboo, and a large rock garden built in the 1930s by Walter Ingwersen, of the eponymous alpine nursery in Sussex. The conservatory is fine, too, and there is a programme of restoration under way to rescue the scroll-design box maze and dell garden. Among the park's fine trees are several sweet chestnuts planted by monks about 700 years ago, now stooping, venerable specimens with portly girth. Helmingham Hall (*q.v.*) is nearby.

Somerleyton Hall

Somerleyton, nr Lowestoft NR32 5QQ TEL. 01502-730224 OWNER Lord and Lady Somerleyton HOURS April–Oct, Thurs, Sun and Bank Holiday Mons, 12.30–5.30p.m. (also Tues and Wed in July–Aug), house 1–5p.m. ENTRANCE £5.20, OAPs £5, children aged 5–16 £2.60, family ticket £14.60 DIRECTIONS 5m NW of Lowestoft on B1074, 7m SW of Yarmouth on A143 WEB www.somerleyton.co.uk

🟥 ♿ Access 🟥 Gift Shop 🟥 Café 🟥 Plants for Sale

Somerleyton Hall has 12 acres of dignified gardens, fragrant in spring when the azaleas and bluebells are in bloom, and pleasantly colourful in summer. The walled garden, at the entrance, has interesting glasshouses with ridge-and-furrow patterned roofs, designed by Sir Joseph Paxton. There are also unusual 'wall-cases' by Paxton along the outer wall, made for growing wall-trained peaches under glass, but now displaying broader ranges of greenhouse plants.

In the grounds beyond there are Victorian shrubberies and fine specimen trees which bring height and shade to the level site. There is a formal rose garden and terrace on the west front, a sunken garden with bedding plant displays by the conservatory tearoom, and a long iron tunnel of roses and wisteria. The yew maze, by Victorian garden designer W.A. Nesfield, has a grassy mount topped by a pagoda at its centre, very popular with visitors.

Local Hero: Humphry Repton

Born at Bury St Edmunds in 1752, Humphry Repton was the son of an excise officer and educated locally, before being sent to Holland, aged 12. Partially adopted by a wealthy and influential family, he grew up in luxurious surroundings and acquired the manners of a cosmopolitan gentleman. Later, unsuccessful business attempts led him to try out his artistic talents as a landscape gardener, and here he found his métier.

Repton's style favoured balustraded terraces and flowerbeds, rather than the pure grass-and-trees approach of his predecessor, Capability Brown (*q.v.*); his famous Red Books illustrated clients' existing gardens, with flap pages that could be overlaid to demonstrate how the grounds could be improved. Handsome, charming and intelligent, he became greatly sought after. Examples of his work can be seen at Holkham Hall (*q.v.*), Tatton Park (*q.v.*), Sheringham and Sheffield Park (*q.v.*).

STANTON

Wyken Hall

Stanton, Bury St Edmunds IP31 2DW TEL. 01359-250287 OWNER K.M. Carlisle HOURS April–Sept, Sun–Fri, 2–6p.m. (the Leaping Hare Vineyard Restaurant is open daily) ENTRANCE £2.50, OAPs £2, children under 16 free DIRECTIONS 9m NE of Bury St Edmunds off A143. Follow brown tourist signs to Wyken Vineyards

🌿 ♿ Access 🌿 Gift Shop 🌿 Café 🌿 Plants for Sale 🌿 2 for 1 Voucher

Wyken Hall is an exquisite Elizabethan manor house, plastered and pargeted in the local vernacular style, and painted the colour of raw salmon, a shade or two more daring than the average Suffolk pink. At the front, several rocking chairs, brought from Mississippi, peer between espaliered apple trees growing on very tall stems, in the manner more usually used for pleached limes. You know the garden will be interesting, for it has twists of originality, while maintaining traditional form. Also at the front is a quincunx pattern of brick-and-flint circles with low box hedging and seasonal infills of flowers.

Beyond, there is a small garden of edibles beside the house, leading to a border of hot colours – scarlet roses, geums and salvias among bronze-leaved impatiens and dahlias, for example. There are three small, linked gardens of traditional, formal design with box and yew hedging, herbs and a dining terrace, a rose garden with central fountain, a kitchen garden and orchard. A nuttery and dell features mown walks through long grasses and wildflowers leading to a young maze of copper-beech hedging. There are also fine old oaks in the grounds. From the wilder areas there are lovely views back to the house, which squats low and content in its wood-enshrouded gardens, while its ornate chimneys attempt to pierce the skyline.

STOWMARKET

Helmingham Hall

Stowmarket IP14 6EF TEL. 01473-890363 OWNER Lord and Lady Tollemache HOURS May–mid-Sept, Sun only, 2–6p.m. Also pre-booked parties or individuals on Wed, 2–5p.m. ENTRANCE £3.75, children £2 DIRECTIONS 9m N of Ipswich on B1077 WEB www.helmingham.com

🟥 ♿ Access 🟥 Gift Shop 🟥 Café 🟥 Plants for Sale

East Anglia possesses more than its fair share of moated properties. Moats were frequently dug in the Middle Ages to protect crops and livestock, or give a house added security. Helmingham Hall is a house of finely patterned brickwork, built in the 15th century. It sits in its own deep-water moat, while another, rectangular moat to one side contains its walled garden. The garden moat is thought to have been made in Saxon times as a secure cattle enclosure, its boundary fence having been replaced by a wall in 1745.

Within those walls lies a garden of outstanding quality, with exuberant herbaceous borders framing kitchen-garden beds of fruit and vegetables; fruit trees are also fanned against the walls. Tunnels over the paths are engagingly garlanded with sweet peas, runner beans and gourds, and the turf paths bring a note of calm order to anchor the abundance of summer colour.

A herb garden on the opposite side of the house features fragrant masses of old roses, lavender, violas and herbs, and there is a skilfully laid-out knot garden in low box hedging. The banks of the moats are awash with daffodils and cowslips in spring, followed by pink clover and ox-eye daisies in the long grass. It is a peaceful, timeless place, utterly in tune with its surroundings. Shrubland Hall (*q.v.*) is nearby.

And also...

Perforated seep-hoses are available by mail order from **Garden Systems, Whitehouse Farm, Grundisburgh, Woodbridge IP13 6RR (tel. 01473-738280)**. They gently leak water into the soil and are a good way to put irrigation exactly where you need it, at the plants' roots (especially effective when used in conjunction with a digital timer). Greenhouse heaters are also sold.

Goldbrook Plants, Hoxne, Eye IP21 5AN (tel. 01379-668770), specialises in hostas (over 400 varieties), hemerocallis and shade-loving perennials. Mail order (send 4 × 1st-class stamps for catalogue). Open April–Sept, Thurs–Sun; Oct–March, Sat–Sun, 10a.m.–5p.m. Closed Jan, Chelsea and Hampton Court Flower Show periods. Off A140, 6m from Diss.

Mill's Farm Plants and Gardens, Norwich Road, Mendlesham IP14 5NQ (tel. 01449-766425/web www.millsfarmplants.co.uk), specialises in garden pinks, with extensive collections of rare old pinks and some of the best modern hybrids – fringed, laced and sweetly scented. Send 5 × 2nd-class stamps for mail order catalogue. Open Feb–Dec, Wed–Mon, 9a.m.–5.30p.m. On A140, ¼m S of Mendlesham turning.

Mr Fothergill's Seeds, Gazeley Road, Kentford, Newmarket CB8 7QB (tel. 01638-751161), sells 1500 varieties of flower and vegetable seeds by mail order. Free catalogue available on request.

Pearl Sulman, 54 Kingsway, Mildenhall, Bury St Edmunds IP28 7HR (tel. 01638-712297), specialises in growing miniature and dwarf pelargoniums, by mail order only (catalogue £1). Also at this address, Brian Sulman (separate business) offers regal pelargoniums by mail (catalogue 50p).

Over 2500 different flower and vegetable seeds are available in the full-colour mail order catalogue of **Thompson & Morgan Seeds,**

Poplar Lane, Ipswich IP8 3BU (tel. 01473-601090). Notable recent introductions include *Agrostemma* 'Ocean Pearl', *Sphaeralcea* 'Los Brisas' and the flavourful main-crop pea 'Rondo'. Their catalogue is also worth combing for interesting species plants.

Michael Loftus ran the well-known Neals Yard Wholefoods in London before leaving to start **Woottens Plants, Blackheath, Wenhaston, Halesworth IP19 9HD (tel. 01502-478258/web www.woottensplants.co.uk)**, in the early 1990s. The nursery offers hardy and half-hardy perennial plants, including pelargoniums, salvias, penstemons, violas, aquilegias, polemoniums and much more. This is a nursery well worth visiting for the excellent range and quality of its plants. There is an extremely informative and beautifully illustrated mail order catalogue costing £4 containing 2000 plants. Open daily, 9.30a.m.–5p.m., garden May–Sept, Wed only. Donation as entrance fee. Off A12, 2m S of Blythburgh, follow signs.

Surrey

London spreads its urban tentacles into the northern reaches of Surrey, and this county is very much commuter-land with frequent rail services into the city. Substantial areas are still rural, however, and little has changed in parts of the wooded Old West Surrey that Gertrude Jekyll wrote about 100 years ago. Wealden Surrey fared much as Wealden Sussex in earlier centuries, where forests were felled for iron smelting. The chalk ridges of the North Downs provide good walking country, including wooded Ranmore Common and the steep escarpment of Box Hill, which was familiar to Jane Austen and her heroine Emma.

Must See

Painshill, Cobham – pleasant strolls through a slice of 18th-century garden history

The Royal Botanic Gardens, Kew, Richmond – three hundred acres of plants on the edge of London

RHS Wisley Gardens, Woking – flagship gardens of the Royal Horticultural Society

Exceptional in Spring

The Isabella Plantation, Richmond

Worth a Visit in Winter

Polesden Lacey, Dorking

Claremont, Esher

Hampton Court Palace, Kingston-upon-Thames

The Royal Botanic Gardens, Kew, Richmond

RHS Wisley Gardens, Woking

BENTLEY

Bury Court

Bentley, Farnham GU10 5LZ TEL. 01420-23202 OWNER John Coke HOURS Phone for details ENTRANCE Phone for details DIRECTIONS A3, then A31 and follow signs to Bentley

🔲 ♿ Access   🔲 Café   🔲 Plants for Sale

The renowned nursery at Bury Court, formerly known as Green Farm Plants, may be closing in 2002 (write or phone for details). I am hopeful, however, that the adjoining garden will remain open, but do phone to check before visiting.

Made in recent years, the garden is on the site of a walled farmyard. The concrete yard and unsightly grain silo have been entirely removed, and in their place is an unusual garden, designed by the prominent Dutch nurseryman, Piet Oudolf, with additional beds planted by the owner. The central area is a cool green lawn, around which several irregularly shaped beds are planted with hardy perennials, grasses and yew topiaries. Cambered paths of Belgian cobblestones provide a number of interesting routes through the garden. One bed is particularly large, sweeping down the length of the garden and displaying bold, chunky species such as eupatorium, asters, hemerocallis, polygonatums, plus stipa and miscanthus grasses. From late summer through autumn it is a rich tapestry of colours and textures derived from the interplay of foliage, flowers and seedheads. A bed at the foot of a sunny barn wall is planted with a collection of cistus species. There is also a prettily planted gravel garden of sedums, eryingiums in variety, lavenders, santolinas and drought-tolerant grasses.

COBHAM

Painshill Landscape Garden

Portsmouth Road, Cobham KT11 1JE TEL. 01932-868113 OWNER Painshill Park Trust HOURS April–Oct, Tues–Sun and Bank Holiday Mons, 10.30a.m.–6p.m. (last adm. 4.30p.m.); Nov–March, Tues–Thurs, Sat–Sun and Bank Holiday Mons, 11a.m.–4p.m. (or dusk if earlier), last adm. 3p.m. ENTRANCE £4.50, OAPs/students £4, accompanied children £2 (under 5s free), pre-booked adult groups of 10 or more £4 per person (not weekends) DIRECTIONS From M25 Jct 10 take A3 towards London, then A245 towards Cobham, garden on right WEB www.painshill.co.uk

🔲 ♿ Access   🔲 Gift Shop   🔲 Café

A long, sinuous route winds its way through this very attractive, 158-acre park, leading you, as its creator intended, through a series of snapshot views, in the early-18th-century style. The route is laid out beside a long, wiggly, 14-acre lake and uphill into woodlands that lead to a slim, four-storey-high gothic tower. This is fantastical and Rapunzel-like, with its crenellations and pointed turret roof (sometimes open on weekends up to the 3rd floor; ask on entry). In 1768 a visitor noted being able to see St Paul's Cathedral, Windsor Castle and many other landmarks, and today (apparently) it is possible to see Canary Wharf, in London's Docklands, from the tower's roof.

The garden's history is fascinating. It is contemporary with Stourhead (*q.v.*) and Stowe (*q.v.*) and was made by one Charles Hamilton, a plantsman, painter and gifted designer, who bought the estate and various neighbouring farms and barren heathland in order to make a 250-acre garden and park. Alas, all of his fortune drained away into his lavish creation over the 35 years that he worked on it. In severe debt, he had to sell Painshill in 1773. It was cherished by a series of owners until the intervention of the Second World War. In 1948 it was sold again, but the new owner split up the estate and much of it became obscured by years of neglect. Fortunately, the classic garden area is now in the hands of a Trust which is running a long-term restoration, rebuilding its bridges and buildings. On the route you will see some of Hamilton's wonderful follies, including a blue-and-white Turkish tent on a hilltop, 'Roman' ruins, designed to inspire a melancholy mood, a Chinese bridge, a sparkly grotto, a 'ruined abbey' and a whimsical gothic temple.

DORKING

Polesden Lacey

Nr Dorking RH5 6BD TEL. 01372-458203/452048 OWNER The National Trust HOURS Grounds open all year, daily, 11a.m.–6p.m. (or dusk if earlier); house late March–early Nov, Wed–Sun and Bank Holiday Mons, 11a.m.–5p.m. ENTRANCE Grounds £4, children £2, family ticket £10; house £3, children £1.50, family ticket £7.50 DIRECTIONS 5m NW of Dorking, from M25 Jct 9 take A24 and follow signs

🌿 ♿ Access 🌿 Gift Shop 🌿 Café 🌿 Plants for Sale

There are renowned flower gardens at Polesden Lacey, but at any time of year, my favourite part of the 30-acre garden is the Long Walk – a broad turf path that runs for quarter of a mile along the hillside, offering panoramic views of the opposite hill and the wooded valley between. It dates from 1761, but Richard Brinsley Sheridan, the play-wright, had it considerably lengthened after he bought the property in 1797.

The flower gardens include a walled rose garden, dissected by lavender and box-edged paths, over which run pergolas of climbing roses. There are clematis here too, and an ancient Chinese wisteria. There are lavenders and irises in profusion, and further flower borders including a grand herbaceous border running for 450ft beneath a sunny wall. The winter garden is small but amazingly cheering and fragrant in the bleakest season, with winter-flowering shrubs, hellebores and carpets of early bulbs.

ESHER

Claremont Landscape Garden

Portsmouth Road, Esher KT10 9JG TEL. 01372-467806 OWNER The National Trust HOURS Open all year, Nov–March, daily, except Mon, 10a.m.–5p.m. (or dusk); April–Oct, Mon–Fri, 10a.m.–6p.m., Sat–Sun and Bank Holiday Mons, 10a.m.–7p.m. ENTRANCE £3.70, children £1.85, family ticket £9.25 (50p discount if travelled by public transport) DIRECTIONS On S side of Esher, on E side of A307

🚻 ♿ Access 🚻 Gift Shop 🚻 Café

Claremont is a wonderful venue for a picnic or a lakeside stroll and has been since the 18th century (bring a hamper, a bottle of wine and good company for a matchless afternoon of tranquillity under its fine trees). Now it is revered by historians as one of the most important examples of the transitional stages between the formal gardens of the very early 18th century and the more naturalistic landscapes that followed in succeeding generations.

Within the 49 acres that survive, it has a spectacular three-acre turf amphitheatre, which the National Trust puts to good use every July as an outdoor auditorium for evening picnics and musical entertainment, and there are numerous woodland paths among camellias and rhododendrons.

Sir John Vanbrugh, Charles Bridgeman and William Kent, the great trio of influential English designers in the early part of the 18th century, each left their mark on the garden. Vanbrugh designed the Belvedere, a hilltop viewing pavilion; the great turf amphitheatre was Bridgeman's work, while we have Kent to thank for the serenely contoured lake and woods. Lord Clive of India bought the estate in 1768 and employed Capability Brown (*q.v.*) to expand and further soften the contours of the garden. Brown brought in some of the fine cedars that thrive in this great garden today.

GUILDFORD

Loseley Park

Nr Guildford GU3 1HS TEL. 01483-304440 (Leisure Department for enquiries); 01483-505501 (information line) OWNER Mr and Mrs M.G. More-Molyneux HOURS Early May–late Sept, Wed–Sat and Bank Holidays (also Sun in June–Aug), 11a.m.–5p.m.; house June–Aug, Wed–Sun, 1–5p.m. ENTRANCE £3, concessions £2.50, children £1.50, garden summer ticket (valid May–Sept for ticket holder and one guest) £15 (house and garden £6, concessions £5, children £3) DIRECTIONS W of A3, 3m SW of Guildford off B3000 WEB www.loseley-park.com

🔲 ⛾ Access   🔲 Gift Shop   🔲 Plants for Sale

Loseley Park is best known for its herd of Jersey cattle, or at least for the fruit yogurts and ice creams the herd's milk yield produces, but there's more. Its Elizabethan stone mansion is set in a pretty park, and a lot of work has been done in the gardens in recent years to make them a major attraction.

The two-and-a-half-acre walled garden, formerly a kitchen garden for the house, is divided into themed areas. They include a rose garden with more than 1000 roses, the beds edged with box hedging, and bold herbaceous borders offering spring bedding and bulbs, followed by splendid late summer colour from heleniums, red-hot pokers, crocosmias, cosmos and dahlias. But the largest area is devoted to a formal fragrant herb garden edged with rope-twist tiles; it is divided into sections featuring dyers' plants, medicinal species, ornamental, cosmetic and wild herbs and a culinary section. The dyers' herbs section is instructive: the popular garden plant *Alchemilla mollis*, or lady's mantle, produces a green dye for wool; *Hypericum perforatum* produces a red silk dye; tagetes makes yellow food colouring and *Galium verum* has long been used to give a yellow tint to cheeses. Woad is a handsome, yellow-flowered herb, not widely grown, but it was used by the ancient Britons to make a deep blue dye for warriors' painted-on tattoos. Light refreshments are served.

KINGSTON-UPON-THAMES

Hampton Court Palace

KT8 9AU TEL. 020 8781 9500 OWNER H.M. The Queen HOURS Park all year, daily; palace all year, Tues–Sun, 9.30a.m.–6p.m., Mon, 10.15a.m.–6p.m. (closes at 4.30p.m., Nov–March) ENTRANCE Parking £3; park free; maze or Privy Garden £2.80, children £1.90; palace £10.80, concessions £8.30, children £7.20, family ticket £32.20 DIRECTIONS On A308 at junction with A309 on N side of bridge over Thames and close to Hampton Court Main Line station WEB www.hrp.org.uk

🔲 ⛾ Access   🔲 Gift Shop   🔲 Café

This is the famous Thames-side palace of Tudor, Stuart and later kings and queens. Its long canal and avenues of trees radiating out from the palace in a *patte d'oie* (goose-foot) design were laid out in the formal French style by Charles II in 1662. They are reminiscent of the fabulous gardens Charles had seen being made at Versailles.

Today, Charles II's creation is overlaid by the splendour that was added by William III and Queen Mary, who came from Holland in 1689. The massive yew pyramids arranged in neat lines in front of the palace were originally small topiary obelisks, but 300 years of growth have thickened them into giant umbrellas in the lawns. Capability Brown (*q.v.*) worked here in 1768 and he is responsible for planting one of Hampton Court's most renowned features, the massive 'Black Hamburgh' grape vine. This gnarled, monster vine in its own glasshouse is said to have roots that reach the Thames. It produces plenty of grapes which are sometimes sold to the public during the months of August and September.

The maze, now slightly bare in places, is being restored over a five-year period, but visitors can still puzzle their way to its heart. The palace's most colourful areas are the enclosed sunken garden, lavishly bedded out for spring and summer; William III's Privy Garden, recently reopened after a massive restoration programme, which is a fabulous baroque garden of swirling parterres, box hedging, yew topiaries and period flowers, with a massive hornbeam tunnel trained over oak trelliswork along one side. Hampton Court is the annual venue of Britain's largest outdoor horticultural show, which is spread over several days in mid-July.

LIMPSFIELD

Titsey Place

Limpsfield RH8 0SD TEL. 01273-407056 (Kate Moisson) OWNER Trustees of the Titsey Foundation HOURS Mid-May–late Sept, Wed, Sun and Bank Holiday Mons, 1–5p.m. Easter Mon: house closed but garden open ENTRANCE £2, children £1 (house and garden £4.50, guided tours only), private visits welcome if booked in advance DIRECTIONS Off the B269 just N of Oxted and M25, from A25 on E side of Oxted, go left into Limpsfield village, after High St turn left on sharp bend into Bluehouse Lane and right into Water Lane, then follow road under M25 through park to walled garden car park

If food and kitchen-gardening are prime seams of interest for you, then a visit to Titsey Place should definitely be in your diary. The 200-acre property, on a south-facing slope of the North Downs, has been in the same family since 1534. Its house contains an art collection, but keeps a low profile as council planners won't allow adequate sign-posting for fear of visitors' cars congesting the narrow local roads. Nevertheless, the one-acre walled kitchen garden has been recently restored at a cost of half-a-million pounds and it is hoped that enough visitors will come to make it financially viable.

Rare peaches and melons are among the ancient fruit varieties cultivated under gleaming glass, along with flowering pot-plants, and there is also an orchid house. The main emphasis, however, is on preserving unusual and nearly-extinct varieties of vegetables – they include over 100 different tomatoes, 70-odd aubergines and around 60 chilli-pepper varieties, as well as sea kale and salads.

Roses and cut-flowers are also grown in the walled area and the 15 acres of gardens around the house include extensive rose beds, Victorian shrubberies, parkland trees and a herbaceous border.

The Shirley Poppy

Shirley, a village now engulfed by urban Croydon, lends its name to an exquisite bloom, bred by local vicar Revd William Wilks 100 years ago from a stray field poppy (*Papaver rhoeas*) found in his garden.

Instead of the usual plain scarlet, this rogue's petals had a halo of white – providing a host of breeding possibilities. From its seeds the Revd Wilks bred generations of poppies, selecting only the best until he achieved an enhanced race bearing white, pastel pinks and double flowers as well as red, all with pale centres. Shirley poppies are still widely sold by seed merchants, although they are not always as true to type as Revd Wilks would have wished.

PIRBRIGHT

Four Aces

Chapel Lane, Pirbright, nr Guildford GU24 0JY TEL. 01483-476226 OWNER Mr and Mrs R. St John Wright HOURS Open several days end of June–early July for National Gardens Scheme, also pre-booked private visits welcome, May–July. Guide dogs only ENTRANCE £2, children free DIRECTIONS 5m NW of Guildford on A322 Bagshot Road. Just before Brookwood arch, directly opposite West Hill Golf Club, turn left into Cemetery Pales. After just under 1m, turn sharp left after village sign into Chapel Lane. Four Aces is the 5th house on the right

🌢 Plants for Sale

Jane St John Wright is passionate about roses and her extremely pretty two-thirds-of-an-acre garden is packed with them, draped over pergolas and arches, filling out borders and mixed with pastel-coloured herbaceous perennials. The style is relaxed and cottagey, with a recently made formal herb garden, two ponds, and terraces studded with pots overflowing with summer flowers. It is a lovely, personal, romantic garden that brings many visitors pleasure every year and has earned Jane requests from friends and neighbours to redesign their gardens.

RICHMOND

Ham House

Ham Street, Richmond TW10 7RS TEL. 020 8940 1950 OWNER The National Trust HOURS House April–Oct, Sat–Wed, 1–5p.m. (last adm. 4.30p.m.); garden open all year, daily, except Thurs–Fri, 11a.m.–6p.m. (or dusk if earlier) ENTRANCE House £6, children £3, family ticket £15; garden £2, children £1, family ticket £5 DIRECTIONS On S bank of River Thames, W of A307 at Petersham; use Sandy Lane. House is walkable from Richmond via Thames towpath (1½m) and is close to Richmond main line and Tube stations

 ⬛ & Access ⬛ Gift Shop ⬛ Café ⬛ Plants for Sale

The splendid house (which is worth seeing – the room stewards are very informative) dates from the 17th century, and its 20-acre gardens are suitably formal to reflect the period style. The Cherry Garden, to one side, is a geometrical parterre of box-edged beds infilled with lavender and santolina (buzzing with bees through the summer), bound by hornbeam tunnels above yew hedging. There are spacious lawns on the south side of the house leading to a 'wilderness' in 17th-century style, with formal hedged enclosures and wildflowers in spring. The terrace beside the house has been recently restored with formal planting, too. The walled garden has a handsome orangery (where refreshments are served); also some fine old trees, a long border of flowers for cutting, and rose beds (of modern varieties) for summer colour.

It is a deservedly popular riverside venue for south-west Londoners, with spacious, well-kept grounds that are pleasant to stroll in at any season.

RICHMOND

The Isabella Plantation

Exceptional in Spring

Richmond Park, Richmond TW10 5HS TEL. 020 8948-3209 OWNER The Crown (tenants: Royal Parks Agency) HOURS Open all year, daily, dawn–dusk ENTRANCE Free DIRECTIONS In southern section of Richmond Park, between Kingston Gate and Robin Hood Gate, car park nearby

⬛ NPC

The Isabella Plantation is an enclosed woodland garden within the great deer park of Richmond which, at over 2500 acres, is one of the largest enclosed parks in Britain. Two of its three ponds, which are now the haunt of wildfowl, were dug in 1861 as watering-holes for livestock; the third pond and a stream were added as part of the more modern development of the woodland garden. It is a tranquil oasis within this 'green lung' of south-west London, and a brilliant spectacle from April to June, with 15 varieties of deciduous azalea and around 40 evergreen Kurume azaleas (a National Collection), plus 50 different species of rhododendron and 120 hybrids in the plantation. These exotic shrubs began to be added in the 1950s, making a garden feature of the natural oak, beech and birch woodland. There is also a heather garden in a small clearing near the largest pond, a bog garden of rushes, gunnera and *Osmunda* ferns, with highlights of flag iris and primulas, and an acer glade, at its most colourful in autumn.

Old Gardening Books Galore

Surrey is well served for reading matter when it comes to gardening, particularly where older books are concerned. **Mike Park, 351 Sutton Common Road, Sutton SM3 9HZ (tel. 020 8641 7796)**, is a Kew-trained horticulturist who exchanges his trowel (for some of the time) to run a business dealing in second-hand and antiquarian gardening books. Gardens, botany, flower arranging and general gardening come within his compass. He regularly sets up a sales stand at the Royal Horticultural Society's monthly Westminster shows, but also buys and sells by mail order (free catalogue on request) and from the above address by appointment only. **Ivelet Books, 18 Fairlawn Drive, Redhill RH1 6JP (tel. 01737-764520/web www.abebooks.com/home/ivelet)**, also buy and sell gardening, botany, landscape architecture and natural history books by mail, and stock many of the classic 20th-century works that are now out of print. They send out two or three catalogues each year (available on request). **Lloyds of Kew, 9 Mortlake Terrace, Kew, Richmond TW9 3DT (tel. 020 8940 2512/web www.lloydsofkew.com)**, faces more or less on to Kew Green, diagonally opposite the main gate of Kew Gardens, close to Kew Gardens main line and Tube stations. This shop also stocks a range of second-hand and antiquarian garden-related books, particularly botanical ones.

The Lutyens and Jekyll Partnership

The partnership of the architect Sir Edwin Lutyens (1869–1944) and plantswoman/writer Gertrude Jekyll (1843–1932) was a fruitful one, and their influence on 20th-century garden design has been profound. They collaborated on the planning of 120 gardens prior to the First World War; Jekyll's contribution was usually in providing planting plans (especially of colour-themed herbaceous borders) to embellish the hard landscaping that Lutyens designed. But there was also an energetic exchange of ideas between these two like-minded people, although they were a generation apart in age.

Both favoured using natural, indigenous materials such as local stone and timbers, and they sympathised with the aims of the Arts and Crafts movement. Both were also highly talented artists in their own fields and were fascinated and charmed by the formal gardens of the Italian Renaissance. Their work still survives to a greater or lesser degree at numerous properties around the country, including Lindisfarne Castle (*q.v.*) in Northumberland, Hestercombe (*q.v.*) in Somerset and here in Surrey, where it all began.

Lutyens designed Miss Jekyll's own house (not open) at **Munstead Wood, Heath Lane, Godalming GU7 1UN (tel. 01483-417867)**, where her garden has been undergoing magnificent restoration work in recent years. It is open several days each year, for the National Gardens Scheme (tel. 01483-211535 for this year's dates). Entrance £2, OAPs £1, children free. Take B2130 from Godalming towards Horsham, after 1m turn left down Heath Lane, garden on right.

RICHMOND

The Royal Botanic Gardens, Kew

Kew, Richmond TW9 3AB TEL. 020 8940 1171 (recorded information)/020 8332 5000 OWNER Ministry of Agriculture, Fisheries and Food HOURS Open all year, daily, 9.30a.m.–4p.m., closing later in summer (up to 7p.m., depending on season) ENTRANCE £6.50, concessions £4.50, under 16s free DIRECTIONS Main gate on Kew Green, S of Kew Bridge; Kew Gardens Tube and Main Line stations are nearby WEB www.kew.org

🌻 ♿ Access 🌻 Gift Shop 🌻 Café

Whether you arrive at the main gate on Kew Green, or the Victoria Gate (with its shop and visitor centre) which is convenient for Kew Gardens station, you will not be far from the chief attractions, Kew's great glasshouses. The Princess of Wales Conservatory has carefully controlled micro-climates ideal for plants from bone-dry deserts as well as those from humid tropical rainforest (do not miss the huge *Victoria amazonica* waterlilies with leaves up to 8ft across). The famous Victorian Palm House is home to yet more weird and wonderful plants from other lands, as is the even prettier Temperate House. Both were designed by Decimus Burton, the gifted Victorian architect.

Yet Kew's 300 acres encompass a great deal more. They were originally two 18th-century royal estates and, although the gardens are steeped in history, they are renowned worldwide for scientific research and their important botanical collections. Kew Palace is a pretty brick house in the Dutch style, with small formal gardens attached and a laburnum arched walkway, lovely in May. There are long walks through the arboretum to the pagoda, and several pretty stone temples are dotted about the grounds. The Marianne North Gallery, some distance from the main attractions, is one of Kew's most fascinating but least-known assets. It is crammed with the astonishing flower and landscape paintings of Miss North, an intrepid woman who travelled through remote parts of the world, usually alone, in the mid-19th century.

The Hileys' Colourful Exotics

Visitors to the Royal Horticultural Society's shows in London and around the country will be familiar with exotic displays by **Brian and Heather Hiley, 25 Little Woodcote Estate, Telegraph Track, off Woodmansterne Lane, Wallington SM5 4AU (tel. 020 8647 9679)**. But the show displays are only a taster; visit the nursery in summer and you are treated to fabulous potted displays of aeoniums and agapanthus, cannas and clivias, pelargoniums and fuchsias, and much else. All are clustered around the old bicycles, well-pumps and other bygones that contribute to the character of this marvellous nursery. There is a mail order catalogue (send 3 × 1st-class stamps) listing their specialist range of tender perennials and grasses. Open all year, Wed–Sat, 9a.m.–5p.m., but phone before visiting between Oct and Easter. Take Woodmansterne Lane from A2022 or A237 and follow signs.

RHS Wisley Gardens

Wisley, nr Woking GU23 6QB TEL. 01483-224234 OWNER The Royal
Horticultural Society HOURS Open all year, Mon–Fri, 10a.m.–6p.m. (or dusk if
earlier), Sat, 9a.m.–6p.m., also Sun for RHS members only ENTRANCE £5,
children £2 (RHS members free) DIRECTIONS 7m NE of Guildford, by A3;
signposted from A3 and Jct 10 of M25 WEB www.rhs.org.uk

🔲 ♿ Access 🔲 Gift Shop 🔲 Café 🔲 Plants for Sale 🔲 NPC

Wisley is the gardeners' Mecca, in all sorts of ways. As the flagship
garden of the Royal Horticultural Society, its 240 acres demonstrate
every conceivable method of gardening and its huge popularity (over
700,000 visitors per year) has led to recent revisions and replanning
which will be undertaken over a period of years. Some people (myself
included) come to saunter through the gardens in all seasons, for
there are always new plants to admire.

The grounds, occupying an undulating site of sandy soil, are graced
by many mature trees, among which are areas devoted to mixed flower
borders, bedding plant displays, heathers, conifers, rhododendrons and
associated plants, Mediterranean plants, fruit trees, vegetable gardens,
small model gardens, hedging plants, wonderful glasshouses, and much
more. The early 20th-century rock garden, on a hillside, is one of the
best of its kind, and there are lovely water gardens below it. There are
also scientific trial grounds which are always interesting, where different
varieties of certain plants are grown together and compared. Another
reason to visit is the extremely well-stocked horticultural and botanical
bookshop, and the plant centre is renowned for its well-grown and well-
cared-for plants, selected with a discerning eye.

Wisley holds National Collections of *Calluna vulgaris*, crocus,
Daboecia, *Epimedium*, *Galanthus* and *Rheum* species and cultivars.

And also...

There is nothing extraordinary about **Chessington Nurseries,
Leatherhead Road, Chessington KT9 2NF (tel. 01372-725638)**,
nothing, that is, until you stroll into the glasshouses at the rear of this
suburban garden centre. This is what makes a visit worthwhile, for
there are indoor plant displays that almost rival those of a major
botanical garden. Citrus trees and passiflora are specialities, but the
whole range of conservatory plants is tremendous. Open all year,
Mon–Sat, 9a.m.–6p.m. (closes at 5p.m. in Jan), Sun, 10a.m.–4p.m. M25
Jct 9, then follow signs to World of Adventures.

Drummonds, 25 Kirkpatrick Buildings, London Road, Hindhead GU26 6AB (tel. 01428-609444/web www.drummonds-arch.co.uk), has an ever-changing selection of architectural antiques and salvage, including old garden ornaments and statuary, iron gates, garden seats, Victorian glass cloches, etc. Great for a rummage around to find something unusual or with a period ambience. Open daily, Mon–Fri, 9a.m.–6p.m., Sat–Sun, 10a.m.–5p.m. On A3 at Hindhead.

The Hannah Peschar Sculpture Garden, Black and White Cottage, Standon Lane, Ockley RH5 5QR (tel. 01306-627269/web www.hannahpescharsculpture.com), is a tranquil, beautifully planted woodland garden with springs and pools, laid out by garden designer Anthony Paul. Its stock of contemporary sculpture changes as pieces are sold, and the gardens themselves are inspiring. Open May–Oct, Fri–Sat, 11a.m.–6p.m., Sun and Bank Holidays, 2–5p.m; other days (but not Mons) and Nov–April by appointment only. Entrance £8, OAPs/students £6, children £5. M25 Jct 9, then S on A24, then A29 to Ockley, right at Cathill Lane into Standon Lane.

Pantiles Nursery, Almners Road, Lyne, Chertsey KT16 0BJ (tel. 01932-872195/web www.pantiles/nurseries.co.uk), specialises in selling really large container-grown trees and shrubs, including unusual and rather exotic varieties, such as dicksonia tree ferns, from Tasmania, and sculptural, weeping cedars. Also bedding plants in profusion. Free catalogue available on request. Open all year, Mon–Sat, 9a.m.–6p.m., Sun, 10a.m.–4p.m. Off A320, 2m S of M25 Jct 11.

Vann, Vann Lane, Hambledon GU8 4EF (tel. 01428-683413), has five acres of idyllic woodland and flower gardens around a Tudor house with later additions. Gertrude Jekyll (*q.v.*) designed its water garden, with a brook flowing through oak woods underplanted with carpets of spring bulbs. There are roses and herbaceous flowers, topiaries, azaleas and a fine pergola walk. Open for 3–4 individual weeks Easter–July, 10a.m.–6p.m.; also private visits by written application. Entrance £3, children 50p. When open for National Gardens Scheme, signposted from A283.

Vernon Geranium Nursery, Cuddington Way, Cheam, Sutton SM2 7JB (tel. 020 8393 7616/web www.geraniumsuk.com), is a specialist grower of pelargoniums (around 1100 varieties) and fuchsias. Plants are dispatched as rooted cuttings, or you can buy pot-grown plants at the nursery. Mail order catalogue £2. Open March–July, Mon–Sat, 9.30a.m.–5.30p.m., Sun 10a.m.–4p.m. M25 Jct 8, then onto Banstead Road, nursery on right.

Winkworth Arboretum, Hascombe Road, Godalming GU8 4AD (tel. 01483-208477), is a hillside woodland with two lakes. It is wonderful in spring when the azaleas and bluebells are in bloom, and spectacular in autumn, with tints of maples, Katsura trees (cercidiphyllum), and mountain ash in great variety. Open all year, daily, dawn–dusk. Entrance £2.70, children £1.35, family ticket £6.75. B2130 from Godalming.

Sussex

MAP NO. 3

F orming a slender lozenge-shape along England's south-eastern coast, Sussex enjoys the contrasts of a wonderful coastline, the chalky spine of the South Downs and the fertile inland sweeps of the Weald, an area once covered with ancient oak forests. Farmland now, the Wealden area is still dotted with tiny hamlets and speckled with ancient ponds. These pools sometimes appear in the middle of nowhere, but are relics of a medieval iron industry where anvils once caused a clamour along the valleys, while the great oaks made prime timbers for warships and fodder for furnaces.

Must See
Nymans, Haywards Heath – richly planted grounds span the seasons for interest
Great Dixter, Northiam – one of the influential gardens of the 20th century

Exceptional in Spring
Wakehurst Place, Ardingly
Leonardslee, Horsham
Petworth House, Petworth
Champs Hill, Pulborough

Exceptional in Summer
West Dean, Chichester
Parham House, Pulborough

Exceptional in Autumn
Denmans, Fontwell
Sheffield Park, Uckfield

Worth a Visit in Winter
Wakehurst Place, Ardingly
Nymans, Haywards Heath
Sheffield Park, Uckfield

Wakehurst Place

Selsfield Road, Ardingly, nr Haywards Heath, West Sussex RH17 6TN
TEL. 01444-894066 OWNER The National Trust, maintained by the Royal
Botanic Gardens, Kew HOURS All year, daily, Nov–Jan, 10a.m.–4p.m.; Feb,
10a.m.–5p.m.; March and Oct, 10a.m.–6p.m.; April–Sept, 10a.m.–7p.m. (last
adm. ¹/₂hr before closing) ENTRANCE £6.50, OAPs £4.50, children free
DIRECTIONS 1¹/₂m NW of Ardingly, on B2028; M23 Jct 10, then A264 towards
East Grinstead, then B2028, garden on right WEB www.rbgkew.org.uk
🌳 ⅄ Access 🌳 Gift Shop 🌳 Café 🌳 NPC

This is a great garden for seeing plants, for its collections – especially
of trees and shrubs – are vast. It is run by Kew's Royal Botanic
Gardens as their second home and, with all its prominent signposting
directing you this way and that, you might get the impression that
it is more about function than aesthetics.

Beside the house is a walled garden of herbaceous flowers and pretty
climbers, and beyond it a very formal garden enclosed by yews. Follow
the signs to the Water Garden and things become more relaxed. There
are sumptuous magnolias on the slopes and, if you're here in spring,
look out for colonies of *Lathraea clandestina*, an unusual parasitic plant,
with flowers the colour of amethyst carpeting the grass at the
streamside. The water gardens have recently been revamped (wonderful
plants but, alas, what happened to the attractive old bridge?). Around
and beyond are woodland walks into the valley and Himalayan glade.
Rhododendrons feature strongly and the gardens contain National
Collections of betula (birches), hypericum, nothofagus (southern beech)
and skimmia. Anyone wanting to keep honey-bees happy should plant
Skimmia × confusa 'Kew Green' which has wonderful, sweet perfume
carrying in the air for yards; at Wakehurst I noted it seems to be the bee
banquet in spring.

Light and airy modern buildings within the grounds house the new
millennium seed bank, a gene bank of the world's seeds, with interesting
exhibits for visitors.

West Dean Gardens

West Dean, Chichester, West Sussex PO18 0QZ TEL. 01243-818210 OWNER
Edward James Foundation HOURS March–Oct, daily, 11a.m.–5p.m. (10.30a.m.,
May–Sept) ENTRANCE £4.50, concessions £4, children £2, family ticket £11, season
ticket £16, family season ticket £40 DIRECTIONS 5m N of Chichester on A286
WEB www.westdean.org.uk
🌳 ⅄ Access 🌳 Gift Shop 🌳 Café 🌳 Plants for Sale

There is a recently restored and deeply impressive two-and-a-half-acre Victorian walled garden in the grounds. With its astounding ranges of flowers, fruits and vegetables and restored working greenhouses, this is now the best part of the garden. Especially so, if you are interested in chillies and peppers – they grow more than 90 different varieties here, and hold an entertaining Chilli Pepper Fiesta one weekend in late summer. Tomatoes also feature strongly. There are interesting displays set up in the walled garden buildings and a tool and mower collection.

In the 35 acres of pleasant ornamental grounds (also under continuous refurbishment and updating), there is a remarkable 100yd-long pergola of stone piers and stout timber cross-beams. It was designed by Harold Peto (*q.v.*) in 1910 and has also been recently restored. It focuses on a pavilion at one end and a formal sunken garden at the other. There are mixed and herbaceous borders, rustic summerhouses and a water garden. If you still want to stretch your legs, there is a two-and-a-quarter-mile circuit walk that climbs through the park to the 45 acres of St Roches Arboretum.

EAST GRINSTEAD

Standen

East Grinstead, West Sussex RH19 4NE TEL. 01342-323029 OWNER The National Trust HOURS March–Oct, Wed–Sun and Bank Holiday Mons, garden 11a.m.–6p.m., house 12.30–4p.m.; garden only Nov–mid-Dec, Fri–Sun, 11a.m.–3p.m. ENTRANCE House and garden £5.50, children £2.75, family ticket £13.75; garden only £3, children £1.50; joint ticket with Nymans Garden (*q.v.*) £9, children £4.50 DIRECTIONS 2m S of East Grinstead, signposted from B2110; use M23 Jct 10 or M25 Jct 6

🌿 Gift Shop 🌿 Café

Standen is the archetypal small country house in the Arts and Crafts style of the late 19th and early 20th centuries. It was designed by the architect Philip Webb, a lifelong friend of William Morris, and much of its interior is decorated with Morris's distinctive floral wallpapers and fabrics. The 12-acre gardens around it were made in the same period, and are the perfect foil to this appealing house. A broad terrace on the south side nestles the house into its hillside surroundings with winding paths to explore the shrubberies westwards up the hillside, and more formal areas to the east; a big slab of lawn directly in front is a light and airy breathing space between the two.

It is a garden of great Wealden views, with intriguing walks among fragrant azaleas, contorted Japanese acers, magnolias and other woodland planting. The formal gardens feature rugosa roses, nepeta and irises enclosed by stepped yew hedging. Notable in this area are the huge 'Annie Elizabeth' and 'Bismarck' apple espaliers, planted 100 years ago.

Croftway Nursery Irises

For a brief couple of weeks in late May and early June, 10 acres of fields near the seaside resort of Bognor Regis are transformed into a Van Gogh landscape of pale blues and mauves, dusky browns, deep reds, mutable pinks, yellows and golds. These are the iris fields of **Croftway Nursery, Yapton Road, Barnham, Bognor Regis, West Sussex PO22 0BG (tel. 01243-552121/web www.croftway.co.uk), between Yapton and Barnham on B2233, leave A27 at Fontwell onto A29, then left onto B2233**, well worth visiting at this time. There is something about irises – the richness of their colours, the delicacy of individual petals, the rigid nobility of their stems, their sweet fragrance and the sheer ephemerality of their flowers – that I find completely intoxicating. Croftway sells over 150 different varieties, including tall bearded, intermediate bearded and dwarf bearded types, and a good range of *Iris sibirica* cultivars. Their Iris Picnic Weekend at the height of flowering time is now an annual event, when over 26,000 plants are in bloom in the fields. (The owner recommends a telephone call near the time, to check bloom status before travelling.) Irises are also sold by mail (dispatched in August and September only). The nursery specialises in hardy geraniums and other hardy perennial plants as well. A catalogue is free on request. Nursery open March–Nov, Mon–Sat, 9a.m.–5p.m., Sun, 10a.m.–4p.m.

FONTWELL

Denmans

Fontwell, nr Arundel, West Sussex BN18 0SU TEL. 01243-542808 OWNER John Brookes HOURS March–Oct, daily, 9a.m.–5p.m. ENTRANCE £2.95, OAPs £2.65, children (4–16) £1.75 DIRECTIONS Turn S off A27, W of Fontwell racecourse (signposted) WEB www.denmans-garden.co.uk

🌼 ♿ **Access** 🌼 **Gift Shop** 🌼 **Café** 🌼 **Plants for Sale**

For the last 20 years this has been the home and garden of John Brookes, internationally renowned garden designer and bestselling author, whose titles include *Room Outside* and *The New Small Garden Book*.

The four-acre garden, delightfully peaceful and now in its maturity, was begun 50 years ago by one Joyce Robinson and her husband, who acquired the Denmans property after the Second World War. John Brookes arrived at a fortunate time to carry on and develop the garden that the ageing Mrs Robinson had begun on a gentle south-facing slope, with free-draining, gravelly soil.

Within its walled garden John Brookes has created an aromatic shrubby herb garden with plantings among the gravels and random pavings, renowned for its relaxed, contemporary look. Beyond are lawns and long-grass wildflower areas, punctuated by maturing trees and boldly swirling and curving island beds filled with 'incidents' of good planting. 'I let the planted areas self seed and then pull out what I don't want to keep,' says Mr Brookes, who tends towards a natural style of planting, flowing and modern, but underpinned by carefully thought out proportions and design. There is a particularly effective 'dry river' of cobble stones, begun by Mrs Robinson and refined by Mr Brookes, which meanders down to a pool at the garden's southern perimeter. An old vinery houses tropical plants and an aviary of budgies and quails. A larger glasshouse, which formerly nurtured the Robinsons' tomato crops, displays a substantial collection of half-hardy plants, mostly from South Africa and Australasia. It's worth looking at the nursery, which features some interesting plants from the garden.

HAYWARDS HEATH

Nymans Garden

Handcrosss, nr Haywards Heath, West Sussex RH17 6EB TEL. 01444-400321 OWNER The National Trust HOURS March–Oct, Wed–Sun and Bank Holiday Mons, 11a.m.–6p.m. or dusk if earlier (last adm. 5.30p.m.); Nov–Feb, Sat–Sun, 11a.m.–4p.m. ENTRANCE House and garden £6, children £3, family ticket £15; joint ticket with Standen (q.v.) £9, children £4.50 DIRECTIONS Signposted off M23/A23, SE of Handcross

 ♿ & Access 🌼 Gift Shop 🌼 Café 🌼 Plants for Sale 🌼 2 for 1 Voucher

Nymans is one of the great gardens of the south-east and another personal favourite of mine. When spring has been mild, the sight of its magnolias can bring tears to the eyes and there is much else to see early on, with its woods flooded by bluebells, extensive use of bulbs – both naturalised and bedded out – and terrific ranges of early-blooming shrubs.

Early summer sees the long grass of the hillside pinetum awash with wildflowers, and in June the small, formal rose garden is at its height of splendour. There are good herbaceous borders in the Top Garden with flowers chiefly in yellow and blue and, at high summer, do not miss the Walled Garden, with its central path ablaze on either side with cosmos, dahlias, salvias, heliotrope and other firework-coloured flowers continuing the splendour until autumn. And there is so much else: a heather and rock garden, Japanese features, a wisteria-drenched pergola, an avenue of majestic limes, sturdy topiary around the romantic ruins of the house. All in all, a garden for all seasons, and one I never tire of visiting.

William Robinson at Gravetye

Gravetye Manor, Vowels Lane, nr East Grinstead, West Sussex RH19 4LJ (tel. 01342-810567), 5m SW of East Grinstead, use M23 Jct 10, then A264 towards East Grinstead, then B2028, is now an extremely luxurious country house hotel and restaurant, but it also has first-class horticultural credentials, as the former home of William Robinson (1838–1935).

Robinson was the most influential and widely read gardening writer of his day – a sort of Geoff Hamilton of the Victorian and Edwardian age – whose seminal work, *The English Flower Garden*, ran to 15 editions during his own lifetime and several more later. He was a prolific writer and publisher of various gardening journals and his approach to wild gardening – using 'perfectly hardy exotic plants under conditions where they will thrive without further care' – pre-empted the current vogue for naturalistic and ecological planting styles by a century.

Born in Ireland and trained at Glasnevin, then Regent's Park, Robinson invested his new-found wealth from publishing in the Elizabethan mansion of Gravetye Manor. He developed its 30-acre gardens with a certain amount of formality near the house and extensive woodland plantings beyond. His gardens have been extensively restored in recent years, but are open only to hotel guests except for a perimeter walk open on Tues and Fri, which is free.

HORSHAM

Architectural Plants

Cooks Farm, Nuthurst, Horsham, West Sussex RH13 6LH TEL. 01403-891772 OWNER Angus White HOURS Open all year, Mon–Sat, 9a.m.–5p.m. ENTRANCE Free DIRECTIONS From A24 Horsham to Worthing road take A272 E for 2m, then take 1st turning left to Maplehurst and Nuthurst, nursery is in Nuthurst, behind the Black Horse pub WEB www.architecturalplants.com
🌿 Nursery 🌿 Mail Order

This is a thoroughly entertaining nursery. It specialises in foliage effects, including plants such as fan palms, banana trees, cycads, bamboos, eucalyptus, puyas, pines, agaves and aralias. 'In the jargon of horticulture, these are knows as "architectural plants",' says the proprietor, Angus White. 'Not because they belong in buildings – although many of them look very fine in the conservatory – but because the plants themselves have their own "architecture" – strong, sometimes spectacular, shapes which bring a distinctive year-round presence to a garden.' The nursery's exotic ambience is enhanced by the colonial-style office (complete with corrugated-iron roof and spacious verandahs) and its own interesting garden, laid out around the office and car parking area. It has a grove of eucalyptus trees, underplanted with bamboos, phormiums, fan-palm trees and other exotic undergrowth, such as *Lobelia tupa*, an exciting, salvia-like plant with red lipstick flowers and big, soft foliage. There is also by far the best loo you will find in any nursery, in a beautifully proportioned wooden building, set on stilts. The nursery's catalogue (free on request) is informative and among the most entertaining you will ever read. Architectural Plants also has a new garden centre at **Lidsey Road Nursery, Woodgate, Chichester, West Sussex PO20 6SU (tel. 01243-545008)**; open daily except Sat, 10a.m.–4p.m. (closed all Bank Holidays except Good Friday).

HORSHAM

Leonardslee Gardens

Exceptional in Spring

Lower Beeding, nr Horsham, West Sussex RH13 6PP TEL. 01403-891212
OWNER The Loder Family HOURS April–Oct, daily, 9.30a.m.–6p.m. ENTRANCE
April and June–Oct, £5; May, Mon–Fri, £6, Sat–Sun, £7 DIRECTIONS 4m SW of
Handcross at Jct of B2110 and A281; leave M23 at Handcross WEB
www.leonardslee.com
🌿 Gift Shop 🌿 Café 🌿 Plants for Sale

See Leonardslee's great trees and famous rhododendrons reflected in its tranquil lakes and it is hard to imagine the scene that would have greeted you 400 years ago. But just think: in the 1580s it was noted that Sussex 'is full of iron mines all over it; for the casting of which there are furnaces...and an abundance of wood is yearly spent; many streams are drawn into one channel, and a great deal of meadow ground is turned into ponds and pools for driving mills by the flashes, which, beating with hammers upon the iron, fill the neighbourhood round about it, night and day with continual noise'.

Today, it is those hammer ponds that furnish the garden so exquisitely with water. The woods grew again and much planting of rhododendrons and other flowering shrubs began in the first half of the 19th century. From 1889 onwards, Sir Edmund Loder, scion of a famous Sussex gardening family, introduced more exotic plants to Leonardslee, and also a herd of Tasmanian wallabies, whose descendants continue to hop about the grounds. Sir Edmund's superb 'Loderi' hybrid rhododendrons were bred here in 1901 and make substantial trees today, bearing huge trumpet flowers, pastel-tinted and sweetly scented. The 240-acre grounds include a fine rock garden, an alpine house, a collection of bonsai trees and a temperate glasshouse, but the real attraction is the chance to stride along its miles of woodland paths and gasp in wonder that heavy industry can leave such a captivating legacy.

Traditional Sussex Trugs

Sussex is the home of the trug, a curved, shallow basket ideal for carting hand-tools, vegetables, fruits or cut flowers through the garden. The word trug derives from the Anglo-Saxon 'trog', meaning boat-shaped, and it is made by steaming and bending slender strips of chestnut and willow. The strips are then riveted firmly to a piece of wood that forms the rim, and another strip wraps around the middle to make a handle. The first Sussex trugs were made in the 1820s by Thomas Smith & Co. of Herstmonceux. They are still made there and marketed as **Sussex Trugs Ltd, Thomas Smith's Trug Shop, Hailsham Road, Herstmonceux, East Sussex BN27 4LH (tel. 01323-832137), on A271 in centre of village**. You can buy them by mail (prices from around £20–£60 incl. postage), or call at the shop, open all year, Mon–Fri, 8a.m.–5p.m., Sat 9a.m.–4p.m.

NORTHIAM

Great Dixter

Dixter Lane, Northiam, nr Rye, East Sussex TN31 6PH TEL. 01797-252878 OWNER Christopher Lloyd OBE HOURS April–Oct, Tues–Sun and Bank Holiday Mons, 2–5p.m.; nursery open all year, 9a.m.–12.30p.m. and 1.30–5.30p.m. ENTRANCE £4.50, children £1 (house and garden £6, children £1.50) DIRECTIONS ½m N of Northiam, turn off A28 at Northiam post office WEB www.greatdixter.co.uk

🌿 Gift Shop 🌿 Plants for Sale 🌿 Nursery 🌿 Mail Order

This garden is famous, partly because it is the lifelong home of plantsman and gardening writer Christopher Lloyd; also because it has been loved, nurtured and developed for nearly a century, or at any rate since Sir Edwin Lutyens (*q.v.*) laid his crisp design on it before the First World War.

Part of its magic is that it seems in a time-capsule, protected by its own grounds and stout hedges from suburban encroachment of the rude world beyond. Even the motor car cannot get near the 15th-century house, for the gardens envelop it and access is only via long and narrow paths. A network of yew hedging and flagstone paths divides Dixter's seven acres into spaces of different character and purpose, demonstrating Lutyens's genius for design, but also his sensitivity to the vernacular buildings of this ancient manor farm.

Within the different areas, planting is dynamic and bold. The most famous view is down the Long Border, a richly planted sunny border filled with mixed annuals, perennials, bulbs, shrubs, small trees and climbing plants (particularly clematis) that perform with brilliant colour over a long season. There are experimental beds of perennial plantings, a kitchen garden, large areas of flower-filled meadow dotted with trees, lots of Edwardian topiaries, informal ponds and a thrilling garden of exotic foliage, with colourful cannas and dahlias. The discreet sunken garden, in a corner between barns and oasts, was designed by Mr Lloyd's father and has yet more lively planting, around a formal pool. There is also an excellent nursery of reasonably priced plants available by mail (catalogue £1).

PETWORTH

Petworth House

Exceptional in **Spring**

Petworth, West Sussex GU28 0AE TEL. 01798-342207 (infoline 01798-343929) OWNER The National Trust HOURS House and pleasure grounds open end March–early Nov, Sat–Wed, 11a.m.–5.30p.m., pleasure grounds also open some weekends in March for spring bulbs, 12 noon–4p.m. (phone for dates); deer park open all year, daily, 8a.m.–sunset (but closes at 12 noon for 3 days in late June for events) ENTRANCE Deer park: free; pleasure grounds: £1.50, children free; house and pleasure grounds: £7, children £4 (under 5s free), family ticket £18 DIRECTIONS In centre of Petworth

🌳 ♿ Access 🌳 Gift Shop

A five-mile-long stone wall runs around the huge deer park of Petworth House. The park, with its majestic serpentine lake, was landscaped by Capability Brown (*q.v.*) and covers 700 acres of undulating grassland peppered with clumps of trees and grazed by deer. It is a great place to come for a long walk and a picnic.

The gardens, or pleasure grounds, near the house, cover 30 acres and are magical through the spring, with grassy walks enlivened by narcissi, primroses, bluebells and fritillaries. Rhododendrons and azaleas bloom among unfurling leaves of Japanese acers and many ornamental trees. The interior of the huge 17th-century mansion house with its art collection is worth seeing, especially J.M.W. Turner's evocative landscape paintings of the park. There is also a restaurant on the premises.

CELEBRITY CHOICE

Stephen Anderton

Presenter of BBC Radio 4's *Growing Places*
and *The Times* gardening correspondent

'I love **Great Dixter** (*q.v.*). The garden hangs around the house so well and, wherever you are in the garden, you are always aware of the house. It's a place that is lived in. The garden's Edwardian layout is formal but also incredibly flexible: things are always changing in the planting. Very few gardens work as hard as this one does at being good in all seasons. There is complicated, hard-working herbaceous detail throughout the year, and in high summer, at a time when many southern gardens are looking worn out, Great Dixter's borders are just starting to get going. Also the planting is very selective; nothing gets past an uncritical eye and the garden has lots of personality stamped on it.'

PULBOROUGH

Champs Hill

Exceptional in Spring

Coldwaltham, Pulborough, West Sussex RH20 1LY TEL. 01798-831868
OWNER Mr and Mrs D. Bowerman HOURS Open for several Weds and Suns in March, May and Aug, for the National Gardens Scheme (Wed, 11a.m.–4p.m., Sun, 2–6p.m.) ENTRANCE £2.50, children free DIRECTIONS From A29 at Coldwaltham turn N towards Fittleworth. Champs Hill is 300yds on right
🚗 ♿ **Access** 🚗 **Plants for Sale**

This is a really unusual heather garden, planted with great conviction – very pretty in spring and spectacular in August. From various seats on its south-facing slope there are panoramic views of the South Downs, with the meanders of the River Arun winding through the valley below. It covers 27 acres on a sandy hilltop, much of the garden being birch, pine and oak woodland, thinned out here and there for plantings of rhododendrons and naturalised bulbs. Around the house there is a significant collection of heathers, about 300 different varieties, most of them being forms of the summer-flowering bell heather (*Erica cinerea*) and ling (*Calluna vulgaris*). Planting is in bold drifts, following the gentle contours of the ground to make large island beds, with turf paths winding through.

PULBOROUGH

Parham House

Nr Pulborough, West Sussex RH20 4HS TEL. 01903-742021 OWNER Parham Park Ltd HOURS April–Oct, Wed–Thurs, Sun and Bank Holiday Mons, 12 noon–6p.m., house 2–6p.m. (last adm. 5p.m.) ENTRANCE Garden only £4, children 50p; house and garden £5.50, OAPs £4.50, children £1, family ticket £11 DIRECTIONS 4m SE of Pulborough on A283

🌿 ♿Access 🌿 Gift Shop 🌿 Café 🌿 Plants for Sale

Parham

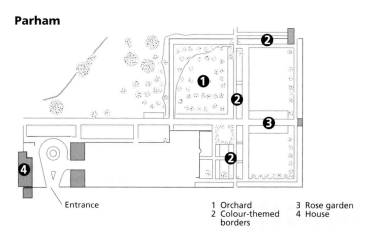

Entrance

1 Orchard
2 Colour-themed borders
3 Rose garden
4 House

A long drive runs through the ancient deer park at Parham, and you immediately know you are somewhere special. The high ridge of the South Downs frowns from a distance and the Elizabethan stone house, with its courtyards and outbuildings, sits like a little village in its fortunate setting. (The house is worth seeing, especially during the mid-July garden festival weekend.)

The seven-acre pleasure grounds behind the house include a brick maze set into the turf (always popular with children) and rambling walks to the lake. The walled gardens are the chief attraction, however. There are sumptuously planted, colour-themed double herbaceous borders of blues, purples and greys in one area; yellows and golds in another; deep purples, pinks and golds in yet another. There are walls garlanded in roses and clematis, an orchard, a kitchen garden, cut-flower borders, a lavender garden, a wendy house with its own garden, flower-filled greenhouses, and further herbaceous borders around the perimeter. Somewhere special indeed.

Flower-arranging courses are also organised, specialising in the abundant but relaxed Parham style.

TICEHURST
Pashley Manor

Ticehurst, East Sussex TN5 7HE TEL. 01580-200888 OWNER Mr and Mrs James Sellick HOURS April–Sept, Tues–Thurs, Sat and Bank Holiday Mons, 11a.m.–5p.m., groups by appointment only ENTRANCE £5.50, OAPs/children £4.50 (under 6s free) DIRECTIONS 10m SE of Tunbridge Wells on B2099 between Ticehurst and A21 (signposted) WEB www.pashleymanorgardens.com
▰ Café ▰ Plants for Sale

The manor is a handsome Tudor house with Jacobean and Queen Anne additions (not open), in a lovely parkland setting. There are shrubberies of rhododendrons and camellias, walled flower gardens, natural springs feeding a series of ponds, and fine views of the Sussex countryside. Tulip time is celebrated with a festival in April and old-fashioned roses (of which there are many here) feature in a mid-summer rose festival each year.

UCKFIELD
Sheffield Park Garden

Nr Uckfield, East Sussex TN22 3QX TEL. 01825-790231 OWNER The National Trust HOURS Jan–Feb, Sat–Sun only, 10.30a.m.–4p.m.; March–Oct, Tues–Sun and Bank Holiday Mons, 10.30a.m.–6p.m. (or dusk if earlier); Nov–Dec, Tues–Sun, 10.30a.m.–4p.m. (or dusk if earlier); last adm. 1 hr before closing ENTRANCE £4.60, children £2.30, family ticket £11.50 DIRECTIONS 5m NW of Uckfield, on E side of A275 (between A272 and A22)
▰ ₺ Access ▰ Gift Shop ▰ Café ▰ Plants for Sale ▰ NPC

The first and only time I have seen a wild mink is when one scampered across the grass and dipped into one of the lakes at Sheffield Park, one autumn. And autumn (particularly mid-October) is the classic time to visit, when the rich scarlets, russets, brilliant golds and deep greens of the surrounding trees are mirrored in its broad waters, their varied silhouettes casting shimmery patterns on a reflected sky. Spring is lovely here too, as rhododendrons and Ghent azaleas (there is a National Collection here) are added to the mix and the woodland glades are awash with bluebells.

The park covers 120 acres and both Capability Brown (*q.v.*) and Humphry Repton (*q.v.*) contributed to its landscaping. Much planting was carried out early this century, however, and the fantastic collection of exotic trees which bring so much colour and shape in every season is largely due to these later plantings. You can take any one of several marked routes, depending on time and energy available, to circuit one or more of the four large lakes. Among the autumn highlights are the scarlet tupelo trees (*Nyssa sylvatica*), equally vivid liquidambars, and the rusty gold swamp cypress and dawn redwood, both of which, unlike most conifers, are deciduous.

And also...

Highdown, Littlehampton Road, Goring-by-Sea, Worthing, West Sussex BN12 6PE (tel. 01903-501054), is a remarkable garden, made in a chalk-pit. The creation of Sir Frederick Stern (1884–1967), it became his experimental ground in seeing which plants could thrive on relentlessly chalky soil. It is well known for its peonies, irises and hellebores, and Stern's book, *The Chalk Garden* (out of print but available from some libraries), is still instructive for anyone gardening on similar ground. Open all year, daily, Dec–Jan, 10a.m.–4p.m.; Feb–March, 10a.m.–4.30p.m.; April–Sept, 10a.m.–6p.m.; Oct–Nov, 10a.m.–4.30p.m. Entrance free, donations welcome. On N of A259.

Holly Gate Cactus Nursery, Billingshurst Road, Ashington, West Sussex RH20 3BB (tel. 01903-892930), is utterly fascinating. It holds one of the largest collections of cacti and succulents in the country, with ravishing display gardens under glass. Cacti and their seeds are available by mail (send 2 × 1st-class stamps for a catalogue). Open daily, 9a.m.–5p.m. Entrance (cacti display only) £2, concessions £1.50. On B2133, ½m from A24.

W. E. Th. Ingwersen Ltd, Birch Farm Nursery, Gravetye, East Grinstead, West Sussex RH19 4LE (tel. 01342-810236/web www.ingwersen.co.uk), is a very traditional and long-established alpine nursery, with plants attractively displayed in cold frames and pans. Bulbs, conifers and some half-hardy plants are also sold. It is a fascinating nursery to browse in and, with its traditional glasshouses, is redolent of times past. Send 2 × 1st-class stamps for a plant list. Open March–Sept, daily, 9a.m.–1p.m. and 1.30–4p.m.; Oct–Feb, Mon–Sat, 9a.m.–1p.m. and 1.30–4p.m. Off B2110, follow signs to Gravetye or Kingscote station; use M23 Jct 10.

Lime Cross Nursery, Herstmonceux, Hailsham, East Sussex BN27 4RS (tel. 01323-833229) is *the* place to go to for conifers – they sell around 300 different kinds, from dwarf species to potentially large trees, and hedging plants in variety. Also a general stock of trees, shrubs and climbers. Free catalogue available on request. Open all year, daily, Mon–Sat, 8.30a.m.–5p.m., Sun, 9a.m.–5p.m. On A271.

Merriments Gardens, Hawkhurst Road, Hurst Green, East Sussex TN19 7RA (tel. 01580-860666), is a well established garden centre with an adjoining four-acre display garden (plus restaurant). The nursery stocks a broad general range of plants and sundries. In the garden there are colourful flower borders, a rock and scree garden, a foliage border and an arched walkway inspired by Claude Monet's at Giverny. Catalogue available for £1.50. Open all year, daily (garden April–Sept), Mon–Sat, 9.30a.m.–5.30p.m., Sun, 10a.m.–5.30p.m. Entrance £3.50, children £2. Just off A21.

Perryhill Nurseries Ltd, Edenbridge Road, Hartfield, East Sussex TN7 4JP (tel. 01892-770377/web www.perryhillnurseries.co.uk), always has lots of interesting plants among its broad range of stock. As well as offering good selections of hardy and half-hardy perennials and fruit, it keeps a well-chosen range of roses, including wild species, hybrid musk and unusual shrub roses. Open March–Oct, 9a.m.–5p.m.; Nov–Feb, 9a.m.–4.30p.m. M23 Jct 10, then E on A264, then 1m N on B2026.

Pots and Pithoi, The Barns, East Street, Turners Hill, West Sussex RH10 4QQ (tel. 01342-714793), sells hand-made, pale-terracotta pots imported from Crete. They have the typical Mediterranean oil-jar shape, some with handles, some delicately patterned; most would make distinctive eye-catchers when well placed in the garden. Open all year, daily, 10a.m.–5p.m. (closing 4p.m. in winter); closed Sat and Sun in Jan. M23 Jct 10, then A264, then B2028 to Turner's Hill, left onto B2110 and on left.

Warwickshire

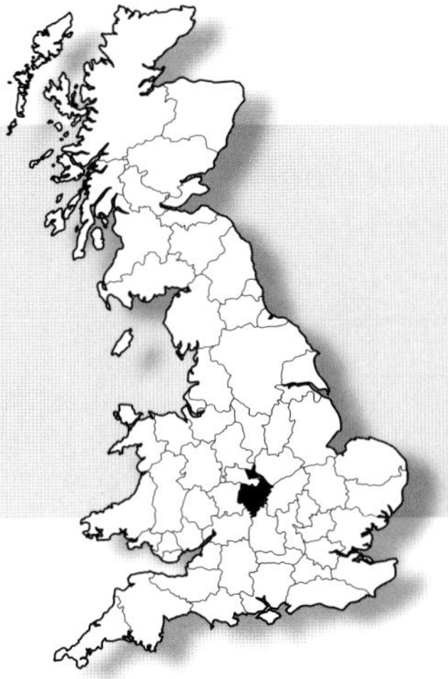

MAP NO. 5

The industrial heartland of Birmingham and the Black Country lies on the north-western edge of this county, yet the gently undulating landscape around Stratford and Warwick seems a world apart. This is a land of fertile pastures, where agriculture still plays a prominent role, and timber-framed houses of earlier centuries survive as testament to the great oak forests which once covered the area. The oaks are no longer plentiful, but fine specimens in the roadside hedgerows are occasional reminders that this region was once heavily wooded.

Exceptional in Summer
Packwood, Lapworth
Ryton Organic Gardens,
  Ryton-on-Dunsmore

Coughton Court

Alcester B49 5JA TEL. 01789-762435 OWNER The National Trust in association with Mrs C. Throckmorton HOURS Mid-March–late April, Sat–Sun; May–Sept, Wed–Sun and Bank Holiday Mons, 11a.m.–5.30p.m.; early Oct, Sat–Sun, 11a.m.–5p.m. ENTRANCE House and garden £6.95, children £3.45, family ticket £21.50; garden only £5.10, children £2.05, family ticket £15.75; walled garden £2.50, under 15s free DIRECTIONS 2m N of Alcester on A435 WEB www.coughtoncourt.co.uk

🚻 ♿ Access 🏵 Gift Shop 🏵 Café 🏵 Plants for Sale

The house dates from the mid-16th century, but the formal gardens around it are barely 10 years old, having been designed by Mrs Throckmorton's daughter. There is a great deal of water in the grounds, with the River Arrow meandering through and providing water for a smaller stream and weir pool. The river bank is planted with moisture-loving perennials; spring flowers and bulbs, including magnificent bluebells, light up the ground under some fine old trees.

The extensive walled garden is part of an ongoing refurbishment programme. It features abundant plantings of perennials and old-fashioned roses, themed areas of red tones and a white garden, an early summer garden, a hot border and a cool border, and long views and vistas.

Charlecote Park

Charlecote, Wellesbourne CV35 9ER TEL. 01789-470277 OWNER The National Trust HOURS Late March–early Nov, Fri–Tues, 11a.m.–6p.m.; house, 12 noon–5p.m. ENTRANCE £5.80, children £2.90 (inclusive ticket, house and garden) DIRECTIONS On N side of B4086, 1m W of Wellesbourne, 5m E of Stratford-upon-Avon, use A46, then B4086; from M40 use Jct 15, then A46 and B4086 WEB www.ntrustsevern.org.uk

🚻 ♿ Access 🏵 Gift Shop 🏵 Café

The house at Charlecote was built in the 1550s, but now little remains of its 17th-century garden with its straight canals and elaborate parterre designs. Capability Brown (*q.v.*) made sweeping alterations to the 240-acre park in the 18th century, but was refused permission to fell the famous avenue of trees.

A century ago, 20,000 bedding plants were produced yearly at Charlecote, used in a series of display beds in the garden forecourt where today there are low-maintenance lawns. Colourful beds and containers are sited near the house, however, and a handsome deer park with trees lies beyond, through which the River Avon flows.

Legend has it that the young William Shakespeare was caught poaching deer here in 1558. Outside the park gates is the **Charlecote Fruit and Flowers Nursery**, offering well-grown and well-displayed perennials, bulbs and alpines.

LAPWORTH

Packwood House Gardens

Lapworth, Solihull B94 6AT TEL. 01564-783294 OWNER The National Trust HOURS Mid-March–Nov, Wed–Sun and Bank Holiday Mons, 11a.m.–4.30p.m. (closes at 5.30p.m., May–Sept); house 12 noon–4.30p.m. ENTRANCE £2.60, children £1.30; house and garden £5.20, children £2.60, family ticket £13; joint ticket with Baddesley Clinton (*q.v.*) £8.50, children £4.25, family ticket £21.25 (gardens only £4.25, children £2.10) DIRECTIONS Off A3400 (2m away, signposted), 2m E of Hockley Heath, 11m SE of central Birmingham

⬛ ♿ Access   ⬛ Gift Shop   ⬛ Café   ⬛ Plants for Sale

From the entrance driveway, you get a tantalising glimpse of Packwood's famous yew topiary, beyond the wall of the 10-acre garden. The yews are trimmed into tall, comfortingly rounded cone shapes of varying heights, set in plain lawns, giving the effect of a crowd of people. Beyond, a spiral path leads up a mount thickly planted with box hedging, the top of which is crowned with a mushroom of yew. This area is known as the Sermon on the Mount.

There are remnants of a formal early 18th-century garden beside the Elizabethan house, with a walled area including bee boles at the foot of the southern wall, and attractive brick gazebos built into each of the four corners. Exceptionally well-grown herbaceous flower borders bring dazzling colour to this garden in the summer. Packwood also possesses an unusually large collection of sundials arranged around the house and garden, presumably because an occupant from an earlier century had an obsession with the passing of time.

LEAMINGTON SPA

Jephson Gardens

The Parade, Leamington Spa TEL. 01926-450000 OWNER Warwick District Council HOURS Open all year, daily, 9a.m.–dusk ENTRANCE Free DIRECTIONS In town centre, main entrance off the Parade, opposite Royal Pump Rooms

⬛ ♿ Access

Royal Leamington Spa has elegant Regency streets and is renowned for its summer floral displays. In its heyday, the rich and famous (including the Duke of Wellington and the actress, Sarah Bernhardt)

came to Leamington to take the waters. The Royal Pump Rooms are close to the entrance of the beautiful Jephson Gardens where 13 acres of grounds are laid out with interesting specimen trees, colourful bedding displays and waterside walks beside the broad River Leam.

RYTON-ON-DUNSMORE

Ryton Organic Gardens

Ryton-on-Dunsmore, Coventry CV8 3LG TEL. 024 7630 3517 OWNER The Henry Doubleday Research Association HOURS Open all year, daily, 9a.m.–5p.m. ENTRANCE £3, concessions £2, under 16s free DIRECTIONS 5m SE of Coventry, by A45 (signposted) WEB www.hdra.org.uk

🌿 ♿ Access 🌿 Gift Shop 🌿 Café 🌿 Plants for Sale 🌿 2 for 1 Voucher

Ryton Organic Gardens

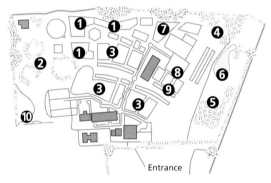

Entrance

1 Animal pens	6 Lake
2 Fruit gardens	7 Paradise Garden
3 Various themed	8 Rose garden
beds and gardens	9 Ornamental kitchen
4 Craftsman's tree	garden
collection	10 Forest garden
5 Conservation area	

This is the national home of organic gardening, with a series of small demonstration plots on a level 10-acre site. The aim is to educate and encourage people to take a chemical-free, eco-friendly approach to gardening, and the results are certainly impressive.

The essence of organic gardening lies in creating a fertile, humus-rich soil environment to provide plants with nourishment, enabling them to build up some resistance to pests and diseases. Composting and mulching have a big role to play in the gardens, and organic methods using barrier pest controls and natural predators are also demonstrated.

Features include a rose garden, an ornamental kitchen garden, herb gardens, rare vegetables, alpine banks, colourful flowerbeds and a forest garden. A recent development is the Geoff Hamilton Paradise Garden, created to celebrate the life of the popular TV gardener, who did so much to further the cause of organic gardening.

Hand-made Terracotta Pots

Whichford Pottery, at Whichford, nr Shipston-on-Stour CV36 5PG (tel. 01608-684416/web www.whichfordpottery.com), 23m from Oxford, take A3400, turn right after Long Compton, has become famous in recent years for its tough, hand-thrown terracotta pots, which are annually turned into magnificent displays at Chelsea and other flower shows. The pottery was founded by Jim Keeling, who now employs more than 20 local people in the business.

Each pot is made by throwing or hand-moulding the blended local clays, then the pots are decorated with swags, basketweave designs, or specially ordered patterns such as family crests, before firing. The Whichford designs have a characteristically flared rim, which allows for greater tolerance of soil expansion during frosty weather; traditional Long-Toms are also very popular. If you cannot get to the pottery (open Mon–Fri, 9a.m.–5p.m., and Sat and Bank Holidays, 10a.m.–4p.m.) there is an excellent mail order catalogue (send 4 × 1st-class stamps), pots being delivered nationwide by carrier.

WARWICK

The Mill Garden

Mill Street, Warwick CV34 4HB TEL. 01926-492877 OWNER Arthur Measures Estate HOURS Easter–Sept, phone for details ENTRANCE Phone for details
🌿 ♿ Access 🌿 Plants for Sale

This one-acre garden beneath the walls of Warwick's famous castle is reached from Mill Street. It is a haven of tranquillity beside the River Avon and includes the old castle mill, complete with water wheel, and views of the ruins of the old town bridge. There are mixed shrub and flower borders and roses and clematis clamber through the trees. The owners will open the garden three or four days a week during the summer months – phone for details.

Warwick Castle

Warwick CV34 4QU TEL. 01926-406600 OWNER The Tussauds Group
HOURS Grounds open all year, daily, April–Oct, 10a.m.–6p.m., Nov–March,
10a.m.–5p.m. ENTRANCE Castle and grounds £11.50, OAPs £8.20, children
£6.75, family ticket £30 DIRECTIONS In the centre of Warwick, signposted and
clearly visible, 2m from M40 Jct 15

🌺 Gift Shop 🌺 Café

Warwick is a handsome town of generously proportioned streets and
houses, its castle generally reckoned the finest medieval example in
the country. Perched picturesquely on a bank above the River Avon,
its grounds were landscaped by Capability Brown (*q.v.*) in the 18th
century. Within the 60-acre gardens, a fine conservatory dating from
1786 houses a model of the famous Warwick Vase – a huge,
beautifully decorated Roman urn. The peacock gardens feature both
real ones and yew topiary imitations, and sumptuous flowers in the
parterre. But the rose garden (made in 1986 from an original Victorian
design of 1868) is exceptional. There are pillars, arches and rope swags
garlanded by climbers and ramblers, with formally arranged beds of
scented shrub roses.

While here, it is worth seeing the amusing waxworks exhibition
displayed through 12 rooms of the castle. It features, in a remarkably
lifelike way, a weekend house party of 1898, but is best seen without
crowds early or late in the day.

And also...

Arbury Hall, nr Nuneaton CV10 7PT (tel. 024 7638 2804), is a
gothicised Tudor/Elizabethan mansion set in 40 acres of parkland, with fine trees and woods awash with spring bluebells.
Rhododendrons, azaleas and a large wisteria provide colour in the
same season, and are followed by displays of roses. The novelist
George Eliot was born on the estate, which featured in her *Scenes
From Clerical Life*. Open Easter–Sept, Bank Holiday Suns and Mons
only, 2–6p.m. Entrance £6, children £3.50, family ticket £14 (garden
only £4, children £2.50). From M6 Jct 3 take A444, signposted from
Nuneaton.

**Baddesley Clinton, Lapworth, Knowle, Solihull B93 0DQ (tel.
01564-783294)**, is an atmospheric, moated manor house, now owned
by the National Trust and little changed since 1634. A modestly
planted walled flower and fruit garden lies to one side. The grounds
include gentle woodland walks around the moat and small lake; a

pleasant walk up to St Michael's church is lined with daffodils in spring, being densely carpeted with bluebells shortly afterwards. Open late Feb, Nov and Dec, Wed–Sun and Bank Holiday Mons, 12 noon–4.30p.m., March–Oct, daily, 12 noon–5p.m. (closes at 5.30p.m., May–Sept); house March–Oct, Wed–Sun and Bank Holiday Mons, 1.30–5p.m. (closes at 5.30p.m., May–Sept). Entrance £5.60, children £2.80, family ticket £14; grounds only £2.80, children £1.40, joint ticket with Packwood House Gardens (*q.v.*) £8.50, children £4.25, family ticket £21.25 (gardens only £4.25, children £2.10). M42 Jct 5, then A41, then A4141 to Chadwick End and follow signs.

The **Shakespeare Birthplace Trust, Henley Street, Stratford-upon-Avon CV37 6QW (tel. 01789-204016/web www.shakespeare.org.uk)**, runs several properties in and around Stratford-upon-Avon, including **New Place/Nash's House** in the town centre (well signposted). This is the site and grounds of Shakespeare's home from 1597 until his death. The Elizabethan-style garden is a reconstruction, with a well-planted and gloriously colourful (although not very authentic) knot garden, surrounded by tunnel walks in Tudor-style trellis work, and further ornamental flower gardens beyond. Open mid-March–mid-Oct, Mon–Sat, 9.30a.m.–5p.m., Sun, 10a.m.–5p.m.; mid-Oct–mid-March, Mon–Sat, 10a.m.–4p.m., Sun, 10.30a.m.–4p.m. Entrance £3.50, concessions £3, children £1.70, family ticket £8.50. **Anne Hathaway's Cottage** is a drive away at Shottery (signposted) on the western side of town, and features a pleasant country cottage garden of box bushes and annual flowers, surrounding the thatched cottage where Shakespeare's wife lived before her marriage. Open mid-March–mid-Oct, Mon–Sat, 9a.m.–5p.m., Sun, 9.30a.m.–5p.m.; mid-Oct–mid-March, Mon–Sat, 9.30a.m.–4p.m., Sun, 10a.m.–4p.m. Entrance £4.50, concessions £4, children £2, family ticket £11.

West Midlands

MAP NO. 5

This strongly urban region encompasses the conurbations of Birmingham, West Bromwich, Walsall and Wolverhampton, areas which expanded very quickly during two centuries of industrialisation. Consequently, the region is surrounded and dissected by busy arterial roads, but beyond the urban sprawl, tranquillity returns suddenly in rural, hidden-away villages. Even the commercial heart of Birmingham becomes a floral feast for a week in mid-June, during the Gardeners' World Live Show, at the National Exhibition Centre.

Worth a Visit in Winter
Birmingham Botanical
  Gardens, Birmingham

Birmingham Botanical Gardens and Glasshouses

Westbourne Road, Edgbaston, Birmingham B15 3TR TEL. 0121-454 1860 OWNER Birmingham Botanical Gardens and Horticultural Society Ltd HOURS Open daily all year, Mon–Fri, 9a.m.–7p.m., Sat, 9a.m.–8p.m., Sun, 10a.m.–8p.m., or dusk if earlier ENTRANCE £5, concessions £2.70, family ticket £13 (£14, Suns and Bank Holiday Mons in summer) DIRECTIONS 1m SW of city centre, signposted locally in Edgbaston; from M5 (3m away) use Jct 3, then take Halley Road, garden on right WEB www.birminghambotanicalgardens.org.uk

🌿 ♿ Access   🌿 Gift Shop   🌿 Café   🌿 Plants for Sale

This wonderful, 15-acre Victorian park is still imbued with its atmosphere of an earlier age, especially when the brass bands play on a Sunday afternoon in the elegant bandstand.

Unlike many other botanic gardens, this was laid out on its creation in the early 1930s as a public amenity and pleasure garden. Its emphasis is on display, which it does magnificently (complete with exotic birds). The steamy glasshouses include a palm house with tree ferns, cycads and orchids; an orangery packed with flowering plants among the citrus trees; a cactus and succulent house; and a fine tropical house, with banana plants, pineapples and a 24ft lily-pool. Outdoors, the tarmac paths gently ramble past shrubberies of rhododendrons, herbaceous borders, roses, marvellous summer bedding displays, fine Victorian rock and scree gardens, and much more.

Wightwick Manor

Wightwick Bank, Wolverhampton WV6 8EE TEL. 01902-761400 OWNER The National Trust HOURS March–Dec, Wed–Thurs, 11a.m.–6p.m., Sat, Bank Holiday Suns and Mons, 1–6p.m., and other days by appointment; house Thurs, Sat and Bank Holidays, 1.30–5p.m. (last adm. 4.30p.m.) ENTRANCE £2.40, children free; house and garden £5.50, children £2.75 DIRECTIONS 3m W of Wolverhampton, up Wightwick Bank (off A454 beside the Mermaid Inn)

🌿 Gift Shop   🌿 Café

Birmingham Botanical Gardens (*q.v.*) are swirly and bright, redolent of the the dawn of the Victorian age, but those at Wightwick Manor, fashioned a couple of generations later, coincide with Victoria's twilight. The 17-acre gardens were laid out from 1887 to 1906 and convey the formal inclinations of the age, with dark yew hedges and topiary, and a formal stone terrace with oak balustrade. Interestingly, this garden is an exact contemporary of those made in Surrey and elsewhere during the Lutyens and Jekyll partnership (*q.v.*), but it lacks the architectural flair of the former and the flower-power of the latter.

The interior of the house gives a better clue to the garden; it is heavily decorated in the Pre-Raphaelite manner, with many original furnishings by William Morris and paintings by Dante Gabriel Rossetti, accompanied by dark, carved panelling and stained-glass windows. Outdoors, the yews form complementary dark walling, as a backdrop to brighter incidents of flowers. There are roses and herbaceous borders, an orchard and, beyond it, rhododendrons gathered around two pools.

And also...

Ashwood Nurseries, Ashwood Lower Lane, Ashwood, Kingswinford DY6 0AE (tel. 01384-401996/web www.ashwood-nurseries.co.uk), have a broad range of plants, but specialise in *Lewisia*, hardy cyclamens, show auriculas and hellebores, for which they are renowned. As well as selling plants, they have an extensive seed list. The colour mail order seed list ($5 \times$ 1st-class stamps) is well presented and instructive. Open daily, Mon–Sat, 9a.m.–6p.m., Sun, 9.30a.m.–6p.m. Off A449 between Kidderminster and Wolverhampton.

Garden Images, Highfield House, Wawensmere Road, Solihull B95 6BN (tel. 0845-130 4321/web www.garden-images.co.uk), produces a free mail order catalogue of gifts for gardeners. It also includes classic tools, dome cloches, plain gardeners' aprons and soft cowhide gloves. The shop at 15 Meer Street, Stratford-upon-Avon, is open Mon–Sat, 9.30a.m.–5p.m., Sun (except Jan–March), 11a.m.–4p.m.

Wiltshire

MAP NO. 2

Farmland dominates Wiltshire; farmland and the great stretch of almost treeless chalk upland that is Salisbury Plain. The rolling Plain is the occasional haunt of Druids (Stonehenge stands proudly upon it) and a vast exercise-ground for the army. Its windswept turf lies as a green mantle over the ancient settlements and tombs of Britain's earliest known inhabitants. From around 5000–2500 years ago this region was the most densely populated in Britain, crossed by the ancient track known as the Ridgeway, which provided a thread of communication from East Anglia to Devon, as they are now known, and the south-west. Today there are infinitely faster road and rail routes linking east and west, but to pause awhile in Wiltshire, especially in its lovely gardens, is worthwhile.

Must See
Iford Manor, Bradford-on-Avon – Harold Peto's own garden, inspired by Italian villas
Stourhead, Stourton – poetically laid out with lakes and temples

Exceptional in Spring
Heale Garden, Middle Woodford

Exceptional in Summer
Westwind, Marlborough

Worth a Visit in Winter
Stourhead, Stourton
Westwind, Marlborough

The Courts

Holt, nr Trowbridge, Bradford-on-Avon BA14 6RR TEL. 01225-782340
OWNER The National Trust HOURS April–mid-Oct, daily, except Sat,
12 noon–5.30p.m. ENTRANCE £4, children £2 DIRECTIONS 3m SW of Melksham,
3m N of Trowbridge, 2½m E of Bradford-on-Avon, on S side of B3107; from
M4 Jct 17 take A350 to Melksham, then B3107

🌑 ₺ Access 🌑 Plants for Sale

The Courts

Entrance

1 Lawns
2 Arboretum
3 Blue and yellow
  gardens
4 Pillar garden
5 Lily-pond
6 Lower pond

From its discreet, narrow entrance, you would not know there is such
a large (seven-acre) and varied garden at The Courts. The elegant
house (not open) was once a law court for the village, where local
cloth weavers could bring their disputes for settlement. Around it,
the gardens offer a maze of contrasting open, lawned areas and
hedge-enclosed mini-gardens of differing moods and colours. Much
of the present layout dates from the 1920s and 1930s, under the
influence of the Gertrude Jekyll style, with colour-themed borders
and lavish use of herbaceous plants contrasted by dark yews. The
formal gardens form an L-shape beside the house and beyond is a
wilder, unstructured area, which has been planted as an arboretum
since the 1950s.

Harold Peto: Wiltshire's Celebrated Garden Maker

Harold Ainsworth Peto (1854–1933) was the fifth son of Sir Samuel Morton Peto, one of the great Victorian railway contractors, whose estate, Somerleyton Hall (*q.v.*), in Suffolk, had formal gardens (by Nesfield) in the Italianate style. Harold Peto became a renowned architect and garden designer whose own work, in turn, was strongly influenced by Italian form. In the 1880s his London architectural practice (in partnership with Ernest George) was one of the most fashionable, and the young Edwin Lutyens (*q.v.*) worked as their assistant for a short while.

Peto's work is noted for its sensitive use of architectural elements, such as terraces, balustrades and stairways, in the broader landscape. His work can be seen here in Wiltshire at Heale Garden (*q.v.*) and his own home, Iford Manor (*q.v.*); and further afield in the partially restored grounds of Easton Lodge (*q.v.*), Essex, at Buscot Park (*q.v.*) in Oxfordshire and at Wayford Manor, Somerset (the last opens, on rare occasions, for the National Gardens Scheme).

BRADFORD-ON-AVON

Iford Manor

Bradford-on-Avon BA15 2BA TEL. 01225-863146 OWNER Mr and Mrs Hignett HOURS April and Oct, Sun and Easter Mon, 2–5p.m., May–Sept, Tues–Thurs, Sat–Sun and Bank Holiday Mons, 2–5p.m. (other times by appointment only) ENTRANCE £3, concessions/children £2.50 (under 10s free, but not permitted at weekends) DIRECTIONS 2m S of Bradford-on-Avon via Westwood, 8m SE of Bath via A36, also signposted from B3109 WEB www.ifordmanor.co.uk

Several elements combine to make this one of the most pleasingly designed gardens in the *Guide*. The ancient Manor itself (not open) is in a fabulous setting, perched above a picturesque meander of the River Frome. A wooded hill rises behind it, bearing traces of Roman settlements. When Harold Peto (*q.v.*) bought the property in 1899, he laid out a series of terraces linked by stone stairways, and added stone loggias and a colonnade to the grounds. Peto was influenced by Italian design (he made frequent excursions to Italy, in search of ancient artefacts and interesting pieces of masonry) and his translation of the idiom into the Wiltshire landscape is deftly and sympathetically executed. A touch of the Riviera (where Peto also made gardens) is added by the planting – which includes wisterias, grape vines, irises, cypress trees and pines.

Peto admired the rigorous approach of Japanese design as well, and added a small Japanese garden to Iford. There are also delightful streamside plantings and small, formal pools on this 20-acre site.

CALNE

Bowood House and Gardens

Bowood, Calne SN11 0LZ TEL. 01249-812102 OWNER The Marquis and Marchioness of Lansdowne HOURS April–Oct, daily, 11a.m.–6p.m. (or dusk if earlier), also rhododendron walks, May–June, daily ENTRANCE House and gardens £6.05, OAPs £5, children £3.80, under 5s £3; rhododendron walks £3.30 (or £2.30 if visiting house as well), children free DIRECTIONS 8m S of M4 Jct 17, 4½m W of Calne, off A4 in Derry Hill WEB www.bowood-estate.co.uk
🔲 Gift Shop 🔲 Café

This stately home covers 200 acres within a huge park laid out by Capability Brown (q.v.). It has lovely parkland and lakeside walks among magnificent trees, with a gushing water cascade, a temple and a hermit's cave within the grounds. The rhododendron walks are open during their flowering season in May and June.

The orangery (now a gallery) was designed by Robert Adam, and in front of it lie formal terraces of rose beds (very bright and cheerful in summer) and neatly clipped columns of yew. There is also a plant centre within the grounds. The family attractions include an extensive adventure playground, a costume gallery in the house and an 18-hole golf course covering 200 acres within the park.

DEVIZES

Home Covert

Roundway, Devizes SN10 2JA TEL. 01380-723407 OWNER Mr and Mrs John Phillips HOURS Open by prior appointment (please phone for details), groups also welcomed by appointment, open occasionally for the National Gardens Scheme charities (phone for dates) ENTRANCE £2.50, children free DIRECTIONS 1m N of Devizes, turn off A361 following signs to Roundway, in village turn left towards Rowde, then on left (signposted)

Think of Wiltshire and chances are you will picture the open landscapes of the chalk Downs. Home Covert is perched 400ft up in the Downs, but on a ridge of greensand, which gives the 33-acre garden an acidic soil unusual in this region. It is a highly skilfully designed plantsman's garden, carved out of an ancient woodland on sloping ground, and packed with unusual shrubs and perennials planted for a succession of colour all year.

Lawns and formal borders around the house give way to grassy paths that lead through plantations of trees and shrubs. The steepness of the site in one area gives some drama to the water garden, with its lake, poolside plantings of colourful primulas, and waterfall. Teas are served and plants are for sale on open days.

MARLBOROUGH

Westwind

Manton Drove, Manton, nr Marlborough SN8 4HL TEL. 01672–515380
OWNER Neil and Jerry Campbell-Sharp HOURS Open by appointment only
ENTRANCE £3 DIRECTIONS From Marlborough take A4 W for 1m, turn left into Manton and bear right past Odd Fellow Arms, then 1st left into Manton Drove, go up hill and on right

 ⅙ Access

Set on a north-facing slope of the Marlborough Downs, this garden has been made over the last 20 years by garden photographer Neil Campbell-Sharp and his wife, Jerry. Both of them are fanatically keen gardeners and plant collectors for, as Neil says, 'Every time we went to photograph a garden, we would buy a plant or swap cuttings and the garden is full of memories of those visits.' The garden's one-and-a-half acres are designed in several themed areas and you can spend ages following the progression from one to another, as each is packed with plants which bring interest into every season.

A cottage garden beside the house features spring and summer flowering perennials, joined by colourful and textural shrubs such as *Cotinus* 'Velvet Cloak', kolkwitzia and *Rubus thibetanus*, which has purple stems coated with a white bloom in winter. Beyond is a small, New England-style vegetable garden with picket fencing and criss-crossed by gravel paths. A hidden-away paved corner with statues and terracotta pots of box topiaries is known as the Italian Terrace. The main sweep of lawn descending from the house is dissected by some spectacular shrub and herbaceous borders, with a fascinating garden of ornamental grasses beside a waterlily pool.

There are roses galore throughout the gardens – roses are a particular passion of the owners – and many rare and beautiful clematis cultivars. The Prayer Garden is a most unusual and inspired feature. It is a yew-hedge-enclosed garden of rose and perennial beds cut into the lawn, with a small, prettily furnished timber summer-house where visitors may retreat in private contemplation. 'If you want to be quiet, right away from it all, you can bring your picnic lunch here and enjoy the seclusion,' says Jerry.

MIDDLE WOODFORD

Heale Garden and Plant Centre

Middle Woodford, nr Salisbury SP4 6NT TEL. 01722-782504 OWNER Mr G. Rasch HOURS Open all year, Tues–Sun, 10a.m.–5p.m. (plant centre opens daily) ENTRANCE £3.25, children £1.50, under 5s free. No dogs DIRECTIONS 4m N of Salisbury, between A360 and A345, signposted locally

🌿 ♿ Access 🌿 Gift Shop 🌿 Plants for Sale 🌿 Nursery

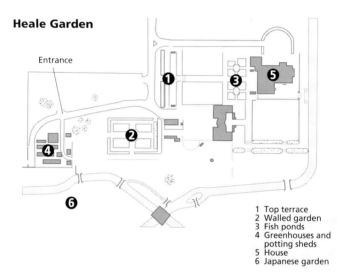

Heale Garden

Entrance

1 Top terrace
2 Walled garden
3 Fish ponds
4 Greenhouses and
  potting sheds
5 House
6 Japanese garden

Tucked away down quiet lanes among the broad loops of the Avon, this is an enchanting, eight-acre garden that really seems to encapsulate 'olde Englande'. Its excellent nursery/specialist plant centre, which also sells antique tools, beckons you on arrival, but ignore the temptation and enjoy the gardens first, for there is much to see.

Broad lawns with trees lead to a formal walled garden, its grass paths delightfully tunnelled with apples and pears, and its beds filled with assorted vegetables and cut flowers. A rose-drenched pergola runs along the southern side. Below it, across the lawns, lies a spectacular Japanese garden, dating from the early years of the 20th century. Four Japanese landscape gardeners were imported to make it, and they diverted the nearby river to create cross-streams, over which lies a traditional teahouse. There is appropriate stream-side planting of acers and willows, irises, cherry trees and sprinklings of spring bulbs. A stone lantern and dark red Nikko bridge complete the scene. Near the house, shrub roses have full rein, with a spectacular, rampant hedge of hybrid musk roses including 'Penelope', 'Buff Beauty' and 'Felicia'. Local designer Harold Peto (*q.v.*) designed the terraced gardens near the house, where mixed shrub and herbaceous borders – and more roses – bring pleasure through the seasons.

STOURTON

Stourhead

Must See

Stourhead Estate Office, Stourton, nr Warminster BA12 6QD TEL. 01747-841152 OWNER The National Trust HOURS Open all year, daily, 9a.m.–7p.m. (or dusk if earlier), closes at 4p.m. for 3 days in late July during concert season; house March–Oct, Sat–Wed, 12 noon–5.30p.m. ENTRANCE £4.80, children £2.60, family ticket £12; house and garden £8.50, children £4, family ticket £20 DIRECTIONS At Stourton, 3m NW of Mere, signposted from A303/B3092

🌿 ዿ Access 🌿 Gift Shop 🌿 Plants for Sale

John Sales, gardens adviser to the National Trust, told me he once received a letter from some people who had visited Stourhead. They wanted their money back, as they had been there, walked around the lake, and could not find any garden. If they were in search of rose beds, flower borders or other more obvious garden features, clearly Stourhead was not for them, as it has none. But it is one of the greatest 18th-century landscape gardens ever made and would certainly feature in my top ten gardens of any kind.

People come to Stourhead for all sorts of reasons: to enjoy the snowdrops and carpets of early bulbs; to see the spectacular rhododendrons in bloom in late spring; for shady woodland walks with plenty of places to pause in summer; or to see the spectacular autumn tints, reflected in the broad 17-acre lake. Others enjoy its scattered buildings, the temples and grotto and allegorical references to Virgil and ancient wisdom. With woodland paths descending the hillside, beautifully composed series of views and fine collections of trees, shrubs and bulbs, it is a 100-acre garden that can be enjoyed at any level and in any season.

STOURTON

Stourton House Garden

Stourton, nr Warminster BA12 6QF TEL. 01747-840417 OWNER Mrs Elizabeth Bullivant HOURS April–Nov, Wed–Thurs, Sun and Bank Holiday Mons, 11a.m.–6p.m. ENTRANCE £3, children 50p DIRECTIONS At Stourton, 3m NW of Mere, signposted from A303/B3092, park in Stourhead (*q.v.*) car park

🌿 ዿ Access 🌿 Café 🌿 Plants for Sale

Lying next door to the restrained landscape park of Stourhead (*q.v.*), this garden, which is full of flowers, could hardly be more different in character. Forming four and a half acres of sub-divided plots around a former Georgian rectory, Stourton House Garden is renowned for its cut-and-dried flowers, which are sold all year round. Many of them are grown in the former kitchen garden, which is devoted to good 'driers' such as helichrysums, delphiniums, golden rod, teasels, achilleas and leeks (which, when left to flower, are as lovely as any of the classier alliums, and make terrific seedheads).

Another enclosed area is bound by Leyland cypress hedges, very effectively clipped into a scalloped pattern along the top, with narrow doorways offering enticing views of further gardens beyond. There are lovely poolside plantings (including carnivorous pitcher plants), wilder, woodland gardens, countless hydrangeas and a spring garden devoted to unusual daffodils.

Lime-loving Plants for Sale

If you have a garden on limy or chalky soil, then a visit to **The Botanic Nursery, Bath Road, Atworth, Melksham SN12 8NU (tel. 01225-706597), on A365 in Atworth, behind the clock tower**, will undoubtedly prove very rewarding. It stocks around 1500 different hardy perennials and shrubs, the vast majority of which will tolerate, or even relish, sinking their roots into alkaline soils. Proprietors Terry and Mary Baker grow much of their stock from seed, with a strong emphasis on wild species, particularly suitable for the more relaxed, ecological styles now in vogue. Some plants on their list you would be unlikely to track down from any other supplier, and the National Collection of *Digitalis* (foxgloves) is held here. Open all year, Fri–Sat, 10a.m.–5p.m. and at other times by appointment only.

And also...

Agralan, The Old Brickyard, Ashton Keynes, Swindon SN6 6QR (tel. 01285-860015), stocks a range of useful gardening products available by mail (catalogue on request). Items include seep-hoses, crop-protection fleeces and mulches, non-chemical pest control including pheromone moth traps; also plant sprayers and accessories. Open all year, Mon–Fri, 9a.m.–5p.m. Ring beforehand for occasional weekend and Bank Holiday openings. M4 Jct 15, then A419, at Spine Road turn left to Ashton Keynes.

The property of **Broadleas Garden, Broadleas, Devizes SN10 5JQ (tel. 01380-722035)** was bought by Lady Anne Cowdray in 1946 and for the last 40 years its nine-acre garden has been developed in a coomb of acidic soil, where camellias, rhododendrons, parrotias and styrax flourish. Springtime is the chief season, when the mature magnolias are at their best and the ground is awash with sheets of early bulbs, rapidly followed by erythroniums (dog's-tooth violet) and trilliums. Although unusual trees and shrubs are the main feature here, readers of the *Guide* have written to me recommending the garden's great charm in summer as well, particularly the border of silver-foliage plants, sunken rose garden, cool woodland walks and superb views. The nursery alongside stocks many unusual plants, including trees and shrubs grown from seeds collected in the wild on botanical expeditions. Open April–Oct, Sun, Wed and Thurs, 2–6p.m. Entrance £3, under 12s free. Off the A360, S of Devizes.

Landford Trees, Landford Lodge, Landford, Salisbury SP5 2EH (tel. 01794-390808/web www.landfordtrees.co.uk), offers a huge range of ornamental broad-leaved trees, hedging plants and conifers (around 600 different species and varieties in all). Many are field-grown (dispatched in winter) but some ranges are also grown in containers and are available any time. Mail order (min. £15) catalogue on request. Open all year, Mon–Fri, 8a.m.–5p.m. M27 Jct 2, then A36 N, take 1st left after junction with B3079 towards Northlands, then left, then right.

Pound Hill House, West Kington, Chippenham SN14 7JG (tel. 01249-782822), is a 15th-century Cotswold-stone house (not open) surrounded by a series of small gardens planted for interest throughout the year with a formidable range of plants. There is an old-fashioned rose garden with clipped box beds, a small Victorian vegetable garden, a water garden, herbaceous borders, a courtyard garden with well-planted pots, containers, and topiary in box and yew. Open March–Oct, daily, 2–5p.m. Entrance £2.50. **Pound Hill Plants** is the owner's family-run business, next door, which specialises in raising alpines, herbaceous perennials, old-fashioned roses and also topiary plants, available from its plant centre (which supplies coffee and home-made cakes as well). Plant centre and garden open Feb–Dec, daily, 10a.m.–5p.m.; nursery open 9a.m.–5p.m. From A46 take A420 towards Chippenham, turn left towards West Kington, on right.

Sherston Parva Nursery, Malmesbury Road, Sherston SN16 0NX (tel. 01666-841066), has a broad range of climbing plants and shrubs suitable for training on walls, including around 100 different clematis and conservatory plants. Also mail order: free catalogue available on request. Open all year, daily, 10a.m.–5p.m. M4 Jct 17, then A429 to Malmesbury, then B4040.

Nurserywoman Derry Watkins specialises in raising half-hardy plants such as choice pelargoniums, salvias, streptocarpus, arctotis and choice gazanias at **Special Plants Nursery, Greenways Lane, Cold Ashton, Chippenham SN14 8LA (tel. 01225-891686/web www.specialplants.net)**. She also runs a series of one-day practical gardening courses in the winter season, on topics such as taking cuttings, pruning, conservatory gardening and container-planting. Open March–Sept, daily, 10.30a.m.–4p.m. and other times by appointment. Garden open by appointment and for NGS. Entrance (garden only) £1.50. M4 Jct 18, then 4m S on A46, past junction with A420, then right.

The Walled Garden Nursery, Horningsham, Warminster BA12 7NQ (tel. 01985-845004), is a one-off. 'We are a small "kitchen-table" business; until now, we have grown, prepared, counted, and packed the seed, sundries and plants by hand,' says proprietor Colin Simpson. Tomatoes are their speciality, offering seeds of around 270 different varieties. They also sell all manner of unusual, historical and just plain weird vegetables, such as tomatillos – a type of physalis used in Mexican cooking. Catalogue free on request.

Westdale Nurseries, Holt Road, Bradford-on-Avon BA15 1TS (tel. 01225-863258/web www.westdalenurseries.co.uk), specialises in bougainvillea (send 4 × 1st-class stamps plus A5 s.a.e. for their list), displayed in a quarter-acre bougainvillea greenhouse. Also pelargoniums in variety and other plants suitable for conservatories. Open all year, daily, 9a.m.–6p.m. M4 Jct 18, then A46 towards Bath, then A363 to Bradford-on-Avon. Leave town on B3107 towards Holt and Melksham, nursery is opposite cemetery.

Worcestershire

This is a prime fruit-growing area, with fertile plains watered by the great Severn and Avon rivers and their tributaries. Market gardening prevails, as roadside farm shops frequently remind you, especially when harvest time arrives for apples and pears. The Georgian town of Pershore derives its name from the quantity of pear orchards that surround it, while the market town of Evesham has medieval buildings and tree-shaded walks beside the Avon. Great Malvern is a handsome spa town, renowned for its bottled water. It lies on the eastern fringes of the Malvern Hills that inspired Edward Elgar, the Victorian composer whose music is so evocative of pastoral Englishness.

Must See
Burford House Gardens, Tenbury Wells – splendid planting in tranquil riverside location

Exceptional in Autumn
Picton Garden, Great Malvern

Worth a Visit in Winter
Burford House Gardens, Tenbury Wells

Books for Gardeners by Mail

St Ann's Books, Rectory House, 26 Priory Road, Great Malvern
WR14 3DR (tel. 01684-562818/web www.st-anns-books.com),
is a treasure trove of books on botany and gardening, both old and
new, listed in their catalogues (two per year on each subject). From
the deeply scientific to the downright obscure, if something you want
is out of print, or you have not found it elsewhere, you might do so
here. (Personal callers only by appointment.)

GREAT MALVERN

The Picton Garden and
Old Court Nurseries

Exceptional
in **Autumn**

Walwyn Road, Colwall, Great Malvern WR13 6QE TEL. 01684-540416
OWNER Mr and Mrs P. Picton HOURS Garden Aug, Wed–Sun, 11a.m.–5.30p.m.,
Sept and 1st 2 weeks in Oct, daily, 11a.m.–5.30p.m., 2nd 2 weeks in Oct,
Wed–Sun, 11a.m.–5p.m.; nursery April–Oct, Wed–Sun, 11a.m.–5p.m. ENTRANCE
£2, children free (nursery free) DIRECTIONS Off A449 on B4218, 3m SW of
Malvern in Colwall village

🌳 ♿ Access 🌳 Plants for Sale 🌳 Nursery 🌳 NPC 🌳 Mail Order

Michaelmas daisy borders were popular in late-Victorian and
Edwardian gardens of the well-to-do, but are a rare sight now. This
two-acre nursery and garden is a tenacious heirloom of that age,
however, and displays these autumnal flowers in the traditional way.

It was begun by Ernest Ballard, a chemist and hobby gardener
who became a nurseryman by default, as a result of his success in
raising exquisite new varieties of *Aster novi-belgii*, also known as New
York asters. Ballard's work here spans the first half of the 20th
century, and in later years he was joined by Percy Picton, who had
gardened at Gravetye Manor for William Robinson (*q.v.*).

New York asters are hard work, needing to be grown from fresh
individual shoots, yearly. They are also prone to soil-borne diseases,
and are grown best in sterilised soil, followed by regular spraying
against mildew. Percy Picton's son, Paul, now runs the nursery and
still grows asters in this way, producing glorious firework explosions
of pinks, mauves, violets, cerise and white, in a dedicated border best
seen in mid-September. He also stocks easy-to-grow species, such as
A. amellus, *A. frikartii* hybrids and the tall *A. novae-angliae* and holds
the National Collection of autumn-flowering asters.

No yellow asters are available yet, but Ernest Ballard came close by crossing white asters with *Solidaster luteus*, which produced weak, yellow-flowered seedlings during the Second World War. While he was out one day, the War-Ag (responsible for wartime food production) arrived to plough up fields for vegetables; unfortunately, they took the wrong patch, and 30 years' work went under the plough. Ballard never really recovered from the incident.

TENBURY WELLS

Burford House Gardens

Tenbury Wells WR15 8HQ TEL. 01584-810777 OWNER Treasures of Tenbury Ltd
HOURS Open all year, daily, 10a.m.–6p.m. ENTRANCE £3.50, children £1
DIRECTIONS 1m W of Tenbury Wells, on A456, 8m from Ludlow WEB
www.burfordhouse.com

🌿 ♿ Access 🌿 Gift Shop 🌿 Café 🌿 Plants for Sale 🌿 Nursery 🌿 NPC
🌿 Mail Order

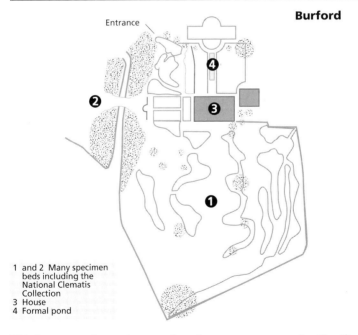

Burford

Entrance

1 and 2 Many specimen beds including the National Clematis Collection
3 House
4 Formal pond

This is a tranquil, spacious garden of seven acres around a dignified Georgian brick house in a lovely setting, beside the River Teme. It was started (and tended for nearly 40 years) by the late John Treasure, a renowned plantsman with a specialist interest in clematis who ran a large and famous clematis nursery to prove it.

There are curvaceous lawns sweeping around large mixed borders, formal and informal pools, and many fine specimen trees and conifers dotted about the grounds. Ornamental grasses and ferns form splendid drifts on the river bank, and the autumn colours of foliage with the sedums, anemones, echinacea and late-flowering clematis are spectacular. Exciting new planting by the present owners is now invigorating the existing layout. Over 200 different clematis (part of a comprehensive National Collection) are available from Burford House Garden Centre in the grounds, and also by mail order.

Herbs in Paradise

The Cottage Herbary, Mill House, Boraston Ford, Boraston, nr Tenbury Wells WR15 8LZ (tel. 01584-781575), 2m E of Tenbury Wells, turn off A456 at Peacock Inn and follow signs. This true cottage garden (Geoff Hamilton featured it in his *Paradise Gardens* television series) covers one and a quarter acres in an idyllic streamside setting on the Worcestershire/Shropshire border. There are old roses, variegated and wild herbs, dyers' plants and much else, all grown organically. Kim Hurst specialises in producing herbs, aromatics, scented foliage and cottage garden plants, many of which are on sale. She also gives informative talks on many aspects of herbs, including herb garden designs, wild herbs and their use, growing herbs organically, pot-pourris and preserving, etc., to garden societies and groups by appointment. Open May–July, Sun only, 11a.m.–5p.m.; weekdays by prior arrangement only. Entrance free, unless it is an NGS Sunday.

TENBURY WELLS

Kyre Park

Kyre, Tenbury Wells WR15 8RP TEL. 01885-410282/410247 OWNER The Sellers Family HOURS Feb–Christmas, daily, 10a.m.–6p.m., nursery 11a.m.–4p.m. (ring to check nursery opening hours Sept–Christmas); Jan, by appointment only ENTRANCE £2, children 50p DIRECTIONS 4m S of Tenbury Wells, off B4214

🌼 ♿ Access 🌼 Café 🌼 Plants for Sale 🌼 Nursery 🌼 NPC 🌼 Mail Order

Kyre Park must have been a very agreeable home in the 18th century. Most of the Georgian house was built onto the shell of a medieval castle. Its park is laid out as a Capability Brown-style landscape garden, overlaying more formal designs. Alas, both house and grounds were badly neglected in recent decades (all the fine fireplaces and fittings in the house were sold) and the park became overgrown. Much clearance and replanting has been carried out more recently under the new owners, and the woods are an ideal habitat for several National Collections of ferns.

The 29-acre park includes pleasant walks around its lakes. Meanwhile, its 18th-century features are gradually being uncovered. Mr Rickard managed to drag me through thickets of brambles and saplings to inspect the remains of a tufa grotto, fed by a spring, which he hopes to restore at some stage.

Most people come here to buy from Rickards Hardy Ferns Nursery, where hundreds of different species and varieties are sold from polytunnels near the car park.

A Walk on the Wild Side

I have known Kim and Phil Westwood for over 12 years and am full of admiration for their latest project at **Crown East Heritage Woodland, Crown East Cottage, Crown East, Bromyard Road, Rushwick WR2 5TR (tel. 01905-425645), 3m W of Worcester, off the A44, on Bromyard Road**. Phil is a woodsman and conservationist, and Kim a great cook. Both are good gardeners. Their unspoilt 10-acre wood is a rare remnant of ancient wildwood, with a natural mix of broad-leaved trees and conifers, plus coppiced hazel and field maple, and abundant primroses, wood anemones and bluebells.

To encourage the wild side of gardening and an enhanced awareness of natural habitats, they run a series of one- and two-day courses through the year, on topics including managing hedgerows and wildlife habitats, coppicing, bird identification and guided woodland walks (including one which ends with a cream tea, and a winter walk which is followed by dinner). Visits by appointment. Cream tea walk £8, Ploughman's lunch walk £12, Woodsman's lunch walk £12, Winter Warmer dinner walk £22.50, children under 10 half price (no non-meal admissions).

And also...

Visit **Cotswold Garden Flowers, office at Gibbs Lane, Ossenham, Evesham WR11 5RZ (tel. 01386-47337); gardens at Sands Lane, Badsey, Evesham WR11 5EZ**. Their speciality is herbaceous perennials, laid out in display gardens and polytunnels in a one-acre field. Free catalogue available on request. Open all year, daily, Mon–Fri, 9a.m.–5.30p.m., Sat–Sun (except Nov–Feb), 10a.m.–5.30p.m. Use M5 Jct 9. Detailed directions available with catalogue.

Fibrex Nurseries, Honeybourne Road, Pebworth CV37 8XP (tel. 01789-720788), specialises in pelargoniums and ivies, holding the NCCPG National Collections for both. It is also well known for hardy ferns. Two catalogues available: send 2 × 1st-class stamps. Open March–July, Mon–Fri, 10.30a.m.–5p.m., Sat–Sun, 12 noon–5p.m.; Aug, Mon–Fri, 10.30a.m.–5p.m.; Sept–Feb (ivies only), Mon–Fri, 10.30a.m.–5p.m. M40 Jct 15 to Stratford-upon-Avon, then B439 to Bidford-on-Avon, then B4632 to Honeybourne.

Hayloft Plants, Little Court, Rous Lench, Evesham WR11 4UL (tel. 01386-793361), offers an interesting range of plug plants, by mail order – useful for anyone lacking the space or time to grow plants from seeds and cuttings. Half-hardy subjects such as argyranthemums, gazanias and arctotis are a speciality, as are a range of penstemons and many other choice species for colourful containers. Mail order only; catalogue free on request.

Madresfield Nursery and Garden Centre, Madresfield, Malvern WR13 5AU (tel. 01684-574066), offers a broad selection of shrubs, trees and herbaceous plants laid out in a Victorian walled garden which still retains its original outbuildings. Open daily, Mon–Sat, 9a.m.–5.30p.m., Sun, 10a.m.–5p.m. From A449, take turning to Madresfield, then 1st on left, nursery on right.

The one-acre walled garden of **Stone House Cottage, Stone, nr Kidderminster DY10 4BG (tel. 01562-69902/web www.shcn.co.uk)**, ingenuously displays a wonderful collection of plants among follies, brick towers and yew hedges. There is also a nursery where you can buy most of the plants you have seen in the gardens. Open March–Sept, Wed–Sat, 10a.m.–5.30p.m., Oct–Feb, by appointment only. Entrance £2.50, children free. Signposted from A448.

Webbs of Wychbold, Wychbold, Droitwich WR9 0DG (tel. 01527-860000), is a huge, well-run garden centre. There are display gardens and a restaurant. Open all year, daily, April–Sept, Mon–Fri, 9a.m.–8p.m., Sat and Bank Holiday Mons, 9a.m.–6p.m., Sun, 10.30a.m.–4.30p.m.; Oct–March, Mon–Sat, 9a.m.–6p.m., Sun, 10.30a.m.–4.30p.m. On A38 outside Wychbold, use M5 Jct 5 and follow signs.

Yorkshire

Yorkshire is the largest county in Britain, with correspondingly broad-ranging, alluring landscapes, from the limestone peaks of the Pennines along the western boundary, to the North York Moors and Cleveland Hills of the east. The Vale of York in the centre is a green, broad plain of rich, alluvial soil, while the south is typified by the hard millstone grit and rich coal seams exploited by industry. Numerous rivers add to the scenic appeal.

For over 300 years Yorkshire has produced memorable gardens, great and small, and outstanding examples of the 18th-century landscape park. The spa town of Harrogate is a horticultural centre for the region, hosting important spring and autumn flower shows in the Valley Gardens and the North of England Showground, while the former Northern Horticultural Society's headquarters are on the outskirts, at Harlow Carr.

Must See

RHS Harlow Carr, Harrogate – Northern showpiece of the Royal Horticultural Society

Fountains Abbey, Ripon – captivating historic landscape garden

Newby Hall and Gardens, Ripon – spectacular 300-yd herbaceous borders

Exceptional in Spring

Parcevall Hall, Appletreewick

Castle Howard, York

Worth a Vist in Winter

RHS Harlow Carr, Harrogate

Fountains Abbey, Ripon

APPLETREEWICK

Parcevall Hall

Skyreholme, Appletreewick, Skipton BD23 6DE TEL. 01756-720311
OWNER Walsingham Trust HOURS April–Oct, daily, 10a.m.–6p.m.; winter by
appointment ENTRANCE £3, children 50p DIRECTIONS 1m NE of Appletreewick,
off B6265 WEB www.parcevallhallgardens.co.uk

Café Plants for Sale

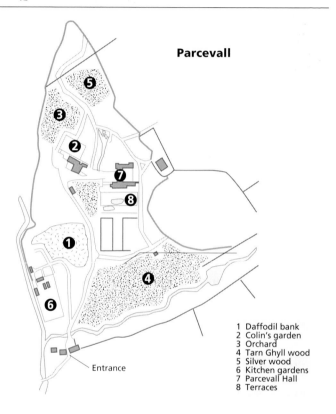

Parcevall

1 Daffodil bank
2 Colin's garden
3 Orchard
4 Tarn Ghyll wood
5 Silver wood
6 Kitchen gardens
7 Parcevall Hall
8 Terraces

Entrance

The 15th-century Hall is hidden away in such a peaceful spot in
Upper Wharfedale that it is used as a centre for quiet retreats. The
16-acre site was bought in 1927 by Sir William Milner, a godson of
Queen Mary, and both house and garden flourished under his
patronage for the next three decades. The garden fell into disrepair
after his death in 1960, but recent restoration work has allowed it to
flourish once more.

The old orchard, awash with daffodils in spring, has been
supplemented by new plantings of historic apple varieties, such as

'Lady Henniker', 'Striped Beefing', 'Cockpit' and 'Gooseberry'. From there, a steep climb provides exquisite views of Middle Wharfedale, washed by stony streams far below. The rock garden was formed in the Carboniferous era, and is watered by a natural spring that feeds a clear pool. Its margins are surrounded by marsh orchids and scented yellow *Primula florindae*. Rhododendrons flourish, in spite of the limestone, due to overlying pockets of acid soil, supplemented over the decades by thick dressings of bracken.

The most architectural part of the garden is a series of terraces and lawns by the house, facing south with spectacular views across the dale to the rocky hill of Simon's Seat. There are also herbaceous borders, lily-ponds and a pergola of climbing roses, a soft focus around the buttressed terraces of pink and buff gritstone.

DONCASTER

The Earth Centre

Denaby Main, Doncaster DN12 4EA TEL. 01709-513933 OWNER The Earth Centre HOURS April–early Nov, daily, 10a.m.–6p.m. (last adm. 4p.m.) ENTRANCE £3.95, concessions/children £2.95 (under 5s free) DIRECTIONS A1(M) Jct 36, then follow signs through Conisbrough to Earth Centre WEB www.earthcentre.org.uk

🚻 ♿ Access 🚻 Gift Shop 🚻 Café

This exciting new 400-acre environmental centre has received one of the Millennium Commission's largest grants and is expected to have cost around £100 million by the time of its completion in 2001. It covers all aspects of environmental issues and has many interactive displays and activities in its range of buildings, but there's also much to interest the gardener.

Visitors begin and end their Earth Centre journey in Solar Point (so named to celebrate the sun's energy), a plaza paved in local York stone, with paths of Bredon gravel from nearby Derbyshire leading off to other areas. In the south-facing 21st-Century Terraced Gardens the white of the limestone-clad terrace walls is designed to reflect solar warmth onto the soil. There are three levels, showing local, national and global organic gardening techniques and produce, grown in a range of soil types. Another area, Forest Gardens, replicates forest conditions with plantings of native woodland species. Gridshells, or shelters, made of green oak and covered with climbers are being used to make the shade canopy, until the planted trees have grown sufficiently. Open parts of this area also feature useful herbs. There are wetland areas, garden ponds, waste-water treatment areas demonstrating uses of algae, wildlife meadows, dry gravel gardens and interesting recycling methods.

The Centre is laid out on the regenerated site of two coal mines. The former coal spoil was spread with clippings and mowings from Doncaster Parks, and sewage sludge, to return it to a fertile soil for planting. It is big on all aspects of recycling and composting, of course, and also in demonstrating water conservation techniques and creating wildlife-friendly habitats. Sixty-two thousand new trees have been planted on the site. Naturally, the food served in the cafés is organic, with as much as possible sourced locally.

CELEBRITY CHOICE

Geoffrey Smith

Panellist of BBC Radio 4's
Gardeners' Question Time

'I spend many a Sunday afternoon at **Fountains Abbey** (*q.v.*) because its landscape garden speaks of the tranquillity of centuries. **Castle Howard** (*q.v.*) is also magnificent; such an immense landscape. Its sheer extravagance is breathtaking.

I also greatly admire the gorgeous herbaceous borders of **Newby Hall** (*q.v.*) and the way they sweep away from the house, down a gentle slope to the river. But, above all others, the garden I love most is **Parcevall** (*q.v.*), 1000ft up in the dales. It's a sublime place and not just because of the plants, although it has a fine collection, but also for the landscape around it. **York Gate** (*q.v.*), at Adel, is second only to Parcevall; it's an intimate family garden, but full of good plantsmanship.'

HARROGATE

RHS Harlow Carr Botanical Gardens

Crag Lane, Harrogate HG3 1QB TEL. 01423-565418 OWNER The Royal Horticultural Society HOURS All year, daily, 9.30a.m.–6p.m. or dusk if earlier ENTRANCE £4, OAPs £3, students £2, children free DIRECTIONS 1½m W of Harrogate town centre on B6162 Otley road WEB www.rhs.org.uk

🅿 ♿ Access 🅿 Gift Shop 🅿 Café 🅿 Plants for Sale 🅿 NPC

The saying goes, 'If it grows at Harlow Carr, it will grow anywhere,' which testifies both to the climate and soil. Formerly the headquarters of the Northern Horticultural Society (which has recently amalgamated with the RHS), the original garden at Harlow Carr was created on 30 acres of pasture leased from Harrogate Council, together with a dilapidated early-Victorian bath-house, built to take advantage of a sulphurous stream. As you would expect of a large demonstration garden run by an organisation, the emphasis is on horticulture and education, without the personal touch of a private garden.

Since its infancy half a century ago, Harlow Carr has expanded to 68 well-maintained acres supporting an astonishing variety of plants in unenviable acid clay exposed to chilly winds. The stream, with bog plants filling its banks, separates the intensively cultivated gardens from the woodland. There are fine rock gardens, a winter garden, and four different themed areas for displaying particular groups of plants. Besides the important trial and demonstration gardens testing new varieties of vegetables and flowers, there are four National Collections of plants, including calluna and rhubarb, as well as dryopteris and polypodium ferns.

LEEDS

York Gate

Back Church Lane, Adel, Leeds LS16 8DW TEL. 0113-267-8240 OWNER The Gardeners' Royal Benevolent Society HOURS May–Aug, Thurs and Sun, 2–5p.m., coach parties by appointment only ENTRANCE £3, children free DIRECTIONS Off A660 Leeds to Otley road, behind Adel church

This celebrated one-acre town garden is ingeniously laid out to provide a great deal of interest, both in design terms and in the variety of plants used. It was made by one family, Mr and Mrs Spencer and their son (alas, all now deceased), from the early 1950s onwards. The gardening tradition continues, however, since Mrs Spencer left the property to the Gardeners' Royal Benevolent Society on her death a few years ago.

Its entrance courtyard is paved with a beautiful circular maze pattern of stone setts and gravel, edged by clipped yews. From here the gardens lead into differently themed areas, underpinned by strong architectural elements and unusual topiaries.

The pool area features moisture-loving plants, including leucojums, astilbes, pachyphragma and lysichitons. Through an open arbour you can pass into a miniature pinetum with a slightly oriental flavour. Beyond it, there are topiarised hollies and an unusual espalier-trained blue cedar tree lining the wall of a long, rectangular canal pool. The herb garden is a memorable set piece, laid out in a long vista framed by yew hedges and bold topiaries and terminating in a fine summerhouse. Another long, hedge-enclosed area is devoted to white flowers, highlighted with grey foliage plants or those with variegated leaves. Spring sees the gardens awash with many kinds of bulbs, but the planting is so rich and varied that there is much to see and draw inspiration from at any time of year. Teas are served on charity days.

The Russell Lupins

George Russell (the fifth son of a shoemaker, he was born in 1857 at Stillington, around 10 miles north of York) worked for many years as a professional gardener in the York region. His private passion was lupins, and he spent more than 20 years on his allotments breeding a new strain bearing large, tightly packed flower spikes in a new range of colours. Word spread and nurserymen and seedsmen from all over the country came to buy his amazing stock. He resisted all offers until one day he finally capitulated and accepted an offer from Jimmy Baker, of Wolverhampton. The new plants caused a sensation when exhibited at the Royal Horticultural Society in 1937 and immediately became a famous and popular strain.

RIPON

Fountains Abbey and Studley Royal

Ripon HG4 3DY TEL. 01765-608888 OWNER The National Trust HOURS Open all year, daily, 10a.m.–5p.m. (7p.m. May–Sept), last adm. 1hr before closing (closed every Fri in Nov–Jan) ENTRANCE £4.50, children £2.30, family ticket £11 DIRECTIONS 4m W of Ripon, off B6265, 8m W of A1 WEB www.fountainsabbey.org.uk
🏵 & Access 🏵 Gift Shop 🏵 Café

The political career of John Aislabie, Chancellor of the Exchequer, burst with the South Sea Bubble in 1720 and he fled, disgraced, to his Yorkshire estate to create a landscape garden. Studley Royal is a garden of trees, sculpted lawns and, above all, differing moods of water. To enjoy Aislabie's intended sequence of surprises in this 800-acre World Heritage site, begin at the discreet entrance at Studley Roger rather than Fountains Abbey, where all the tourists are directed, which is like starting a meal with the pudding.

At the entrance the River Skell plunges over the cascade into a huge lake. But stand on the bridge and you will see that, before its liberation, the water runs along the orderly confines of a formal canal, beside which smooth lawns form a level, semicircular sward. Cut into the turf, like precise shapes lifted from rolled-out pastry, lie the silent moon ponds: a perfect circle flanked by symmetrical crescents, reflecting the dark woods and temple behind.

More eye-catching temples are placed around the gardens, but the most compelling one long predates the garden, being the ruins of the Cistercian Fountains Abbey. Glimpsed through the trees, its melancholy tower and crumbling gothic arches invite further exploration and you can follow the river upstream to the abbey ruins. The abbey's 800-year-old mill has recently been renovated, too. Fountains was initially a place of austerity and toil, yet by the 13th century its estates were producing around 30,000lb of wool per year, for a rich and powerful monastic empire. The waters of the Skell skirt its foundations much as the distant generations of Aislabies would have known it.

RIPON

Newby Hall and Gardens

Nr Ripon HG4 5AE TEL. 01423-322583 OWNER R.E.J. Compton
HOURS April–Sept, Tues–Sun and Bank Holiday Mons, 11a.m.–5.30p.m.; house 12 noon–5p.m. ENTRANCE £5, OAPs £4, children £3.50, family ticket £16 (2 adults, 2 children), £19.50 (2 adults, 3 children); house and garden £6.80, OAPs £5.80, children £4, family ticket £21 (2 adults, 2 children), £25 (2 adults, 3 children) DIRECTIONS Off B6265 between Boroughbridge and Ripon, 4m W of A1(M) WEB www.newbyhall.com

🚗 ♿ Access 🚗 Gift Shop 🚗 Café 🚗 Plants for Sale 🚗 NPC
🚗 2 for 1 Voucher

When John Claudius Loudon (the Geoff Hamilton of the early 19th century) visited Newby Hall in 1837, he could find little to praise: 'A mass of flower beds…extremely ill placed [with] nothing to recommend them and it is seen at a glance that they have no business where they are.'

Ninety-odd years later, the 30-year-old Major Edward Compton turned much of the garden's 25 acres into a golf course, an entertaining diversion while his vast plantings of shelter trees were growing (for shelter is needed to fend off the persistent winds hurling across the moors). This accomplished, he began his master plan, which is largely the layout you now see. If Loudon were to come back today, he would surely report very differently, for this is one of the most richly planted and thoughtfully laid-out gardens in the country.

The double herbaceous borders are famous, running – spectacularly – for 300yds down a gentle slope to the River Ure, forming the main axis from the house. To either side are intimate, enclosed gardens of varying themes, that were inspired by Lawrence

Johnston's garden at Hidcote Manor (*q.v.*) in Gloucestershire. Sylvia's Garden features flowering plants chiefly for spring and early summer, and the rose pergola is draped in assorted climbing varieties, leading to an Edwardian rock garden designed by the indefatigable Ellen Willmott (*q.v.*). From there, a curving pergola suspends springtime tresses of laburnum flowers. There are fine trees, old-fashioned roses and autumn foliage shrubs in great variety, and the richness of planting is largely due to the skills and enthusiasm of the present owners, Robin Compton (Major Edward's son) and his wife, Jane, who have also brought in new sculpture exhibits recently. Newby Hall also holds a National Collection of cornus.

Apples of the North

R.V. Roger Ltd, The Nurseries, Pickering YO18 7HG (tel. 01751-472226), 26m N of York, 1m S of Pickering, on A169, stocks a huge range of plants, including roses, trees, hedging, conifers, heathers, shrubs, climbers, herbaceous plants and fruit, available from the plant centre and also by mail (catalogue £1.50). Fruit is a speciality, particularly apples which grow well in the north, of which over 60 varieties on a range of rootstocks are offered, grown in their own field. Since 'Cox's Orange Pippin' is intolerant of cold conditions, Anthony Roger recommends the self-fertile dessert apple 'Sunset' as a substitute. He also suggests 'Newton Wonder' (also self-fertile), 'Fortune', a mid-season variety for picking in September, and 'Balsam', one of his favourites, which should be picked in November and is ready to eat from February. His other favourites are 'Epicure', 'because it is so delicious', and 'Brownlees Russet', 'the best russet to grow in the north'. As they are field grown, the bulk of the fruit is dispatched between November and March, while dormant. Apple Day (21 October) is celebrated at the nursery with fruit tastings, displays, and experts who will identify visitors' own fruit and offer advice on growing. Open daily, 9a.m.–5p.m. (Sun, 1–5p.m.).

WETHERBY

Bramham Park

Wetherby LS23 6ND TEL. 01937-846002 OWNER Mr G. Lane Fox
HOURS April–Sept, daily, 10.30a.m.–5.30p.m. (closed 1 week in June); house by appointment only ENTRANCE Grounds only £4, OAPs/children £2, under 5s free
DIRECTIONS 10m NE of Leeds, take A1 to Bramham and follow signs to Thorner
🅿 ♿ Access 🅿 2 for 1 Voucher

The 66-acre historic gardens are famed for being a very rare surviving example of the French style of Le Nôtre, having been laid out in the very early 18th century. There is a geometric arrangement of straight avenues cut through woodland, flanked by high beech hedges. The park is said to be haunted by riderless horses that fled from the Battle of Bramham Moor in 1408. They were witnessed by the present owner's father, Colonel Francis Lane Fox, during the 1930s. He thought he heard the local hunt riding across the park and held open a gate for them to pass, but nobody came, and when the sound of galloping hooves died away, he realised he had heard the horses. There are miles of walks to stretch your legs, punctuated by statues, temples, obelisks and formal ponds. The flower gardens near the house are confined to an Edwardian design of formal rose beds and a herbaceous border, providing shots of summer colour in what is otherwise a serene, green landscape.

YORK

Castle Howard

Exceptional in Spring

Nr York YO60 7DA TEL. 01653-648333 (recorded message) or 01653-648444 OWNER Castle Howard Estates Ltd HOURS Mid-March–Oct, daily, 10a.m.–6p.m. (last adm. 4.30p.m.), grounds all year, daily, 10a.m.–6p.m. (or dusk if earlier) ENTRANCE £4.50, OAPs/children £2.50; house and grounds £7.50, OAPs £6.75, children £4.50, family ticket £19.50 (2 adults, 2 children), £24 (2 adults, 3 children), £28.50 (2 adults, 4 children) DIRECTIONS 14m NE of York, from A1 take A64 towards Malton and follow signs WEB www.castlehoward.co.uk

🖍 ⅄ Access 🖍 Gift Shop 🖍 Café 🖍 Plants for Sale 🖍 Nursery 🖍 Mail Order

The creation of three men – the 3rd Earl of Carlisle, the gentleman-architect John Vanbrugh and his brilliant assistant Nicholas Hawks-moor – Castle Howard is a fascinating example of how an owner managed to enjoy and shape a vast landscape in the last days of the 17th century. Horace Walpole captured the essence of it in 1772: 'Nobody told me that I should at one view see a palace, a town, a fortified city, temples on high places, woods worthy of being each a metropolis of the Druids, the noblest lawn on earth fenced by half the horizon and a mausoleum that would tempt one to be buried alive... I have seen gigantic places before but never a sublime one.' In the early 1980s it featured in the television adaptation of *Brideshead Revisited*.

Wear comfortable shoes and allow plenty of time to explore the Temple of the Four Winds, the Roman bridge and Hawksmoor's mausoleum, the outstanding set pieces in the huge 1000-acre park. Ray Wood, on the east side of the house, is a 20-year-old naturalistic garden of rhododendrons, bluebells and specimen trees planted within an older woodland. Fountains by Nesfield remain in the formal gardens in front of the house, and there is a large collection of old-fashioned and species roses in the old walled kitchen gardens.

Sheep Shears – for Trim Topiary

Burgon & Ball Ltd, La Plata Works, Holme Lane, Sheffield S6 4JY (tel. 0114-233 8262/web www.burgonandball.com), has been producing agricultural tools since 1730, but its sheep shears are no longer confined to trimming livestock. The sharp blades and single-handed action have proved useful to topiarists for trimming evergreen sculptures in box and yew with precision. The shears come in two sizes, and are available by mail order. The firm also produces the Bay Tree Collection of unusual and decorative garden objects, included in a free full-colour mail order catalogue, from the above address.

And also...

Brodsworth Hall, Brodsworth, Doncaster DN5 7XJ (tel. 01302-722598), is a Victorian stone mansion in classical Italian style, fascinating for its well-preserved interior. It gives a good insight into the Victorian country house life. The 15-acre gardens are landscaped in high Victoriana with dense shrubberies, symmetrical bedded-out flower gardens, a mystical quarry garden with natural cliffs and artificial rockwork decked with ferns, and a box-edged rose garden, with iron pergola. Open April–Oct, Tues–Sun and Bank Holidays, 1–6p.m. (closes at dusk in Oct); garden open at 12 noon (last adm. 5p.m.). Garden only Nov–March, Sat–Sun, 11a.m.–4p.m. Entrance £5, concessions £3.80, children £2.50; garden only £2.60, concessions £2, children £1.30 (Sat–Sun, Nov–March, £1.60, £1.20 and 80p). Leave A1(M) at Jct 37, take A635 towards Barnsley and follow signs.

If you like delphiniums, you'll love **8 Dunstarn Lane, Adel, Leeds LS16 8EL**, home of retired Liberal MP Richard Wainwright. His two-acre garden is famous for its collection of delphiniums, laid out in three 225ft-long herbaceous borders created over 60 years ago by his father. More than 60 different varieties are displayed in the gardens, which open at peak time for a couple of Sunday afternoons in July. For this year's dates phone the NGS (01483-211535). Entrance £2, children free.

Carthusian monks founded **Mount Grace Priory, Staddlebridge, Northallerton DL6 3JG (tel. 01609-883494)**, in 1398, living as hermits in four-roomed cells, each with its own garden. One has been carefully reconstructed with a garden of raised beds featuring herbs. Also on the 11½-acre site is an Arts and Crafts-style house built at the turn of the century, incorporating earlier buildings, and a one-acre Victorian garden of stepped terraces and shrubberies. Open April–Oct, daily, 10a.m.–6p.m. (last adm. 5.30p.m.), 5p.m. in Oct; Nov–March, Wed–Sun, 10a.m.–4p.m. (closed 1–2p.m. in winter). Entrance £2.90, concessions £2.20, children £1.50 (English Heritage and National Trust members free, except for special events). No dogs allowed. 12m N of Thirsk, 7m NE of Northallerton, on A19.

Norton Conyers, nr Ripon HG4 5EQ (tel. 01765-640333), was visited by Charlotte Brontë in 1839 and provided the inspiration for Thornfield Hall in *Jane Eyre*. Its two-and-a-half-acre 18th-century walled garden contains herbaceous borders, a historic orangery and pick-your-own fruit in season, plus a small plant sales area specialising in unusual hardy plants. The garden is open every Sun and Bank Holiday Mons, Easter–Sept and daily for one week in early July, 11.30a.m.–5p.m., house 2–5p.m. (phone first to check hours). Entrance (garden) free (except charity days, £2.50), (house) £3, concessions £2.50. A1, then A61 towards Ripon, then right towards Melmerby.

Tree enthusiasts will enjoy the 85 acres of **Thorp Perrow Arboretum, Bedale DL8 2PR (tel. 01677-425323),** home to over 2000 tree species, including National Collections of ash, oak, walnut and lime. It is a pleasant place for springtime walks, particularly when thousands of daffodils and bluebells are in bloom, and in autumn when tree foliage tints can be spectacular. Open daily all year, dawn–dusk. Entrance £3.50, OAPs £2.50, children £2. Leave A1 at Leeming Bar and follow signs to Bedale, then 2m S on B6268.

The Valley Gardens, Valley Drive, Harrogate (run by Harrogate Council, tel. 01423-500600), are on a 42-acre site on the south-western side of the town centre, opposite the famous Royal Pump Room. They convey the civic pride of this prosperous spa town, with colourful and precise formal bedding for spring and summer, and a long dahlia border for late summer and autumn, a pleasing place to walk off lunch or tea taken at **Betty's**, the famous tearoom nearby. Gardens open all year, 24 hours a day. Entrance free.

NORTHERN IRELAND

Ards and Down

S peaking as someone used to the crowded south-east of England, I find one of the great joys of visiting gardens in Ards and Down is the tranquillity to see and photograph them at leisure. There is no doubt that the region is under-visited while harbouring some priceless horticultural jewels.

It is a rural region of small hills, stony outcrops and quiet lanes; friendly, relaxing and endlessly rewarding for anyone who takes a pleasure in plants and an undisturbed landscape. Strangford Lough, an inland sea enclosed by the Ards Peninsula, is famous for migrating and nesting birds, seals and other wildlife, but several fine gardens are also positioned on its shores.

Must See

Mount Stewart, Newtownards – quirky and interesting design, well planted

Exceptional in Spring

Castlewellan National Arboretum, Castlewellan
Rowallane, Saintfield

Worth a Visit in Winter

Rowallane, Saintfield
Castle Ward, Strangford

CASTLEWELLAN

Castlewellan National Arboretum

The Grange, Castlewellan, Forest Park BT31 9BU **TEL.** 028 4377 8664
OWNER Dept of Agriculture and Rural Development, N. Ireland **HOURS** Open
all year, daily, 10a.m.–4p.m. **ENTRANCE** £3.80 cars, £10 mini-buses **DIRECTIONS**
25m S of Belfast, 4m NW of Newcastle, by A24

🍴 ♿ Access 🍴 Café

Castlewellan Arboretum is famous for raising the eponymous golden-leaved Leyland cypress (which, you cannot help noticing, is extensively used as garden hedging in the region). The Arboretum sits on sloping ground on the northern side of the beautiful Mourne Mountains, four miles inland from the sea. Its tree collection, spread over 108 acres, was begun more than 100 years ago by the Annesley family, and the acidic soil supports a classic cocktail of rhododendrons, camellias, South American and Antipodean trees and shrubs, arranged within the extensive walled gardens and around the lakeside. Walks here at any time of year are rewarding, but spring and autumn are the most spectacular for their floral and foliage bounty respectively, while the many white-flowered eucryphias are a summer speciality. The Arboretum has also recently opened a new hedge maze, which they claim is the largest of its type in the world.

NEWTOWNARDS

Mount Stewart House and Gardens

Portaferry Road, Newtownards BT22 2AD **TEL.** 028 4278 8387/8487
OWNER The National Trust **HOURS** Gardens April–Sept, daily, 11a.m.–6p.m.,
Oct, Sat and Sun, 11a.m.–6p.m., March, Sun only, 2–5p.m., St Patrick's Day,
11a.m.–6p.m.; house Easter period, daily, April and Oct, Sat–Sun and Bank
Holiday Mons, May–Sept, Wed–Mon, all 1–6p.m. (last adm. 5p.m.) **ENTRANCE**
£4, children £2, family ticket £8.50; house and garden £4.50, children £2.25,
family ticket £9.75 **DIRECTIONS** 15m SE of Belfast on A20

🍴 ♿ Access 🍴 Gift Shop 🍴 Café 🍴 2 for 1 Voucher

Some gardens are remarkable for their plant collections, some for their rigorous design, and others are special for the particular atmosphere imbued by their makers. Mount Stewart combines all of these three assets and is among the most memorable of the hundreds that I have visited for this *Guide*.

The 80-acre garden was chiefly laid out during the 1920s by Edith, Marchioness of Londonderry. Edith, known to her close friends as 'Circe, the Sorceress', was a remarkable woman by any standards: an influential political hostess, she founded the Women's Legion in

1915 which provided jobs for women while men were away fighting and greatly improved the status of women in the workplace. Following the First World War, Edith spent much of her time at Mount Stewart and refurbished the house interiors as well as giving ex-servicemen employment in laying out the formal gardens.

The Italian garden on the south front of the house comprises richly planted formal parterres (best in summer) modelled on those of Dunrobin Castle, Sutherland, Edith's childhood home. Beyond is the Spanish garden, with rills and formal pool, surrounded by impressive arcaded hedges of Leyland cypress. The sunken garden on the west side was laid out according to plans sent by post from Gertrude Jekyll (*q.v.*), although its plantings of yellow and orange, blue and purple flowers and foliage is largely to Edith's specification. Mount Stewart's gardens were deeply personal to Edith and are imbued with symbolism; its shamrock garden, enclosed by yew hedges, contains a topiarised Irish harp in yew and a ground pattern featuring the Red Hand of Ulster, planted seasonally with scarlet flowers. The Dodo terrace features cast-concrete animals from The Ark, a dining club regularly hosted by Edith in London. All Ark members had amusing or apposite nicknames, often referring to animals: Edith's philandering husband was Charley the Cheetah, Winston Churchill was called Winnie the Warlock, while the financier and journalist William Astor was Billy the Goat.

Mount Stewart's sheltered position, dependable rainfall and lime-free soil have all encouraged rapid growth of rare and sub-tropical plants in the formal gardens and glorious rhododendrons and magnolias in the surrounding woodlands and lakeside. Edith's extravagant spending on their creation hardly dented her husband's vast coal-mining fortune. An interesting, little-known mark of Edith's independent nature is that she had a twining snake tattooed up her left leg while visiting Japan in 1904. It remained a private foible until hemlines were raised in the 1920s and '30s, whereupon its discovery caused a sensation.

SAINTFIELD

Rowallane

Saintfield, Ballynahinch BT24 7LH **TEL.** 028 9751 0131 **OWNER** The National Trust **HOURS** Open all year, daily, May–Sept, 10a.m.–8p.m.; Oct–April, 10a.m.–4p.m. **ENTRANCE** £3, children £1.25, family ticket £7 (Nov–mid-March, free) **DIRECTIONS** 11m SE of Belfast, 1m S of Saintfield, on A7 **WEB** www.nationaltrust.org.uk

🔲 ♿ Access 🔲 Café 🔲 NPC 🔲 2 for 1 Voucher

With Rowallane and Mount Stewart (*q.v.*) in reasonably close proximity, you can witness, in one day, two completely opposing forces in garden-making – formal and naturalistic. Each has its own sense of place, with Mount Stewart's reflecting and responding to the formal house it surrounds, while Rowallane's 52-acre garden moulds itself to the landscape. It could hardly do otherwise, for Rowallane sits firmly in drumlin land, an undulating, rocky landscape formed in the Ice Age, leaving bare rocks and smooth boulders pushing up through pockets of acidic soil.

'My son always calls it eiderdown country, because it looks buttoned-down,' says Rowallane's head gardener, Mike Snowden, and the description is apt. The only formal area at Rowallane is the walled kitchen garden, but even that is now given over to naturalistic plantings of primulas and meconopsis threaded among specimen shrubs and trees, including a towering *Magnolia veitchii*, spectacularly in bloom in spring. The point of Rowallane is its plant collections, of endless fascination to any keen gardener, while its gentle contours and thoughtful planting make it a pleasure for anyone. You can saunter at random through woods and glades, among the flowering shrubberies, or tiptoe between the boulders in the rock garden.

Most visitors come to see the fine collection of rhododendrons, between mid-April and mid-June, assembled by the garden's makers, the Revd John Moore in the last half of the 19th century and his nephew, Hugh Armytage Moore, in the first half of the 20th. Rowallane has also produced many of its own distinctive plant varieties, including the hybrid *Hypericum* 'Rowallane', *Chaenomeles* × *superba* 'Rowallane', and a crocosmia, viburnum, primula and meconopsis. A summer highlight of the walled garden is its National Collection of penstemon hybrids (around 65 of the large-flowered cultivars). The property was farmed before the arrival of the Revd Moore and its small, stone-walled fields and domestic atmosphere add to the garden's friendly character.

STRANGFORD

Castle Ward

Strangford, Downpatrick BT30 7LS **TEL.** 028 4488 1204 **OWNER** The National Trust **HOURS** House open Good Friday–Sun after Easter, daily, rest of month Sat–Sun only, June–Aug, daily, except Thurs, Sept–Oct, Sat–Sun only, 1–6p.m. (last adm. 5p.m.); grounds open daily all year, dawn–dusk **ENTRANCE** £3, children £1.50, family ticket £7.50; parking £3 **DIRECTIONS** On S shore of Strangford Lough, 7m NE of Downpatrick, on A25, 1½m W of Strangford village

🔳 ঝ Access 🔳 Gift Shop 🔳 Café

Castle Ward

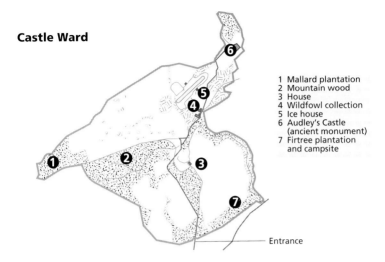

1 Mallard plantation
2 Mountain wood
3 House
4 Wildfowl collection
5 Ice house
6 Audley's Castle
  (ancient monument)
7 Firtree plantation
  and campsite

Entrance

Glorious views of the seawater inlet of Strangford Lough, fine woodland walks and a pleasing, intimate Victorian garden of exotics are some of the pleasures of a visit to the 700-acre estate of Castle Ward. (There is also a four-week opera season in June and a Gilbert and Sullivan opera in September.) Owing to the mild local climate, the parkland trees grow into magnificent specimens, their feet bathed in seas of bluebells in late spring.

The sunken garden, on the north side of the house, is walled and formal, with sculpted lawns enclosing beds of roses and seasonally bedded-out flowers. Castle Ward's cabbage palms in this area have formed stout-trunk trees that bring a vertical emphasis, while tender exotics such as *Beschorneria yuccoïdes* and fasciculations take advantage of the sheltering walls and surrounding forest trees.

Visit the extraordinary house; it is an entertainingly schizophrenic mix of classical austerity on its south-western front and a contrasting gothick style on the north-east, due to the opposing tastes of its creators, Bernard Ward (later Lord Bangor) and his wife, Lady Anne. The curious his-'n'-hers arrangement continues indoors, too. 'Mr Ward is building a fine house,' wrote Mrs Delany, while visiting in 1762, 'but...it is a pity it should not be judiciously laid out. He wants taste and...his wife is so whimsical that I doubt her judgement. If they do not do too much they can't spoil the place, for it hath every advantage from nature that can be desired.' From the point of view of sunlight, Lady Anne perhaps drew the short straw in taking the north-east elevation, but she did have, at least, compensating spectacular views of the undulating park and distant Lough.

And also...

Ballyrogan Nurseries, The Grange, Ballyrogan, Newtownards BT23 4SD (tel. 028 9181 0451, evenings only), are open by appointment with Gary Dunlop, the proprietor, who holds the National Collections of crocosmia, celmisia and euphorbia in his rugged and rocky three-acre garden. Send 2 × 1st-class stamps for a catalogue of his extensive list of nursery plants, which can be ordered by mail.

Carraig Beag, 1 Cloughey Road, Portaferry, Newtownards BT22 1ND (tel. 028 4272 8777), covers two-thirds of an acre, at the southern end of Strangford Lough. The home of Mrs D. Wallace, it features extensive planting, including two ponds with associated planting for seasonal interest. Open by appointment only, May–Aug. Entrance £2, children free, reduced rates for parties of 20 or more.

Roses are the speciality at **Dickson Nurseries Ltd, 42a Milecross Road, Newtownards BT23 4SS (tel. 028 9181 2206)**. This firm was founded in 1836 and many well-known 20th-century roses have been bred here, including 'Grandpa Dickson', a yellow hybrid tea, and the popular patio rose 'Sunseeker'. The nursery is open Mon–Thurs, 8a.m.–12.30p.m. and 1–5p.m., and Fri, 8a.m.–12.30p.m. A mail order list of roses is free on request. Off A20, 11m SE of Belfast.

9 Portaferry Road, Greyabbey BT22 2RU (tel. 028 4278 8351), the first house on the shore side of Portaferry Road, on the shores of Strangford Lough, is near the famous Mount Stewart gardens (*q.v.*). Here is a delightful, private seaside garden divided into richly planted, individual sections by Mrs Betty Brittain, who is pleased to show visitors round, by appointment. Entrance £2, OAPs £1, children free, reduced rates for parties of 20 or more.

Seaforde Gardens and Tropical Butterfly House, Downpatrick BT30 8PG (tel. 028 4481 1225), boast the National Collection of eucryphia, as well as a hornbeam maze and a large, walled garden (part of which is a commercial nursery raising over 700 different trees and shrubs, and there is a Butterfly House with tropical plants). There is also a tearoom and the gardens are accessible to the disabled. All is set within eight acres of a lovely landscape park with fine mature trees and rhododendrons. Open Easter–Oct, Mon–Sat, 10a.m.–5p.m., Sun, 1–6p.m., Nov–March, Mon–Fri, 10a.m.–5p.m. Entrance for garden £2.50, children £1.50; tropical Butterfly House and garden £4.30, children £2.50, family ticket £12. Off A24, 20m S of Belfast (signposted).

Belfast and Antrim

MAP NO. 8

It is a deeply ingrained part of Irish hospitality to ensure that everyone is well fed and watered, and I enjoyed a hearty meal and a few beers in good company at the amazing Crown Liquor Saloon (a gas-lit, exotically tiled Victorian pub) in Belfast on my first day here – a good start. Beyond the city, the landscape is undulating, small farmland, with wooded glens and a spectacular coastline, particularly at the Giant's Causeway where some 40,000 steps formed from basalt columns, as a result of the even cooling of volcanic lava 60 million years ago. Harebells, thrift and sea campions eke out a living on the windy headlands, while pyramidal orchids and burnet roses cling to the dunes of Murlough Bay, watching over Scotland's Western Isles, just a few miles away by sea.

Worth a Visit in Winter
Belfast Botanic Gardens,
  Belfast

Belfast Botanic Gardens

Botanic Avenue, Belfast BT9 1JP **TEL.** 028 9032 4902 **OWNER** Belfast City
Council Parks Dept **HOURS** Open all year, daily, 8a.m.–sunset **ENTRANCE** Free
DIRECTIONS In the University area, about a 10-minute walk from Donegall
Square, between University and Ulster Museum, access from University Road,
Botanic Avenue, Agincourt Avenue, Colenso Parade and Stranmillis
Embankment

🅿 ♿ Access 🅿 Café

The city of Belfast built its wealth on the traditional industries of
shipbuilding, rope-making, linen and tobacco, and an enjoyable couple
of hours can be spent in its Botanic Gardens, which reflect the boom
times of the Victorian age. The gardens were founded in 1828 and cover
around 28 acres; they are partly formal, with seasonal bedding set into
broad lawns, and contain 5000 different plants with special collections
of Irish-raised cultivars and *Bromeliaceae* (the tropical plant family which
includes pineapples). There are fine herbaceous borders and a rose
garden with around 8000 plants, but the glasshouses are the highlight
of a visit. The restored palm house, built in the mid-19th century, is one
of the finest and earliest surviving examples of curvilinear glass and
cast ironwork with a gracefully domed roof, while the Tropical Ravine
House nearby offers views from a balcony into a more steamy jungle
of ferns, bananas, waterlilies and vines from the tropics (pull the chain
to operate the waterfall!).

Within the Botanic Gardens lies the fascinatingly eclectic Ulster
Museum, with exhibits ranging from Irish antiquities to modern art,
to treasures from a wreck of the Spanish Armada.

Patterson's Spade Mill

751 Antrim Road, Templepatrick BT39 0AP **TEL.** 028 9443 3619 **OWNER** The
National Trust **HOURS** Easter Bank Holiday, daily, 2–6p.m.; April, May and
Sept, Sat, Sun and Bank Holidays only, 2–6p.m.; June–Aug, daily, except
Tues, 2–6p.m. **ENTRANCE** £3, children £1.25, family ticket £7.25 **DIRECTIONS** 3m
E of Templepatrick on A6 (Belfast–Antrim road)

🅿 ♿ Access 🅿 Mail Order

Comparatively few people have seen a garden spade being made by
hand, but it is fascinating, and a visit to this time-capsule cottage
industry is well worthwhile; you can buy a spade to take home or
order one tailored to your own measurements.

At least 171 different types of spade have been recorded in Ireland, their shapes having evolved to suit different types of terrain; a winged spade is suitable for cutting out blocks of peat, whereas the Annalong spade is designed with a taper to wedge into stony soils. Six different styles are regularly made at Patterson's now, the typical model having a long, fairly narrow blade, useful for digging in confined spaces – for example, in well-stocked flowerbeds where you want to avoid disturbing surrounding plants.

All the spades start as a 4in × 2in × ¾in block of steel, which is heated and hammered into shape before being riveted to an ash shaft. It is hot, noisy, heavy work, with the vast hammer being driven by water from the River Ballygowan and the dusty air in the dimly lit mill filled with the blended smells of oil, metal and wood shavings.

And also...

Redcot, 35 King's Road, Belfast BT5 6JG (tel. 028 9079 6614), is a two-and-a-half-acre garden with mixed plantings of shrubs and trees, and double herbaceous borders extending 100ft, plus woodland, wild areas and a fernery. Open by appointment with Mr and Mrs Knox Gass. Entrance £2.50, children free.

SCOTLAND

Central Scotland

This region encompasses the areas previously known as Fife, Lothian and Tayside, parts of which are now fragmented into unitary authorities. South of the Firth of Forth lies Edinburgh, the Heart of Midlothian, with its castle perched on a core of ancient volcanic rock. North of the Forth lies the ancient Kingdom of Fife with its pleasantly undulating farming landscape, sandy coastline and attractive fishing villages. Dunfermline was once the seat of the Scottish monarchy, but Fife's great claim to fame now is the university town of St Andrews, home of the Royal and Ancient Golf Club. Perthshire and Kinross, with Angus, occupy the former Tayside. It has a lush greenness and a picturesque hardiness with ancient, wind-blasted granite hills and broad, forested glens. There are deep inland lochs fed by countless mountain burns, and tough wildflowers survive the harsh conditions of moorland and scree.

Must See
Drummond Castle, Crieff – breathtakingly bold formality
Royal Botanic Garden, Edinburgh – diverse plant collections overlooking Edinburgh city

Exceptional in Spring
Bolfracks Garden, Aberfeldy
Branklyn Garden, Perth

Worth a Visit in Winter
Royal Botanic Garden, Edinburgh

ABERFELDY

Bolfracks Garden

Aberfeldy, Perthshire PH15 2EX **TEL.** 01887-820207 **OWNER** Contact Mr D. Hutchinson **HOURS** April–Oct, daily, 10a.m.–6p.m. **ENTRANCE** £2.50, children under 16 free **DIRECTIONS** 2m W of Aberfeldy on A827 towards Kenmore

This four-acre garden is in a lovely situation overlooking the Tay river valley, famous for its whisky distilleries and salmon fishing. (You can take a scenic one-and-a-half-mile woodland walk from nearby Aberfeldy to the Falls of Moness, which inspired Burns to write a song, *The Birks of Aberfeldy*.) The Bolfracks walled garden features mixed borders of trees, shrubs and perennials. There are also, as in so many of the gardens of Scotland, masses of roses, both old and modern, for a long season of blooms.

A woodland garden with peat walls and a natural stream provide the setting for many rhododendrons, azaleas, primulas and meconopsis, and sheets of naturalised bulbs. Cluny House Gardens (*q.v.*) is close by, on the eastern side of Aberfeldy.

James Grieve and his Plants

James Grieve joined Dicksons Nursery in Edinburgh in 1859, where he became involved with plant hybridisation while managing the nursery. His particular interests in plant breeding were concerned with achimenes, carnations, phlox, rhododendrons and violas, but his name is most familiar today for the well-known apple that is named after him.

The apple 'James Grieve' is renowned for its excellent sweet flavour, well-balanced acidity and use as both a dessert apple and a cooker (the latter when used fresh). It arose as a seedling, open pollinated from 'Pott's Seedling' or from 'Cox's Orange Pippin', and was introduced to the trade by Dicksons in 1893. In 1897 it received an Award of Merit from the Royal Horticultural Society, followed by a First Class Certificate in 1906. It is an ideal fruit for northern gardens where summers are cooler and allow the fruits to develop at a steady pace, but is not a good choice in the humid west of the country, where it may develop canker.

BALERNO

Malleny Garden

Balerno, nr Edinburgh, Lothian EH14 7AF **TEL.** 0131-449 2283 **OWNER** The
National Trust for Scotland **HOURS** April–Oct, daily, 9.30a.m.–7p.m.,
Nov–March, daily, 9.30a.m.–4p.m. (house not open) **ENTRANCE** £2
DIRECTIONS In Balerno, off A70 Edinburgh–Lanark road, 7m from Edinburgh
⬛ ⅙ Access ⬛ NPC

Covering just three acres, this is a pretty, summery garden attached
to a 17th-century house. Its group of four yew trees, clipped like
slender mushrooms on stalks, are 400 years old and dominate the
garden, standing in huddled conversation beside smooth lawns.
There are fine herbaceous borders, 12ft deep and sumptuously
planted, and the National Collection of 19th-century shrub roses.
To see this garden at its best, visit around mid- to high summer.
The garden also houses an important National Collection of bonsai.

CRIEFF

Drummond Castle

Crieff, Perthshire PH7 4HZ **TEL.** 01764-681257 **OWNER** Grimsthorpe &
Drummond Castle Trust Ltd **HOURS** Easter and May–Oct, daily, 2–6p.m. (last
entry 5p.m.) **ENTRANCE** £3.50, OAPs £2.50, children £1.50 (under 5s free)
DIRECTIONS 2m S of Crieff, off A822
⬛ ⅙ Access

The spectacular gardens of Drummond Castle lie in a level valley
bottom, made all the more dramatic because you get an aerial view
first, from the castle's courtyard, high up on a ridge of rock towering
over the valley. The symmetrical parterres are laid out with neat
swirls and lines of low, box hedging, partly infilled with gravel and
partly with brilliant roses and summer bedding. Topiarised
variegated hollies, green and golden columns of yew and cypress,
and mop-headed, purple-leaved acers and plums bring vertical
accents into the pattern, and all is immaculately maintained.

The garden was laid out in the 1830s, but in the highly wrought
style that prevailed in the 17th century. At the heart of the parterre is
a celebrated sundial, made by John Mylne, master mason to Charles I,
dating from around 1630. The vegetable and fruit gardens and
glasshouses beyond a beech hedge at the rear are also worth visiting,
and the trees in the surrounding woods and park are unusually large
and beautiful.

There is partial wheelchair access.

Culross Palace

Culross, Fife KY12 8JH **TEL.** 01383-880359 **OWNER** The National Trust for Scotland **HOURS** Phone for details **ENTRANCE** Phone for details **DIRECTIONS** On A985, 4m E of Kincardine Bridge, 12m W of Forth Road Bridge **WEB** www.nts.org.uk

🖼 **Gift Shop** 🖼 **Café**

Culross is a well-preserved medieval village with narrow, cobbled streets, picturesquely set on the north shore of the River Forth. Its palace was not a royal residence but home to a wealthy merchant; tour the atmospheric rooms, with beautifully painted timber ceilings, to set the scene before venturing into the garden.

At the rear, the garden rises in steep terraces, covering barely one acre of ground. It is laid out in medieval style, in a series of rectangular raised beds containing culinary, medicinal and dyers' herbs, with some salads and vegetables. Although the planting is not exclusively devoted to plants used in medieval Scotland, the period flavour is preserved with timber boards edging the beds, and woven willow hurdles and a rustic willow tunnel providing part of the framework. I visited on a bright, summer's day when the crunchy paths were quite dazzling; on closer inspection they turned out to be crushed seashells, making a fine contrast to the soft green herbs.

Hill of Tarvit Mansion House

Cupar, Fife KY15 5PB **TEL.** 01334-653127 **OWNER** The National Trust for Scotland **HOURS** Garden (summer) 9a.m.–9p.m., (winter) 9a.m.–4.30p.m.; house Easter, May and Sept, daily, 1.30–5.30p.m., July–Aug, daily, 11a.m.–5.30p.m., Oct, Sat–Sun, 1.30–5.30p.m. **ENTRANCE** House and garden £5, concessions/children £4, family ticket £14; garden £2 and £1, by honesty box **DIRECTIONS** Take A92 to Cupar, then 2m S on A916 **WEB** www.nts.org.uk

🖼 ♿ **Access** 🖼 **Gift Shop** 🖼 **Café**

Terraces of broad lawns follow the gentle contours of the site around Hill of Tarvit's Mansion House. The grey-stone, symmetrical house was built during the Edwardian age, in 1906, for one Frederick Sharp, a financial tycoon and art collector, whose ancestors made their fortune turning jute into sackcloth, greatly in demand for sandbags during the American Civil War.

The four-acre garden, like the house, was designed by Sir Robert Lorimer, a prominent local architect, in the contemporary formal style prevailing. The setting is deliberately green, with neat yew hedges and topiaries framing the lawns on the south side, and an interesting series of yew buttresses seemingly 'supporting' a retaining wall beside the lowest terrace, which is reached via a grand stone stairway.

A south-facing wall, enclosing the gardens on the north side of the house, provides shelter for a long herbaceous border in the Edwardian style, punctuated with flowering shrubs such as roses, philadelphus and buddleias. From here you can enter the woodland garden, through a fine gateway, and climb the steep path up to the monument on Tarvit Hill, where you will be rewarded with breath-taking panoramic views.

David Douglas – Our Man in America

David Douglas (1798–1834) was one of several intrepid Scottish plant hunters whose pioneering journeys have helped to enrich our gardens. Born at Scone, Perthshire, he was the son of a stonemason. His childhood fascination for natural history led him early into a botanical career, beginning at Scone Palace, in the gardens of Lord Mansfield. Work followed in the botanic garden of Glasgow University, where he caught the attention of W.J. Hooker, the regius professor. Douglas joined Hooker on botanising expeditions through the highlands, which led to trips much further afield for the Royal Horticultural Society. He made three expeditions to America, which was at that time still largely unexplored and inhabited by the indigenous tribes of American Indians. In the tradition of the great plant hunters of the 19th century, his journeys involved great hardship and danger. Tough and resourceful, Douglas survived encounters with grizzly bears, fevers, shortage of food, harsh climates and unfriendly Indians. His explorations led him deep into country which had never encountered a white man, and on one occasion his canoe capsized, leaving him to be spun through a whirlpool before being tossed onto a bank, having lost his irreplaceable journals and 400 plants. Alas, on his third expedition he paused in the Hawaiian islands where his body was found in a pit trap, having been gored by a wild bull.

In his short life Douglas gathered 20,000 plant specimens and introduced around 200 new species which are now widely grown in Britain. They include many American pines, the grand fir *Abies grandis*, the Douglas fir *Pseudotsuga menziesii*, the fabulous *Arbutus menziesii* with its cinnamon-coloured peeling bark, and the aromatic Californian 'headache' tree, *Umbellularia californica*.

The Scotch Thistle

Scotland embraces the thistle as its emblem flower, and at Drummond Castle *(q.v.)* the distinctive outline of this flower has been adapted to wonderful effect in the layout of the garden's great parterre. The emblematic use of the thistle dates from the Middle Ages, when it was adopted by Stuart kings in their heraldic coats of arms. It is thought that the thistle was seen to be a suitable mascot, being tough, durable and defiant, or perhaps because of its prickly aggressiveness.

There is some debate over which particular species of thistle is the appropriate one. Certainly the cotton thistle, *Onopordum acanthium*, is decorative enough and makes a fine garden plant where there is room for it. Out of a base rosette of large, silver-grey leaves the leafy flower stem rises to a towering 7–8ft, making this biennial a wonderful spectacle in the flower border. Its neat heads of typical purple thistle flowers are handsome, although small in comparison to the great eruption of foliage. The spear thistle, *Cirsium vulgare*, is another candidate for the title of Scotch thistle, bearing classic thistle flowers above fearsomely thorny stems and foliage. It is certainly the more ubiquitous wildflower of the two, and the more likely to have been adopted early on, although for garden purposes its ornamental charms are limited except for use in 'wild' areas of naturalised flowers.

EDINBURGH

Royal Botanic Garden

Must See

20a Inverleith Row, Edinburgh, Lothian EH3 5LR **TEL.** 0131-552 7171 **OWNER** Dept of Agriculture and Fisheries for Scotland **HOURS** Daily, Nov–Jan, 9.30a.m.–4p.m.; Feb and Oct, 9.30a.m.–5p.m.; March and Sept, 9.30a.m.–6p.m.; April–Aug, 9.30a.m.–7p.m. **ENTRANCE** Free, donations welcome **DIRECTIONS** 1½m N of city centre, at Inverleith, just off A902 **WEB** www.rbg.org.uk

🌺 ♿ **Access** 🌺 **Gift Shop** 🌺 **Café** 🌺 **Plants for Sale**

This is a centre for botanical research, for which it has a worldwide reputation, but it is also a thrilling garden for visitors. The higher parts of the garden enjoy fabulous views of the city, and its 70 acres include every type of plant imaginable. There is an extensive and beautifully laid-out rock garden, a large collection of heathers, a spectacular herbaceous border (backed by very tall beech hedging), excellent demonstration gardens and examples of different types of hedging trees and wonderful glasshouses. These contain large collections of plants from the humid tropics and arid deserts.

The locally acidic soils nurture many rhododendron species and other plants of the Far East, chiefly grown from seed collected in the wild. Look out for the lovely oriental herbaceous flowers such as the Himalayan poppies, variously petalled in bright blues, reds, yellows and white according to their species. Future generations of botanists and horticulturists learn their craft here, and the standard of maintenance is very high.

FALKLAND
Falkland Palace

Falkland KY15 7BU **TEL.** 01337-857397 **OWNER** The National Trust for Scotland **HOURS** April–Oct, Mon–Sat, 10a.m.–5.30p.m., Sun, 1.30–5.30p.m. (last adm. 4.30p.m.), groups at other times by appointment **ENTRANCE** £5, concessions £4, family ticket £14; garden only £2.50, concessions £1.70 **DIRECTIONS** On A912, 11m N of Kirkcaldy **WEB** www.nts.org.uk

🌿 ⚬ Access 🌿 Gift Shop

The palace was built between 1501 and 1541 by James IV and James V. It was the country residence of Stewart kings and queens (including Mary Queen of Scots), who hunted deer and wild boar in the surrounding forest. The three-acre garden, however, dates from the 1940s and 1950s, and is chiefly the work of garden designer Percy Cane, who laid out herbaceous borders around the broad lawns and planted trees and shrubs to extend interest through the seasons. Roses garland the old garden walls and summer herbs and delphiniums are a popular spectacle. The royal tennis court, reputedly the world's oldest, is still used.

FORFAR
House of Pitmuies

Guthrie by Forfar, Angus DD8 2SN **TEL.** 01241-828245 **OWNER** Mrs Farquhar Ogilvie **HOURS** Easter–end Oct, daily, 10a.m.–5p.m. **ENTRANCE** £2.50, children under 12 free **DIRECTIONS** Off A932, 6½m E of Forfar

🌿 Plants for Sale

There are beautiful walled gardens beside the house, leading to an informal riverside walk. Pride of place goes to the semi-formal gardens with a series of long borders of delphiniums and roses – a spectacular highlight of the gardens in July and early August – plus other plantings of herbaceous flowers. Other fine features include a collection of fruit of special interest, glasshouses and conservatories, an alpine meadow and a cool woodland garden with riverside walks – prettiest in spring when the naturalised bulbs and rhododendrons are in bloom. The 18th-century house is closed, except by prior appointment, but you can visit the unusual turreted doo-cot (dovecote) and gothic-style wash-house. Fruit from the garden is offered for sale when ripe.

MUSSELBURGH

Inveresk Lodge

24 Inveresk Village, Musselburgh, East Lothian EH21 7TE **TEL.** 01721-722502 **OWNER** The National Trust for Scotland **HOURS** April–Oct, Mon–Fri, 10a.m.–6p.m., Sat–Sun, 12 noon–6p.m.; Nov–March, Mon–Fri, 10a.m.–4.30p.m., Sun, 2–5p.m. **ENTRANCE** £2, concessions £1, by honesty box **DIRECTIONS** Off A6124, S of Musselburgh, 6m E of Edinburgh **WEB** www.nts.org.uk

⬤ ♿ Access

Inveresk is an attractive and unusual village, dating chiefly from the late 17th to early 18th centuries, but built on the site of what was once a large Roman camp. Its name derives from the Celtic terms Inver (at the mouth of) and Esk (water). Seventeenth-century Inveresk Lodge (not open) is the oldest house in the village and its pretty gardens, which *are* open, are laid out in informal terraces on a steep slope. As well as many herbaceous plants and grasses there is a border of shrub roses, a selection of climbing roses and plenty of trees, shrubs and flowers which bring interest right through the autumn. A large Edwardian conservatory houses pot plants and an interpretation exhibit.

The village itself is also well gardened. The splendidly gabled, former merchant's home, Shepherd House, has an intensively planted, one-acre walled garden, with potager, ponds and fountains, an alpine wall, parterres and a large collection of tulips. It is occasionally open to the public for special charity days (tel. 0131-665 2570 for dates) and by prior appointment.

PERTH

Bell's Cherrybank Gardens

Cherrybank, Perth, Perth and Kinross, Tayside PH2 0PF **TEL.** 01738-627330 **OWNER** Guinness UDV **HOURS** Easter–Sept, Mon–Sat, 10a.m.–5p.m., Sun, 12 noon–4p.m., and by appointment at other times **ENTRANCE** £3, under 18s free

⬤ ♿ Access ⬤ Café ⬤ Gift Shop ⬤ Plants for Sale ⬤ NPC

These gardens occupy a wedge-shaped piece of undulating ground around the headquarters of Arthur Bell & Son, on the south-west side of Perth. They are immaculately maintained and comprise an important National Collection of heathers (around 1000 different varieties are grown here), planted in generous drifts between snaking paths and neat lawns. A natural burn flows into the garden from the Glasgow Road, providing an ideal source of water for the garden's pools and fountains. The tapestries of colour are particularly good in late summer, the prime flowering period, but there are many spring- and early summer-flowering species here, too.

George Forrest – Our Man in China

Like David Douglas (*q.v.*) and Robert Fortune (*q.v.*), both of whom preceded him, George Forrest (1873–1932) was a tough, lone Scot with an unquenchable thirst for finding plants in far-flung lands. Born in Falkirk, Forrest worked as a chemist's apprentice before going to Australia, where he travelled and worked for 10 years. On his return to Scotland he took employment in the Herbarium of the Royal Botanic Garden, Edinburgh, but within a year he was travelling in the high mountains of Yunnan province, in north-west China.

Chinese explorations occupied his time for the next 28 years, in a total of seven major expeditions which also took him to upper Burma and Tibet. Many popular garden plants were first brought to Britain by Forrest, including *Pieris forrestii*, many exquisite rhododendron species, primulas in great variety, camellias, gentians, berberis, buddleias, cotoneasters and mahonias. Today it is hard to imagine the potential perils of looking for plants. Forrest narrowly escaped with his life in 1905 when marauding Tibetan monks hunted down his collecting party and murdered all but one of them. Hampered by lack of food, an injured and painful foot and travelling under darkness, Forrest spent 10 days retreating back to safety.

More than 30,000 plant specimens were gathered on his journeys and returned to Edinburgh. George Forrest died in Yunnan province, of heart failure, while out shooting grouse.

PERTH

Branklyn Garden

116 Dundee Road, Perth, Perth and Kinross, Tayside PH2 7BB **TEL.** 01738-625535 **OWNER** The National Trust for Scotland **HOURS** March–Oct, daily, 9.30a.m.–7p.m. **ENTRANCE** £3, concessions/children £2, family ticket £8 **DIRECTIONS** Take A9 to Perth, cross Queen's bridge, turn right down Dundee Road, garden on left after ½m **WEB** www.nts.org.uk

🌿 & Access 🌿 Gift Shop 🌿 Plants for Sale 🌿 NPC

Covering just under two acres, this richly stocked plantsman's garden on Perth's outskirts was begun in 1922 by plant enthusiasts John and Dorothy Renton, on the site of a former orchard. The garden has a solidly mature but well-kept feel and, despite the fact that it has not been in private ownership since 1967 (when it was passed to the National Trust for Scotland), it is intimate and informal.

Its specialities are rhododendrons, alpines, hardy herbaceous plants of the Far East and colourful swathes of spring bulbs. Spring and early summer are its greatest months, but autumn sees the brilliant russet and golden tints of numerous acers and azaleas. Look for the National Collection of *Cassiope* – dwarf evergreen shrubs related to rhododendrons and heathers.

Gentians: Blue Alpine Gems

Ian Christie, Ann Christie and Ian Martin run **Christie's Nursery, Downfield, Main Road, Westmuir, Angus DD8 5LP (tel. 01575-572977/web www.christiealpines.co.uk), on A926, 1m W of Kirriemuir, 6m W of Forfar**. This alpine specialist nursery sits 500ft up, on the northern rim of the fertile Strathmore valley, below the spectacular Angus Glens. 'Without a doubt this is one of the finest natural beauty spots in Britain, and we can guarantee an unlimited supply of clean fresh air,' say the Christies. They also supply a huge range of tough alpine plants which thrive in that air, and hold the National Collection of *Gentiana* (nearly 200) of which around 50 different species and cultivars are on sale. Few gardeners are resistant to the charms of gentians, especially the true blue kinds and those with pyjama-striped trumpet flowers. Broadly speaking, most of the spring-flowering gentians are sun-lovers, requiring neutral to limy, sharply draining soils; the autumn-flowerers tend to need peaty, acid soil which retains some moisture, and a position that doesn't bake in midday sun. Meconopsis, primulas, alpine rhododendrons and trilliums are also well represented in the nursery. A mail order catalogue is available on request. Open March–Oct , Mon and Wed–Sat, 10a.m.–5p.m., Nov–Feb, by prior appointment only.

PITTENWEEM

Kellie Castle and Garden

Pittenweem, Fife KY10 2RF **TEL.** 01333-720271 **OWNER** The National Trust for Scotland **HOURS** Open all year, daily, 9.30a.m.–sunset; castle May–Sept, Easter and weekends, 1.30–5.30p.m. **ENTRANCE** £2, concessions £1, by honesty box; castle and garden £5, concessions £4, family ticket £14 **DIRECTIONS** From A917, 3m NW of Pittenweem village, on B942 (signposted) **WEB** www.nts.org.uk

🌳 ⅀ Access 🌳 Gift Shop 🌳 Café

Kellie Castle

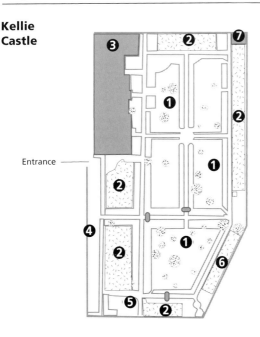

Entrance

1 Lawns
2 Fruit and vegetable gardens
3 Castle
4 Lawn terrace
5 Yew-enclosed secret garden
6 Cut flowers
7 Robert Lorimer's summerhouse

A pretty, pleasing, utterly peaceful walled garden of one and a half acres, snuggling under the castle's massive bulk of buff-grey stone. My first impression upon entering through the gate in the garden wall was of a distinctly feminine nature, and it wasn't surprising to discover that the head gardener is a woman, Kathy Sayer, who has maintained it organically since arriving in 1990.

Knee-high box hedges line the gravelled paths which run around the garden's perimeter, dividing it into three main sections, with fruit tree-studded lawns filling the centre. The garden's chief function has always been to produce fruit, vegetables and flowers for the house. There are also many old roses (around 90 different varieties), and a pair of low hedges of the crimson-and-white striped *Rosa gallica* 'Versicolor' (*Rosa mundi*), reputed to have been here for over 100 years. Poppies and peonies, lupins, lavatera and dame's violet all contribute to the abundant beauty, and self-sown flowers are allowed to stay *in situ* wherever possible. Kathy Sayer's hens are regularly allowed to roam the garden, assisting the organic slug-control.

A two-storey summerhouse in one corner of the garden was designed by the Arts and Crafts architect, Sir Robert Lorimer – Kellie Castle was his family's summer home in the late 19th and early 20th century.

And also...

Early spring bulbs entice local visitors to **Cambo Gardens, Cambo Estate, Kingsbarns, St Andrews, Fife KY16 8QD (tel. 01333-450054/web www.camboestate.com)**. Created around the Cambo Burn, the Victorian walled garden also sports old roses and a recently laid-out ornamental potager; there are plants for sale, too. Open all year, daily, 10a.m.–dusk. Entrance £2.50, children free. On A917.

Cluny House Gardens, by Aberfeldy, Perthshire PH15 2JT (tel. 01887-820795), has a plantsman's woodland garden specialising in rhododendrons, candelabra primulas, meconopsis and other acid-loving plants from the Far East in a romantically wild setting. Particularly lovely in spring and autumn. Open March–Oct, daily, 10a.m.–6p.m. Entrance £3, children free. Leave A9 at Ballinluig and take A827 towards Aberfeldy, after 6m turn off to Strathtay and continue for 3½m.

The original 'Pleasance' gardens at **Edzell Castle, Edzell, nr Brechin, Angus, Tayside DD9 7UE (tel. 01356-648631)**, were laid out in 1604 and, although they fell to rack and ruin, were reinstated in the 1930s in their 17th-century style. There are rose beds, box edging, plus box and yew topiaries contained within walls that are decorated with sculptured stone panels and niches. Open April–Sept, daily, 9.30a.m.–6.30p.m.; Oct–March, Mon, Tues, Wed and Sat, 9.30a.m.–4.30p.m., Thurs, 9.30a.m.–12.30p.m., Sun, 2–4.30p.m. Entrance £2.80, concessions £2, children £1 (under 5s free). Leave A90 near Brechin, then 6m on B966 and follow signs from Edzell. **2 for 1 Voucher**

Glamis Castle, Glamis, by Forfar, Angus, Tayside DD8 1RJ (tel. 01307-840393/web www.glamis-castle.co.uk), is a turreted, pink-sandstone palace that was a childhood home of Queen Elizabeth the Queen Mother. An 18th-century landscape park surrounds the castle; its two-acre, Italian-style garden features herbaceous borders contained within stout yew hedges, with a formal fountain and ornamental gazebos. There is also an interesting sundial in the grounds and a newly opened pinetum. Open end March–late Oct, daily, 10.30a.m.–5.30p.m. (10a.m.–5.30p.m. July–Aug), last adm. 4.45p.m. Entrance £6.20, OAPs £4.70, children £3.10, family ticket £17; grounds only £3.10, concessions £1.60. On A94 between Forfar and Perth.

Glendoick Garden Centre, Glendoick, Perth, Tayside PH2 7NS (tel. 01738-860260), specialises in rhododendrons, azaleas and other ericaceous shrubs (particularly enkianthus and kalmia), with primulas and meconopsis. There is also a comprehensive mail order catalogue (send £2) for orders exceeding £35-worth of plants. Open all year, daily, 9a.m.–5p.m. (9a.m.–6p.m. in summer). Entrance free. 7m from Perth on A90.

Kinross House, Kinross, Perth and Kinross, Tayside KY13 8ET (tel. 01577-862900), is a late 17th-century mansion surrounded by four acres of beautifully proportioned, formal walled gardens. The walls themselves are decorated with statuary and ornamental gates, and within their enclosure are sumptuous herbaceous borders, some colour-themed, with roses, yew hedges and lovely views over the loch. Open May–Sept, daily, 10a.m.–7p.m. Entrance £2, children 50p. Leave M90 at Jct 6, then at Kinross turn right at roundabout, garden on left (signposted).

St Andrews Botanic Garden, Canongate, St Andrews, Fife KY16 8RT (tel. 01334-477178/476452/web www.botanicgardens.co.uk), on the western side of town, straddles the meandering waters of Kinness Burn. It is part of the historic university, with specialised alpine and rock gardens, a lake and woodland garden, including rhododendrons and azaleas. The interesting glasshouses shelter tropical plants and orchids, cacti and alpines. Open daily, 10a.m.–7p.m. (closes 4p.m. Oct–April). Entrance £2, concessions/children £1. Signposted from A91.

The University of Dundee Botanic Garden, Riverside Drive, Dundee, Tayside DD2 1QH (tel. 01382-647190), is a teaching institution, with systematic beds of plants grouped by their families, but is interesting and well prepared for visitors, too. There are areas set aside to demonstrate plant communities for different habitats, drought-resistant plants, carnivorous ones, interesting glasshouses, fine trees and a lake. Open all year, Mon–Sat, 10a.m.–4.30p.m. (closing 3.30p.m. Nov–Feb), and Sun, 11a.m.–4p.m. (closing 3p.m. in winter). Entrance £2, OAPs/children £1, family ticket £5. A92 towards Dundee city centre, then along Riverside Drive, at roundabout follow signs to the university, garden on right.

Dumfries and Galloway

MAP NO. 8

A site of varying landscapes – the desolate inland region of the Glenkens, with its mountains, lochs and waterfalls, the hilly pastures of Dumfriesshire, and the low, sea-enveloped terrain of West Galloway, which reaches out to the north-east stretches of Ireland, just a short boat-crossing away. It is more usual for people to pass through the region, *en route* to Glasgow or Carlisle, but there are some renowned horticultural highlights. The sheltered coastal gardens thrive thanks to the warming influence of the Gulf Stream, which creates a milder, but wetter climate than other parts of Scotland.

Exceptional in Spring

Castle Kennedy, Stranraer

Threave Garden, Castle
  Douglas

Worth a Visit in Winter

Threave Garden, Castle
  Douglas

CASTLE DOUGLAS

Threave Garden

Castle Douglas DG7 1RX **TEL.** 01556-502575 **OWNER** The National Trust for Scotland **HOURS** March and Nov–Dec, Wed–Sun, April–Oct, daily, 9.30a.m.–sunset; walled garden and glasshouses 9.30a.m.–5p.m.; visitor centre and shop, 9.30a.m.–5.30p.m. **ENTRANCE** £4.50, children £3.60, family ticket £12.50 **DIRECTIONS** Off A75, 1m W of Castle Douglas, 19m W of Dumfries, follow signs to Threave **WEB** www.nts.org.uk

🌿 &. Access 🌿 Gift Shop 🌿 Café 🌿 Plants for Sale

Of the 1200 acres of the Threave estate, 64 are devoted to gardens. There is plenty of labour to keep them up to scratch, for this is the National Trust for Scotland's own training school for full-time gardeners. Threave is particularly famous for its spring displays of daffodils (around 200 different varieties), which carpet the lawns surrounding the Victorian red-sandstone mansion house. However, there is much else to see through the year, in the mixed borders, peat and rock gardens and, especially, the old walled kitchen garden, with its Victorian glasshouses, traditional herbaceous borders, assorted vegetables and trained fruit.

KIRKCUDBRIGHT

Broughton House

12 High Street, Kirkcudbright DG6 4JX **TEL.** 01557-330437 **OWNER** The National Trust for Scotland **HOURS** April (or Easter if earlier)–Oct, daily, 1–5.30p.m. (July–Aug, 11a.m.–5.30p.m.) **ENTRANCE** £3.50, concessions/children £2.50 **DIRECTIONS** In Kirkcudbright town centre, off A711/A755 (signposted)

Broughton House

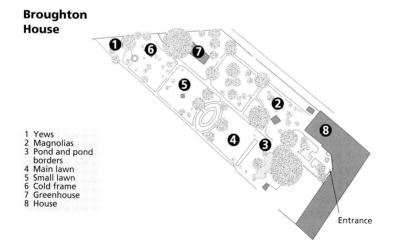

1 Yews
2 Magnolias
3 Pond and pond borders
4 Main lawn
5 Small lawn
6 Cold frame
7 Greenhouse
8 House

Entrance

Kirkcudbright (pronounced Ker-coobree) is a handsome coastal town, formerly a busy port, with broad streets of elegant Georgian and Victorian terraced houses and cottages (and plenty of places to stay). Situated at the head of the River Dee estuary, its harbour shelters fishing and leisure boats. It has been compared to Cornwall's St Ives, since both enjoy a mild climate and a soft light that has attracted artists in droves. In the centre of town, Broughton House belonged to the renowned Scottish artist E.A. Hornel in the early decades of the 20th century. Its one-and-a-half-acre garden is a curious hybrid of Scottish country garden and oriental styles, and leads down to the Dee estuary. Behind the grey stone 18th-century town house there are broad lawns and exuberant herbaceous borders, with a jolly mix of mallows, marguerites, montbretia and pot-marigolds, penstemons, poppies and persicaria. They are joined by Japanese cherry trees and waterlily pools with stepping-stones. The peaceful artist's home is now a museum of his and other painters' work.

STRANRAER

Castle Kennedy Gardens

Exceptional in Spring

Stair Estates, Rephad, Stranraer DG9 8BX **TEL.** 01776-702024 **OWNER** Earl of Stair **HOURS** April–Sept, daily, 10a.m.–5p.m. **ENTRANCE** £3, OAPs £2, children £1, free for disabled **DIRECTIONS** 5m E of Stranraer from A75, left at Castle Kennedy village and 1m down private drive (signposted)

🌿 **Gift Shop**   🌿 **Café**   🌿 **Plants for Sale**

With its long avenues of dark trees, imposing, pointed turrets and views of the deep waters of the Black Loch, this 75-acre site can be a slightly spooky place in gloomy weather. It is lifted by spectacular spring colour from the rhododendrons, and is interesting on several counts.

The original gardens were laid out by the 2nd Earl of Stair in the early 18th century. He was a Field Marshal and British Ambassador to France, and laid out the gardens with military precision in a series of formal rides and cross-axes, using the man- and horsepower of the Royal Scots Greys and Inniskilling Fusiliers. Several rides meet at the Round Pond, a circular pool packed with lilies in a two-acre site. A monkey puzzle avenue, over 100 years old, leads from the pool towards the castle, thought to be the tallest and finest avenue of its type in Britain. A smooth bowling green and sculpted turf terraces are part of the early gardens landscaped by the soldiers, and the garden boasts many specimen trees of terrific size which flourish in the mild, moist climate. The garden's rhododendron collection enjoys international renown (many hybrids were actually bred here) and some of the oldest were grown from seed brought back by Sir Joseph Hooker from the

Himalayas in the mid-19th century. There is also a walled garden of herbaceous flowers beside the ruins of the 15th-century Castle Kennedy.

STRANRAER

Logan Botanic Garden

Port Logan, Stranraer DG9 9ND **TEL.** 01776-860231 **OWNER** Royal Botanic Garden, Edinburgh **HOURS** March–Oct, daily, 9.30a.m.–6p.m. **ENTRANCE** £3, concessions £2.50, children £1, family ticket £7 **DIRECTIONS** 14m S of Stranraer off B7065

 &. Access   Gift Shop   Café   Plants for Sale   2 for 1 Voucher

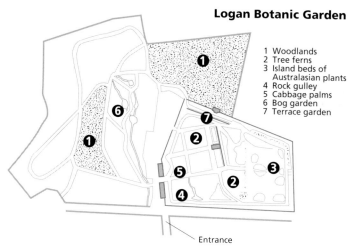

Logan Botanic Garden

1 Woodlands
2 Tree ferns
3 Island beds of Australasian plants
4 Rock gulley
5 Cabbage palms
6 Bog garden
7 Terrace garden

Entrance

The 14-mile stretch of road south of Stranraer down the Mull of Galloway is dull and featureless, making the arrival at Logan Garden all the more pleasing, for you suddenly step into a 10-acre sub-tropical oasis that takes full advantage of the warming Gulf Stream climate. It has much in common with Tresco Abbey Gardens (*q.v.*) on the Isles of Scilly, for it is rich in plants from the southern hemisphere which can be grown outdoors in few other parts of Britain.

There are Chatham Island forget-me-nots from the South Pacific Ocean, bearing clear blue flowerheads and large, pleated leaves, South African daisies in variety and rare trees from Chile. The cabbage palms are memorable, forming avenues of 40ft-high trees, while tree ferns and huge fan palms add to the tropical scenery. Anyone interested in plants will find it hard to tear themselves away on a fine summer's day. Enjoy its tranquillity, for the remote location ensures that overcrowding from visitors is never a problem. The food in the garden's Salad Bar was also good on my visit.

Poppies from the Far East

If there is one time of year when I envy gardeners in the cooler, northern stretches of the UK, it is in late spring–early summer, when the vivid, blue-petalled Himalayan poppies (*Meconopsis* species) are in bloom. They relish the cool climate and moisture-laden atmosphere of the north-west and are a feature of **Craigieburn Garden, Craigieburn House, by Moffat DG10 9LF (tel. 01683-221250), from M74 Jct 15 take A708, at Moffat go towards Belkirk for 2m, then on left**. Woodland and moisture-loving plants are the speciality and unusual species of meconopsis can be bought from the plant shop and admired within the recently developed, eight-acre show garden beside it. Open Easter–Sept, Sat–Sun, 12.30–6.30p.m. Entrance £2.50.

And also...

The two-and-three-quarter-acre, 17th-century walled garden at **Cally Gardens and Nursery, Gatehouse of Fleet, Castle Douglas DG7 2DJ (tel. 01557-815029)**, offers many rare and unusual species among the 3500 plants listed in its catalogue (send 3 × 1st-class stamps). Herbaceous perennials, particularly geraniums, agapanthus, crocosmias and grasses are a speciality, and many plants on offer have been grown from seed recently collected on expeditions to far-flung corners of the world. Open Easter–early Oct, Sat–Sun, 10a.m.–5.30p.m., Tues–Fri, 2–5.30p.m. Entrance £1.50. From A75 take Gatehouse Road, after 2m turn left into Cally Palace Hotel entrance and follow signs to the walled garden.

Elizabeth MacGregor, Ellenbank, Tongland Road, Kirkcudbright DG6 4UU (tel. 01557-330620), specialises in unusual herbaceous perennials, particularly violas and violettas, of which she offers over 100 different varieties (send 4 × 1st-class stamps for a catalogue). Open to visitors May–Oct, Fri–Sat and Mon, 10a.m.–5p.m. On A711, 1m N of Kirkcudbright.

Old and new fruit varieties are the speciality of **J. Tweedie Fruit Trees, Maryfield Road Nursery, Maryfield, nr Terregles, Dumfries DG2 9TH (tel. 01387-720880)**. New varieties currently available include 'Pax' gooseberry, 'Canada Red' rhubarb, and dwarf cherry trees on Edabriz rootstocks. Send a s.a.e. for the mail order catalogue. Open by appointment only.

Highland

Nothing impresses so much in this region as the overpowering presence of the ancient mountains. It is a landscape of awesome rock faces, smoothed and pared down by distant ice ages, where volcanic remains have left craggy peaks. Rainfall is very high throughout the region and year, while persistent winds prune trees into asymmetrical shapes. It is the domain of hardy sheep which nonchalantly graze the roadsides. But there are splendid gardens here, too, and excellent nurseries, in this sparsely populated area in the far north of Scotland.

Must See
Inverewe Garden, Poolewe –
   awesome plant collection in
   windswept coastal setting

Exceptional in Spring
Armadale Castle, Sleat

Exceptional in Summer
Cawdor Castle, Nairn

Sea View Garden

Durnamuck, Dundonnell, Wester Ross IV23 2QZ **TEL.** 01854-633317
OWNER S. and I. Nelson **HOURS** Mid-May–mid-Sept, daily, 10a.m.–6p.m.
ENTRANCE £1, children free **DIRECTIONS** Signposted off A832 Gairloch–
Dundonnell road at Badcaul for 1m

🌿 ♿ Access 🌿 Plants for Sale

Sea View is an intimate, half-acre cottage garden, laid out since 1990,
surrounding a stone crofter's cottage overlooking Little Loch Broom.
Its owners, Simone and Ian Nelson, came from the Lake District to settle
here in 1989 and, while Ian paints watercolour landscapes, Simone
develops the garden, which was previously virgin heathland, now made
fertile with tons of composted manure. Hedges of griselinia and
escallonia help to filter persistent winds. There are also raised beds of
alpines and seasonal perennials, a heather bed, pond and bog area, a
narrow border of herbaceous plants, and a small kitchen garden with
raised vegetable beds and fruit trees. All is well maintained, and the
bright day of my visit belied the extreme difficulties of making any sort
of garden here, where work is often delayed by weeks of steady rain.

Lochalsh Woodland Garden

Lochalsh House, Balmacara, by Kyle of Lochalsh, Ross-shire IV40 8DN
TEL. 01599-566325 **OWNER** The National Trust for Scotland **HOURS** All year,
daily, 9a.m.–sunset **ENTRANCE** £2, concessions/children £1 **DIRECTIONS** Off A87,
3m E of Kyle of Lochalsh

Lochalsh Woodland Garden is more woodland than garden, its
craggy slopes covered with heather, seedling birches and pines, and
bracken. It enjoys a peaceful position overlooking the waters of Loch
Alsh and is a pleasant place for a picnic.

Many of the mature oaks, larches and pines on its 13 acres were
planted around 1887 as a shelterbelt to Lochalsh House (not open).
There are rhododendrons scattered through the woods, mainly
slightly tender varieties planted by E.H.M. Cox of Glendoick (*q.v.*) in
the early 1960s, from wild seed collected in the Himalayas. The
position is outstanding, warmed by the influence of the Gulf Stream,
and enjoys views of the Sound of Sleat and parts of Skye. The National
Trust for Scotland calls this 'very much a garden in the making', and
they are extending the plantings of hydrangeas, fuchsias, bamboos,
ferns and rhododendrons.

Primulas Galore at Ardfearn

Many of the customers who buy from **Ardfearn Nursery, Bunchrew, Inverness IV3 6RH (tel. 01463-243250), 4m W of Inverness, by A862**, select their plants from a mail order catalogue, but this is a nursery worth visiting if you are in the area. This open, breezy site is ideal for raising healthy, extremely hardy plants, and the nursery stocks a broad selection of alpines and rock-garden plants from all over the world. Primulas are a speciality (around 90 different species and varieties are grown here), with gentians, celmisias and assorted small shrubs and conifers suited to the acid soils that prevail in this region. Open all year, daily, 9a.m.–5p.m. Mail order Oct–March

NAIRN

Cawdor Castle

Cawdor, by Nairn IV12 5RD **TEL.** 01667-404615 **OWNER** The Dowager Countess of Cawdor **HOURS** May–mid-Oct, daily, 10a.m.–5.30p.m. (last adm. 5p.m.) **ENTRANCE** £3.20; castle and grounds £6.10, OAPs £5.10, children £3.30 **DIRECTIONS** 6m SW of Nairn, on B9090, off A96 **WEB** www.cawdorcastle.com
 Access Gift Shop Café

Cawdor and Inverewe (*q.v.*), the latter way over to the west, are the jewels in the Highlands' horticultural crown. The former is sumptuously filled with herbaceous borders and roses galore, formally laid out in symmetrical patterns on level ground beside the castle. There are lavender-edged beds with roses filling out the centres; long borders packed with traditional seasonal flowers, including peonies, lupins, delphiniums, heleniums, penstemons and campanulas in a glorious explosion of summer colour; broad lawns, beautiful trees and plenty of seats for the weary (easily seen, for they are painted bright red).

Away from the main show gardens is a less-visited secret garden with a holly maze bordered by laburnum tunnels. Beyond is a beautifully made, box-edged herb garden, and a yew-enclosed white garden with modern central fountain. Around these are colour-graded Jekyll-style herbaceous borders leading through cool blues and yellows into warmer reds and plum colouring. Everything is maintained to a very high standard.

Perennials by the Loch

Like Ardfearn Nursery (*q.v.*), **Abriachan Nurseries, Loch Ness Side, by Inverness IV3 8LA (tel. 01463-861232), 9m SW of Inverness, on A82, ignoring side roads marked to Abriachan**, enjoys a splendid location. It overlooks the deep, dark waters of Loch Ness and offers an extensive nursery, and two acres of gardens to explore within 10 acres of hazel woodland. Margaret and Donald Davidson came here 17 years ago and have built up a solid reputation for producing a wide range of well-grown perennials, both hardy and half-hardy. There are campanulas, a huge selection of primulas (which thrive in the hazel woods), helianthemums, many geraniums, peonies and other old-fashioned border plants. Hardy penstemons thrive (due to the protective influence of the loch), and rosemary does exceptionally well on the free-draining, acidic, sandy soil. There is also a lively and informative mail order catalogue (send 4 × 1st-class stamps). Open Feb–April and Oct–Nov, daily, 9a.m.–5p.m., April–Sept, daily, 9a.m.–7p.m. Entrance to garden £2, children 20p. (The site is on a hill and is not disabled-friendly.)

ORD

An Acarsaid

Ord, Teangue, Isle of Skye IV44 8RN **TEL.** 01471-855218 **OWNER** Mrs E. McInnes **HOURS** Open Easter–Oct, daily, 12 noon–5.30p.m. **ENTRANCE** Donations to charity **DIRECTIONS** On the waterfront at Ord, 5m from A851 along unclassified, single-file track

An Acarsaid (The Anchorage) is a neat, white bungalow, the retirement home of Eileen and the late Ranoull McInnes. It lies in an uncompromisingly exposed position perched on a limestone crag, facing the Atlantic ocean and merciless winds. It is what I would call a plantsman's garden with atmosphere – impossible to avoid the latter, due to its incredible location – and gentle humour thrown in for good measure. The two-acre garden is spread along a steep, rocky hillside and makes creative use of the natural stone to hand, which Ranoull McInnes fashioned into stairways, low walls and cobblestone paths. Near the seaward entrance is a fabulous animal skeleton cemented into the garden wall, bearing the legend Each Uist Earballach (Ranoull McInnes was a Gaelic-speaking native of Skye), and further description reveals the creature as being Hydro Equus Extendus, a rare, long-tailed water horse related to the Loch Ness

Monster. (I won't spoil your fun in guessing what the skeleton really is, but the McInneses had me fooled for a long time about this!)

A thoughtfully numbered route leads through the garden past a rock bank of primulas, saxifrages, aquilegias, mountain avens and other alpines to the front garden, which is home to an eclectic collection of roses, spring and summer bulbs, meconopsis, hardy geraniums, ferns and much else. A handsome mountain ash is beautifully garlanded with white-flowered 'Wedding Day' roses and an unnamed scarlet climbing rose. The clifftop woodland garden is a semi-wild area, leading through a shrubbery to a viewpoint of Skye's spectacular Cuillin mountains, which are marked out on a display board for identification, although their peaks are often masked by clouds and tempestuous rain. Tough plants eke a living out of the shallow soil of this weather-blasted garden. It is a place which has an unruly character entirely appropriate to its setting.

POOLEWE

Inverewe Garden

Must See

Poolewe, Wester Ross IV22 2LG **TEL.** 01445-781200 **OWNER** The National Trust for Scotland **HOURS** Open all year, daily, 9.30a.m.–9p.m. (closes 5p.m. mid-Oct–March) **ENTRANCE** £5, OAPs/children £4, under 5s free, family ticket £14 **DIRECTIONS** On A832 by Poolewe, 6m N of Gairloch **WEB** www.nts.org.uk

   ⟐ Ġ Access ⟐ Gift Shop ⟐ Café ⟐ Plants for Sale ⟐ NPC

On my first visit to Inverewe I arrived at 8p.m., and had this fabulous garden all to myself, just me – and millions of midges. Be sure to arrive liberally doused with repellent; the gardeners wear netted headgear on still days, when midges are a serious problem.

Since a three-mile labyrinth of paths winds through the garden, you can lose yourself in the richly planted woodland featuring large collections of rhododendrons, eucalyptus, olearias and many other plants of the southern hemisphere, which thrive here due to the warming influence of the Gulf Stream. Among them are woodland perennials in variety, lily-pools, bold drifts of candelabra primulas and shuttlecock ferns. The gardens also contain the National Collections of *Brachyglottis* (shrubby *Senecio*), olearia and rhododen-dron (Barbatum series).

The house front is enlivened by a curved herbaceous border, spectacular from June to August, and below is a rock garden sloping down to the shore. The sunny walled garden also faces the sea and displays a sumptuous blend of herbaceous and annual flowers, vegetables, fruit and pergolas draped with climbing roses and clematis. The garden was made by Osgood Mackenzie in the latter half of the 19th century. Seeing all its rich variety, it is hard to believe that when Mackenzie arrived the estate was a treeless wasteland. It lies at 57.8°N, closer to the Arctic Circle than St Petersburg and most of Labrador, and on one of the world's most windswept coastlines. It is also exceptionally well maintained. Garden Cottage Nursery (*q.v.*) is nearby, and good meals are served at the Poolewe Hotel, on the opposite shore of the loch.

The Ancient Scots Pine

When caught in low-angled sunlight the scaly, buff-orange bark of *Pinus sylvestris*, the Scots pine, lights up in a fiery glow, heightening the contrast with its clouds of dark green needle-foliage.

The ancient Caledonian Pine Forest is said to be the only true native forest in Britain, although only parts of it remain in scattered clumps through the Highland region. The trees, often characterfully mis-shapen, sparsely populate the hillsides here and there, rising out of coarse mats of springy heather.

In medieval times the scene was quite different. The native pines and birches spread in a great forest across the Highlands from Perth to Ullapool. Alas, wholesale felling of trees began in the late 17th century to supply charcoal for a thriving iron industry and timbers for warships and construction purposes.

Scots pines were planted as waymarkers for drovers' routes through England in the 18th century. They were invaluable for signalling where grazing and rest places could be found.

Some replanting of indigenous pines has been carried out in the Highlands in the last two decades, but fenced protection from grazing deer and sheep is needed for them to thrive. In unfenced areas there is now little or no natural regeneration of the once great forest and therefore it is dying out.

SLEAT

Armadale Castle Gardens

 Exceptional in Spring

Sleat, Isle of Skye IV45 8RS **TEL.** 01471-844305/844227 **OWNER** Clan Donald Lands Trust **HOURS** Gardens open all year; Visitor Centre (which has a good café) April–Oct, daily, 9.30a.m.–5.30p.m **ENTRANCE** £4, concessions/children £3, donation box in winter **DIRECTIONS** At S end of Skye on A851 (single-track road), 14m S of Broadford; or by ferry, in summer, from Mallaig on the mainland to Ardvasar **WEB** www.cland.demon.co.uk

🚻 ♿ Access 🎁 Gift Shop ☕ Café 🌱 Plants for Sale

Armadale Castle Gardens

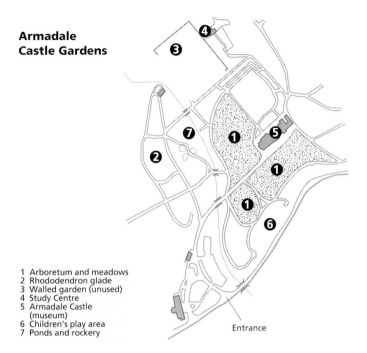

1 Arboretum and meadows
2 Rhododendron glade
3 Walled garden (unused)
4 Study Centre
5 Armadale Castle (museum)
6 Children's play area
7 Ponds and rockery

Entrance

This fine garden lies in the Sleat (pronounced slate) peninsula, in the far south of the Isle of Skye. There are 40 acres of gardens and woodland within the vast (20,000-acre) Clan Donald Lands estate. They include new ponds with a rock garden in an informally landscaped area with winding paths in turf and gravel. A long, luxuriantly planted, traditional herbaceous border lies in a sheltered position beyond the tree-speckled lawns behind the ruined castle. Above the border is a terraced walk beside a raised bed featuring hypericums and sages, sedum, santolina and phygelius. The trees at Armadale are magnificent, especially the mossy beeches, and there are many rhododendrons, including recently planted specimens. Wildflowers are a feature in the many areas of long grass and meadow, with colonies of orchids under the wych-elms.

The property enjoys fabulous easterly views of the mountains of the mainland and the waters of the Sound of Sleat. While you're here, do visit the Study Centre, where interesting exhibitions are held each year, and a new museum featuring the history of the clan and the castle.

Attadale Gardens

Strathcarron, Wester Ross IV54 8YX **TEL.** 01520-722217 **OWNER** Mr and Mrs E. Macpherson **HOURS** April–Oct, Mon–Sat, 10a.m.–5.30p.m. **ENTRANCE** £3, children £1 **DIRECTIONS** On A890 between Strathcarron and South Strome

🌿 ♿ Access 🌿 Plants for Sale

The 20-acre gardens are laid around Attadale House, on the edge of a vast Highland estate. Although the gardens are on level ground, steep hills and cliffs rise up sharply along the north-eastern edge, the lowest slopes of which contain a rhododendron walk above a water garden, which runs in a series of lily-filled ponds alongside the drive. There are further woodland walks leading to a small, formal sunken garden, a box-edged herb and kitchen garden, and a rhododendron dell. The gardens lie in a spectacular landscape, although visitors may find the persistent sheep flies are a problem in summer.

And also...

Brin Herb Nursery, Flichity, by Farr, Inverness IV2 6XD (tel. 01808-521288/web www.sageweb.co.uk), stocks over 300 varieties of herbs and wildflowers grown at 700ft above sea level, with bulbs, salads, cut herbs and strawberries in season. There are also well-labelled display gardens, a restaurant specialising in herb-flavoured food and teas, and seeds for sale. Open Mid-March–Oct, Mon–Sat, 9.30a.m.–6p.m., Sun, 2–5p.m. Entrance free. On B851 to Fort Augustus, 7m W of A9, 9m S of Inverness.

The entrance drive to **Dochfour Gardens, Inverness IV3 8GY (tel. 01463-861218)**, winds through a mature wood of larches, firs, birch and beech at the foot of craggy hills overlooking Loch Ness. The 17-acre gardens are set among topiarised yew hedges, with lavender-edged rose beds, a herbaceous border and a kitchen garden (with pick-your-own strawberries in season). But it is the trees here that impress most, particularly a fine deodar near the house (not open). A delightful water garden has spreading parrotias and Japanese acers beside a bank of rhododendrons and meconopsis. Open April–Sept, Mon–Fri, 10a.m.–4p.m. Entrance £1.50, OAPs and children £1. Off A82, 5m SW of Inverness.

Dunvegan Castle, Dunvegan, Isle of Skye IV55 8WF (tel. 01470-521206/web www.dunvegancastle.com), is a fortress stronghold dating from the 13th century that has been continuously inhabited by the chiefs of the Clan MacLeod. There are 10 acres of 18th-century gardens with rhododendron woodlands and impressive natural waterfalls. Some garden walks end at the castle jetty, where boat trips can be taken from spring to autumn to a seal colony in Loch Dunvegan. Open all year, daily, mid-March–Oct, 10a.m.–5.30p.m., Oct–mid-March, 11a.m.–4p.m. Entrance to castle and garden £5.50, OAPs £5, children £3; gardens only £3.80, children £2. From A863 go through Dunvegan, castle on left.

Garden Cottage Nursery, Tournaig, Poolewe, Achnasheen, Wester Ross IV22 2LH (tel. 01445-781777), stocks a wide range of plants in an informal garden setting, surrounded by trees and wild rhododendrons. Shrubs suited to the west coast, with primulas and moisture-loving plants, are their speciality. Many of the plants seen at Inverewe can be bought here; there is also a mail order catalogue (send 4×2nd-class stamps). Nursery only open Easter–Oct, Mon–Sat, 10.30a.m.–6p.m. A9, then A835, then A832, nursery is 1½m N of Inverewe.

The Hydroponicum, Achiltibuie, Ullapool IV26 2YG (tel. 01854-622202/web www.thehydroponicum.com), is a purpose-built growing environment where modern, soil-less growing methods are used in conjunction with heat and sunlight. Bananas, grapes, citrus fruits, figs and giant blackberries flourish in the solar-heated, insulated growing houses, and strawberries are picked from April to September. Access is for guided tours only. The fruits are used in the adjacent café. Open Easter–Oct, daily, 10a.m.–6p.m., last guided tour 5p.m. (tours at 12 noon and 2p.m. only in Oct). Tour £4.75, concessions £3.50, children £2.75, under 5s free, family ticket £12.50. Signposted from A835, 25m N of Ullapool.

Little Leckmelm Shrubbery and Arboretum, by Ullapool, Wester Ross IV26 2RH (Ullapool Tourist Information tel. 01854-612135), is a tranquil woodland best seen at rhododendron time, although it has some splendid trees too, including a magnificent weeping beech. It was laid out in the 1870s, but from 1940 it lay unattended for 45 years until the present owners began a programme of scrub clearance and restoration. Open April–Sept, daily, 10a.m.–6p.m. Entrance £2, children free, by honesty box (no coaches). S of Ullapool, signposted from A835.

Moray and Aberdeenshire

MAP NO. 8

This area (until recently known as Grampian) encompasses tracts of the spectacular heather-clad Grampian Mountains – snow-capped throughout the winter, and worn by wind and ice – the scenic valley of Royal Deeside, the fishing harbours of the North Sea coast and the handsome, sparkly-granite town of Aberdeen, the 'silver city by the silver sea'. The region is also famous for its culinary heritage: the salmon and trout of its magnificent rivers, the fine Aberdeen Angus cattle and plentiful distilleries of Scotland's most famous export, its whisky. There are also numerous medieval castles, bearing witness to clan wars but, thankfully, some of them are now more pleasingly surrounded by magnificent gardens.

Must See
Pitmedden Garden,
  Pitmedden – crisp formality
  corseting riotous summer
  colour

Exceptional in Summer
Crathes Castle, Banchory

BANCHORY

Crathes Castle

Banchory, Aberdeenshire AB31 5QS **TEL.** 01330-844525 **OWNER** The National Trust for Scotland **HOURS** Castle April (or Good Friday if earlier)–Oct, daily, 10.30a.m.–5.30p.m., last adm. 4.45p.m. (closes at 4.30p.m. in Oct); garden and grounds all year, daily, 9.30a.m.–sunset **ENTRANCE** £7, concessions/children £5; garden £4.50 and £3 **DIRECTIONS** On A93, 3m E of Banchory and 15m W of Aberdeen **WEB** www.nts.org.uk

🌳 & Access   🌳 Gift Shop   🌳 Café   🌳 Plants for Sale

Since the four-acre walled garden is divided into eight separate, themed areas, unquestionably making it one of Scotland's finest summer gardens, visitors should allow plenty of time to explore it. They are divided partly by old stone walls and partly by magnificent yew hedges dating from 1702, out of which rise bulging topiaries, which greatly add to the garden's appeal.

There are herbaceous borders in variety, and the planting was partly inspired by the writings of Gertrude Jekyll (*q.v.*) and William Robinson (*q.v.*) at the turn of the century, both of whom advocated a looser, freer style of planting than had been seen in rigidly formal Victorian gardens of the late 19th century. Some borders are colour-schemed white and cream, there is a garden of blue flowers, a well-stocked rose garden and a golden garden featuring golden-foliage and yellow-flowered plants. The traditional herbaceous borders are sumptuously planted in the Edwardian manner. The restored glasshouses contain an important collection of old-fashioned Malmaison carnations with peony-like clove-scented flowers in a spectrum of pastel pink tints.

The grey-walled castle, in the north-west corner, towers over these highlights. Also see the exquisite 16th-century painted ceilings, coloured with natural pigments, featuring heroes of the past. Drum Castle (*q.v.*) is close by, on the road to Aberdeen.

BANCHORY

Drum Castle

Drumoak, by Banchory, Kincardine and Deeside, Aberdeenshire AB31 5EY **TEL.** 01330-811204 **OWNER** The National Trust for Scotland **HOURS** Grounds open all year, daily, 9.30a.m.–dusk; castle Easter–May and Sept, daily, 1.30–5.30p.m., June–Aug, daily, 11a.m.–5.30p.m., Oct, Sat–Sun, 1.30–5.30p.m. (last adm. 4.45p.m.) **ENTRANCE** Castle, gardens and grounds £6, OAPs/children £4.40, family ticket £16.50; gardens/grounds £2 and £1.30 **DIRECTIONS** Off A93 (signposted), 3m W of Peterculter, 10m W of Aberdeen, 8m E of Banchory **WEB** www.nts.org.uk

🌳 & Access   🌳 Gift Shop   🌳 Café

Drum Castle's solid, square tower is one of the three oldest tower houses in Scotland, dating from the late 13th century, although it has been added to over succeeding centuries. It is enveloped by green pastures and magnificent specimen trees, but the main interest for gardeners is the distant two-and-a-quarter-acre walled garden which has been recently redesigned to display a comprehensive collection of old roses, within a formal framework, best seen at mid-summer.

Beyond it, the grounds include the Old Wood of Drum, 117 acres of ancient natural oakwood, one of the few remaining relics of a vast forest which once covered the lower slopes of the Dee Valley. The forest, which has existed since the last glaciation (10,000 years ago), was used as royal hunting ground from the mid-13th century onwards. Any time of year is rewarding for following the well-marked woodland walks among its oaks, birches and Scots pines, although bright days in spring and autumn show it in particularly beautiful light.

KENNETHMONT
Leith Hall and Garden

Huntly, Aberdeenshire AB54 4NQ TEL. 01464-831216 OWNER The National Trust for Scotland HOURS Hall and grounds Easter and May–Sept, daily, 1.30–5.30p.m., Oct, Sat–Sun, 1.30–5.30p.m.; garden and grounds all year, daily, 9.30a.m.–sunset ENTRANCE Hall and grounds £4.40, concessions/children £2.90, family ticket £13.50; garden and grounds only £2, concessions/children £1.30, family ticket £5.30 DIRECTIONS On B9002, 1m W of Kennethmont, 7m S of Huntly WEB www.nts.org.uk
🚩 ₺ Access 🚩 Café

The springs of the region's peaty hills and the meltwaters off the mountains to the south and west provide a well-watered landscape, famous for its malt whiskies, but Leith Hall, set in a 286-acre estate, offers abundance of a different kind. Sumptuous summer planting schemes and an air of Edwardian grandeur permeate the gardens. The Hall dates from 1650, and lies on the site of a Benedictine monastery (it is thought that a specimen yew on the property dates from the monks' occupation in medieval times). Nothing remains of the 17th-century formal gardens that were laid out with the house, for the grounds were landscaped-over during the 19th century to bring parkland up to the house walls.

The five-acre West Garden is an Edwardian creation, retaining much of its original layout and boasting splendid herbaceous borders which run from the garden gates up to the top of the garden, and are crossed by another path, also lined with herbaceous flowers. The northern, inland position of the property lays it open to mean, cold winters and a relatively short season of summer glory. The rose-beds feature tough varieties of the hybrid Scots briar, *Rosa pimpinellifolia*, such as 'Glory of Edzell' and 'Ormiston Roy', which have replaced less hardy roses that could not survive the winters here. The rock garden also dates from the early 20th century, and is not a collection of alpines, but a gathering of bulbs, low shrubs and herbaceous plants among rocky outcrops and gravel mulches.

The East Garden is a formal, two-acre, partially-walled area of Victorian origin. Little of the original design has survived, but its south-facing slope is now devoted to organically cultivated fruits (including old Scottish apple varieties) and vegetables. Flowers for cutting line the grass paths.

PITMEDDEN

Pitmedden Garden

Must See

Pitmedden, Ellon, Aberdeenshire AB41 7PD **TEL.** 01651-842352 **OWNER** The National Trust for Scotland **HOURS** May–Sept, daily, 10a.m.–5.30p.m. (last adm. 5p.m.) **ENTRANCE** £5, concessions/children £4, family ticket £14 **DIRECTIONS** On A920, 1m W of Pitmedden village and 14m N of Aberdeen; from Aberdeen use A90, then B999 to Pitmedden and follow signs **WEB** www.nts.org.uk

🌿 ♿ Access 🌿 Gift Shop 🌿 Café 🌿 Plants for Sale

Here is a classic, eight-acre, formal garden of green boxwood parterres laid out partly in swirling embroidery patterns, and partly with heraldic designs, in the French-influenced style favoured by wealthy landowners in the 17th century. Although the original garden did not survive in succeeding centuries (it had long been ploughed up in favour of fruit and vegetables), a suitably formal design was reinstated by the National Trust for Scotland in the 1950s.

Between the low hedges, the patterns are filled in each year with 40,000 colourful seasonal bedding plants, in blocks of single colours. They are planted out in May, creating a glorious sight at high summer. There are three miles of box hedging to be clipped each year; besides forming the swirling embroidery patterns, they also spell out mottoes of the Seton family who lived at Pitmedden: 'Sustento Sanguine Signa' (With blood I bear the standard), states one, surrounding the Seton family crest. Also of interest on this 120-acre estate are Pitmedden's sundials, its sturdy pair of garden pavilions and collections of old varieties of tree fruits.

And also...

Brodie Castle, Brodie, Forres, Moray IV36 2TE (tel. 01309-641371/web www.nts.org.uk), has long been famous for its daffodils, for the owner in the late 19th and early 20th century produced over 400 new varieties on the estate, during its heyday. The collection is once more being established at the castle, and presently around 100 Brodie-raised varieties can be seen in the castle's 175 acres of grounds during spring, particularly in April and early May. Between July and October you can buy their daffodils (which are unavailable anywhere else in the world) in person or by mail order. Open (garden) all year, daily, sunrise–sunset, (castle) April–Sept, Mon–Sat, 11a.m.–5.30p.m., Sun, 1.30–5.30p.m., Oct, Sat–Sun. Entrance free, castle £6, concessions £4.50, family ticket £16.50. Signposted from A96 at Brodie.

James Cocker & Sons, Whitemyres, Lang Stracht, Aberdeen AB15 6XH (tel. 01224-313261/web www.roses.uk.com), is an old-established rose nursery, founded in 1841. Among the classic, top-selling roses bred here are 'Alec's Red', 'Glenfiddich' and 'Silver Jubilee'. Cocker's mail order rose catalogue (updated each May), offering over 300 varieties, is free on request, or call at the nursery and garden centre, open daily, 9a.m.–5.30p.m.

Scottish Borders

The gentle landscape of the Borders features green, undulating hills, broad dales and old drovers' roads which make stimulating walking country. There are two tweeds to note, the famous river washing through the region and the local cloth fashioned from the wool of countless sheep roaming the surrounding hills. Wool production has been an important industry for many centuries, although these days finer wools are imported for the softest fabrics. Melrose is an unassuming, small town, famous for its sublime ruin, a 12th-century Cistercian abbey, which Sir Walter Scott maintained should be visited in moonlight. Just south of Melrose, the three-peaked volcanic outcrops of the Eildon Hills loom over Tweeddale, offering outstanding views of the now peaceful borderlands.

Must See
Mertoun Gardens,
  St Boswells – high quality
  walled garden in great
  riverside location

Exceptional in Spring
Lamberton Nursery,
  Lamberton
Dawyck Botanic Garden, Stobo

Exceptional in Summer
Manderston, Duns
Floors Castle, Kelso
Bughtrig Garden, Leitholm

DUNS

Manderston

Exceptional in Summer

Duns TD11 3PP **TEL.** 01361-883450 **OWNER** Lord Palmer **HOURS** Mid-May–Sept,
Thurs, Sun and Bank Holiday Mons, 2–5.30p.m. (parties welcome at other
times by appointment) **ENTRANCE** House and grounds £6, children £3;
grounds only (including gardens, stable and dairy) £3.50, children £1.50
DIRECTIONS 2m E of Duns on A6105 **WEB** www.manderston.demon.co.uk
🌸 Gift Shop 🌸 Café

Manderston

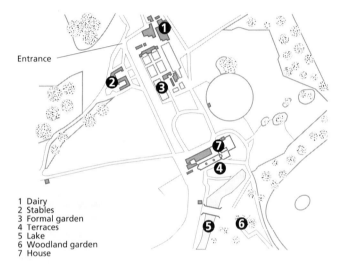

Entrance

1 Dairy
2 Stables
3 Formal garden
4 Terraces
5 Lake
6 Woodland garden
7 House

This is an interesting 56-acre garden, with a definite feel of 'jam
yesterday'. It was built at *vast* expense at the dawn of the 20th
century with lavish stone terraces and balustrades in the Edwardian
style. The huge walled kitchen garden is, alas, sealed off and no
longer in production and the once glorious network of glasshouses
alongside it has mostly disappeared. Curiously, though, the staging
and heating pipes are still in place, and some of this area is
decorated with potted plants as though the glass was still there.
There is a peony border for early summer and beds of dahlias look
jolly in August.

The formal gardens that lead on from here are in the Italianate
style with a luxuriant rose pergola and clipped hedges separating

terraces of symmetrical beds with fountains and bedded-out flowers. A herbaceous border lies to one side and a long walk stretches out on the other, through impressive beds displaying lines of *Galtonia candicans*, scarlet roses and dwarf dahlias – a brilliant show in late summer. There are more formal terraces on the lake side of the house, solidly packed with red roses, hostas and variegated topiary.

Old gardens that were as lavish as this one must be a millstone around the necks of their owners, since armies of staff would have been employed a hundred years ago, and it must be a daunting task for the small staff today, who manage some areas well at the expense of others. Large amounts of funds will surely be needed at some stage to fix the massive stonework which is going out of kilter here and there on the terraces, but in the meantime, enjoy this rare survivor of the 'Golden Afternoon' of the Edwardian age. And while you're here, don't miss the wonderful stables, reported in *Country Life* magazine in 1914 as being 'almost perfection in their arrangement' and remaining so to this day.

ECKFORD

Teviot Water Garden

Kirkbank House, Eckford, Kelso, Roxburghshire TD5 8LE **TEL.** 01835-850734 **OWNER** Mr and Mrs Denis Wilson **HOURS** April–Sept, daily, 10a.m.–5p.m., also by appointment at other times **ENTRANCE** Free (donations for garden upkeep) **DIRECTIONS** Between Kelso and Jedburgh on A698 (ignore signs to Eckford village)

🌿 Gift Shop 🌿 Café 🌿 Plants for Sale

Set on a north-west-facing bank of the River Teviot, this enterprise consists of three attractions: the Teviot Smokery, the Water Gardens and an adjoining shop specialising in aquatic plants and sundries. The water garden is accessed by steep, narrow paths on the river bank, winding through narrow, terraced areas planted with moisture-loving perennials, grasses and bamboos. At the foot of the garden, a path leads onto pleasant riverside walks with small interpretation displays explaining the wildlife and waterfowl in the area. The gardens are occasionally host to sculpture exhibitions, providing a relaxed and informal setting for the work of many different artists. The small aquatic centre sells pond and bog plants, also fish, pebbles and other sundries. The smokery deals in fresh local produce such as trout, eels and wild game, brined and smoked over oak chips.

JEDBURGH

Monteviot

Jedburgh, Roxburghshire TD8 6UQ **TEL.** 01835-830380 **HOURS** April–Oct, daily, 12 noon–5p.m. **ENTRANCE** £2, children under 14 free **DIRECTIONS** 4m from Jedburgh, turn off A68 on to B6400 to Nisbet, N of Jedburgh, entrance second turning on right

▣ ♿ Access ▣ Plants for Sale

A box-edged parterre filled with culinary herbs lies next to the house (not open), and is the oldest part of the garden, enjoying views of the River Teviot below. At a lower level there is a terraced rose garden where stone walls help contain the heady, rosy fragrances of mid-summer, and this area, too, enjoys marvellous valley views. In the 1960s the garden designer, Percy Cane, designed a formal lawned and stepped area, the River Garden, that runs right down to the water's edge; its encircling beds are well stocked with mixed plantings of shrubs, small trees and perennials for a tapestry of colour through the seasons.

The garden's arboretum and pinetum contain exceptionally good specimen trees, dating from the latter half of the 19th and early 20th century. There is also a delightful water garden, crossed by three linked timber bridges, fed by a natural spring and surrounded by rhododendrons and lush waterside perennials. Please note that there is only limited wheelchair access to the garden.

KELSO

Floors Castle

Exceptional in Summer

Kelso, Roxburghshire TD5 7SF **TEL.** 01573-223333 **OWNER** The Duke and Duchess of Roxburghe **HOURS** Early April–end Oct, daily, 10a.m.–4.30p.m. **ENTRANCE** £5.50, concessions £4.25, children £3.25 (under 5s free), family ticket £15; grounds only £3 **DIRECTIONS** Follow signs in Kelso, Floors is on NW side of town **WEB** www.roxburghe.bordernet.co.uk

▣ ♿ Access ▣ Gift Shop ▣ Café ▣ Plants for Sale

Kelso is an attractive town with cobbled streets and handsome buildings and on its west side stands magnificent Floors Castle – said to be the largest inhabited house in Scotland. It is spread out on the north side of the meandering River Tweed's broad valley. Its park, dotted and wooded with fine trees, is on generally level ground. For the garden lover, the main interest is in its walled garden, set well away from the castle.

Within the walled area (at its best in high summer) there are several points of interest, including a rose border (of hybrid teas) and a range of glasshouses growing flowering plants for the house. There is a long herbaceous border planted for early to mid-summer splendour with lupins, geraniums, campanulas, etc. Beyond it, the central double herbaceous borders are long, very traditional and generously planted with phlox, thalictrum, echinops, achilleas, coreopsis, sidalcea and much else, well staked against the wind, and with pillar roses trained along swagged chains behind each border. Further borders feature delphiniums in one area and a blue-and-mauve theme elsewhere. Beside the walled garden a brand-new parterre, in traditional French 18th-century style, has been made to celebrate the millennium. It features the linked initials of the Duke and Duchess of Roxburghe (G, V & R), with a ducal coronet and a double M for the year 2000, laid out in turf and gravel, with some box topiary highlights.

Top marks to Floors for the well-thought-out visitor facilities. The garden is delightful and well kept, with friendly staff in the small garden centre. The coffee shop attached to the walled garden serves excellent home-made food (including good lunches) and has the poshest loos (complete with Molton Brown soaps) I have come across.

Border Alpines

English gardeners in the north find it handy to nip over the border into Scotland, to browse through **Lamberton Nursery, No. 3 Lamberton, Berwickshire TD15 1XB (tel. 01289-308515/web www.mcbeath.clara.net), close to the A1, immediately north of the border at Lamberton**. This new enterprise has been set up by Ron McBeath, formerly of Edinburgh's Royal Botanic Garden. Its speciality is in producing new, rare and unusual plants suitable for the rock and alpine garden, the peat and woodland garden, or the sunny border. Specialist interests cover the *Liliaceae*, *Arisaema*, *Roscoea*, *Primula* and *Meconopsis* species and other related plants, especially those that originated in the Himalayas and China. Much of the stock is raised from seed gathered on recent plant-hunting expeditions, so if you want something your friends haven't got, you'll more than likely find it here. Part of the development of the nursery includes a display garden in the making, with rock and water features. The McBeaths have also, rather thoughtfully, set up an aviary and small animal area, so that accompanying children need not be bored if their prime interest is not alpine gardening! Open April–Oct, daily, 10a.m.–5p.m., and at other times by appointment. Groups are welcomed by appointment. There is a mail order list, available on request.

A Fortune – from All the Tea in China

Tea drinking is so firmly embedded in British culture that it seems strange that only 150 years have passed since the secrets of tea cultivation were learned from the Chinese. For this we have to thank Robert Fortune (1812–80), one of several fearless Scottish plant hunters who risked life and limb in search of new plants.

Fortune was born in Berwickshire and worked at Edinburgh's Royal Botanic Garden before heading south to run the indoor plants section of the Horticultural Society's garden at Chiswick. At the end of the first Opium War, China started to open up to foreign trade and Fortune began an expedition in 1842 in search of peonies, bamboos, 'the plant which produces rice paper' (*Tetrapanax*), kumquats and other exotics. For the salary of £100 per year, plus £500 for expenses, he risked the wrath of the suspicious Chinese nurserymen and resisted attacks from pirates. His second trip to China in 1848 was for the East India Tea Company. As the tea industry was a closely guarded secret by the Chinese, Fortune disguised himself as a Chinaman from a distant province in order to learn the necessary information and acquire tea plants (*Camellia sinensis*). He was then able to supply the Company with 2000 young tea plants, 17,000 germinated seedlings and half a dozen Chinese expert tea-makers.

Several more expeditions to the Orient proved equally successful. As well as acquiring more tea, Fortune returned with many now familiar garden plants, including Japanese anemones, the winter-flowering honeysuckle *Lonicera fragrantissima*, weigela, pompom chrysanthemums, tree peonies, primulas, forsythia and brilliantly coloured azaleas.

LEITHOLM

Bughtrig Garden

Near Leitholm, Coldstream, Berwickshire TD12 4JP **TEL.** 01890-840678 **OWNER** Major General and the Hon. Mrs Charles Ramsay **HOURS** Mid-June–mid-Sept, daily, 11a.m.–5p.m., or by appointment **ENTRANCE** £2, children £1 **DIRECTIONS** ½m E of Leitholm on B6461

 Access

This is an intimate, very well-kept garden, enclosed mainly by hedges rather than walls, and lying quite close to the elegant Georgian house (not open). Within its two-and-a-half acres there are further hedges sub-dividing the plot into productive kitchen and flower gardens, planted to be of interest at different times over the summer season. A straight, turf walk, enclosed by 6ft-tall copper beech hedges, is devoted to displays of pastel-coloured lupins down one side and a mixed herbaceous border with roses on the other. (The dark purple lupins and deep red roses look particularly effective against the copper beech foliage.) Elsewhere, gravel paths lead the way through box-edged beds displaying shrub roses, more herbaceous flowers and blocks of colour from bedded-out annuals such as white lavatera and dwarf sweet peas (both of these are very effective). There are dahlia beds and borders, old fruit trees, soft fruits, cordon-trained sweet peas and nice old greenhouses. In other words, this is a formal and colourful garden with old-fashioned charm.

MELROSE

Abbotsford

Melrose, Roxburghshire TD6 9BQ TEL. 01896-752043 OWNER Dame Jean Maxwell-Scott HOURS Mid-March–Oct, daily, 9.30a.m.–5p.m. (Suns in March–May and Oct, 2–5p.m.); walled kitchen garden June–Oct only ENTRANCE £4, children £2 DIRECTIONS On B6360 between A7 and A68

  ♦ Access   ♦ Gift Shop   ♦ Café   ♦ 2 for 1 Voucher

Sir Walter Scott, the Scottish novelist and poet (and author of *Ivanhoe*) bought this property, on the banks of the Tweed, in 1812 and lived here for the next 20 years, until he died. During his time here, Scott demolished the existing house (Cartley Hall) and built a grand new mansion with turrets and stepped gables, renaming it Abbotsford. You can look around the ground floor of the property, which includes Scott's library, but if you want to see the best bit of the gardens go in mid-August, when the splendour of the walled garden is unveiled each year.

Around the house there are lawned courtyards, simply designed, with topiary yews formally positioned. An open stone colonnade separates one terrace from another, and is lined with a run of deep red 'Frensham' roses – a variety which looks very good in the gloom of a cloudy day. The walled garden's *pièce de résistance* is a joyful double border of bedded-out late summer flowers, including dahlias, cosmos, antirrhinums, nicotiana, heliotrope, etc. Rose arches over the cross-axis support cascades of 'Minnehaha' roses, and the rest of the walled area is devoted to a productive kitchen garden with rows of cut flowers and herbaceous beds beside the walls.

MELROSE

Priorwood Garden

Melrose, Roxburghshire TD6 9PX **TEL.** 01896-822493 **OWNER** The National Trust for Scotland **HOURS** April–Dec, Mon–Sat, 10a.m.–5.30p.m., Sun, 1–5.30p.m. (closes at 4p.m., Oct–Dec) **ENTRANCE** £2 **DIRECTIONS** Between A68 and A7 (signposted) in Melrose, adjacent to the Abbey **WEB** www.nts.org.uk

🌑 ⴕ **Access** 🌑 **Gift Shop** 🌑 **Plants for Sale**

Priorwood Garden

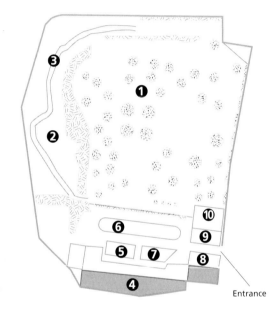

1 Orchard
2 Woodland
3 Woodland path
4 Dried flower display
5 Allium bed
6 Herbaceous border
7 Annuals raised under glass
8 Cottage garden
9 Shrub border
10 Annual bed

Entrance

Priorwood has an unusual walled garden, overlooked by Melrose Abbey's 15th-century ruins. Most of the plants are grown for the purpose of cutting, for dried flower arrangements. There are flat-headed achilleas and spiky, metallic blue globes of echinops, poppies and alliums producing attractive seed-pods, and spires of blue delphinium. Several hundred different plants are grown and dried on this three-acre site and are also on sale in the property's shop. Beside it, the extensive orchard contains a collection of historic apple varieties which illustrate the history of the apple in cultivation. This inspired the *Priorwood Orchard Recipe Book* (on sale in the shop), which features suggestions ranging from apple sorbet and toffee apple pudding to jam and cider.

Harmony Garden, St Mary's Road, Melrose TD6 9LJ (tel. 01721-722502), also NTS, is a couple of hundred yards along the road. It enjoys good views of Melrose Abbey and the Eildon Hills. Within its walled garden there is a productive kitchen area, a small herbaceous border and shrubberies surrounding a lawn. It's not worth going out of your way to see, but is a pleasant place to stroll to if you are in Melrose and visiting Priorwood and the Abbey. Open April (or Easter if earlier)–Sept, Mon–Sat, 10a.m.–5.30p.m., Sun, 1.30–5.30p.m.

ST BOSWELLS

Mertoun Gardens

St Boswells, Melrose, Roxburghshire TD6 0EA **TEL.** 01835-823236 **OWNER** The Duke of Sutherland **HOURS** April–Sept, Sat–Sun and Bank Holiday Mons, 2–6p.m. **ENTRANCE** £2, OAPs £1.50, children 50p **DIRECTIONS** 2m NE of St Boswells on B6404, 2½m from A68

 ♿ Access

Mertoun provides exceptionally satisfying garden-visiting. The 26-acre grounds are beautiful, framed with magnificent trees, set beside the River Tweed. The sloping, three-acre walled garden is especially good; one path rises through an old orchard and the perimeter paths are lined with crisp box hedging, enclosing vegetables and herbs in neat rows, and abundant bushes of summer fruits. Fan-trained pears, plums and apples make productive use of the attractive stone walls, and less hardy fruits – figs and peaches – are nurtured in the traditional way under glass. There are borders of peonies, irises, delphiniums, lupins and other old-fashioned flowers, and cut-flower beds devoted to gladioli, for which the garden and its gardener are renowned.

Like so many Scottish gardens, spring sees an explosion of colour from rhododendrons and azaleas, and the alpines and waterside plants. The grounds are laid out informally, with a burn running through to join the Tweed that marks the southern boundary. An unusual feature in the garden is a circular dovecote dated 1576, thought to be the first to have been built in Scotland to provide fresh meat through the winter.

STOBO

Dawyck Botanic Garden

Stobo, Peeblesshire EH45 9JU **TEL.** 01721-760254 **OWNER** Royal Botanic Garden, Edinburgh **HOURS** Mid-Feb–mid-Nov, daily: March–Sept, 9.30a.m.–6p.m.; mid-Feb and Oct–mid-Nov, 10a.m.–4p.m., other times by appointment **ENTRANCE** £3, concessions £2.50, children £1 (under 5s free), family ticket £7 **DIRECTIONS** 8m SW of Peebles, on B712 (signposted)

 Gift Shop Café Plants for Sale 2 for 1 Voucher

This is a lovely woodland site, breathtaking in spring and autumn, run by the Royal Botanic Garden in Edinburgh as one of their satellite gardens – they also run Logan Botanic Garden (*q.v.*) near Stranraer, and Benmore Botanic Garden (*q.v.*) at Benmore, Argyll. Trees are the thing at Dawyck, which is famous for the Dawyck beech, *Fagus sylvatica* 'Dawyck' (sometimes listed as 'Fastigiata'), an unusual columnar form of beech which was raised here before 1850.

Some of the oldest larches here date back to plantings around 1725, and many of the assorted conifers have achieved over 100ft in height. Also note the introduction of colourful rhododendrons and other flowering shrubs, and the masses of spring bulbs, especially narcissi. A new feature of the garden is a plants trail with rare Scottish plants. The lovely woodland walks ramble through the steep slopes above a tributary of the River Tweed, accompanied by the music of water gushing down the rocky cascades.

And also...

The Hirsel, Coldstream, Berwickshire TD12 4LP (tel. 01890-882834), is an all-year-round garden. There are snowdrops and aconites followed by massed daffodils in spring. Rhododendrons and azaleas bloom through late May and June, and rose beds and shrub borders bring summer colour, followed by various autumn tints and berries. The grounds are also well known for being a visiting and nesting site for numerous migrant birds. Open all year, daily, dawn–dusk. Entrance £2 per car. Off A697 at Coldstream.

Kailzie Gardens, Kailzie, by Peebles, Peeblesshire EH45 9HT (tel. 01721-720007), features a substantial walled garden within its 20 acres, with a mixture of kitchen produce, lawns, ornamental plantings and a fine glasshouse. There are roses, double herbaceous borders and flowers for drying. The woodland area features walks among rhododendrons, primulas and Himalayan blue poppies and the garden hosts snowdrop days in February. Open all year, daily, 11a.m.–5.30p.m. (10a.m.–4p.m., mid-Oct–mid-March). Entrance £2.50, children 75p. On B7062, 2½m E of Peebles.

The gardens of **Mellerstain, Mellerstain House, Gordon TD3 6LG (tel. 01573-410225)**, were laid out in the early 20th century by Reginald Blomfield, proponent of the formal garden style. There are balustraded terraces ornamented with roses and topiary, and fine views of the Cheviot Hills to the south. Beyond the formal gardens is a well-treed landscape park with a lake. Open Easter and May–Sept, Sun–Fri, 12.30–5p.m. (last adm. 4.30p.m.), garden closes at 6p.m. Entrance £2; house and garden £5, concessions £4.50, children £2. Leave A68 at Earlston and follow signs for 5m.

Western Scotland

MAP NO. 8

This large region encompasses Argyll, Ayrshire, Dumbartonshire and the industrial and cultural conurbation of Glasgow and the Clyde. Loch Fyne, a sea loch, is famous for its seafood, particularly smoked kippers, and for the lovely gardens of Crarae. It is a land of clan castles and wonderful landscape, with unpredictable weather. Ayrshire attracts visitors for its links golf courses as much as its seaside resorts, Troon and Turnberry being the most famous. From the latter, and from nearby Culzean Castle, you have good views of Ailsa Craig, the offshore island and seabird sanctuary, whose name is commemorated in popular varieties of onion and tomato.

Must See

Ardchattan Priory Garden, Connel – location, location, location, as they say, and varied plants

An Cala, Easdale – rich planting and serenity despite inhospitable location

Exceptional in Spring

Brodick Castle, Brodick

Achnacloich, Connel

Glenarn, Helensburgh

Crarae Glen Garden, Minard

Angus's (Barguillean) Garden, Taynuilt

Exceptional in Summer

Geilston Garden, Cardross

Worth a Visit in Winter

Culzean Castle Country Park, Maybole

Crarae Glen Garden, Minard

Kinlochlaich House Garden

Appin, Argyll and Bute PA38 4BD **TEL.** 01631-730342 **OWNER** Mr and Mrs D.E. Hutchison and Miss F.M. Hutchison **HOURS** Open all year, daily, Mon–Sat, 9.30a.m.–5.30p.m., Sun 10.30a.m.–5.30p.m. (or dusk if earlier) **ENTRANCE** £1.50 **DIRECTIONS** Midway between Oban and Fort William on A828 **WEB** www.kinlochlaich-house.co.uk

🌿 ♿ Access 🌿 Nursery

The coast road from Oban to Fort William is dangerously scenic, with views of the mountains and offshore islands (Port Appin, nearby, is worth a quick detour on a fine day). At Kinlochlaich House the walled garden near the house is the only bit that is open to view, and it is unusual, being of octagonal design. It was built at the same time as the house, around 1790, to provide the house with its supply of fruit and vegetables. Apparently (like many gardens in the Highlands situated on thin soil over hard rock), the walled garden's soil probably came from Ireland as ship's ballast. Most of the walled area has been turned into a garden centre, specialising in plants suitable for the local climate. Although we are some way north here, the garden is on the west coast and enjoys the mild influence of the Gulf Stream. About one-quarter of the garden is planted ornamentally, with shrubberies set into lawns, featuring rhododendrons, azaleas, primulas, heathers and herbaceous plants.

Appin House, a couple of miles further north on the A828, is now divided into holiday apartments but its garden, made in the 1960s, has a rockery, a flower border and many spring bulbs and shrubs. It enjoys magnificent views of the Lynn of Lorne and the islands of Shuna, Lismore and Mull. Open mid-April–mid-Oct, daily, 10a.m.–6p.m. for Scotland's Gardens Scheme. Entrance £1.50, OAPs £1, children free (collecting box).

Brodick Castle

Exceptional in Spring

Brodick, Island of Arran KA27 8HY **TEL.** 01770-302202 **OWNER** The National Trust for Scotland **HOURS** Garden and country park, all year, daily, 9a.m.–dusk; castle and walled garden April–Oct, daily, Nov–Dec, Fri–Sun, 11a.m.–4.30p.m. (3.30p.m. in winter), walled garden closes at dusk **ENTRANCE** £2.50, concessions £1.70; castle and grounds £6, concessions £4, family ticket £13.50 **DIRECTIONS** Car ferry from Ardrossan to Brodick (55 mins), then A481 N for 2m, signposted from Brodick **WEB** www.nts.org.uk

🌿 ♿ Access 🌿 Gift Shop 🌿 Café 🌿 Plants for Sale 🌿 NPC

Brodick's red-sandstone castle sits above a sheltered bay on the east side of the Island of Arran. It is protected from south-westerly gales by the massif of the Arran mountains, which add considerably to the drama of the 200-acre site. There has been a fortress here for at least 1000 years, although the castle dates from the 13th to 19th centuries. Its walled garden was built in 1710, and today is planted in Victorian style, with carpet bedding, copious roses and summer-flowering perennials and annuals. The woodland gardens are famous for their National Collections of rhododendrons, which were rapidly accumulated during the 1920s and 1930s by Mary Louise, the 6th Duchess of Montrose, who lived in the castle and took a huge interest in its garden until her death in 1957. Rambling paths descend the hillside to the seashore, taking in the beauty of spring-flowering shrubs, pools of cobalt-blue poppies and luscious waterside plantings of primulas and gunnera. There is also a pretty, rustic summerhouse and a restored ice house in the grounds; the gardener gives weekly guided walks during the summer months.

CAIRNDOW

Ardkinglas Woodland Garden

Cairndow, Argyll and Bute PA26 HB **TEL.** 01499-600261 **OWNER** Mr John Noble/Ardkinglas Estate **HOURS** All year, daily, dawn–dusk **ENTRANCE** £2, under 16s free **DIRECTIONS** Off A83 Loch Lomond to Inveraray road, through Cairndow village (signposted)

The point of coming here is to see the garden's 'champion trees' – those deemed to be either the tallest or broadest of their kind in the British Isles, as officially measured for the Tree Register. There are no less than five champion conifers at Ardkinglas, all of them clearly labelled and located near the woodland footpaths, although it is fun to try to pick them out yourself, at a distance. They include a specimen Western red cedar (*Thuja plicata*), a grand fir (*Abies grandis*), a golden Sawara cypress (*Chamaecyparis pisifera* 'Plumosa Aurea'), a particularly impressive European silver fir (*Abies alba*) and a Patagonian cypress (*Fitzroya cupressoïdes*). Much restoration work has been going on in the woodland, which is light and airy, with good but steep paths, and peppered with rhododendrons which relish the local conditions.

Situated at almost sea level on the northern shore of Loch Fyne, the Ardkinglas Estate enjoys a mild climate due to its waterside setting, although it is frowned over by bare mountains and hills. The original, designed landscape was laid out in the late 18th century, but the woodland garden with its splendid trees came a little later, reflecting the golden age of the 19th-century plant collectors gathering specimens in distant lands. There is an average rainfall here in excess of 100in and this, together with the free-draining, fertile, sandy loam of the site, has provided ideal conditions for the woodland to thrive. Even if you don't like conifers, you can't help being impressed by the mightiness of these trees and you will find yourself looking skywards a good deal. There are no facilities in the woodland itself, but the Ardkinglas Estate's specialist plant centre, shop and café are situated 2m further north on the A83 at Clachan, where you will also find the Loch Fyne Oyster Bar (tel. 01499-600264), which serves excellent food all day.

CARDROSS

Geilston Garden

Cardross, Dumbarton G82 5EZ **TEL.** 01389-841867 **OWNER** The National Trust for Scotland **HOURS** April–Oct, daily, 9.30a.m.–5p.m. **ENTRANCE** £2 **DIRECTIONS** On A814 at west end of Cardross, 18m N of Glasgow

Geilston

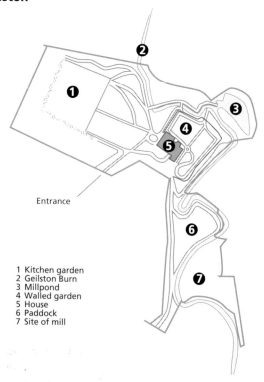

1 Kitchen garden
2 Geilston Burn
3 Millpond
4 Walled garden
5 House
6 Paddock
7 Site of mill

This property is one of the small country houses and estates that evolved along the banks of the Clyde as trading and industry developed in Glasgow. In the 18th century it belonged to a merchant family who made their money importing tobacco from Virginia; later it was owned by a Glasgow iron merchant.

An avenue of red-twigged lime trees leads up to the gardens, and your first stop should be the very well-ordered kitchen garden near the car park. Here are long, privet-hedged walks and vistas on a gently sloping hillside, with lupins and delphiniums in one bed and brilliant dahlias in another, plus flowers for cutting. Sweet peas and runner beans are in orderly rows and the soft fruits and vegetables are well maintained. There is a short walk to the sloping walled garden adjoining the house (not open), where you will find smooth lawns, box-edged paths, and multicolour beds of hybrid tea and floribunda roses. A splendid herbaceous border, filled with marguerites, phlox, lychnis, sedums, echinops and much else, leads to greenhouses, brimming with tomatoes and pelargoniums. Beyond the walled garden are lovely woodland walks beside Geilston Burn and its millpond, with simple timber bridges crossing the stream. This is a very nice garden; well-kept, very peaceful, with old-fashioned charm and quite a personal feel, although it is no longer privately owned.

CLACHAN-SEIL

Ardmaddy Castle Garden

Balvicar, by Oban, Argyll and Bute PA34 4QY **TEL.** 01852-300353 **OWNER** Mr and Mrs C. Struthers **HOURS** Open all year, daily, dawn–dusk **ENTRANCE** £2, children 50p **DIRECTIONS** Near Clachan-Seil, from A816 take B844 towards Easdale and follow signs

  ♿ Access   Plants for Sale

The castle sits in a prominent location above its large walled garden, where there are well-tended beds of fruit and vegetables lined with low box hedging. (Home-grown produce is on sale at the potting shed near the garden entrance during the main season.) There are also extensive shrub and flower borders and lawns within the walled area, including a collection of potentillas. A gate at the far end opens into beautiful woodland gardens, with a stream running through, leading to bluebell woods containing some mature rhododendrons planted more than 50 years ago. The property is in a stunning location, enjoying views of the sea and low hills on the Isle of Seil. The small Willowburn Hotel and Restaurant (tel. 01852-300276), at nearby Clachan-Seil, is a quiet and friendly base for exploring this picturesque region.

CONNEL

Achnacloich

Connel, Oban, Argyll and Bute PA37 1PR **TEL.** 01631-710221 **OWNER** Mrs J.Y. Nelson **HOURS** April–Oct, daily, 10a.m.–6p.m. **ENTRANCE** £1.50, OAPs £1, children free **DIRECTIONS** 3m E of Connel off A85, N of Oban

🟫 ⚬ Access 🟫 Plants for Sale

An insignificant lane beside a railway bridge leads to Achnacloich, but the grey stone early-Victorian house (not open), with its pointed turret, turns out to occupy a commanding position beside the L-shaped Loch Etive. Close to the house is an enormous Douglas fir tree, dating from the 1840s, and one of the first of its kind to be planted in Britain. There are plenty of woodland walks through glades of rhododendrons, magnolias and other spring-flowering shrubs, accompanied by daffodils, bluebells and primulas in the first half of the year. In the old garden, rustic bridges lead a picturesque way across the bulrushed Duck Pond.

The walled garden, of local stone, dates from when the house was built and is sheltered to the east by a fine wood of old Scots pines. Part of the walled area continues to produce vegetables and some fruit, but, like so many of the labour-intensive areas of large, old properties, it is no longer staffed to the levels that were intended when it was built, and parts are neglected. There are lovely views, however, and it is a most pleasant place to stroll on a fine day at any time of year.

CONNEL

Ardchattan Priory Garden

Oban, Argyll and Bute PA37 1RQ **TEL.** 01631-750238 **OWNER** Mrs Sarah Troughton **HOURS** April (or Easter if earlier)–Oct, daily, 9a.m.–6p.m. **ENTRANCE** £2 (by donation) **DIRECTIONS** 10m N of Oban, take A85, cross Connel Bridge and turn first right on Bonawe road

🟫 ⚬ Access 🟫 Café 🟫 Plants for Sale

This peaceful, most attractive garden surrounds Ardchattan Priory (not open), the second oldest inhabited house in Scotland, built in 1230 for monks of the Vallescaulian order and updated in the 16th century, after the Reformation. It occupies a glorious, level position on the north shore of Loch Etive, and is planted to provide something

Ardchattan

1 Wildflowers and
  sorbus trees
2 Shrub garden
3 Daffodils and
  autumn shrubs
4 Monk's Walk
5 Herbaceous border
6 Shrub border
7 Rock garden
8 Priory
9 Chapel ruins
10 Monk's Pond

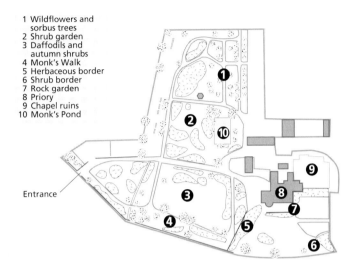

Entrance

of interest in every season. Shrubs and trees in grass near the entrance lead on to a wild garden, informally planted with 180 different shrubs including many roses, over 30 different varieties of sorbus trees, rhododendrons, azaleas and many bulbs and wildflowers. The Monk's Walk, on the loch side, is lined by 400-year-old trees, leading to open lawns in front of the priory, and the more formally gardened area. Here there is a curving herbaceous border, a rock garden, rose beds, a bed of peonies and day lilies, and more shrubs. You can also visit the ruins of the old chapel and burial ground at the eastern edge of the property. Ardchattan is worth visiting simply to see its location, but the garden, although not sophisticated or manicured, seems like a piece of heaven on a fine day.

COVE

Linn Gardens

Cove, Dunbartonshire G84 0NR **TEL.** 01436-842242 **OWNER** James and Jim Taggart **HOURS** Open all year, daily, dawn–dusk; nursery open daily, 11a.m.–5p.m. **ENTRANCE** £3, OAPs £2.50, students £2, under 12s free **DIRECTIONS** ⅔m N of Cove village, take A814, then B833

🌿 Nursery

If you're in the area and fancy making a detour along the Rosneath Peninsula on the Firth of Clyde, this garden makes interesting visiting for the plant-aholic. But be warned, if you're the sort of person who likes everything ship-shape, neat and tidy, then give this one a wide berth.

It is a plantsman's garden gone mad – or at least gone wild – and is rather romantically jungly (be prepared to lose your way occasionally, along the narrow and sometimes steep paths). Numerous routes climb the hillside, reaching a house at the top, perched above a cliff and some formerly formal areas (rather weedy), with a rectangular pond and small outhouses. Linn house (not open) was built in 1860 by one William Martin, a Glasgow leather merchant and bootmaker (apparently the boots Sir Edmund Hillary wore to climb Everest were made by the Martins). Today it is engulfed in vines and roses, and an enterprising phygelius which has reached the house roof. An effective planting combination in this area is the purple grape vine (*Vitis vinifera* 'Purpurea') with pink, daisy-flowered *Mutisia oligodon* twining through. Many different plants have colonised the terrace, below which thickets of yuccas, assorted grasses and crocosmia lead you back down the hill.

There are bamboos and waterfalls, a rock-face studded with self-sown *Primula capitata*, still pools, exotic woods of cabbage palms, a hidden-away cottage, rhododendrons galore and much else – some 6000 different species and cultivars. The very extensive range of plants is due to Dr James Taggart, who has lived here since 1971 and, with his son, runs a nursery of unusual plants, situated at the garden entrance.

EASDALE

An Cala

Ellenabeich, Easdale, Isle of Seil, Argyll and Bute PA34 4RF **TEL.** 01852-300237 **OWNER** Sheila and Thomas Downie **HOURS** April–Oct, daily, 10a.m.–6p.m. **ENTRANCE** £1.50 **DIRECTIONS** 16m SW of Oban, from A816 take B844, following signs to Easdale, next to Inshaig Hotel

🧽 **2 for 1 Voucher**

The layout of this wonderful garden dates from the 1930s and is the most northerly creation of Thomas Mawson, the landscape architect who did much work in the Lake District. It forms a horseshoe shape, facing straight onto the Atlantic ocean at the front, enjoying dramatic sea views, and rising on a steep cliff face at the rear. Waterfalls tumble down the cliffs and feed meandering streams and pools. A narrow path of steep slate steps climbs up into the cliff, leading to larch woods. Pines, escallonias and elms all help to give shelter to the garden which is frequently battered by salty gales off the sea. Within its smooth, broad lawns there are richly planted beds of herbaceous perennials, roses, blue hydrangeas, azaleas and other flowering shrubs. Large, spreading cherry trees, primulas and orchids contribute to the spring show. Dry-stone walls, paths and a terrace make use of the abundant slate in the neighbourhood, and there are lots of seats thoughtfully positioned at viewpoints up and down the garden. By any standards it is a very good garden, and all the more remarkable for its uncompromising and remote position.

HELENSBURGH

Glenarn

Rhu, Helensburgh, Dunbartonshire G84 8LL **TEL.** 01436-820493 **OWNER** Michael and Sue Thornley and family **HOURS** Late March–late Sept, daily, dawn–dusk **ENTRANCE** £2, children £1 **DIRECTIONS** In Rhu, off A814, 2m N of Helensburgh (signposted), limited parking outside garden gate

Glenarn

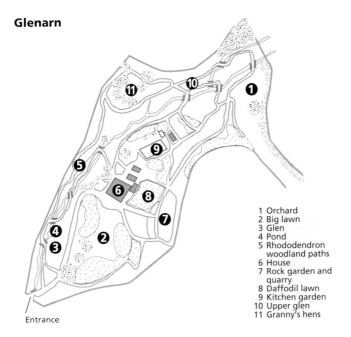

1 Orchard
2 Big lawn
3 Glen
4 Pond
5 Rhododendron woodland paths
6 House
7 Rock garden and quarry
8 Daffodil lawn
9 Kitchen garden
10 Upper glen
11 Granny's hens

Entrance

Occupying a mild position above the Gare Loch, around 25 miles north-west of Glasgow, this old, ten-acre garden must have been a difficult one to restore, being a natural woodland on steeply sloping ground with hard whinstone outcrops. Glenarn's house (not open) was built in the late 1830s by the MacGeorge family, who began planting rhododendrons, including species collected by plant hunter Joseph Hooker at Sikkim, in 1849. A large specimen *Rhododendron falconeri* dates from this expedition and occupies a commanding position near the house.

In 1927 another family took on the property and planted rhododendrons, magnolias and other Far Eastern treasures in great quantity, from seed collected by Frank Kingdon-Ward and Ludlow and Sherriff among others. By the time the present owners arrived, in 1983, the garden was 150 years old and in need of some thinning-out and restoration, a project that has been a labour of love (and occasional frustration) ever since, as their garden diary records. 'October 1998: Floods, storms, tempests and one night the water overflowed from the surrounding gardens and fields into Glenarn, roared down the glen, taking the paths with it and dumping them in the pond. Digging the stones out and putting them back on the paths was a tedious business...'

Spring is the best season to enjoy the garden's steep woodland paths, ducking and winding through big oaks and sycamores, lit up here and there by the brilliant flowers of the introduced shrubs and rashes of spring bulbs. An open area devoted to a new kitchen garden neatly demonstrates the sort of fencing required to keep out roe deer and rabbits. A rock garden and quarry face above the daffodil lawn is the latest project undergoing restoration.

KILCHRENAN

Ardanaiseig Garden and Hotel

Kilchrenan, Argyll and Bute PA35 1HE **TEL.** 01866-833333 **OWNER** Mr Bennie Gray **HOURS** April–Oct, 9a.m.–8p.m. **ENTRANCE** £2, children 50p (collection box in car park) **DIRECTIONS** 21m N of Oban, take A85 to junction with B845, follow road to Kilchrenan Inn, then left into single-track road for 3m

Remote and romantically situated at the north end of Loch Awe, Ardanaiseig Garden can be reached by sea plane or helicopter or, more prosaically, via the lonely road through the sheep-grazed moors. This is an old garden, currently undergoing gradual restoration, but with several points of interest. The house, now a splendid country house hotel, was built for James Archibald Campbell in the 1830s by William Burn, a well-known Edinburgh architect. Formerly known as New Inverawe, it was bought by Sir John Ainsworth in 1880, who changed the name to Ardanaiseig. Its 100 acres of gardens, forest and woodland walks include a substantial tree collection planted by Campbell, with the rest of the gardens laid out by the Ainsworths. (A tree list and map, marking 72 significant species, is available from the hotel for those who are interested.) There is nothing to see in the walled garden, which is not yet restored, but the grounds make pleasant walking, with views of the splendid peak of Ben Cruachan and the deep waters of the loch. The hotel serves excellent coffee and teas.

MAYBOLE

Culzean Castle Country Park

Maybole, South Ayrshire KA19 8LE **TEL.** 01655-884455 **OWNER** The National Trust for Scotland **HOURS** Garden and country park, all year, daily, 9a.m.–dusk; castle, Visitor Centre, etc., April–Oct, daily, 10.30a.m.–5.30p.m. **ENTRANCE** £4, concessions/children £3, family ticket £10; castle and grounds £8 and £6, family ticket £20 **DIRECTIONS** 12m S of Ayr, 4m W of Maybole, from A77 take A719 **WEB** www.nts.org.uk

🔥 ♿ Access 🔥 Gift Shop 🔥 Café 🔥 Plants for Sale

Culzean enjoys a majestic site, its castle rising out of the clifftop, with the sea raging on the rocks below. It is the National Trust for Scotland's most visited property (with around 230,000 visitors per year), offering 563 acres of undulating parkland, with lovely lakes and woods. The elegant castle and its home farm were designed by Robert Adam in the late 18th century (worth seeing for the magnificent armoury display and Adam's virtuoso Oval Staircase), and there are pretty features dotted about the grounds, including a beautifully restored camellia house, and a fine fountain of stylised dolphin and oyster-shell design.

The 30-acre gardens include a large, walled area, partly used for plant sales, with a range of glasshouses set beside glorious double herbaceous borders. Also within the walled gardens are wilder, shrubby areas, with specimen trees and broad lawns for picnics. Beside the castle, the formal, terraced gardens feature tender plants that are nurtured by the mild, coastal position and reflected warmth of the stone walls.

MINARD

Crarae Glen Garden

Exceptional in Spring

Crarae, Inveraray, Argyll PA32 8YA **TEL.** 01546-886614/886388 **OWNER** The Crarae Garden Charitable Trust **HOURS** All year, dawn–dusk (9a.m.–6p.m. in summer); Visitor Centre 10a.m.–5p.m. **ENTRANCE** £2.50, children aged 5–16 £1.50, family ticket (2 adults, 2 children) £7 **DIRECTIONS** On A83, 11m S of Inveraray, on W side of Loch Fyne **WEB** www.crarae-gardens.org

🔥 Gift Shop 🔥 Café 🔥 NPC

The natural and exotic come together at Crarae to create a wondrous experience: dramatic Highland landscape mixed with choice plants from the Far East. A burn runs through the steep ravine that is the focus of the 100-acre garden. Informal paths wind around the valley sides and occasionally cross it, by timber bridges.

The garden was made in the first half of the 20th century by Lady Grace Campbell, aunt of the celebrated plant hunter Reginald Farrer, followed by her son, Sir George Campbell. Farrer introduced many rhododendron species to Britain, and to Crarae, following his journeys to Kansu in 1914 and upper Burma in 1919. Other gardening friends contributed seeds and plants to the garden through the succeeding decades, and Sir George maintained two incontrovertible maxims: 'Never plant too close, but allow room for natural development,' and 'Always try to ensure that the plants look natural in their setting.'

Spring is glorious here, not only with the rhododendrons, for there are many other acid-loving shrubs and perennials threaded through the gardens. Autumn brings spectacular leaf tints from a multitude of trees. Recent additions include a Scottish Clan Garden, featuring plants attributed to the clans of Argyll and the Isles, and a Millennium Forest Project is in progress to create 50 acres of native woodland. The garden also contains a neolithic burial chamber, part of a 4500-year-old cairn, and the National Collection of *Nothofagus*.

TAYNUILT

Angus's (Barguillean) Garden

Exceptional in Spring

Barguillean Farm, Taynuilt, Argyll and Bute PA35 1HY TEL. 01866-822254
OWNER Mr Sam Macdonald HOURS Open all year, daily, 9a.m.–6p.m.
ENTRANCE £3, children free DIRECTIONS Take A85 at Taynuilt, turn S at Taynuilt Hotel towards Glen Lonan and follow signs for 3m

From a big parking area on the hilltop, you go through the garden gate into an enchanting, nine-acre woodland of lichen-encrusted oak and birch trees, sheltering rhododendrons (many of them labelled) and deciduous azaleas, plus other flowering shrubs, primulas and conifers. Informal paths mown through the turf wander this way and that down the hillside, to an 11-acre loch, extensively covered with waterlilies. There are plenty of rustic benches to sit on and take in the views (including mighty Ben Cruachan and Glen Etive) and a picnic area is provided with seat-tables. The garden was begun in 1957, in memory of Angus Macdonald, a journalist killed in Cyprus in 1956, and was created by his mother. Its development continues and it is said to have the largest collection of North American rhododendron hybrids in the west of Scotland – no mean feat, in a region where substantial rhododendron gardens are almost two-a-penny.

Bill Mackenzie and his Yellow Clematis

I had the honour and pleasure of meeting the late Bill Mackenzie on several occasions, thanks to the renowned plantswoman Valerie Finnis, who introduced us. I recall Bill's soft Argyllshire accent and the thrill of seeing his eponymous clematis in bloom, in his own garden.

Bill Mackenzie was truly a link with the past, for he first went to work at Edinburgh's Royal Botanic Garden in 1928, at the tail end of the golden age of plant hunting, when George Forrest and Frank Kingdon-Ward were still sending back hitherto unknown plants from China. 'It was a golden age,' Bill had told me, 'with many thousands of new plants that had never been seen before coming in by the barrowload. We were overwhelmed. It wasn't just an ounce or two of seed of each new plant, but pounds of it in many cases. You sowed what you could, pricked off what you could and the rest went to the tip. Such terrible waste, but it was far too much material for us to handle.'

After the Second World War Bill was appointed curator of the Chelsea Physic Garden (*q.v.*) and became friends with Valerie Finnis, who was in charge of alpine plants at Waterperry Gardens (*q.v.*) in Oxfordshire. During a visit to Waterperry, Bill spotted a yellow clematis seedling and, he recalled, 'the next thing I knew, Valerie had it up at the Royal Horticultural Society's show and got an award for it'. She named it 'Bill Mackenzie'. The desirable, bright yellow clematis is renowned for its vigour and generous amounts of lantern-like flowers produced from high summer well into autumn, followed (and often accompanied) by silky, silvery seedheads. It is a hardy, easy-to-grow climber, flowering best when planted deeply into rich, well-manured soil, in a bright position.

And also...

Arduaine Garden, Arduaine, by Oban, Argyll PA34 4XQ (tel. 01852-200366/web www.nts.org.uk), holds an important collection of rhododendron species, sheltered by large trees planted 100 years ago. Its position on the west coast allows it to enjoy the warming influence of the Gulf Stream, enabling a range of slightly tender plants to be grown. There are rambling woodland walks, best seen in spring, and the garden possesses lily-pools fed by natural springs, beside which are lush plantings of ferns, irises and blue poppies. The Loch Melfort Hotel, next door, provides comfortable accommodation. Open all year, daily, 9.30a.m.–sunset. Entrance £3, concessions/children £2, family ticket £8. Off A816, 20m S of Oban.

Bargany Gardens, Old Dailly, Girvan, South Ayrshire KA26 9QL (tel. 01465-871249), consist of pleasant woodland, best seen at rhododendron time for the colourful displays among good specimen trees and conifers. There are also good spring bulb displays, a lily-pond and a rock garden. Open May, Sat–Mon, 10a.m.–5p.m. Entrance £2, under 12s free. Leave A77 at Girvan, take B734, garden 4m on left.

Barwinnock Herbs, Barrhill, by Girvan, Ayrshire KA26 0RB (tel. 01465-821338/web www.barwinnock.com), specialises in producing culinary, medicinal and fragrant-leaved plants, all organically grown, for collection and by mail. (Catalogue free on request.) Open April–Oct, daily, 10a.m.–6p.m. Signposted from A714, S of Girvan.

Benmore Botanic Garden, Benmore, Dunoon, Argyll PA23 8QU (tel. 01369-706261), covers 140 acres and is run by the Royal Botanic Garden, Edinburgh, as a satellite garden, specialising in plants appropriate to the setting. Formerly known as Younger Botanic Garden, it is famous for its extensive ranges of flowering trees and shrubs, rhododendrons and conifers. Its renowned avenue of tall wellingtonia trees was planted in 1863; there are also good examples of monkey-puzzle trees, which grow well in this region. A new courtyard garden has opened recently. Garden open March–Oct, daily, 9.30a.m.–6p.m. Entrance £3, concessions £2.50, children £1, family ticket £7. On A815, 7m N of Dunoon. **2 for 1 Voucher**

The extensive woods and 1860s pinetum at **Blairquhan Castle, Straiton, Maybole, Ayrshire KA19 7LZ (tel. 01655-770239/web www.blairquhan.co.uk)**, can be viewed along its three-mile private drive beside the River Girvan. Its walled kitchen garden has been skilfully redesigned with ornamental plantings replacing vegetable crops. Open mid-July–mid-Aug, daily, except Mon, 2–6p.m. (last adm. 4.45p.m.). Entrance £5, OAPs £4, children £3 (house and garden). A77, then B7045.

Finlaystone Country Estate, Langbank, Renfrewshire PA14 6TJ (tel. 01475-540505/web www.finlaystone.co.uk), was designed in 1900 and has been enhanced over the years, with 10 acres of gardens and another 70 of mature woodlands dissected by walks. There are traditional herbaceous borders beside neat lawns, mature shrubberies and fine views of the River Clyde, a garden of fragrance and a bog garden among its delights. Open all year, daily, 10.30a.m.–5p.m.; house open by appointment only. Entrance £3, OAPs/children £2. On A8, W of Langbank and 10m W of Glasgow Airport.

Glasgow Botanic Garden, 730 Great Western Road, Glasgow G12 0UE (tel. 0141-334 2422), has lovely greenhouses and conservatories with displays of plants from the tropics as well as desert plants and those from the temperate regions. They include the vast National Collection of begonias, amounting to around 240 species and 130 cultivars, plus the National Collections of *Dendrobium* orchids and *Dicksoniaceae* (tree ferns). Outdoors there are fine herbaceous borders, good specimen trees, a rock garden, a lake, topiaries and a scented rose garden. Owned by City of Glasgow Council. Open all year, daily, 7a.m.–dusk (glasshouses, 10a.m.–4.45p.m., closing 4.15p.m. in winter). On A82 and close to Hillhead underground station.

Greenbank Garden, Flenders Road, Clarkston, Glasgow G76 8RB (tel. 0141-639 3281/web www.nts.org.uk), has three acres of walled garden, and 13 of policies surrounding an elegant Georgian house built in 1764 for a Glasgow merchant. The attractive garden demonstrates the wide range of ornamental plants that can be grown in the region; there are annuals, perennials, shrubs, trees and rock garden plants. Open all year, daily, 9.30a.m.–sunset. Entrance £3.50, concessions £2.50, National Trust members free. Off Mearns Road in Clarkston, use M77 Jct 3, then A726.

WALES

Mid Wales

This region is covered by the large county of Powys. Quiet, gentle hills of green pasture and sheep are a feature of its landscape, dotted with small market towns and villages of Tudor timber and Georgian brick. Reliable breezes blowing in from the south and west power small forests of windmills on some of the higher ground, while the water run off from the Cambrian Mountains in the west helps to fill the deep reservoir of Lake Vyrnwy, supplying water to distant Liverpool. The area is more popular with walkers than gardeners, and the famously scenic Offa's Dyke Path runs along the region's eastern edge.

Must See

The Dingle Nurseries and
  Garden, Welshpool – expert
  handling of a difficult site
Powis Castle, Welshpool –
  outstanding historic setting
  with sumptuous terraced
  beds

Worth a Visit in Winter

The Dingle Nurseries and
  Garden, Welshpool

Glansevern Hall Gardens

Berriew, Welshpool, Powys **TEL.** 01686-640200 **OWNER** G. and M. Thomas
HOURS May–Sept, Fri–Sat and Bank Holiday Mons, 12 noon–6p.m. **ENTRANCE**
£3, concessions £2, children free **DIRECTIONS** Take A483 S from Welshpool,
after 5m entrance is on left by bridge over River Rhiew (signposted)

🌑 ♿ Access 🌑 Café 🌑 Gift Shop 🌑 Plants for Sale

Glansevern Hall is a handsome late-Georgian house (not open), set
in 15 acres of Victorian pleasure grounds, which include a four-acre
lake. It lies in a gloriously peaceful position on the banks of the River
Severn, with streams running through the grounds. When the present
owners arrived nearly 20 years ago, much of the garden was over-
grown and neglected, so they carried out a steady programme of
dredging the lake and removing dead trees, weeds and rubble. In the
process they have uncovered a Victorian tufa-lined grotto and rock
garden, and turned an abandoned pig-pen into a walled garden lined
with climbing roses, such as 'Handel', 'Albertine', and 'Constance
Spry'. Roses – 'Paul's Himalayan Musk' – also adorn an arbour set
on a tiny island in the lake, framing a classically inspired statue. The
water gardens are lushly planted with primulas, hostas, ferns, arum
lilies and foxgloves. There are also herbaceous beds of mixed
perennials and more roses.

Whimble Nursery

Kinnerton, Presteigne, Powys LD8 2PD **TEL.** 01547-560413 **OWNER** Elizabeth
Taylor **HOURS** April–mid-Oct, Wed–Sun, 10.30a.m.–5.30p.m. **ENTRANCE** Free
DIRECTIONS Take A44, then B4357, then B4372 to Kinnerton (signposted)

🌑 Nursery

It is mainly walkers and cyclists who venture west from the Border
town of Presteigne into the glacier-smoothed hills of mid-Wales,
peppered with remote sheep farms and watered by countless streams,
but there is the odd gem, such as this small nursery specialising in
cottage-garden flowers, which attracts other visitors. Around 800ft
above sea level, but within the shadow of the 2000ft-tall eminences
of Bache Hill and Whimble, self-taught nurserywoman Elizabeth
Taylor produces well-grown hardy plants, particularly aquilegias,
campanulas, geraniums, penstemons, pinks and violas, many of
which are displayed in a small garden at the nursery entrance. She
concentrates on unusual plants which have caught her eye. Send s.a.e.

for a plant list (without descriptions) or 5 × 1st-class stamps for a catalogue, but bear in mind there is no mail order service.

MACHYNLLETH

Centre for Alternative Technology

Machynlleth, Powys SY20 9AZ **TEL.** 01654-702400 **OWNER** Centre for Alternative Technology **HOURS** Open all year, daily, 10a.m.–5.30p.m. (4p.m. in winter) **ENTRANCE** £7, concessions £5, children £3.60, family ticket £20 (discounts for arrival by public transport or bicycle) **DIRECTIONS** 3m N of Machynlleth on A487 **WEB** www.cat.org.uk

🔲 ♿ Access 🔲 Gift Shop 🔲 Café 🔲 Plants for Sale

This research centre for development and education in alternative technology is also a major visitor attraction for the region, with much to interest forward-thinking gardeners. It is sited in a former slate quarry, with plenty of wind and water at its disposal to drive turbines and provide power, but not so much in the way of sunshine to feed its solar energy panels, although they do their bit. The soil is thin and poor, very slatey of course, but over the years it has been enriched, where needed, by extensive applications of composts. Its gardened areas demonstrate how to grow plants organically in a variety of situations, and the edibles it produces are used in the restaurant and staff canteen. The demonstration gardens show composting and mulching trials, crop rotations which help the soil to stay in good heart and deep bed systems which require no digging but rely on worms and soil organisms to do all the work. The 'suburban garden' is popular with visitors who enjoy its mix of cottage-garden plants, soft fruits and vegetables grown on a scale most people can identify with. The 'sunken garden' is a tiny backyard area crammed with containers. Wildlife gardening, organic pest control, companion planting and solar-powered fountains are among the interesting aspects shown by this ecologically conscientious community.

WELSHPOOL

The Dingle Nurseries and Garden

Welshpool, Powys SY21 9JD **TEL.** 01938-555145 **OWNER** Nursery, A. and K. Joseph, garden, R. and B. Joseph **HOURS** Open all year, Wed–Mon, 9a.m.–5p.m. **ENTRANCE** £1.50 (donated to charity); nursery free **DIRECTIONS** 3m N of Welshpool; take A490 (direction Llanfyllin) for 1m, turn left at sign for Dingle Nursery or Frochas, then left again after 1¾m (signposted) **WEB** www.dinglenurseries.co.uk

🔲 Nursery 🔲 2 for 1 Voucher

Dingle Garden

Entrance

1 Secret gravel garden
2 Scree garden
3 Woodland planting,
  including azaleas
  and acers
4 Informal woodland
  planting
5 Large ornamental
  pool
6 Lawn
7 House

Centuries-old sheep farms and ancient oak woods surround this thriving four-acre garden and nursery, created by Barbara and Roy Joseph. Under the distant gaze of Moel y Golfa, the Bald or Stony Hill, the Dingle reflects in miniature some of the dramatic features of its surroundings. The garden's paths zig-zag down its rugged slopes, and a small, natural stream fills a big pool at the bottom. An astonishing range of plants is packed into the garden to bring colour and interest in every season, with each bed carefully colour-themed for harmonious juxtaposition of flower and foliage tints. The adjoining nursery is renowned for its range of well-grown plants, especially trees, shrubs and conifers, but there is no catalogue or mail order.

WELSHPOOL

Powis Castle

Welshpool, Powys SY21 8RF **TEL.** 01938-557018 **OWNER** The National Trust
HOURS April–June, Sept–Oct, daily, except Mon–Tues, July–Aug, daily, except Mon, 11a.m.–6p.m. (but open Bank Holiday Mons), last adm. ½hr before closing; castle 1–5p.m. **ENTRANCE** £5, children £2.50 (under 5s free), family ticket £12.50; castle and garden £7.50, children £3.75, family ticket £18.75
DIRECTIONS 1m S of Welshpool, turn right off A483 from Welshpool

🌺 **Gift Shop** 🌺 **Café** 🌺 **Plants for Sale** 🌺 **NPC**

My first visit to Powis Castle was on an unseasonally cold and grim day one spring, but it is in the power of the garden to win you over, whatever the weather, with its velvety wraps of yew hedging and warmly tinted, red sandstone fortress. A return more recently, in contrast, basked in semi-tropical weather, brought out the richness of the planting for which Powis is so well known.

Powis is one of the treasures in the National Trust's horticultural crown, a garden on the grand scale, but not only impressive by its size – 33 acres; the setting is magnificent, its terraces run in deep, parallel steps down the hillside and are extensively planted, and the garden speaks of centuries of care and development. The retaining walls of the terraces feature clouds of blue ceanothus, late-flowering phygelius, and abutilons; the herbaceous beds are an opulent, Edwardian mix of classic border plants such as monkshoods, asters, crocosmias and red-hot pokers, and there are imaginatively planted containers, too.

Huge, irregular domes of clipped yew dribble over the wall of the top terrace; they began life as small, pointed topiaries lining the stairway in the original 17th-century garden, but now form a soft green cushion around the castle's foundations. Spare some time, too, to see the lower formal gardens with their pyramidal apple trees, vine tunnel and roses, and the grassy slopes ornamented with specimen trees. A tiny National Collection of *laburnum* is also held here.

CELEBRITY CHOICE

Stephen Lacey
Author, journalist and a presenter
of BBC2's *Gardeners' World*

'**Powis Castle** (*q.v.*) is practically on my doorstep, so I go there quite a lot at all times of year and all times of day. It's amazingly scenic and I love driving through the park. There is a lushness in the west of Britain, because of the rain, that you don't get in the east; Powis has a fertile feel to it with things growing buxomly. It is a rich source of planting ideas and the planting changes quite a lot from year to year. Colours in the planting are quite intense and the borders have helped me to develop a taste for strong colours, such as the scarlets and oranges of crocosmias. Unlike many gardens, this one gets better and better as the season progresses and is really good in August, not only from the flowers; you get other things, such as the great showers of rose-hips from *Rosa glauca* and *R.* "Highdownensis", and you will often see magnificent sunsets there.'

And also...

The 18th-century farmhouse (not open) of **Bedw Hir, Gwenddwr, Powys (tel. 01982-560714)**, is situated 900ft above sea level, on a south-facing slope, with gardens extending to over four acres with breathtaking views of the Black Mountains. It features beds of hardy and unusual perennials, a wildflower meadow, shrubs and trees in the lawns, an old orchard and lovely water gardens, including a pond with marginal and moist soil plantings. Open April–early Nov, Wed, 11a.m.–7p.m. (for NGS), May–Oct, Mon and Fri, 11a.m.–7p.m., also by appointment at other times. Entrance £2, children free. Take A470, at Erwood, 6m S of Builth Wells, follow signs to Gwenddwr, at top of hill take left fork, after ¼m turn right uphill after Fron Farm, Bedw Hir is next left.

Gregynog Hall, Tregynon, nr Newtown, Montgomery. This site has been inhabited since the 12th century and the present property, an early 19th-century, black-and-white house, is owned by the University of Wales. Its large grounds feature extensive woodlands with marked walks and beautiful trees and are best seen in spring to admire the rhododendrons, azaleas and many bulbs. The sunken lawns in front of the house are associated with an unfinished 18th-century design by William Emes, a Derbyshire landscaper who also did some work at Powis Castle (*q.v.*) and Erddig (*q.v.*). There are 19th-century fountains, specimen shrubs in the dell, and an impressive indented hedge of crisp, golden yew marking the bank between the upper and lower lawned terraces. Much of its planting interest is due to sisters Elizabeth and Margaret Davies, who lavished their attention on the garden between 1920 and 1939. A descriptive leaflet is available. Open all year, daily, dawn–dusk. Entrance free, collection box for donations. From Newtown take A483 towards Welshpool, turn W on B4389 towards Bettws Cedewain, continue for 7m, go through Tregynon, entrance on left.

A group of medieval buildings makes up the delightful **Tretower Court, Tretower, Crickhowell, Powys NP8 1RF (tel. 01874-730279)**. A relatively new medieval garden, laid out in 1991, now complements the Court and has been planted as authentically as possible to illustrate the typical garden of a wealthy commoner in the mid-15th century. Visit in summer to enjoy the tunnel arbour and small pavilion draped in vines, roses and honeysuckle; the enclosed gardens feature trelliswork, turf seats, fragrant herbs, irises, lilies, fountains and a chequerboard pattern of flowerbeds. Open late March–late Oct, daily, March and Oct, 10a.m.–4p.m., April–May and Sept, 10a.m.–5p.m., June–Aug, 10a.m.–6p.m. Entrance £2.50, OAPs/concessions £2, family ticket £7. Off A40, 3m outside Crickhowell (signposted).

North-east Wales

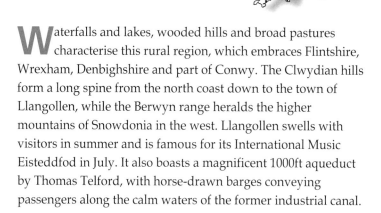

MAP NO. 4

Waterfalls and lakes, wooded hills and broad pastures characterise this rural region, which embraces Flintshire, Wrexham, Denbighshire and part of Conwy. The Clwydian hills form a long spine from the north coast down to the town of Llangollen, while the Berwyn range heralds the higher mountains of Snowdonia in the west. Llangollen swells with visitors in summer and is famous for its International Music Eisteddfod in July. It also boasts a magnificent 1000ft aqueduct by Thomas Telford, with horse-drawn barges conveying passengers along the calm waters of the former industrial canal.

Exceptional in Spring
Chirk Castle, Wrexham

CHIRK

Chirk Castle

Chirk, Wrexham LL14 5AF **TEL.** 01691-777701 **OWNER** The National Trust
HOURS End March–Oct, Wed–Sun and Bank Holiday Mons, gardens
11a.m.–6p.m. (5p.m. in Oct), castle 12 noon–5p.m. (4p.m. in Oct)
ENTRANCE £5.60, children £2.80, family ticket £14; garden only £3.40 and
£1.70 **DIRECTIONS** ½m W of Chirk village, off A5, 8m S of Wrexham,
signposted from A5 and A483

■ ♿ Access ■ Gift Shop ■ Café

The yew hedges at Chirk are the signature feature of the gardens, for
they appear as stout and impenetrable as the castle's walls and have
suitably castellated tops to echo the masonry. Forming an enclosure
to the terraced lawns, the yews also provide much-needed shelter on
this staggering, hilltop site.

The castle, finished around 1310, was used to survey the
movements of the defeated Welsh tribes along the English border.
The surrounding six-acre, 18th-century park and gardens speak of
more recent, peaceful times, with topiaries and terraced lawns, a
sunken garden featuring old hybrid tea and floribunda roses, and a
long, wavy border planted with flowering shrubs. Here, the azaleas,
flowering cherries and lilacs are a glorious feature of spring, with the
magnolias, dogwoods and rhododendrons that have been planted
since the last war by Lady Margaret Myddelton.

Hilltop Trees from Down Under

Everything you have ever wanted to know about eucalyptus, the
gum trees of Australasia, is contained in the excellent catalogue from
**Celyn Vale Nurseries, Allt-y-Celyn, Carrog, Corwen, Denbigh-
shire LL21 9LD (tel. 01490-430671), off A5 between Corwen
and Llangollen**. They grow here in six acres on the hillside, 800ft
up, and the proprietor, Andrew McConnell, has made extensive
studies of the hardiness of different species in recent years. His plants
are raised from seed obtained from wild plants growing in very cold,
exposed habitats which ensures the hardiness of his stock, comprising
some 50 different eucalyptus species and about 10 acacias from
Australia and Tasmania. Plants are generally sold by mail, but you
can browse and buy direct from the nursery (open March–Oct,
Mon–Fri, 9a.m.–4p.m.), although telephone appointments are
appreciated.

LLANGOLLEN

Plas Newydd

Hill Street, Llangollen, Denbighshire LL20 8AW **TEL.** 01978-861314
OWNER Denbighshire County Council **HOURS** Garden all year, daily,
dawn–dusk; house Easter–Oct, daily, 10a.m.–5p.m. **ENTRANCE** £2.50, children
£1.25, family ticket £6; garden free **DIRECTIONS** From A5 to Llangollen, turn
up Hill Street (signposted)
 & Access

**Plas
Newydd**

1 Stables
2 Bardic stones
3 Topiary garden
4 House
5 Lady Eleanor's Bower
6 Bards' Memorial
7 River Cuffleymen
8 Stone font

Entrance

The Ladies of Llangollen – Eleanor Butler and Sarah Ponsonby –
came to Plas Newydd in 1780, having run away from their Irish
homes and, over the next 50 years, created one of the most famous
and talked about gardens in the Romantic style. (Famous visitors
included Wordsworth, Shelley, Sir Walter Scott, Dr Darwin and his
son, Charles, and the Duke of Wellington.) According to Prince
Pückler-Muskau, who visited them in 1828, they 'took it into their
heads to hate men, to love only each other, and to live from that
hour in some remote hermitage…neither lady has ever passed a

night out of their cottage…[and] no one presentable travels to Wales unprovided with an introduction to them'.

Influenced by the 19th-century writer Sir Uvedale Price, and Rousseau, they transformed the four acres surrounding their lonely cottage by planting shrubberies, glades of white lilacs for romantic, moonlit walks, thickets of 'Lilaks [sic], Laburnums, Seringas [sic], White Broom, Weeping Willow, Apple Trees, poplar'; they assembled gnarled and twisted tree branches into summerhouses, balustrades and naturalistic bridges to cross the River Cuffleymen. Mosses, ferns and salvaged stone remnants from nearby Valle Crucis Abbey add to the Romantic idyll.

The river in its ravine, mature forest trees and sombre, weeping conifers continue to capture some of the spirit of the place, in spite of a good deal of building now occupying the surrounding landscape. Subsequent owners have added flowerbeds around the house and some marvellous topiaries in green and golden yew.

The Ladies added three ornately carved timber porches to the house front (for which they held a 'Porch Warming Party'), and it is well worth seeing the house interior too, which has further examples of the Ladies' self-confessed 'oak carving mania'. Alas, the house is no longer crammed with curiosities, as it was in their day. Pause, too, to enjoy the views of Castell Dinas Brân, the Trevor rocks and Berwyn Mountains that so enchanted the Ladies and inspired their gardening.

WREXHAM

Erddig

Nr Wrexham LL13 0YT **TEL.** 01978-355314 **OWNER** The National Trust
HOURS Late March–end Oct, daily except Thurs and Fri (but open Good Friday), 11a.m.–6p.m., July–Aug, 10a.m.–6p.m., Oct, 11a.m.–5p.m.; house 12 noon–5p.m. (4p.m. in Oct), last adm. 1 hour before closing **ENTRANCE** £3, children £1.50; house and garden £6, children £3, family ticket £15
DIRECTIONS 2m S of Wrexham, signposted from A525 and A483
▓ ঙ **Access** ▓ **Gift Shop** ▓ **Café** ▓ **NPC**

The list of wall fruits originally planted in the formal, early 18th-century gardens of Erddig features such specialities as 'Kanatian Peach', 'Blew Perdrigon Plumb', 'Scarlett Newington Netorn', 'Gross Blanquett Pare' and 'Orange Apricock', to name a few. Fruit continues to be an important theme of the gardens at Erddig, for the National Trust has restored the near-derelict gardens to something approaching their former glory, and searched out old varieties grown in the period.

There are pyramid-shape apple trees, and further fruits in formal plantations and splayed against the extensive walls; Portuguese laurels are clipped into mophead shapes to imitate orange trees in white timber Versailles tubs, and the formality is completed by broad lawns and a central, rectangular canal.

It is a spacious, airy, two-and-a-half-acre garden, not especially intimate or atmospheric, but great for long walks in the park, especially when the daffodils are in bloom, while the National Collection of ivy invites closer scrutiny of the shadiest of the garden's walls. The house and outbuildings on this 1700-acre estate feature interesting exhibits of the upstairs/downstairs lifestyle, and there are riding stables, and a timber workshop producing well-made garden furniture for sale.

Home-grown Saffron by Mail

Once a flourishing industry in 16th-century England, saffron (obtained from *Crocus sativus*) is not popularly grown today, but Caroline Riden produces both the corms and the harvested aromatic strands on her farm. The crocuses need a sunny spot and free-draining, manured, slightly alkaline soil, and should be planted from June to August, while dormant. For a mail order form and cultivation details, send a s.a.e. to **Caroline Riden, Caer Estyn Farm, Rhyddyn Hill, Caergwrle, Wrexham LL12 9EF (tel. 01978-761558)**. Open by appointment only.

And also...

Anyone interested in the formal four-acre Victorian gardens of W.A. Nesfield should visit **Bodrhyddan Hall, Rhuddlan, Denbighshire LL18 5SB (tel. 01745-590414)**. A magnificent parterre beside the south front of the house is laid out in elegant scrolls and other patterns in low box hedging, seasonally infilled with bedding plants in blocks of single colours. Among the artefacts to be seen indoors is a 3000-year-old Egyptian mummy. Open June–Sept, Tues and Thurs, 2–5.30p.m. Entrance £4, children £2. A55, then A525, turn right at both roundabouts in Rhuddlan, hall on left.

Dibley's Nurseries, Llanelidan, Ruthin, Denbighshire LL15 2LG (tel. 01978-790677), specialises in streptocarpus, the tender Cape primrose that comes in glorious shades of violet and blue-mauve, and tints from red to pink to white. A frequent medal winner at the

Royal Horticultural Society's shows, the nurseries are open daily, April–Sept, 10a.m.–5p.m., or you can order by mail (free extensive catalogue available on request). A525, then B5429 towards Llanelidan, turn left at crossroads, nursery on left.

Visitors are welcomed by prior appointment to **Donadea Lodge, Babell, nr Caerwys, Flintshire CH8 8QD (tel. 01352-720204)**. The long, narrow gardens are laid out beside an attractive, white-rendered and slate-roofed house. A special feature is the rather grand avenue of lime trees marching beside a dry stone wall and a length of lawn, where clumps of daffodils and grape hyacinths light up the spring. Clematis (around 80 different varieties) garland walls and shrubs and clamber into the trees, bringing colour through the seasons. The main event of summer is provided by countless shrub and climbing roses, including the vigorous rambler 'Bobbie James' and reliable flowerers such as 'Goldfinch' and blush pink 'Felicia'. Since a good deal of this garden, 700ft above sea level, receives shade (from the limes and many other trees and shrubs), shade-loving perennials are used in variety, as well as variegated-leaved shrubs which help to bring shots of light into the mixed borders here and there. Open May–July, daily, by pre-arranged appointment. Entrance £2, children 20p. Turn off A541 Mold to Denbigh road at Afon-wen, signposted Babell, at T-junction turn left, garden on right; from A55 take B5122 to Caerwys, then 3rd turn on left.

North-west Wales

MAP NO. 4

This is a land steeped in myths and heroes, more frequently trodden by walkers and climbers than by gardeners, for the 845 square miles of the Snowdonia National Park is the region's dominating feature. It is a landscape of pale, moisture-laden air, brooding peaks veiled in mist and shadow, and deep cauldrons filled with chill waters cascading from the glacial highlands. The weather can change from brightness to gloom in an instant, and has the power to inspire similar mood changes in the visitor; at such times the frequent roadside invitations to nearby farms, to take tea, are especially welcoming. Both houses and gardens make use of the local Ffestiniog slate, a stone of mutable beauty and sheen, like a magpie's wing.

Must See

Plas Brondanw,
   Penrhyndeudraeth –
   skilfully handled formality
   in the mountains

Exceptional in Spring

Plas Newydd, Isle of
   Anglesey
Bodnant, Colwyn Bay

ISLE OF ANGLESEY

Plas Newydd

Llanfairpwll, Anglesey LL61 6DQ **TEL.** 01248-714795 **OWNER** The National Trust **HOURS** Easter–end Oct, Sat–Wed, 11a.m.–5.30p.m.; house 12 noon–5p.m.; rhododendron garden April–early June only; woodland walk and marine walk open all year **ENTRANCE** £4.80, children £2.40, family ticket £11.80; garden only £2.50, children £1.25 **DIRECTIONS** A5, then A4080 towards Brynsiencyn, gardens on left

🔲 ♿ Access 🔲 Gift Shop 🔲 Café 🔲 2 for 1 Voucher

This property, the National Trust's Plas Newydd, is not to be confused with Plas Newydd in Denbighshire (*q.v.*) and the Ladies of Llangollen. It lies above the narrow, yacht-speckled channel of the Menai Strait (you can embark on historic cruises from Plas Newydd) and gazes south-east across the water to Snowdonia's handsome peaks. Humphry Repton (*q.v.*) worked here on improving the gardens, followed by the first Marquess of Anglesey and his descendants. The 169-acre gardens offer pleasingly informal walks among an impressive collection of flowering trees and shrubs.

Many plants from the southern hemisphere flourish here in the mild micro-climate. The far-flung rhododendron garden, nearly a mile's walk from the house, is a naturalistic woodland filled with marvellous specimens, but is open only from April to early June, during the flowering season.

COLWYN BAY

Bodnant Garden

Tal-y-Cafn, Colwyn Bay, Conwy LL28 5RE **TEL.** 01492-650460 **OWNER** The National Trust **HOURS** Mid-March–Oct, daily, 10a.m.–5p.m. **ENTRANCE** £5.20, children £2.60 **DIRECTIONS** 8m S of Llandudno and Colwyn Bay, off A470 (signposted), use A55, then A470 **WEB** www.oxalis.co.uk/bodnant

🔲 Gift Shop 🔲 Café 🔲 Plants for Sale 🔲 NPC

Bodnant is largely the combined result of two families, the owner's and the gardener's, working in tandem through the 20th century. (Head gardener Martin Puddle is the third generation of Puddles to take charge of the garden, for his grandfather arrived in 1920, to work for the 2nd Lord Aberconway.)

The story begins with Henry Davis Pochin, an industrial chemist and inventor, who discovered how to turn soap white. He bought the estate in 1874 and planted its famous laburnum walk and the exceptional conifers in the Dell. His grandson, Henry (later, the 2nd Lord Aberconway), invested heavily in the garden during the early part of the 20th century, and we must thank him for the fine terraced upper gardens with lawns around the house, and the great collections of woodland plants. (From the terraces, note the fine views of the Snowdonia mountains to the west.)

While the upper gardens are restrained and formal, with flower and rose borders and neat lawns, by far the most exciting part is the Dell, a steep valley carved by a tributary of the River Conwy, where the sound of rushing torrents adds to the spectacle. The south-west-facing hillside of thin, acidic soil is home to countless rhododendrons and magnolias which flare up in starbursts of white, pink, yellow and red between the bare branches of woodland trees. Bodnant is also home to National Collections of *Encryphia*, magnolia and *Rhododendron forrestii* hybrids. Many of the old conifers now form skyward pillars reaching up through the valley, while winding paths and timber bridges invite further exploration.

The 90-acre garden's most interesting building is the attractive Pin Mill, at the end of a formal canal in the upper gardens. It was an early 18th-century garden lodge, which became a pin factory and then a tannery, before being brought stone-by-stone all the way from Gloucestershire to take up its present, more dignified employment.

The Conwy Seed Fair

If you have seeds to sell, or seeds to buy, why not book a date in the diary to visit the **Conwy Seed Fair,** a springtime event held on 26 March every year. This, and the Conwy Honey Fair (held annually on 13 September) are the last surviving ancient fairs in the North Wales town of Conwy. They are among the oldest fairs in the British Isles, dating back more than 700 years to the Royal Charters of King Edward I in 1278, when the inhabitants of Conwy and its environs were granted permission to sell their produce within the city's walls without paying a trading charge. Originally Conwy enjoyed several other days of free trade – horse, butter and wool fairs – but the seeds and honey are the lone survivors. Local beekeepers now organise both fairs, held in Conwy High Street, which is closed to traffic for the day. Stallholders are still entitled to set up stalls free of charge. The Seed Fair is not confined only to the bartering of seed, however. Gardening goods of many kinds are on offer, including plants, pots and tubs, gardening tools and produce from the garden, plus food, drinks and crafts. Information and stall details are available from **Peter McFadden, Aberconwy & Colwyn Beekeepers' Association, Ynys Goch, Ty'n y Groes, Conwy LL32 8UH (tel. 01492-650851)**.

PENRHYNDEUDRAETH

Plas Brondanw

Llanfrothen, Gwynedd LL48 6SW **TEL.** 01766-770814 **OWNER** Portmeirion Foundation **HOURS** Open all year, daily, 9a.m.–5p.m. **ENTRANCE** £2, children 50p **DIRECTIONS** 3m N of Penrhyndeudraeth, off A4085, on the Croesor Road **2 for 1 Voucher**

Plas Brondanw

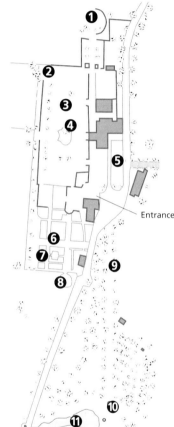

1 North belvedere
2 Viewpoint gateway
3 Lawns
4 Stone-balustraded terrace with large holm oak
5 House
6 Topiary gardens with herbaceous flowers
7 Pool
8 Apollo belvedere
9 Uphill walk to folly
10 Viewing tower folly
11 Water cascade

Formal gardens do not feature strongly in Wales; the nation's gardeners more usually respond to the mountainous topography and acid soils by taking a naturalistic approach. Not only is Plas Brondanw a notable exception, but it is one of the most enchanting gardens you will see anywhere, although it is little known.

The estate was given to 25-year-old Clough Williams-Ellis in 1908 as a birthday present from his father. 'Nothing, just then, could possibly have been more ecstatically welcomed by me,' he recalled. A young architect with vision, and strongly imbued with the contemporary Arts and Crafts style, Williams-Ellis plotted the garden, a long, narrow strip of about three acres, dividing it into hedged rooms punctuated by slender columns of Italian cypress, which fare surprisingly well here.

This is an intimate, domestic and comfy garden, set against the awesome backdrop of the Snowdonia mountains. Its tiered yew topiaries are exceptionally fine, with deep crowns recalling traditional Welsh hats; the walls of local stone and slate shimmer in metallic mauves and browns in the rain, but transport the garden into Mediterranean mode when the sun shines.

Flowers do not feature strongly, for this is chiefly a garden of green architecture and reflective pools, but with its vistas directing your gaze to the summits of Moel Hebog and Cnicht in the distance, fancy blooms close to hand would seem an irrelevance.

There is a pleasant walk, on the other side of the road, up a steep hill to a folly look-out. Williams-Ellis was in the Welsh Guards when he got married in 1915, but, always an individualist, requested a ruin as a present from his fellow officers, instead of the usual silver salver. After the war he turned the gift of a pile of stones into the present viewing tower.

Plant Hunters' Plants

Sue and Bleddyn Wynn-Jones are so smitten with plants from the Far East that they regularly go on expeditions to Taiwan, Korea and the Himalayas to collect wild seed. The results of their travels are among the rarefied list of plants sold in their nursery, **Crûg Farm Plants at Griffiths Crossing, nr Caernarfon, Gwynedd LL55 1TU (tel. 01248-670232), 2m NE of Caernarfon, take A55, then A487 Caernarfon–Bangor Road**. Shade-loving plants are a speciality, and the list of hardy cranesbill geraniums which tops 300 includes many species unavailable elsewhere. The National Collection of *Coriaria* – unusual shrubs and sub-shrubs renowned for their colourful berries – is held here, with 11 species and three cultivars. If you like to seek out rare plants to fox your friends, a visit here is a must (allow plenty of boot-space for purchases). Much of the stock is also on view in the walled display gardens. Open end Feb–late Sept, Thurs–Sun and Bank Holiday Mons, 10a.m.–6p.m. There is no mail order, but for their extensive plant list send a s.a.e. with 2 × 2nd-class stamps.

Buxton's Blue Geranium

'A pearl beyond price' is how the influential plantsman, Graham Stuart Thomas, describes *Geranium wallichianum* 'Buxton's Variety' in his seminal work, *Perennial Garden Plants*. It thus went on to everybody's wish-list and is now widely grown, but its origins lie here, in forested Betws-y-coed on the River Conwy. Edmund Charles Buxton (1838–1925) came from Hendon, but moved to Coed Drew, Betws-y-coed, to plant a hillside garden in the spectacular but uncompromising landscape of Snowdonia. Buxton's clear blue geranium is invaluable for its long season of bright blue button flowers with white eye, prolific in bloom and backed by attractive foliage that takes on blood-red tints as the season progresses. It arose in his garden from the more mauve-tinted Himalayan species of *G. wallichianum*. E.C. Buxton is also remembered in a desirable, pale yellow anthemis.

PENRHYNDEUDRAETH

Portmeirion

Penrhyndeudraeth, Gwynedd LL48 6ET **TEL.** 01766-770228
OWNER Portmeirion Ltd **HOURS** Open all year, daily, 9.30a.m.–5.30p.m.
ENTRANCE £5, OAPs £4, children £2.50, family ticket £12 **DIRECTIONS** Off A497 at Minffordd between Penrhyndeudraeth and Porthmadog **WEB** www.portmeirion.wales.com

🌿 Gift Shop 🌿 Café 🌿 Plants for Sale 🌿 2 for 1 Voucher

Next time I come here I shall check into the rather splendid Portmeirion Hotel (which runs the village) and spend a little longer in this enchanting and eccentric place. Set into approximately 175 acres of woodland gardens on the seashore, Portmeirion is best known as the location for the cult TV series, *The Prisoner*. It was designed by the rich and talented architect Clough Williams-Ellis (see Plas Brondanw, *q.v.*), to accommodate 'like-minded and highly civilised persons'. He invited an eclectic mix of artists, philosophers, left-wing sympathisers, scientists and writers to take up residence and, during his lifetime, many did.

The village is speckled with fan palms, cabbage palms and Italian cypress trees, all of which flourish because of the warming influence of the Gulf Stream. Rhododendrons, fuchsias and hydrangeas add to the ice-cream hues of the delightful, painted buildings.

Try to see Portmeirion on a sunny day, to capture the essence of Riviera frivolity, so incongruously set between the broad estuary sands of Traeth Bach and the veiled, misty mountains of Snowdonia.

And also....

Bodysgallen Hall, Llandudno, Conwy LL30 1RS (tel. 01492-584466), is a luxurious country-house hotel of pink sandstone, mainly Jacobean, with deeply impressive, walled gardens, part of the 214 acres of land, open to residents and diners. There is a symmetrical box parterre filled with fragrant herbs, a rockery with cascade and a walled rose garden featuring white and pale yellow flowers that glow in the fading light of a summer's evening. The productive kitchen garden supplies food for the restaurant, and there are also extensive woodland walks – a fabulous place for a special-treat weekend, with Bodnant Garden (*q.v.*) just a few miles up the road. Open all year, daily. Entrance free to patrons of the hotel. On A470, near Llandudno.

You need to make an excursion down the slender Lleyn Peninsula to reach the National Trust's **Plas-yn-Rhiw, Pwllheli, Gwynedd LL53 8AB (tel. 01758-780219)**. Here is an intimate and rambling cottage garden, just ¾ acre, with stout box hedges and simple topiaries, narrow and bumpy stone paths, and an eclectic mix of flowering and foliage plants with bulbs. Its feminine nature, with the emphasis on fragrance, is due to the three Keating sisters and their mother, who bought the handsome stone farmhouse and surrounding hillside in 1938, with the clear intention of preserving it for later generations to enjoy. Open end March–mid-May, Thurs–Mon; mid-May–Sept, Wed–Mon; Oct, Sat–Sun, 12 noon–5.30p.m.; also part of Feb for snowdrop days. Entrance (garden only) £2, children £1, snowdrop days £2.50. Take A499 from Pwllheli, then B4413, at Botwnnog follow signs to Plas-yn-Rhiw.

Sundialman at Cae Gwyn, Capel Curig, Betws-y-coed, Conwy LL24 0DH (tel. 01690-720288), specialises in hand-made garden sundials in engraved brass and slate, and armillary spheres. An illustrated catalogue is available on request (send a s.a.e.), but commissions and restorations are also undertaken. Open by appointment only.

South Wales

MAP NO. 4

This region encompasses the reinstated Monmouthshire, the county of Wales that is south-easternmost (for some years known as Gwent) and the industrial heartland of Glamorgan. With its industrial heritage and strong associations with mining, this is the most densely populated part of Wales. From the 18th century onwards, the famous Rhondda Valleys provided work for thousands in the (now defunct) mines, but at a price, for the beautiful landscape draining the southern edge of the Brecon Beacons rapidly became scarred by industry, as dark and satanic as the mountain waters were sweet and pure. Monmouthshire is garlanded on its eastern boundary by the beautiful meanders of the Wye Valley and the ancient chase of the Forest of Dean. The valley and the ruins of the Cistercian Tintern Abbey inspired William Wordsworth to 'thoughts of more deep seclusion' and they continue to enchant visitors to this day.

Exceptional in Spring
Clyne Gardens, Swansea

Exceptional in Summer
Veddw House, Devauden

Exceptional in Autumn
Dyffryn Gardens, Cardiff

CARDIFF
Dyffryn Gardens

Exceptional in Autumn

St Nicholas, Cardiff CF5 6SU **TEL.** 029 2059 3328 **OWNER** Vale of Glamorgan Council **HOURS** Open all year, daily, April and Sept–Oct, 10a.m.–5p.m., May, 10a.m.–6p.m., June–Aug 10a.m.–7p.m., Nov–March, 10a.m.–dusk (no facilities available) **ENTRANCE** April–Oct £3, concessions £2, family ticket £6.50, Nov–March free **DIRECTIONS** M4 Jct 33, then A4232, then A48 towards Cowbridge, turn left and follow signs **WEB** www.dyffryngardens.org.uk

🌿 ♿ Access 🌿 Gift Shop 🌿 Café 🌿 Plants for Sale

The renowned Edwardian landscape architect, Thomas Mawson, laid out the 55 acres of gardens around Dyffryn's splendid mansion. Close to the house the formal gardens, with symmetrical, seasonal flower-beds and enclosed garden rooms set to one side, tie the architecture of the mansion seamlessly into its grounds. On the south side, a broad lawn with central water canal and lily-pond creates a grand setting, enhanced by topiary and formal planting. There is a rose garden, a glasshouse of exotic orchids, a herbaceous walk, a classical garden with fountain inspired by those excavated at Pompeii, and a rotunda of yew. The wilder gardens and arboretum beyond the formal areas contain many fine specimen trees and shrubs, dating from the days of the great plant hunters earlier this century. Japanese maples are a feature of the oak woods.

DEVAUDEN
Veddw House

Exceptional in Summer

Veddw, Devauden, Monmouthshire NP16 6PH **TEL.** 01291-650836 **OWNER** Anne Wareham and Charles Hawes **HOURS** Easter–Sept, Sun and Bank Holiday Mons, 2–5p.m. by appointment only **ENTRANCE** £2.50, children £1 **DIRECTIONS** Devauden is on B4293, almost midway between Chepstow and Monmouth (signposted when open)

🌿 ♿ Access

The four acres of Veddw House gardens are varied and colour-themed. Two acres around the house are divided by formal and informal hedging of box, yew, beech and cotoneaster into a variety of separate gardens and colour borders. In spring the meadow, full of small bulbs, is a major feature. This is bordered on one side by a formal vegetable garden where two flower borders – one full of roses, the other herbaceous – contain the brick and gravel paths, which define beds where cabbages mingle with clipped box and standard 'Iceberg' roses.

Veddw House Gardens

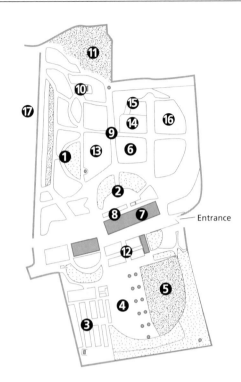

1 Wild garden
2 Crescent border
3 Vegetable garden
4 Meadow
5 Orchard
6 Garden under development
7 House
8 Conservatory
9 Yew walk
10 Ruined cottage
11 Hazel copse
12 Front garden
13 Reflecting pool
14 Cornfield
15 Addison garden
16 Grasses parterre
17 Charles' wood

The conservatory provides protection for a range of tender and exotic plants and offers a view of the crescent border, filled with flowering perennials and shrubs. On the hillside beyond is a developing garden, featuring grasses and low-growing perennials. The yew walk, with a *trompe l'oeil* urn, leads to a small hazel copse, with a ruined cottage, and then on to two acres of woodland walks.

NEWPORT

Tredegar House and Park

Newport NP10 8YW **TEL.** 01633-815880 **OWNER** Newport County Borough Council **HOURS** Easter–July and Sept, Wed–Sun, Aug, daily, Oct, Sat–Sun, all 11.30a.m.–4p.m. **ENTRANCE** House and garden £4.95, OAPs £3.65, children £2.25, family ticket £12.95; garden only free, audio tour £1 **DIRECTIONS** 2m from Newport, signposted from M4 Jct 28 and A48

🚻 ♿ Access 🎁 Gift Shop ☕ Café

The walled gardens at Tredegar have been undergoing restoration since important archaeological evidence of formal, Tudor gardens was unearthed. A tracing of an early 17th-century plan shows that the house (also open) was surrounded on two sides by a series of walled enclosures roughly following the present ones, with a 'great gate' into 'the great bowling greene', a wilderness or maze with a corner arbour, a garden plot 'contrived in walks and borders for trees and flowers', and three orchards with 550 trees planted 'dyamond wise'.

Part of the old layout was covered for 200 years by a thick layer of soil from the excavated lake (made *c*.1790), and archaeological investigations revealed an intricate layout of paths, beds, a small mount and a pair of parterres in front of the orangery. The main central path was of coal dust, bordered with crushed seashells; the patterns of the parterre were formed with different materials such as crushed lime mortar, seashells, brick and coal dust. These have been reinstated, along with espalier fruit trees and box hedging.

The 90-acre park dates from the late 18th century, and one of its avenues, predating the naturalistic Landscape movement, has managed to survive. Deep 19th-century herbaceous borders line the central cedar garden.

The Bishop's Famous Dahlia

Many gardeners value the brilliant scarlet blooms and deep bronze foliage of *Dahlia* 'Bishop of Llandaff', which originated in this region. Llandaff was an ancient cathedral city perched on the banks of the River Taff, but is now swallowed up in the conurbations of Cardiff. Local nurseryman Fred Treseder, who came from Cornwall, spent 50 years dabbling in breeding new dahlias. When his friend, Bishop Hughes of Llandaff, admired a new red dahlia, the nurseryman promptly named it after him. It was awarded an Award of Merit by the Royal Horticultural Society in 1928 and became widely grown during the following decade. In 1936 *The Spectator* declared that it was 'the most popular flower of the moment in many parts of England'. Plant fashions come and go, and 'Bishop of Llandaff' faded into obscurity for many years, but its current vogue is partly due to a revived interest in strongly coloured flowers and a trend towards creating 'hot' borders, like those at Hidcote (*q.v.*).

SWANSEA

Clyne Gardens

Mumbles Road, Black Pill, Swansea SA2 9DU **TEL.** 01792-298637
OWNER Swansea City Council **HOURS** All year, daily, dawn–dusk **ENTRANCE** Free
DIRECTIONS 3m W of Swansea, on coast road

NPC

This beautiful, 50-acre, woodland garden is best seen in spring. The local acid soil nurtures many fine rhododendrons, notably the large-leaved Falconera types, of which there is a National Collection here (the gardens also hold National Collections of acid-loving pieris, enkianthus and triflora rhododendrons). There are sumptuous magnolias, gunneras and candelabra primulas at the streamside, and fragrant azaleas creating a delightful place for a springtime stroll. Refreshments are served during the peak season, in May.

And also...

Creta Cotta Pots and Urns, Jubilee Cottage, Penrhos, nr Raglan, Monmouthshire NP15 2LE (tel. 01600-780416), are hand-made to traditional designs in terracotta from Crete. Sizes vary from a few inches to over 4ft in height. There are also fuchsias and herbs for sale. Open weekends, 10a.m.–6p.m., at other times by appointment. Telephone for price list. From A40/A449 exit for Raglan, turn right towards Dingestow, then left towards Tregare, at T-junction turn left past church, then right towards Penrhos, then right again past church, turn right at fork, then left at T-junction, left again and cottage is on left; 4m from A40.

Penhow Nurseries, St Brides Netherwent, Penhow, Nr Newport, NP4 3AU (tel. 01633-400419). I discovered this nursery from their marvellous display at the Chelsea Flower Show. It specialises in *Diascias* and perennial Nemesias, those pastel-coloured stalwarts of summer containers and hanging-baskets, and their ranges of both these genera are outstanding. There is a catalogue and mail order (minimum order £16). The nursery opens daily, 9a.m.–6p.m. through the main season. Between Newport and Chepstow on A48; follow signs to Penhow Castle, nursery is on S side of A48, opposite the Rock and Foutain Inn.

Penpergwm Lodge, Abergavenny, Monmouthshire NP7 9AS (tel. 01873-840208). This is a lovely, three-acre, formal garden with mature trees, hedges and lawns, a potager of unusual plants and vegetables, an apple and pear pergola and south-facing terraces featuring sun-loving plants. There is also a nursery alongside, specialising in unusual hardy perennial plants. Catriona Boyle's School of Gardening, now in its 16th year, is run from here. Open Easter–Sept, Thurs–Sun, 2–6p.m. Entrance £2, children free. Private visits and parties welcome. From Abergavenny take B4598 towards Usk, after 3m turn left opposite King of Prussia pub, garden on left.

Plantasia, Parc Tawe, Swansea, West Glamorgan SA1 2AL (tel. 01792-474555), is a tropical oasis covering 1900sq yds laid out under a glass pyramid in a modern shopping centre in the middle of Swansea. Its steamy environment contains one of the finest collections of tropical plants in Britain (excluding the larger botanical gardens), holding around 1400 different species and cultivars. There is also a tropical butterfly house, a wildlife room with snakes, lizards, tarantulas and scorpions and a large colony of leaf-cutting ants, and an aquarium. Open all year, Tues–Sun and Bank Holidays (daily in June–Aug), 10a.m.–5p.m. Entrance £2.50, children £1.75. A short walk from city centre.

West Wales

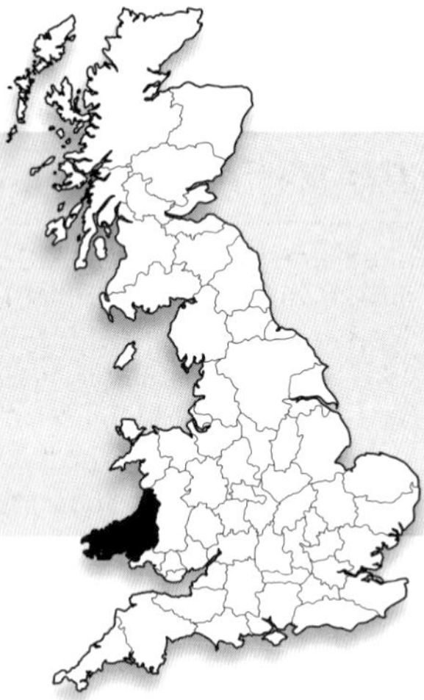

MAP NO. 4

Britain's smallest national park is situated here, along the Pembrokeshire coast, and the area encompasses dramatically beautiful stretches of coastline, with steep cliffs and tiny, offshore islets. Prehistoric monuments scattered through the region provide evidence of thousands of years of human occupation, and the area is steeped in myths and Arthurian legend. Fishing continues to be an important source of livelihood around the coast, with seafood a local speciality (try the Carew oysters, or crabs and lobsters brought in at Milford Haven). Further inland, things have been happening along the scenic valley of the Tywi river. Aberglasney Gardens have been rescued from the undergrowth and restored and the 18th-century landscape park of Middleton Hall has recently reopened its gates to unveil the new National Botanic Garden for Wales. So there are two more reasons to come to this enchanting (and delightfully uncrowded) corner of Wales.

Worth a Visit in Winter
Hilton Court, Haverfordwest
Dinefwr Park, Llandeilo

CARMARTHEN

The National Botanic Garden of Wales

Middleton Hall, Llanarthne, Carmarthenshire SA32 8HG **TEL.** 01558-668768
OWNER Trustees of the NBGW **HOURS** April–Feb, daily: April–Aug,
10a.m.–6p.m., Sept–Oct, 10a.m.–5.30p.m., Nov-Feb, 10a.m.–4.30p.m. (last
adm. 1hr before closing) **ENTRANCE** £6.50, concessions £5.20, children £3,
family ticket £16 **DIRECTIONS** On A48, between Llandeilo and Carmarthen **WEB**
www.gardenofwales.org.uk

🔴 ♿ Access 🔴 Gift Shop 🔴 Café 🔴 Plants for Sale

This large project, several years in the making, is applying a new
persona to an existing historic garden and park. Around £43 million
has been put forward to build a premier botanic garden for Wales,
half of it provided by the Millennium Commission and National
Lottery Funds.

The original park, of 568 acres, was landscaped in 1789 by one
William Paxton, who had made his fortune in India and returned to
Wales with an idea of how to spend it. In the middle of the park he
built an imposing neo-classical house and devoted a good deal of
money and effort to bringing a dramatic waterscape to the site.
Streams were dammed to make a chain of lakes meandering from
one end of the park to the other, crossed by bridges and enlivened
by waterfalls and cascades. Water was piped all over the park and
gardens and Paxton intended turning his estate into a spa, so he built
various bathing buildings, too. After Paxton died in 1824, his spa
buildings disappeared. In 1931 the mansion was demolished
following a great fire, and much of the great park returned to nature,
with the lakes silting up.

The new project has involved restoring Paxton's lakes, repairing
and enhancing the woodlands, with many new tree plantings, and
bringing in various themed gardens around the park. They include
a Welsh Habitat Garden – nothing to do with Conran's shops, but
landscaped with local stones and plants; a display of medicinal and
useful herbs; a science centre; a 'fossil quarry'; a 'genetic garden'
comparing naturally occurring and laboratory-mutated plants, and
much else. The chief eye-catcher, however, is a huge, domed glasshouse designed by Sir Norman Foster, built on the site of the old Hall,
and housing a living collection of Mediterranean plants, with
interpretation exhibits. Aberglasney Gardens (*q.v.*) and Dinefwr Park
(*q.v.*) are nearby.

Hilton Court Gardens and Crafts

Roch, Haverfordwest, Pembrokeshire SA62 6AE **TEL.** 01437-710262
OWNER Mr and Mrs P. Lynch **HOURS** March–Feb, daily, 10a.m.–5.30p.m., closed
in Jan **ENTRANCE** Garden £1 **DIRECTIONS** A487 St David's road from
Haverfordwest; approx. ¾m beyond Simpson Cross, look for sign to Hilton
on left **WEB** www.hiltongardensandcrafts.co.uk

🌀 ♿ Access 🌀 Gift Shop 🌀 Café 🌀 Plants for Sale 🌀 Nursery

This attractive garden and plant centre adjoins an early 18th-century
house on an old estate, and is a treat for anyone holidaying on the
scenic Pembrokeshire coast. Water features strongly, for the existing
stream has been used to fill a chain of lakes, where the mid-summer
highlight is a spectacular display of waterlilies and other aquatic
plants. These include impressive stands of *Gunnera manicata*, bearing
leaves expanding to 8ft or more, on sturdy, thorny stems.

Within Hilton Court's 11 acres of garden (which have been created
only over the last 10 years or so), there are pleasant walks among fine
flowering trees and shrubs which provide interest over a long season.
The property's close proximity to the sea means the garden centre
specialises in plants tolerant of strong winds and a salt-laden
atmosphere.

Picton Castle Garden

Haverfordwest, Pembrokeshire SA62 4AS **TEL.** 01437-751326 **OWNER** Picton
Castle Trust **HOURS** Garden and gallery April–Oct, Tues–Sun, 10.30a.m.–5p.m.;
castle April–Sept, Tues–Fri, Sun and Bank Holiday Mons (guided tours only)
ENTRANCE Garden and gallery £3.95, OAPs £3.75, children £1.95; castle,
garden and gallery £4.95, OAPs £4.75, children £1.95 **DIRECTIONS** 4m E of
Haverfordwest, just off the A40 **WEB** www.pictoncastle.co.uk

🌀 ♿ Access 🌀 Gift Shop

The rather romantic-looking castle, with a crenellated roof and
bulging towers, was built in the 13th century and retained its
external appearance when the interior was remodelled in the 18th
century. Its 40 acres of grounds include extensive woodland areas
well stocked with rhododendrons and azaleas, areas of wild
flowers and some fine trees. The walled garden features masses of
herbs, hardy perennial flowers and a central pond with fountain.
The gallery hosts temporary art exhibitions and garden events
include spring and summer horticultural shows. There is also a
restaurant.

LLANDEILO

Aberglasney Gardens

Llangathen, Carmarthenshire SA32 8QH **TEL.** 01558-668998 **OWNER**
Aberglasney Restoration Trust **HOURS** Open all year, April–Oct, daily,
10a.m.–6p.m., Nov–March, Mon–Fri and 1st Sun in month, 10.30a.m.–3p.m.
ENTRANCE £5, OAPs £4, children/disabled £2.50, family ticket £12 **DIRECTIONS** 3m
W of Llandeilo on A40, go S at Broad Oak junction (signposted) **WEB**
www.aberglasney.org

🌳 ♿ Access 🌳 Gift Shop 🌳 Café 🌳 Plants for Sale

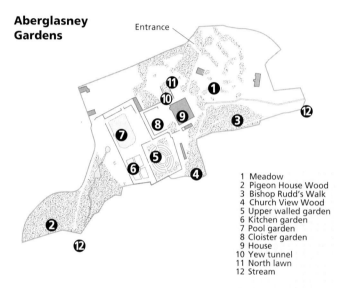

Aberglasney Gardens

Entrance

1 Meadow
2 Pigeon House Wood
3 Bishop Rudd's Walk
4 Church View Wood
5 Upper walled garden
6 Kitchen garden
7 Pool garden
8 Cloister garden
9 House
10 Yew tunnel
11 North lawn
12 Stream

Aberglasney is one of several fine and ancient estates strung like
pearls along the captivating broad valley of the River Tywi, in a
region of fine scenery and uncluttered, well-made roads. It is known
to have been an important manor in medieval times, passing down
the generations of a prominent Welsh family until it was sold to
the Bishop of St David's Cathedral in Pembrokeshire around 1600.
The Bishop and his son spent a great deal of money making lavish
gardens and building massive arcaded walls.

The property underwent alternating periods of good and bad fortune
in succeeding centuries and was all but lost under brambles and thickets
of trees until a rescue job began in 1995. An awesome restoration project,
costing £3.5 million, means you can once again stroll along its parapet
walk which gives aerial views of the walled gardens, one designed by

Penelope Hobhouse in a formal style sympthetic to the Bishop's time here, and featuring colourful perennial flowers. There is a rectangular lake with a central island, an area devoted to vegetables and soft fruit, an ancient yew tunnel and lovely streamside woodland walks. The restoration is an ongoing programme, so don't expect it all to be complete, but it makes an interesting visit.

The Tenby Daffodil

Wales possesses both the daffodil and the leek as its national flowers, the former being worn by many in buttonholes on St David's Day (1 March). The origins of this custom are unclear, but the south-west corner of Wales certainly has a species all of its own, the Tenby daffodil (*Narcissus pseudonarcissus* ssp. *obvallaris*). Bearing clear yellow flowers on short, sturdy stems, the Tenby daffodil was first documented by the Welsh botanist R.A. Salisbury in 1796. It appeared reliably and abundantly in fields and pastures of Carmarthenshire and Pembrokeshire, particularly around Tenby, every spring. Once word of its beauty and novelty caught the attention of gardeners and bulb suppliers, the wild plants began to be dug up by the cartload.

The plant was harvested almost to extinction during the 19th century, and in 1894 the Cardiff Naturalists' Society observed that teams of bulb collectors had scoured the greater part of south Pembrokeshire 'for several seasons in a vigorous attempt to meet the phenomenal demand'. Ruthless gathering of bulbs for the retail trade was followed by the ploughing up of grasslands during two world wars and the continued use of land for intensive farming. In its wild state, the Tenby daffodil became very scarce indeed, although it survived in gardens, hedgebanks and churchyards.

Recent years have seen renewed efforts by the local authorities to re-establish their indigenous flower. Now, happily, the area of Tenby is once again bathed in the brilliant gold of its handsome narcissus in springtime. Gardeners wanting to obtain bulbs of *N. p.* ssp. *obvallaris* can find them on the lists of a few select bulb specialists, including **John Shipton (Bulbs), Y Felin, Henllan Amgoed, Whitland, Carmarthenshire SA34 0SL (Tel. 01994-240125)**. Open by appointment only. For a mail order catalogue, send a s.a.e.

LLANDEILO

Dinefwr Park

Llandeilo, Carmarthenshire SA19 6RT **TEL.** 01558-823902 **OWNER** The National Trust **HOURS** March–Oct, Thurs–Mon, 11a.m.–5p.m. (last adm. 4.30p.m.); parkland also Nov–end March, Thurs–Mon, dawn–dusk **ENTRANCE** £2.80, children £1.40, family ticket £7 **DIRECTIONS** Just W of Llandeilo via A40 **WEB** www.nationaltrust.org.uk

🅿 ♿ Access ☕ Café

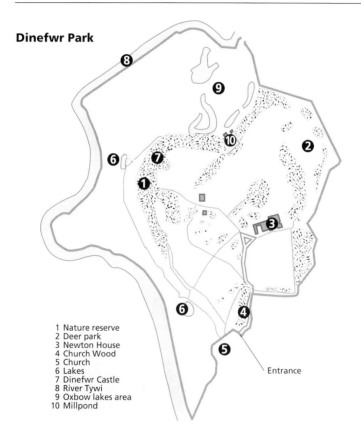

Dinefwr Park

1 Nature reserve
2 Deer park
3 Newton House
4 Church Wood
5 Church
6 Lakes
7 Dinefwr Castle
8 River Tywi
9 Oxbow lakes area
10 Millpond

Entrance

If you're in the area to see Aberglasney Gardens (*q.v.*) or the National Botanic Garden of Wales (*q.v.*), it is worth calling in at Dinefwr Park to compare and contrast these lovely estates strung along the Tywi river valley, in an area gouged and smoothed by a great glacier in the Ice Age. There isn't much of a garden here, but the park, with its scattered woods and great oak trees, makes interesting and scenic walking.

In 1775 Capability Brown (*q.v.*) came to Dinefwr and wrote that 'Nature has been truly bountiful and art has done no harm.' He produced several plans (not carried out) although there are six clumps of trees in the park that are attributed to him, and one path, to the remains of 12th-century Dinefwr Castle, is known as Brown's Walk.

Several viewpoints give you good sightings of the lazily meandering Tywi, which has left a series of oxbow lakes in the park, designated as Sites of Special Scientific Interest for their wildlife habitats. There are good interpretation leaflets available which explain how this beautiful landscape was fashioned by nature, as Brown pointed out. A walled garden in the grounds is privately owned, but often open to the public, though it isn't the reason you would come here.

And also...

Not to be confused with a property of the same name at Welshpool, Powys, **The Dingle, Dingle Lane, Crundale, Haverfordwest, Pembrokeshire (tel. 01437-764370)**, is an 18th-century country gentleman's home (not open) with a sumptuously planted three-acre garden, with plenty of interest for wildlife in a semi-naturalistic setting. It includes a rose garden and rose walk, water gardens, secret hidden-away places to explore and many unusual shrubs and herbaceous plants. There is partial wheelchair access only and plants are for sale at the adjoining small nursery. Heathfield Lodge (*q.v.*), and Picton Castle (*q.v.*), are close by. Open all year, daily, summer 8.30a.m.–6p.m.; winter 10a.m.–4p.m. Entrance £2.50, children free. Off B4329, 2m NE of Haverfordwest.

Heathfield Lodge, Wiston, Haverfordwest, Pembrokeshire SA62 4PT (tel. 01437-731200), is a peaceful hillside garden with excellent views, made over the last 25 years. Natural springs which water the site have been used to create habitats for moisture-loving plants in variety. There are also summer borders, a collection of young trees and plants for sale. Partial wheelchair access only. Open June–Aug, Sun–Mon, 1–6p.m. Entrance £2, children free. Take A40 to Haverfordwest, then turn right through Crundale following signs to Wiston and on left.

Penlan-Uchaf Farm, Fishguard, Pembrokeshire SA65 9UA (tel. 01348-881388). Situated in an exposed position near the top of the Gwaun Valley, this bright and colourful garden, on steep terrain, features an alpine garden and masses of bulbs for spring interest, herbaceous perennials and climbing sweet peas through summer, plus annuals, bedded-out fuchsias and pelargoniums. There are also fragrant herbs and wildflowers planted into raised beds, accessible to wheelchair users and the blind. Teas are provided and plants are for sale. Partial wheelchair access only. Open April–mid-Nov, daily, 9a.m.–dusk. Entrance £2, children 50p. From Fishguard take B4313 towards Narbeth, after 7m go left following signs to Cwm Gwaun and Gwaun Valley (Pontfaen), farm is next to Sychpant Forest car park.

Upton Castle, Pembroke Dock, Pembrokeshire SA72 4SE (tel. 01646-651782), is mainly a woodland garden and park, planted chiefly for spring interest, with a collection of mature rhododendrons, camellias and magnolias, plus many specimen trees. There are also woodland walks to the river. Refreshments are for sale and there is wheelchair access. Open April–Oct, Sun–Fri, 10a.m.–5p.m. (please phone to check times before visiting). Entrance £1.20, children 60p, family ticket £3 (season tickets available). Off A477, 2m NE of Pembroke, turn right in Cosheston, castle signposted on left.

The Walled Garden at Pigeonsford, nr Llangranog, Cardiganshire, SA44 6AF (tel. 01239-654360), is quite near the beautiful sandy beach of Penbryn. It is actually much more than a walled garden; within its one-acre Georgian walled area there are fruits and vegetables plus herbaceous flowers and shrubs in variety, basking on a south-facing slope. There are also fourteen acres of shrubberies, woodland and riverside walks and picnic areas. A maze of maize (sweetcorn) is planted for late summer interest. Plants, vegetables and fruit are for sale in season. Open Easter–end Oct, daily, 10a.m.–6p.m. Entrance £2.50, children 50p. From Cardigan take A487 towards Aberystwyth, at crossroads at Pentregat turn onto B4321 towards Pontgarreg, follow signs for Urdd Centre and ski slope, ³⁄₄m past Pontgarreg turn left at crossroads, entrance on right.

Six of the Best

Among all these fabulous gardens, it is very difficult to select any of them as 'the best'. All of them have been chosen for the *Guide* for their particular merits, but it has been an honour (and a somewhat daunting task) to select half a dozen gardens that are outstanding in each of the following categories. So here goes, these are six of the best, and I hope you will agree when you visit them.

Best Large Gardens

Beth Chatto Gardens   Essex

Forde Abbey   Somerset

Holker Hall   Cumbria

Mount Stewart   Ards and Down

Nymans   Sussex

Stourhead   Wiltshire

Best Small Gardens

Bide-a-Wee Cottage   Northumberland

Bughtrig   Scottish Borders

Crossing House Garden   Cambridgeshire

Herterton House   Northumberland

Turn End   Buckinghamshire

Broughton House   Dumfries and Galloway

Best Town Gardens

Eccleston Square   London

Kensington Roof Garden   London

The Courts, Holt   Wiltshire

University of Oxford Botanic Garden
Oxfordshire

Royal Botanic Garden, Edinburgh   Central
Scotland

York Gate   Yorkshire

Best Seaside Gardens

An Cala   Western Scotland

Coleton Fishacre   Devon

Headland   Cornwall

Inverewe Garden   Highland

The Old Vicarage, East Ruston   Norfolk

Tresco Abbey Garden   Cornwall

Best Organic Gardens

Hatfield House   Hertfordshire

Kellie Castle   Central Scotland

Ryton Gardens   Warwickshire

Snowshill   Gloucestershire

Westwind   Wiltshire

Yalding   Kent

Best for Family Visits

Alton Towers   Staffordshire

Bicton Park   Devon

Centre for Alternative Technology   Mid
Wales

The Earth Centre   Yorkshire

Port Lympne   Kent

The Living Rainforest   Berkshire

National Plant Collections

The National Plant Collections are held in gardens throughout the British Isles. They are administered by the National Council for the Conservation of Plants and Gardens (NCCPG), which aims to 'conserve, document, promote and make available Britain's great biodiversity of garden plants for the benefit of horticulture, education and science'. Most of the work is done on a voluntary basis by enthusiasts and Collection Holders run their collections at their own expense. Listed below are the specialist collections held at gardens featured in *The Garden Lovers' Guide*.

Asplenium scolopendrium   Sizergh Castle, Cumbria

Aster amellus, A. cordifolius and A. ericoïdes   Upton House, Oxfordshire

Astilbe   Holehird, Cumbria; Marwood Hill Gardens, Devon

Azara   Trelissick, Cornwall

Begonia   Glasgow Botanic Gardens, Western Scotland

Bergenia   Cambridge University Botanic Garden, Cambridgeshire

Bletilla   Pinchbeck, Lincolnshire

Brachyglottis   Inverewe, Highland

Buddleja   Longstock Park, Hampshire

Buxus   Langley Boxwood Nursery, Hampshire

Calluna   Harlow Carr Botanic Gardens, Yorkshire

Calluna vulgaris   RHS Wisley Garden, Surrey

Carpinus   Sir Harold Hillier Gardens and Arboretum, Hampshire

Carpinus betulus   Beale Arboretum, Hertfordshire

Cassiope   Branklyn Garden, Central Scotland

Catalpa   Cliveden, Buckinghamshire

Ceanothus   Eccleston Square, London

Ceanothus (deciduous types)   Knoll Gardens, Dorset

Celmisia   Ballyrogan Nurseries, Ards and Down

Chamaecyparis lawsoniana   Bedgebury National Pinetum, Kent

Cimicifuga   Bridgemere Nurseries, Cheshire

Cistus   Chelsea Physic Garden, London

Citrus   Reads Nursery, Norfolk

Clematis   Burford House Gardens, Worcestershire

Conifers (dwarf and slow-growing)   Savill and Valley Gardens, Berkshire

Coriaria   Crûg Farm Plants, North-west Wales

Cornus   Newby Hall Gardens, Yorkshire; Sir Harold Hillier Gardens and Arboretum, Hampshire; Rosemoor Gardens, Devon

Corylus   Sir Harold Hillier Gardens and Arboretum, Hampshire

Corylus (cobnuts and filberts)   Brogdale Horticultural Trust, Kent

Cotoneaster   Sir Harold Hillier Gardens and Arboretum, Hampshire

Crocosmia   Ballyrogan Nurseries, Ards and Down; Lanhydrock, Cornwall

Crocus   RHS Wisley Garden, Surrey

× **Cupressocyparis**   Bedgebury National Pinetum, Kent

Cystopteris   Sizergh Castle, Cumbria

Daboecia   RHS Wisley Garden, Surrey

Dendrobium   Glasgow Botanic Garden, Western Scotland

Dianthus (Malmaison types)   Crathes Castle, Moray and Aberdeenshire; J.M. Marshall, Gloucestershire

Dicksoniaceae (tree ferns)   Glasgow Botanic Garden, Western Scotland

Digitalis   The Botanic Nursery, Wiltshire

Dryopteris   Harlow Carr Botanical Gardens, Yorkshire; Sizergh Castle, Cumbria

Elaeagnus   Beale Arboretum, Hertfordshire

Enkianthus   Clyne Gardens, South Wales

Epimedium   RHS Wisley Garden, Surrey

Erica   Bell's Cherrybank Garden, Central Scotland

Erodium   R.V. Roger Nurseries, Yorkshire

Erythronium   Greencombe, Somerset

Eucryphia   Bodnant Garden, North-west Wales; Seaforde Gardens, Ards and Down

Euphorbia   The Grange, Ballyrogan, Ards and Down; University of Oxford Botanic Garden, Oxfordshire

Fagus   Kirkley Hall, Northumberland

Ferns   Savill and Valley Gardens, Berkshire

Ficus   Reads Nursery, Norfolk

Fragaria × ananassa (strawberry)   Brogdale Horticultural Trust, Kent

Fraxinus (but not excelsior cvs)   Thorp Perrow Arboretum, Yorkshire

Fritillaria (European spp.)   Cambridge University Botanic Garden, Cambridgeshire

Galanthus   RHS Wisley Garden, Surrey

Gaultheria (inc. Pernettya)   Greencombe, Somerset

Gentiana   Christie's Nursery, Central Scotland

Geranium   Catforth Gardens, Lancashire; Cambridge University Botanic Garden, Cambridgeshire

Grevillea   Pine Lodge, Cornwall

Hamamelis   Sir Harold Hillier Gardens and Arboretum, Hampshire

Hedera   Erddig, North-east Wales; Fibrex Nurseries, Worcestershire

Heliotropium   Hampton Court Palace, Surrey

Hemerocallis   The Nursery Further Afield, Oxfordshire

Hoheria   Abbotsbury Sub-tropical Garden, Dorset

Hosta (modern hybrids)   Ann and Roger Bowden, Devon; **(small-leaved)** Apple Court, Hampshire

Hyacinthus orientalis   9 Rosemary Road, Waterbeach, Cambridgeshire

Hydrangea   Holehird, Cumbria

Hypericum   Harlow Carr Botanical Gardens, Yorkshire; Wakehurst Place, Sussex

Ilex   Savill and Valley Gardens, Berkshire; Rosemoor Garden, Devon

Inula   Tatton Park, Cheshire

Iris (award-winning bearded cvs)   Myddelton House, London and Middlesex

Iris ensata   Marwood Hill Garden, Devon

Juglans (excl. regia cvs)   Thorp Perrow Arboretum, Yorkshire

Juniperus   Bedgebury National Pinetum, Kent

Laburnum   Powis Castle, Mid Wales

Lamium   Monksilver Nursery, Cambridgeshire

Lavandula   The Scented Garden, Dorset Downderry Nursery, Kent Norfolk Lavender, Norfolk

Ligustrum   Sir Harold Hillier Gardens and Arboretum, Hampshire

Liriodendron   West Dean Gardens, Sussex

Lithocarpus   Sir Harold Hillier Gardens and Arboretum, Hampshire

Lonicera (spp. and primary hybrids)   Cambridge University Botanic Garden, Cambridgeshire

Lysimachia   Cotswold Garden Flowers, Worcestershire

Magnolia   Savill and Valley Gardens, Berkshire; Bodnant Garden, North-west Wales; Caerhays Castle Garden, Cornwall

Mahonia   Savill and Valley Gardens, Berkshire

Malus   Brogdale Horticultural Trust, Kent; Granada Arboretum, Jodrell Bank, Cheshire; Hyde Hall, Essex

Meconopsis   Craigieburn Garden, Dumfries and Galloway

Mentha   Iden Croft Herbs, Kent

Narcissus   Broadleigh Gardens, Somerset

Narcissus (Brodie cvs)   Brodie Castle, Moray and Aberdeenshire

Nothofagus   Crarae Garden, Western Scotland; Wakehurst Place, Sussex

Nymphaea   Bennett's Water Gardens, Dorset; Stapeley Water Gardens, Cheshire; Kenchester Water Gardens, Herefordshire

Olearia   Inverewe Garden, Highland

Origanum   Iden Croft Herbs, Kent; Hexham Herbs, Northumberland

Osmunda   Sizergh Castle, Cumbria

Paeonia (spp. and primary hybrids)   Hidcote Manor, Gloucestershire

Papaver (annual poppies)   Thompson & Morgan, Suffolk

Paris   Crûg Farm Plants, North-west Wales

Pelargonium   Fibrex Nurseries, Worcestershire

Penstemon (large-flowered cvs)
Rowallane Garden, Ards and Down

Pernettya   Valley Gardens, Berkshire

Phormium   Mount Stewart, Ards and Down

Photinia   Sir Harold Hillier Gardens and
Arboretum, Hampshire Trelissick, Cornwall

Phygelius   Knoll Gardens, Dorset

Picea   Ardkinglas Woodland Garden, Western
Scotland

Pieris   Clyne Gardens, South Wales; Savill and
Valley Gardens, Berkshire

Pinus (excl. dwarf cvs)   Sir Harold Hillier
Gardens and Arboretum, Hampshire

Platanus   Mottisfont Abbey, Hampshire

Polypodium   Harlow Carr Botanical Gardens,
Yorkshire; Kyre Park, Worcestershire

Polystichum   Greencombe, Somerset;
Holehird, Cumbria

Potentilla fruticosa   Webbs of Wychbold,
Worcestershire

Primula (Asiatic types)   Cluny House Gardens,
Central Scotland; **(Cortusoïdes/Farinosae)**
Plant World Botanic Gardens, Devon; **(auricula,
show/alpine)** Martin Nest Nurseries,
Lincolnshire

Prunus (cherries and plums)   Brogdale
Horticultural Trust, Kent

Pseudopanax   Ventnor Botanic Garden, Isle of
Wight

Pyrus (perry pears)   Brogdale Horticultural
Trust, Kent

Quercus   Sir Harold Hillier Gardens and
Arboretum, Hampshire

Rheum (culinary varieties)   RHS Wisley
Garden, Surrey

Rhododendron (Ghent azaleas)   Sheffield
Park Garden, Sussex; **(Glenn Dale azaleas)**
Savill and Valley Gardens, Berkshire; **(Kurume
azaleas)** Isabella Plantation, Surrey; **(Barbatum
series)** Inverewe Garden, Highland; **(spp.)** Savill
and Valley Gardens, Berkshire; **(Falconera
types)** Clyne Gardens, South Wales; **(Falconera
types)** Brodick Castle, Western Scotland; **(Falconera
types)** Brodick Castle, Western Scotland;
(Grandia types) Brodick Castle, Western
Scotland; **(Maddenia types)** Brodick Castle,
Western Scotland; **(Triflora types)** Clyne
Gardens, South Wales; **(forrestii hybrids)**
Bodnant Garden, North-west Wales

Ribes (blackcurrants and gooseberries)
Brogdale Horticultural Trust, Kent; **Ribes
(species and primary hybrids)** Cambridge
University Botanic Garden, Cambridgeshire

Rodgersia   Hadspen Garden, Somerset

Rohdea japonica   Apple Court, Hampshire

Rosa (19th-century shrub roses)   Malleny
Garden, Central Scotland; **(Pre-1900 shrub
roses)** Mottisfont Abbey, Hampshire; **(spp. and
cvs)** The Gardens of the Rose, Hertfordshire;
(spp.) Peter Beales Roses, Norfolk; **(historical
European roses)** University of Birmingham
Botanic Garden, West Midlands

Rubus idaeus   Brogdale Horticultural Trust,
Kent

Ruscus   Cambridge University Botanic Garden,
Cambridgeshire

Salix   Westonbirt Arboretum, Gloucestershire

Salvia   Pleasant View Nursery, Devon; **(tender
salvias)** Kingston Maurward Gardens, Dorset

Sambucus   Wallington Garden,
Northumberland

Sarcococca   Capel Manor, London and
Middlesex

Sarracenia   Marston Exotics, Herefordshire

Saxifraga (European spp.)   Cambridge
University Botanic Garden, Cambridgeshire;
(Kabschia and Engleria) Waterperry Gardens,
Oxfordshire

Scabiosa caucasica   Hardwick Hall,
Derbyshire

Skimmia   Wakehurst Place, Sussex

Sorbus   Granada Arboretum, Jodrell Bank,
Cheshire; **(S. aria and micromeles)** East
Durham and Houghall Community College,
Durham; **(S. aria and micromeles)** Winkworth
Arboretum, Surrey

Streptocarpus   Dibley's Nurseries, North-east
Wales

Styracaceae   Holker Hall, Cumbria

Taxus   Bedgebury National Pinetum, Kent

Thalictrum   Bridgemere Garden World,
Cheshire

Thuja   Bedgebury National Pinetum, Kent

Thymus   Hexham Herbs, Northumberland

Tilia   Thorp Perrow Arboretum, Yorkshire

Tulbaghia   Marwood Hill Gardens, Devon

Tulipa (spp. and primary hybrids)
Cambridge University Botanic Garden,
Cambridgeshire

Vaccinium   Greencombe, Somerset

Viburnum   Hyde Hall, Essex

Vinca   Monksilver Nursery, Cambridgeshire

Vitis vinifera   Brogdale Horticultural Trust,
Kent; Reads Nursery, Norfolk

Woodwardia   Apple Court, Hampshire

Outstanding Tree Collections

If you enjoy trees in their great variety, then look out for the following gardens and arboreta. Some, such as Ardkinglas Woodland Garden in Scotland, feature Champion Trees – deemed to be the largest examples of their kind in the British Isles. Others, such as Westonbirt Arboretum and Kew Gardens, are exceptionally beautiful in spring and autumn, for the blossoms and tinted leaves of their deciduous collections. See individual entries for more detailed information.

Alton Towers   Staffordshire

Ardanaiseig Garden   Western Scotland

Ardkinglas Woodland Garden   Western Scotland

Arduaine Garden   Western Scotland

Batsford Arboretum   Gloucestershire

Beale Arboretum   Hertfordshire

Bedgebury Pinetum   Kent

Benmore Botanic Garden   Western Scotland

Bicton Park Gardens   Devon

Biddulph Grange   Staffordshire

Caerhays Castle Garden   Cornwall

Castle Howard   Yorkshire

Castle Kennedy and Lochinch   Dumfries and Galloway

Castlewellan National Arboretum   Ards and Down

Cholmondeley Castle   Cheshire

City of Bath Botanic Gardens   Avon district

Crarae Glen Garden   Western Scotland

Dawyck Botanic Garden   Scottish Borders

Drummond Castle   Central Scotland

Exbury Gardens   Hampshire

Forde Abbey   Dorset

Holker Hall   Cumbria

Killerton   Devon

Knightshayes Court   Devon

Little Leckmelm Shrubbery and Arboretum   Highland

Monteviot   Scottish Borders

Muncaster Castle   Cumbria

Ness Botanic Gardens   Cheshire

Nymans Garden   Sussex

Pencarrow   Cornwall

RHS Wisley Gardens   Surrey

Royal Botanic Garden, Edinburgh   Central Scotland

Royal Botanic Gardens, Kew   Surrey

Savill Garden, The   Berkshire

Sheffield Park   Sussex

Sir Harold Hillier Gardens and Arboretum   Hampshire

Tatton Park   Cheshire

Thorp Perrow Arboretum   Yorkshire

University of Birmingham Botanic Garden   West Midlands

Valley Gardens, The   Berkshire

Wakehurst Place   Sussex

West Dean Gardens   Sussex

Westonbirt Arboretum   Gloucestershire

Winkworth Arboretum   Surrey

Organic Gardens

Interest in organic methods of gardening is booming. Going organic is safer for pets and wildlife and, these days, is a very popular option for growing fruit and vegetables for our own consumption, too. The gardens listed below are a selection of the best places to see organic gardening in action. At other properties you may find that a small part of the grounds (the kitchen garden area, for example) is gardened organically.

An Cala   Western Scotland

Audley End (walled garden)   Essex

Barnsdale   Leicestershire and Rutland

Centre for Alternative Technology   Mid Wales

Cerney House Garden   Gloucestershire

Cholmondley Castle (kitchen garden)   Cheshire

Culross Palace   Central Scotland

Edmondsham House   Dorset

Gilbert White's House (kitchen garden)   Hampshire

Glebe Cottage Plants   Devon

Greencombe   Somerset

Hatfield House   Hertfordshire

Kellie Castle   Central Scotland

Leith Hall (kitchen garden)   Moray and Aberdeenshire

Naturescape   Nottinghamshire

Pendle Heritage Centre   Lancashire

Period Plants Nursery   Berkshire

Pureland Relaxation and Meditation Centre   Nottinghamshire

Ryton Organic Gardens   Warwickshire

Sea View Garden Gallery   Highland

Snowshill Manor   Gloucestershire

Sticky Wicket   Dorset

The Cottage Herbary   Worcestershire

The Earth Centre   Yorkshire

Titsey Place   Surrey

Trebah Garden   Cornwall

Westwind   Wiltshire

Willow Lodge (kitchen garden)   Gloucestershire

Yalding Organic Gardens   Kent

MAPS

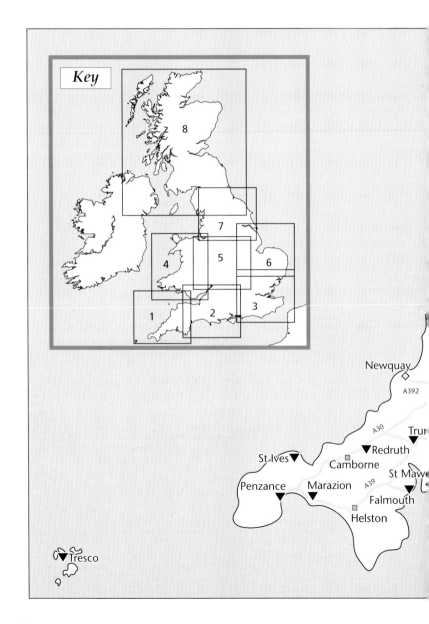

Key

8

7

4

5

6

1

2

3

Newquay

A392

A30

Trur

Redruth

St Ives

Camborne

St Maw

Penzance

Marazion

A39

Falmouth

Helston

Tresco

Map 1

▼ Main Entry ◇ And also…

0   10   20 miles

Port Talbot ■
Bridgend ■
Porthcawl ■

Ilfracombe ■
Porlock ▼
A39

A361
A39
A396

▼ Barnstaple

■ Bideford
A361
▼ Warkleigh

Hartland ◇
A39
Great Torrington ▼
A388
A386
A377
Tiverton ▼

A3072

DEVON

◇ Sticklepath
Exeter ■

A30
A388
▼ Drewsteignton
Christow ◇

A39
A395
A38
A380

▼ Padstow
CORNWALL
A388
Buckland Monachorum
Teignmouth ■
Newton Abbot ▼
Torquay

◇ Washaway
A390
▼ Yelverton
Dartington ◇

Bodmin ■
A38
A386
Rattery ▼
Paignton ■

A30
A391
◇ Lostwithiel
Saltash ■
PLYMOUTH
Brixham ■
A379

St Austell ▼
Cuddra ◇
Fowey
Plympton ■
Kingswear ▼

A390
▼ Polruan
Torpoint

▼ Penteway
A379
Salcombe ▼

© MAPS IN MINUTES™ (1999)

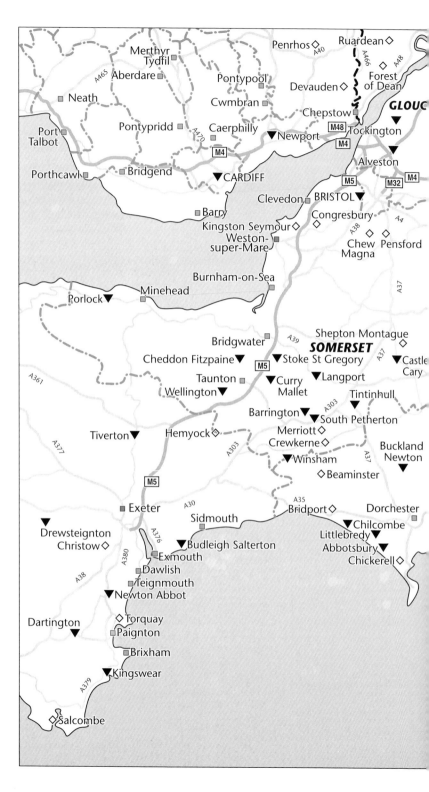

Map 2

▼ Main Entry ◇ And also...

0   10   20 miles

© MAPS IN MINUTES™ (1999)

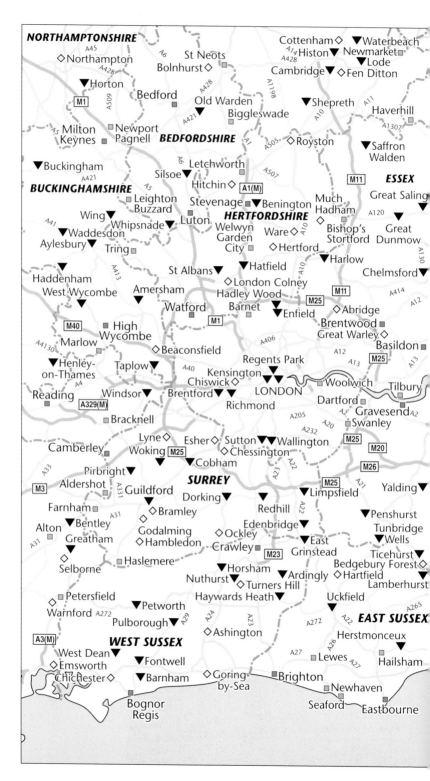

NORTHAMPTONSHIRE

◇ Northampton

A45

A6

Cottenham ◇   ▼ Waterbeach

A14 Histon ▼ Newmarket ■

Cambridge ▼ ◇ Fen Ditton   ▼ Lode

A428

St Neots

Bolnhurst ◇   ■

▼ Horton

A509

A428

A421

A6

A1198

A11

▼ Shepreth

Bedford ■   Old Warden   Biggleswade

A421

A10

Haverhill

A1307

Milton Keynes ■   ■ Newport Pagnell

A5

BEDFORDSHIRE

A1

A505   ◇ Royston

▼ Saffron Walden

▼ Buckingham

A421

A6   Letchworth

Silsoe ▼   Hitchin ◇

A507

M11

ESSEX

BUCKINGHAMSHIRE

A5

Leighton Buzzard ■   Stevenage ■ ▼ Benington

A1(M)

Much Hadham ■

Great Saling ▼

A120

Wing ▼   Whipsnade ▼

A41

Waddesdon ▼   Tring ■

Aylesbury ▼

Luton ■

HERTFORDSHIRE

Welwyn Garden City ■

Ware ◇

A10

◇ Hertford

Bishop's Stortford ■

Great Dunmow ■

A130

▼

Haddenham

West Wycombe ▼

A413

Amersham

St Albans ▼   ▼ Hatfield

◇ London Colney

Hadley Wood ▼

▼ Harlow

A10

Chelmsford ▼

A414

M11

A12

Marlow   ■ High Wycombe

M40

A4130

◇ Beaconsfield

Watford ■   Barnet ■

M1

▼ Enfield

M25

◇ Abridge

Brentwood ■

Great Warley ◇

M25

A12

A13

Basildon ■

▼ Henley-on-Thames

Taplow ▼

A40

Regents Park ▼▼

Kensington ▼

Chiswick ◇   ▼▼

LONDON

A406

A13

Reading ■

A329(M)

Windsor ▼   Brentford ▼▼

Richmond

◇ Woolwich ■

Dartford ■

Tilbury ■

A2 Gravesend A2

A4

■ Bracknell

A205

A2

■ Swanley

Camberley

A33

Lyne ◇   Esher ◇   Sutton ▼▼ ▼ Wallington

Woking   M25

A20

A232

M25

M20

M26

Pirbright ▼

Aldershot ■

M3

A331

Cobham ▼

Chessington ◇

A23   A22

SURREY

A21

Yalding ▼

Guildford ■   Dorking ▼

▼ Limpsfield

M25

Farnham ■

A31

◇ Bramley

Redhill

A22

▼ Penshurst

Tunbridge Wells

Alton   ▼ Bentley

A31

Greatham ▼

Godalming ◇   ◇ Hambledon

◇ Ockley

Edenbridge ▼

▼ East Grinstead

M23

Bedgebury Forest ◇

Ticehurst ▼

◇ Selborne

■ Haslemere

Crawley ◇

◇ Hartfield

Lamberhurst

▼ Horsham

Nuthurst ▼ ◇ Turners Hill

▼ Ardingly

Uckfield

A265

◇ Petersfield

▼ Petworth

Haywards Heath ▼

▼

EAST SUSSEX

Warnford   A272

A24

A23

A272

A22

Pulborough ▼

A29

A3(M)

◇ Ashington

Herstmonceux

A26

West Dean ▼

WEST SUSSEX

A27

■ Lewes   A27

Hailsham ■

◇ Emsworth

Chichester ◇   ▼ Barnham

▼ Fontwell

◇ Goring-by-Sea

■ Brighton

■ Newhaven

Bognor Regis

Seaford   Eastbourne ■

Map 3

▼ Main Entry ◇ And also...

0   10   20 miles

© MAPS IN MINUTES™ (1999)

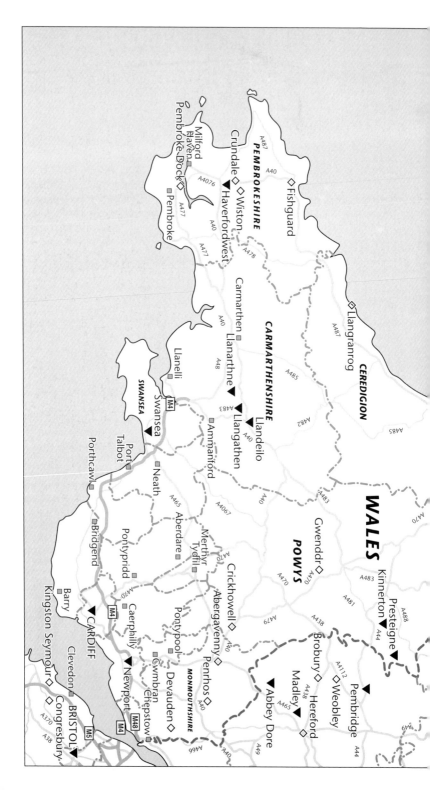

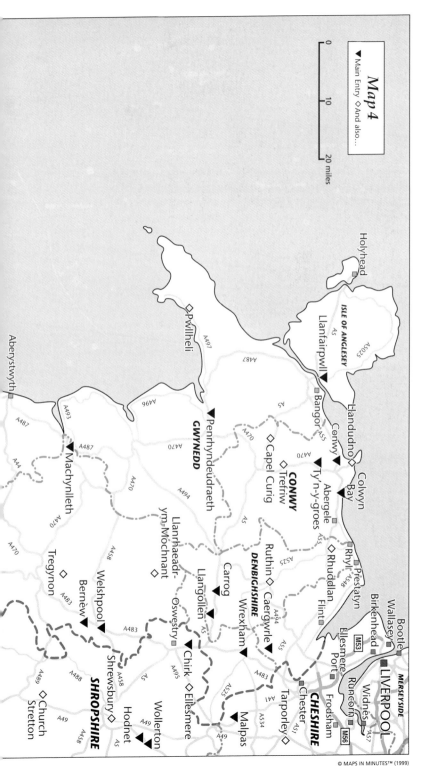

Map 4

▼ Main Entry ◇ And also....

0   10   20 miles

Holyhead

ISLE OF ANGLESEY

A5

A5025

Llanfairpwll ▼

Bangor ■

A55

A5

A487

A497

Pwllheli ◇

A496

A470

GWYNEDD

A470

A494

Penrhyndeudraeth ▼

Aberystwyth ■

A487

A493

A487

Machynlleth ▼

A44

A470

A470/A44

Tregynon ◇

A458

Bernew ◇

Welshpool ▼

A483

Llanrhaeadr-ym-Mochnant ◇

A5

Capel Curig ◇

◇ Trefriw

CONWY

A470

Abergele ▼

Ty'n-y-groes ▼

Conwy ▼

A55

Llandudno ◇

Colwyn Bay ◇

A55

Rhyl ■

A548

Prestatyn ■

Rhuddlan ◇

A525

Ruthin ◇

DENBIGHSHIRE

Caergwrle ◇

A494

Carrog ▼

A5

Llangollen ▼

Wrexham ▼

A5

A483

A495

Chirk ▼

◇ Ellesmere

Oswestry ■

A483

A5

Shrewsbury ◇

A458

A488

SHROPSHIRE

A49

Church Stretton ◇

A489

A49

Hodnet ▼

Wollerton ▼

A49

A53

A41

A483

A525

Malpas ▼

A49

Tarporley ▼

A534

A51

Chester ■

CHESHIRE

Frodsham ■

Ellesmere Port ■

M53

A57

Runcorn

Widnes ■

M56

Flint ■

A55

A548

LIVERPOOL

Bootle

Wallasey

Birkenhead ■

Bebington

MERSEYSIDE

© MAPS IN MINUTES™ (1999)

Map 5

▼ Main Entry   ◇ And also…

0   10   20 miles

DERBYSHIRE

NOTTINGHAMSHIRE

RUTLAND

LEICESTERSHIRE

WARWICKSHIRE

NORTHAMPTONSHIRE

BUCKINGHAMSHIRE

OXFORDSHIRE

Bakewell
Dronfield M1
Worksop
Retford
Staveley
▼ Chesterfield
Lincoln
Doddington ◇
◇ Bakewell
Clay Cross
Mansfield
Matlock
Sutton in
Ashfield
Kirkby in
Ashfield
▼ Newark-
on-Trent
Ripley
Hucknall
◇ East Stoke
▼ Tissington
Ilkeston
Ashbourne
◇ Ednaston
▼ Clifton
▼ NOTTINGHAM
DERBY
Langar ◇
Grantham ▼
Elvaston ◇
Long Eaton
Belvoir ▼
▼ Ticknall
Burton upon
Trent
Loughborough
Melton
Mowbray
Gunby ▼ ◇ Thistleton
Ashby-de-la-Zouch
Coalville
Cossington
◇ Essendine
◇ Lichfield
Syston ◇
Oakham ▼
Tamworth
LEICESTER
Stamford
Sutton
Coldfield
Hinckley
M69
Market
Harborough
Corby
Nuneaton ◇
M42
Bedworth
M1
North Kilworth
◇ Solihull
COVENTRY
M6
Melchbourne
▼ Lapworth
▼ Ryton-on-Dunsmore
Rugby
▼ Cottesbrooke
M40
WARWICKSHIRE
M45
▼ Guilsborough
Rushden
Warwick ▼
Leamington Spa
Daventry
◇ Northampton
Bolnhurst ◇
Alcester Charlecote
◇ Stratford-
upon-Avon
Canons
Ashby
▼ Horton
Bedford
▼ Chipping Campden
M1
Alkerton ▼
Banbury ▼
Milton
Keynes
Newport
Pagnell
Whichford
Mixbury ◇
▼ Buckingham
Silsoe ▼
◇
Moreton-in-Marsh
BUCKINGHAMSHIRE
M1
Toddington
Leighton
Buzzard
Steeple Aston ▼
M40
Bicester
Wing ▼
Luton
Woodstock ▼
Whipsnade ▼
Burford ◇
Witney
Kidlington
Aylesbury ▼
Tring
Oxford
▼ Wheatley
St Albans ▼
Cerney
◇ Lechlade
OXFORDSHIRE
West Wycombe
Amersham ▼
Kelmscott ◇

© MAPS IN MINUTES™ (1999)

Goole

M18

Thorne

M180

Scunthorpe

M181

M180

Immingham

Grimsby

Cleethorpes

A15

A18

Nettleton ◇ A46

A159

A15

A16

A1031

Gainsborough

A631

A631

Hemswell ▼

Louth ▼

A16

A52

Harpswell ▼

A46

Retford ■

A158

A156

A57

A1

Doddington ◇ ■ Lincoln

LINCOLNSHIRE

A158

A52

A617

A46

Newark-
on-Trent ▼
◇ East Stoke

A15

A17

A16 A17

Boston ■

A1

A17

A52

Langar ◇

A52

Grantham ▼

Belvoir ▼

A52

Heacham ▼

A606

A607

Melton
Mowbray

A1

A15

Pinchbeck ▼ ◇ Weston

Spalding ■ A151

Grimston ◇

A607

Gunby ▼ ◇ Thistleton

A12

King's
Lynn ■

A10

RUTLAND ◇ Essendine

A16

Wisbech ▼

Wimbotsham

Oakham ▼

A606

Stamford ■

A47

A47

A1122

Downham
Market ■

A47

A6003

A43

◇ Peterborough

A605

March ■

A10

A141

A6

A427

A6116

A1

A1107

Market
Harborough ■ Corby ■

Prickwillow ◇

CAMBRIDGESHIRE

Ely

▼ Cottesbrooke

A14

A14

Huntingdon ■

A10

A14

▼ Guilsborough

A45

◇ Melchbourne

St Ives ■

Hemingford Grey ▼

◇ Burwell

NORTHAMPTONSHIRE ■ Rushden

Cottenham ◇ ▼ Waterbeach

◇ Northampton

A6

St Neots

A14

A428

Histon ▼

A428

Bolnhurst ◇ ■

Cambridge ▼ ◇ Fen Ditton

▼ Horton

A428

A1198

M11

M1

A509

Bedford ■

Old Warden ▼

A10

▼ Shepreth

A11

Haverhill ■

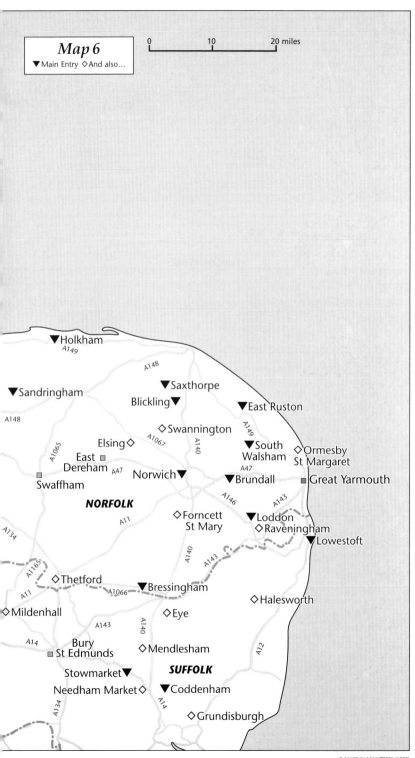

Map 6

▼ Main Entry ◇ And also…

0   10   20 miles

▼Holkham
A149

▼Sandringham

A148

A148 ▼Saxthorpe

Blickling▼

▼East Ruston

◇Swannington

A1067

Elsing ◇

A1065

A149

A140

▼South
Walsham

◇Ormesby
St Margaret

East ▪
Dereham A47

A47

▪
Swaffham

Norwich▼

▼Brundall

▪ Great Yarmouth

NORFOLK

A146

A143

A11

◇Forncett
St Mary

▼Loddon
◇Raveningham

A134

A140

A143

▼Lowestoft

A1165

◇Thetford

A1066

▼Bressingham

A11

◇Halesworth

◇Mildenhall

◇Eye

A140

A143

A14

Bury
▪ St Edmunds

◇Mendlesham

A12

SUFFOLK

Stowmarket▼

A134

Needham Market◇

A14

▼Coddenham

◇Grundisburgh

Map 7
▼ Main Entry ◇ And also...

0   10   20 miles

SUNDERLAND
Houghton le Spring
Peterlee
A19
Hartlepool
A689
Redcar
Middlesbrough
A66
A171
A172
Whitby
A684
A169
A171
◇Northallerton
A19
A170
Pickering▼
A170
Scarborough
A168
A64
A165
A1(M)
A166
A614
(A166)
Bridlington
Knaresborough
A19
A59
York▼
▼Wetherby
A64
A1035
A165
A58
Tadcaster
A19
A163
A1079
Beverley
Garforth
A1
A614
A164
A63
Castleford
A63
Selby
M62
HULL
M62
Pontefract
Goole
A15
Wakefield
M18
Hemsworth
A67
Thorne
Scunthorpe
Immingham
M180
M181
M180
A18
Grimsby
SOUTH
◇Doncaster
Nettleton ◇
A46
YORKSHIRE ▼Conisborough
A159
A15
A16
Rotherham
A1(M)
Gainsborough
A631
SHEFFIELD
A631
◇▼Hemswell
A57
◇
A156
A46
Louth▼
ronfield M1
Blyth
Harpswell
Staveley
Worksop
Retford
A158
A619
A1
A57

© MAPS IN MINUTES™ (1999)

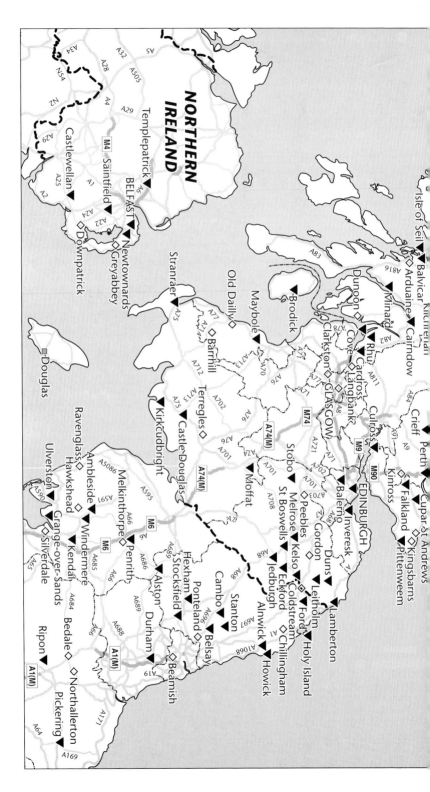

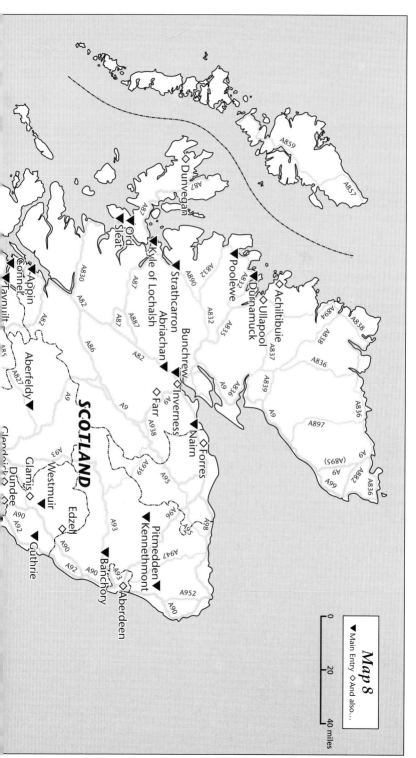

Map 8
▼ Main Entry ◇ And also…

SCOTLAND

Dunvegan
Ord
Sleat
Kyle of Lochalsh
Strathcarron
Abriachan
Bunchrew
Poolewe
Durinamuck
Ullapool
Achiltibuie
Appin
Connel
Taynuilt
Aberfeldy
Farr
Inverness
Nairn
Forres
Glamis
Westmuir
Edzell
Dundee
Guthrie
Pitmedden
Kennethmont
Banchory
Aberdeen

0   20   40 miles

© MAPS IN MINUTES™ (1999) © Crown Copyright

Index

Ideas, advice and inspiration

The Garden Lovers' Guide to Britain

2 FOR 1 OFFER
ONE ADULT FREE WITH ONE FULL PAYING ADULT

Abbotsbury Sub-tropical Gardens Dorset

BBC Gardeners' World VALID UNTIL END OF OCTOBER 2003

The Garden Lovers' Guide to Britain

2 FOR 1 OFFER
ONE ADULT FREE WITH ONE FULL PAYING ADULT

Abbotsford Scottish Borders

BBC Gardeners' World VALID UNTIL END OF OCTOBER 2003

The Garden Lovers' Guide to Britain

2 FOR 1 OFFER
ONE ADULT FREE WITH ONE FULL PAYING ADULT

An Cala Western Scotland

BBC Gardeners' World VALID UNTIL END OF OCTOBER 2003

The Garden Lovers' Guide to Britain

2 FOR 1 OFFER
ONE ADULT FREE WITH ONE FULL PAYING ADULT

Arley Hall Gardens Cheshire

BBC Gardeners' World VALID UNTIL END OF OCTOBER 2003

The Garden Lovers' Guide to Britain

2 FOR 1 OFFER
ONE ADULT FREE WITH ONE FULL PAYING ADULT

Benmore Botanic Garden Western Scotland

BBC Gardeners' World VALID UNTIL END OF OCTOBER 2003

The Garden Lovers' Guide to Britain

2 FOR 1 OFFER
ONE ADULT FREE WITH ONE FULL PAYING ADULT

Bicton Park Botanical Gardens Devon

BBC Gardeners' World VALID UNTIL END OF OCTOBER 2003

The Garden Lovers' Guide to Britain

2 FOR 1 OFFER
ONE ADULT FREE WITH ONE FULL PAYING ADULT

Bramham Park Yorkshire

BBC Gardeners' World VALID UNTIL END OF OCTOBER 2003

The Garden Lovers' Guide to Britain

2 FOR 1 OFFER
ONE ADULT FREE WITH ONE FULL PAYING ADULT

Brook Cottage Garden Oxfordshire

BBC Gardeners' World VALID UNTIL END OF OCTOBER 2003

The Garden Lovers' Guide to Britain

2 FOR 1 OFFER
ONE ADULT FREE WITH ONE FULL PAYING ADULT

Capel Manor Middlesex

BBC Gardeners' World VALID UNTIL END OF OCTOBER 2003

The Garden Lovers' Guide to Britain

2 FOR 1 OFFER
ONE ADULT FREE WITH ONE FULL PAYING ADULT

Catforth Gardens Lancashire

BBC Gardeners' World VALID UNTIL END OF OCTOBER 2003

Terms and conditions:

1. This voucher must be surrendered upon admission.
2. Photocopies of this voucher will not be accepted.
3. The voucher cannot be used for group parties or in conjunction with any other offer.
4. There is no cash alternative.
5. The voucher is valid only during official opening times. See p.395 for more information.

Terms and conditions:

1. This voucher must be surrendered upon admission.
2. Photocopies of this voucher will not be accepted.
3. The voucher cannot be used for group parties or in conjunction with any other offer.
4. There is no cash alternative.
5. The voucher is valid only during official opening times. See p.103 for more information.

Terms and conditions:

1. This voucher must be surrendered upon admission.
2. Photocopies of this voucher will not be accepted.
3. The voucher cannot be used for group parties or in conjunction with any other offer.
4. There is no cash alternative.
5. The voucher is valid only during official opening times. See p.52 for more information.

Terms and conditions:

1. This voucher must be surrendered upon admission.
2. Photocopies of this voucher will not be accepted.
3. The voucher cannot be used for group parties or in conjunction with any other offer.
4. There is no cash alternative.
5. The voucher is valid only during official opening times. See p.406 for more information.

Terms and conditions:

1. This voucher must be surrendered upon admission.
2. Photocopies of this voucher will not be accepted.
3. The voucher cannot be used for group parties or in conjunction with any other offer.
4. There is no cash alternative.
5. The voucher is valid only during official opening times. See p.90 for more information.

Terms and conditions:

1. This voucher must be surrendered upon admission.
2. Photocopies of this voucher will not be accepted.
3. The voucher cannot be used for group parties or in conjunction with any other offer.
4. There is no cash alternative.
5. The voucher is valid only during official opening times. See p.412 for more information.

Terms and conditions:

1. This voucher must be surrendered upon admission.
2. Photocopies of this voucher will not be accepted.
3. The voucher cannot be used for group parties or in conjunction with any other offer.
4. There is no cash alternative.
5. The voucher is valid only during official opening times. See p.242 for more information.

Terms and conditions:

1. This voucher must be surrendered upon admission.
2. Photocopies of this voucher will not be accepted.
3. The voucher cannot be used for group parties or in conjunction with any other offer.
4. There is no cash alternative.
5. The voucher is valid only during official opening times. See p.338 for more information.

Terms and conditions:

1. This voucher must be surrendered upon admission.
2. Photocopies of this voucher will not be accepted.
3. The voucher cannot be used for group parties or in conjunction with any other offer.
4. There is no cash alternative.
5. The voucher is valid only during official opening times. See p.186 for more information.

Terms and conditions:

1. This voucher must be surrendered upon admission.
2. Photocopies of this voucher will not be accepted.
3. The voucher cannot be used for group parties or in conjunction with any other offer.
4. There is no cash alternative.
5. The voucher is valid only during official opening times. See p.201 for more information.

The Garden Lovers' Guide to Britain

2 FOR 1 OFFER
ONE ADULT FREE WITH ONE FULL PAYING ADULT

Chatsworth
Derbyshire

Gardeners' World
VALID UNTIL END OF
OCTOBER 2003

The Garden Lovers' Guide to Britain

2 FOR 1 OFFER
ONE ADULT FREE WITH ONE FULL PAYING ADULT

Church Hill Cottage Gardens Kent

Gardeners' World
VALID UNTIL END OF
OCTOBER 2003

The Garden Lovers' Guide to Britain

2 FOR 1 OFFER
ONE ADULT FREE WITH ONE FULL PAYING ADULT

Compton Acres
Dorset

Gardeners' World
VALID UNTIL END OF
OCTOBER 2003

The Garden Lovers' Guide to Britain

2 FOR 1 OFFER
ONE ADULT FREE WITH ONE FULL PAYING ADULT

Dalemain House and Gardens Cumbria

Gardeners' World
VALID UNTIL END OF
OCTOBER 2003

The Garden Lovers' Guide to Britain

2 FOR 1 OFFER
ONE ADULT FREE WITH ONE FULL PAYING ADULT

Dawyck Botanic Garden
Scottish Borders

Gardeners' World
VALID UNTIL END OF
OCTOBER 2003

The Garden Lovers' Guide to Britain

2 FOR 1 OFFER
ONE ADULT FREE WITH ONE FULL PAYING ADULT

Dingle Nurseries and Garden Mid Wales

Gardeners' World
VALID UNTIL END OF
OCTOBER 2003

The Garden Lovers' Guide to Britain

2 FOR 1 OFFER
ONE ADULT FREE WITH ONE FULL PAYING ADULT

Edzell Castle and Garden
Central Scotland

Gardeners' World
VALID UNTIL END OF
OCTOBER 2003

The Garden Lovers' Guide to Britain

2 FOR 1 OFFER
ONE ADULT FREE WITH ONE FULL PAYING ADULT

Furzey Gardens
Hampshire

Gardeners' World
VALID UNTIL END OF
OCTOBER 2003

The Garden Lovers' Guide to Britain

2 FOR 1 OFFER
ONE ADULT FREE WITH ONE FULL PAYING ADULT

The Gardens of the Rose
Hertfordshire

Gardeners' World
VALID UNTIL END OF
OCTOBER 2003

The Garden Lovers' Guide to Britain

2 FOR 1 OFFER
ONE ADULT FREE WITH ONE FULL PAYING ADULT

Glen Chantry
Essex

Gardeners' World
VALID UNTIL END OF
OCTOBER 2003

Terms and conditions:

1. This voucher must be surrendered upon admission.
2. Photocopies of this voucher will not be accepted.
3. The voucher cannot be used for group parties or in conjunction with any other offer.
4. There is no cash alternative.
5. The voucher is valid only during official opening times. See p.173 for more information.

Terms and conditions:

1. This voucher must be surrendered upon admission.
2. Photocopies of this voucher will not be accepted.
3. The voucher cannot be used for group parties or in conjunction with any other offer.
4. There is no cash alternative.
5. The voucher is valid only during official opening times. See p.82 for more information.

Terms and conditions:

1. This voucher must be surrendered upon admission.
2. Photocopies of this voucher will not be accepted.
3. The voucher cannot be used for group parties or in conjunction with any other offer.
4. There is no cash alternative.
5. The voucher is valid only during official opening times. See p.75 for more information.

Terms and conditions:

1. This voucher must be surrendered upon admission.
2. Photocopies of this voucher will not be accepted.
3. The voucher cannot be used for group parties or in conjunction with any other offer.
4. There is no cash alternative.
5. The voucher is valid only during official opening times. See p.111 for more information.

Terms and conditions:

1. This voucher must be surrendered upon admission.
2. Photocopies of this voucher will not be accepted.
3. The voucher cannot be used for group parties or in conjunction with any other offer.
4. There is no cash alternative.
5. The voucher is valid only during official opening times. See p.419 for more information.

Terms and conditions:

1. This voucher must be surrendered upon admission.
2. Photocopies of this voucher will not be accepted.
3. The voucher cannot be used for group parties or in conjunction with any other offer.
4. There is no cash alternative.
5. The voucher is valid only during official opening times. See p.397 for more information.

Terms and conditions:

1. This voucher must be surrendered upon admission.
2. Photocopies of this voucher will not be accepted.
3. The voucher cannot be used for group parties or in conjunction with any other offer.
4. There is no cash alternative.
5. The voucher is valid only during official opening times. See p.147 for more information.

Terms and conditions:

1. This voucher must be surrendered upon admission.
2. Photocopies of this voucher will not be accepted.
3. The voucher cannot be used for group parties or in conjunction with any other offer.
4. There is no cash alternative.
5. The voucher is valid only during official opening times. See p.368 for more information.

Terms and conditions:

1. This voucher must be surrendered upon admission.
2. Photocopies of this voucher will not be accepted.
3. The voucher cannot be used for group parties or in conjunction with any other offer.
4. There is no cash alternative.
5. The voucher is valid only during official opening times. See p.126 for more information.

Terms and conditions:

1. This voucher must be surrendered upon admission.
2. Photocopies of this voucher will not be accepted.
3. The voucher cannot be used for group parties or in conjunction with any other offer.
4. There is no cash alternative.
5. The voucher is valid only during official opening times. See p.165 for more information.

The Garden Lovers' Guide to Britain

2 FOR 1 OFFER
ONE ADULT FREE WITH ONE FULL PAYING ADULT

Goodnestone Park Gardens Kent

Gardeners' World
VALID UNTIL END OF OCTOBER 2003

The Garden Lovers' Guide to Britain

2 FOR 1 OFFER
ONE ADULT FREE WITH ONE FULL PAYING ADULT

Holker Hall Gardens Cumbria

Gardeners' World
VALID UNTIL END OF OCTOBER 2003

The Garden Lovers' Guide to Britain

2 FOR 1 OFFER
ONE ADULT FREE WITH ONE FULL PAYING ADULT

How Caple Court Herefordshire

Gardeners' World
VALID UNTIL END OF OCTOBER 2003

The Garden Lovers' Guide to Britain

2 FOR 1 OFFER
ONE ADULT FREE WITH ONE FULL PAYING ADULT

Knoll Gardens Dorset

Gardeners' World
VALID UNTIL END OF OCTOBER 2003

The Garden Lovers' Guide to Britain

2 FOR 1 OFFER
ONE ADULT FREE WITH ONE FULL PAYING ADULT

Logan Botanic Garden Dumfries and Galloway

Gardeners' World
VALID UNTIL END OF OCTOBER 2003

The Garden Lovers' Guide to Britain

2 FOR 1 OFFER
ONE ADULT FREE WITH ONE FULL PAYING ADULT

Mannington Hall Gardens Norfolk

Gardeners' World
VALID UNTIL END OF OCTOBER 2003

The Garden Lovers' Guide to Britain

2 FOR 1 OFFER
ONE ADULT FREE WITH ONE FULL PAYING ADULT

Mount Stewart Ards and Down

Gardeners' World
VALID UNTIL END OF OCTOBER 2003

The Garden Lovers' Guide to Britain

2 FOR 1 OFFER
ONE ADULT FREE WITH ONE FULL PAYING ADULT

Muncaster Castle Gardens Cumbria

Gardeners' World
VALID UNTIL END OF OCTOBER 2003

The Garden Lovers' Guide to Britain

2 FOR 1 OFFER
ONE ADULT FREE WITH ONE FULL PAYING ADULT

Newby Hall and Gardens Yorkshire

Gardeners' World
VALID UNTIL END OF OCTOBER 2003

The Garden Lovers' Guide to Britain

2 FOR 1 OFFER
ONE ADULT FREE WITH ONE FULL PAYING ADULT

Nymans Garden Sussex

Gardeners' World
VALID UNTIL END OF OCTOBER 2003

Terms and conditions:

1. This voucher must be surrendered upon admission.
2. Photocopies of this voucher will not be accepted.
3. The voucher cannot be used for group parties or in conjunction with any other offer.
4. There is no cash alternative.
5. The voucher is valid only during official opening times. See p.72 for more information.

Terms and conditions:

1. This voucher must be surrendered upon admission.
2. Photocopies of this voucher will not be accepted.
3. The voucher cannot be used for group parties or in conjunction with any other offer.
4. There is no cash alternative.
5. The voucher is valid only during official opening times. See p.173 for more information.

Terms and conditions:

1. This voucher must be surrendered upon admission.
2. Photocopies of this voucher will not be accepted.
3. The voucher cannot be used for group parties or in conjunction with any other offer.
4. There is no cash alternative.
5. The voucher is valid only during official opening times. See p.113 for more information.

Terms and conditions:

1. This voucher must be surrendered upon admission.
2. Photocopies of this voucher will not be accepted.
3. The voucher cannot be used for group parties or in conjunction with any other offer.
4. There is no cash alternative.
5. The voucher is valid only during official opening times. See p.160 for more information.

Terms and conditions:

1. This voucher must be surrendered upon admission.
2. Photocopies of this voucher will not be accepted.
3. The voucher cannot be used for group parties or in conjunction with any other offer.
4. There is no cash alternative.
5. The voucher is valid only during official opening times. See p.217 for more information.

Terms and conditions:

1. This voucher must be surrendered upon admission.
2. Photocopies of this voucher will not be accepted.
3. The voucher cannot be used for group parties or in conjunction with any other offer.
4. There is no cash alternative.
5. The voucher is valid only during official opening times. See p.373 for more information.

Terms and conditions:

1. This voucher must be surrendered upon admission.
2. Photocopies of this voucher will not be accepted.
3. The voucher cannot be used for group parties or in conjunction with any other offer.
4. There is no cash alternative.
5. The voucher is valid only during official opening times. See p.79 for more information.

Terms and conditions:

1. This voucher must be surrendered upon admission.
2. Photocopies of this voucher will not be accepted.
3. The voucher cannot be used for group parties or in conjunction with any other offer.
4. There is no cash alternative.
5. The voucher is valid only during official opening times. See p.346 for more information.

Terms and conditions:

1. This voucher must be surrendered upon admission.
2. Photocopies of this voucher will not be accepted.
3. The voucher cannot be used for group parties or in conjunction with any other offer.
4. There is no cash alternative.
5. The voucher is valid only during official opening times. See p.295 for more information.

Terms and conditions:

1. This voucher must be surrendered upon admission.
2. Photocopies of this voucher will not be accepted.
3. The voucher cannot be used for group parties or in conjunction with any other offer.
4. There is no cash alternative.
5. The voucher is valid only during official opening times. See p.337 for more information.